The Sahmat Collective: Art and Activism in India since 1989

Jessica Moss and Ram Rahman

SMART MUSEUM OF ART
The University of Chicago

This catalogue is published in conjunction with the exhibition
The Sahmat Collective: Art and Activism in India since 1989
Curated by Jessica Moss and Ram Rahman
Smart Museum of Art, The University of Chicago
February 14–June 9, 2013

By Jessica Moss and Ram Rahman with essays by Prabhat Patnaik, Madan Gopal Singh, William Mazzarella, Geeta Kapur, Karin Zitzewitz, and Rebecca Zorach.

The Sahmat Collective: Art and Activism in India since 1989 is made possible by The Smart Family Foundation, Helen Zell, and the Efroymson Family Fund, a CICF Fund. Additional support is provided by Larry and Marilyn Fields, Barbara Fosco, The Fosco Family Foundation, and Lisa and Michael Kornick.

The University of Chicago
5550 South Greenwood Avenue
Chicago, Illinois 60637
773.702.0200
smartmuseum.uchicago.edu

 Distributed by the University of Chicago Press.

ISBN 978-0-935573-53-4

Design and typesetting: Jason Pickleman, the JNL graphic design
Editor: Amy Teschner
Printing: Everbest

Library of Congress Cataloging-in-Publication Data

The Sahmat Collective : Art and Activism in India since 1989.
pages cm
Catalogue published in conjunction with the exhibition *The Sahmat Collective: Art and Activism in India since 1989.* Curated by Jessica Moss and Ram Rahman, Smart Museum of Art, February 14-June 9, 2013.
Includes bibliographical references.
ISBN 978-0-935573-53-4 (pbk.)
1. Arts--Political aspects--India--Exhibitions. 2. Arts, Indic--Exhibitions. 3. Safdar Hashmi Memorial Trust--Exhibitions. I. David and Alfred Smart Museum of Art.
NX180.P64S24 2013
709.54'5607477311--dc23
2012042908

FRONT COVER
M. Sovan Kumar bicycling his work *Mobile Shelter* at the opening event for *Art on the Move*, Delhi, March 18, 2001.

BACK COVER
Safdar Hashmi performing in a Janam street play, ca. late 1970s. Photo courtesy Janam archive.

OPPOSITE
Images and Words exhibition in Delhi, April 12, 1991.

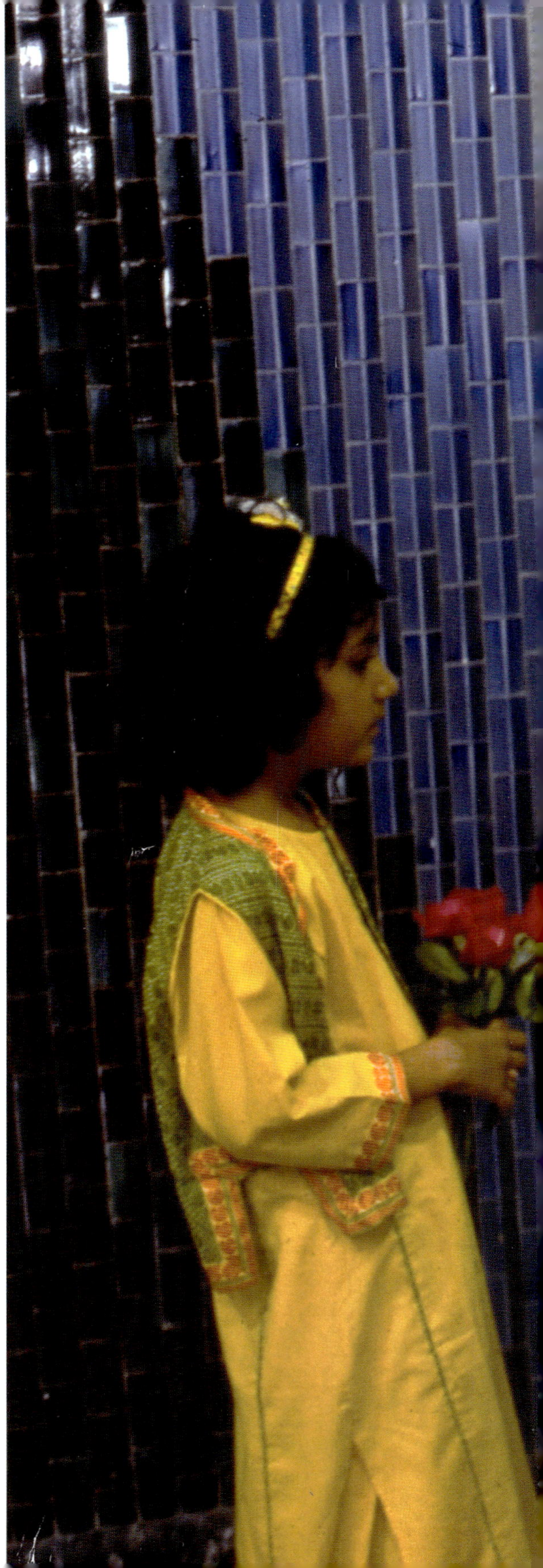

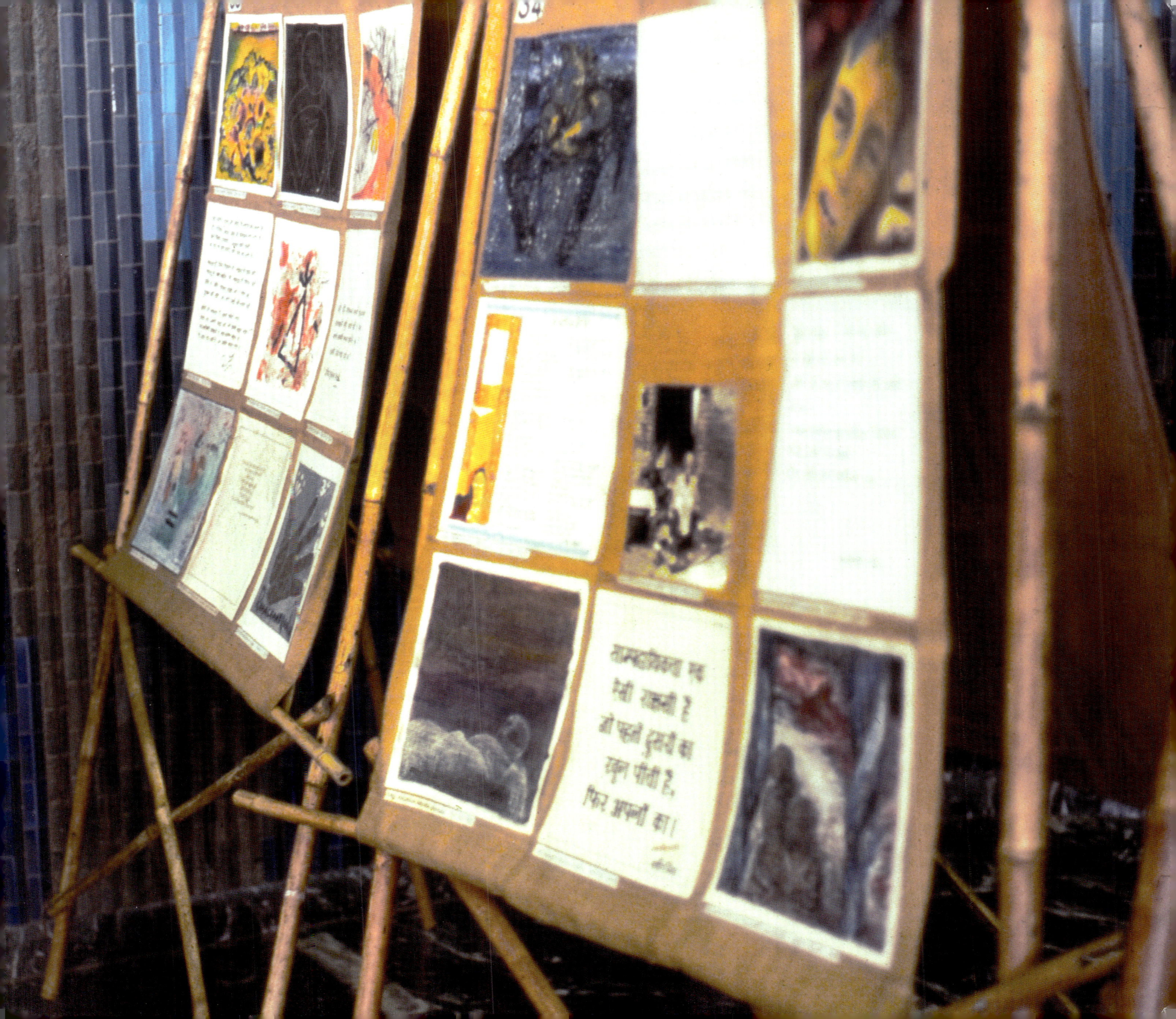
साम्प्रदायिकता एक
ऐसी राक्षसी है
जो पहले दूसरों का
खून पीती है,
फिर अपनों का।

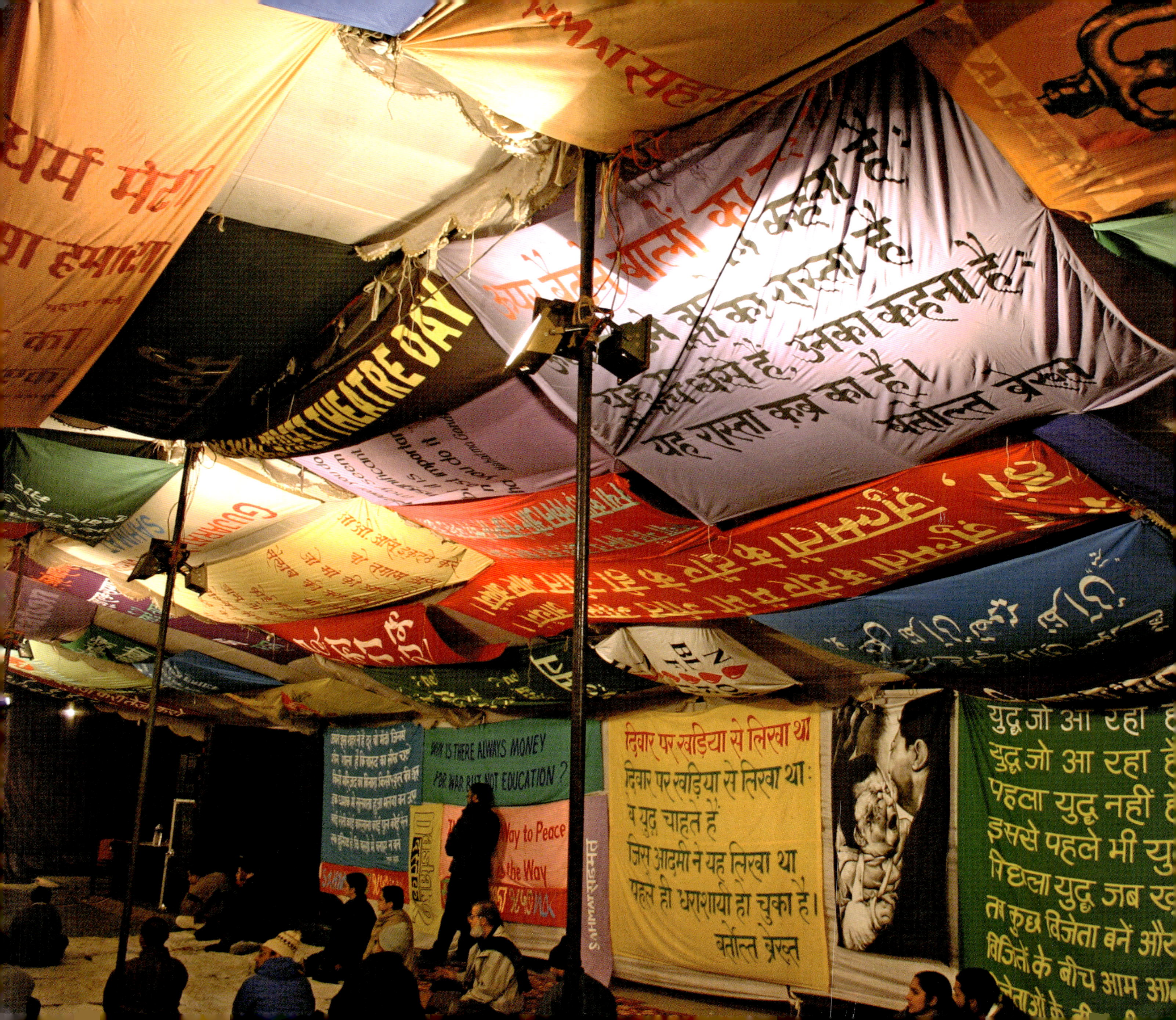

STREET THEATRE DAY
WHY IS THERE ALWAYS MONEY
FOR WAR BUT NOT EDUCATION ?
दिवार पर खड़िया से लिखा था
दिवार पर खड़िया से लिखा था:
वे युद्ध चाहते हैं
जिस आदमी ने यह लिखा था
पहले ही धराशायी हो चुका है।
बर्तोल्त ब्रेख्त
SAHMAT सहमत

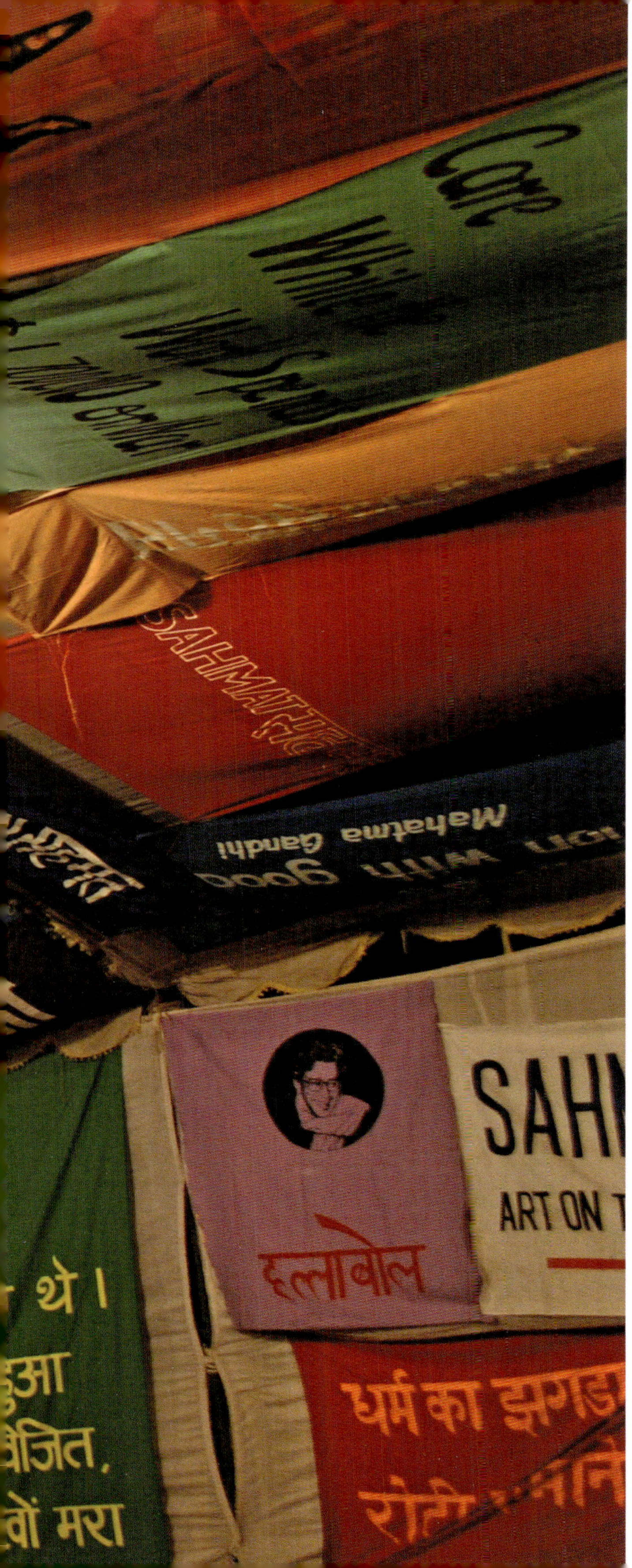

Sahmat's emergence in 1989 resulted in, numerically speaking, extraordinary participation by the entire breadth of India's artists, from academy-style painter to classical singer, from alternative filmmaker to community theatre enthusiast, from Communist Party griot to small-town photo-journalist. Sahmat's interventions quickly laid out a new mode of artistic operation in the Indian context, bringing on board waves of voluntary conscripts from the art world, the intelligentsia and "cultural workers" who embraced Sahmat as a national platform for anti-state and progressive dissent. By the time of its "Anhad Garje" [meaning "unborn, boundless, raging sound"] campaign of 1993—its quickfire response to the Babri Masjid demolition, when all other elements of civil society and the state seemed paralysed—Sahmat was routinely pulling off tremendous logistical feats on a national scale, straddling events in several different cities (up to 30 at a time) with input and involvement from hundreds, even thousands, of artists. From certain standpoints, this made Sahmat into the largest-ever voluntary collective of artists coming together to share a single political platform.

—Arindam Dutta

From "SAHMAT, 1989–2004: Liberal Art Practice Against the Liberalised Public Sphere," in *Cultural Dynamics* (London; Thousand Oaks, CA; and New Dehli: SAGE Publications, 2005), 199.

◄ Interior of performance tent, *Safdar Hashmi Memorial, The Making of India*, January 1, 2004.

PROJECTS

ESSAYS

Foreword

The Smart Museum of Art at the University of Chicago is proud to present *The Sahmat Collective: Art and Activism in India since 1989*. Together this publication and the exhibition it accompanies document an extraordinary movement, an artists' collective born out of revulsion to a galvanizing moment of political violence. While a number of leading Indian artists have received individual attention in the United States in recent years, this project focuses on an entirely different approach to art-making in India and thus asserts a very different conception of its potential. Certainly it is a story worth telling, and it resonates as part of two complementary arcs in the Smart Museum's contemporary art programming over the last decade: the first devoted to exploring the work of artists who tackle complex social issues in their work and the other devoted to groundbreaking studies of contemporary Asian art, particularly in China, a field in which the Smart Museum and the University of Chicago were early and consistent leaders. *The Sahmat Collective* builds on this foundation and moves into new territory, focusing on a significant trend in contemporary art, in a country that demands our attention.

We take it for granted that artists will comment powerfully and provocatively on political and social issues. With their uniquely personal means of confronting the world and expressing their responses to it, they can frame problems in revelatory and unexpected ways, forcing us to confront what we might wish to avoid and compelling us to act. Yet the very familiarity of our assumptions about the ongoing ability of artists to raise our consciousness has dimmed our appreciation of the forces that drive them to do so. This blind spot is perhaps most prevalent among those of us who live in wealthy and relatively placid societies where dissent generally carries little risk and societal challenges are less plainly in view.

Since its inception, the Sahmat collective has embraced the power of joint action across classes and religions, involving artists of considerable renown alongside those whose artistic talents might rarely even be acknowledged, let alone given free reign. In a vast and populous country whose democratic ideals are nevertheless riven by fault lines of religion, power, wealth, and class, the work of Sahmat has become a dynamic and insistent force for change, embracing secular and egalitarian values while rendering ineffectual the old distinctions between high and low art. Sahmat is an exhilarating, vital movement; we seek to explore here not only its story but also its significance.

This project had its origin with the ambition of the Smart Museum's associate curator of contemporary art, Jessica Moss, to capitalize upon the legacy of the last decade of contemporary art exhibitions at the Smart while charting new territory by shifting our attention to India. As all involved can readily attest, she has worked with enormous dedication, energy, and good cheer over several years to launch this project on its course undaunted by the challenges, overseeing every element involved in bringing it to successful fruition. We owe her our profound thanks. Early on, Moss encountered Ram Rahman, a founder of the Sahmat collective and one of its long-time curators, whose knowledge of this material is unequaled. The Sahmat archives constitute a remarkable trove too little known outside India, and thus this project was born. The value of Ram Rahman's assistance and enthusiasm for this venture proved essential, and we are grateful.

We have also counted on a host of colleagues in India for assistance of all types, first among them Ram Rahman's colleagues in Sahmat: Rajendra Prasad, Indira Chandrasekhar, Ashok Kumari, Lalit Narayan (Bunty) and Naresh. Their generosity and helpfulness have overcome the geographical distance that separates Chicago from New Delhi; it has been a privilege to work with them. In addition, we are deeply grateful to the lenders who have supplemented Sahmat's archive—Anil Chandra, Tasneem Zakaria Mehta, Peter Nagy, Lalit Nirula, Priya Paul, Lekha and Anupam Poddar, Inder Salim, Vivan Sundaram, and Julie Walsh, as well as Gallery Espace, New Delhi, and Talwar Gallery, New York—and agreed to part with precious works of art in order to round out the exhibition's narrative. And to the many artists, both famous and lesser-known, involved with the Sahmat collective over the more than twenty years of its existence, we can only offer admiration for their passion and commitment to their cause, as well as gratitude that they should have shared these qualities with us through their work.

At the University of Chicago, the project had the benefit of a series of exhibition workshops—a standard practice over the last several years for all major exhibitions at the Smart Museum—in which a range of faculty members from the University's renowned South and Southeast Asian Studies departments as well as scholars from a range of disciplines—including history, anthropology, music, cinema and media studies, international studies, literature, and the visual arts—participated, helping both to shape the exhibition and its related programming, informing their development in ways too numerous to count. These workshops provided ample evidence of the astonishing resource that colleagues at a great university can be when one seeks to deepen the investigation of complex interdisciplinary topics. To the participants, some of whom have also contributed essays to this volume, we express our heartfelt thanks and admiration.

This volume makes an important contribution to our understanding of an exciting and important movement in contemporary art in India thanks to the insightful essays provided, in addition to project co-curators Jessica Moss and Ram Rahman, by Geeta Kapur, Madan Gopal Singh, William Mazzarella, Prabhat Patnaik, Karin Zitzewitz, and Rebecca Zorach. We are grateful to them all.

At the Smart Museum, this project has involved nearly all the staff, and they have performed with their extraordinary if customary professionalism. A few merit special recognition here. Stephanie Smith, deputy director and chief curator, has been an inspiring and thoughtful mentor to Jessica Moss, and her thinking has done much to give form to this project. Michael Christiano has led the Museum's Department of Education and Interpretation in developing a wide range of exhibition programming, including partnerships across the University and with the Eye on India festival, to whose organizers Sanjoy Roy, Anuradha Behari, and Karim Ahamed we also offer thanks. Steven Rosofsky has produced engaging videos combining footage from Sahmat's archive with new interviews with their artists and organizers. Angela Steinmetz, head registrar, has coordinated complex shipping arrangements from India and across the country for the exhibition tour and worked with Rudy Bernal and Ray Klemchuk on the installation of the exhibition. Warren Davis, director of development and external relations, and his colleague Kate Nardin have worked tirelessly to see that the resources needed to mount this project were made available. And, as is customary at the Smart Museum, where talented students make invaluable contributions every day, a number of them have proven irreplaceable in bringing this project to life, including curatorial interns Kimberly Mims and Nandini Ramakrishnan.

We are also deeply grateful to the project's financial supporters, without whom it could never have come into being. Thanks are owed to the Smart Family Foundation, which has been exceptionally generous, as it has on so many occasions before. Helen Zell provided lead support at a critical time, demonstrating her visionary commitment to important work in Chicago. It is a privilege to have the support of the Efroymson Family Fund, a CICF Fund, with additional support from Larry and Marilyn Fields, Barbara Fosco through the Fosco Family Foundation, and Lisa and Michael Kornick.

Finally, it is a pleasure to acknowledge our colleagues who are participating in the exhibition's national tour. Their interest and support has been gratifying. At the Ackland Art Museum at the University of North Carolina, Chapel Hill, we thank Emily Kass, director, and Peter Nisbet, chief curator, who were immediately enthusiastic about the exhibition as part of a celebration of Indian culture in the Research Triangle.

In providing a fascinating look at a remarkable art movement, *The Sahmat Collective: Art and Activism in India since 1989* demonstrates the profound potential of art that arises from a desire to confront intractable social issues. Sahmat's work—its many generous acts of art-making in the cause of activism—has captured our attention, and will continue to exert its influence on Indian society with ramifications that extend far beyond the borders of the subcontinent. We at the Smart Museum are proud to share this compelling material with a wide audience in the United States.

Anthony Hirschel
Dana Feitler Director
Smart Museum of Art
The University of Chicago

The Sahmat Collective: Art and Activism in India since 1989

Founded in 1989, Sahmat is a contemporary artists' collective created in and for India. While fomenting discussion and activism around politically charged topics, the Delhi-based collective catalyzes the production and display of artworks to advance artistic freedom and secular, egalitarian values. The initial urge to form Sahmat came as a response to the death of Safdar Hashmi, a political activist, actor, playwright, and poet who was fatally attacked by political thugs during a street theatre performance in January 1989. Sahmat is both an acronym for the Safdar Hashmi Memorial Trust, and the Hindi word for "in agreement."

Sahmat's history of exhibitions, performances, and publications bears out their mission of advocating for "the essentially pluralist and democratic spirit of creative expression." Presenting a unified voice of resistance against censorship and intolerance, the members of Sahmat have created a rich range of interdisciplinary performances and projects—from informal, street-side traveling shows to cultural protests and dynamic conceptual exhibitions. The artists, actors, poets, musicians, and scholars of the original group, joined by a growing roster of artists, have had an indelible impact on Indian culture, and many of the artists who have been deeply involved with Sahmat during its more than twenty-year history are now recognized as among the country's most influential voices.

The Sahmat Collective: Art and Activism in India since 1989 offers an in-depth look at the work produced by this group of artists and their urgent belief that art can propel political change and culture can reach across boundaries of class. As an exhibition, it begins with the collective's founding in January 1989 and continues through a series of case studies of key projects extending to the present day. This catalogue adopts the same format, showcasing a selection of Sahmat's undertakings with a combination of vivid imagery, reprints of historic texts and press coverage, and recollections and observations with the group's artists, project coordinators, and participants. The myriad voices in the catalogue reflect the dynamic, collaborative spirit of Sahmat.

Indeed, pluralism and interdisciplinary forms of expression are paramount to Sahmat, whose foremost principle has been to counter India's divisive politics, as recalled in events on these pages. In contemporary India, "communalism" designates conflicts between extremists of religious communities, similar to the way the term "sectarian" is used in an American context. As Rebecca Zorach explains in her essay in this volume, "The term *communalism* has specific resonance in South Asia, where it refers to ethnic or religious nationalism: the political and sometimes violent privileging of one particular community." Political parties are generally considered to play an important role in stimulating, supporting, and suppressing communal tendencies in India. Politics there saw a right-wing upsurge of Hindu majoritarian communalism in the 1990s, which was also Sahmat's most active and activist period to date. From the destruction of the Babri Masjid (Babur's Mosque) in 1992 by Hindu nationalist activists to the Gujarat riots in 2002, communal tension—specifically between Hindus and Muslims—has led to terrible violence and devastation.

In the face of such intense conflict, Sahmat has used the arts not only to voice resistance but also to work toward unity. They often draw inspiration from the medieval Sufi-Bhakti movement, which was based on Islamic and Hindu traditions and led by mystic poets across India. An egalitarian people's practice of reaching the divine through individual action, without the intercession of a priest in a temple or a *mullah* in a mosque, Sufi-Bhakti offers a tradition of resistance to orthodoxies. Its attributes—individual responsibility, resistance, collaboration across traditions and cultures, and caring for others—have influenced both specific Sahmat programs and its overall ethos. Sahmat has used verses of Sufi-Bhakti poetry on posters and spotlighted them through performance events, most notably *Anhad Garje* (1992) and *Muktnaad* (1993), which drew national attention with its all-night series of performances in Ayodhya, the first time people came to the city in a form of protest since the mosque's destruction.

As seen from the more than one thousand people who attended *Muktnaad*, one of Sahmat's strengths has been its ability to bring together people from different backgrounds and disciplines on a shared platform. Recognizing that art operates within a broad field, Sahmat has extended its cultural and activist initiatives by collaborating with academics and scholars on symposia and publications, advancing critical conversation around key social issues such as the interpretation of history in the education system. They have also engaged audiences apart from the academic and artistic communities, for instance by inviting auto-rickshaw drivers to participate in their 1992 project *Slogans for Communal Harmony* by writing verses on unity and brotherhood, and then putting those messages on their vehicles in a lively contest of word and design. The participants then drove those decorated auto-rickshaws in procession throughout Delhi.

From its origins Sahmat has shown a steadfast belief in the importance of involving youth. They have produced children's books written by Safdar Hashmi and illustrated by contemporary artists (which have been translated into many languages and printed in the hundreds of thousands for wide distribution throughout India), brought mobile exhibitions to schools, held workshops for children, and distributed posters and broadsheets to university and student groups around the country. In efforts to reach future generations and stop the spread of suspicion, fear, hostility, and intolerance, Sahmat has repeatedly demonstrated their passionate belief in India's touted slogan *Unity in Diversity*.

The Sahmat Collective: Art and Activism in India since 1989 is the group's most comprehensive retrospective exhibition, and the first to present its full range of activist action and artistic experimentation to a US audience. (Although well established in India's artistic, academic, and activist circles, only a few of Sahmat's projects have been shown outside of India.[1]) To aid in contextualizing Sahmat's activities and the artwork produced for them, a timeline following these pages offers an overview of relevant events in India and the compelling ways that Sahmat responded. This timeline does not capture the full breadth of the collective's undertakings—omitting many symposia, seminars, conventions, press conferences, protests, meetings, book releases, plays, and other activities—but it collects in one place the variety of events noted throughout this book.[2] This view of Sahmat's production also highlights the ways that art and politics can inform one another, and the role the arts can play to voice resistance and activate social change.

We wish to extend our deepest gratitude to those who have helped make this book possible. Thank you to all of the artists for sharing your work with us. Special thanks to the contributing authors for their illuminating essays: Geeta Kapur, William Mazzarella, Prabhat Patnaik, Madan Gopal Singh, Karin Zitzewitz, and Rebecca Zorach. We are also grateful to all those who allowed their texts to be reprinted or provided new texts for this project: Aijaz Ahmad, Atul Dodiya, Nicola Durvasula, Arindam Dutta, Tapati Guha-Thakurta, Irfan Habib, Qamar Azad Hashmi, Ranjit Hoskote, Geeta Kapur, M. Sovan Kumar, Sadanand Menon, Sukumar Muralidharan, Peter Nagy, Prabhat Patnaik, Chaitanya Sambrani, Teesta Setalvad, K. G. Subramanyan, Vivan Sundaram, and Sitanshu Yashaschandra, as well as posthumously, Safdar Hashmi, Rummana

Hussain, Ravinder Kumar, Satyajit Ray, Bhisham Sahni, and Habib Tanvir. And thank you to those who participated in interviews and provided their thoughtful observations and recollections: Rajinder Arora, Vijay Bagodi, Jatin Das, Astad Deboo, Arunkumar H. G., Inder Salim, Subodh Gupta, Moloyashree Hashmi, Sohail Hashmi, Zarina Hashmi, Romi Khosla, Nalini Malani, Shubha Mugdal, Veer Munshi, Pushpamala N., Manu Parekh, Madhvi Parekh, Dadi Pudumjee, Mona Rai, M. K. Raina, Gigi Scaria, Mithu Sen, Parthiv Shah, Nilima Sheikh, Gulammohammed Sheikh, and Vivan Sundaram. This catalogue would not have been possible without the tireless efforts of Rajendra Prasad and Indira Chandrasekhar and we are profoundly grateful. Additional thanks go to Parthiv Shah, Rajinder Arora, and those in the Sahmat office: Ashok Kumari, Lalit Narayan (Bunty), and Naresh for managing, researching, and photographing the archive.

My deepest thanks go to my incredible colleagues at the Smart: Michael Christiano, Sarah Mendelsohn, Kim Mims, Kate Nardin, Sara Patrello, Stephanie Smith, and Angela Steinmetz—your invaluable contributions have shaped this project and made working on it a pleasure. In developing the exhibition, we held a series of exhibition planning workshops and meetings that engaged the expertise of the University's renowned South and Southeast Asian studies faculty as well as scholars from a range of disciplines—including history, anthropology, music, and the visual arts. Thank you to Michael Burt, Tarini Bedi, Jamie Bender, Dipesh Chakrabarty, Leela Gandhi, Theaster Gates, David Hays, Rochona Majumdar, Kaley Mason, William Mazzarella, James Nye, Srikanth (Chicu) Reddy, and Rebecca Zorach for participating in those conversations, which helped guide not only this publication but also the exhibition, its interpretation, and related programming.

I'd like to reiterate Tony's thanks to those who believed in and supported this project, I am sincerely grateful for your generosity. Special thanks to The Smart Family Foundation, Helen Zell, Adnaan Hamid and Elissa Efroymson and the Efroymson Family Fund, Larry and Marilyn Fields, Barbara Fosco, and Lisa and Michael Kornick. My profound thanks go to Jason Pickleman for this vibrant design and Amy Teschner for her patient and thoughtful editorial acumen.

And finally, a huge thanks goes to my co-curator Ram Rahman—your creativity and passion has fueled this project. My heartfelt gratitude goes to Ram and everyone from the Sahmat collective: thank you for sharing your world of ideas and actions, an incredible archive, and deeply personal stories and works of art. They not only tell an inspiring story of creativity and courage, they prove that art has the power to unify citizens and drive change.

Jessica Moss
Associate Curator of Contemporary Art
Smart Museum of Art
The University of Chicago

1. The exhibition *Hum Sab Ayodhya* (We Are All Ayodhya) toured Columbia University, the University of Amherst, the Massachusetts Institute of Technology, and University of California, Berkeley in 1993–94. Other presentations of Sahmat's work in the United States have included a version of *Postcards for Gandhi*, which was exhibited at Bose Pacia Gallery in New York in 1995 and as a street exhibition at the South Street Seaport in New York in 1996. Further, *Dust on the Road*, a collaborative exhibition with Hoopoe Curatorial that showcased Sahmat's work alongside Canadian contemporary artists, toured Canada in 2000.

2. For a more complete account of Sahmat's activities, see *Sahmat 20 Years 1989–2009: A Document of Activities and Statements* (New Delhi: Sahmat, 2009), and their website: www.sahmat.org.

A Journey of Resistance

When Sahmat was formed in the emotional aftermath of Safdar Hashmi's murder, it was decided at the very outset that it would be an artist-run collective and not an affiliate of the Communist Party of India (Marxist), although many in the founding group were Safdar's comrades in the party. This decision has allowed Sahmat the freedom to conceive and execute innovative projects, sometimes at lightning speed, and Prabhat Patnaik in his essay writes in some detail about this unique space that the group created in the progressive left. Of course Sahmat could never have survived without the support of the CPI(M), its cadre and organizational affiliates. Its first office was located in the enclosed verandah of a flat allotted to the writers' organization of the party, and the current office is in the garage of a CPI(M) member of Parliament's residence. Yet Sahmat's independence from party diktat has allowed for the participation of people with varying political beliefs, all essentially progressive.

Art as activism in India was fostered mainly by the Communists in the 1940s. It was the vision of the general secretary of the then undivided Communist Party of India (CPI), P. C. Joshi, that writers, artists, and performers should be involved in direct political action, which led to the founding of the Indian Progressive Writers' Association (PWA) in 1936 and the Indian People's Theatre Association (IPTA) in 1942. Both were directly affiliated to the CPI. In fact the party had set up a commune in Bombay of performers, actors, and writer members of IPTA and PWA, which functioned from 1943 to 1947—until the official ties between these organizations and the party were severed after Joshi was ousted as general secretary. The event that led to the formation of IPTA and provided the motivation for its incredible reach across India was the Bengal Famine of 1942. It was also the famine that prompted Joshi to recruit two visual artists, the photographer Sunil Janah and the illustrator Chittaprosad, to work for the party's newspaper *People's War*, and move them from Calcutta to the commune in Bombay; their official affiliation with the party also ended in 1947 after Joshi's ouster. But those five years of intense cultural action had a lasting impact on cultural developments in India after independence. The idea of "Unity in Diversity"—of the unity of a people's culture cutting across the multiple religious, caste, and class identities of the subcontinent—was propagated by the Communists in the 1940s. After the dissolution of IPTA in 1947 many of them moved to Delhi and found employment in various government cultural departments set up after independence, including All India

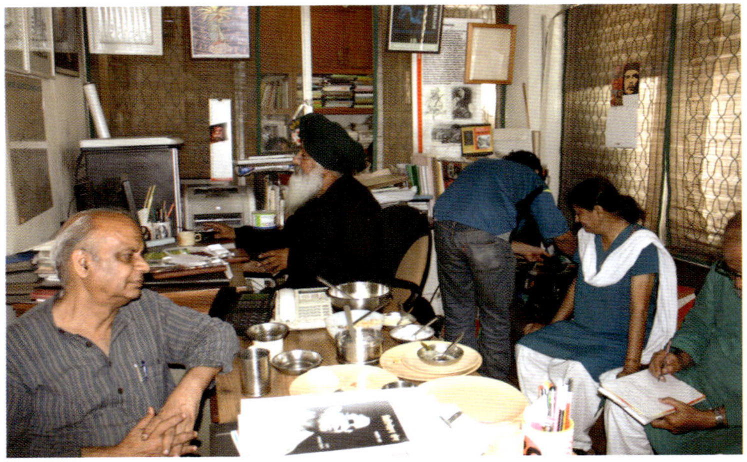

Rajendra Prasad on the left, Madan Gopal Singh on the computer. Old Sahmat office, Vitthalbhai Patel House, New Delhi. Remnants of the lunch always available to any who walk in, and two telephones, crucial instruments in Sahmat's functioning, 2009.

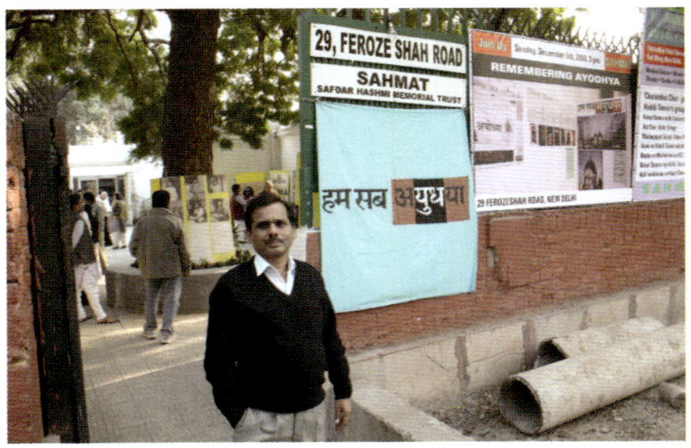

View of the current Sahmat office, the garage in the left background. *Hum Sab Ayodhya* mounted in the driveway, December 6, 2009

Radio. It was through them that the cultural ideas of the left movement became central to the national cultural ethos of the newly independent, "Nehruvian" India.

Sahmat's direct link to IPTA was through Bhisham Sahni, the writer, and Habib Tanvir, the theatre director. Both had also worked closely with Safdar Hashmi, and they served as the first and second chairpersons, in succession, of Sahmat. If the Bengal famine was a moment that galvanized IPTA, the demolition of the mosque in Ayodhya in 1992 played a similarly central role in Sahmat's trajectory and led it into a more activist phase. It also served to broaden the base of the collective to include historians, archeologists, and social scientists. Sahmat's Ayodhya initiatives and the attacks on them led to its national prominence, in ways it had never imagined. By staying the course and keeping up the struggle and resistance through the arts, the collective has managed to survive and remain relevant.

Sahmat likes to define itself as a "platform." Open-ended and inclusive, it has helped to create and maintain the space for cultural resistance. It is on this platform that the historian, even the archeologist, can be a cultural activist. With right-wing politics in India striving hard to restrict cultural space and freedom from within, and the equally massive assault from the globalized economic and mono-cultural interests coming from the outside, it has become even more crucial to defend that space for resistance.

Sahmat's January 1 memorials to Safdar have given a space to performing artists to experiment and extend the boundaries of their practices. The rock band Indian Ocean recorded their performance live at one such memorial on Safdar Hashmi Marg (Road) in Delhi and released it as their first album (*Desert Rain*, 1997). I remember the avant-garde theatre/political cabaret performer Maya Rao charging onto the stage carrying a dead fish, disrupting and evicting the classical singer Shubha Mudgal and her stunned musicians, while an equally shocked audience looked on. It was only as her act played out that we realized the subtext of her piece—attacks on freedom of expression. At another memorial we presented art history lectures on the artists M. F. Husain and Chittaprosad and photographer Sunil Janah in between performances of revolutionary songs, in a highly successful experiment.

This exhibition and the accompanying book have been an ambitious undertaking. To represent in a gallery the work of the Sahmat collective, which straddles so many diverse fields, was a daunting task. It is a credit to the interest, persistence, and immense hard work that Jessica Moss and her colleagues at the Smart Museum have invested in this project, that it has been possible to expose the work to a US audience. There have been exhibitions of contemporary Indian art in the United States before, but none that has presented the interactions among contemporary art, society, and politics in the subcontinent in such a focused manner. The exhibition and book present artworks that have been shown in galleries, but also many that have been shown in vastly different public spaces. Unusually for an exhibition of art, work in other public mediums—posters, pamphlets, books, and tent banners—are also on view, mediums that have helped expand the field of contemporary art-making and that have rarely found space in the discourse on Indian contemporary art.

In its art projects Sahmat has consistently attempted to break away from accepted and conventional formats of art-making and display. As the Indian art scene has fallen victim to the globalized art market and the pressures of the aesthetic associated with international biennial exhibitions, the Sahmat platform has provided a space for showing and making art that speaks to more personal and local concerns. The art in the Sahmat archive and the pieces kindly loaned by our collector friends present a journey of contemporary Indian art over the last two decades—a journey in which many artists shifted from figuration to more conceptual installation and assemblage. Sahmat's projects also reflect the camaraderie and community spirit of the Indian art scene, where artists of different generations and philosophical outlook still have a close-knit sense of community and purpose. These projects are parts of larger initiatives that include lectures, performances, publications, and symposia. We have tried to convey that larger context in the exhibition and the catalogue.

The Sahmat Collective: Art and Activism in India since 1989 evolved out of the exhibition *Image, Music, Text: 20 Years of Sahmat* that I curated for the collective, which was shown at Jamia Millia Islamia University in New Delhi in 2009. Neither that show nor the present one could have been accomplished without the meticulous archiving done by the group, led by Rajendra Prasad, universally known as "Rajen." Rajen prefers to remain in the wings of the main stage, but as mentor, ideologue, and guiding spirit, no one has wielded a more formidable influence on the artists, historians, social scientists, and musicians whose work you see here—all through the telephone in his hand. The inspired editing of the texts by the eagle-eyed Indira Chandrasekhar in all our projects has extended to this volume too.

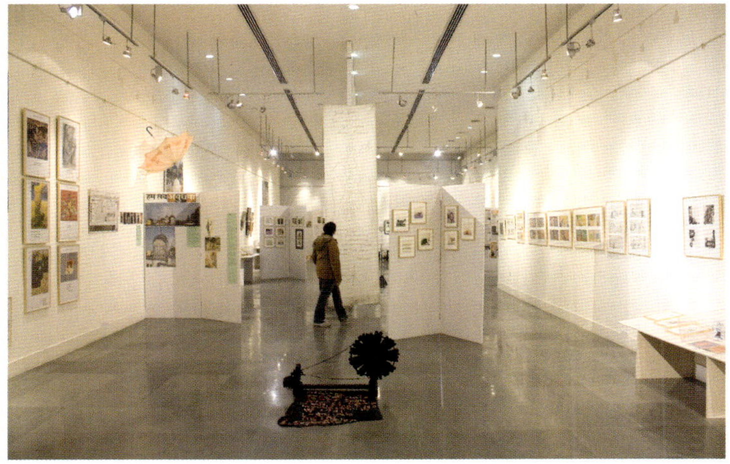

Installation view of *Image, Music, Text: 20 Years of Sahmat*, at the M. F. Husain Gallery, Jamia Millia Islamia University, New Delhi, 2009.

The complexities of India's ethnic, racial, religious, and linguistic mix, as well as the nuances and complexities of the politics that form the context of this work, may be hard to follow, but we have tried our best to make it easier to unravel. For the American viewer, it may help to see these works in the context of the "culture wars" as they are playing out in India, not too unlike those that have been playing out in the United States. The central position of the Ayodhya mosque demolition may also be better understood in reference to the psychic trauma caused to the American nation by the 9/11 attacks. For us, Ayodhya was the same.

Ram Rahman
Photographer and a Member of Sahmat's Founding Group

Timeline

An overview of relevant events in India (in purple) and the compelling ways that Sahmat responded (in red).

1857

India's First War of Independence (the Sepoy Revolt) against British rule.

1947

August 15: India gains independence from British colonial rule. The partition of the subcontinent results in the creation of two independent nation-states, India and Pakistan. The partition is marked by massive migration and violent displacement of large sections of the population, causing over a million deaths.

Jawaharlal Nehru assumes office as prime minister of independent India's first government, led by the Congress Party.

1948

January 30: Mohandas Karamchand Gandhi, the foremost leader of India's struggle for independence from British rule, is assassinated by Nathuram Godse, a Hindu nationalist activist.

1950

January 26: The Constitution of India comes into effect. India becomes a republic.

1957

The first elected Communist government comes to power in the southern Indian state of Kerala, with E. M. S. Namboodiripad as chief minister.

1964

Jawaharlal Nehru dies. Gulzarilal Nanda serves as caretaker prime minister for a few days, until the election of Lal Bahadur Shastri.

The Communist Party of India (Marxist) / CPI(M) is formed by a breakaway faction at the Seventh Congress of the Communist Party of India / CPI, held in Calcutta.

The Vishwa Hindu Parishad / VHP (World Hindu Council) is formed. VHP is the religious wing of the Sangh Parivar, a group of organizations that work in favor of Hindu-majoritarian nationalism. The VHP becomes a major promoter of the Hindu identity movement (*Hindutva*) within and outside India.

1966

Indira Gandhi is chosen as leader of the Congress government after the sudden demise of Lal Bahadur Shastri.

1967

Non-Congress governments are formed in several Indian states after the general elections, weakening the hold of the Congress Party, which remains in power at the center.

1970–71

Following a civil war in Pakistan, East Pakistan emerges as the independent, secular nation-state of Bangladesh.

1975

June 26: In the wake of widespread political opposition to the Congress government, strikes and protests across the country, and an Allahabad High Court judgment pronouncing Indira Gandhi's election to office in 1971 as null and void, President Fakhruddin Ali Ahmed, upon request by Prime Minister Indira Gandhi, declares a State of Internal Emergency under Article 352 of the Indian Constitution, citing threats to national security and a weakened economy as the reasons. The 21-month period of the emergency, one of the most controversial times in the history of independent India, witnesses suspension of civil liberties and imprisonment of hundreds of thousands of political opponents. It is lifted on March 21, 1977.

1977

A coalition of opposition parties called the Janata Party, led by Morarji Desai as prime minister, assumes power after winning the election, breaking the hold of the Congress Party at the center for the first time since independence. The Jan Sangh, a right-wing Hindutva party, merges with the Janata Party.

1980

The Congress Party, led by Indira Gandhi, comes back to power, winning the election with a large majority. The Janata Party splits; the Jan Sangh leaves the coalition to establish itself as the Bharatiya Janata Party (BJP). The BJP emerges as India's second largest political party, on a right-wing political platform.

1984

Prime Minister Indira Gandhi is assassinated in Delhi by her Sikh bodyguards in retaliation against the military operation (Operation Bluestar) targeting Sikh militants at the Golden Temple, Amritsar. Her death leads to large-scale violence and attacks against the Sikh community at large, especially in Delhi.

Rajiv Gandhi, Indira Gandhi's son, is elected with a massive majority. The Congress Party government led by him as prime minister continues until 1989.

1988

The telecast of serials based on the Hindu epics *Ramayana* and *Mahabharata* creates a revivalist cultural ambience.

1989

January 1: Safdar Hashmi and his street theatre group Jana Natya Manch (Janam) are attacked in Sahibabad, on the outskirts of Delhi, while performing a play. Hashmi is fatally injured.

January 2: Hashmi dies in a hospital in New Delhi. People march in protest from the Supreme Court to Rabindra Bhavan (where the government-run national academies of art, literature, music, and dance are located).

January 3: Hashmi's funeral takes place; large numbers join the funeral procession in Delhi.

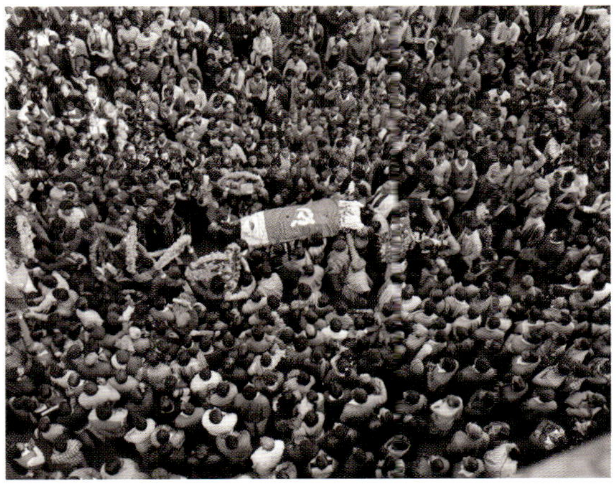

January 4: March from Rabindra Bhavan, New Delhi, to Sahibabad, where Janam performs their unfinished play of January 1.

January 5: Silent march from Shivaji Park, Minto Road, Delhi, to the residence of the Union Home Minister, Buta Singh.

January 9: Meeting of artists and cultural activists at Rabindra Bhavan, New Delhi, after a torchlight procession. The demand is raised at the meeting that College Street, at the Mandi House circle (the cultural hub of the city), be renamed Safdar Hashmi Marg (Road).

January 12: Actor Shabana Azmi reads protest statement against Hashmi's murder at the awards ceremony of the 12th International Film Festival of India, held at Siri Fort Auditorium, New Delhi.

January 24: The University of Calcutta confers posthumous Honorary D. Litt. (Doctor of Letters) degree on Safdar Hashmi.

February: **The Safdar Hashmi Memorial Trust (Sahmat) and Committee are formed.**

April 12: Sahmat gives a call for Hashmi's birthday to be observed as **National Street Theatre Day** all over the country. National Street Theatre Day, observed every year since then, continues to focus attention on the street theatre movement. Sahmat produces a new poster annually to distribute to street theatre groups throughout India.

April 12–16: Sahmat holds a five-day cultural festival, ***Safdar Samaroh* (Safdar Festival),** and an **art exhibition and auction, *Artists Alert*,** in New Delhi. Sahmat releases children's books based on Hashmi's writings, illustrated by contemporary artists.

September 13–16: Sahmat organizes a festival of street theatre, ***Chauraha* (Crossroads),** in New Delhi.

Proponents of Hindu nationalism launch a movement, with support from the BJP, for the demolition of a historic mosque of the medieval era, Babri Masjid (Babur's Mosque), in the north Indian city of Ayodhya, to reclaim the site as Ramjanmabhoomi (the birthplace of the Hindu god-king Rama, whose story is told in the *Ramayana*). The Vishwa Hindu Parishad spearheads the movement.

The Indian government bans the import of copies of Salman Rushdie's book *The Satanic Verses*, in response to angry protests from Muslims.

1989–91

The Congress Party loses its majority in the general election and two successive non-Congress governments, led by V. P. Singh first and then Chandrashekhar, come to power. Under V. P. Singh's prime ministership (1989–90), an attempt is made to implement the 10-year-old recommendations of the Mandal Commission, aimed at affirmative action in favor of the backward classes and castes by reserving seats and creating quotas in educational institutions and public sector jobs; the move is met with widespread opposition and agitation from upper-caste groups.

1990

January 1: Sahmat initiates the ***Safdar Hashmi Memorial*,** which has been held annually ever since to commemorate the day of the attack against Safdar Hashmi and Janam. A protest march is held from Rabindra Bhavan, New Delhi, to Sahibabad, where a street play is performed and there is a display of paintings, including a 44-foot-long collective painting made by artists.

January 2: Sahmat pays homage to Hashmi with recitations of poetry, readings, and music and dance performances at Rabindra Bhavan, New Delhi. College Street at the Mandi House circle is renamed Safdar Hashmi Marg (Road).

October–November: Sahmat organizes ***Janotsav* (People's Festival)**—a month-long series of community-based cultural workshops, performances and exhibitions, conducted at Mangolpuri, a resettlement colony in Delhi.

1991

Indian politics witnesses a right-wing upsurge. BJP president L. K. Advani begins his 36-day-long *Rath Yatra* (literally, "chariot procession/journey") on September 25, described by the BJP as a *dharam yatra* (holy pilgrimage). It engenders violence and communal riots all along its route.

January 1: Sahmat initiates the campaign ***Artists Against Communalism (AAC)*,** with a 17-hour cultural sit-in and performances at Safdar Hashmi Marg, New Delhi. Similar programs are held on January 30, 1991, on the anniversary of Mahatma Gandhi's assassination, in the cities of Aligarh, Bangalore, Baroda, Hyderabad, Mumbai, and Patna.

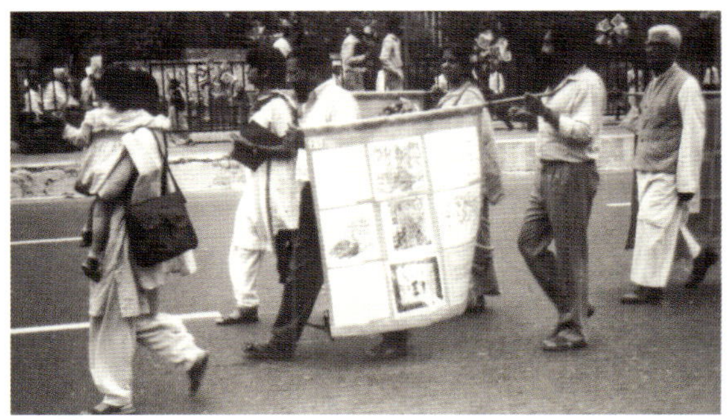

April 12: Sahmat presents the exhibition ***Images and Words,*** as part of the ***AAC*** campaign, involving more than 400 painters, writers, and photographers. The exhibition travels to 30 cities and then tours 40 schools in Delhi over the following year.

April 21–30: Exhibition of photographs made by children of Mangolpuri during *Janotsav*, at National Centre for Performing Arts, Bombay.

May: Rajiv Gandhi is assassinated in Tamil Nadu, during his election campaign.

November 10–25: Sahmat organizes ***Chauraha*** **(Crossroads), an All-India Street Theatre Workshop,** in New Delhi. Around 100 street theatre activists interact among themselves and with leading practitioners of theatre and other art forms.

1991–96

Congress-led government comes to power at the center with P. V. Narasimha Rao as prime minister.

1992

January 1: Sahmat presents ***Slogans for Communal Harmony,*** a public art project involving auto-rickshaw drivers in a contest to create slogans for communal harmony in New Delhi. In March, a similar contest of slogans for communal harmony is conducted in Bombay, involving the city's taxi drivers.

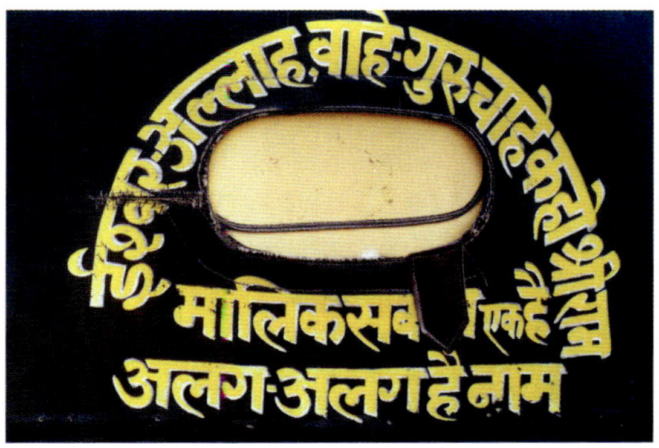

March 9–17: Sahmat presents several AAC events in Bombay including a 12-hour cultural sit-in and concert (March 14) at Shivaji Park; ***Images and Words*** exhibition and auction; street plays by Jana Natya Manch; film screenings; and a seminar on "Culture and Communalism."

May 14: Sahmat hosts a symposium on **"Freedom of Expression and Growing Intolerance."**

December 6: Babri Masjid (Babur's Mosque) in Ayodhya is demolished by Hindu nationalist activists during a rally-turned-riot at the culmination of the Ramjanmabhoomi movement. Widespread communal riots erupt around the country, including bloody riots in Bombay (December 1992–January 1993) and in Surat, Ahmedabad, Kanpur, Delhi, and other cities.

December 7–13: Sahmat holds a cultural protest against the demolition of the Babri Masjid at Safdar Hashmi Marg in New Delhi with protest music, poetry recitations, and installations and street painting by artists. Manjit Bawa and Paramjit Singh create the painting *Kaun Mara?* (Who Died?) on site.

December 25, 1992–January 1, 1993: Sahmat presents ***Anhad Garje*** (a phrase from the poet Kabir that roughly translates to "the silence reverberates"), a program inspired by the Sufi-Bhakti traditions, in New Delhi, Bombay, Surat, Valod, Baroda, Ahmedabad, and Lucknow. It includes concerts by classical musicians and folk singers, lectures by eminent scholars, and film screenings.

1993

Sahmat publishes a series of posters titled ***In Defense of Our Secular Tradition***, juxtaposing verses from Sufi-Bhakti poetry with paintings by some of India's best-known contemporary artists.

August 9: Sahmat presents an exhibition titled ***Hum Sab Ayodhya*** (**We Are All Ayodhya**) that explores the multifaceted history, geography, culture, and life of the people of Ayodhya. The exhibition is on view in 17 Indian cities.

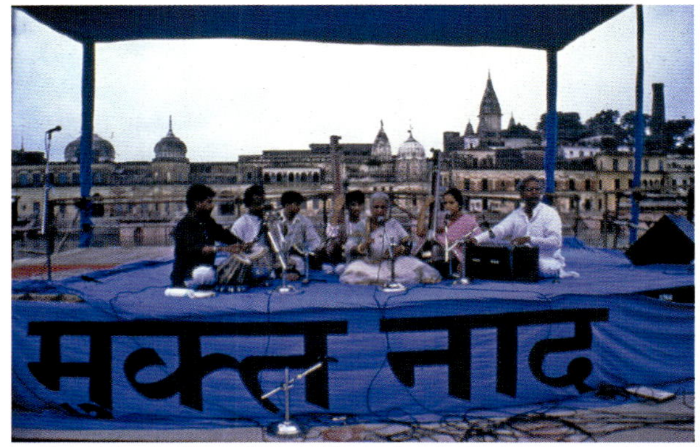

August 14–15: Sahmat organizes ***Muktnaad*** (Free Sound/Liberated Sound), a night of performances on the banks of the Sarayu at Ayodhya, in an effort to break the siege of the Hindutva forces through creative, rather than political action.

August 21: The "Ram-Katha" panel, delineating different versions of the *Ramayana* of the *Hum Sab Ayodhya* exhibition is confiscated from Teen Murti House, New Delhi; Sahmat files a case to revoke the confiscation order.

Assembly elections between 1993 and 1995 signal a major shift in Indian politics favoring a competitive multi-party system. The field consists of many smaller parties that represent the substantial ethnic, social, and regional diversity of India.

1994

January 1: Sahmat presents ***Safdar Hashmi Memorial: In Defense of Our Secular Tradition.***

January 30: Sahmat publishes ***Punchline: Cartoons Against Communalism***, a book of cartoons against communalism drawn from the period three months prior to and three months after the demolition of the Babri Masjid. More than 30 cartoonists participate in a seminar to discuss the specifics of the genre. An exhibition titled ***Punchline*** that comprises a selection of the cartoons is displayed in various schools in Delhi and travels to 25 cities in India.

April 13: Sahmat commemorates the **75th anniversary of the Jallianwala Bagh massacre,** which marked a turning point in the national movement for independence. The program includes the release of a poster; readings by actor Zohra Sehgal, film director Saeed Mirza, theatre director Ramgopal Bajaj, and Professor Malini Bhattacharya; and a performance of the play *Baghe Jallian* (once banned by the British), directed by M. K. Raina and performed by schoolchildren.

June 19: The Bajrang Dal (a hardline youth wing of the VHP) attacks the *Punchline* and *Hum Sab Ayodhya* exhibitions at a venue in Pune and destroys exhibition panels. The exhibition travels on to Ahmedabad with a fresh set of panels.

October: India's Supreme Court refuses to advise the central government on the bitter religious dispute between Hindus and Muslims regarding the mosque-temple site at Ayodhya. However, the Supreme Court upholds the government's takeover of the site.

1995

January 1: Sahmat presents ***Safdar Hashmi Memorial—Manas Bana: A Tribute to Mahatma Gandhi.***

October 2: Sahmat presents ***Postcards for Gandhi,*** commemorating the 125th anniversary of Mahatma Gandhi's birth.

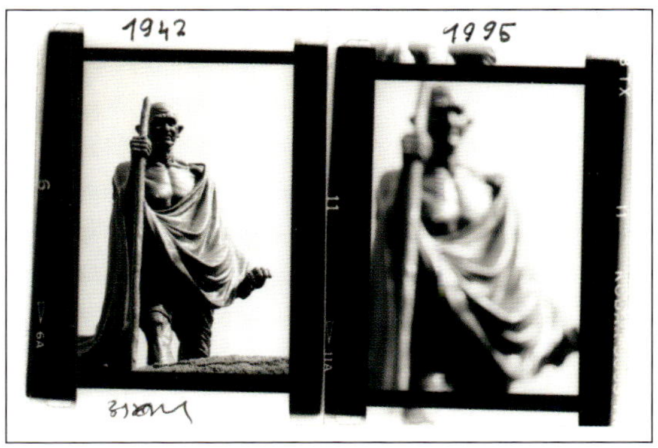

December 16: Sahmat organizes a protest meeting against the ban on Salman Rushdie's novel *The Moor's Last Sigh*, with public readings from the book.

1996

January 1: Sahmat presents ***Safdar Hashmi Memorial: Parwaaz.***

The BJP emerges as the single largest party in Parliament for the first time. Prime Minister Atal Behari Vajpayee cannot muster a majority, however, and the government falls after 13 days. United Front governments are formed by a coalition of parties opposed to the BJP, with H. D. Deve Gowda and then I. K. Gujral as prime minister, during 1996–98.

A campaign orchestrated by Hindu chauvinists is launched against India's most prominent modern artist, M. F. Husain (1915–2011). Sahmat organizes a protest march in New Delhi, which is attended by prominent politicians.

1997

January 1: Sahmat presents ***Safdar Hashmi Memorial: In Defense of Our Secular Tradition.***

May 11: Sahmat organizes an event celebrating the **140th anniversary of the 1857 Sepoy Revolt.** Classical singers and rock bands perform, setting old folk songs on the revolt to their own music. Large numbers of schoolchildren paint during a "paint sit-in."

September 11–20: Sahmat organizes ***Gift for India,*** an exhibition of 200 gift boxes made by artists from within and outside India, celebrating 50 years of India's independence.

1998

January 1: Sahmat presents ***Safdar Hashmi Memorial: In Defense of Our Secular Tradition***. Sahmat publishes a pledge to fight communalism, citing the assassination of Gandhi and the demolition of Babri Masjid in Ayodhya as instances of bigotry.

May: Mention in Parliament of ***Secularism Alert,*** a dossier prepared by Sahmat, by Rashtriya Janata Dal leader and Member of Parliament Lalu Prasad Yadav.

1998–2004

Atal Behari Vajpayee leads the National Democratic Alliance (NDA), a BJP-led coalition government, as prime minister.

1998

May: Hindutva groups mount attack on M. F. Husain's Mumbai residence. Sahmat holds a press conference to condemn the attack and an artists' delegation submits a memorandum to the president of India.

December: Hindutva groups attack iconic Hindi film actor Dilip Kumar's residence in Mumbai. Sahmat organizes a candlelight protest meeting at Home Minister L. K. Advani's New Delhi residence.

December 27–31: Sahmat organizes ***Dastak,*** a convention on secular cultural action.

1999

January 1: Sahmat presents ***Safdar Hashmi Memorial: In Defense of Our Secular Tradition.***

August 16–23: Sahmat produces ***Harvest of Hatred,*** a 38-panel poster exhibition documenting the attacks by right-wing communal forces on civil society, minorities, and cultural freedom. The exhibition travels to the cities of Nagpur, Jhansi, Bhopal, Kanpur, and Sihora over the next month.

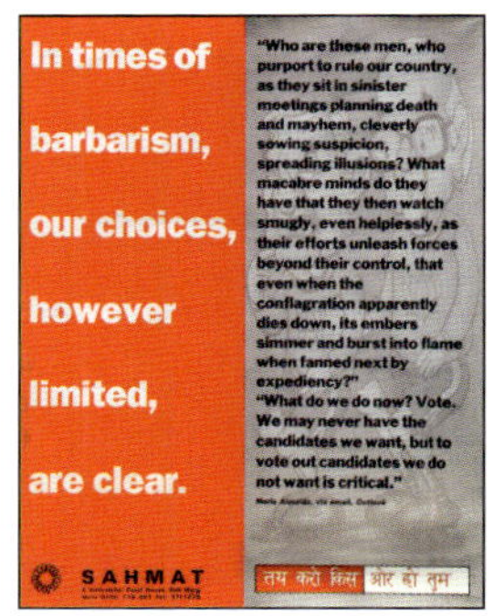

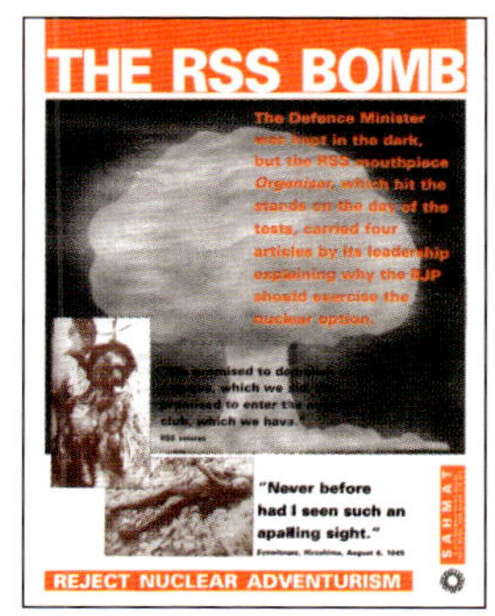

September 24–October 1: Hunger strike by Shabnam Hashmi at Gandhi Maidan, Lucknow, to protest a BJP attack on Sahmat Rangmanch (a theatre group started by Sahmat) while performing a street play against the communal politics of the BJP.

2000

January 1: Sahmat presents ***Safdar Hashmi Memorial: Tribute to freedom fighter Udham Singh.***

June 23–September 4: Hoopoe Curatorial presents ***Dust on the Road,*** an exhibition that showcases Sahmat's projects alongside works by Canadian artists, presenting it in five cities in Canada.

2001

January 1: Sahmat presents ***Safdar Hashmi Memorial.***

March–April: Sahmat organizes ***Art on the Move,*** a mobile exhibition. Artists are invited to submit proposals using ready-made vehicles as bases for sculptures that are taken around different locations in New Delhi.

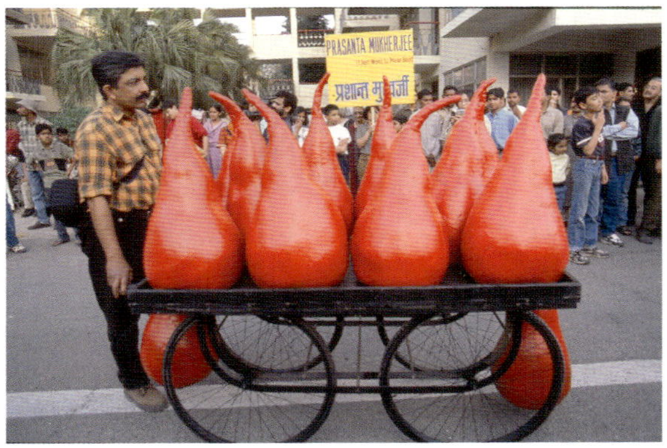

July 17: A Delhi High Court judgment lifts the ban on the Ram Katha panel in Sahmat's *Hum Sab Ayodhya* exhibition.

August 4–6: Sahmat organizes a convention on the **"Communalization of Education"** in New Delhi. More than 600 delegates, including education ministers from several Indian states, attend; the convention discusses the Hindu-nationalist education policy that the BJP-led government has been pursuing since it came to power in 1999.

September 11: Muslim terrorists attack the World Trade Center in New York City and the Pentagon in Arlington, Virginia. In October the United States retaliates by launching the War on Terror and invading Afghanistan.

2002

January 1: Sahmat presents ***Safdar Hashmi Memorial: Against War.***

February: Around 59 Hindu pilgrims and activists who were returning from Ayodha die aboard the Sabarmati Express when a mob sets one of the train cars on fire in Godhra, Gujarat. The incident triggers widespread violence against and brutal killing of hundreds of Muslims across the state.

March 1: Best Bakery, a business operated by a Muslim family in Vadodara, Gujarat, is attacked and burned by a mob of Hindutva activists, killing 14 (12 Muslims, 2 Hindus). The legal case is widely viewed as a test case for human rights and justice in India.

April 26–27: Sahmat (with *Communalism Combat*, Mumbai) presents **"Punish the Guilty: Testimony of Survivors":** testimonies by about 40 survivors from relief camps in Gujarat. A delegation including victims of the Gujarat violence meets President K. R. Narayanan. Sahmat also presents ***Listen to the Survivors—Genocide in Gujarat 2002,*** an exhibition of photographs from Gujarat by Sahir Raza, at Vitthalbhai Patel House, New Delhi.

December 23, 2002–January 4, 2003: Sahmat presents the exhibition ***Ways of Resisting: 1992–2002,*** at Lalit Kala Akademi Galleries, Rabindra Bhavan, New Delhi.

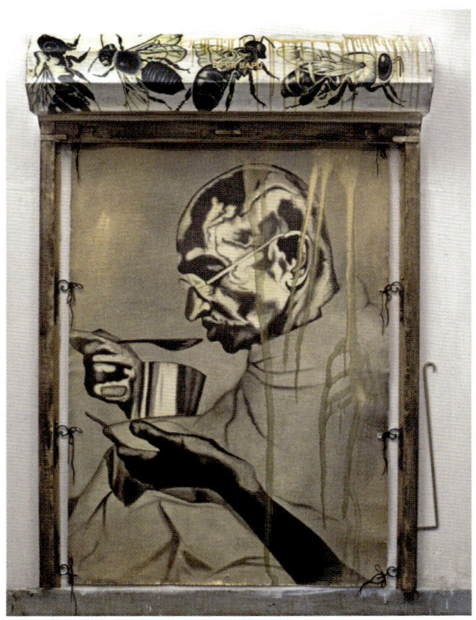

2003

January 1: Sahmat presents ***Safdar Hashmi Memorial: Ways of Resisting.***

February 26: Sahmat holds a meeting and press conference to protest the unveiling of a portrait of right-wing ideologue and leader V. D. Savarkar in Parliament House.

March 8: Sahmat organizes a meeting and press conference to critique the court order of the Lucknow Bench of Allahabad High Court directing the Archaeological Survey of India (ASI), to excavate the Babri Masjid site in Ayodhya.

April 12: On National Street Theatre Day, Sahmat organizes ***Dharti ko Aman Chahiye* (The World Needs Peace) anti–Iraq War program:** artworks, street play by Janam, anti-war readings, songs, poetry, and performances.

April 17: Sahmat holds a meeting and press conference on the destruction of the Baghdad Museum.

April 27: Sahmat holds a meeting and press conference on **"Gujarat: A State under Siege"** (with *Communalism Combat*).

June 17: Sahmat holds a meeting and press conference to discuss issues raised by the ASI's excavation of the Babri Masjid site.

July 11: Bhisham Sahni, eminent writer and chairman of Sahmat, passes away.

July 16: Sahmat hosts a condolence meeting for Bhisham Sahni.

August 29: Sahmat organizes a meeting and press conference to discuss the ASI report on excavation of the Babri Masjid site.

September 1: Sahmat organizes a meeting to protest attacks on Habib Tanvir and Naya Theatre, on the occasion of Habib Tanvir's 80th birthday.

October 9: Sahmat holds a protest meeting against attacks on Habib Tanvir and Naya Theatre; Janam and Act One stage plays.

November 2: Sahmat presents *The Making of India* in Chennai (with Asian College of Journalism and Swaralaya): exhibition, seminar, and an evening of Sufi-Bhakti music and dance performances.

November 3: The judgment is handed down in Safdar Hashmi's case, 14 years after his murder. The accused, Mukesh Sharma and 12 others, are found guilty by a Ghaziabad court.

December 29: Sahmat holds a seminar on "The Making of India," in New Delhi.

2004

The first United Progressive Alliance (UPA), a coalition government led by the Congress Party, with Manmohan Singh as prime minister, comes to power after the general election, ending the rule of the BJP-led NDA government.

January 1: Sahmat presents ***Safdar Hashmi Memorial: The Making of India.***

January 6–12: Sahmat presents ***The Making of India*** exhibition.

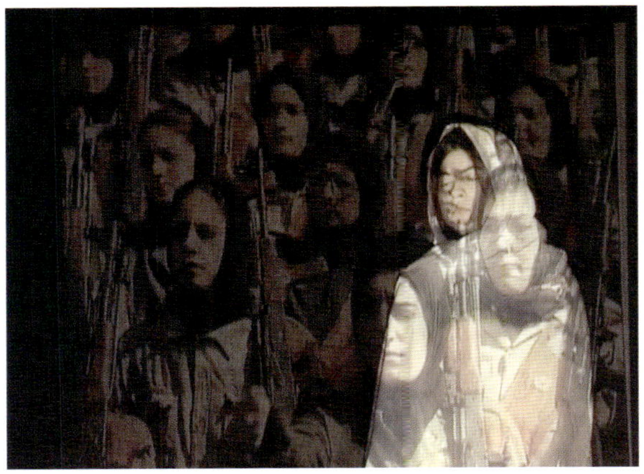

January 31: Sahmat holds a protest meeting against destruction by the VHP and Bajrang Dal of paintings by M. F. Husain and Chitrabanu Majumdar in the Golden Art Gallery of Art and Textiles, Surat.

February 21: Sahmat holds a protest meeting against attacks on culture (with Janvadi Lekhak Sangh); poster and book release, *Barbarians at the Gate.*

April 10–12: Sahmat celebrates **National Street Theatre Day** on Safdar's 50th birthday with a lecture, "Republic of Hunger" by Utsa Patnaik; book release, *Republic of Hunger*; and street plays by Naya Theatre and Janam.

June 11: Sahmat holds a convention demanding withdrawal of "saffronized" NCERT (National Council of Educational Research and Training) textbooks.

July 5: Sahmat holds a symposium on **"India: An Economic Agenda for 2004."**

October 19: Sahmat organizes a convention to deliberate issues arising from the proposed draft for the Employment Guarantee Act.

November 13: Sahmat holds a symposium on **"Justice in Gujarat."**

2005

January 1: Sahmat presents ***Safdar Hashmi Memorial: Commemorating Munshi Premchand's 125th Birth Anniversary.***

February 10–27: Sahmat presents an exhibition and symposium on iconic Urdu and Hindi writer Premchand at Jamia Millia Islamia University, New Delhi.

March 12: Sahmat commemorates the ***75th Anniversary of Gandhi's Dandi March (Salt Satyagraha)*** with an exhibition, symposium, book release of *Dhundhle Padchinh*, a Dandi March poster, and music by Vidya Shah.

April 14–17: Sahmat holds a convention in support of Gujarat victims: **"Flashback–2002–Gujarat Genocide" (with *Communalism Combat*).**

May 25: Sahmat holds a convention on undoing the anti-secular legacy of the BJP/NDA regime: **"The Unfinished Agenda in Education and Culture."**

August 6: Sahmat holds **"Debating Education I,"** a convention on school education, demanding revision of the National Curricular Framework.

September 24: Sahmat holds **"Debating Education II,"** a convention on higher education.

2006

January 1: Sahmat presents ***Safdar Hashmi Memorial: 75th Anniversary of the Dandi March.***

May 8: Sahmat leads a delegation of artists to meet Home Minister Shivraj Patil, in support of artist M. F. Husain.

September 2: Sahmat hosts **"Iconography Now: Rewriting Art History,"** a symposium in support of M. F. Husain and against communal assaults on art and culture in India, coinciding with the release of a book of essays under the same title.

November: The Report of the Sachar Committee (a committee set up by Prime Minister Manmohan Singh) on the social, economic, and educational status of Muslims in India is released. It is the first official attempt since India's independence to conduct a systematic, data-based survey of the status of a minority community.

2007

January 1: Sahmat presents ***Safdar Hashmi Memorial: 150th Anniversary of the 1857 Revolt.***

January 30–February 5: Sahmat organizes ***Making History Our Own,*** an exhibition celebrating 60 years of India's independence and the 150th anniversary of the 1857 Revolt.

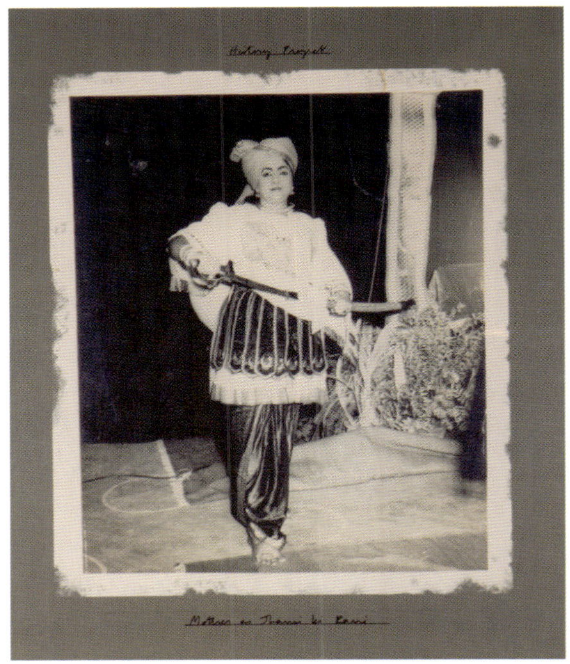

February 22–24: Sahmat holds a seminar on **"India Independent: Economics, Politics & Culture"** (with *Social Scientist*).

April 12–19: Sahmat's exhibition ***Making History Our Own*** is on view at its second venue, the Women's Press Club of India, New Delhi.

May 14: Sahmat holds a protest meeting at Rabindra Bhavan, New Delhi, against the right-wing attack on students and faculty of the Faculty of Fine Arts, M.S. University of Baroda, Vadodara, Gujarat.

Bomb explosion in Samjhauta Express, a train service that connects New Delhi, India, to Lahore, Pakistan. Of the 68 fatalities, most are Pakistanis. It is thought to be the work of a Muslim militant group until 2012, when investigations reveal that Hindutva extremists were responsible for the bombing.

October 2: Sahmat organizes a street festival on the lawns of Vitthalbhai Patel House in New Delhi to celebrate **M. F. Husain's 92nd birthday.** The location is near Husain's mural of Jawaharlal Nehru on the wall of the Council of Scientific and Industrial Research building, which was done in the early 1960s.

2008

January 1: Sahmat presents ***Safdar Hashmi Memorial: Jashn-e-Dauran, Envisioning the Modern*** with talks on the works of M. F. Husain, photographer Sunil Janah, and artist Chittaprosad, and renderings of IPTA songs.

May 19: Sahmat organizes a meeting on the M. F. Husain judgment delivered by Delhi High Court; book release, *Maqbool Fida Husain . . . Petitioner.*

July: Government of India signs a nuclear deal with the United States. Left parties withdraw support to the Congress-led United Progressive Alliance (UPA) government in protest.

August 22–25: Sahmat organizes an exhibition of reproductions of M. F. Husain's works and photographs of Husain by other artists at the Vitthalbhai Patel House lawns, in protest against his absence at the India Art Summit. The exhibition is vandalized on August 24.

August 26–September 2: Sahmat presents the Husain exhibition at Jamia Millia Islamia University, New Delhi.

September 1: Sahmat inaugurates the program ***Of Resonance and Resistance: 20 Years of Sahmat,*** with Habib Tanvir's 85th birthday celebration, a panel discussion, and songs by Naya Theatre.

October–November: Sahmat presents the program *Of Resonance and Resistance: 20 Years of Sahmat*: Sufi-Bhakti music concerts by Madan Gopal Singh, Shubha Mudgal, Dhruv Sangari, Rekha Raj, Deepak Castelino, Pritam Ghoshal, and Sunanda Sharma.

2009

January 1: Sahmat presents ***Safdar Hashmi Memorial: 20 Years of Sahmat.***

January: Sahmat presents lectures by Akeel Bilgrami on "Some Threats to Democratic Culture," and Arindam Dutta on "Media, c. 1993."

January 15–February 14: Sahmat produces ***Image, Music, Text: 20 Years of Sahmat,*** a retrospective exhibition, at M. F. Husain Art Gallery, Jamia Millia Islamia University, New Delhi. Music concerts by Madan Gopal Singh, Rekha Raj, Vidya Shah.

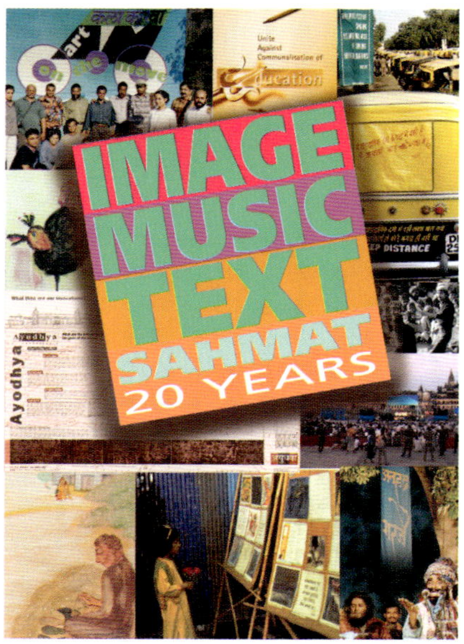

March: The Congress Party–led UPA wins a majority in the general election and comes back to power.

June 8: Theatre personality Habib Tanvir, chairman of Sahmat, passes away.

June 10: Sahmat holds a meeting: **"Remembering Habib Tanvir."**

August 8: Sahmat holds a convention: **"Debating Education 4: The Neoliberal Thrust in Education."**

August 24: Sahmat presents a lecture by Geeta Kapur: "Exile of M. F. Husain."

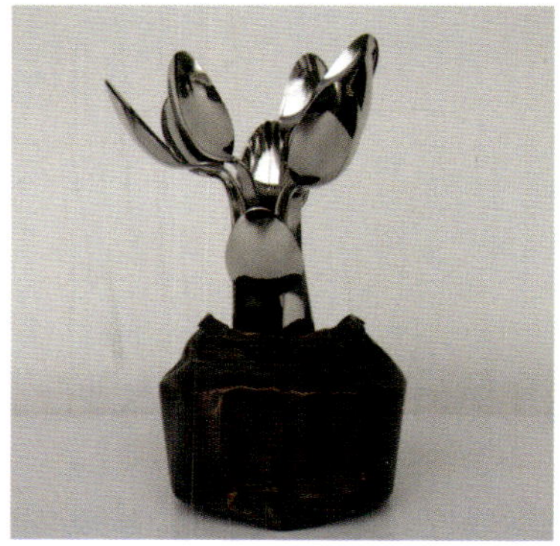

September 17–24: Sahmat organizes the exhibition ***For Husain at 94,*** at M. F. Husain Art Gallery, Jamia Millia Islamia University, New Delhi.

November 7: Sahmat hosts a lecture by Ram Rahman: "Sunil Janah: Photographing India in the 1940s and '50s."

November 19: Sahmat hosts the program ***Remembering Faiz Ahmad Faiz*** on the eve of Faiz's 25th death anniversary; Shubha Mudgal sings.

November 25: Sahmat hosts a lecture by Geeta Kapur, in memory of Rummana Hussain: "Rummana's Question: is it what you think?"

December 6: Sahmat's exhibition *Hum Sab Ayodhya* is remounted.

2010

January 1: Sahmat presents ***Safdar Hashmi Memorial.***

July 28: Sahmat hosts symposium **"Unravelling Hindu Terror."**

August 28: Sahmat hosts symposium **"Kashmir/Culture?"**

September 17: Sahmat organizes ***Husain @ 95,*** a celebration of M. F. Husain's 95th birthday, at Jamia Millia Islamia University, New Delhi.

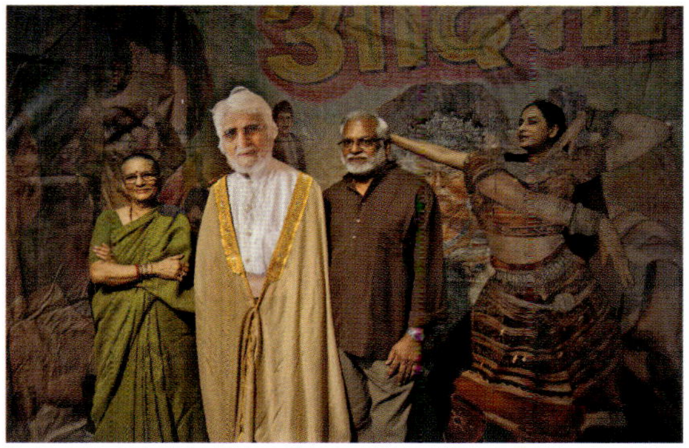

December 6–8: Sahmat hosts an all India seminar on **"Fact and Faith: Democracy after the Ayodhya Verdict"** (with *Communalism Combat* and *Social Scientist*).

2011

January 1: Sahmat presents ***Safdar Hashmi Memorial:*** **Faiz Ahmad Faiz birth centenary celebration.**

June 9: M. F. Husain passes away in London at the age of 95.

July 2: Sahmat presents ***Husain Utsav*** **(Festival): Tribute to M. F. Husain.**

August 12: Sahmat hosts a seminar: **"Marxism Today."**

September 17: Sahmat hosts **M. F. Husain's birthday celebration** at Jamia Millia Islamia University.

October 13–15: Sahmat organizes an all India seminar to commemorate 75 years of the Progressive Cultural Movement in India: ***"Awaaz Do!"*** **(Raise Your Voice!).**

December 17: Sahmat presents a symposium on **"Redefining the Secular in Indian Society."**

2012

January 1: Sahmat presents ***Safdar Hashmi Memorial:*** celebration of the centenaries of three progressive Hindi poets: Kedarnath Singh, Shamsher Bahadur Singh, and Nagarjun.

February 27: Sahmat organizes a meeting to observe the 10-year anniversary of the genocide in Gujarat.

April 12: Sahmat celebrates National Street Theatre Day with the release of the book *Balraj and Bhisham Sahni: Brothers in Political Theatre* and a music concert by Madan Gopal Singh.

May–June: Sahmat celebrates Rabindranath Tagore's birth centenary: ***Tagore Tells and the Patua Paints,*** an exhibition of artworks illustrating three of Tagore's stories for children, made by *patuas*, traditional visual artists from Bengal, and the release of the three illustrated books in English, Hindi, and Bengali.

September 17: Sahmat organizes ***Imaging a Legend,*** an exhibition of photographs in tribute to M. F. Husain, Jamia Millia Islamia, New Delhi.

September 28–29: Sahmat presents **"Celebrating 100 Years of Manto,"** a seminar on Saadat Hasan Manto with participation from writers and scholars from Pakistan and India.

October 11: Sahmat (with Act One and Parcham) organizes ***Sangharsh ke Geet,*** an evening of protest music, with the release of a music DVD of Parcham's new collection of songs, and performances by Parcham, Madan Gopal Singh, Jasbir Jassi, and Harpreet.

2013

January 1: Sahmat presents ***23rd Safdar Hashmi Memorial.***

February 14: ***The Sahmat Collective: Art and Activism in India since 1989*** opens at the Smart Museum of Art at the University of Chicago.

1989 Sahmat's Beginnings

On January 1, 1989, Safdar Hashmi—political activist, actor, playwright, poet—and his theatre group, Jana Natya Manch, were violently attacked while performing a street play in Sahibabad, an industrial area on the outskirts of Delhi. The play, titled *Halla Bol!* (Raise Your Voice!), was being performed as part of a campaign in support of a workers' strike. Hashmi died of his injuries the next day.

Hashmi was thirty-four years old when he died. Like many young men and women of his generation in India, Hashmi was deeply committed to secularism and egalitarianism—principles that drove the nation's struggle for independence from British colonial rule. After completing graduate work in literature he began an academic career, but soon his interest in theatre merged with his growing political commitment and he became a full-time political activist. During the late 1970s and 1980s, Hashmi moved close to the Left, eventually becoming a member of the Communist Party of India (Marxist). He simultaneously embraced political theatre and street theatre, and led the growth of the Jana Natya Manch (popularly known by its abbreviated form *Janam*, meaning "birth" in Hindi) into a forum of democratic and accessible theatre aimed at political change.

Hashmi's brutal, politically motivated death aroused a spontaneous, nationwide wave of revulsion, grief, and resistance, transforming him from outspoken political artist to a lasting symbol of the very values that his murderers had sought to crush.

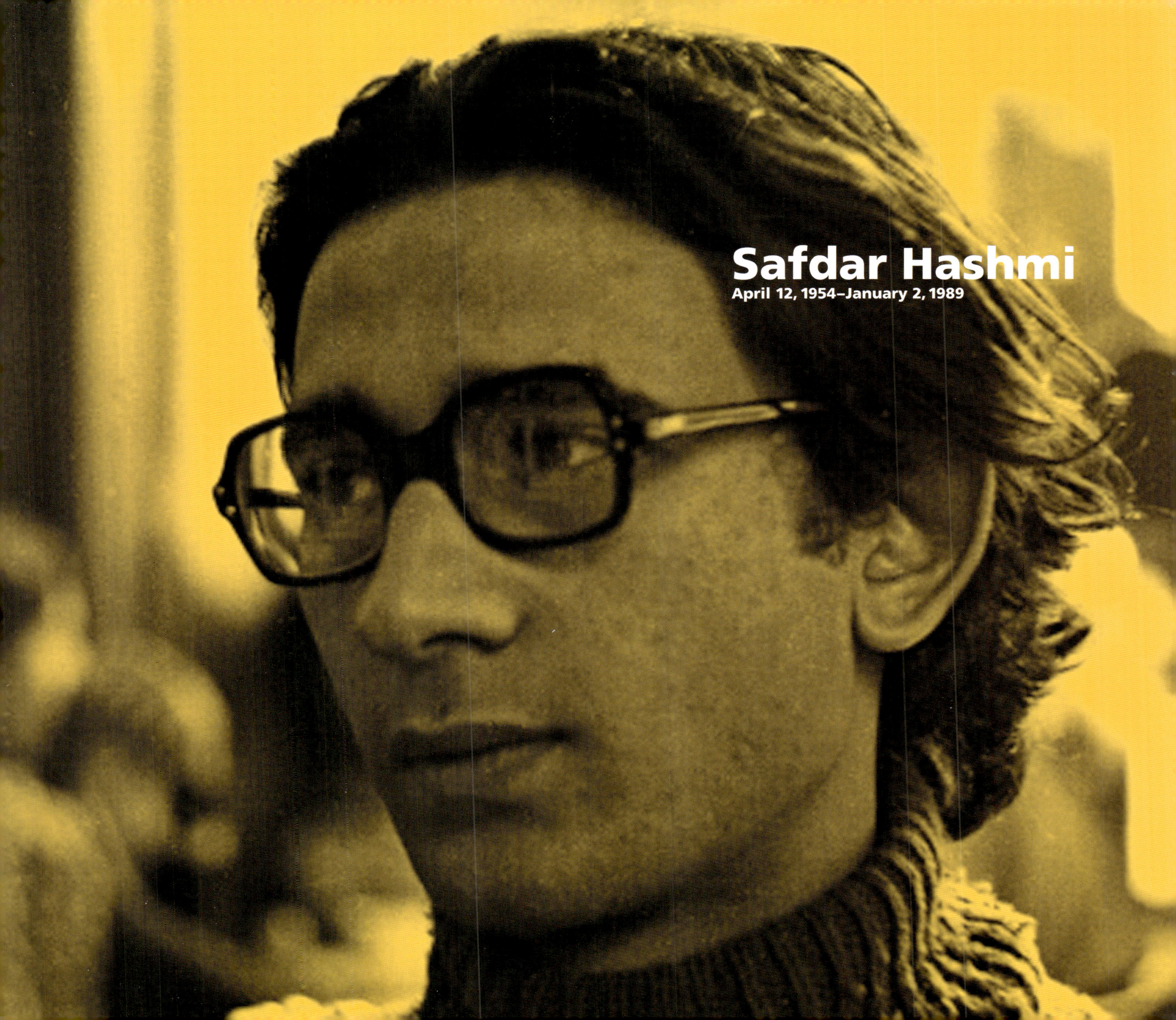
Safdar Hashmi
April 12, 1954–January 2, 1989

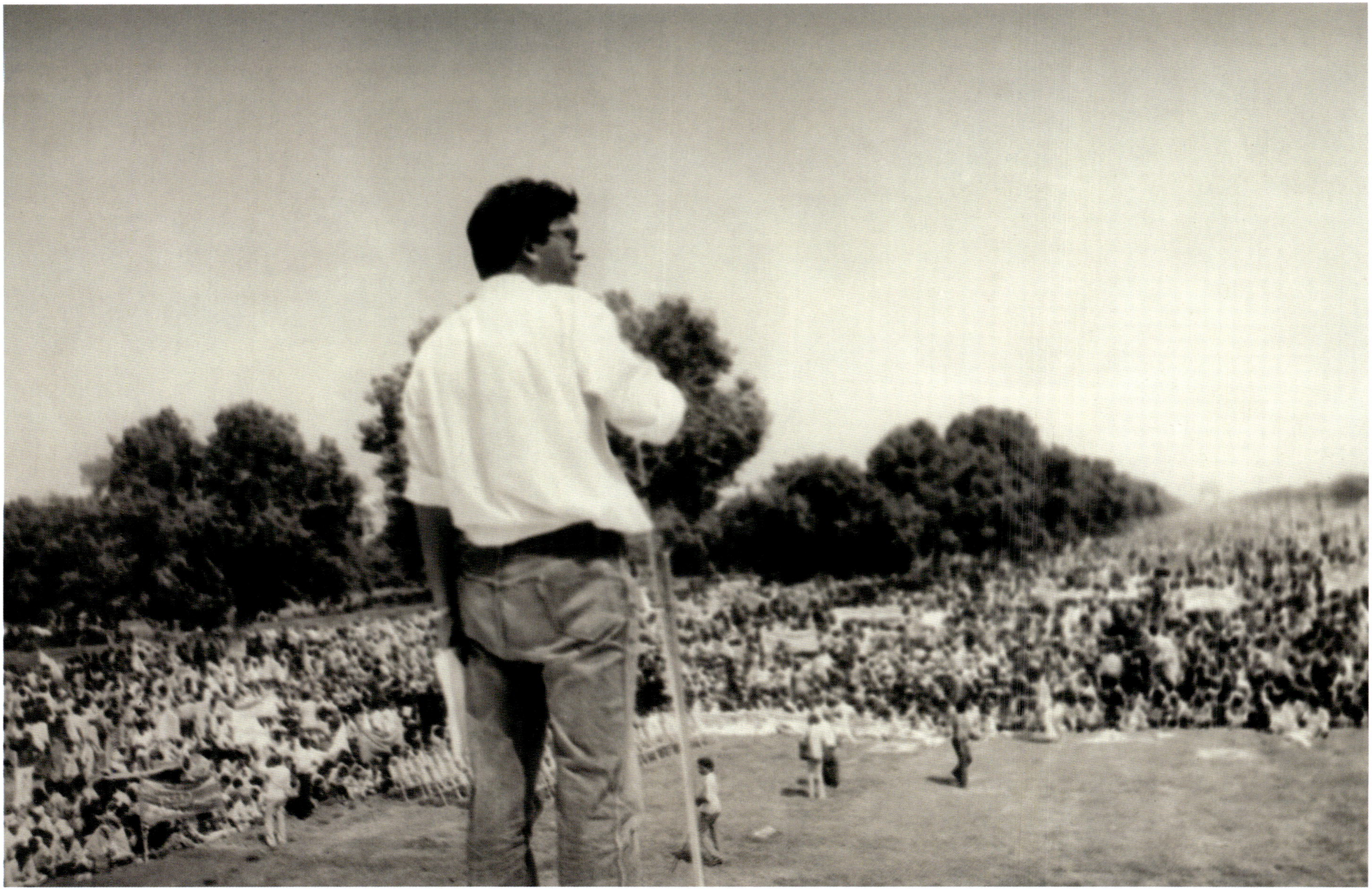

Safdar Hashmi at a political rally, ca. 1980s. Photo courtesy Janam archive.

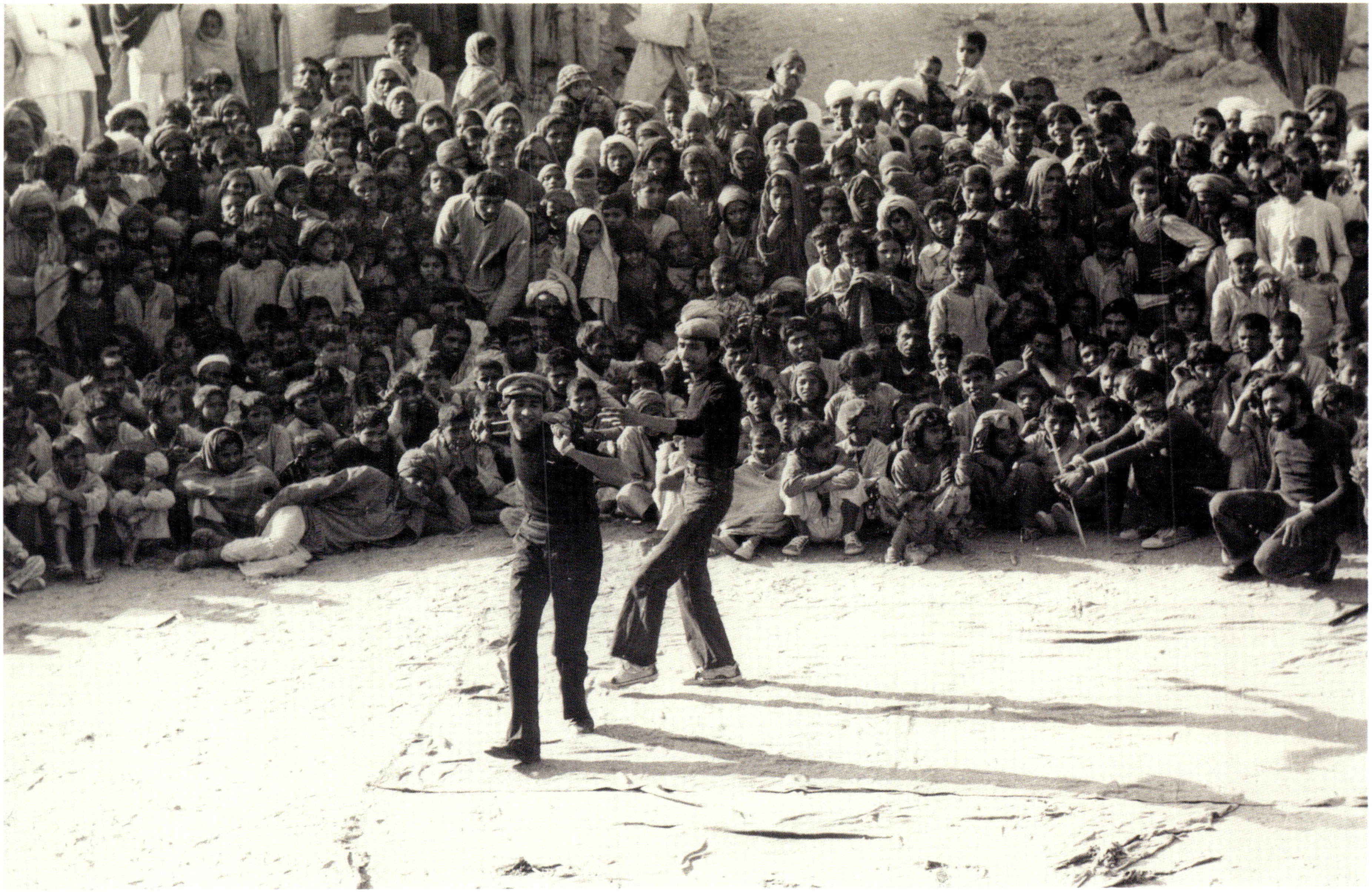

Safdar Hashmi (front) performing in the Janam street play *Aaya Chunav* (The Elections Are Here), Hissar, Haryana, 1981. Photo: Surendra Rajan, courtesy Janam archive.

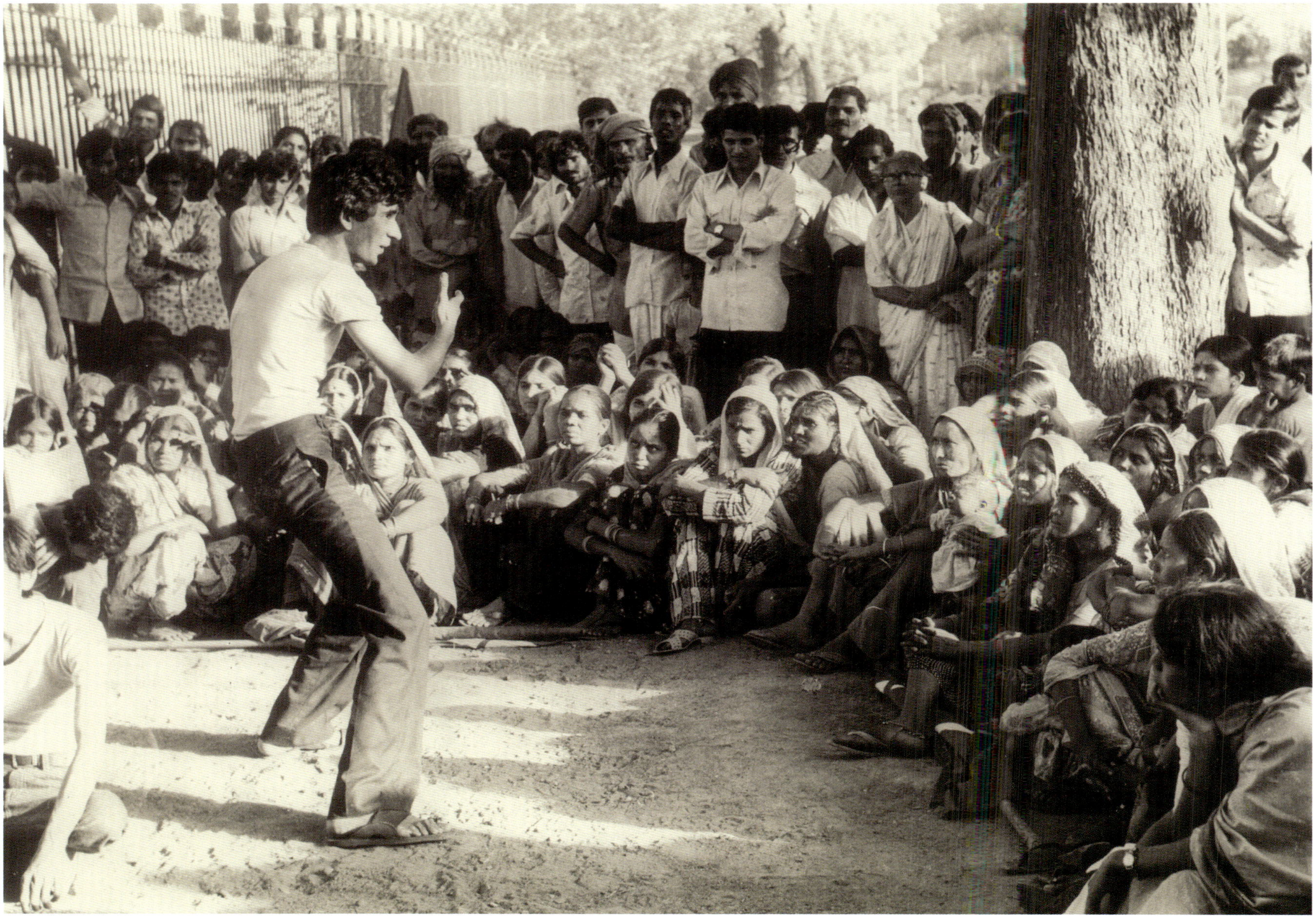

Safdar Hashmi performing in a Janam street play, ca. late 1970s. Photo courtesy Janam archive.

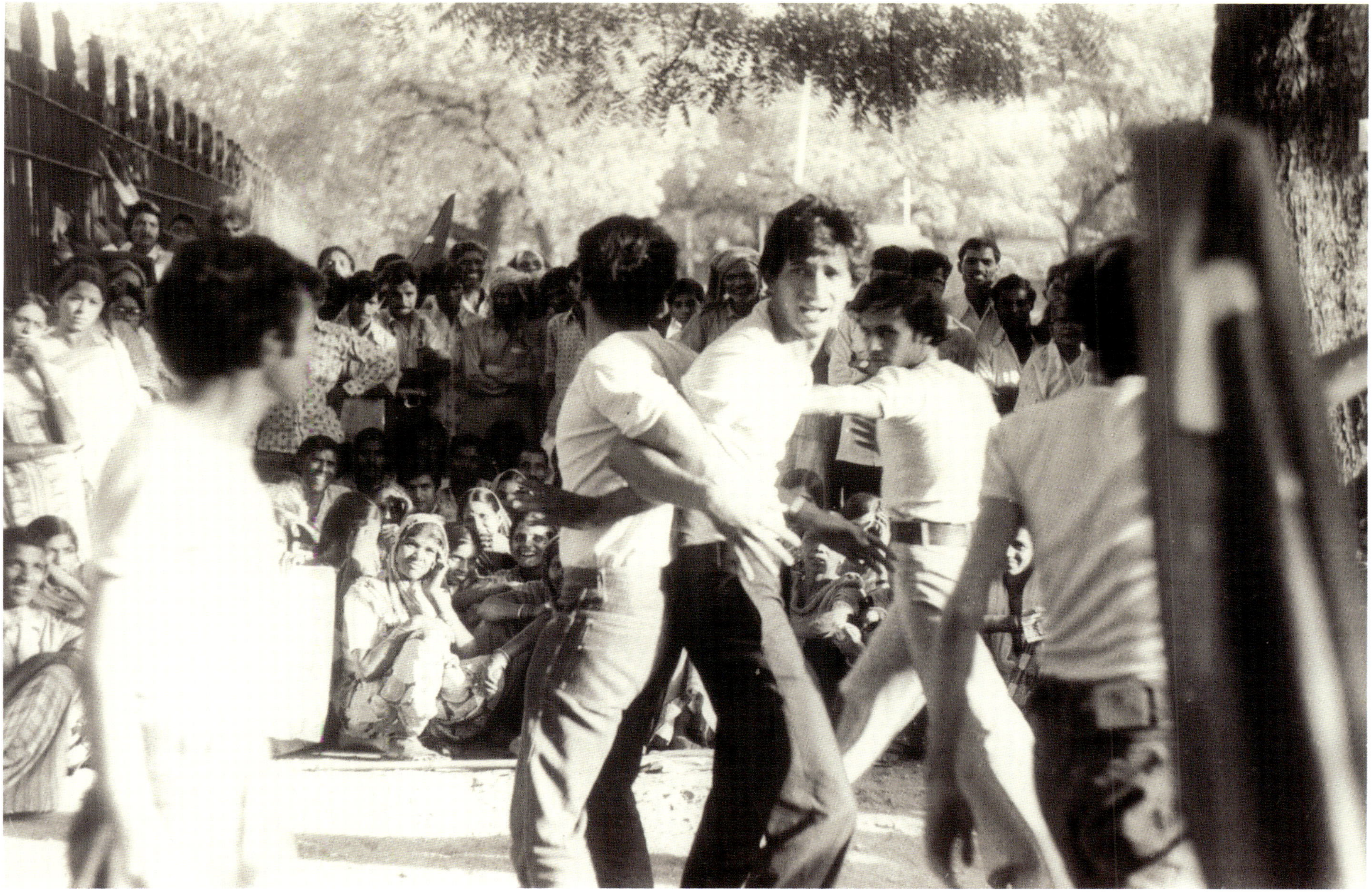

Safdar Hashmi (center) performing in a Janam street play, ca. late 1970s. Photo courtesy Janam archive.

Qamar Azad Hashmi

Excerpt from Qamar Azad Hashmi, *The Fifth Flame*, translated from Urdu by Madhu Prasad and Sohail Hashmi (Delhi: Penguin Books, 1997).

Safdar Hashmi amar rahe! Long live Safdar Hashmi! The slogan reverberates through the cold, grey January morning. The pain has spread. It flows like the flag, red with the blood of countless young martyrs, that covers and protects his body like a loving friend. The pain has spread. Like gold tested in the fire, it purifies the spirit. There is a single pledge. Comrade, your name, your actions, your commitment, will never be forgotten. Your courage brings strength to these arms today. Your love will envelop us, today and in the future. We will not give up hope. Though you no longer walk beside us, your laughter and your songs will rise again from our throats, and when we advance to new revolutionary goals, your example will be there for us, encouraging us to forge further ahead. Comrade, farewell!

The streets of Delhi, accustomed to the sound of Safdar's light-hearted step, to the music of his voice and his laughter, are silent and stunned. With a thunderous crash the crystal has shattered. It splinters with a brittle brilliance. The fragments will never become whole again. What has happened cannot be undone. The funeral procession moves on. The sorrow spreads; it reaches out and touches everyone, and everything. Heartbroken but determined, thousands accompany the mortal remains of a beloved friend and revolutionary on his last journey, and then, eternal rest. Safdar, vibrantly alive, is no more. No one seems to understand what has happened. No one is able to make sense of it. What do we do now? What am I to do now? I cannot think, cannot feel any more. But life, like death, is an eternal truth. One has to live, for oneself, for others, for realizing Safdar's ideals. Wipe your tears, comrades. Lift your torches. Light the flames. Bid farewell to Safdar today. Wear his image round your neck and let the world know that Safdar will not be forgotten. The leaping flames of the *mashaal* [torch] tear away the veil of darkness. Light spills into the streets. Run out into those streets and sing the songs he loved so well. We will not mourn Safdar. We will remember him in celebration.

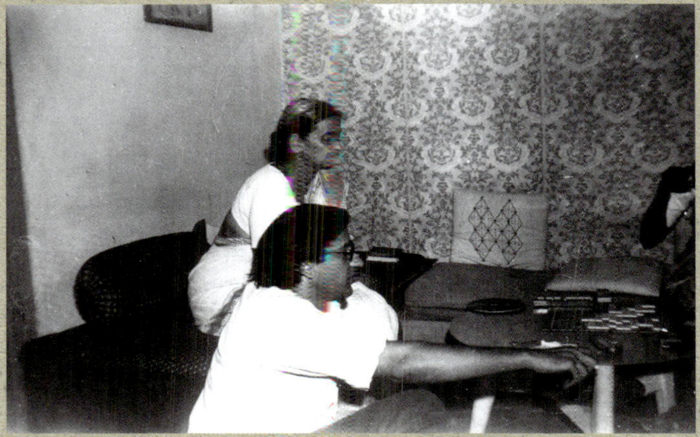

Safdar Hashmi with his mother, Qamar Azad Hashmi.

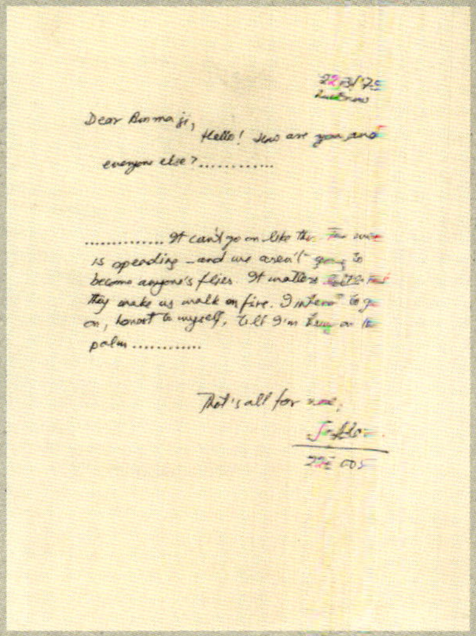

Letter from Safdar Hashmi to his mother, Qamar Azad Hashmi, dated March 22, 1979.

Hello! How are you and everyone else?............

...........It can't go on like this. The web is spreading—and we aren't going to become anyone's flies. It matters little that they make us walk on fire. I intend to go on, honest to myself, till I'm hung on the palm.............

That's all for now,
Safdar

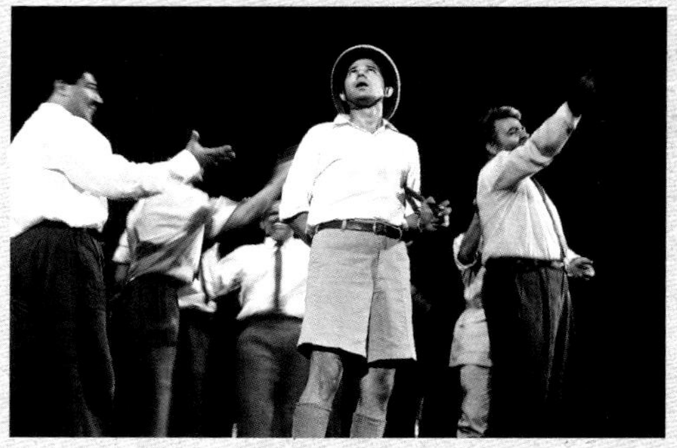

Safdar Hashmi (center) in the play *Motey Ram ka Satyagraha*, (The Resistance of Motey Ram), directed by Habib Tanvir for Janam, 1988. In a staging of the play in 1989, after Hashmi's death, Habib Tanvir played the same role.

Habib Tanvir

Translated excerpt from Habib Tanvir, "Safdar Hashmi: Some Personal Reminiscences," in *Safdar* (Hindi) (Delhi: Rajkamal Prakashan, 1989).

A theatre artist and a revolutionary—roll them inseparably into one—that was Safdar Hashmi. His father was a colleague of mine; we both worked at the Soviet Information Department in Delhi for a time. One day when Safdar was 18 or 19, his father brought him to meet me. He said the boy was my fan and he was following in my footsteps. He had seen all my plays and decided he would be in theatre. He added that he had started acting and "was turning quite red," referring to Safdar's political activities as an emerging student leader. It is one of the greatest ironies of our times that just when Safdar had indeed begun to mature as a revolutionary artist, he was so brutally snatched away from the scene. Revolution and art were both ingrained in his nature, and with courage, integrity, and discipline, he went about acquiring an awareness of human affairs. This included adequate knowledge of the humanities and the social sciences, which he diligently began to study right from his student days. His general knowledge was vast, and his mastery of the languages Urdu, Hindi, and English was amazing. It was a pleasure to talk to him on any subject. . . .

As an activist, Safdar worked under impossible conditions. I witnessed quite a few of his street plays performed in the far-flung congested colonies of Delhi on mushy ground and in extremely oppressive weather. From traveling early in the day to performing at various places and returning late at night, it must have been rough-going all along. To have a lucrative job as Safdar did and carry on like this day after day, it must take some love of the people and some dedication.

He wrote the scripts for these plays about day-to-day issues concerning various sections of the working people, wrote songs for them, often set them to tunes himself, and participated in them as singer, actor, and director. That was some activity, and it continued for not less than ten years without pause.

He wrote verses beautifully but never thought much of himself as a poet. He directed and then apologized that he did not know how. He acted so well, but he considered himself a non-actor. He was a leader who never thought himself to be one. He was imbued with an exquisite sense of humor and laughed at all things laughable all the time. He had only to make an entry into a household and the atmosphere was electrified and all sunshine. These were some of the qualities that made him into a leader—qualities seldom seen in most others. After ten years of street theatre activity, Safdar turned back to have another look at what he called the mainstream of theatre. Sometimes he called it the proscenium theatre as opposed to street theatre. He had practised it for quite a few years a long time ago. He said he had almost forgotten all he had learned from it and felt alienated. He wanted to return to it, if only to carry on his street theatre with greater skill. He chalked out a program of action. The first step was to get me to direct a play for his group. The result was the production of *Motey Ram ka Satyagraha*, a dramatization of a short story by Hindi writer Munshi Premchand, last July [1988]. The next steps included drama workshops with M. K. Raina, Bansi Kaul, and others. . . .

I have never enjoyed working in such close cooperation with another artist more. I have never witnessed a more humane leader—a leader having a stronger hold over a motley group of actors from all walks of life, with different political opinions. I have not come across a more effective teacher of political action. There is a general false notion about revolutionaries being mere firebrands. The human service, insight, genuine sympathy, and sheer good nature, which all help to make a genuine revolutionary are often forgotten. Safdar stood to correct this notion through his life's work. I recall my need last July for medical attention at Safdarjung Hospital for a patient, one of my artists. When I mentioned this, Safdar sent young medical students to the patient's residence, arranged check-ups with doctors at the hospital, and remained with me and the patient for hours during those long and dreary check-ups. And all this during a time when he was neckdeep in work. I was amazed at his acquaintance and influence with ever so many medicos in most of the major hospitals of Delhi. Such popularity, as we well know, comes from give-and-take, involving at some level some personal service. I consider this an important aspect of Safdar's revolutionary nature. . . .

Safdar's murder was committed in broad daylight and deliberately. He was attacked while performing his play *Halla Bol* in Sahibabad district, Ghaziabad, the afternoon of New Year's Day. The next evening, at about 10 pm he succumbed to his injuries. . . . His injuries were multiple and they were all head injuries inflicted by *lathis* [sticks carried by Indian police] and crowbars. He was attacked by a mob with the intent to kill and they apparently took their time in doing the job to the finish, while the police connived either by ignoring or by keeping themselves deliberately away.

It was his death that revealed to us the extraordinary extent of his popularity. What is more, it is his death that now seems to work the miracles he had only aspired for in his life. He lived and died for one cause: to change our society for the better. It is impossible to conceive greater consistency. If that result is achieved through his death, he would not have died in vain. If Safdar's death can really bring all artists and intellectuals together and get them to align with the oppressed working people in a solid front, he would not have died in vain.

MOLOYASHREE HASHMI

The working-class movement was on the upswing in the mid-1980s. The workers of Delhi went on a one-day strike in 1986, a three-day strike in 1987, and a seven-day strike in 1988. This was the biggest working-class action in the history of Delhi's labor movement. When Safdar learned that the Centre of Indian Trade Unions (CITU, the trade union organization connected to the Communist Party of India [Marxist]), of which he was a member, was planning a seven-day strike, he was very excited. There was never a doubt that Janam would do a play for this.

The play that emerged, *Chakka Jaam* (The Wheels Grind to a Halt), was largely written by Safdar, but he was also able to get one or two younger members of the group to contribute ideas, and a couple of the scenes were not even written by him. The play was wonderful—funny, innovative, and rousing. The workers loved it. The play became a huge hit with them. The strike itself was a huge success (though not because of the play!). The movement made many tangible gains.

After the strike, Safdar suggested we update the play to the post-strike situation. This version of the play was called *Halla Bol!* (Raise Your Voice!), and we began performing this version in mid-December 1988. The performance on January 1, 1989 was a part of this series.

In Sahibabad, Ghaziabad, the satellite town of Delhi where the attack took place, the capitalists, with help from criminal elements, had threatened and on occasion attacked our trade union comrades. As a matter of fact, some of the capitalists were themselves criminals! So the attack on Janam took place in this overall context.

After nearly two decades municipal council elections were taking place in Ghaziabad. The play began that morning fairly uneventfully. Midway through, though, the attackers (who we later learned were connected to the then-ruling party at the center) arrived in an election procession and insisted on passing through the very spot where we were performing. Safdar and a couple of our trade union comrades spoke to them, and it looked as if the matter was resolved. But it turned out to be a feint: they had retreated only to get their iron rods and other weapons. Before we knew what was happening, a full-scale attack was upon us. Naturally, everybody ran in whatever direction they could. Safdar led the largest group, about seven or eight actors and some comrades, to the nearby office of the CITU. The attackers followed us there, and in trying to ensure that everybody else could flee to safety, Safdar was caught. He was dragged to the spot of the performance and beaten repeatedly on his head, and left for dead. Three of our actors reached that spot some time later and managed to take him to the hospital. Safdar never regained consciousness, and he died in hospital the following day, January 2, 1989.

Safdar was cremated on January 3. About 15,000 people marched that day in protest. Then, on January 4, Janam returned to the spot of the attack and completed the disrupted play. Again, thousands of people came out in support. The next day there was a silent march through the downtown area of Delhi, which culminated in a massive condolence meeting. It was here that the first announcement of a trust being formed in his memory was made.

SOHAIL HASHMI

For about two years before he died Safdar had been planning to raise funds to create a space where politically committed young women and men could come together to train in theatre, music, writing, filmmaking, and other forms of agitational propaganda. He was unhappy with the quality of material that the progressive cultural movement was producing and wanted to create a center of excellence. He was not prepared to accept the argument that because the cultural movement of the working class had limited resources, it should make do with what was available. In Safdar's eyes making do was an argument that only led to mediocrity, and he did not want to make any compromise on quality.

Safdar Hashmi (right) with brother Sohail Hashmi and their nephews.

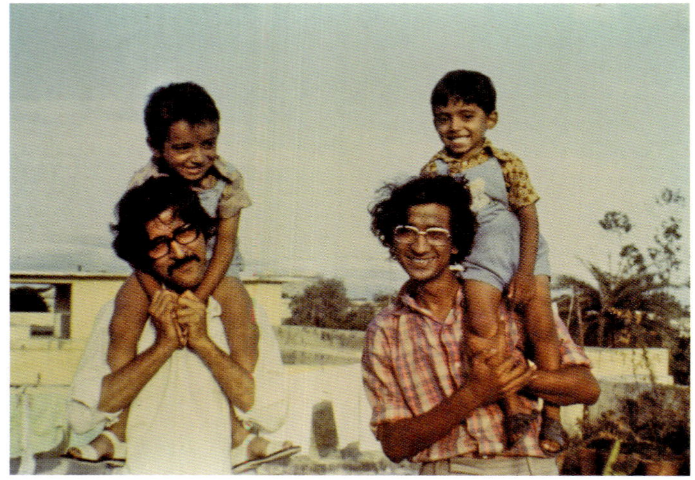

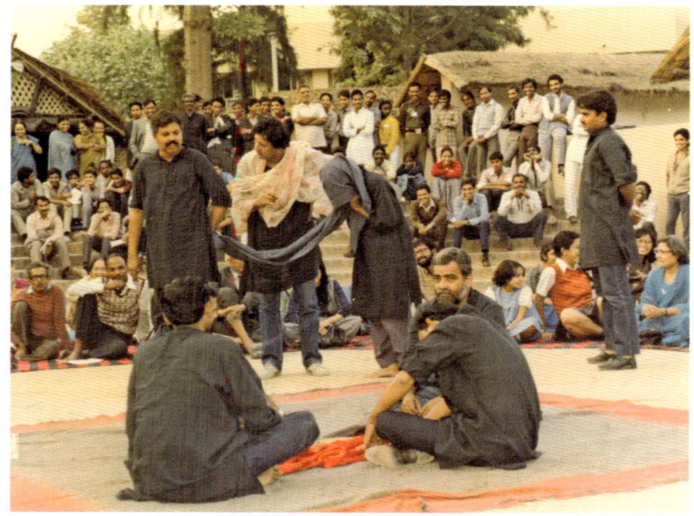

Safdar Hashmi (in shawl) performing in *Aurat* (Woman) at Pragati Maidan in Delhi, 1986.

►
RAM RAHMAN
Safdar Hashmi's Funeral Procession, January 3, 1989, Vitthalbhai Patel House, New Delhi, photograph, dimensions variable.

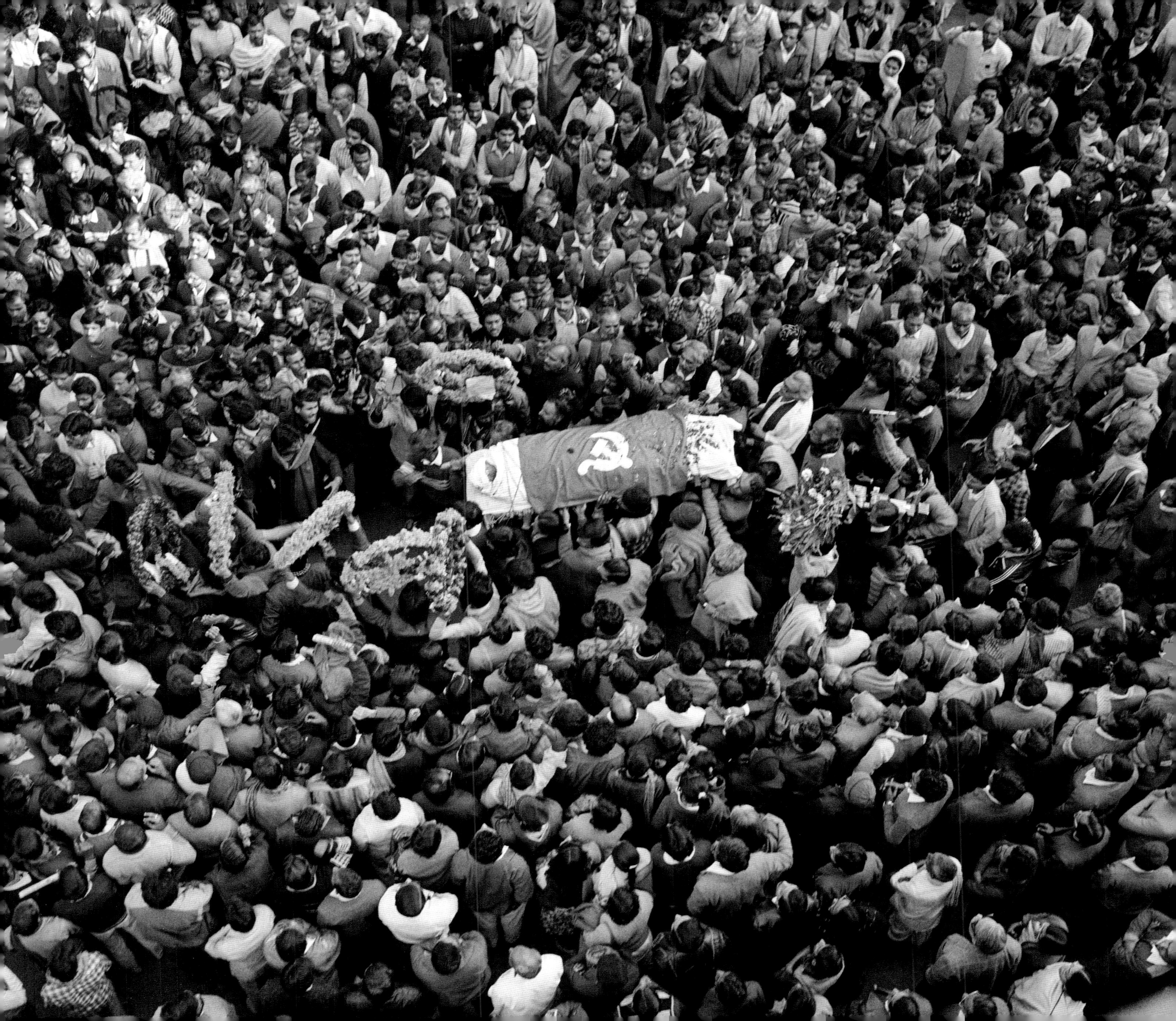

1989

The Founding of Sahmat

The spontaneous anger generated by Safdar Hashmi's murder soon grew into a resolve among artists, writers, scholars, filmmakers, theatre artists, and cultural activists to resist all forces that threaten the right to freedom of creative expression in India. In February 1989, within weeks of Hashmi's death, a group of them came together to form Sahmat—the Safdar Hashmi Memorial Trust and Committee. From its inception, Sahmat has been a collective of, and a platform for, individuals with a broadly shared political perspective best described as politically Left. Through their works of art, exhibitions, public events and performances, and publications, members of Sahmat have joined forces against communalism—the influences of religious fundamentalism and sectarianism in sociopolitical life. As art historian Geeta Kapur puts it,

> **"Sahmat has worked to build solidarity among artists and intellectuals on questions of conscience in current politics, especially in the areas of communalism. It has attempted, more ambitiously, to build a movement where an alert consciousness will anticipate fundamentalist tendencies in our national cultural life and provide a platform for those of us who should want to intervene in the social processes through our own practice."[1]**

1. From "Sahmat," in *Sahmat 1989–1999* (New Delhi: Sahmat, 1999).

Many of India's best known artists, writers, and intellectuals have been associated with Sahmat alongside younger creative individuals and activists, all as "Friends of Sahmat." Sahmat has remained a broad-based collective in the best sense of the term, not bound by rules of association or membership of any kind. Indeed the success of Sahmat's initiatives and reach is perhaps partly explained by its open-door, voluntary nature—a spirit captured by the meaning of the Hindi word *sahmat* itself: "in agreement."

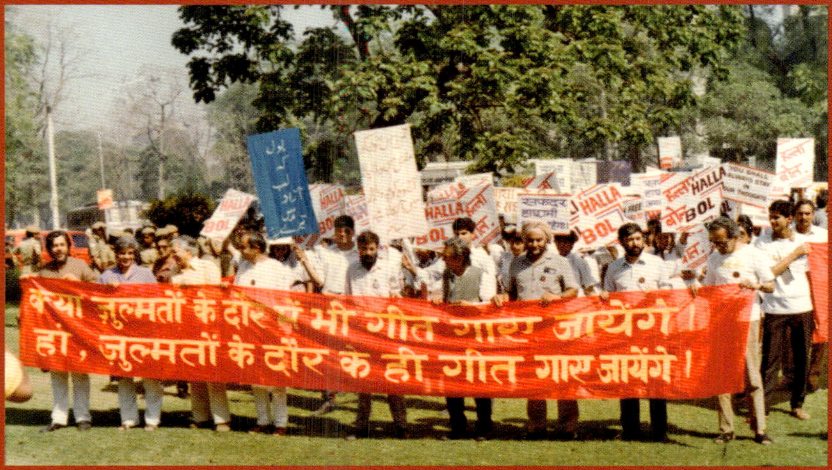

Marchers holding a banner with lines by Bertolt Brecht in Hindi, *Kya zulmaton ke daur mein bhi geet gaye jaayenge? / Haan, zulmaton ke daur ke hi geet gaaye jaayenge* (And will there be singing in the dark times?/ Yes, there will be singing of the dark times), *Safdar Samaroh*, April 1989. Front row (from left to right): filmmaker Saeed Mirza, artists Vivan Sundaram and Krishen Khanna, curator Martand Singh, unidentified, writer Bhisham Sahni, Mahip Singh, unidentified, theatre director Habib Tanvir.

The first trustees of Sahmat were

Bhisham Sahni (chairman), Habib Tanvir (who became chairman in 2003, after Bhisham Sahni passed away), G. P. Deshpande, Vivan Sundaram, M. K. Raina, Sohail Hashmi, and Moloyashree Hashmi (managing trustee).

The founding group also included

Rajinder Arora, Rati Bartholomew, Manmohan Bawa, Rajeev Bhargava, Tani Bhargava, Fiyaz Butt, Romesh Chander, Anil Chandra, Kumi Chandra, Indira Chandrasekhar, Qamar Azad Hashmi, Shabnam Hashmi, Geeta Kapur, Romi Khosla, Sashi Kumar, Radhika Menon, Madhu Prasad, Rajendra Prasad, Dadi Pudumjee, Ram Rahman, Gauhar Raza, Parthiv Shah, Shamshad, and Madan Gopal Singh. At weekly Thursday meetings of this original group, most of the initial activities of Sahmat were conceived, approved, and executed.

The current trustees of Sahmat (as of 2012) are

Irfan Habib (chairman), Vivan Sundaram, M. K. Raina, Sohail Hashmi, Moloyashree Hashmi, Ram Rahman, and Madan Gopal Singh. Shabnam Hashmi served as secretary of Sahmat until 2002, and Ashok Kumari has been functioning as the secretary from 2002 to the present.

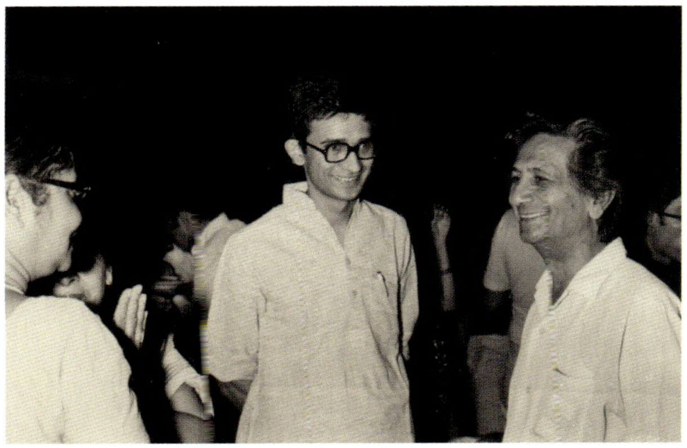

Safdar Hashmi (center) with Bhisham Sahni (right).

Bhisham Sahni

Everything Safdar did and stood for—the values, the ideals, and the activities with which Safdar was associated and where he was investing every ounce of his energy—was all dedicated in the service of our society. He was doing it neither for self-promotion, nor for publicity, nor for earning material comforts for himself. His aim was to expose the internal contradictions of our society. He was fighting, struggling for social justice.

Translated excerpt from Bhisham Sahni, "A Few Words," in *Safdar* (Hindi) (Delhi: Rajkamal Prakashan, 1989).

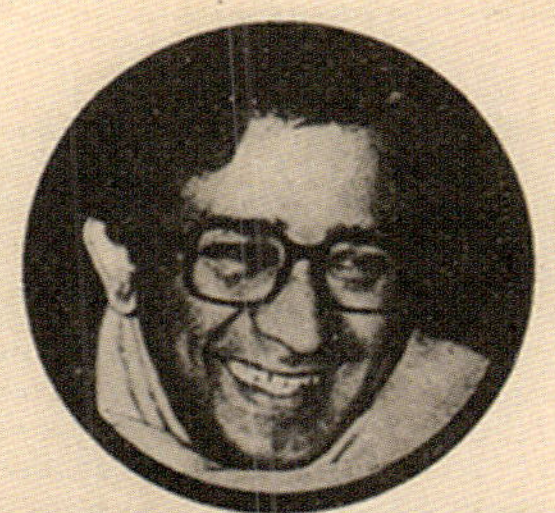

SAFDAR HASHMI 12 April 1954 – 2 January 1989

A prominent theatre activist of the country, Safdar Hashmi, died on 2 January 1989 at Ram Manohar Lohia Hospital as the result of a murderous attack by goondas.

On 1 January he had gone to Sahibabad (Ghaziabad), with other members of the Jan Natya Manch, the street theatre group of which Safdar was the convenor, to stage a play titled 'Halla Bol'. While the play was being performed the goondas attacked the group and Safdar was fatally injured. Showing immense courage, Safdar bore the brunt of the attackers' violence, and ensured that the other members of the group got to safety. Born on 12 April 1954 in Delhi, Safdar did an M.A. in English from St. Stephen's College, Delhi University, in 1975. During his university years he became a member of the SFI and then joined the IPTA, only to leave in protest against plays being performed on the Congress platform at a time when the pre-Emergency, authoritarian attacks on the people had already begun. He was one of the founders of the Jan Natya Manch (Janam) in 1973. In 1976 he became a member of the CPI(M). After brief stints at teaching at Zakir Hussain College, Delhi, the universities at Srinagar, Garhwal and Srinagar, Kashmir, and as Press Information Officer at the West Bengal Information Centre, Safdar became a full-time theatre activist and party worker from December 1983. By this time Janam had acquired national prominence in the cultural sphere with plays such as *Machine*, *Aurat*, *Gaon Se Shahar Tak*, *Raja Ka Baja* and *Hatyare*. Safdar wrote the songs for these plays and contributed greatly to the scripts, which dealt with the burning issues of the times, concerning exploited sections among the people. Largely due to Safdar's untiring efforts, Janam has played a major role in the creation of an all-India street theatre movement. Safdar's creativity went beyond Janam. He has written poems and plays and done sketches and masks for children, designed hundreds of posters, written scripts and directed short films for television, written on culture and theatre for the national newspapers and the SFI journal Student Struggle . He was one of the main organizers of the Committee for Communal Harmony and its activities to counter the rise of communal, fundamentalist and divisive forces. He has also organised a number of seminars and workshops on theatre and culture. His dream of a nationwide democratic cultural movement envisaged the organisation of a 'Janotsav' to counter the government-sponsored Apna Utsav's mythification of folk culture and its propagation of decadent values. Safdar's political commitment and artistic creativity, combined with a keen sense of fun and irreppressible friendliness and warmth, made him extremely popular among all those he worked with. With his death the CPI(M), the Jan Natya Manch, the cultural movement and the democratic and secular forces of the country have lost a beloved friend, a talented artist and a committed political activist.

Leaflet distributed in large numbers at the protest meeting at Rabindra Bhavan on January 9, and at the awards function of the 12th International Film Festival of India, Siri Fort Auditorium, New Delhi, on January 12, 1989, by actor Shabana Azmi and director John Schlesinger.

M. K. RAINA

There was outrage in the city of Delhi, and protests in every part of India. Safdar's funeral stunned the government. There were industrial workers, theatre people, students, housewives, musicians, artists, political leaders, and the general public walking in this miles-long funeral procession. It was anger against a brutal act committed by political goons that brought them out on the street. It was about freedom of expression and artistic freedom. The funeral procession made its way along fifteen kilometers, and all along the way there were thousands of people who were waiting to catch a last glimpse of a man they perhaps had not even known when he was alive. I think it was a mark of respect to a fallen actor, a dramatist, a poet, and a political worker. His funeral procession also revealed how Safdar had touched numerous lives in his short life of thirty-four years.

Through meetings and long discussions in the days immediately following his death, we decided that we should form a trust in Safdar's name that would be dedicated to the cause that he held dear, which broadly meant celebrating India's tradition of cultural diversity through communal harmony and equality.

MOLOYASHREE HASHMI

In 1989–90, when I was actively associated with Sahmat, I remember that the small "office" was a place people came to regularly—as indeed they do, to date—so that it became a sort of hangout for progressive artists and intellectuals. There was a tremendous energy. There would be a meeting every Thursday, which anyone could attend. A lot of the planning for future events was done in those meetings. A certain kind of open, democratic participation was (and is) the hallmark of Sahmat's functioning.

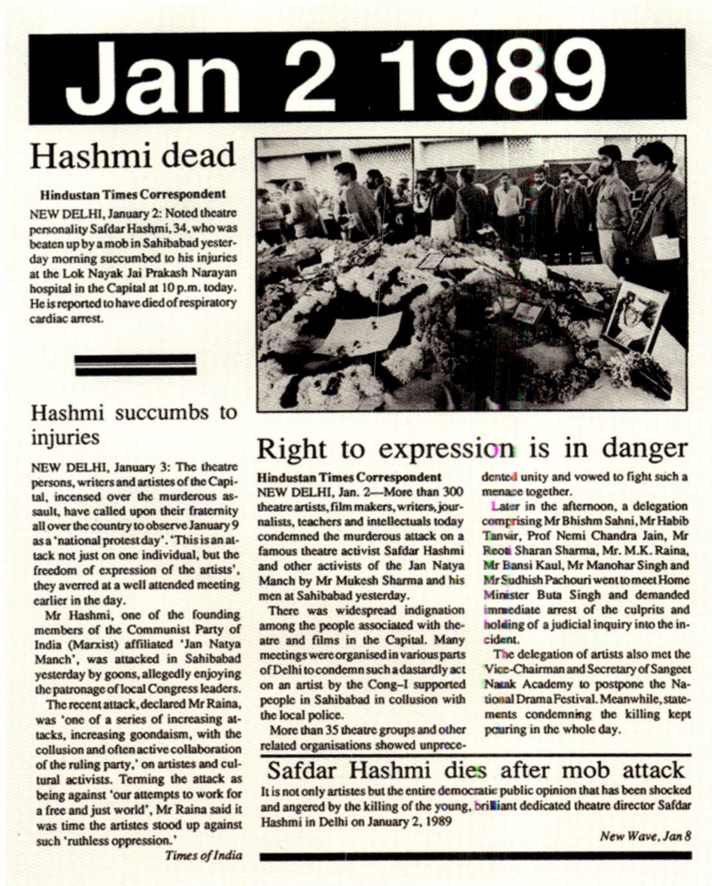

Jan 2 1989

Hashmi dead

Hindustan Times Correspondent

NEW DELHI, January 2: Noted theatre personality Safdar Hashmi, 34, who was beaten up by a mob in Sahibabad yesterday morning succumbed to his injuries at the Lok Nayak Jai Prakash Narayan hospital in the Capital at 10 p.m. today. He is reported to have died of respiratory cardiac arrest.

Hashmi succumbs to injuries

NEW DELHI, January 3: The theatre persons, writers and artistes of the Capital, incensed over the murderous assault, have called upon their fraternity all over the country to observe January 9 as a 'national protest day'. 'This is an attack not just on one individual, but the freedom of expression of the artists', they averred at a well attended meeting earlier in the day.

Mr Hashmi, one of the founding members of the Communist Party of India (Marxist) affiliated 'Jan Natya Manch', was attacked in Sahibabad yesterday by goons, allegedly enjoying the patronage of local Congress leaders.

The recent attack, declared Mr Raina, was 'one of a series of increasing attacks, increasing goondaism, with the collusion and often active collaboration of the ruling party,' on artistes and cultural activists. Terming the attack as being against 'our attempts to work for a free and just world', Mr Raina said it was time the artistes stood up against such 'ruthless oppression.'

Times of India

Right to expression is in danger

Hindustan Times Correspondent

NEW DELHI, Jan. 2—More than 300 theatre artists, film makers, writers, journalists, teachers and intellectuals today condemned the murderous attack on a famous theatre activist Safdar Hashmi and other activists of the Jan Natya Manch by Mr Mukesh Sharma and his men at Sahibabad yesterday.

There was widespread indignation among the people associated with theatre and films in the Capital. Many meetings were organised in various parts of Delhi to condemn such a dastardly act on an artist by the Cong–I supported people in Sahibabad in collusion with the local police.

More than 35 theatre groups and other related organisations showed unprecedented unity and vowed to fight such a menace together.

Later in the afternoon, a delegation comprising Mr Bhishm Sahni, Mr Habib Tanvir, Prof Nemi Chandra Jain, Mr Reoti Sharan Sharma, Mr. M.K. Raina, Mr Bansi Kaul, Mr Manohar Singh and Mr Sudhish Pachouri went to meet Home Minister Buta Singh and demanded immediate arrest of the culprits and holding of a judicial inquiry into the incident.

The delegation of artists also met the Vice-Chairman and Secretary of Sangeet Natak Academy to postpone the National Drama Festival. Meanwhile, statements condemning the killing kept pouring in the whole day.

Safdar Hashmi dies after mob attack

It is not only artistes but the entire democratic public opinion that has been shocked and angered by the killing of the young, brilliant dedicated theatre director Safdar Hashmi in Delhi on January 2, 1989

New Wave, Jan 8

Printed booklet with press reports of Safdar Hashmi's death, 1989.

NILIMA SHEIKH

The murder of Safdar Hashmi shook the artist community to the core, and the outrage brought about a unique bonding. An informal camaraderie and kinship turned into a political collective—political for many of us not because of alignment to specific political parties, but because there was a public agenda against injustice and a need to find a language that communicated an urgent need for agency. So it was a collective that needed to be wide and artists/artistes from all the arts found each other in an attempt to work together collectively. However professionalism and excellence remained a determined choice, because the core organizers of Sahmat were committed and leading artists/artistes/academics themselves, and it was understood that it was through commitment to excellence in their professions that the battle had to be won. And each of us chipped in to do the tasks we could.

MITHU SEN

When Safdar Hashmi was murdered, I was a teenaged first-year student in a faraway art college in Bengal, but I remember how I reacted and wanted to scream loudly. Many years later, when I came to Delhi after finishing my studies, I found Sahmat there and saw how it had started screaming against injustice in life. After that I got involved with Sahmat.

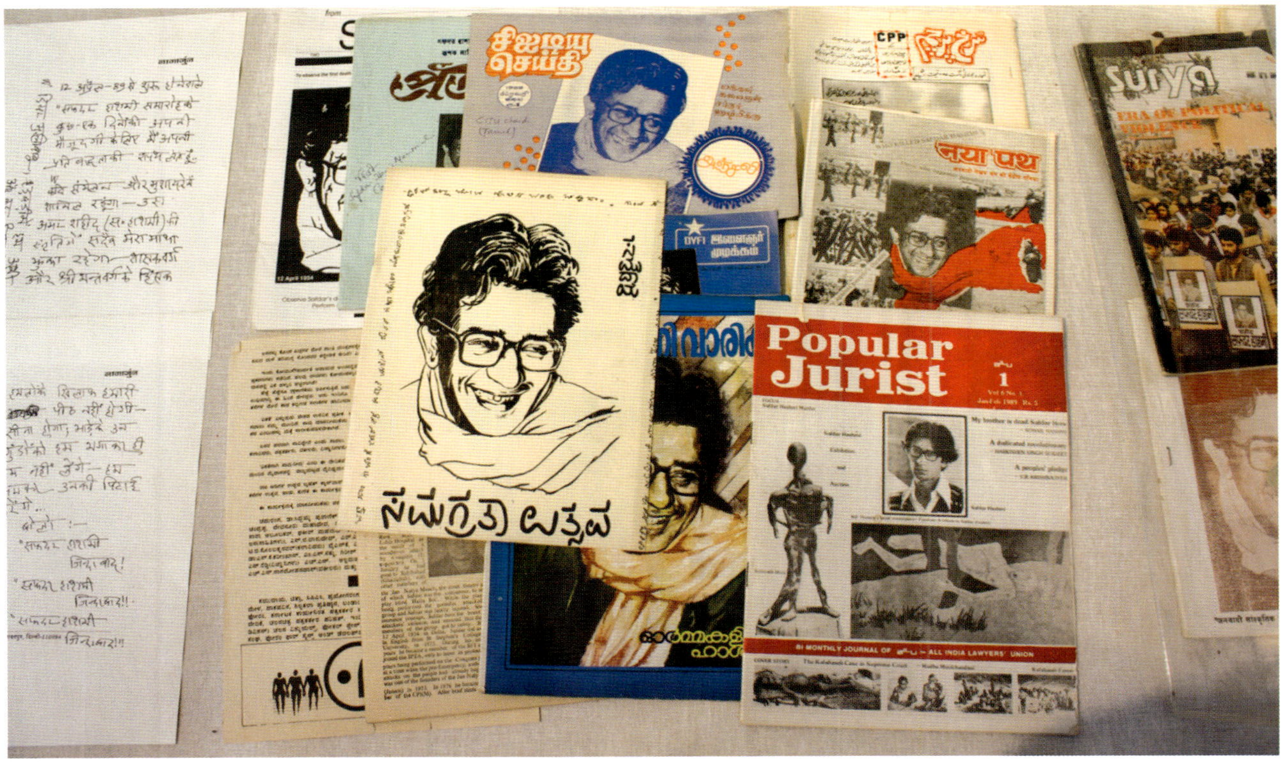

Journals and magazines in different languages from across India mark Hashmi's passing, 1989.

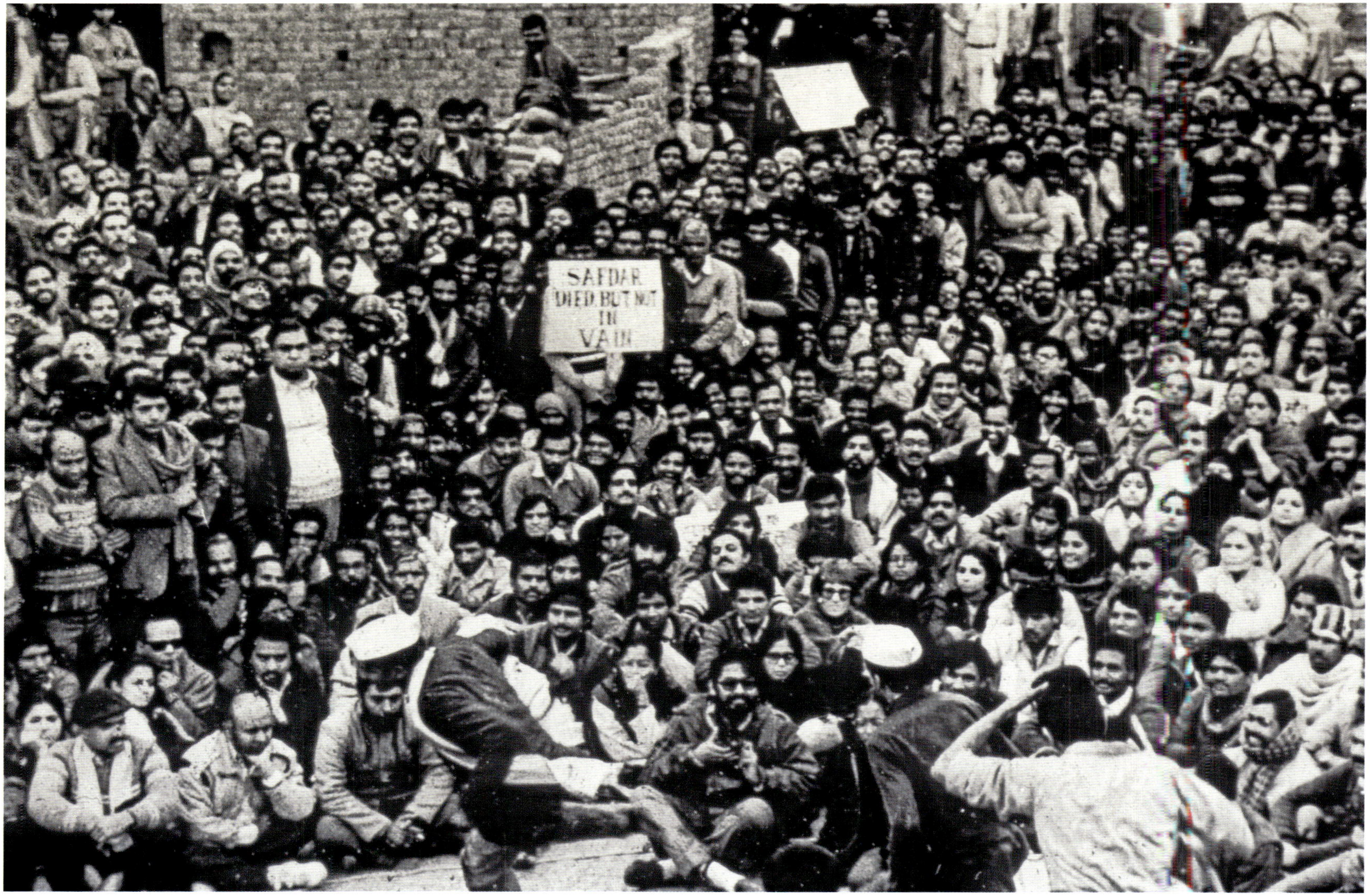

Crowd watches Janam complete their performance of
Halla Bol! (Raise Your Voice!) in Sahibabad, January 4, 1989.

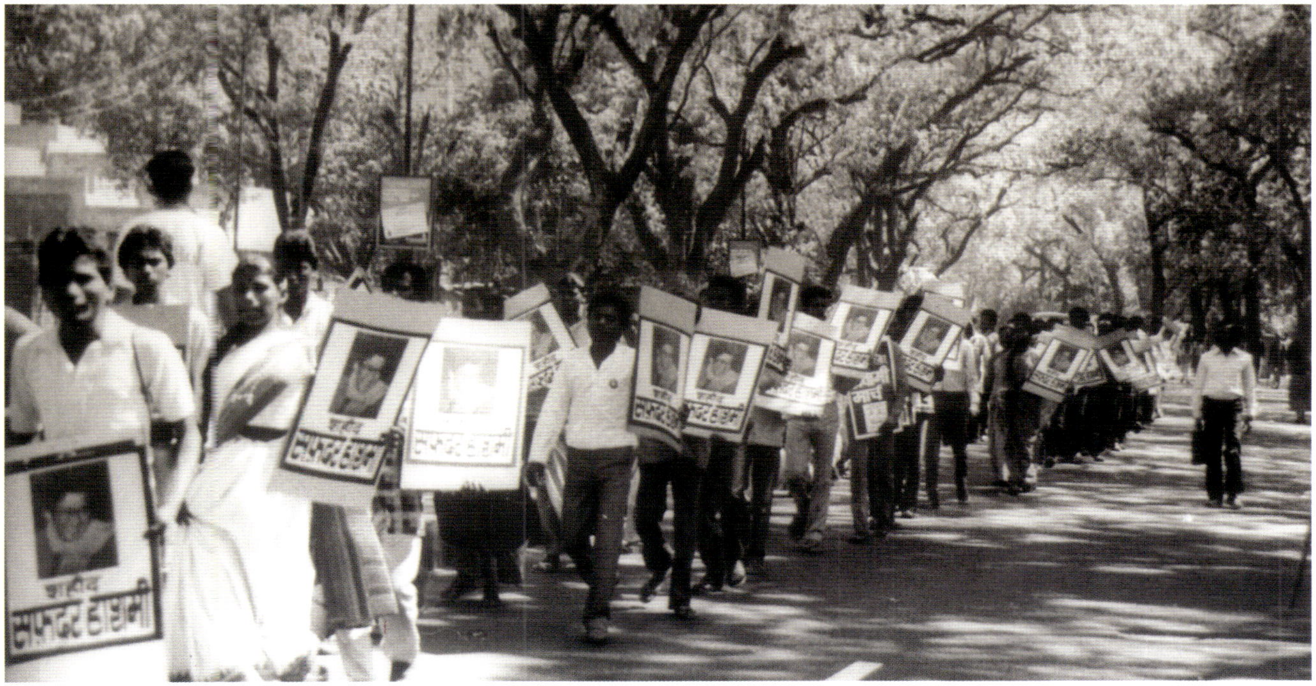

Silent march from Shivaji Park, Minto Road, to the home minister's residence, New Delhi, January 5, 1989.

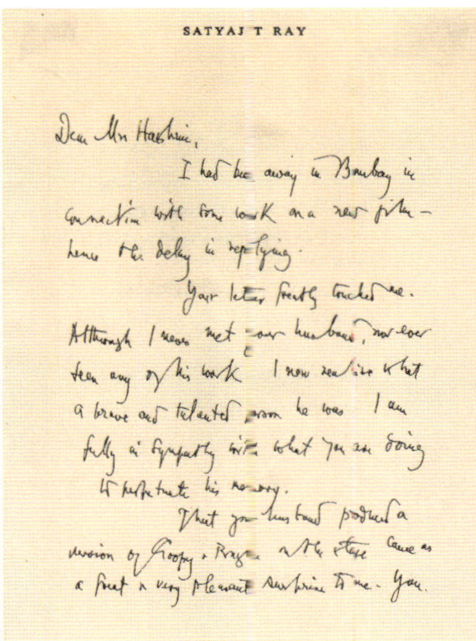

SATYAJIT RAY

Dear Mrs Hashmi,

I had been away in Bombay in connection with some work on a new film – hence the delay in replying.

Your letter greatly touched me. Although I never met your husband, nor ever seen any of his work I now realise what a brave and talented person he was. I am fully in sympathy with what you are doing to perpetuate his memory.

That your husband produced a version of Goopy & Bagha on the stage came as a great & very pleasant surprise to me. You

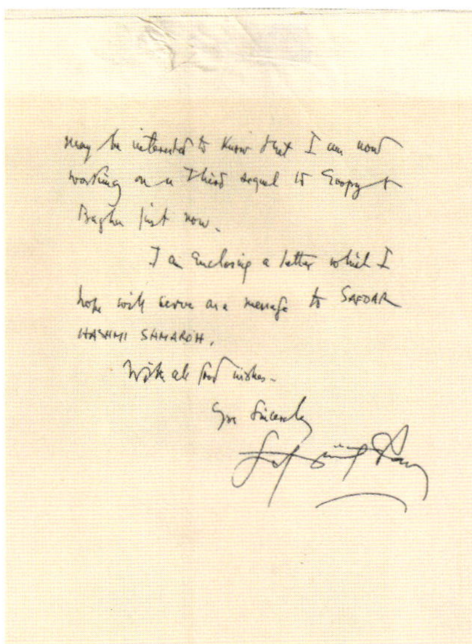

may be interested to know that I am now working on a third sequel to Goopy & Bagha just now.

I am enclosing a letter which I hope will serve as a message to SAFDAR HASHMI SAMAROH.

With all best wishes.

Yours sincerely,

Satyajit Ray

Letter to Moloyashree Hashmi from filmmaker Satyajit Ray.

I had been away in Bombay in connection with some work on a new film—hence the delay in replying.

Your letter greatly touched me. Although I never met your husband, nor ever seen any of his work, I now realize what a brave and talented person he was. I am fully in sympathy with what you are doing to perpetuate his memory. That your husband produced a version of Goopy and Bagha on the stage came as a great and very pleasant surprise to me. You may be interested to know that I am now working on the third sequel to Goopy and Bagha just now.

I am enclosing a letter which I hope will serve as a message to Safdar Hashmi Samaroh. With all best wishes,

Yours sincerely,
Satyajit Ray

1989

Safdar Samaroh and *Artists Alert*

April 12–16, 1989

As its first major program, Sahmat held a five-day cultural festival, *Safdar Samaroh* (Safdar Festival), in New Delhi from April 12 to 16, 1989. With specially choreographed performances of classical and modern dance by Durga Lal, Madhavi Mudgal, and Astad Deboo, a theatre production, a presentation with life-size puppets by Dadi Pudumjee, poetry readings, feature film screenings, a screening of the documentary *Safdar* made by Sashi Kumar, and a seminar on street theatre, the festival marked the beginning of a process of involving artists in collective action through their different creative mediums.

To help establish operating funds for its future endeavors, Sahmat put out a call to artists to donate works for a five-day exhibition titled *Artists Alert*, to be followed by an auction. More than a hundred painters, sculptors, and photographers contributed works, most of which were specially created for the project.

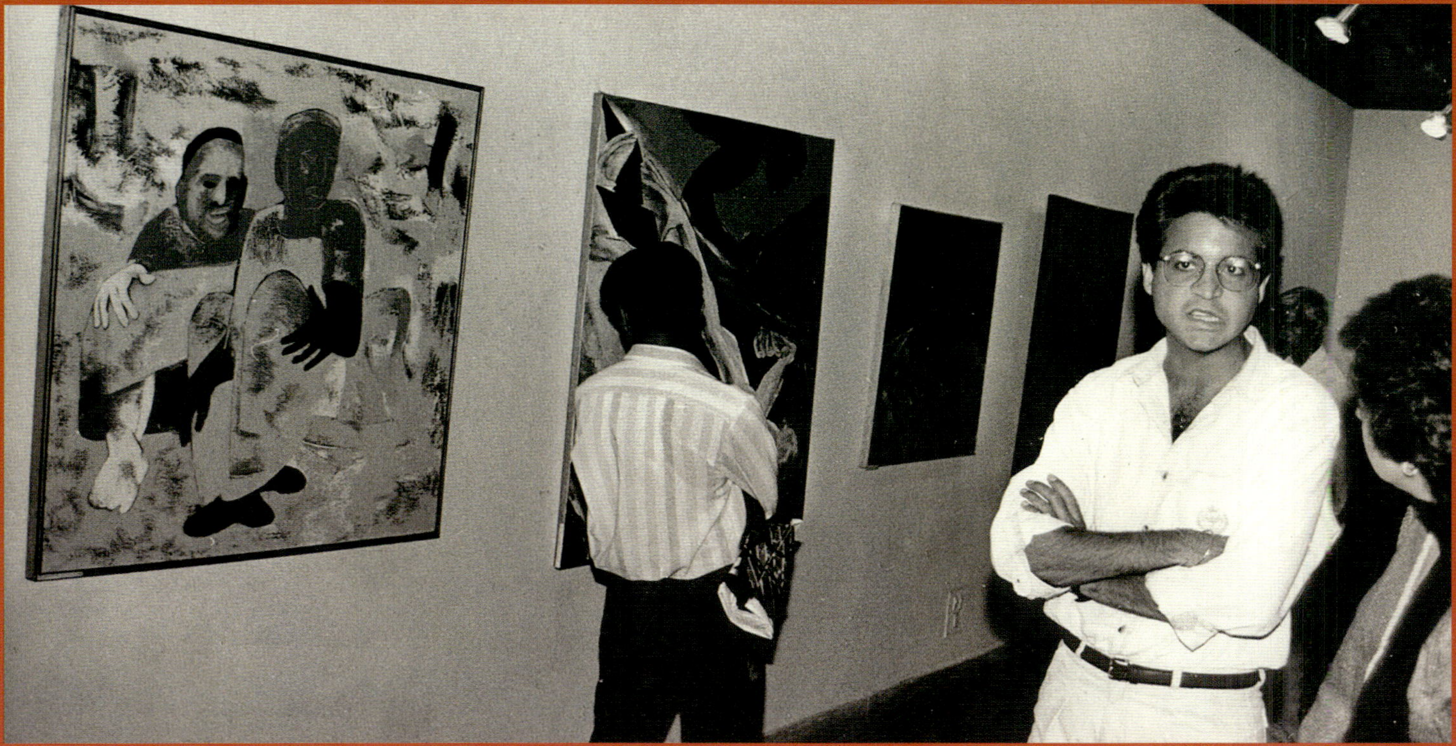

Artists Alert, exhibition view, Lalit Kala Akademi Galleries, Rabindra Bhavan, New Delhi, April 12, 1989.

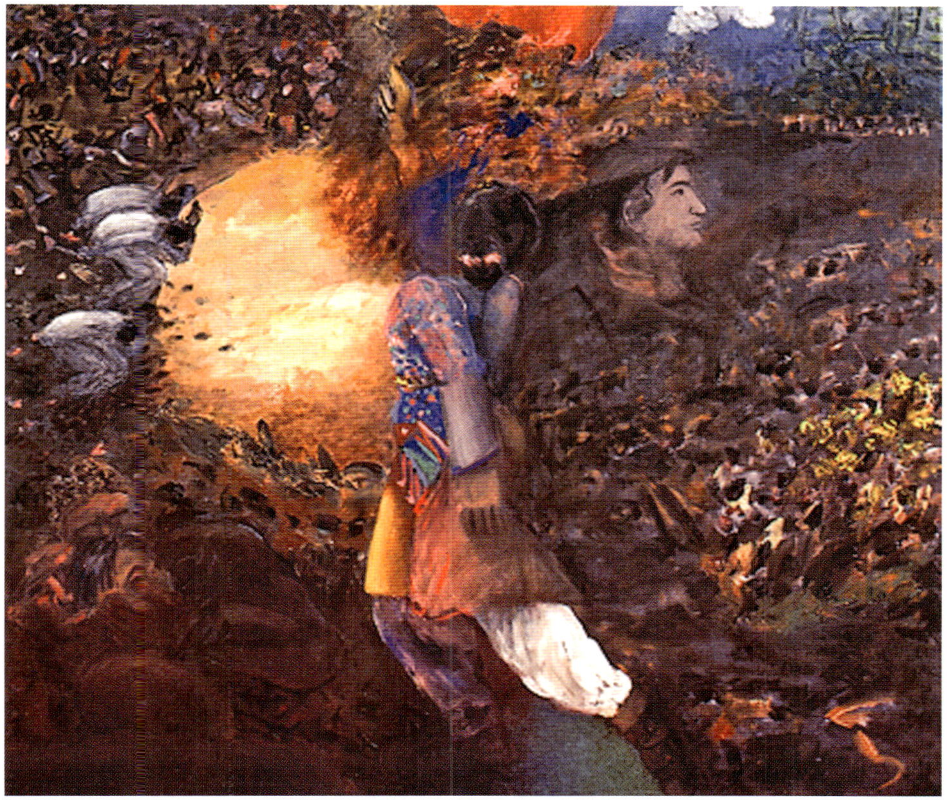

CLOCKWISE FROM TOP LEFT

VIVAN SUNDARAM
Safdar and Moloyashree, 1989,
oil on canvas, 53 7/8 x 59 7/8 inches.

ALTAF
Murder on the Pavement, 1989,
oil on canvas, 36 x 36 inches.

ARPITA SINGH
Pink Flowers, Yellow Flowers, 1989,
oil on canvas, 87 x 77 inches.

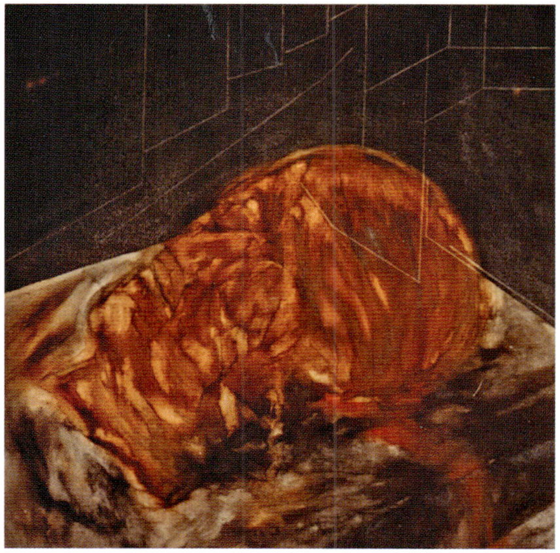

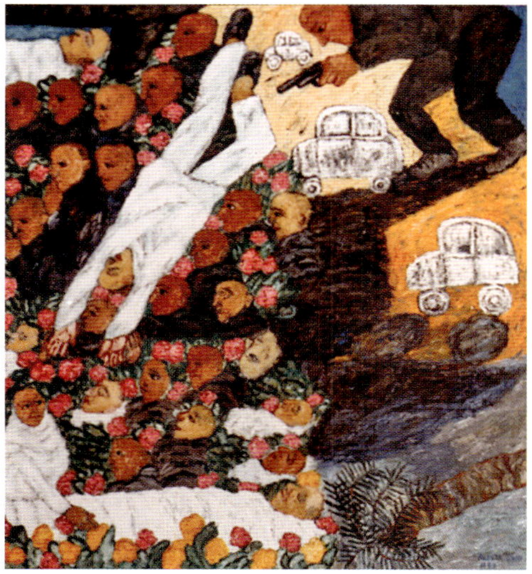

Geeta Kapur

Excerpt from Geeta Kapur, "Artists Alert," in the catalogue *Artists Alert: An Exhibition of Painting, Sculpture, Graphics and Photography* (New Delhi: Sahmat, 1989).

This exhibition and auction are not, for once, a charity event, nor are they meant to boost the art market—and the two kinds of shows are often the flipside of the same coin, as those who recognize these mechanisms well know. There are no simple ways for artists to survive, yet they must do more; they must intervene in the system that alienates them. Interrupting the routine of survival and success, there are causes that bring artists together. Fortunately, there is still a sense of community and, on occasion, a sense of solidarity among Indian artists. This is such an occasion: the murder of a fellow-artist. It is the murder of a theatre person on location, while at work, and so it is a violation of the very profession of an artist even as it is a political murder.

Safdar Hashmi was of course a theatre activist with a political purpose. He was a communist, and his group was performing a street play to support a wage increase for industrial workers where the issue was precisely the right to speak, the right of the worker to assert his/her minimum needs, to express his/her identity as a worker, through solidarity and action. The play was called *Halla Bol!* The worker's right is a long way away perhaps, but the artist's right of expression is taken for granted in a democratic society both because this is a publicized feature of liberal culture and because artists are rendered innocuous anyway in that culture. Can the artist say anything that can upset money or state power?

If it needed Safdar among us to die in order to recall that an artist is not so innocuous, then we must pay a certain price for this awareness. That price may be as private as self-reflection in which we allow our convictions to be put to the test. But Safdar's terrible sacrifice should also make us face up to the present, to become historically alert. And make us recognize that there are times when you have to close ranks with your fellow-artists and raise your voice. It is not only a question of the freedom of expression, though in all societies this still claims many sacrifices before it is won. The question is to make your identity and your practice sufficiently complex so that it is not easily appropriated or easily destroyed by antagonist forces. It may sometimes mean that an artist chooses to intensify his or her solitude, challenging the pragmatic rules of conduct. This is a difficult choice too, and we should know how to honor art. But there are other ways to challenge the given circumstances, opposite ways: to break the isolation of a specialist role that our societies prefer, to engage in multifarious forms of creativity to demystify art practice. The subject-matter of art need not, must not, become uniform or populist, but it is important to create alternative forums in which further acts of public intervention are possible.

The letters and messages that have come to Sahmat from a hundred or so artists who have agreed to participate in this exhibition and auction are a testimony to the quality of concern of Indian artists. They want to link hands round the figure of Safdar, though he was in some ways different. He was a theatre activist and a communist. These messages are themselves material to think about in regard to the Indian art situation. Somnath Hore, that remote and ailing artist who has sustained his commitment to the Left over several decades, gives a moving little bronze called *Comrades*—a man holding in his arms a comrade who has fallen—and he writes, "Hashmi died a revolutionary death. One should take care to see that this does not become a cushion for somebody else's comforts. . . . yet people cannot live by frustration; they have to look forward to a healthy and meaningful life." Meera Mukherjee, an intractable presence in the Indian art scene, comes forth and gives an affirmative bronze image of people's solidarity (made on the occasion of a demand by young artists for better art education facilities in Calcutta) called Andolan. Other artists—Arpita Singh, Altaf, Shamshad, Jatin Das, Suhas Roy, Vivan Sundaram—make a motif of Safdar's death in terms of their own work. A reticent artist like Prabhakar Barwe simply says that he is *sahmat* (in agreement) after the motto of the Safdar Hashmi Memorial Trust. And almost everyone says that they are grateful to be asked to show their solidarity through giving a work.

The works make an exhibition, the exhibition is put to auction, the money raised will go towards Sahmat projects including, among other things, opportunities for artists to diversify their practice, to participate in collective activity, and build up alternative structures of communication and action.

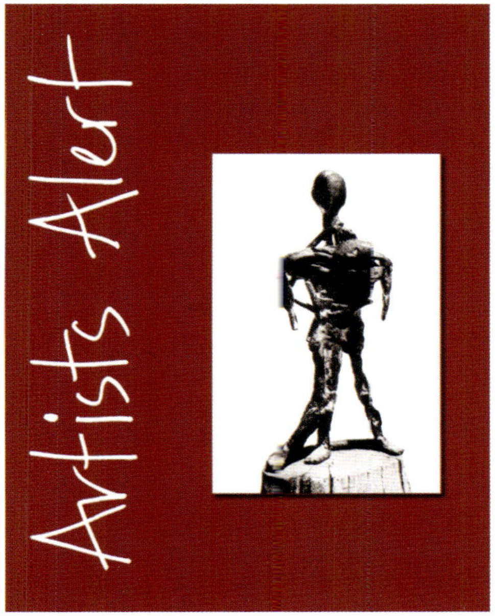

Cover for *Artists Alert* catalogue (New Delhi: Sahmat, 1989), with a reproduction of Somnath Hore, *Comrades*, 1984, bronze. Book and cover design: Parthiv Shah.

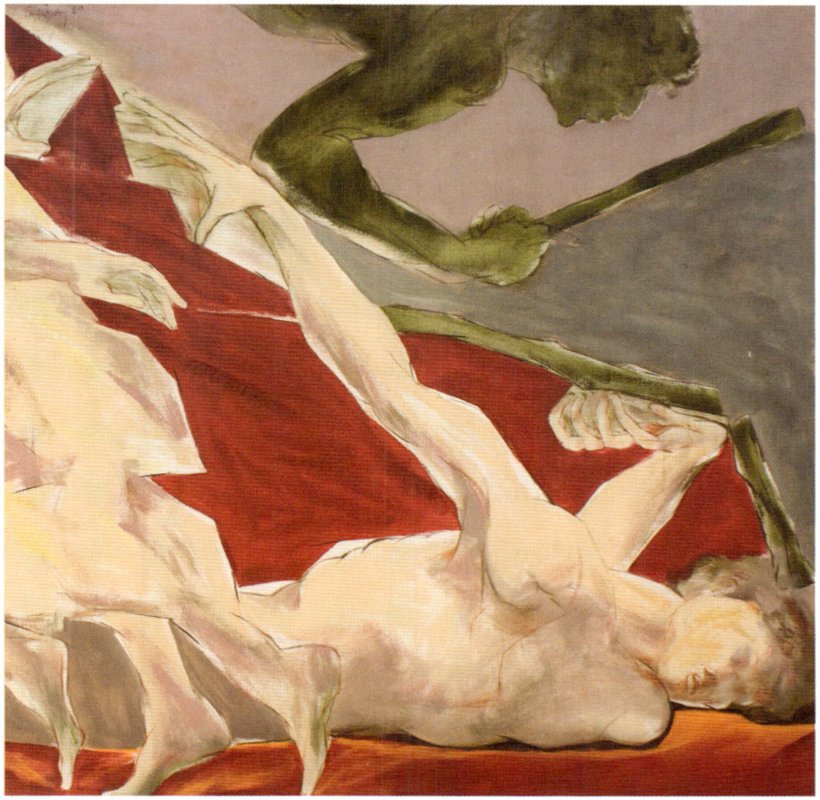

JATIN DAS
In Memory of Safdar Hashmi, 1989, oil on canvas, 48 x 48 inches.
Collection: Anil Chandra.

VIVAN SUNDARAM

One idea behind *Artists Alert* was to raise funds for Sahmat. Since it followed the Sotheby's auction in Bombay, which was a marker of the change that took place in terms of the art market, there was, in one sense, an interest or excitement then about artworks being auctioned. The auction was successful and Sahmat formed a financial base from which to start work.

Artists Alert signaled that artists were willing to come forward and be named in the public domain, and that they wanted to contribute their works in solidarity. The show was not curated; we accepted all the work that was submitted.

JATIN DAS

I was one of the artists associated with the initial days of Sahmat, along with many others. Though I normally do not paint on events, after the death of Safdar I did a large oil on canvas, which was auctioned and the proceeds went to Sahmat. I think Sahmat is one of the few organizations in the country through which artists can voice their opinions regarding art and art practice fearlessly, and pursue the concern for genuine freedom of expression. The ideology of Sahmat does not interfere with our individual practices as artists.

1989

National Street Theatre Day

April 12, 1989

A few months after his death in 1989, Sahmat declared Safdar Hashmi's birthday, April 12, National Street Theatre Day. The response was overwhelming: across the country more than 30,000 street plays were performed, new scripts written, inactive theatre groups reactivated, and new groups formed. National Street Theatre Day, observed every year since, continues to focus attention on the street theatre movement in India—free, public performances, often with a political or social message. Every year on April 12, Sahmat releases a new thematic poster, distributing it to street theatre groups and activists across India. Many of the posters have featured poems or images of Safdar Hashmi; some have celebrated centenaries of writers (Bertolt Brecht in 1998 and Faiz Ahmed Faiz in 2010); and others have been statements of protest—against the Iraq war (2003), against right-wing attacks on free speech in India (1999, 2009), and as calls for justice for the victims of the 2002 Gujarat riots (2002, 2005, 2012). The posters include a blank space on which local groups can write, print, or paste the details of their events, thus unifying all the performances that occur that day throughout India.

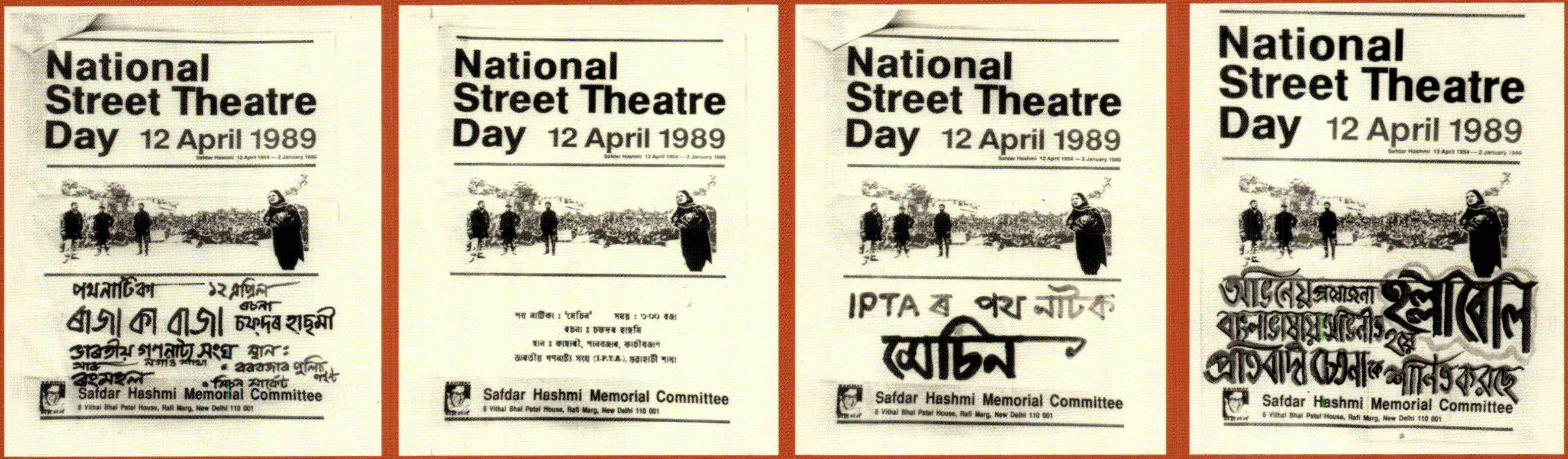

Posters for the first National Street Theatre Day with insertions from various local performance groups, 1989.

►
Protest march by street theatre artists on the first National Street Theatre Day, April 12, 1989, in Assam.

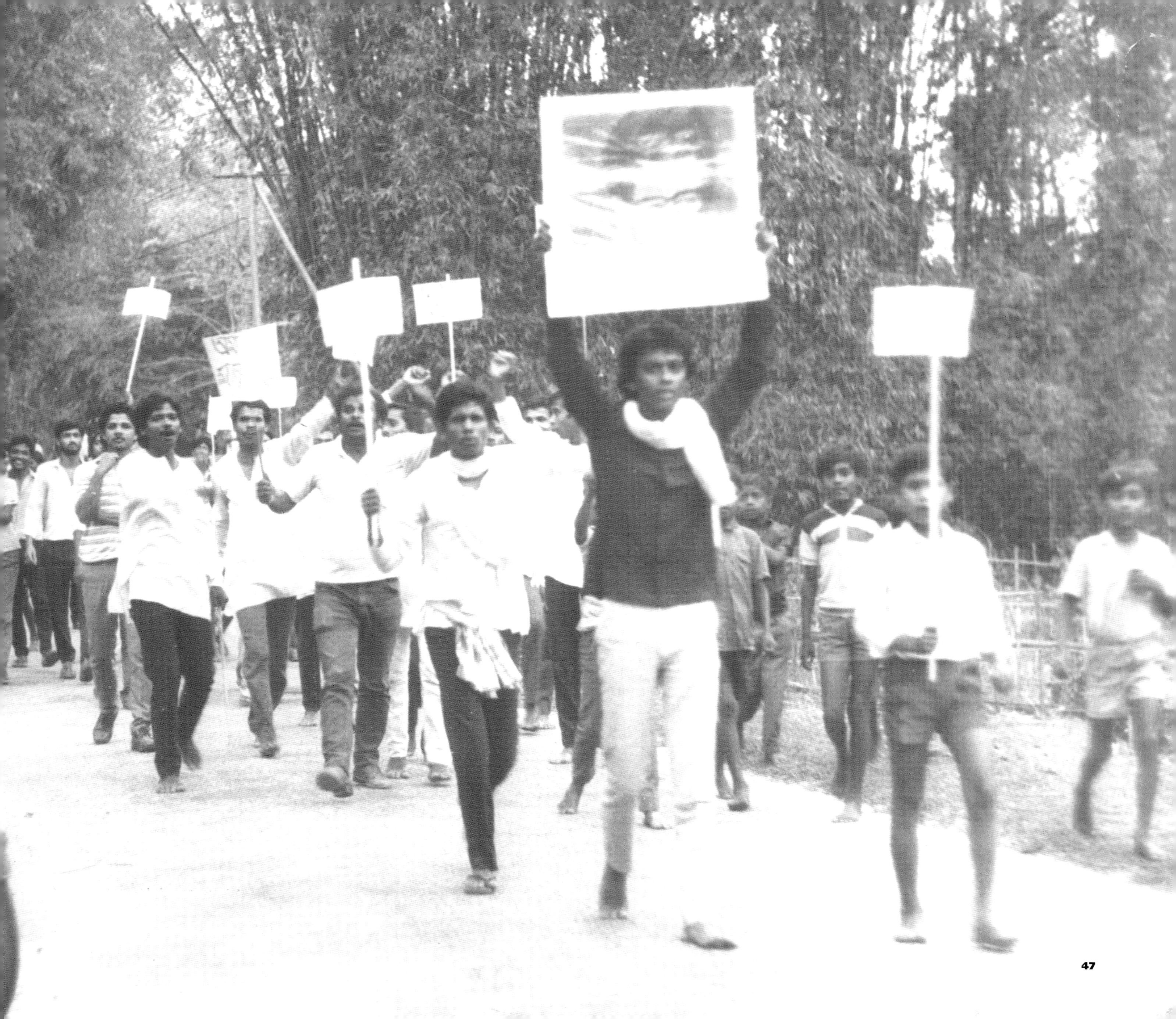

On Street Theatre

Safdar Hashmi

Excerpt from Safdar Hashmi, *The Right to Perform* (New Delhi: Sahmat, 1989).

The occasion may be a strike or an agitation or a mournful day after a manmade tragedy...the location may be a factory gate, a pavement, a busy marketplace, a barn, a school playground, a park in a residential area or any open space available . . . street theatre artists reach out to people . . . to inform and agitate them into action . . . it is people's theatre in the true sense.

The most definite origin of this form of theatre can be traced back to the presentation of Mayakovsky's *Mystery Bouffe* in Moscow on the first anniversary of the October Revolution, in 1918. This theatre became a vital tool of the Soviet revolutionaries' propaganda in the later years. Shows incorporating interpretations of important events and social phenomena went to the people, at their places of work and residences.

Though street theatre has escaped media attention, it has made its space among working-class people in many areas. This has, however, resulted in a conflict between proponents of street theatre and proscenium theatre. The former accuse the latter of being cultural renegades whose theatre is only for a select, "high-nosed" group, lacking social relevance. Hardcore proscenium proponents, on the other hand, condemn street theatre saying that it is only politics, too simplistic and crude to be considered a form of art at all.

What is desirable is that proscenium theatre should imbibe some of the spirit of the street theatre and the special skills developed within it, and street theatre people need to learn a lot from their counterparts in terms of finesse in performance. This is desperately required if street theatre is to be safeguarded because its very "handiness" is allowing it to be used by people who are not even familiar with its basic philosophies.

Street theatre, however, is here to stay. An effective tool of change in our society, it is also, slowly but surely, making a place of its own as a valid form of art.

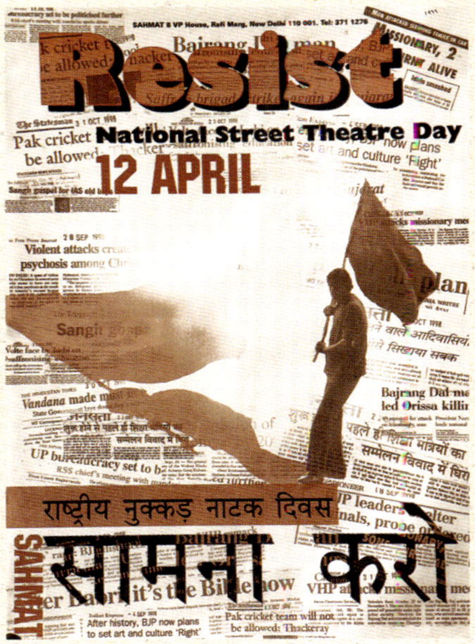

National Street Theatre Day poster, 1999, 19 x 14 inches.
Design: Ram Rahman.

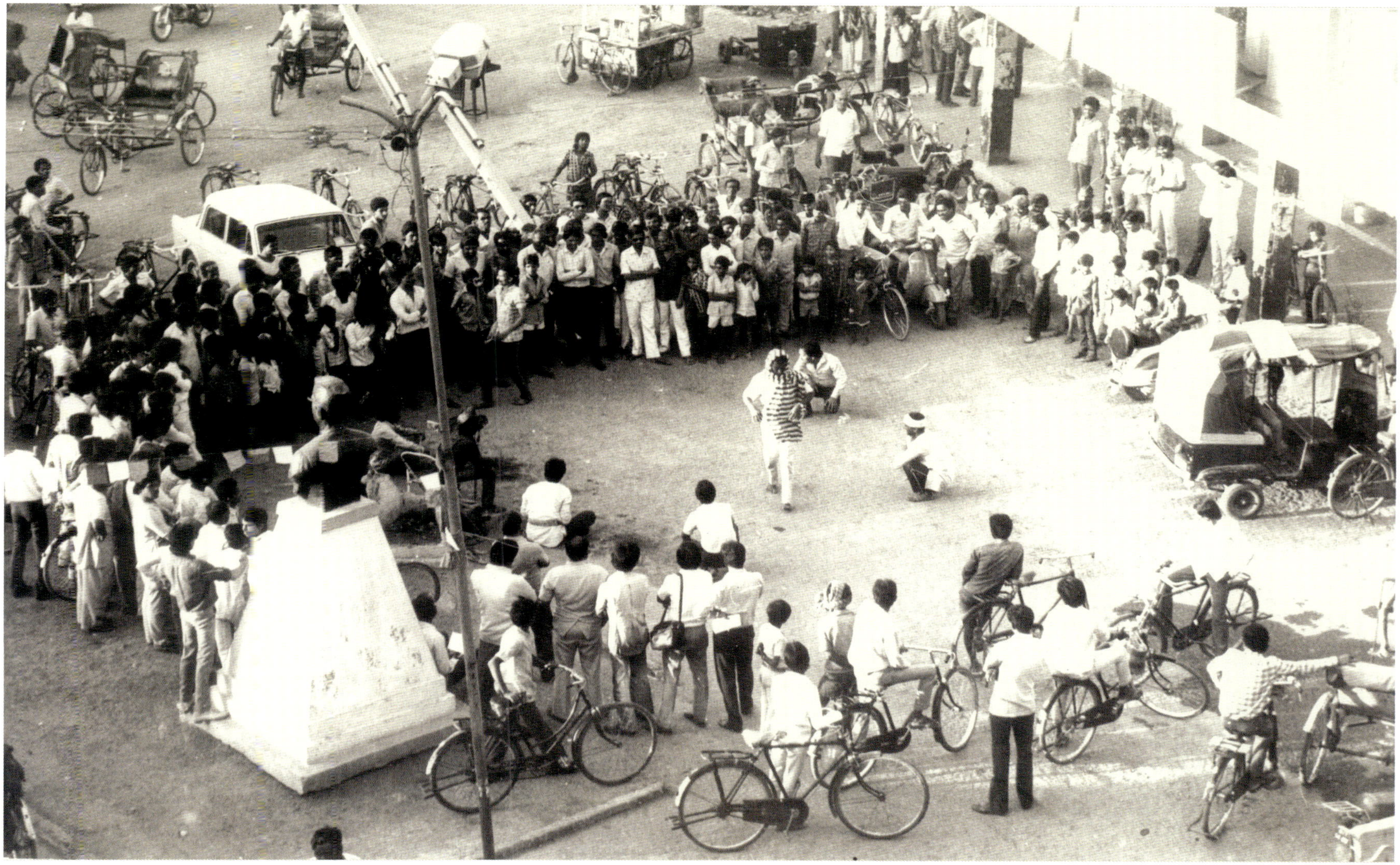

Performance by Indian People's Theatre Association (IPTA), Bilaspur, Madhya Pradesh, April 12, 1989.

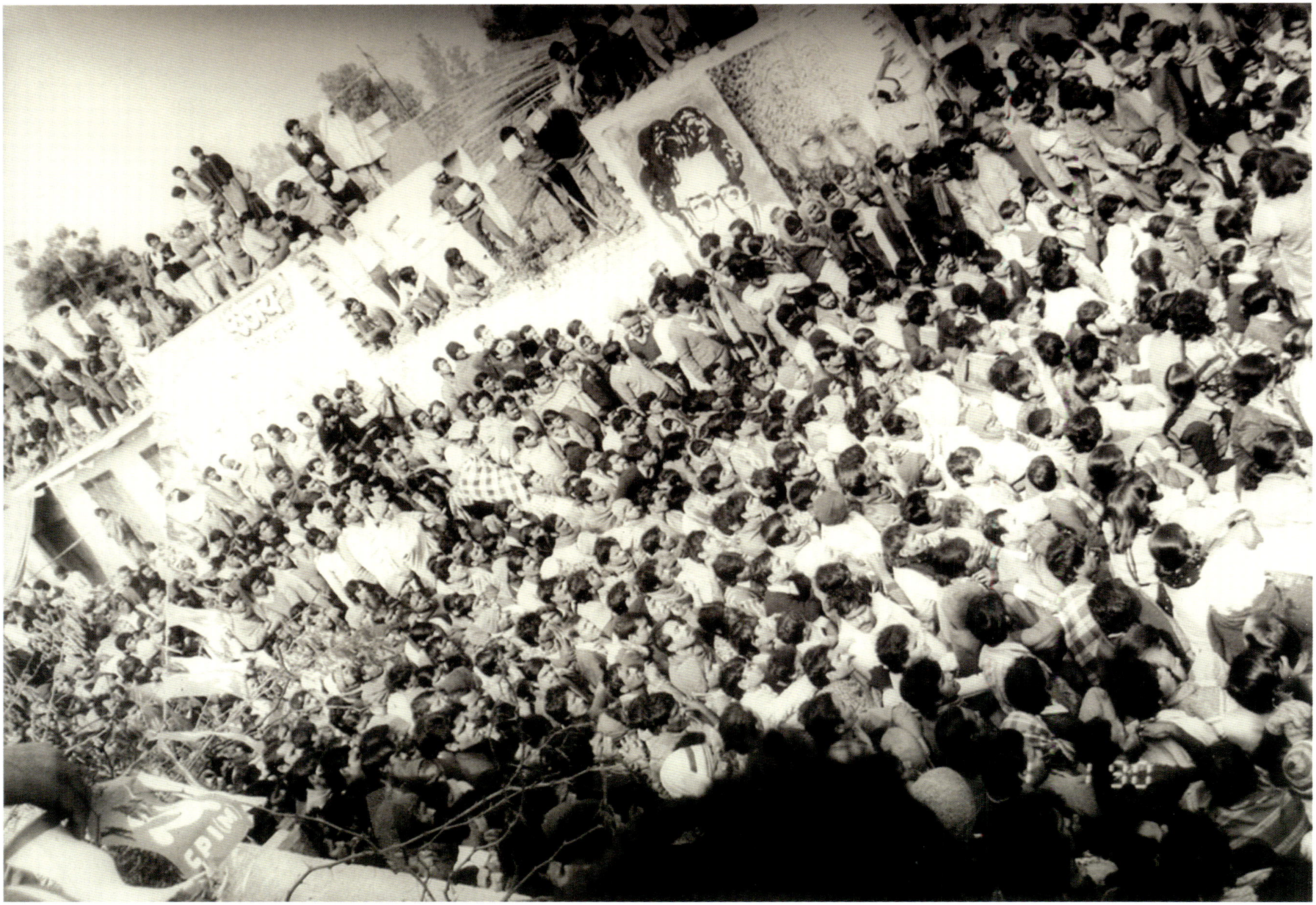

Audience at a performance by Janam on the first anniversary of Safdar Hashmi's death, Jhandapur, Sahibabad, January 1, 1990.

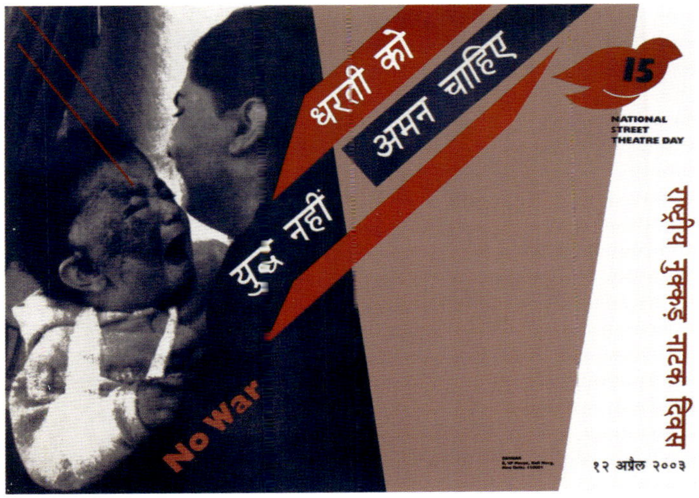

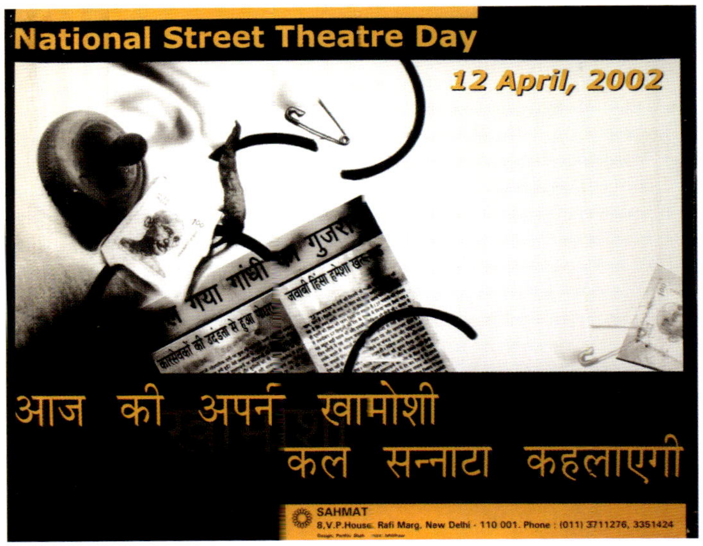

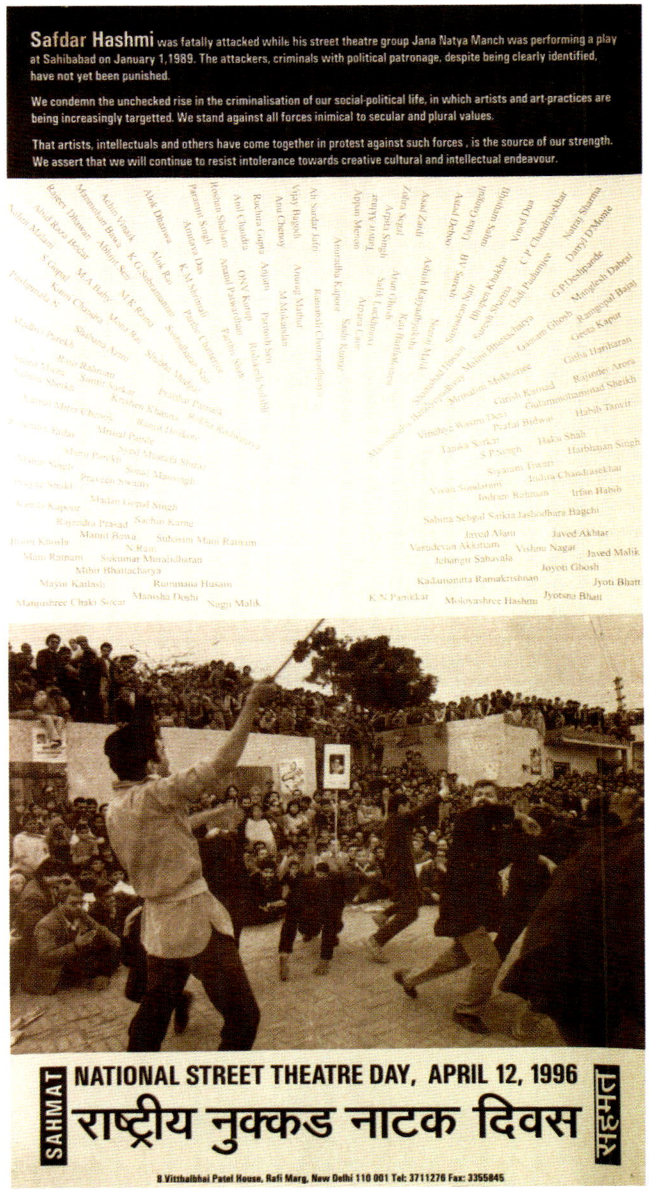

CLOCKWISE FROM TOP LEFT

National Street Theatre Day poster, 2003, 14 x 19 inches. Design: Ram Rahman.

National Street Theatre Day poster, 1996, 22 x 11½ inches. Design: Ram Rahman.

National Street Theatre Day poster, 2002, 14 x 19 inches. Design: Parthiv Shah.

SOHAIL HASHMI

In the early 1970s, when Janam started doing street theatre, there was a lot of criticism from practitioners of proscenium theatre. Throughout this period, Safdar kept up a dialogue with theatre artistes, both through discussions and in his writings. He argued that it was not the form of its presentation—whether it was staged inside an auditorium or in an amphitheatre, whether the audience sat on three sides or on all sides—that mattered: theatre should be seen for what it says, and for engaging its audience critically and creatively. Safdar refused to condemn or undermine other forms of theatre, though he was very critical of the so-called traditional theatre that was, in the name of preserving traditional forms, presenting and privileging antiquated, feudal, and retrograde social relations and forms of class domination.

MOLOYASHREE HASHMI

On the first National Street Theatre Day, April 12, 1989, Sahmat organized a festival of street theatre titled *Chauraha* (Crossroads). A number of street theatre groups from across the country came to participate. We organized their performances centrally of course, but also in several *bastis* and residential or office complexes. It was exciting to watch each other's work, to interact, and to learn from each other.

PARTHIV SHAH

The reach and dissemination of some of Sahmat's posters has been thrilling for me as the creator! Safdar Hashmi's birthday is celebrated as National Street Theatre Day all across India. Many street theatre groups in the country create new performances and perform them on that day. Most of these groups are small and don't have the resources to print posters or publicity material for their plays, and so I designed a poster that was printed and sent by Sahmat to theatre groups all across rural, semi-urban, and urban India. The design had a blank space for each group to add details of their own performance. This served to give the event a pan-India feel, and also a consistency where all the groups felt that they were connected with each other across India on that day.

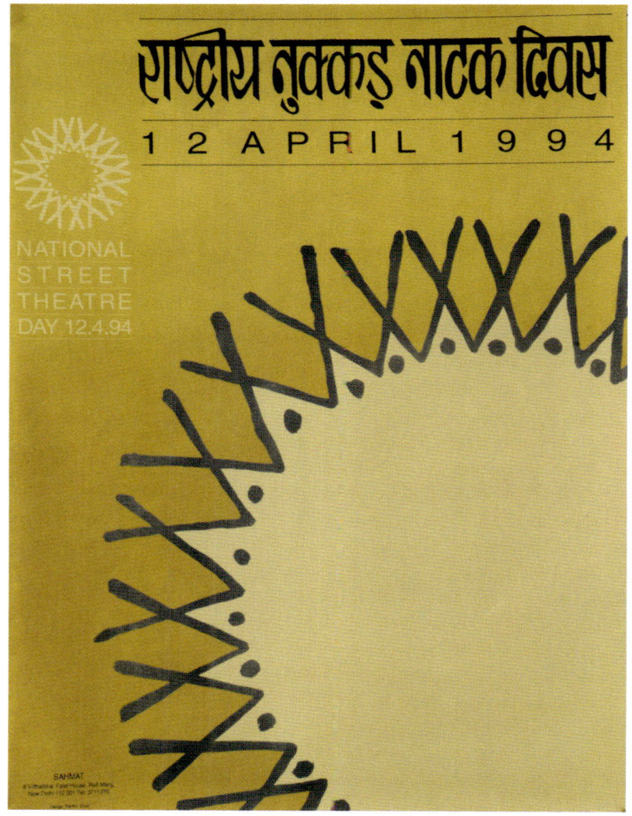

National Street Theatre Day poster, 1994. 22 x 16½ inches. Design: Parthiv Shah.

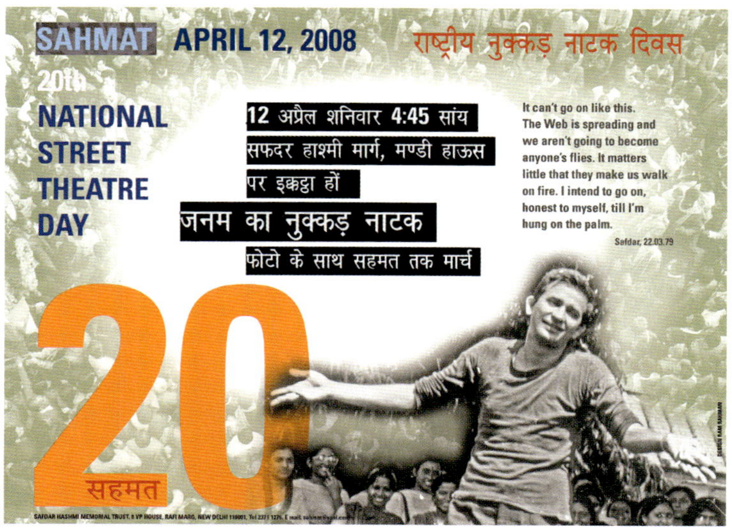

National Street Theatre Day poster, 2008, 14 x 19 inches. Design: Ram Rahman.

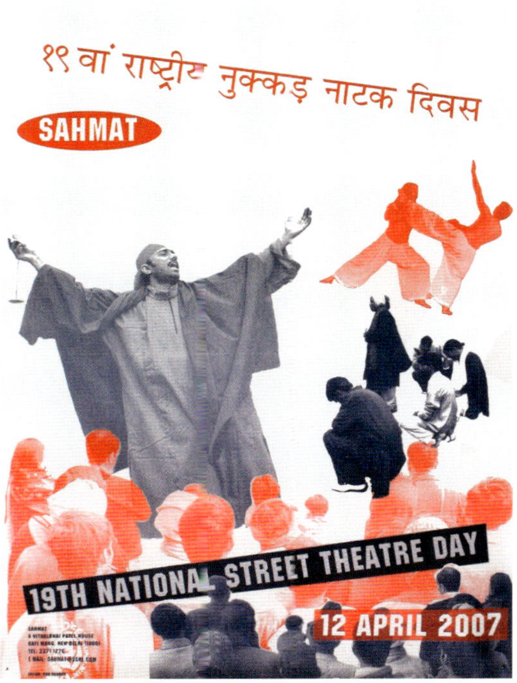

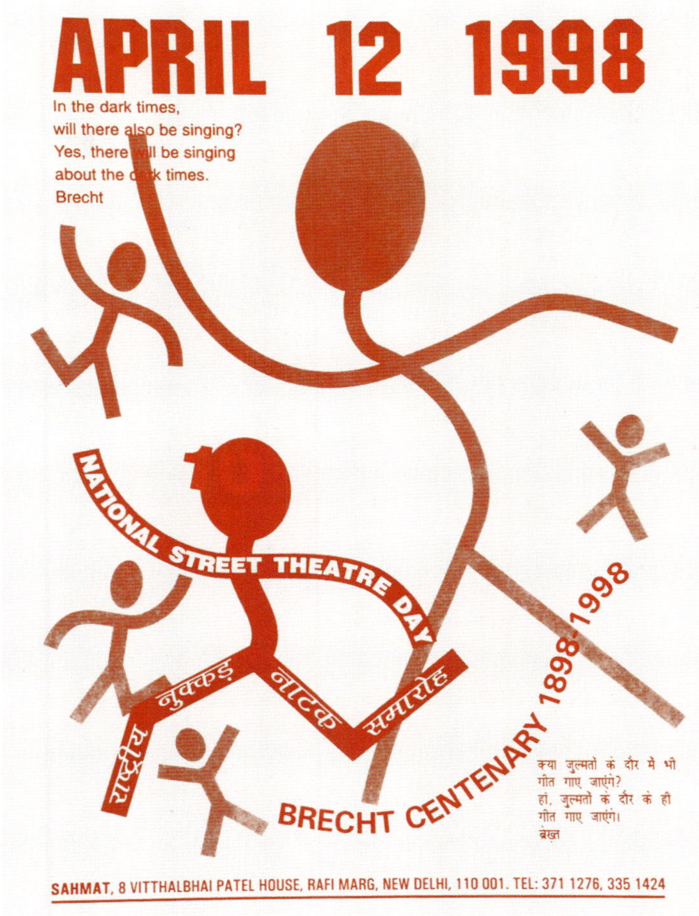

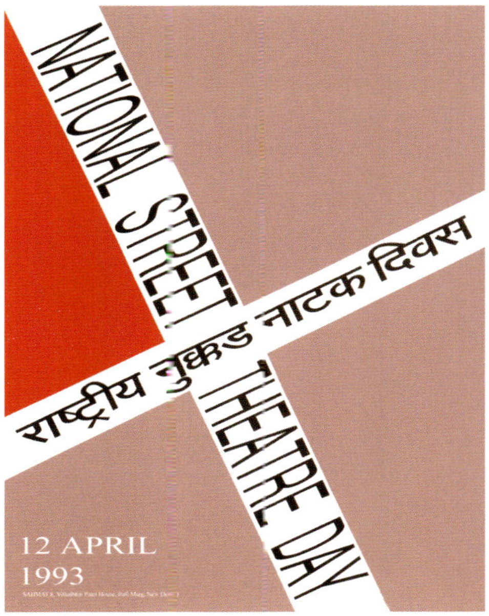

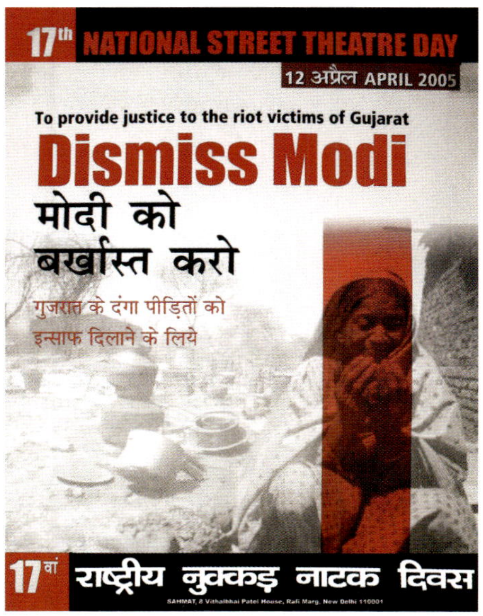

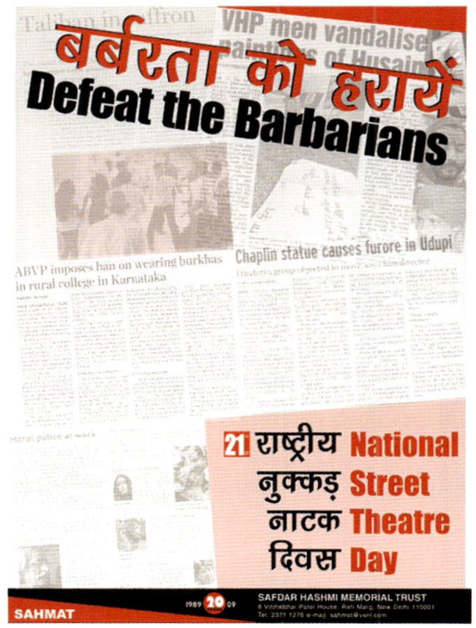

CLOCKWISE FROM TOP LEFT

National Street Theatre Day poster, 2007, 19 x 14 inches. Design: Ram Rahman.

National Street Theatre Day poster, 1998, 21 x 15½ inches. Design: Ram Rahman.

National Street Theatre Day poster, 2009, 19 x 14 inches. Design: Rajinder Arora.

National Street Theatre Day poster, 2005, 22 x 17 inches. Design: Rajinder Arora.

National Street Theatre Day poster, 1993, 19 x 14 inches. Design: Parthiv Shah.

1990 *Janotsav*

Janotsav (People's Festival) consisted of a series of community-based cultural workshops and interactive programs conducted at Mangolpuri, a resettlement colony in Delhi, from October 8 to November 11, 1990. The idea for the festival originated with Safdar Hashmi. Committed to a view of culture that integrates artistic skills with concern for the oppressed and the goal of a life of dignity for all, Hashmi had envisioned *Janotsav* not as an event staged for passive audiences but as a process that would generate a popular and participatory cultural movement. After Hashmi's death, Sahmat developed the concept of *Janotsav* through discussions and workshops, with an aim to help build an inclusive culture by promoting interactions and encounters among the residents of Mangolpuri and practitioners of various art forms.

Over the course of a month, about one hundred artists worked with children and adults from the Mangolpuri community during workshops that produced collaborative works of theatre, visual arts, and music. Residents also viewed works and performances that artists brought to Mangolpuri. While exposing the community to a variety of urban art forms and practices, *Janotsav* helped to demystify art-making by inviting members of the community into the creative process. In addition to imparting skills to those who participated in the workshops, *Janotsav* provided an opportunity for vigorous interactions among the artists and members of the community.

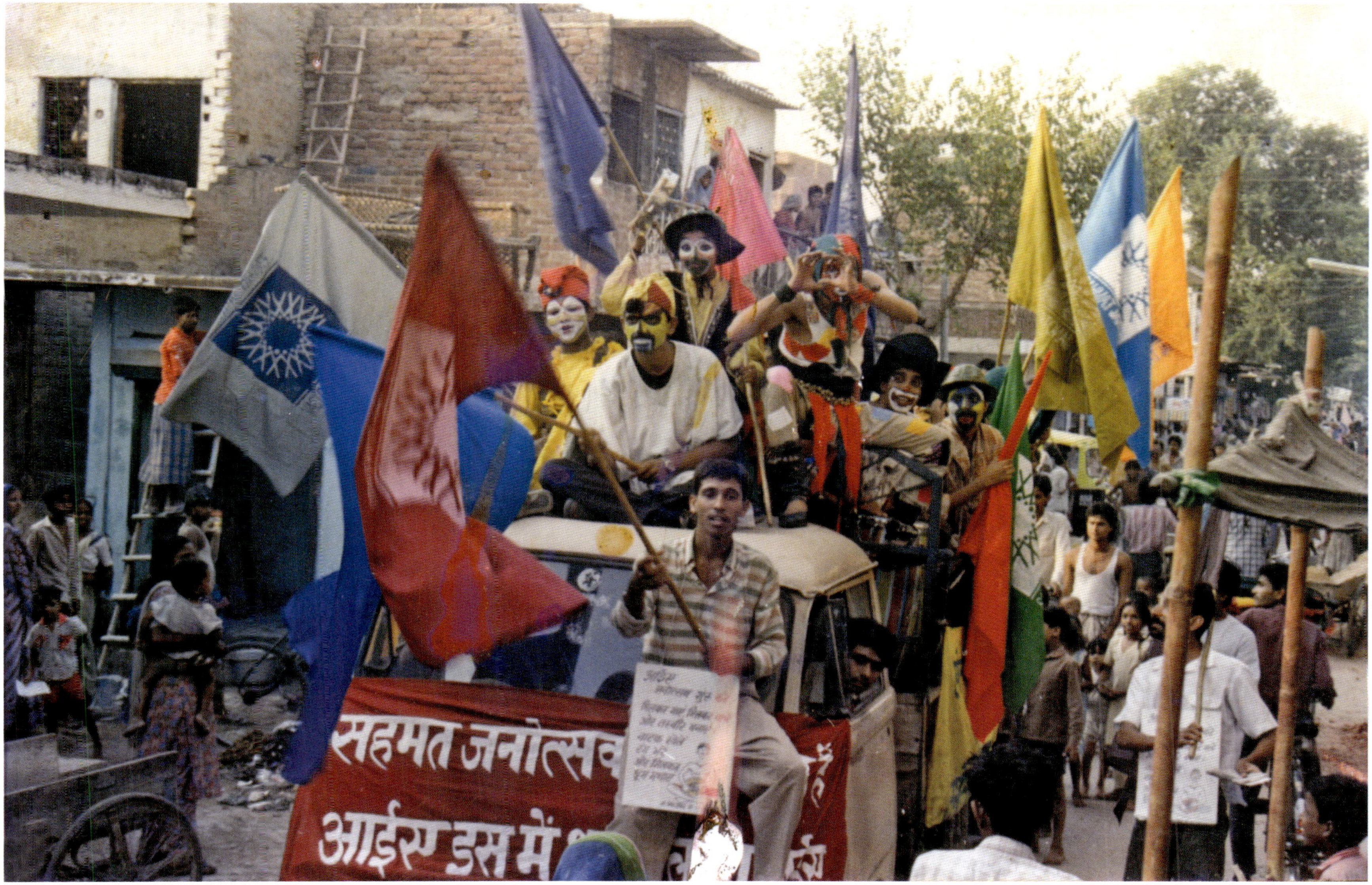

Students of the National School of Drama join theatre workshop participants from Mangolpuri atop a truck to announce *Janotsav* events.

Janotsav

MOLOYASHREE HASHMI

Sahmat has organized a number of events and activities that reached out to the working people and members of the lower middle class. I remember in particular the Janotsav, a "people's festival," organized in 1990 in Mangolpuri, a large and teeming resettlement colony in west Delhi. The inspiration for this came from Safdar. He had dreamt of such a festival in which the best Indian artists would take their art to the people and in turn also create art with them.

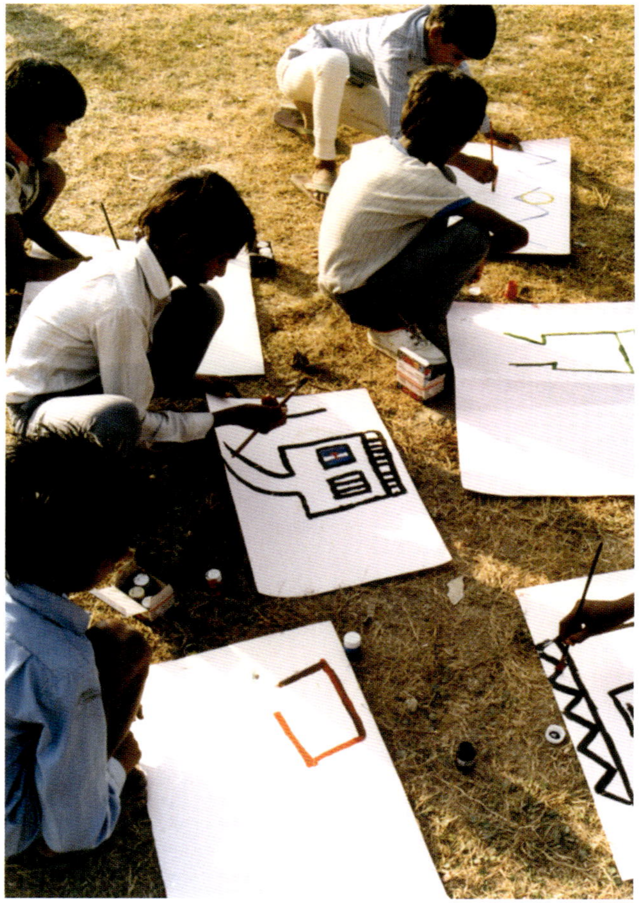

Children's painting workshop in Mangolpuri.

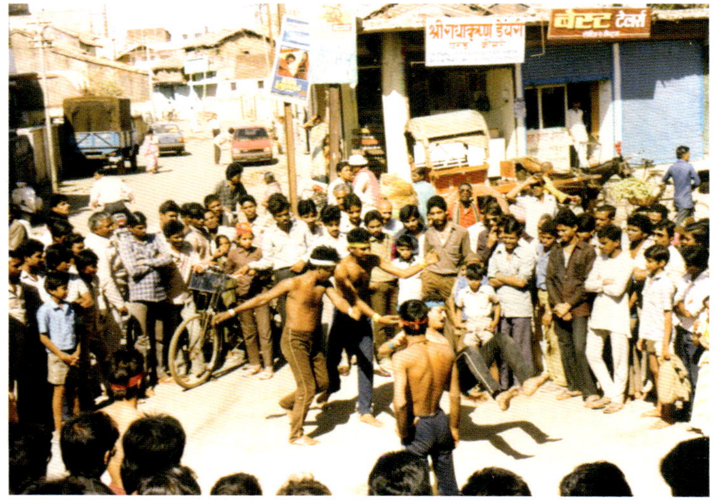

A street theatre performance in progress at Mangolpuri.

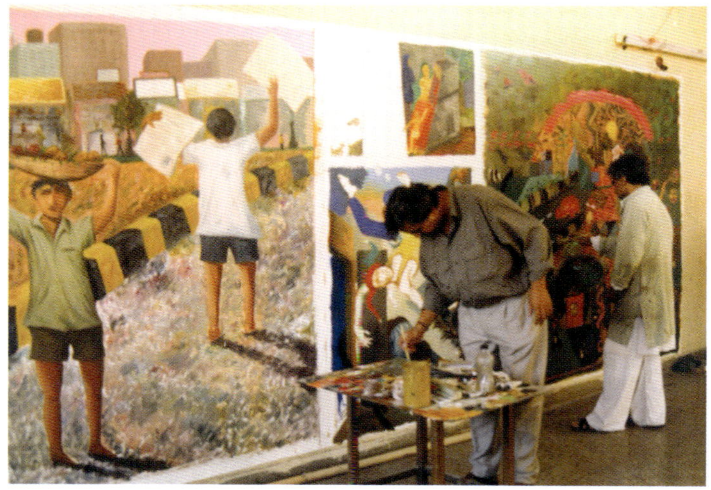

Artists Shamshad (left) and Vivan Sundaram (right) give finishing touches to their canvases on the wall of the *baraat ghar* (community center) in Mangolpuri.

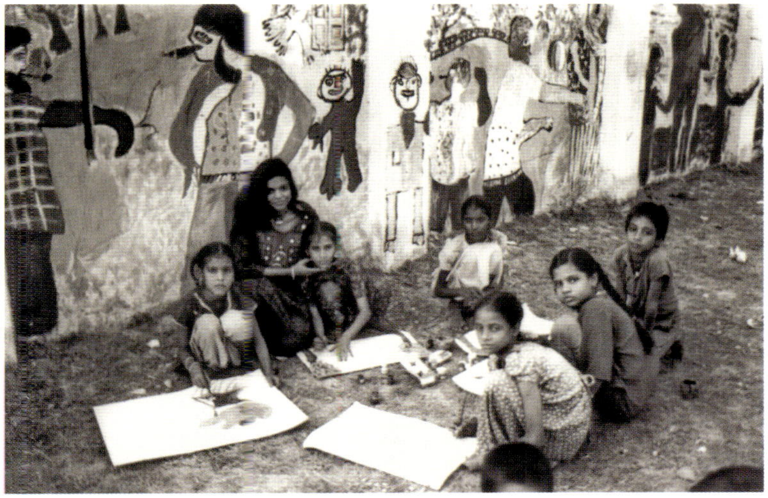

Children of Mangolpuri at a painting workshop.

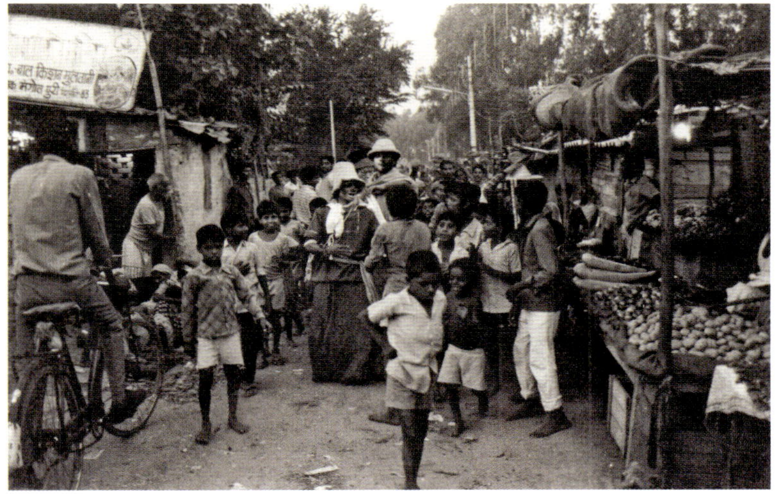

Theatre workshop participants with painted faces on the streets of Mangolpuri.

VIVAN SUNDARAM

Janotsav was, I think, a really early but important project because we went out to a slum resettlement colony. This was in a place called Mangolpuri. After the slums in Delhi had been demolished in the mid-1970s, the occupants had been resettled in areas at the edge of the city where they were given twenty-five-square-yard plots of land, and Mangolpuri was one of these areas. To go to a working-class area of this kind and work there was very exciting and stimulating.

We all felt that it was important to move out of familiar spaces that we know, and to connect with some aspect of a living community space. And that's why we chose Mangolpuri. The area had some members of the CPI(M) [Communist Party of India (Marxist)] who lived there, so we thought there would be some local people who could, in a sense, help us make contact with the community. Here's an interesting aside: some of these comrades found that what we were doing as art didn't quite fit in with whatever ideas and notions they had of art. They felt this art-making and the art that resulted was not what people would understand and so we would alienate them. But then, you could see how all the young people who came to our workshops were excited and enthusiastic, and eager to participate.

There was this huge energy with people from across different disciplines . . . there was theatre going on and artist's workshops and workshops with children and so on. I helped to organize the painting workshop, which culminated in an exhibition.

There was this community center hall where we set up large canvases on the walls, and one of my intentions was to get the local people to paint alongside. And so, while I made my painting, they worked on it as well. There were two persons in particular who were quite talented, though they had never painted before. They did these large paintings with considerable confidence, and they got very involved with the fact that there were a few painters painting and that they could paint alongside them. And, in that same space, one of our finest theatre directors, Habib Tanvir, was also rehearsing, with both actors from his group and local people. So, there were crossovers: that space was both a kind of collective painting studio and a theatre rehearsal-cum-performance space.

For the exhibition, we got the artists to contribute works as they would for a normal exhibition, but it was held in this working-class area. We created a large stage and we also had theatre and music performances. Also, there was this community center—called the *baraat ghar*, which local people hire for weddings—where we had our temporary office, and artists painted murals all along the walls of this fairly large area. There were at least eight to ten artists who were doing that apart from those who were painting on canvas inside.

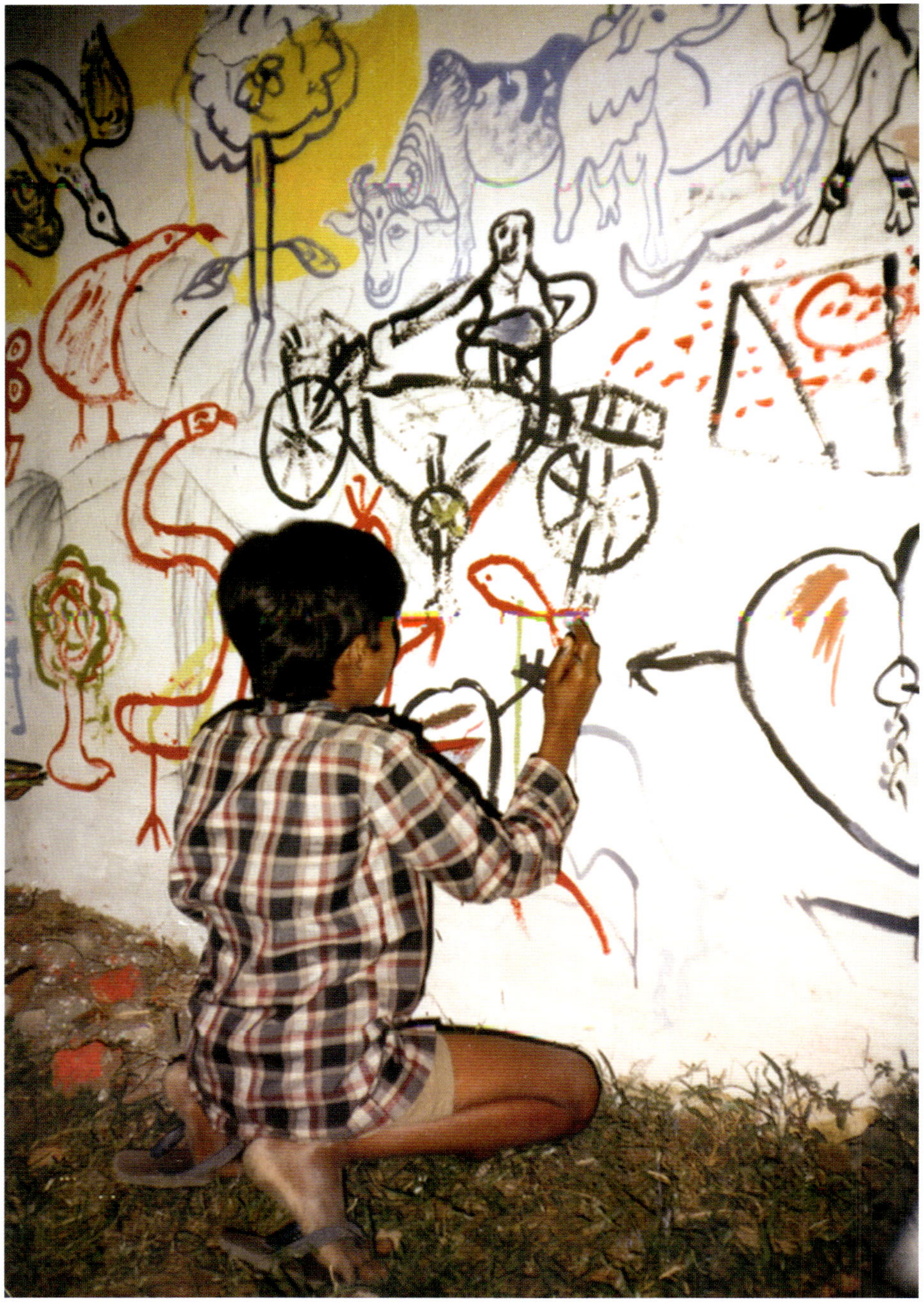

A young artist at work on the environment wall mural that was created by children working with artists Gurpreet, Orijit, and Prithvijit.

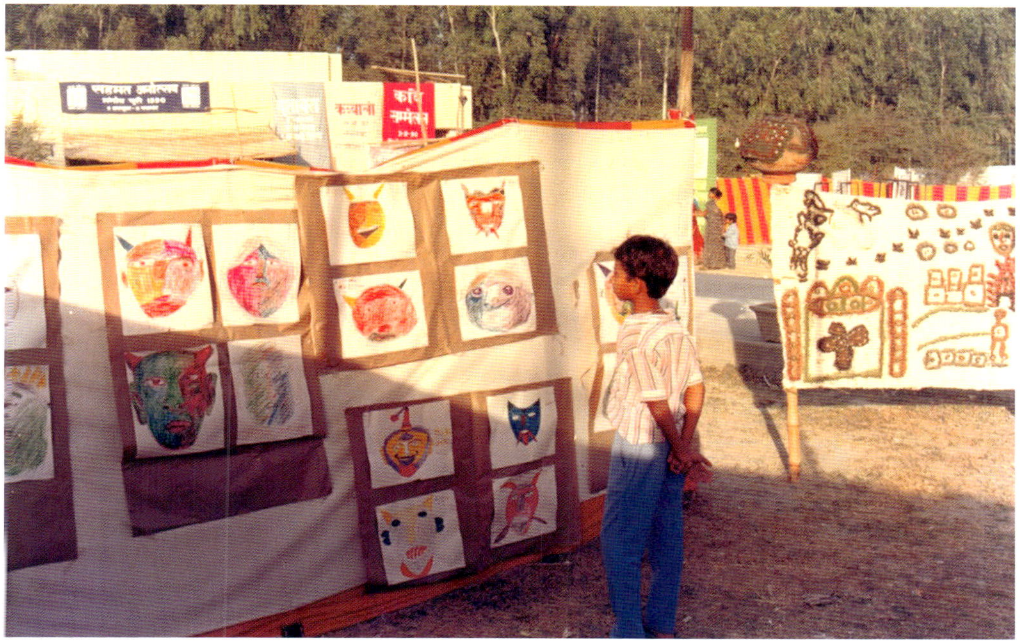

Children's paintings on display during *Janotsav* at Mangolpuri.

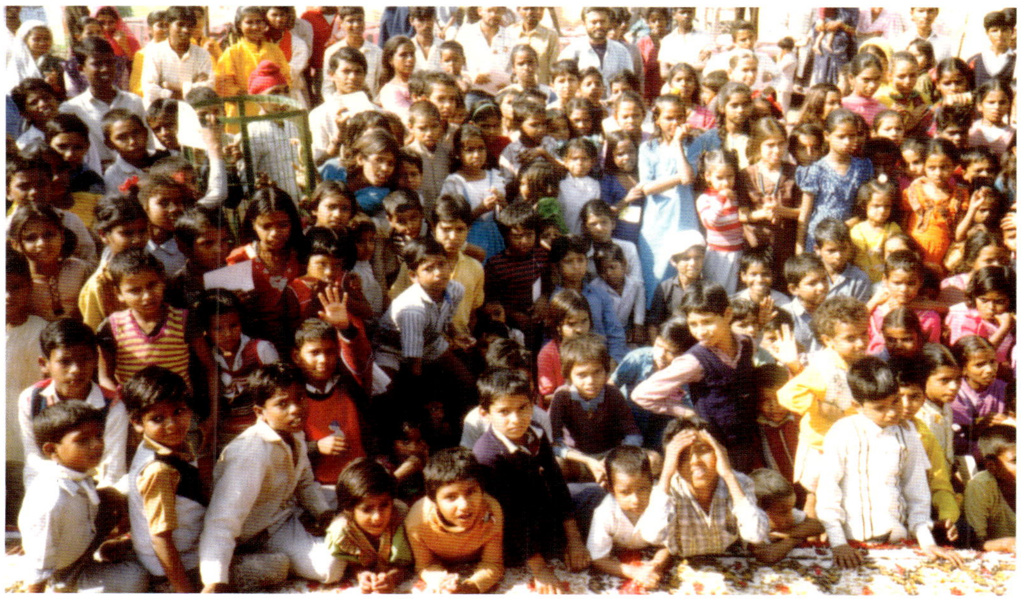

Children of Mangolpuri watch a performance during *Janotsav*.

PARTHIV SHAH

Mangolpuri was an intense four-week experience. I went there every day to the community center, *baraat ghar*, where the children would come and a lot was shared under this one roof. This was part of a larger workshop that involved wonderful artists from other fields such as the legendary theatre person Habib Tanvir.

I did a photography workshop where I gave cameras to about fifty young children in the age group of around eight to fifteen. This was the first time these participants had ever held a camera, and they printed their photographs in a makeshift dark room in a kitchen at the community center. For the children, learning how to shoot, develop, process, and print photographs, as well as the sheer joy of working with us, was a fantastic experience. This was the first time they had a tool that allowed them to choose, select, and capture images to show others. For me, too, given my interest in understanding how people see and what they perceive, this was a most fascinating exercise. The photographs they printed were shown first in the community and then exhibited at a prestigious venue in Mumbai, at the Center for Photography as an Art Form, NCPA.

The experience raised several important questions: of representation, perception, artistic freedom, of transcending stereotypical hierarchies of art and its presentation.

Photographs made by children of Mangolpuri in a photography workshop conducted by Parthiv Shah.

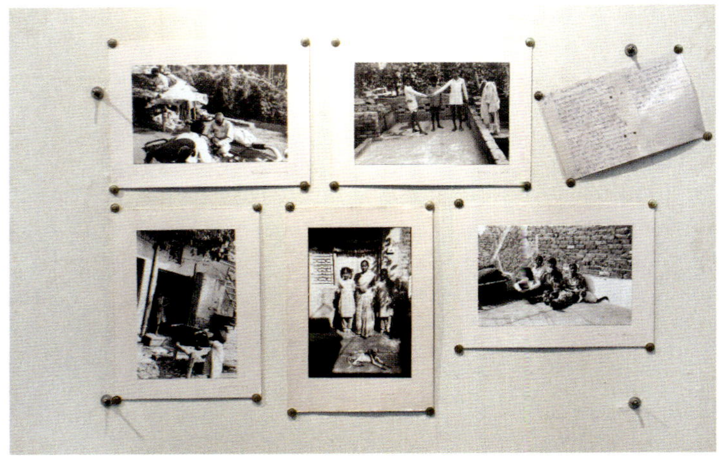

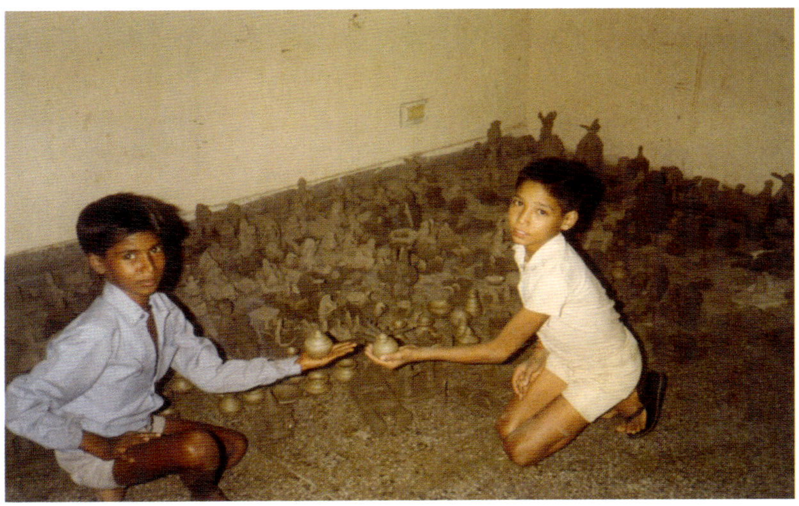

Children hold up terracotta works they made in a workshop conducted by sculptors Soman and Pramod.

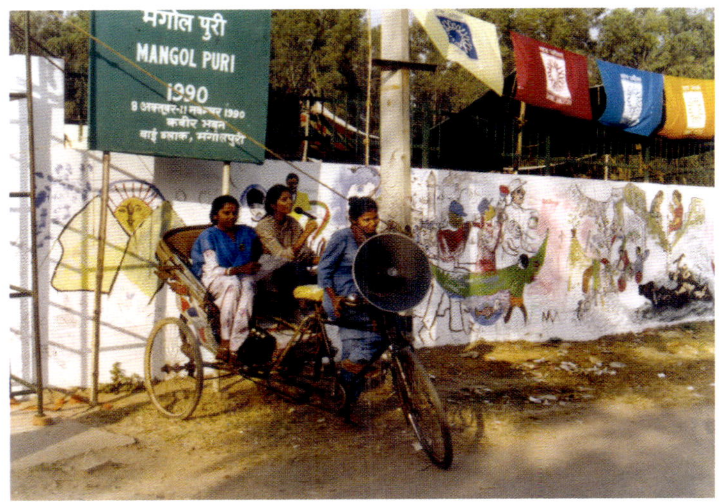

Volunteers seated in a cycle-rickshaw fitted with a speaker.

A Unique Folk Festival

Madhu Prasad

Excerpt from "A Unique Folk Festival," *Sunday Herald*, *Deccan Herald*, Bangalore, November 18, 1990.

The chatter and excitement of the children, the noise, bustle, dust . . .

Nothing extraordinary, one would think, for Mangolpuri, a sprawling resettlement colony located in west Delhi. Yet, the Sahmat *Janotsav*, already a month into its activities here, is truly extraordinary.

A novel experiment in setting up sustained interaction between professional artistes and creative persons and the residents of Mangolpuri, the impact of the Janotsav is clearly tangible. From three little used and ill-cared for *baraat ghars*, which now house numerous workshops, emanate the sounds, colors and rhythms of a joyous creativity. . . .

A visit to the K Block *baraat ghar* is an exhilarating experience. Brightly colored banners featuring the *Janotsav* emblem are prominently displayed at the gate. As we enter, *shamianas* mark out the workspace of the terracotta workshop being conducted by sculptors Soman and Pramod. Over 90 participants, working in two shifts, are producing reliefs. There is an infectious sense of involvement as we watch a ten-year-old boy working swiftly and without hesitation, unwilling to leave despite the fact that it is past eight o'clock and getting dark and cold outside. The work drying on the floor is impressive, displaying both imagination and skill. Within a day or two, Soman will teach the children to "fire" their creations with cowdung cakes. Work has already started on another project: a terracotta mural is being created in a corner of the L Block park, as part of an adventure playground that is being developed there.

Across the courtyard, a group of boys and girls are working on lino sheets. So far they have been drawing on paper; today for the first time it is lino sheets and tools for scooping out areas to be left plain, bringing the designs out in relief, ready for printing. Anandamoy Banerji and Sushanta Guha, who are conducting the workshop, have with great difficulty restricted the numbers, for careful supervision is essential with novices using scooping knives for the first time.

We enter the central hall of the *baraat ghar* to find a theatre workshop in process, which was initially conducted by Madhusree Dutta and now by Habib Tanvir. A number of young men and women are involved in rehearsing a production to be mounted in the culminating days of the *Janotsav*. At six in the evening this hall resounds with the sound of dancing feet, as Krishna from the Bhumika Dance Troupe engages a group of aspiring dancers. . . . The walls of the central hall display several canvases. Vivan Sundaram's painting has delighted everyone. On a textured background characteristic of his style, Mangolpuri teenagers have constructed their own painting.

Just outside the hall, Dadi Pudumjee and Randhir Khare's puppetry workshop is on in full swing. Participants have started from scratch, making their own puppets and storyline. . . . With unemployment, bribery and corruption emerging as major themes, an enormous pair of hands has been integrated into the script. A grasping, greedy presence, these hands follow the puppets, intervening in the action all the time. On the lawns, Arun Kumar, Jitendra and Kishore enjoy the boisterous antics of the participants in their mask-making workshop. They have brought bright pieces of cloth to don the beautiful *papier-mâché* masks they have made in the workshop and are preparing to participate in the weekend programe with students of the National School of Drama.

The door is closed. A small red light is on outside. Parthiv Shah's photography group is developing the first set of film rolls that they have used. The students cannot quite believe that they have been allowed to take the cameras with them, so that they can explore and choose the subjects they would like to shoot. The results are surprisingly good; many are to be used right away in the *Mangolpuri Samachar*, a tabloid being produced by the journalism workshop conducted by Kumi Chandra and Brijendra.

Children dominate the Y Block *baraat ghar*, which also houses the *Janotsav* office. Pal Sahib, with years of experience at Bal Bhavan, creates magic as he brings together paper, paint and scores of eager hands and minds that even in school have no access to these. Sonya Verma and Bulbul Sharma also handle art workshops with the young ones. The group working with Orijit, Prithvijit, and Gurpreet has almost completed their environment wall mural, while Sumantra Sengupta has provided the motivation for covering the walls of the once drab *baraat ghar* with paintings that flow into a mural that continues beyond the gates and out onto the street.

Theatre, music and dance workshops are also held here. Ashish Ghosh runs the children's theatre workshop, while Rakesh, Joy, and Sudhanva handle the two street theatre groups with young men and women. Dinesh Khanna is producing a play with yet another group. Kajal Ghosh and Amit Sengupta are training young vocalists. Viswakant's dance workshop, one of the earliest to settle down to a rigorous routine, is more than ready for its first public performance.

The list of activities seems never-ending, but the *Janotsav* is moving to a close. We watch two 15-minute video films: on riot-affected Punjabi families in Mangolpuri, and on price rise. Produced entirely by local participants in the workshop conducted by CENDIT, they are authentic, visually attractive and competently made. Our attention is riveted to the little screen as we listen to a young woman from Mangolpuri. Mobile of face and strong in her conviction that those who appear to have nothing will show the world what they are capable of achieving, she seems to epitomize the spirit expressed through every phase and activity of Sahmat's *Janotsav*.

1989–
1990

Children's Books

Safdar Hashmi wrote numerous poems, stories, and plays for children, and as a body of work they reflect a lesser-known aspect of his creative work. Within a year of its formation, Sahmat published ten books for children based on these texts, which were illustrated by both emerging and established artists. Eight were based on individual poems by Hashmi: *Ped* (Tree), illustrated by Mickey Patel; *Red Flower*, illustrated by Mona Rai; *Bansuriwala* (Flute Player), illustrated by Arpita Singh; *Holi* (Holi, the Indian festival of colors), illustrated by Mohandas N. N.; *Gadbad Ghotala* (Topsy-Turvy World), illustrated by B. V. Suresh; *Bagh ki Sair* (A Walk in the Garden), illustrated by Vasudevan Akkitham; *Kitaben* (Books), illustrated by Surendran Nair; and *Saare Mausam Acchhe* (All Seasons Are Wonderful), illustrated by Nilima Sheikh. One was a collection of Hashmi's poems, titled *Duniya Sabki* (The World Belongs to Everyone), and one a collection of plays, titled *Natak ki Duniya* (The World of Plays), both illustrated by Bindia Thapar.

Conceived as a collaborative project to bring together images by artists and texts by writers in the format of a printed book, the success of this series prompted Sahmat, in later years, to commission and publish several more artist-illustrated books for children.

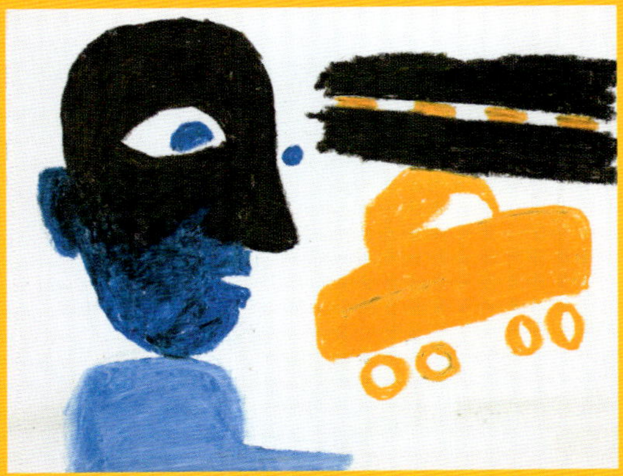
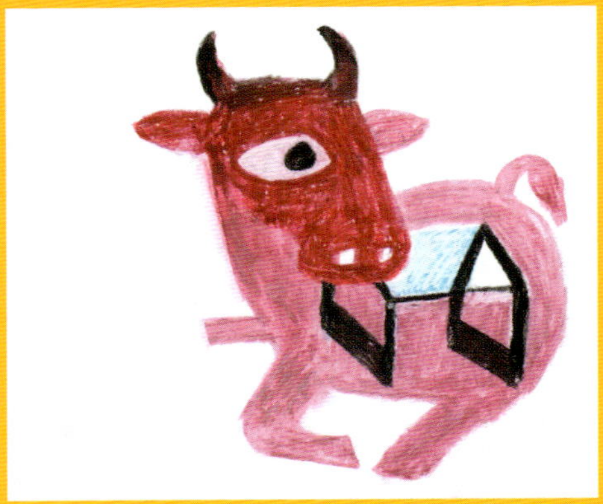
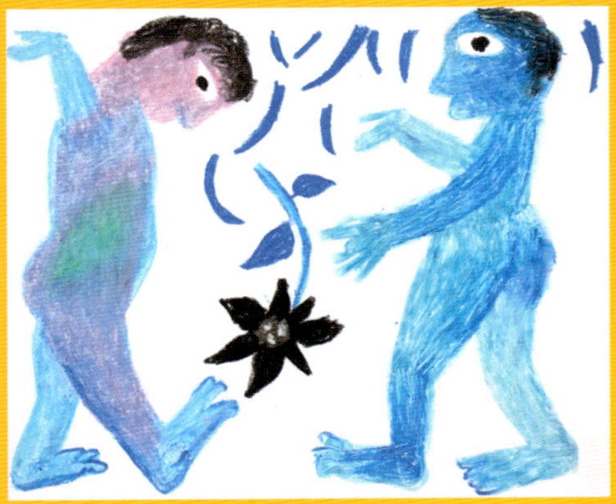

B. V. SURESH
Gadbad Ghotala, 1989, oil pastel on paper, 11 x 14 inches.

It was also one of the first instances of contemporary Indian artists contributing to such a project, contrasting the prevailing convention in Indian publishing of employing professional illustrators for children's books. The books reinforce Sahmat's commitment to disseminating progressive art across boundaries of class, religion, and age. They have been reprinted multiple times and translated into several Indian languages. Hundreds of thousands of copies of the various editions have been—and continue to be—sold. This popularity may reflect their dual nature: though outwardly simple and whimsical, the books tell stories of harmony and acceptance.

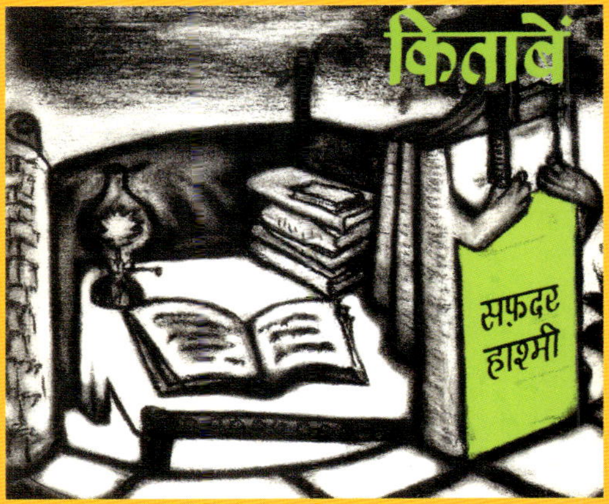

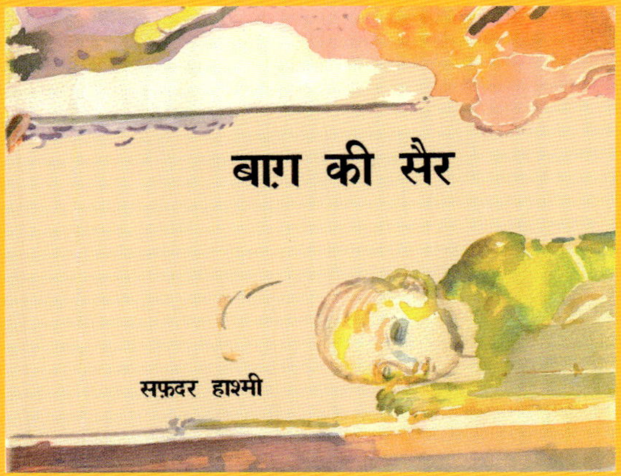

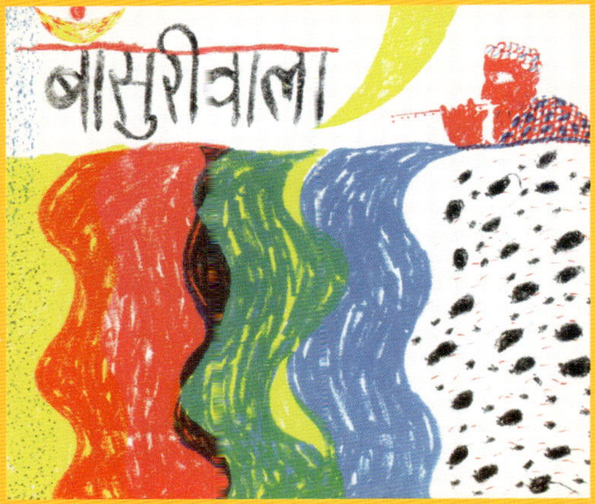

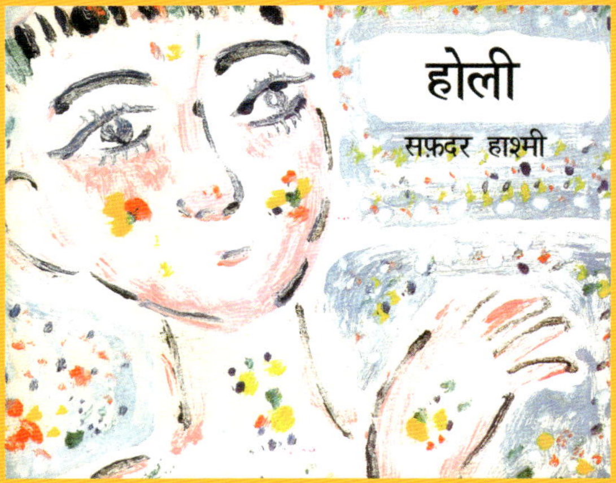

CLOCKWISE FROM TOP LEFT

Cover of *Kitaben* (Books) by Safdar Hashmi, illustrated by Surendran Nair, 1989.

Cover of *Bagh ki Sair* (A Walk in the Garden) by Safdar Hashmi, illustrated by Vasudevan Akkitham, 1989.

Cover of *Holi* by Safdar Hashmi, illustrated by Mohandas N. N., 1989.

Cover of *Bansuriwala* (Flute Player) by Safdar Hashmi, illustrated by Arpita Singh, 1989.

NILIMA SHEIKH

Illustrations for *Saare Mausam Acchhe* (All Seasons Are Wonderful), 1990, diptych, watercolor on paper, 7 x 17 inches each.

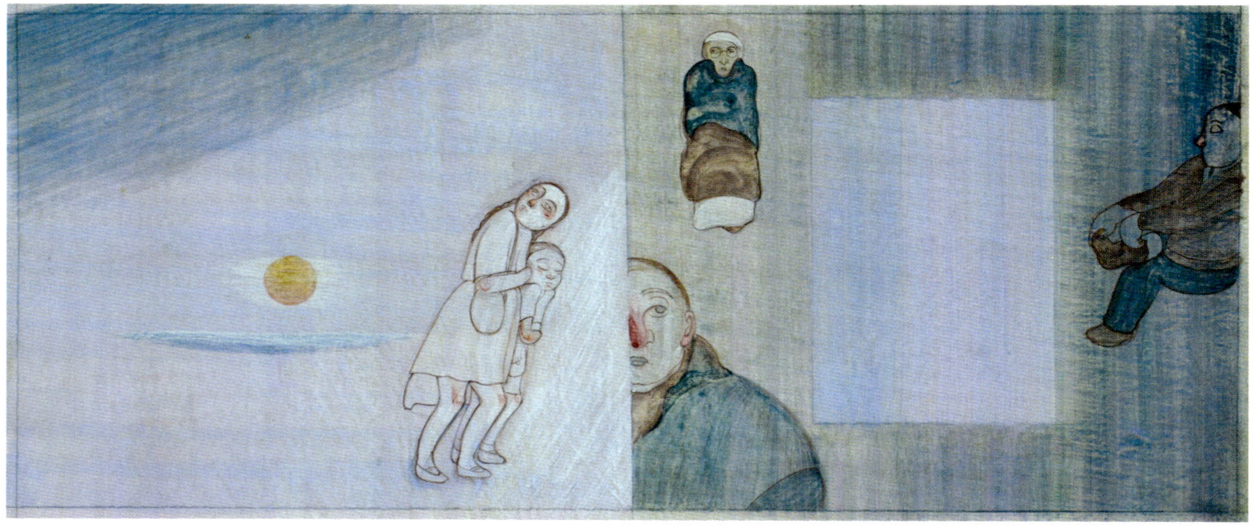

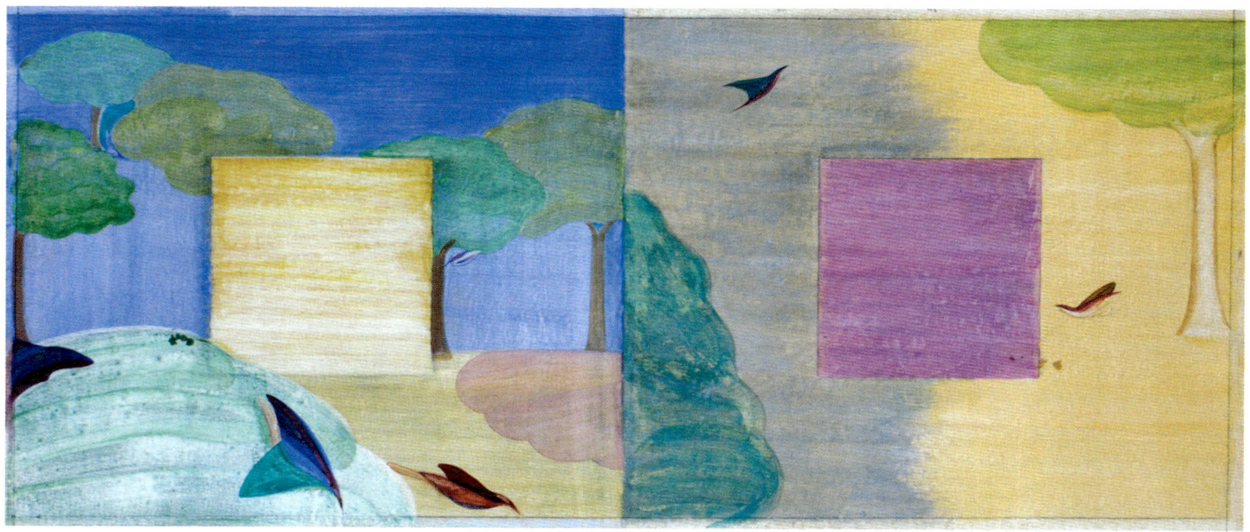

Illustrating one of Safdar's poems for children challenged me. I had to develop my visual language for the specific needs and understanding of children. Having used text as a catalyst and component in my paintings since 1984, I had already designed and illustrated a book for children, but when the idea of publishing Safdar Hashmi's poems for children was raised and Vivan Sundaram assumed the responsibility of overseeing the project, I felt I could extend myself. The pleasure of matching the joyous humanism of the poem has stayed with me. I had been working since the mid-1970s, after the birth of my children, with the intimate life of the neighborhood, in Baroda where I lived and in Himachal Pradesh where we had a family home. And I used to tease in anecdotes and recognizable personas to make the works come alive for my children. So *Saare Mausam Acchhe* (All Seasons Are Wonderful), a poem about shared

NILIMA SHEIKH

Illustrations for *Saare Mausam Acchhe* (All Seasons Are Wonderful), 1990, diptych, watercolor on paper, 7 x 17 inches each.

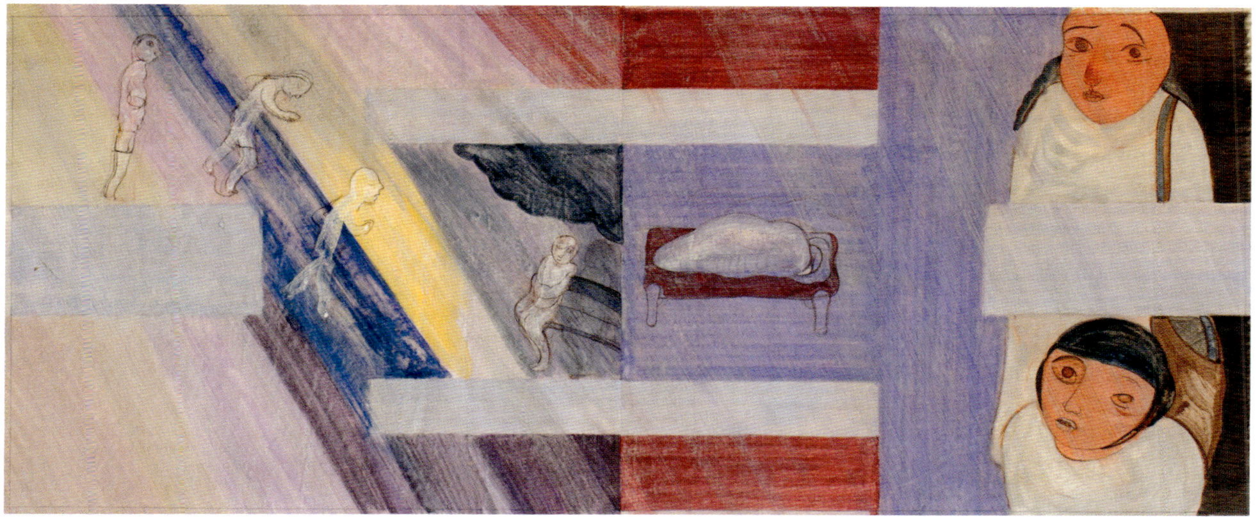

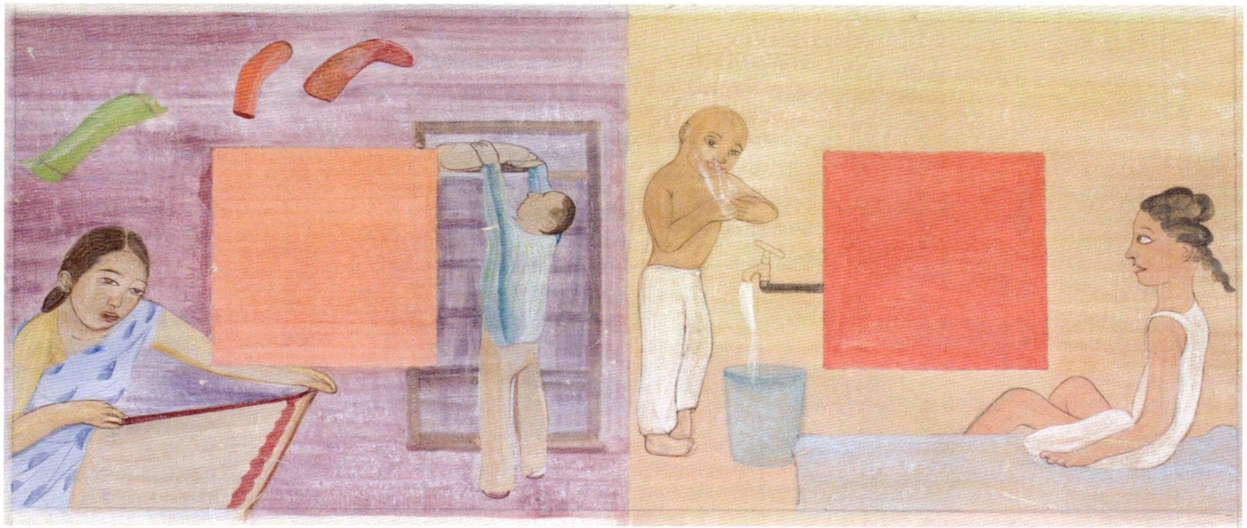

neighborhood spaces, came at the right time for me. My objective was to see that children, not just mine, had access to the poem about changing seasons, and to the extended family life of mothers, sisters, domestic animals, neighbors at leisure and at work—masons, cobblers, the washerman and his wife. My collaboration with contemporary and past poets and writers has continued, notably in the last decade with the Kashmiri poet Agha Shahid Ali. Hesitant to take the plunge into the complex worlds of Kashmir, to which I wanted to bring some visibility, I was led by the hand, so to speak, by the poetry of the poet who saw himself as marked/martyred by the pain of his homeland.

Illustrating poems has allowed me to borrow words for what I could not paint and paint what was left unsaid, besides trying to match painting to poetry. —N. S.

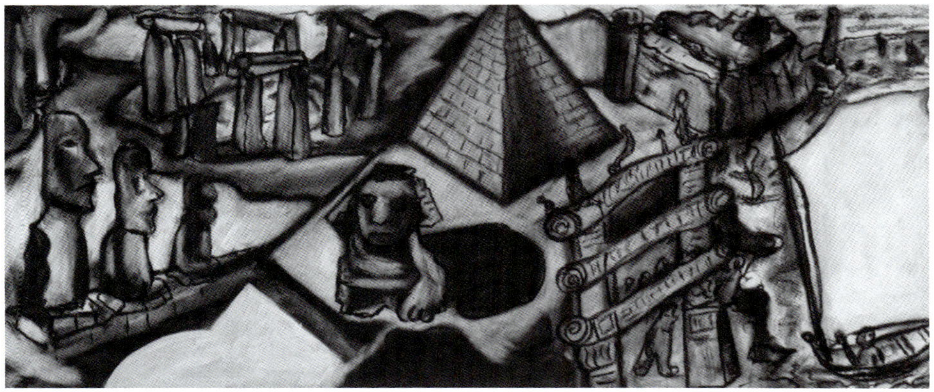

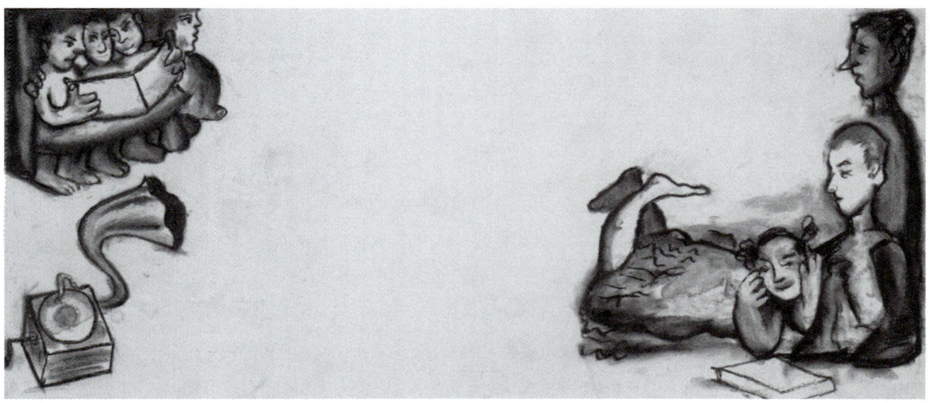

SURENDRAN NAIR
Illustrations for *Kitaben* (Books), 1989, charcoal on paper, 7 x 17 inches each.

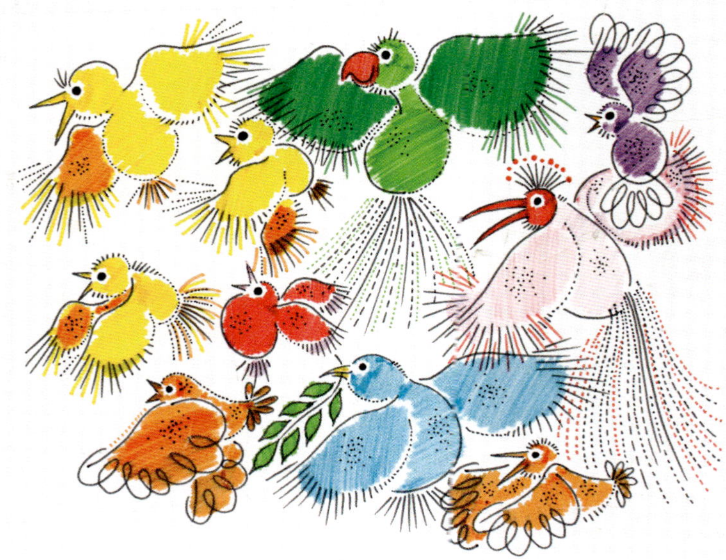

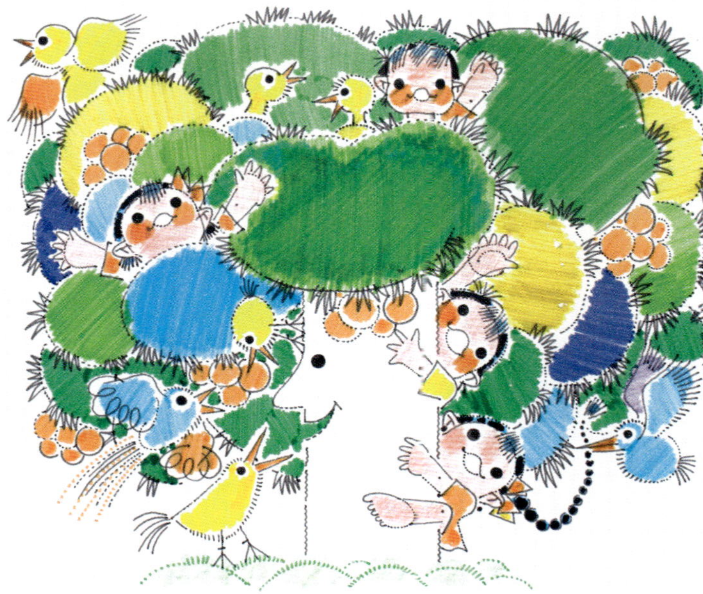

MICKEY PATEL
Illustrations for *Ped* (Tree), 1989, ink and color on paper, 7 x 9½ inches each.

MONA RAI
Illustration for *The Red Flower,* 1989, watercolor on paper, 7 x 8 inches.

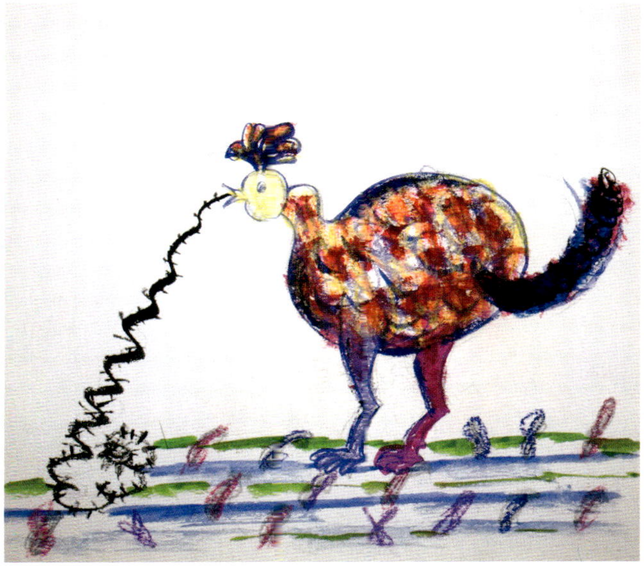

Cover of *The Red Flower* by Safdar Hashmi, illustrated by Mona Rai, 1989.

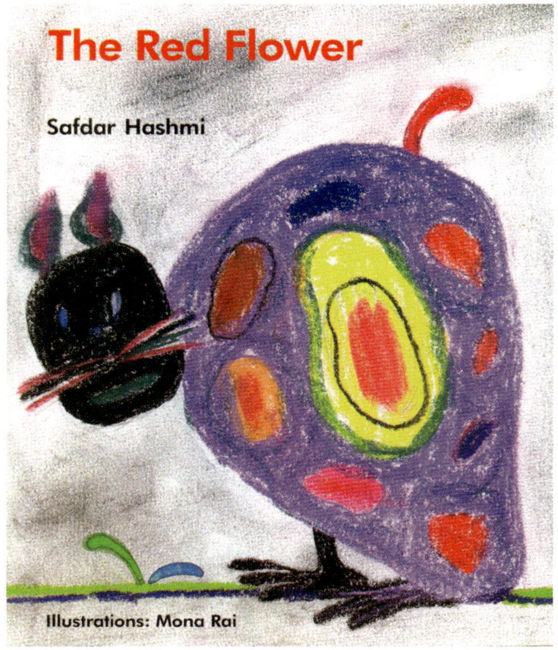

Safdar Hashmi's *The Red Flower* offers a parable of interaction between animals and nature. As the red flower wilts in distress from a worm in her petals, her friend the sun hides in the clouds, unhappy that he cannot help the flower. To show his solidarity, the wind stops blowing. A rooster is unable to crow in the stuffy air. Finally a frog helps the rooster realize that he can pluck out the worm from the flower, which he does, restoring order to all. The story ends with optimism: "It is easy to sit and cry when things go wrong somewhere. But if someone has the sense and cares to make an effort, things will come right again. And all shall be happy and gay."

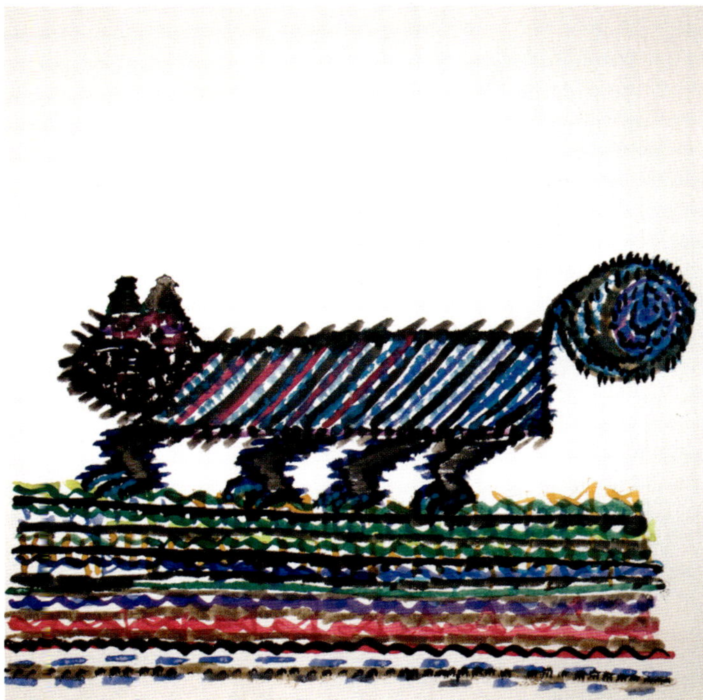

MONA RAI
Illustration for *The Red Flower,* 1989, watercolor on paper, 7 x 8 inches.

When Vivan told me that he'd like me to do the book I was very excited because I had not done a thing like that earlier. . . . I'm very fond of children and I've also done some teaching assignments teaching art and French. I was in a dilemma as to how to start it or how to handle it, because my style of working is very different and very abstract. Then as I read the story and thought about it, it kind of got moving by itself. Once I started to do it, I really enjoyed it. It was fun. —M. R.

1991–
Ongoing

Artists Against Communalism

Artists Against Communalism Campaign

With a seventeen-hour sit-in at Safdar Hashmi Marg (Road), New Delhi, on January 1, 1991, accompanied by performances in music, dance, and theatre, Sahmat launched the campaign *Artists Against Communalism (AAC)*. Seeing a rapidly escalating threat of communalism—forces of religious fundamentalism and sectarianism in sociopolitical life—Sahmat members chose an unconventional form of protest. Rather than using standard methods such as marches and strikes to express the creative community's opposition to such forces, they asserted the plural and composite nature of India's cultural traditions by providing a shared platform for a rich variety of India's performing arts. From emerging to established senior artists, the participants' enthusiasm stretched the event from twelve to seventeen hours, in spite of the cold New Year's Day. The positive response of the *AAC* audience and the extent of the media's coverage indicated both a vast potential for promoting secularism through art, and the possibility of reaching popular audiences with a wide range of art practices, ensuring that the performances became a recurring program of Sahmat. It went on to travel to several cities across India.

Sahmat produced similar programs as part of the larger *Artists Against Communalism* campaign: a commemoration of Mahatma Gandhi's assassination was held in six cities on January 30, 1991, and *Images and Words*, an ambitious mobile exhibition that traveled to thirty cities around the country. The following year, also under the *AAC* banner, Sahmat held *Slogans for Communal Harmony*, one of the largest public art projects to have been organized in India at the time.

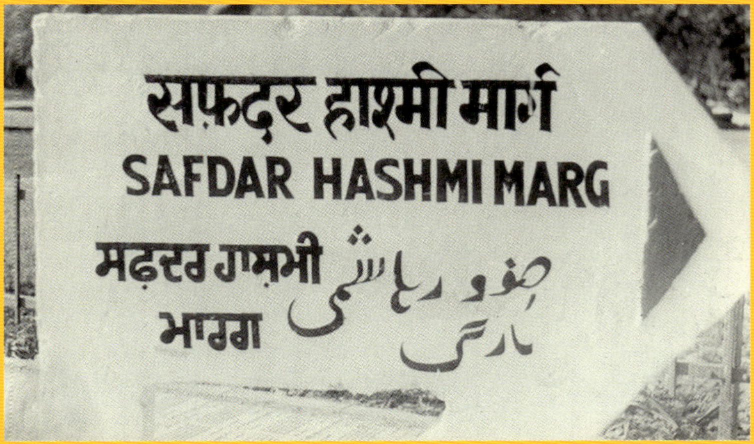

College Street at Mandi House in New Delhi was renamed as Safdar Hashmi Marg (Road) on January 2, 1990, after public campaigning. The road was blocked off for Sahmat to use as the site for the annual January 1 *Safdar Hashmi Memorial* for years to come.

► Classical dancers Raja and Radha Reddy, waiting to perform for *Artists Against Communalism*, Safdar Hashmi Marg, January 1, 1991.

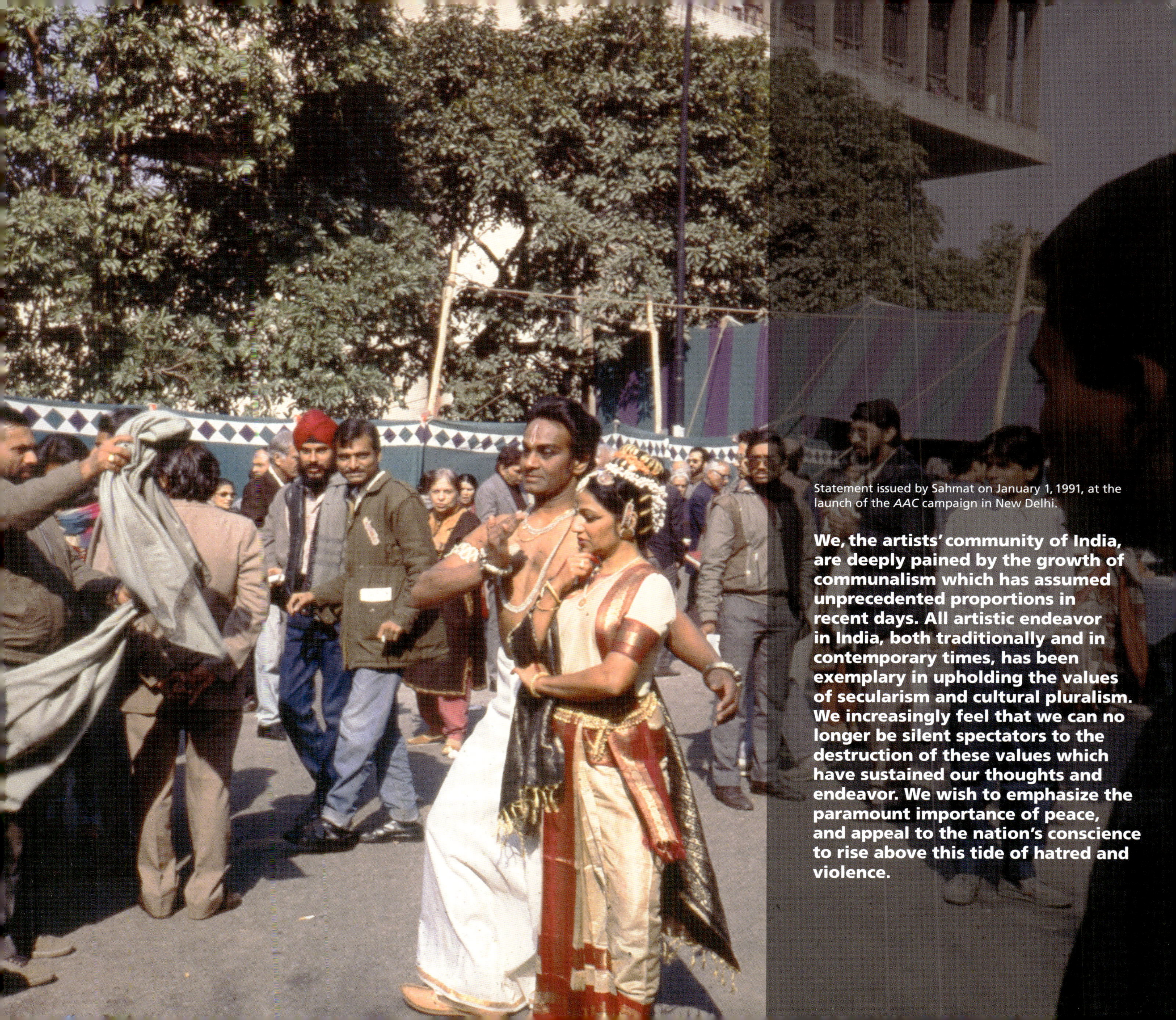

Statement issued by Sahmat on January 1, 1991, at the launch of the *AAC* campaign in New Delhi.

We, the artists' community of India, are deeply pained by the growth of communalism which has assumed unprecedented proportions in recent days. All artistic endeavor in India, both traditionally and in contemporary times, has been exemplary in upholding the values of secularism and cultural pluralism. We increasingly feel that we can no longer be silent spectators to the destruction of these values which have sustained our thoughts and endeavor. We wish to emphasize the paramount importance of peace, and appeal to the nation's conscience to rise above this tide of hatred and violence.

PUSHPAMALA N.

Well, I have been an organizer only in Bombay (Mumbai). This was for the first *Artists Against Communalism* festival in 1992 when I was the curator and organizer of the visual art section. I conceived the idea and organized long banners against communalism painted by Mumbai artists, which were hung on either side of the stage. I also selected artist Tyeb Mehta's painting as a large backdrop for the stage. Besides of course, being involved in the general organization, our flat in Prabhadevi, Mumbai, was the project's headquarters.

ASTAD DEBOO

Performing on the stage for Sahmat is something I look forward to every year, which brings me along with other varied artists both from the performing world and the visual world, and even writers and scholars, who are all there with a single focus on secularism. Being there through the years has become like a family reunion. . . . It has also enriched me as an individual and my practice. Performing on a stage that is not really a proscenium stage and each of us coming on stage one after the other facilitate a sense of sharing and interaction among the various artists and the audience. At the same time the audience comes with an open mind: it's not like sometimes when you are performing in a proper theatre and there are people who come with a preconceived notion. Once I'm on stage I am there, and I am not really perturbed by the fact that there are no proper lights, for instance, because I have an attentive audience. For me, that's more important. I am able to communicate my work, through my dance, to the audience.

Contemporary dancer Astad Deboo performs at *Artists Against Communalism* in Bombay, March 14, 1992.

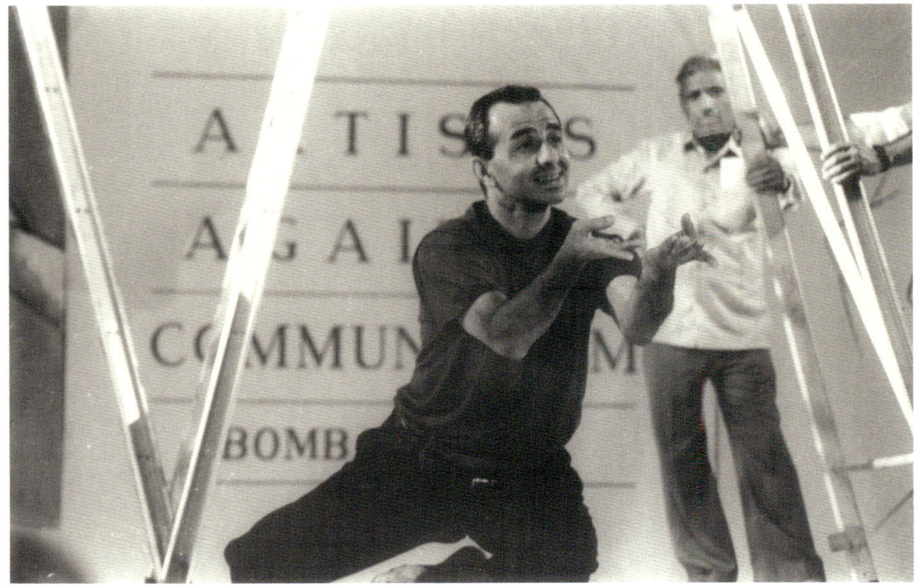

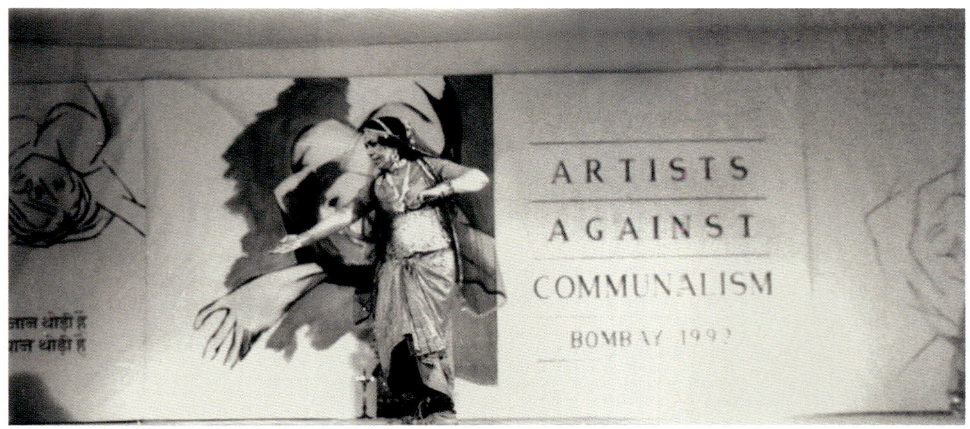

Classical Kathak dancer Sitara Devi performs at *Artists Against Communalism* in Bombay, March 14, 1992. Backdrop banner painted by Tyeb Mehta.

Classical Hindustani musician Hariprasad Chaurasia performs at *Artists Against Communalism*, Bombay, March 14, 1992. Backdrop banner painted by Tyeb Mehta.

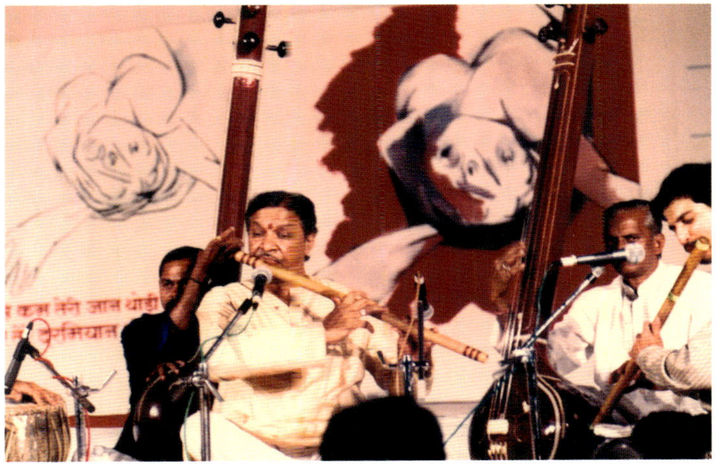

SHUBHA MUDGAL

I was first invited to perform for Sahmat's *Artists Against Communalism* initiative on January 1, 1991. The invitation was extended by S. Kalidas and Sabina Sehgal, who were closely associated with Sahmat's activities and were also students of Hindustani classical music. As I reached the venue for the performance and waited for my turn to go on stage and perform, I was struck by the solidarity that the presence of so many creative people and artistes conveyed. There were celebrated painters, music maestros, filmmakers, theatre persons, activists, scholars. I was familiar with some of them, but I was ignorant of the work and eminence of others there. Each one expressed solidarity with the cause in one way or another. Some, like me, just came quietly and performed or painted. Others spoke with eloquence and brilliance and passion, and I still remember that day quite vividly because there was this unforgettable energy and creative charge in the atmosphere. I think it was that vitality and sense of community that fascinated me and led to an association with Sahmat that is now over two decades old and still going strong.

Since my first performance for Sahmat in 1991, I have composed and set to tune verses that are relevant to the issues that Sahmat is dedicated to. I'm not sure I can claim that music can always be a force for social change. When members of one community are brutalizing members of another community, I can't claim that a song will stop them from barbaric acts of violence. But I do know that music offers me the only way I know of registering my protest, however humble. I may not have sung obvious words (against communalism), but I have sung here for the banner and that, in itself, is a contribution toward the issue.

TYEB MEHTA

Falling Figure (detail), banner painted for *Artists Against Communalism* in Bombay, 1992, 120 x 120 inches.

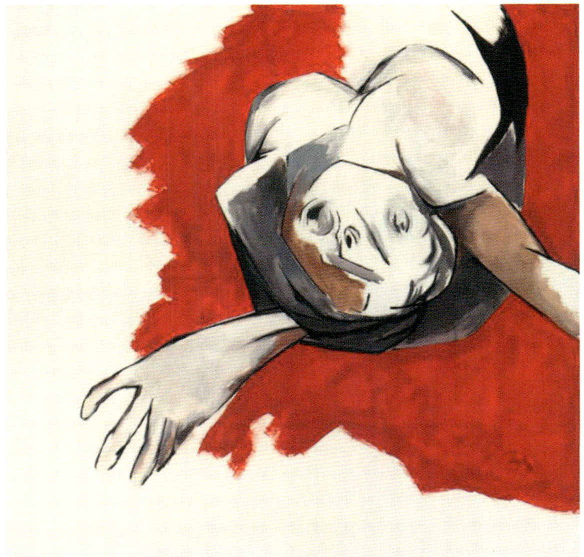

DADI PUDUMJEE

My participation in Sahmat has been very important to me, though I was far more involved in the beginning than in more recent times. I have been exposed to many different artists and writers through Sahmat: the chance to participate in discussions on freedom of expression, India's judicial processes, issues of history, and the interpretation of history in contemporary politics made me rethink my work. It made me aware of my own thinking process and where I stand as an artist and individual.

The last time I performed for Sahmat with my puppets was a few years ago, but one of the first times—possibly in the first Safdar Hashmi festival—was the piece *Failed to be Human*, based on a poem by Randhir Khare.

Art must be seen and heard by all and at various spaces wherever possible, not just confined to closed spaces, and Sahmat provides that alternative space.

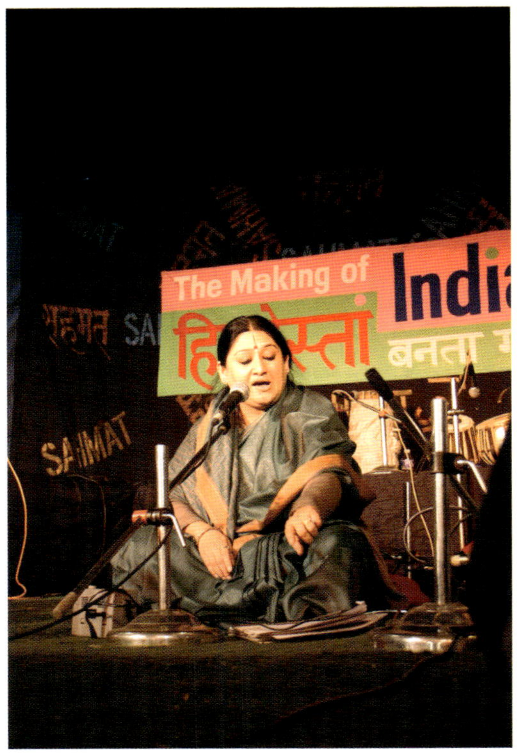

Shubha Mudgal sings at event for *The Making of India*, Delhi, January 1, 2004.

Bhisham Sahni

Excerpt from foreword to *Artists Against Communalism* (New Delhi: Sahmat, 1992).

To my mind, the primary social concern of an artist, writer or cultural worker in India at this time is to confront, with all his or her talent and involvement, the growing communal menace which is threatening to tear apart the very fabric of our national entity. Each passing day brings awful news. People have begun to give credence to the mischievous formulation that ethnic self-assertion is the order of the day and is the natural outcome of earlier historical developments, that India is only a conglomeration of diverse, mutually hostile, ethnic, religious and social groups which had been brought together and given a semblance of unity under the British Raj, but which are now falling apart. Examples are cited from the situations prevailing in other countries to prove the validity of this formulation. This view is being deliberately projected in India to give legitimacy to the separatist activities and to weaken our resolve to fight and overcome these separatist forces. But for us in India, this is not a new formulation; the British rulers often had recourse to it whenever the freedom struggle gained momentum.

But the fact remains that the communal menace is growing. Every now and then vicious riots break out in one town or another, taking a toll of hundreds of innocent lives. In such a gloomy situation, the activities of our secular-minded artists and writers are like a gleam of light. It is heartening to find that this virus of communalism has not affected our cultural workers. The artists and writers have, by and large, adhered to our rich, humanistic traditions and condemned communalism in no uncertain terms. Not only that, many of them have come out and are actively engaged in fighting this menace.

And in this campaign against communalism, the role and the contribution of Sahmat—a name sanctified by the sacrifice of our brilliant and dedicated artist Safdar Hashmi—has been a truly inspiring one. It has been and continues to be a vanguard role. We would like to invite you most fervently to join this campaign against communalism, and make it still more effective with your creative involvement in its activities. You will not regret it.

Contemporary dancer Navtej Johar and singer Madan Gopal Singh perform at *Safdar Hashmi Memorial*, Delhi, January 1, 2007.

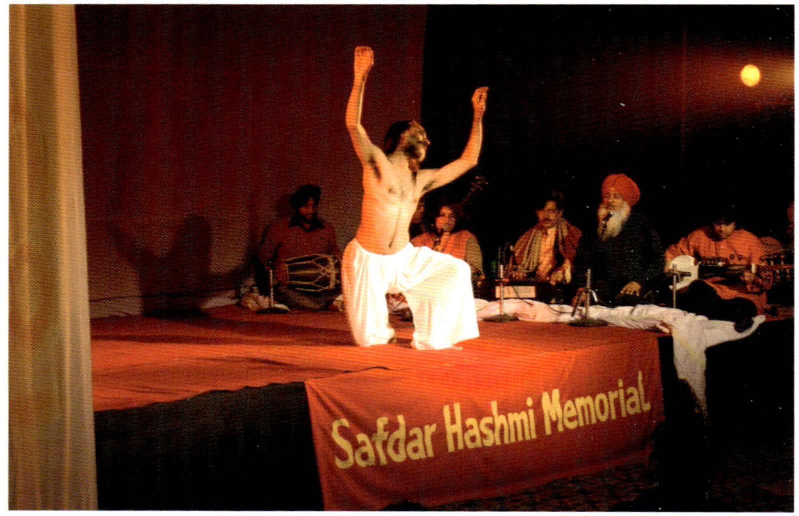

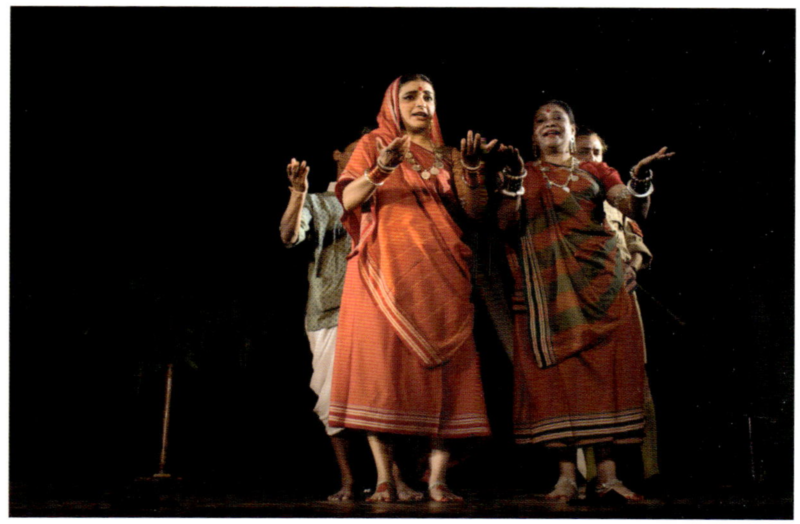

Nageen Tanvir (left) and other members of Habib Tanvir's theatre group, Naya Theatre, staging *Charandas Chor* in Delhi, January 1, 2010.

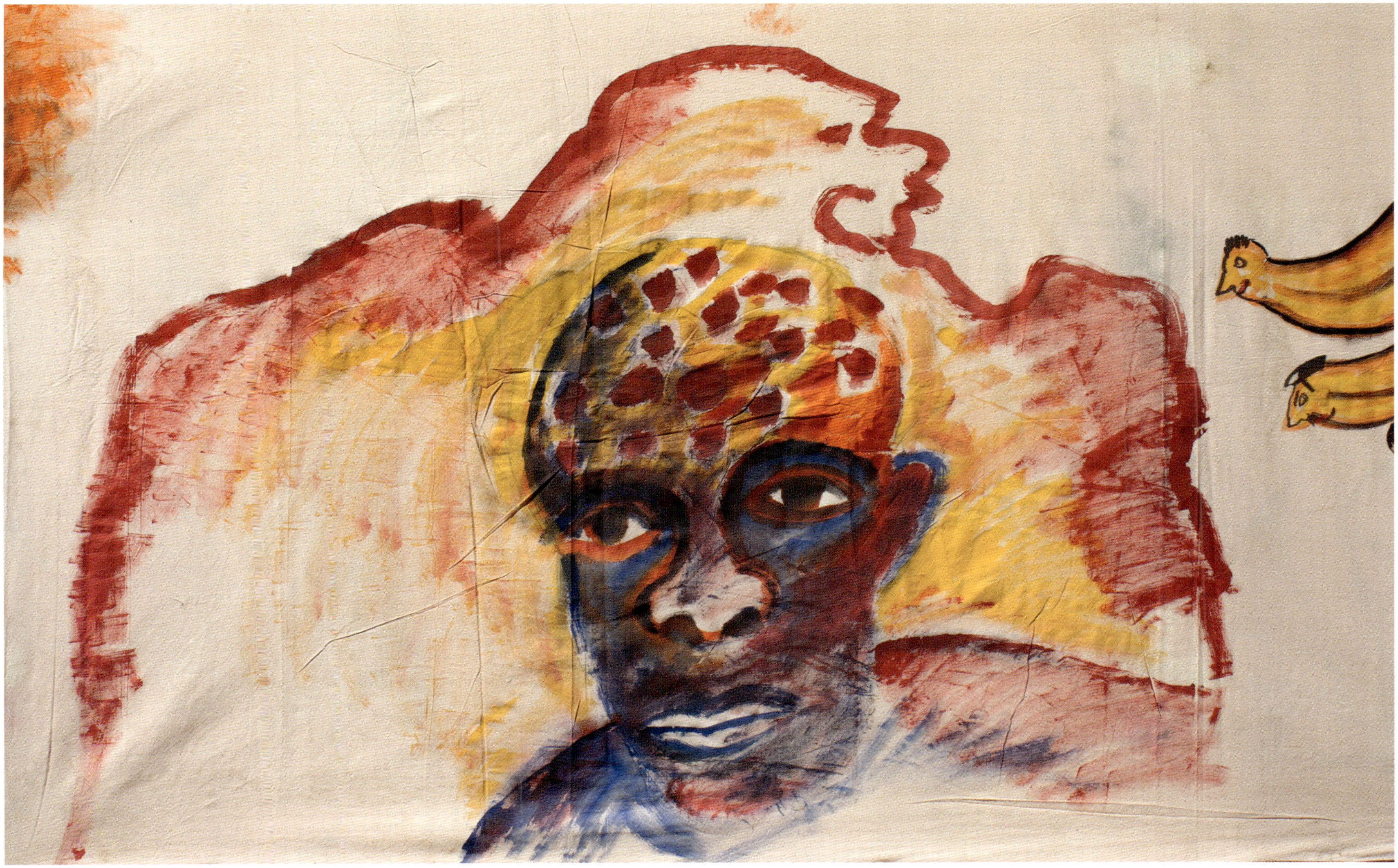

BHUPEN KHAKHAR
Banner painted for *Images and Words* in Baroda, 1992, 36 x 48 inches.

SHABNAM HASHMI

Excerpt from "A statement for secularism," *The Independent*, Bombay, February 19, 1993.

Today if one does not speak out against communal forces the artist's freedom too will be curtailed. Sahmat being a cultural organization cannot stop riots. Nor do we claim to be doing political or relief work. But we can mobilize both artists and the common man to come together and speak out against communal forces. From time to time we have been accused of convincing the convinced but that's not wholly true. An organization like Sahmat is doing its own bit by reaching out to people through culture and helping them continue in this direction by offering them a sense of purpose. That is equally important.

The Economic Times, New Delhi, April 1 1992

Artists Against Communalism

Strain of sweet secular music

Over a hundred leading artistes collected under SAHMAT's banner, in Bombay in mid-March, to signal once again the integrative powers of art. **Roshan Shahani** *on the moving experience.*

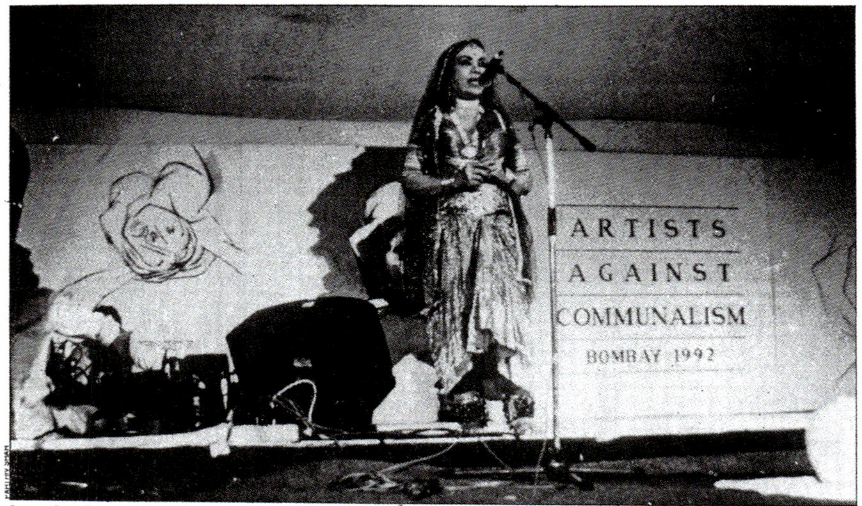

Lengendary danseuse Sitara Devi at the Shivaji Park 'happening' in Bombay: collectivising artistes in the cause of cultural pluralism

TURN BY TURN, they came and performed. India's classical musicians, interspersed with dancers, poets and painters, beckoned by the *pukaar* from the Safdar Hashmi Memorial Trust — SAHMAT — to join the tide of the movement of *Artists Against Communalism*.

On the performance stage, Tyeb Mehta's talisman painting — the eloquent falling figure looming large as a sonorous elegy in line — provided the backdrop to the 12 hours of *bandish* raga and a myriad *layas* released at Shivaji Park, with the moon as deity witness to the melting of the heirarchies of age, status and mode of performance.

•••

If we are seeking unities, our musical traditions certainly show us a way. Here were the performers; they appeared like meteors on a dulcet night as we gave ear to the Rudra Veena — the first musical instrument of civilisation played upon in the beginning of time by Shiva himself — now in the hands of the young **Baha-uddin**, scion of the great Dagar musicians.

He induces it to sing, carefully amplified with high tech mikes and a volume projector box that allow its low *meend* to be heard in an open, public space. It was a whiff of *dhrupad* as Baha-uddin paved the way for his brethren from Delhi, the proud **Fahimuddin Dagar, Zahiruddin Dagar** and son, **Wasifuddin** who ignited the pre-dawn *gagan* with their resounding mnemonics and a devotional incantations.

Image, text and music. A conjoined awareness of these is inevitable on such occasions. You warm up to the realisation that the great Dagar family is one of the repositories of ancient Indian temple music, and 20 continuous *peedhis* (generations) have nurtured the *dhrupad* in its present form.

We realise that are in a mess — up to our ears — when we go about categorising music as Islamic or Hindu. Have not the *dhrupad* and the *khayal* refused to manifest themselves as monolithic structures without the bind of religious world-views? Did not they grow on the breath of individuals from various communities? Does not history tell us that the vitality of the *khayal* is owed to disparate musical streams that fed it?

As the Sanskrit scholar, Mukund Lath said succinctly, Indian music is "a system of possibilities". Who can, in the name of religion, stake exclusive claims on it and force it into the straitjacket of a single colour?

The night of solidarity was the night of the moon. Some artistes had put a thought behind tune and text. Others gave random renditions from a repertoire. It did not seem to matter either way, for a heritage is a heritage when it resonates with humanism. The musician doesn't have to make explicit the alignment to a cause. It emerges in the tradition which he moves with his own temperament.

That pleading, beseeching address to a lover, or to a divinity, is the underlying erotic-devotional thread that weaves its way about in the *cheez*. Cogitations upon love can become reflections on sacrifice, surrender and protest.

Think of Faiz Ahmad Faiz and his call to revolution through a language cradled in the erotic, and Akhtari Bai's musicalisation of his poetry. It is an address which moves ideas on gender and relationships. The dichotomies of man-woman, east-west, faith and betrayal are given over to the cadences of a vast philosophy of love. It is music that humbles you to pay obeisance to the knowledge that particularities are to be understood as part of the ocean of storms that encloses our cosmos.

Shobha Gurtu as a *thumri* and ghazal singer has been assigned, by chance and circumstances, to replace Begum Akhtar. When she let go on *Nazariyan Laage Nahin Kahin Aur*, she maintained an emotional pitch and presented a possibility of imagining an event or a general crisis. The richness of the *bol-baant*, the proportion of a *swara* given to word, its stretch and pull open the doors to a new world.

Considering *swara* on another plane, **Shiv Kumar Sharma** prologued his *dogri geet* and Mishra Pahadi *dhun* on the santoor with his opinion that *swara* was *Ishwar*, that it was universal and that his Kashmir folk song had travelled and moved with him over the continents. The melody left behind the worlds in which it was first composed, he said. It became passages of sound and suggested the landscape for those wanting to hear history in a song.

Amjad Ali Khan stood out prominently amongst those who wished to articulate their thoughts in this event. He reminded everyone of the zig-zag nature of musical development as it coursed through Hindu and Islamic and other minds and gave an example of the bonding of *guru* and *shagird* — that of Swami Haridas and Miyan Tansen.

In the few moments given to him to spell out his Darbari Kannada (Tansen's raga), he magnanimously gave the space of a few *avartanas* to his young tabla accompanist, **Anuradha Pal**, who blazed away on a *teen-taal* while he was content to strum out a *mukhada*. The *ustaad* seemed sensitive to the wider context of secularism.

But it was Pandit Jasraj who spoke most militantly and appealingly. As though to stave off the silence of artistes, he exhorted the cognoscenti and the writers to give him a poem to put to music.

Religious identity was a matter of surface, he explained. We have to know ourselves after we have crossed the preoccupations with such ordinary matters. He plunged into a characteristic invocation to his gods before he neatly outlined his own *bandish* which has the refrain *Mero Allah Meharbaan* and the line, *Maan Leejiye Tu Shyam* emerging from the body of this composition.

After this, he made a prayer out of a massive Kabir configuration which describes brotherhood and the even radiance that spreads over a soil that can hold together a diversity that is mankind. He ended with a *gurbaani geet* saying he'd been through *gurdwaras* and temples in Punjab, contributing to integration through the country's rich casket of compositions.

SAINT poets like Nanak, Kabir, Surdas, Meera, Tukaram come naturally to the mind of the musician desiring both philosophical reflection and an identity with common people. The poetry of clairvoyance, as that of Kabir, was given musical sophistication by Kumar Gandharva and now, every *shishya* or admirer of Kumar Gandharva sings Kabir within that set language of lilt and call that came to be the bardic vision in Hindustani music.

When **Shubha Mudgal** charged her recital with this language, she could not bring significance to the composition — from the Nathpanthi sect, also a Kumar Gandharva favourite — having slowed down the *laya* which the late singer used to maintain as the steady pulse of his music.

Neela Bhagwat's Kafi *tappa* rendered in a folk Punjabi dialect and the Amir Khusro *tarana* were explored for their inherent meanings — the words, the raga and the rhythm. The *tappa* in the folk classical Pushto *taal* has an invocatory *Allah Di Kasam* and the *tarana* has the voice of Amir Khursro conducting polemics with word and note in the Persian language. "People call me an idol worshipper, but I do not care for these criticisms," is a fiery, ruminative line in the heart of the *tarana*.

Khusro was born of a Turkish father and a Brajbasi mother, according to Dr Ashok Ranade, who points out his importance as a professional song writer. Khusro had served under seven rulers and was pulled in different directions of music-making with his various patrons. It could be said that *khayal* singers owe a lot to him not just by way of poetry but, for the secular world view and the fine correspondence of musical form with literary content.

Renewing the musical traditions with contemporary poetry or raga modifications and new structures has been the demand of classical music. Its social context has been widened and differentiated with the *dhyan* of the *gurus* and the

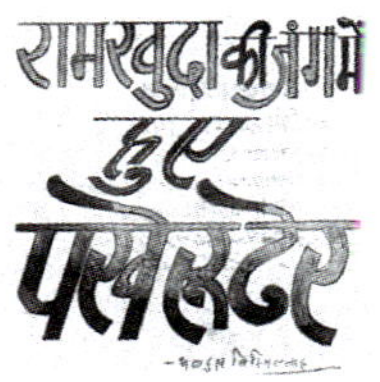

gelling of a tradition in a *gharana* or a discreet *khandaan*.

When Ravi Shankar or Pandit Jasraj, Amjad Ali, Kumar Gandharva or Hariprasad Chaurasia and others gave the dignity of classical form to new melodies and verse for the cause of altruism or national integration and peace, they marked the *chalan* and pace and *shakal* of a raga with their musical grain.

Ravi Shankar's *Prashanti*, whose recording he played to the audiences at Shivaji Park, is a simple hymn to peace in raga Yaman. The hymn has to be considered in the context of our present atmosphere of strife and communal conflagration. It serves as a moving signature from the rarefied *jagat* of the music world and heightens the interaction between art and society.

The point to consider is the position of the artist, writer or musician surrounded, asphyxiated by the disease of communalism. It is simplistic to take a view that is diametrically opposite to that of communalism. The artist will only end up visualising the problem in terms of clothes and rituals and names of gods.

Surely, the concern for integration and equality lies beneath these appurtenances. That night many of the poets read out expressionistic forms of poetry which referred to struggle and crisis in general, to human endeavour and pride. **Ali Sardar Jaffrey**'s *Haathon ka Tarana* could be looked upon as a paen to human creativity.

When Pandit Jasraj makes *allah* his own in his self-composed *bandish*, appealing to his mercy, he is artistically appropriating a culture which contains magnificent humanitarian ideas and a practise epitomised in this image of mercy and grace. Many *bandish* compositions in the *khayal* gather in this appeal to the *karim rahim* or *kartaar*. It is a call for peace within the self and outside as well as, a call for the spread of compassion.

In the largely erotic *shringaar*-based compositions of the *khayal* which, on the surface, describe the pain of separation of the waiting *nayika*, the grand vision of reaching out towards an Almight may not be visible. But, we know that a musician can convert the restless night of a lover into the unrest of a season, through a pause upon a word and its melodification in rhythm.

Sultan Khan hugged his instrument to his ample chest and poured forth a delectable Rajasthani *geet* in a husky, timbred voice, supporting himself with the pliant twang of his *durlabh saaz* — exquisitely curlicued phrases in raga Desh.

And, **Dhruba Ghosh** who looked like he was merely going to oblige the audience with his Kedaara in Jalad Ektaal, launched into a baul song and made his tribute to the night of the moon — it had settled like the orb of a *bindu* on the top of the performing stage. Dhruba's Bengali folk tune rose to meet it with its vivid description of the quest for a guru and knowledge.

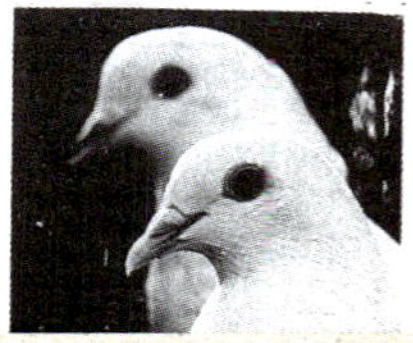

"Strain of Sweet Secular Music," report on *Artists Against Communalism* program in Bombay, *The Economic Times*, April 1, 1992.

MAIL TODAY
News for the new world
Mail Today, New Delhi, Saturday, January 2, 2010

SAHMAT'S TRIBUTE TO THE SPIRIT OF HASHMI

Creative collective's fest keeps the flame of an ideal burning

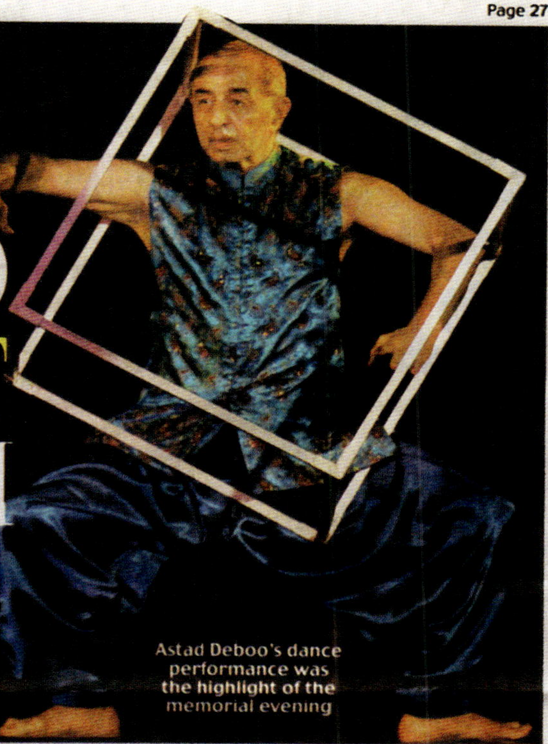

Astad Deboo's dance performance was the highlight of the memorial evening

K. ASIF

By **Archana**

IN THE RECENT past, whenever SAHMAT, the Safdar Hashmi Memorial Trust, has held events in support of the exiled master of modern Indian art, M.F. Husain, it has had to face attacks by right-wing fundamentalists. The attacks have been so frequent that the media has viewed each SAHMAT gathering as a potentially headline-garnering event. Mercifully for those associated with this organisation of artists, intellectuals and social activists, its 21st memorial for Safdar Hashmi at VP House on Rafi Marg passed off without any incident on Friday.

It was on January 1, 1989, that theatre actor/political activist Safdar Hashmi and Jan Natya Manch troupe were attacked by hoodlums carrying *lathis* and firearms. The group was staging a street play at Sector IV, Sahibabad. Hashmi, who was then 34, sustained head injuries to which he succumbed later.

Photographer Parthiv Shah, one of the founder members of SAHMAT, said that the organisation was one of its kind simply because it was a collective of artists. "You can have an association of engineers, journalists and doctors, but artists? Their egos are too big for that. That's why SAHMAT is unique; despite fights, we have gone on and on," he said.

But has SAHMAT's activism seen a decline in the recent years? M.K. Raina, another founder member and theatre director-actor, had the answer. He said, "One can't remain at the top of the pyramid all the time. An organisation does have its moments of highs and lulls. But you can't ignore the way SAHMAT has been able to keep the M.F. Husain issue as a burning topic. On his last birthday, we forced the government to react on his exile."

The memorial event began with a play on contemporary politics by the Haryana Gyan Vigyan Samiti, Rohtak, and wrapped up in the evening with the staging of the acclaimed Habib Tanvir play, *Charandas Chor*. It was performed by the late director's Naya Theatre Group, led by his daughter Nageen.

In between, there were vocal recitals by Rekha Raj, Vidya Shah and Madan Gopal Singh, and a contemporary dance performance by Mumbai's Astad Deboo. Deboo's act was dedicated to the late artists Tyeb Mehta and Manjit Bawa, who passed away last year, and Rumanna Hussain, whose 10th death anniversary was observed last year.

> "Safdar was very different because he came from a family that has chosen to stand up and be heard."
> **— Qamar Azad Hashmi, mother**

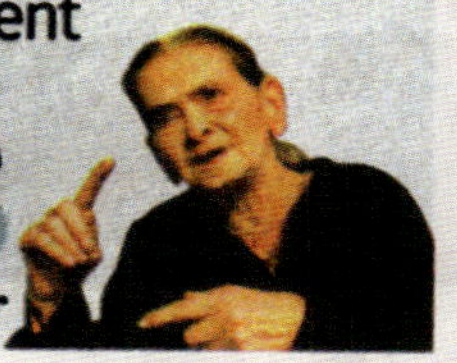

The spirit of Hashmi was palpable at the venue, and one could sense an electrifying energy all around. For one person, though, it was a very personal occasion, and a sombre reminder of "that day in 1989". That was Hashmi's mother, Qamar Azad Hashmi.

"It may sound clichéd but not a single day has passed since 1989 when I have not missed Safdar," said the 84-year-old matriarch.

DELHI AFTER dusk

"Safdar was very different because he came from a family that has chosen to stand up and be heard across generations," she said, before deciding to close up. "There's so much to talk about but it will take up a lot of time and who has the patience today?"

She signed off by saying that the fact that her late son was "different and loved by all" was proved by the number of absolute strangers who had been inspired by his ideals since his death. For SAHMAT, that has been the big achievement.

archana.khare@mailtoday.in

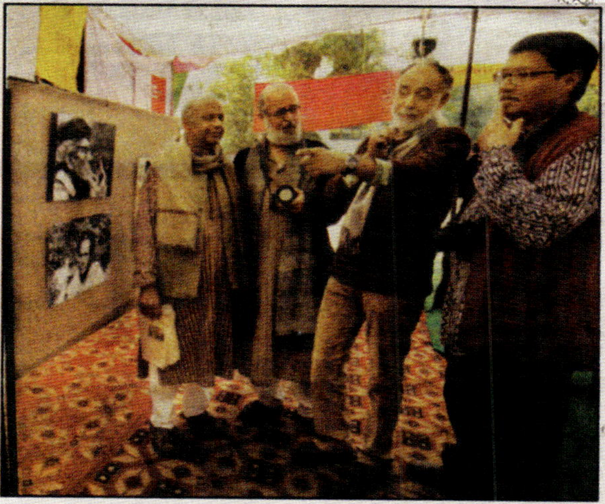

(From left) SAHMAT's leading members Rajan Prasad, Sohail Hashmi, M.K. Raina and Ram Rahman in front of a display of the late Habib Tanvir's photographs at VP House, Rafi Marg.

"Sahmat's Tribute to the Spirit of Hashmi," report on the *Safdar Hashmi Memorial* program, *Mail Today,* New Delhi, January 2, 2010.

1991–1992

Images and Words

As part of the ongoing *Artists Against Communalism* program, Sahmat organized *Images and Words*, an exhibition including works by over 400 artists, writers, poets, theatre persons, and filmmakers. The contributions took the form of eleven-by-eleven-inch canvases, which were then incorporated into three-by-three-foot panels for exhibition (nine canvases on each panel). From its opening in New Delhi on April 12, 1991, until its conclusion in Bombay on March 16, 1992, the exhibition traveled to thirty cities followed by a tour of forty schools in Delhi.

The panels gave concrete and tangible expression to the idea of secularism and cultural plurality. By reinterpreting symbols of tradition and opposing hegemonic cultural stereotypes, they addressed the issue of communal divisiveness head-on. Through participation in the *AAC* campaign visual artists who usually worked alone and in private spaces found an opportunity to express themselves in a more public way. Their work was viewed by audiences who had often not been exposed to such art forms. The exhibition allowed for private exploration of social issues while also manifesting a collective expression of concern.

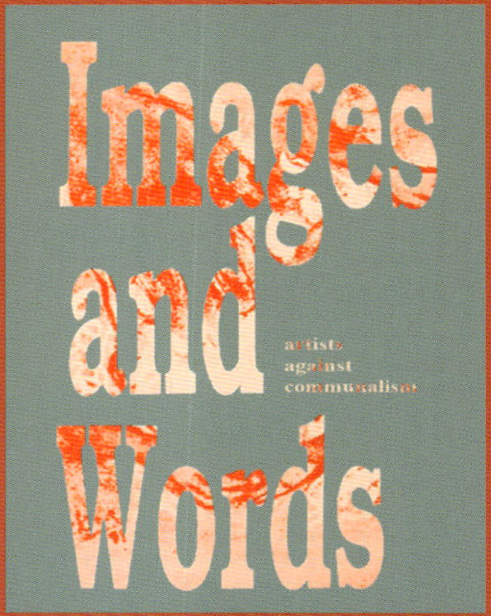

Cover of *Images and Words* catalogue. Design: Parthiv Shah.

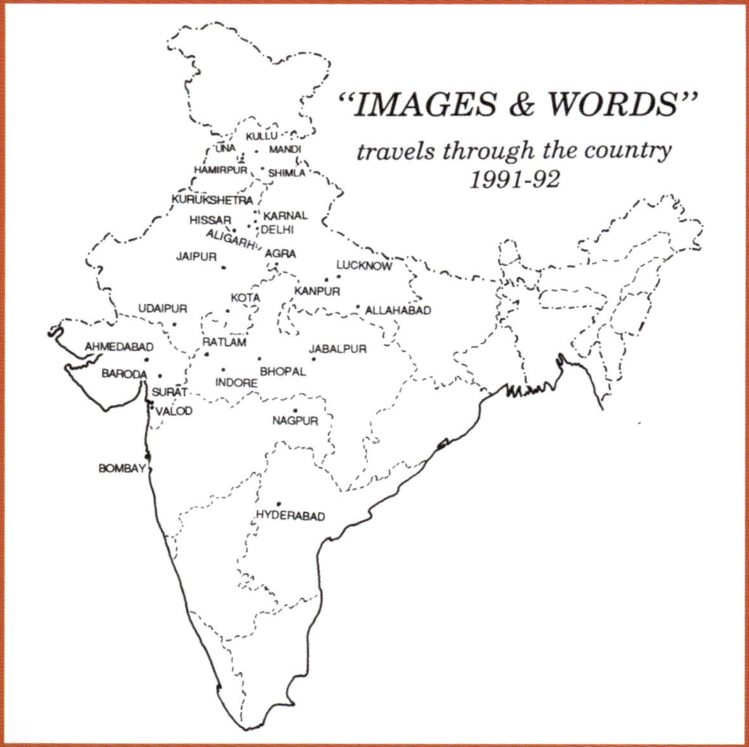

Map showing areas in India where *Images and Words* traveled.

Images and Words, Delhi, April 12, 1991.

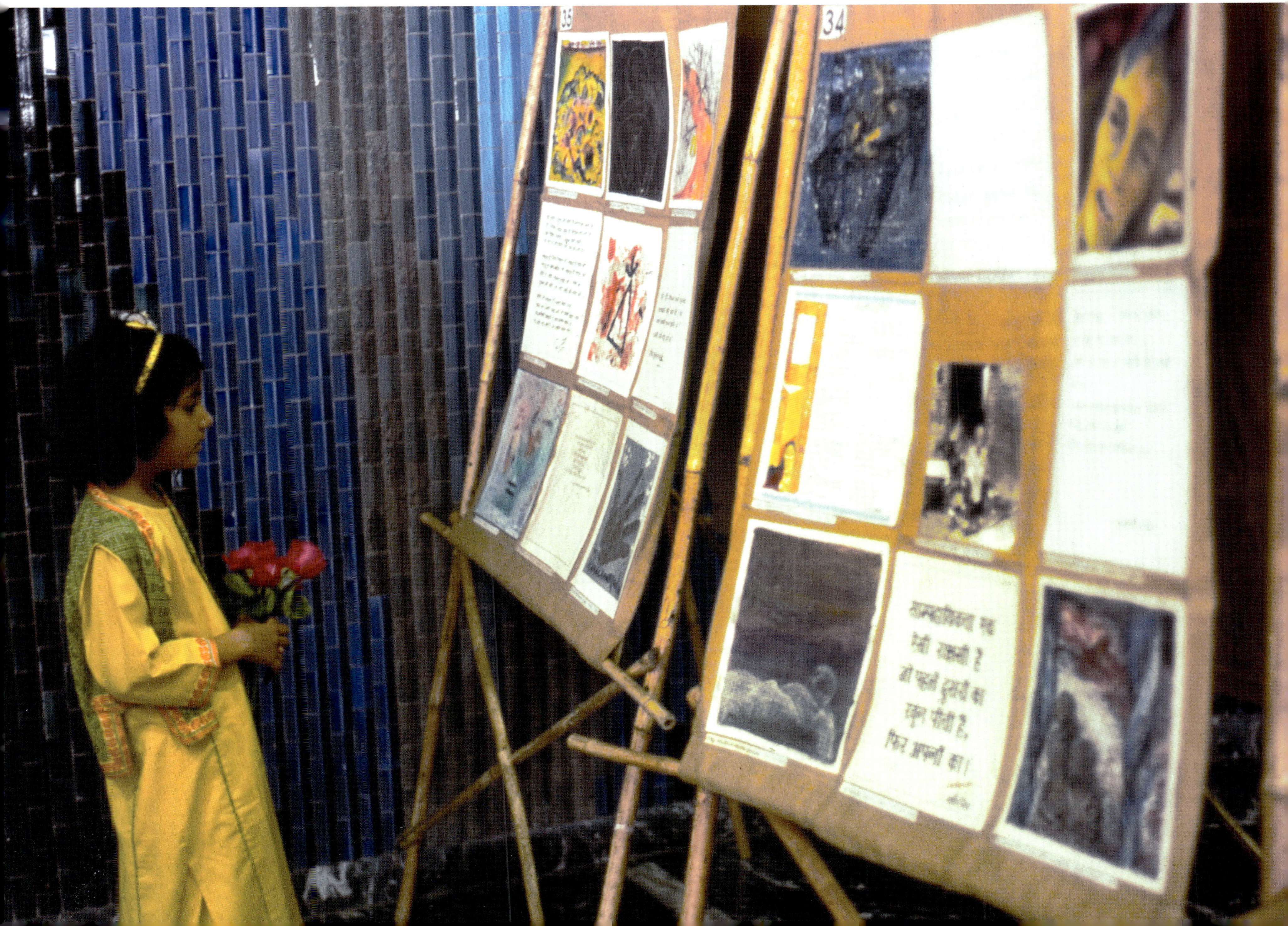

VIVAN SUNDARAM

Images and Words was one of our first projects. The format, which had an agitprop aspect to it, was my idea. There were works by artists and a few photographers, and texts by poets and writers—mainly in Hindi, Urdu, and English. And Orijit Sen designed a very efficient format for display made of bamboo sticks such that it could be easily disassembled and transported. We had a bus in which the exhibition traveled, and it was presented in at least forty locations in Delhi—at street-crossings and squares, in universities and schools. It is possibly the most viewed and visited exhibition ever in independent India. In a sense it was a traveling show, and we got terrific responses from the people.

The varied images were expressive in different ways. Some of them were directly political, some more poetic. The poems more directly expressed some of the themes of conflict. It is easier to deal with the communal problem in writing, to state a secular perception of what would be common to Hinduism and Islam, whether through poetry or other kinds of text. So I think that if you were inclined to read the texts, to read a poem, to read a few lines of it, you would get a sense of the theme—I mean we tried to organize the words and images in some sense, but it was a bit of free association with none of them illustrating the other. On the street, when hundreds of people were looking at it, they would see one image, then another. They would read a bit of a poem, whether it was in Hindi, English, or Urdu . . .

LEFT AND RIGHT
Images and Words, Delhi, April 12, 1991.

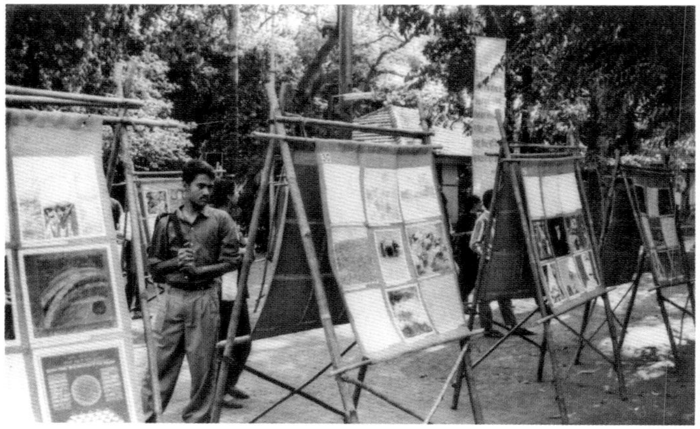

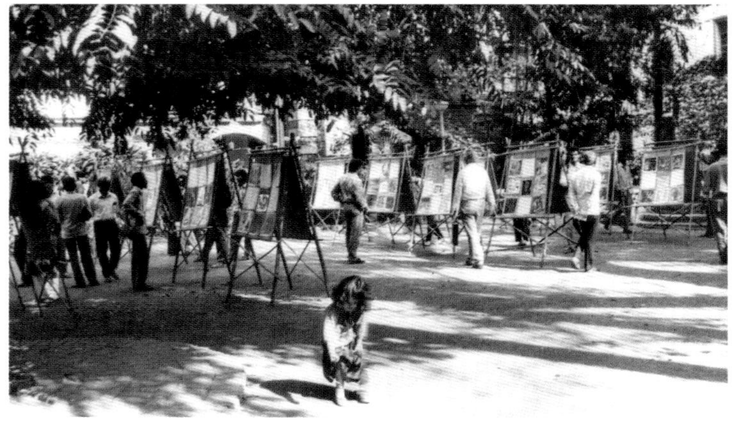

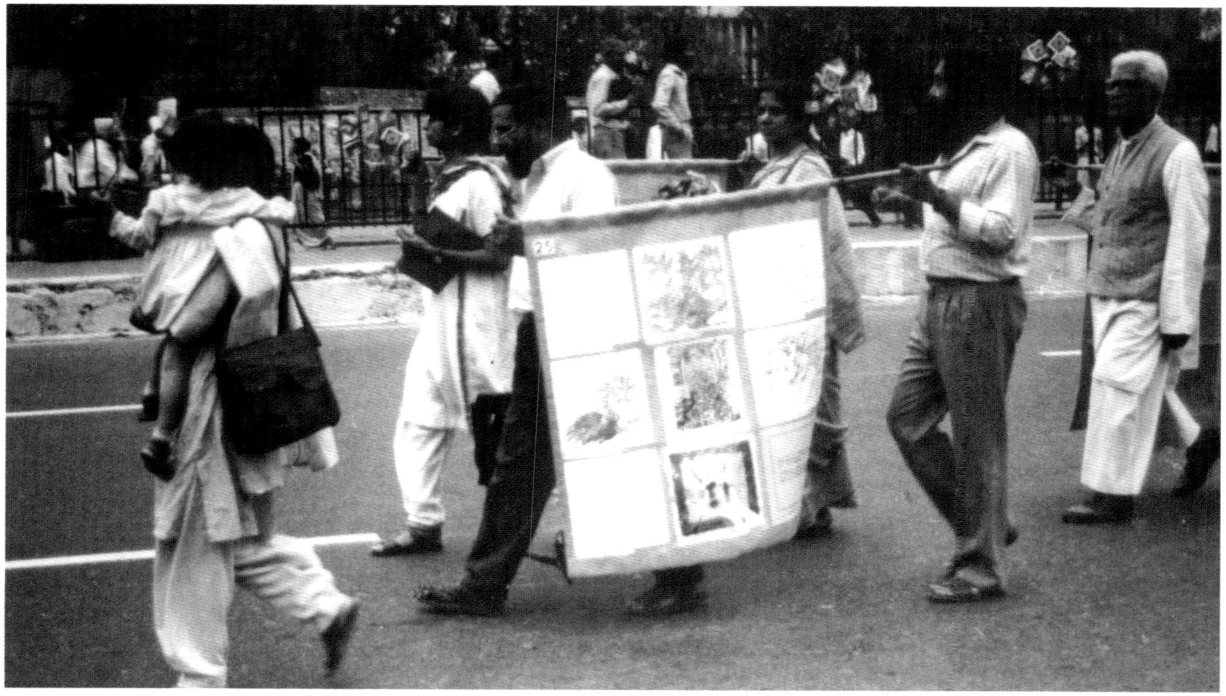

Images and Words carried in procession from Delhi Gate to Safdar Hashmi Marg, Delhi, April 12, 1991.

Images and Words at Jamia Mill a Islamia University, Delhi, January 1999. In the background, Rekha Raj sings Sufi poetry from Punjab.

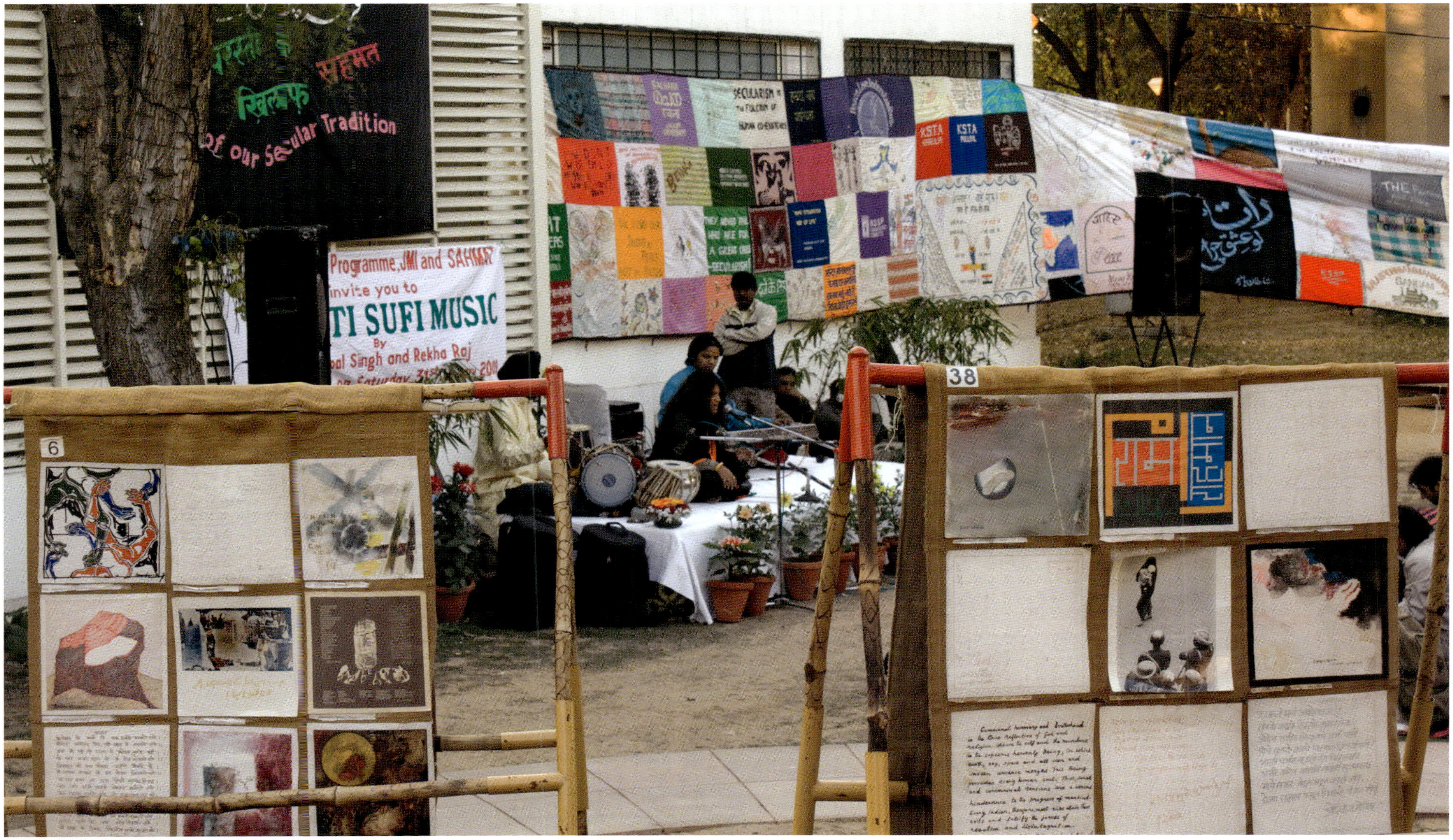

SOHAIL HASHMI

The exhibition, inaugurated in Delhi on April 12, 1991, Safdar's birth anniversary, traveled to thirty cities before reaching Bombay in mid-March 1992. At each location there were activities organized around the exhibition, ranging from on-the-spot painting to poster-making workshops, theatrical performances, poetry readings, songs of protest, setting up of book stalls, etc. The exhibition went to working-class areas and to schools and colleges, and at each place people received it differently. Workers, especially those who could read, spent a long time reading the text: school and college students copied the texts in their notebooks. In fact the catalogue of the exhibition was a hot-selling item as long as it lasted because many grass-roots organizations wanted to use the poems and texts as slogans against religious intolerance.

The auction, too, was in keeping with the spirit of the exhibition. Individual works were not being auctioned. Rather, each entire panel was on auction, and people had to bid for all the nine works that appeared on it.

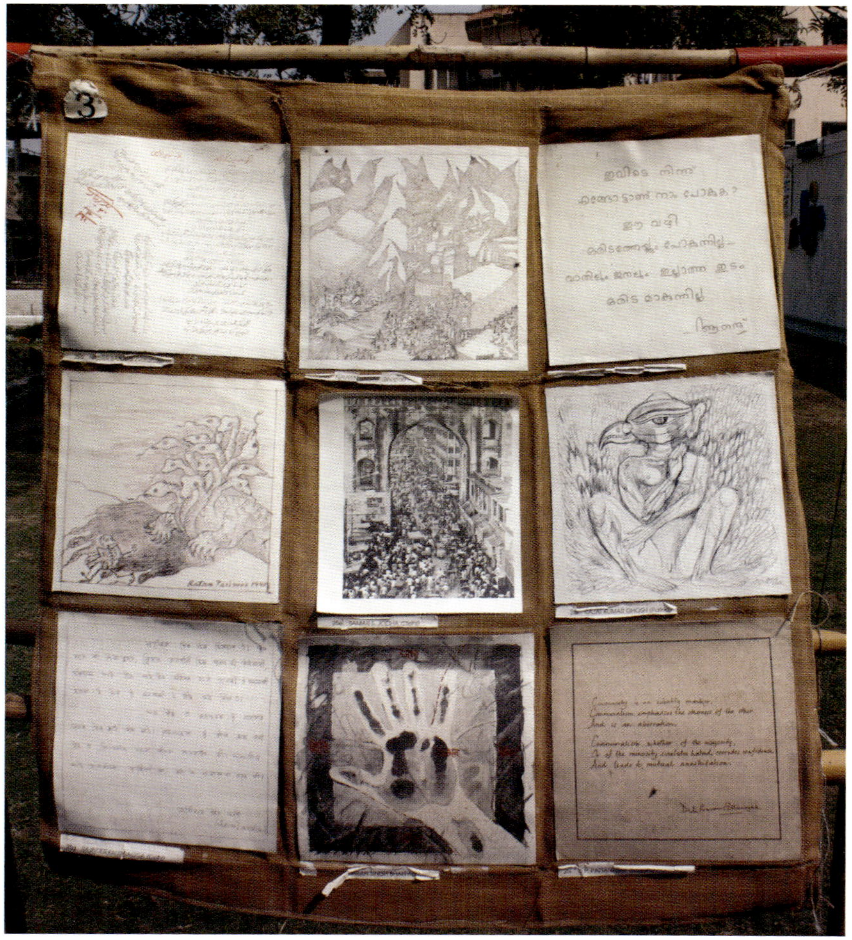

Panel from *Images and Words*, 1991, mixed media, 36 x 36 inches. Work by (from left to right and top to bottom): Nazeer Banarsi, Naveen Sagar, P. Sachidanandan (Anand), Ratan Parimoo, Samar Jodha, Rajat Kumar Ghosh, Rajinder Kaur Bagga, Harcharan Singh Bhatty, and D. P. Pattanayak.

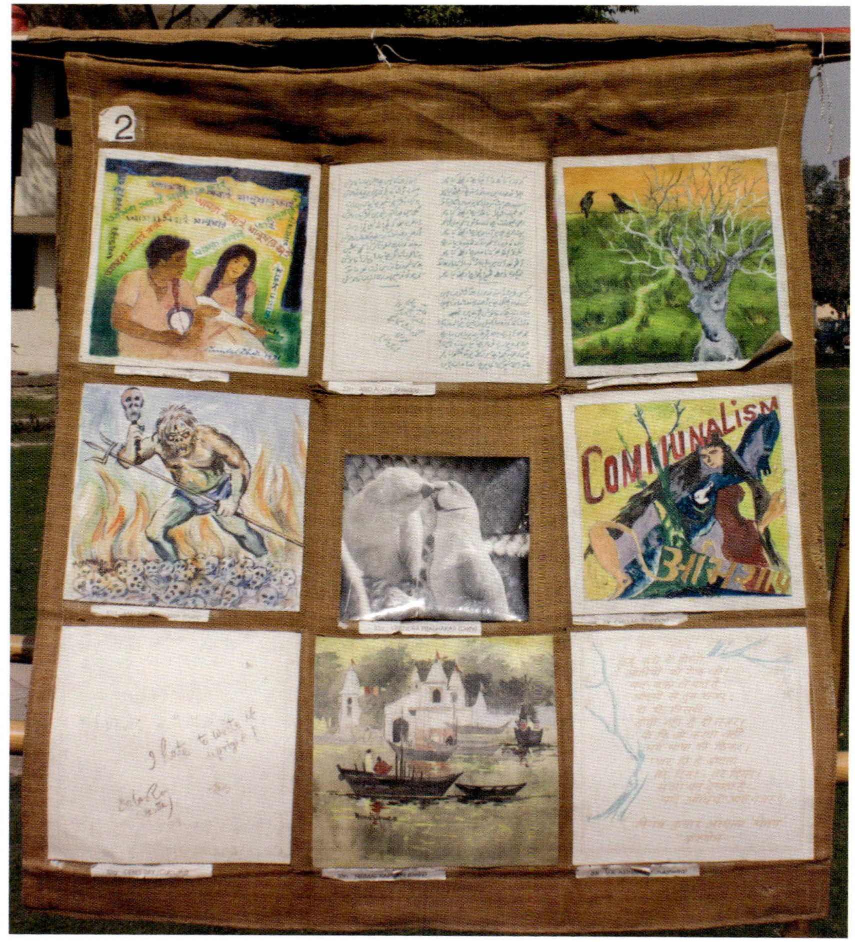

Panel from *Images and Words*, 1991, mixed media, 36 x 36 inches. Work by (from left to right and top to bottom): Ramlal Dhar, Abid Alami, Prayag Jha, Manmohan Bawa, Virendra Prabhakar, J. K. Chillar, Debes Ray, Nirmal Kapoor, and V. K. Asthana.

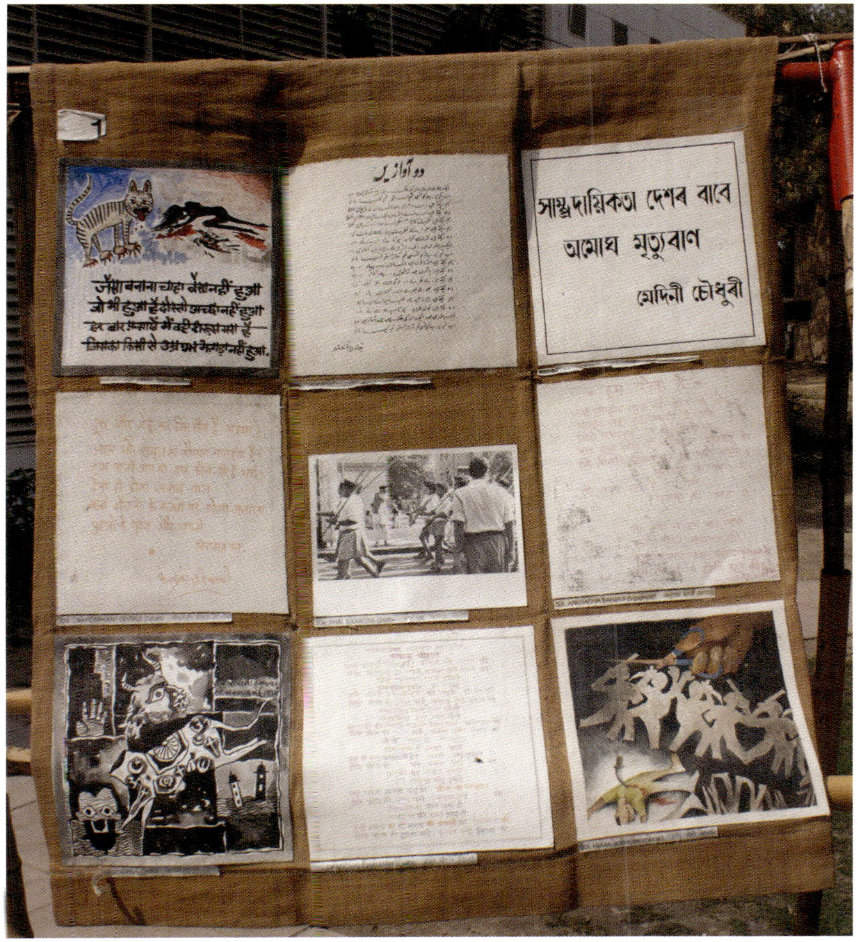

Panel from *Images and Words*, 1991, mixed media, 36 x 36 inches. Work by (from left to right and top to bottom): Vinod Tiwari, Javed Akhtar, Medini Choudhry, Chandrakant Devtale, Phal S. Girotia, Anuradha Banerji, Jagdish Nandwana, Chanchal Chauhan, and Hema Joshi.

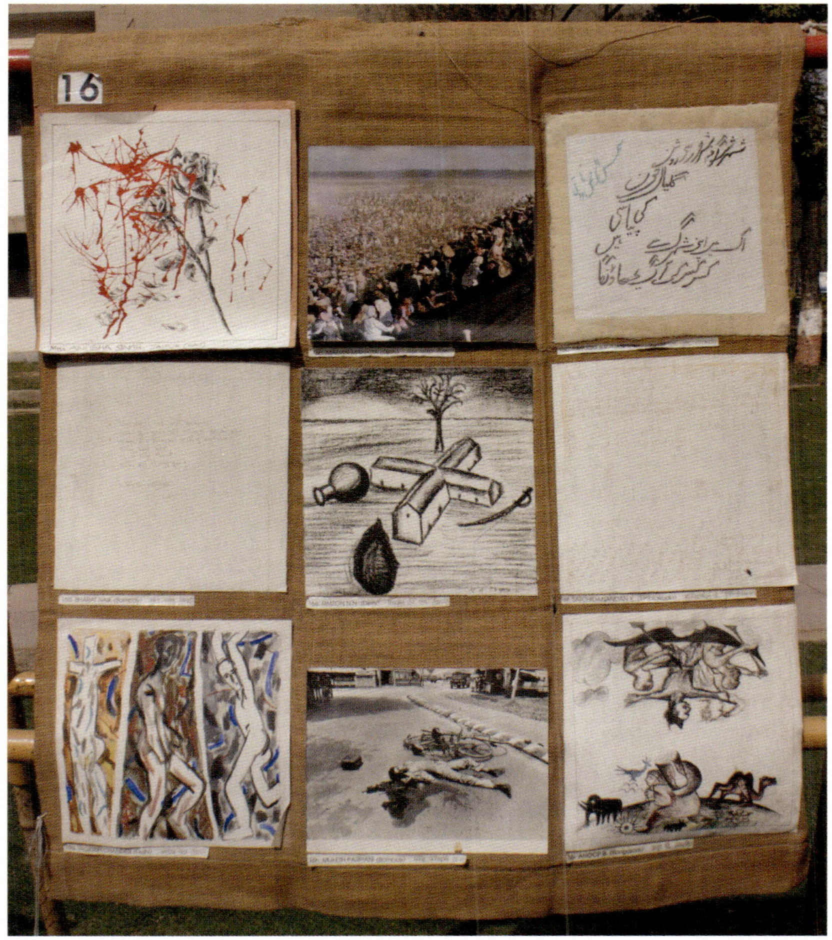

Panel from *Images and Words*, 1991, mixed media, 36 x 36 inches. Work by (from left to right and top to bottom): Anubha Singh, Madan Mahatta, S. R. Faruqui, Bharat Naik, N. N. Rimzon, K. Satchidanandan, Jagdish Chander, Mukesh Parpiani, and Anup B.

1992

Slogans for Communal Harmony

On January 1, 1992, Sahmat invited auto-rickshaw drivers in Delhi to participate in a competition—they were asked to create or select poems about brotherhood and communal harmony and paint the poems on the backs of their vehicles, to be judged on their content and design. This request resulted in one of the biggest public art projects mounted in India to date; hundreds of auto-rickshaw drivers sacrificed a day's fares and came together for a procession from Delhi's Safdar Hashmi Marg to India Gate. The diverse group of drivers—Sikhs, Hindus, and Muslims among them—wrote pithy appeals for unity. The winning poems included: *Deeds and not birth make a man great*, by Ramesh Kumar; *Slogan shouting and politicking cannot give any happiness. This comes from brotherhood*, by Ramnivas; and *Everyone feels hungry and needs bread to satisfy that hunger. Neither hunger has any religion nor does bread know any such barriers*, by Devnath Sahni. Judges on behalf of Sahmat included theatre director Ram Gopal Bajaj, artist Krishen Khanna, and architect Romi Khosla; theatre director and actor M. K. Raina awarded cash prizes to the winners. The poems remained visible for years after the event—not only on the auto-rickshaws but also painted on street-side fences and projected as slides in movie theatres.

Sahmat repeated the project in Mumbai in March 1992, only this time using the city's taxis and taxi drivers (since auto-rickshaws are not permitted in downtown Mumbai). Actor Shabana Azmi and poet Javed Akhtar judged the contest there.

►
India is a golden bird
India my motherland is great
May it shine like gold

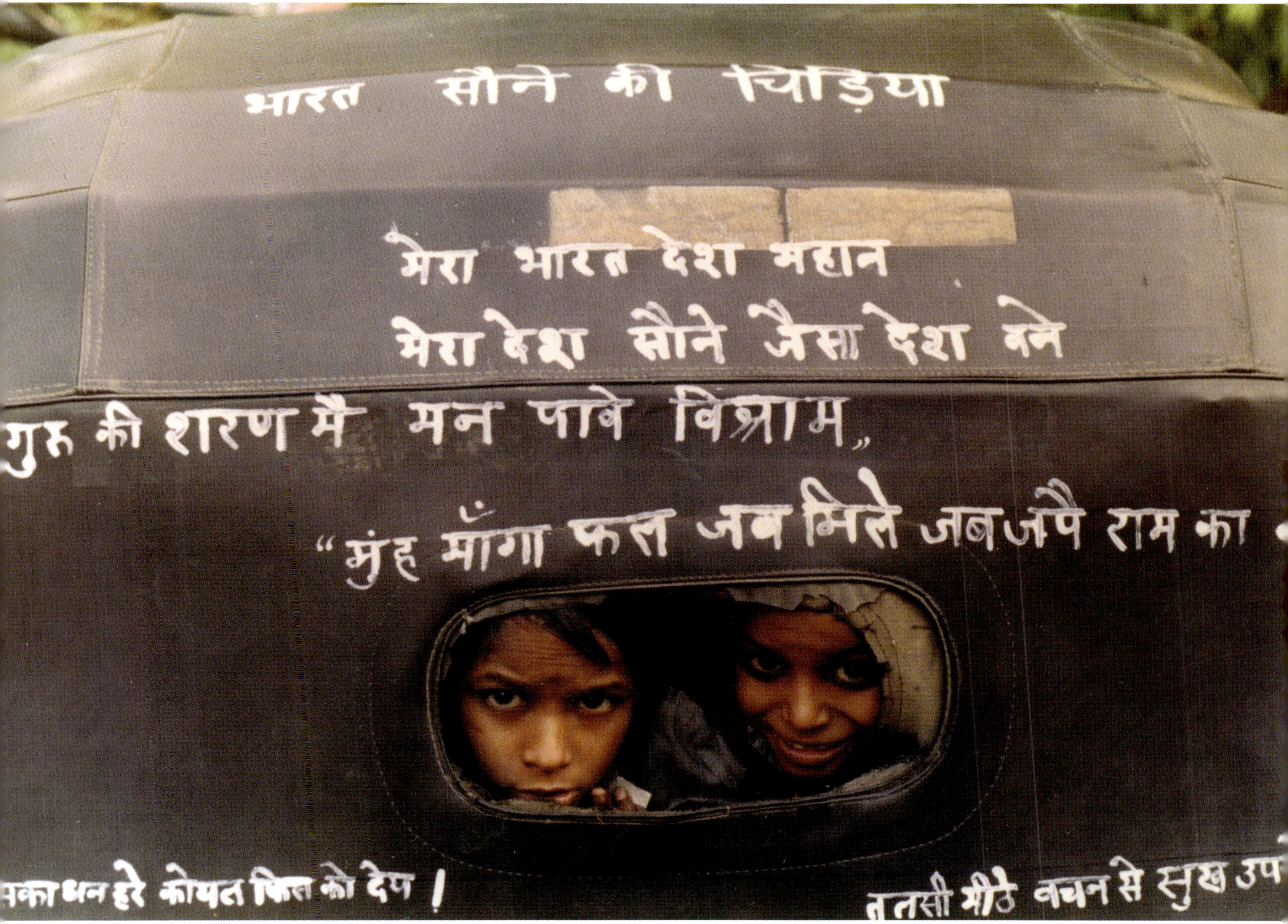

भारत सौने की चिड़िया
मेरा भारत देश महान
मेरा देश सौने जैसा देश बने
गुरु की शरण मै मन पावे विश्राम„
“मुंह माँगा फल जब मिले जबजपै राम का
का धन हरे कोयल किस को देय !
तुलसी मीठे वचन से सुख उप

Just as the faith of the passenger matters little to the driver,
as all have to be delivered home
Similarly, for the unity of a nation, the faith of the citizens matters little
Hindus, Muslims, Sikhs, Christians, all have to be embraced

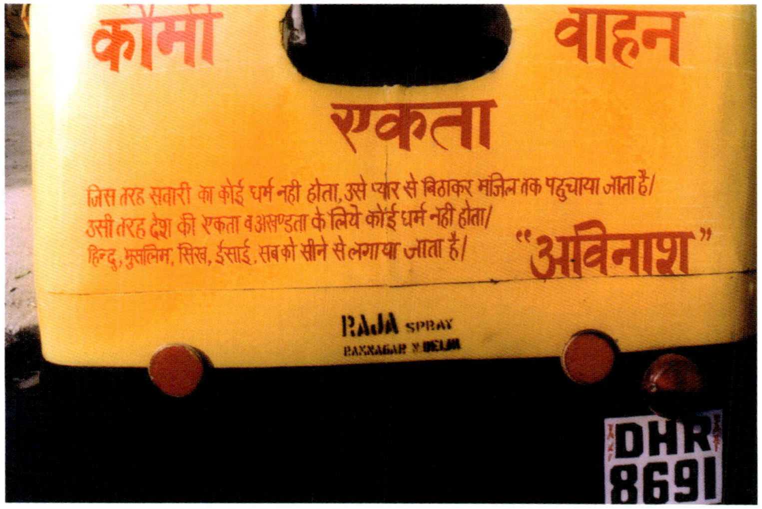

Sikhs, Hindus, Muslims, Christians, Ahoms and Tamils
Whoever resides in India is an Indian

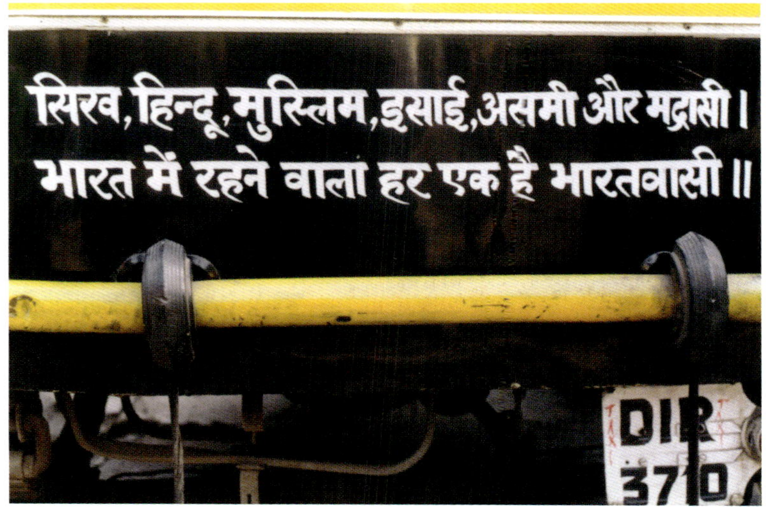

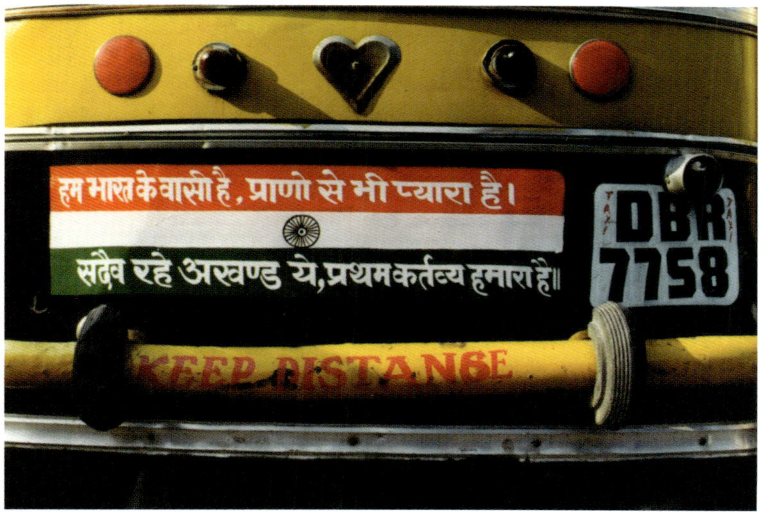

India is where we live, and we love it more than life
To see that it remains united must be the aim of our life

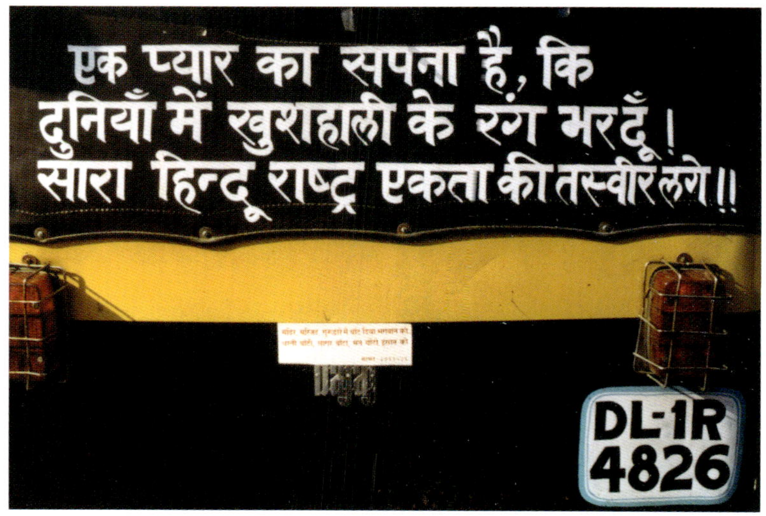

I have a dream of love
That the world of love be filled with colors of joy
And all of India be a picture of unity

If we live like brothers
Who can divide us?
With love, unity, pride in the nation
We will progress, together, all of us

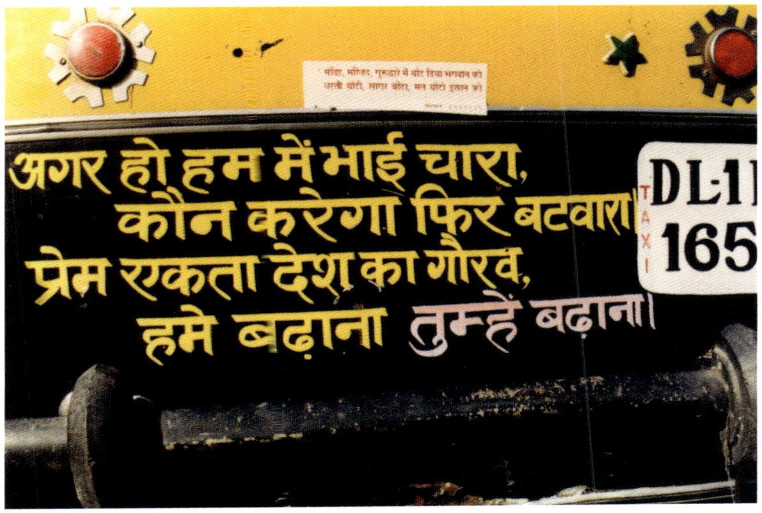

We will establish the message of peace, unity and brotherhood
Children of one God, we will remain united as Indians

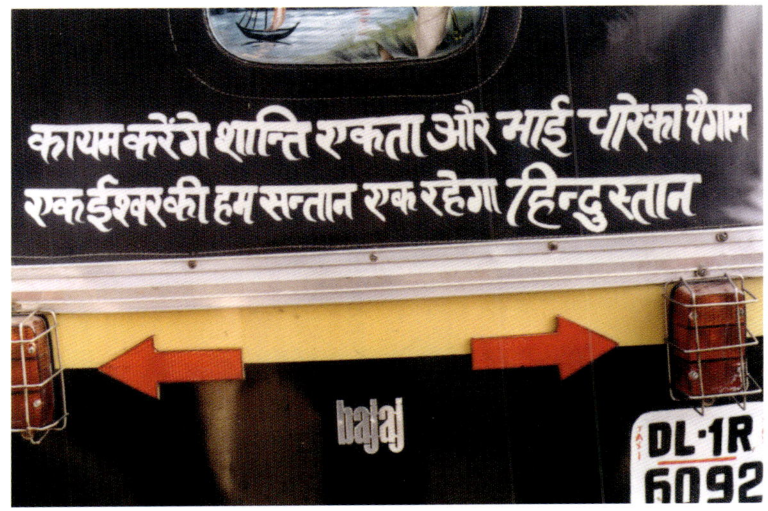

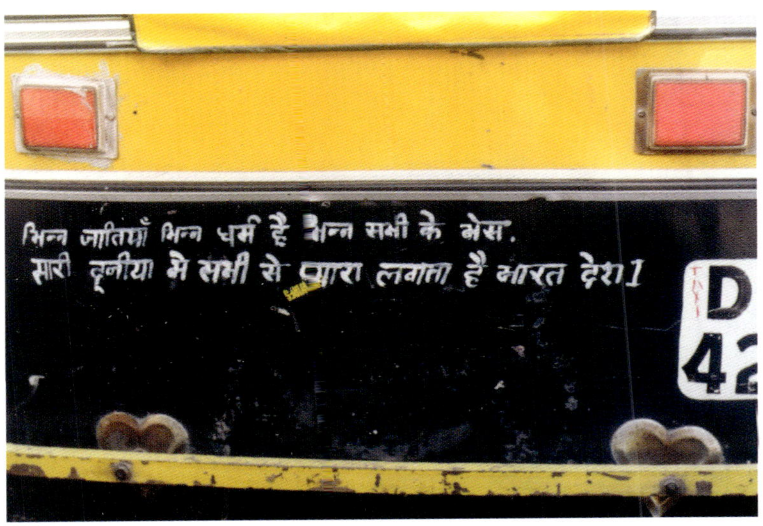

We as India come from different communities, we dress differently and follow different faiths
There is no land as lovely as India in the whole world.

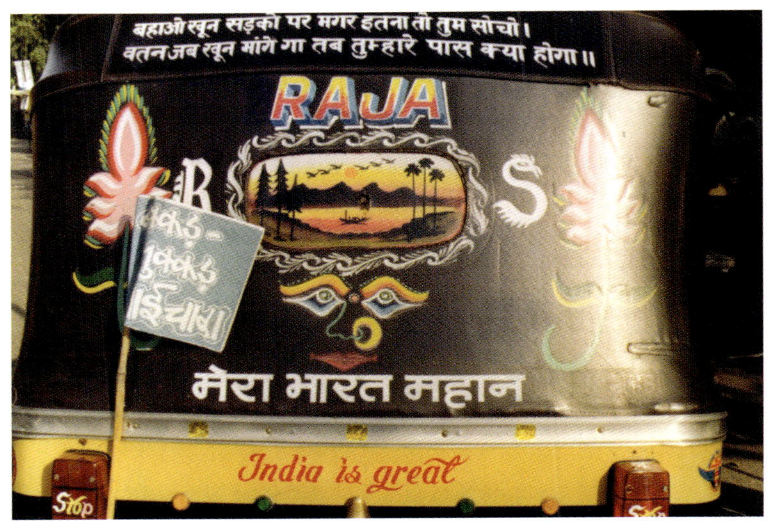

Go ahead and drench the streets in blood
But what will you do when the nation needs it?

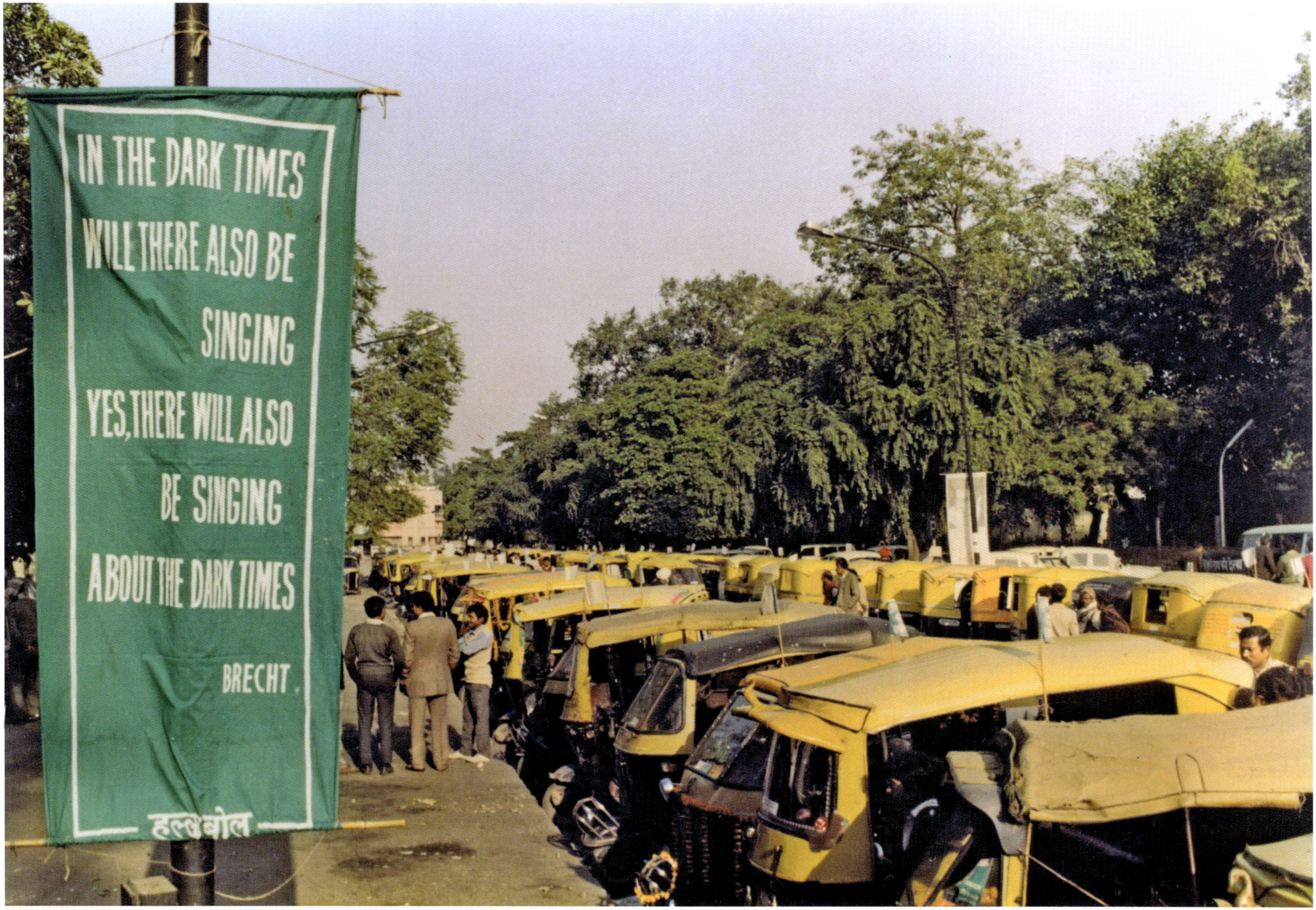

Auto-rickshaws lined up at Safdar Hashmi Marg, Delhi, for the slogan judging, January 1, 1992.

Driving home the message of peace

Our Staff Reporter

For the auto-rickshaw drivers in the Capital, it was an unusual beginning of the new year. Hundreds of them gathered at Mandi House,the cultural epicentre of Delhi, with verses of peace and communal amity written on their vehicles.

It was a contest, organised by the Safdar Hashmi Memorial Trust (SAHMAT) to mark the third death anniversary of Safdar Hashmi who was brutally killed while performing a street play in Sahibabad, three years ago.

There were three first prizes of Rs 3,000 five second prizes of Rs 2,000 and 10 third prizes of Rs 1,000. A jury, comprising theatre director Ram Gopal Bajaj architect Romi Khosla and painter Krishen Khanna judged the merit of each verse, which was first photographed and then presented before the jury.

A procession was later taken to India Gate where the prizes were given away by theatre director-cum-actor M K Raina. The first prize winners were Ram Niwas from Lakshmi Nagar, Dev Nath Sahani from Gol Market and Ramesh Kumar from Ambedkar Nagar.

The programme this time differed in character from the cultural artists sit -in against communalism, organised by the SAHMAT on January 1, last year.

The campaign started in December last year with almost 40,000 pamphlets distributed in different parts of the Capital and an appeal from the SAHMAT to the auto drivers to participate in the contest.

Scooter drivers drove up to the venue much before the scheduled time on Wednesday morning. By noon the number neared 200. Instead of the usual artists' or~intellectuals' meet, Mandi House witnessed a rare gathering of auto-drivers, who spoke a different language.

They explained the need to counter communalism and strengthen ties of brotherhood and unity. Notwithstanding the cryptic remark of one of the drivers about the cash incentive being the chief propelling factor in the participation, the slogans were a testimony to the creativity and ingenuity of the writers.

'Cheap' has become the way of life in the country, with blood cheaper than milk', read the verses of Wariyam Singh, who went on to ask, " Except the bureaucrats and the insane, who can laugh freely today?".

Yet another verse read," Every communal carnage takes toll of people, who never knew enemies". The participants unanimously proclaimed that this was the first time that they have been encouraged to participate in such a programme.

Said Dev Kumar of East Delhi," It is not the inaam, but the issue of creating awareness against communalism, which is important. "A resident in the Capital since 1967, the opportunity as perceived by Mr Kumar, is truly unique, having come after 24 long years.

"Had Maxwell Pereira allowed , we would write such slogans on every auto-rickshaw," he added. There were many to endorse him.

The auto-drivers spoke at length about the need to propagate a message of sanity, in a country, rocked by divisive politics. They asserted, "The politicians alone are responsible for the present tensions."

"Driving home the message of peace," *The Patriot,* New Delhi, January 2, 1992.

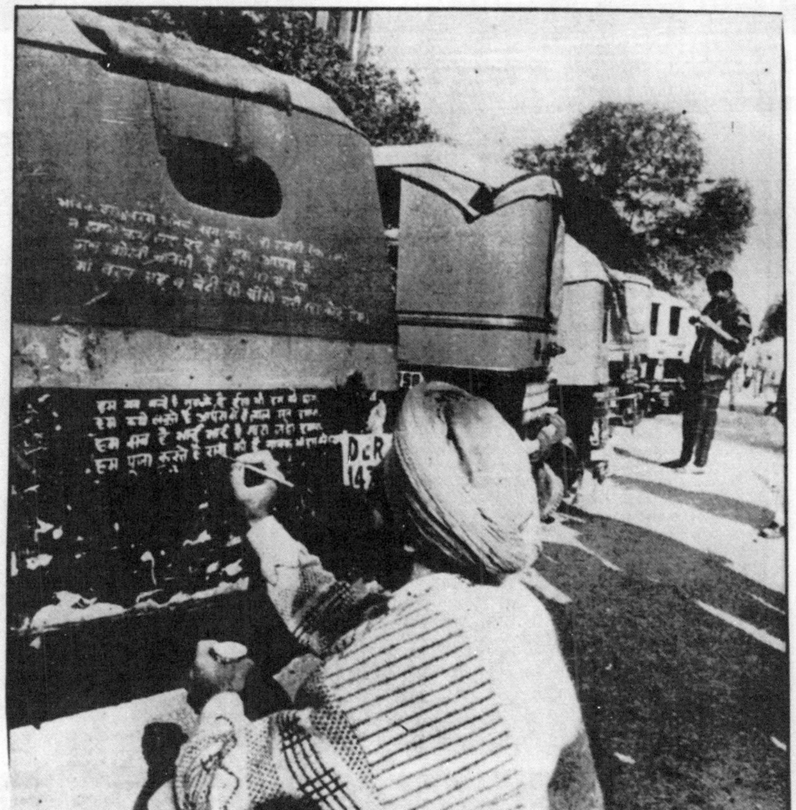

A three-wheeler driver giving the final touches to his entry participating in a contest for slogans against communalism organised by the Safdar Hashmi Memorial Trust in the Capital on Wednesday. — TOI

The Times of India, January 2, 1992.

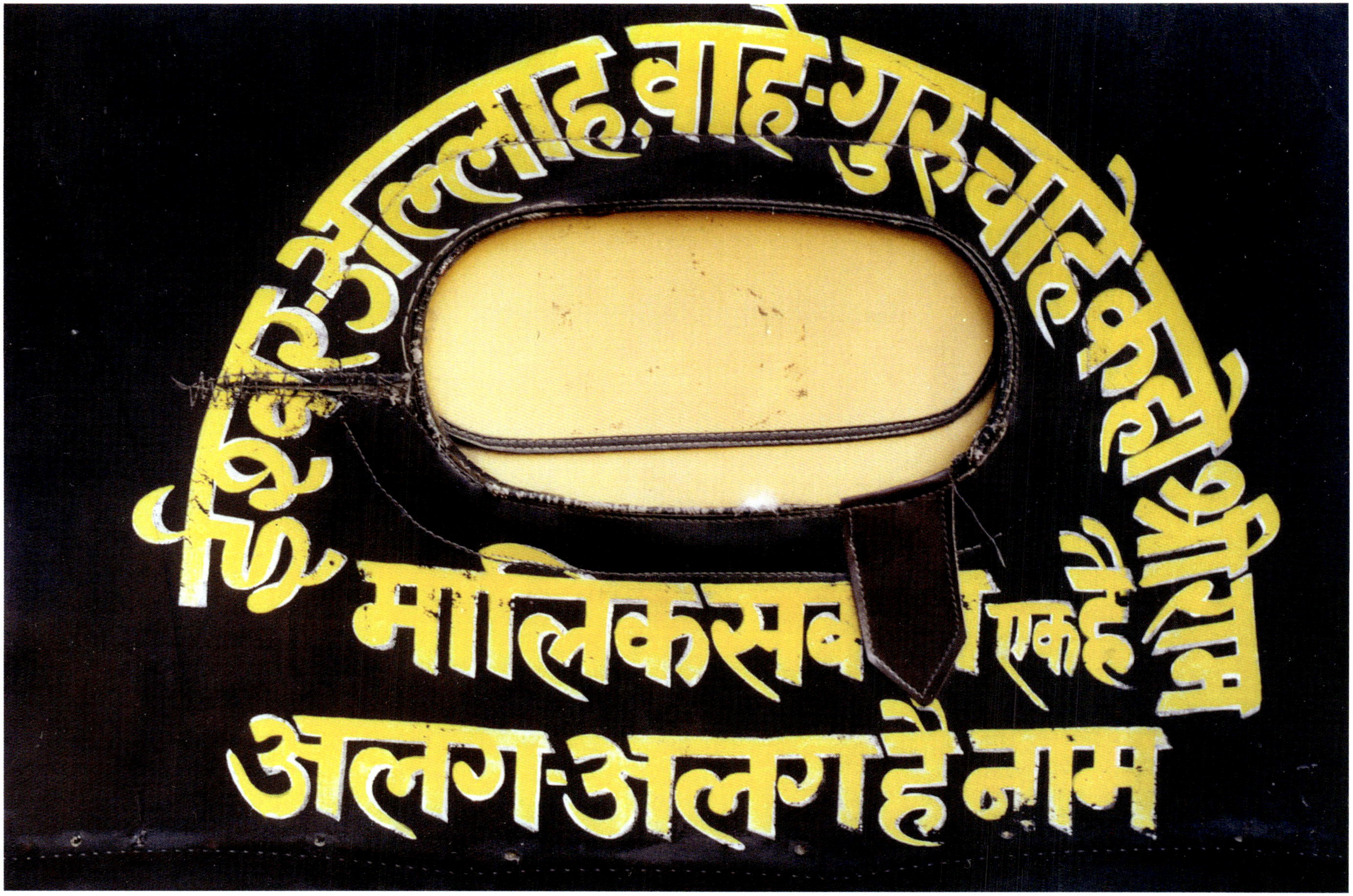

Call Him Ishwar, Allah, Wahe-Guru, or Shri Ram, if you will
These are but different names for the one creator

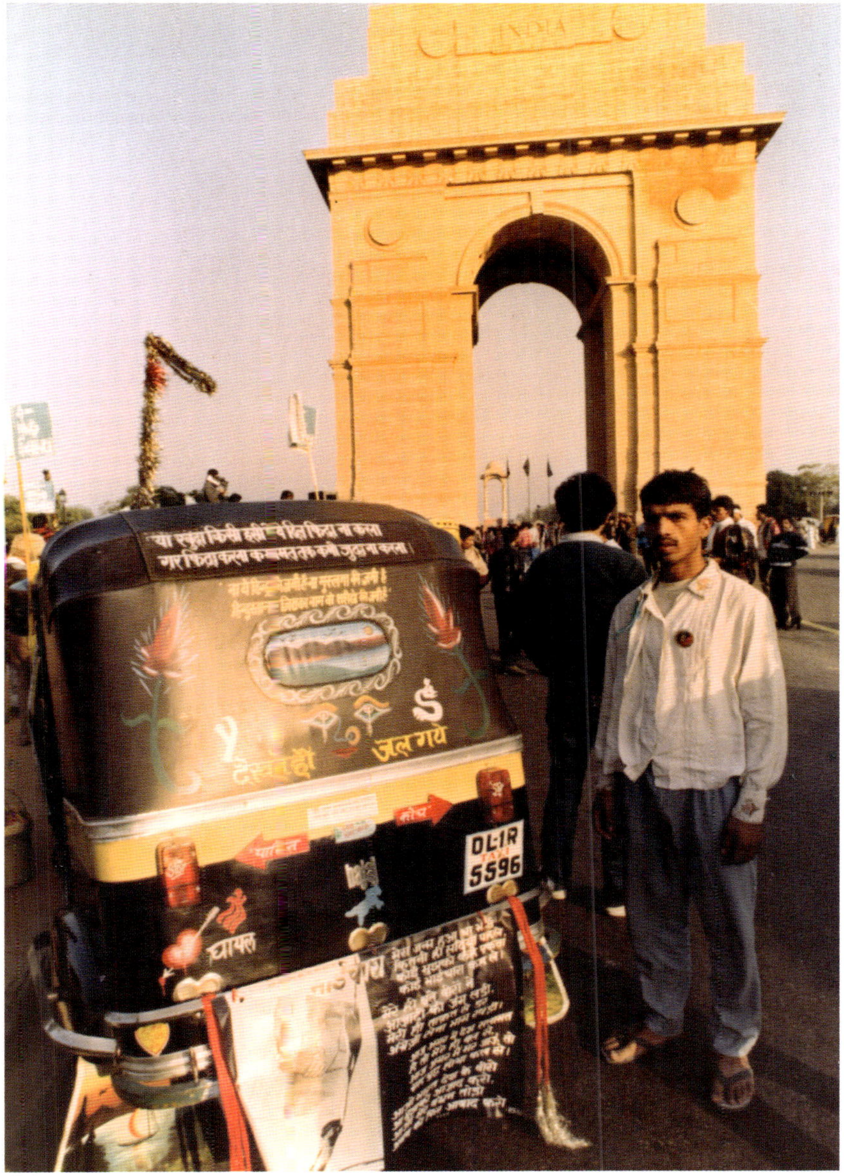

A prize-winning auto-rickshaw driver, Ramnivas, at India Gate in Delhi, January 1, 1992.

Slogan shouting and politicking cannot give any happiness. This comes from brotherhood.

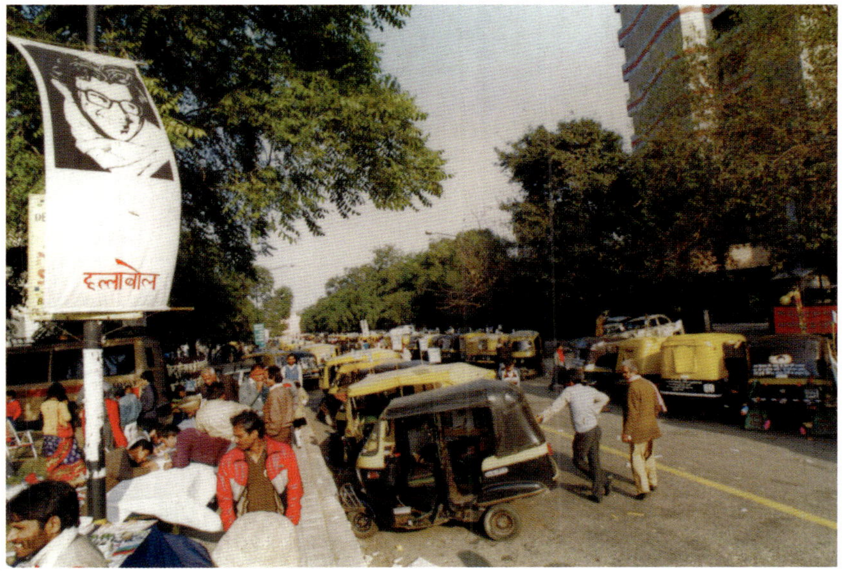

Auto-rickshaws lined up at Safdar Hashmi Marg for the slogan judging, under a banner depicting Hashmi.

Anil Chandra of Sahmat with an auto-rickshaw driver.

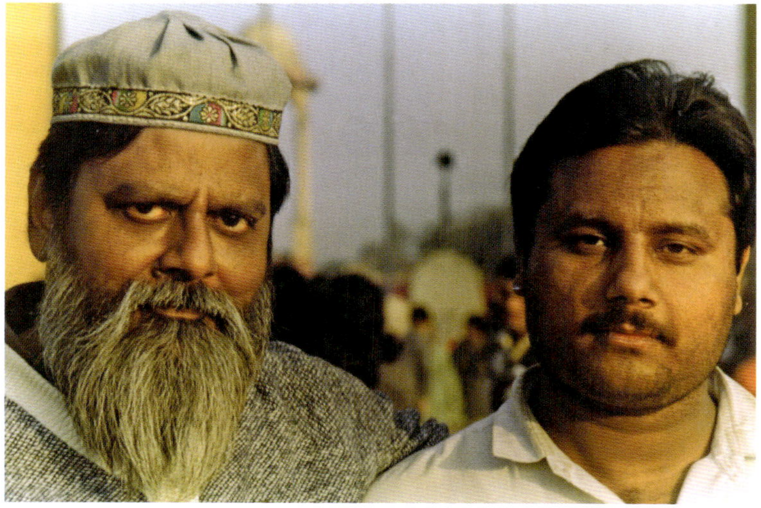

Architect Romi Khosla (in jacket), one of the judges, faces a television crew surrounded by competing auto-rickshaw drivers.

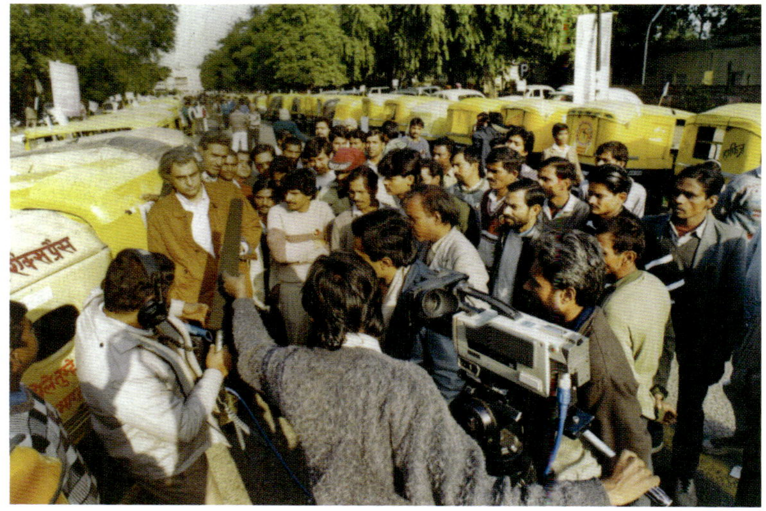

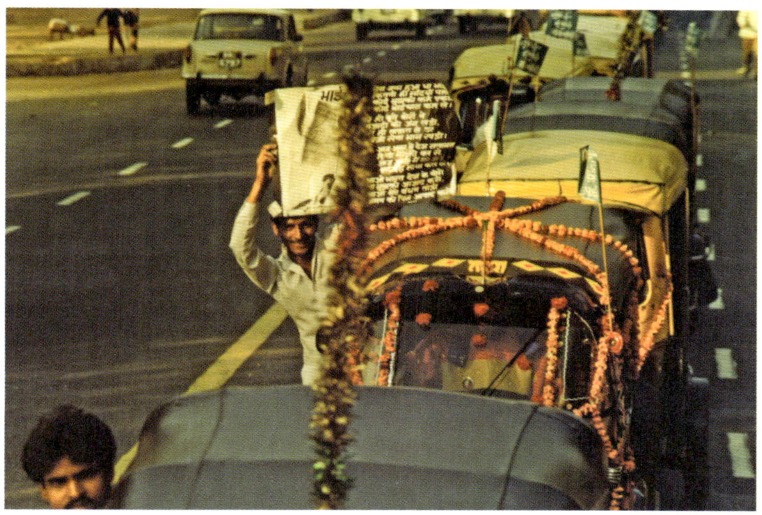

An auto-rickshaw driver displays a Sahmat poster during the procession down the streets of Delhi.

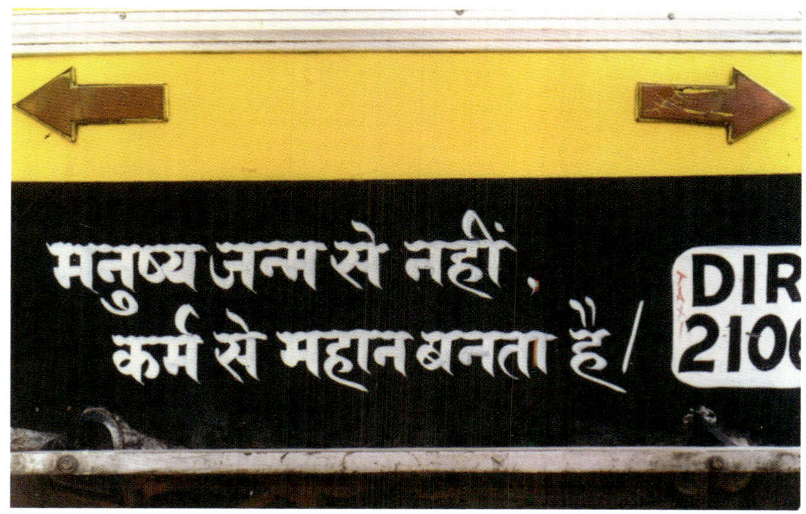

Deeds and not birth make a man great
by Ramesh Kumar, one of the prize-winning entries.

SOHAIL HASHMI

In India, trucks and buses primarily, but also taxis and auto-rickshaws, often have lines of poetry or verses inscribed on their vehicles. These bits of rhyming text are normally painted on the backs of the vehicles. The carefully chosen texts convey the drivers' attitude toward life, their angst, their sense of injustice, and their frustrations. Many write the names of their loved ones on their vehicles, some adorn them with names and pictures of gods and goddesses, and others use photographs of film stars.

A couple of years after the formation of Sahmat, even as communal passions were being roused on a daily basis and the BJP was harping on avenging imagined atrocities of the past, we began discussing how to intervene at the level of popular culture, and the idea of trying to involve auto-rickshaw drivers was discussed. We decided to print a small leaflet that addressed auto drivers; the text consisted of a simple message that roughly ran along these lines:

The auto driver earns a living by taking strangers to their destinations; the religion of the passenger makes no difference to him, nor should his religion make a difference to the passenger, but if both begin to be selective about who they would travel with, both will suffer.

The leaflet concluded with the message: "Auto drivers write all kinds of poetry on their vehicles. Why don't you write something in your own words, that carries a message of brotherhood?" The leaflet invited them to assemble at Safdar Hashmi Marg on January 1, 1992. (From 1990 the first day of the year has been observed by Sahmat as "Safdar Memorial" and a day-long program of music, dance, theatre, and art is held to observe the day Safdar was attacked; it has become a landmark cultural event of Delhi.)

The idea of approaching auto drivers came about for several reasons. Auto drivers are like daily wagers; they have to be out working every day. Most do not own their vehicles and rent them out from the owners on a daily basis. Any disruption of work is very difficult for them; in situations of riots, they become easy targets for hooligans and mobs. For all these reasons, we thought that they would be open to the idea of carrying the message of communal harmony. Another reason we thought of auto drivers was that once a slogan is written on an auto-rickshaw, it would be seen across the city. For writers and artists involved in the project it was a unique opportunity to interact creatively with people with whom they had never had this kind of exchange.

Once the vehicles had been painted and the judges had made their selection, all the autos traveled in a procession to India Gate and lined up along one of the radial roads where the prizes were announced and given away, amid much clapping and slogan-shouting.

Taxi drivers in Bombay with one of the judges, actor Shabana Azmi (second from right), and Sahmat secretary Shabnam Hashmi (right), March 14, 1992.

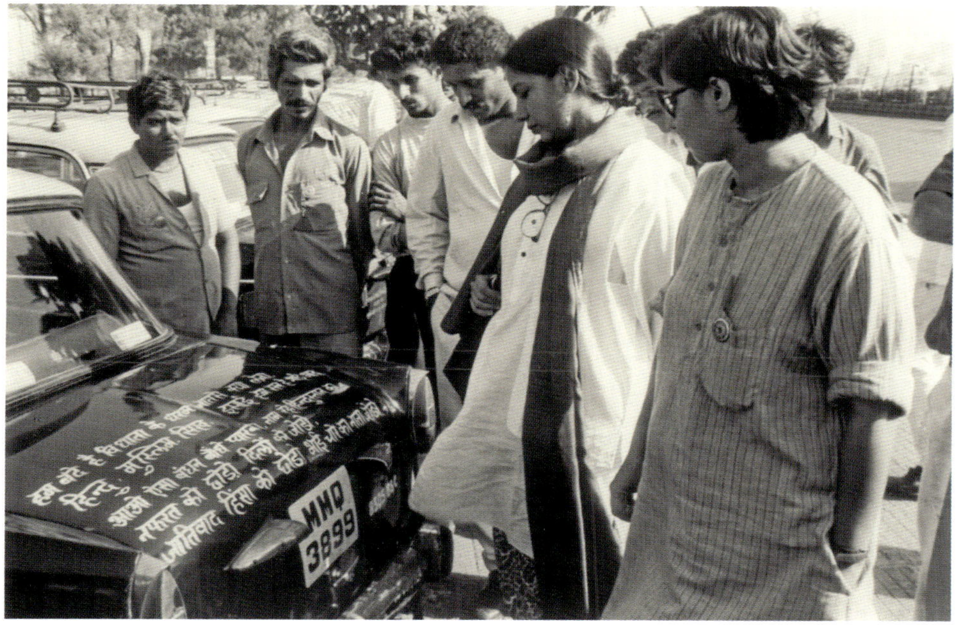

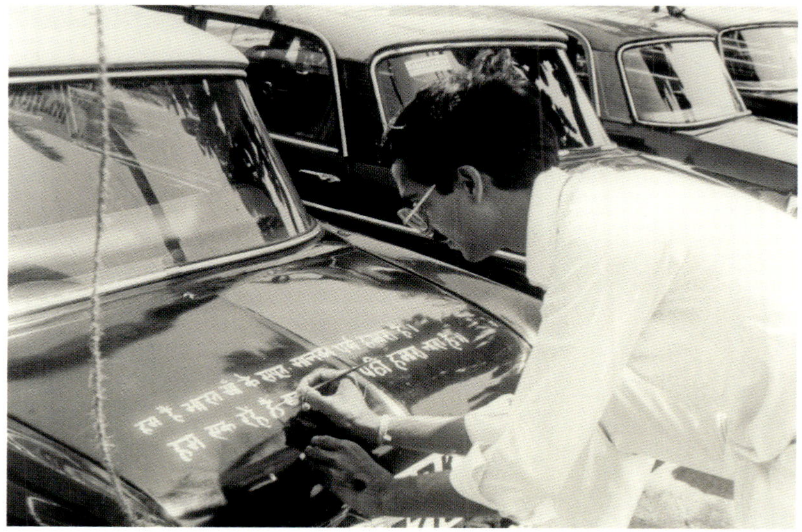

A taxi driver gives the finishing touches to his poem, Bombay, March 14, 1992.

1992–
Ongoing

Ayodhya: Demolition of the Babri Masjid and After

On December 6, 1992, a violent mob of Hindutva activists demolished the sixteenth-century Babri Masjid (Babur's Mosque) in Ayodhya. This destructive act marked the culmination of a movement launched by the Hindu Right to redress an alleged historical injustice—namely, the demolition of a Hindu temple to build the mosque—and to reclaim the site of Ayodhya, which these fundamentalist groups regarded as the birthplace of the Hindu god Rama.

Sahmat responded immediately and at length, with a yearlong series of events. The morning after the demolition, a delegation of artists, intellectuals, and activists from Sahmat met the president of India, Shankar Dayal Sharma, to call for both the arrest of the perpetrators and the immediate dismantling of any newly constructed temple on the ruins of the mosque. Sahmat also printed hundreds of thousands of copies of a poster carrying the exhortation *Aaj koi naara na hoga, sirf desh bachaana hoga* (There shall be no slogans today, our only task is to save the nation), which was plastered on walls throughout the streets of Delhi and distributed as newspaper inserts in many areas of the capital. At the end of that week the collective also held a sit-in on Safdar Hashmi Marg, defying judicial orders imposed to restrict public gatherings. Poets read poetry, singers sang, and painters painted on the street—among them Manjit Bawa, who made *Kaun Mara?* (Who Died?).

This video grab shows the last dome of the Babri Masjid before its destruction, December 6, 1992.

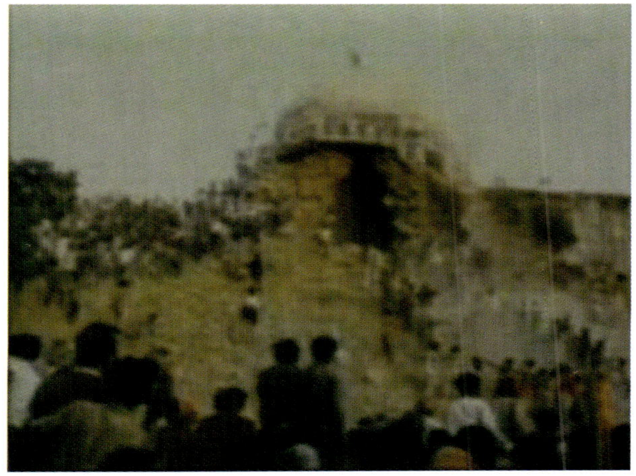

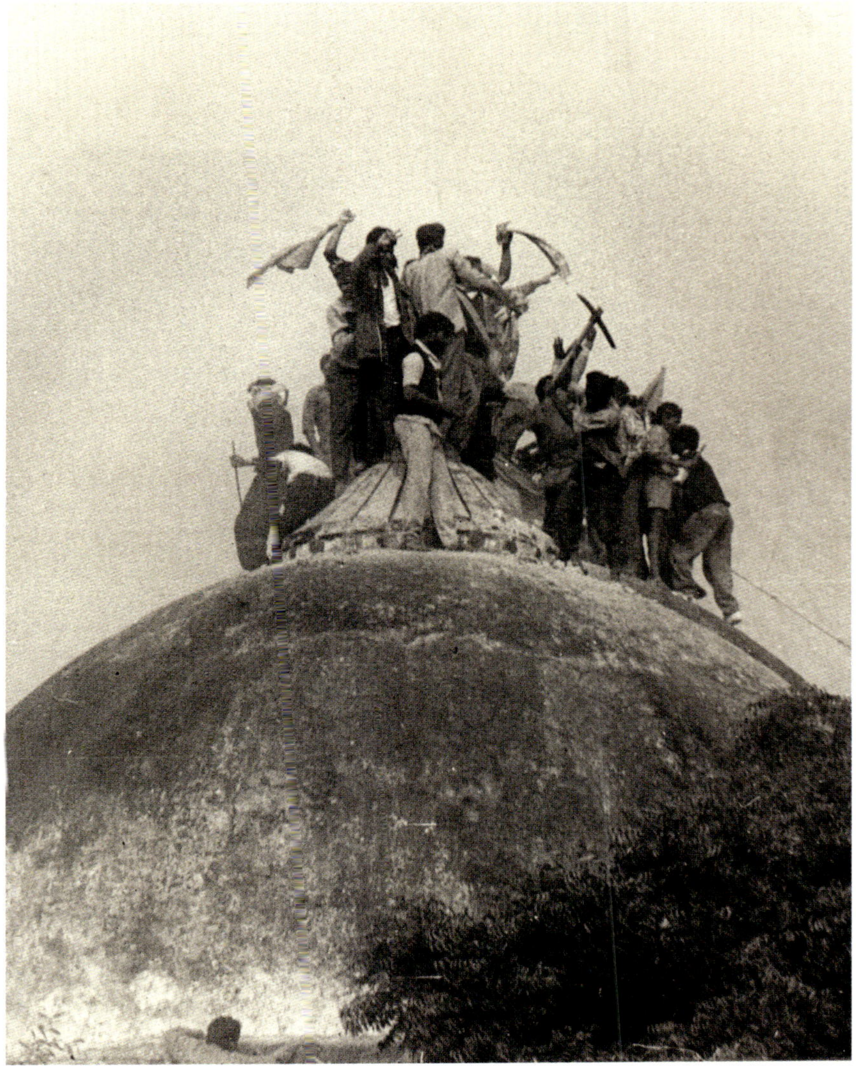

Right-wing stormtroopers begin the demolition of the Babri Masjid, December 6, 1992.

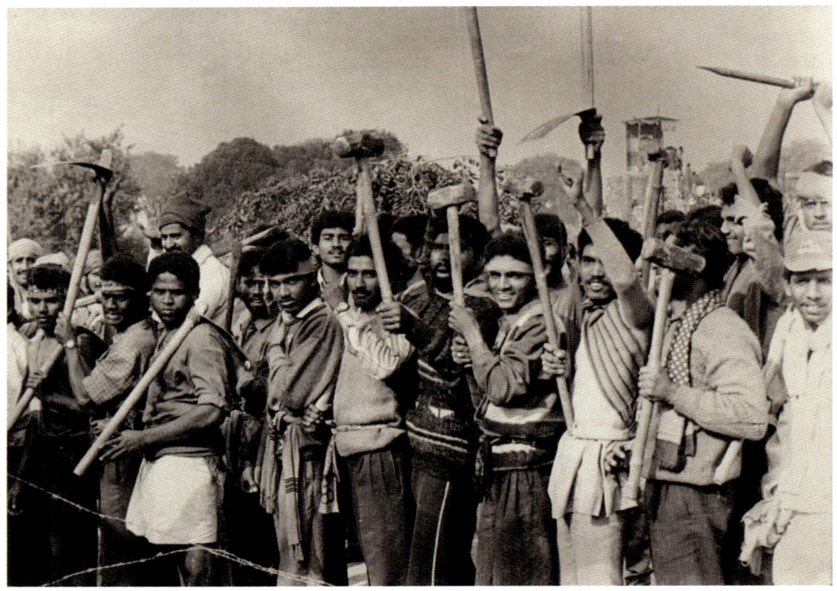

Right-wing storm troopers preparing to attack the mosque, December 6, 1992. Photo: Pravin Jain.

Painted on the street during a protest gathering organized by Sahmat just days after the demolition of the Babri Masjid, *Kaun Mara?* (Who Died?) is a highly unusual work by the artist Manjit Bawa (1941–2008). The subject, based on the Hindu myth of god Vishnu assuming the form of Narasimha, the man-lion, is immediately recognizable. In the story, King Hiranyakashipu, blinded by hubris and the belief that he is indestructible, smashes a pillar in his palace to see if god really resides everywhere, as asserted by his son Prahlad who is a devotee of Vishnu. Vishnu emerges from the pillar in the form of Narasimha and disembowels the king, laying him across his lap. In referring to this terrifying myth, the artist offers an interpretation of the destruction of the Babri mosque that is at once deeply personal and universal. As Manjit Bawa completed the painting in rough strokes, landscape painter Paramjit Singh joined in to paint the background and roiling skies, making it a unique canvas painted by two eminent contemporary artists of India.

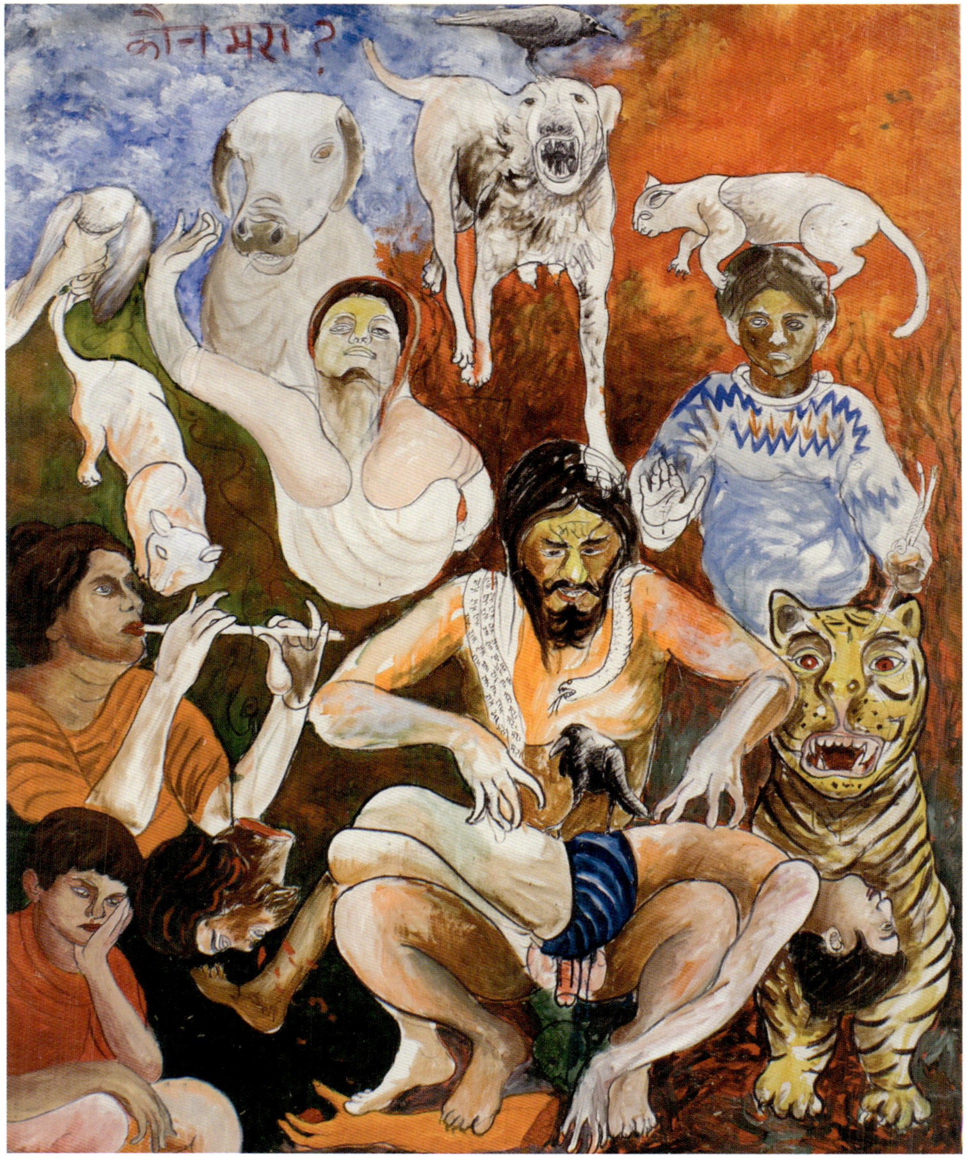

Manjit Bawa, *Kaun Mara?* (Who Died?), background painted by Paramjit Singh, December 10, 1992, acrylic on canvas, 70 x 60 inches.

MADAN GOPAL SINGH

For a while Manjit had been working on a small drawing that depicted him with his son Ravi on his lap. Initially, it seemed like the depiction of an affectionate bond between a physically challenged son and a doting magician of a father. . . . Manjit's daughter, Bhawna, could be seen close to the periphery immersed in her own world of a child's innocent play. It was a peaceful drawing to begin with. I saw it becoming grim and ominous as Advani's Rath Yatra threateningly went around the country, leaving a trail of blood and gore. The child in his father's lap was beginning to now look listless, almost dead. The father had a deadly dagger in his hand. The entire landscape of the family—and in Manjit's work the family is always the landscape—was beginning to acquire a filicidal tonality. The mother was looking away, forlorn, playing a flute. The little girl continued to play innocently. The child being literally killed on his father's lap could also be seen now sitting aside witnessing his own sacrificial offering. The animals, birds, and reptiles—always so endearing in a seamless ecology in Manjit's work—now not only began to stand as witnesses to this clearly foregrounded violence, but also lost their sense of being spontaneously incorporated within the landscape. The entire mise-en-scène acquired the appearance of a disturbing group photograph where each element was carefully arranged in a disharmony of existence.

THE TIMES OF INDIA, NEW DELHI, SATURDAY, DECEMBER 12, 1992 **CAPITAL**

Artists hold protest

The Times of India News Service

NEW DELHI, December 11.

IN a logic reminiscent of the advocates of the Ram Mandir at Ayodhya, the city police tried in vain today to persuade some 500 artists, writers, photographers and other intellectuals to shift the venue of their protest meet from the Safdar Hashmi Marg (near the Mandi House circle) to a "less prominent and sensitive" area.

The meet had been planned as early as Monday, and prominently announced in all the major dailies. The city police too had been informed in a letter about the nature of protest -- paintings, photographs, songs and street plays. But the venue and time had been ignored until the even was underway this evening. After viewing Manjit Bawa's canvas, the Ayodhya photographs compiled by Ram Rehman, and hearing the soulful singing of Madan Gopal Singh and Susmit Bose, the police were too perplexed to use force.

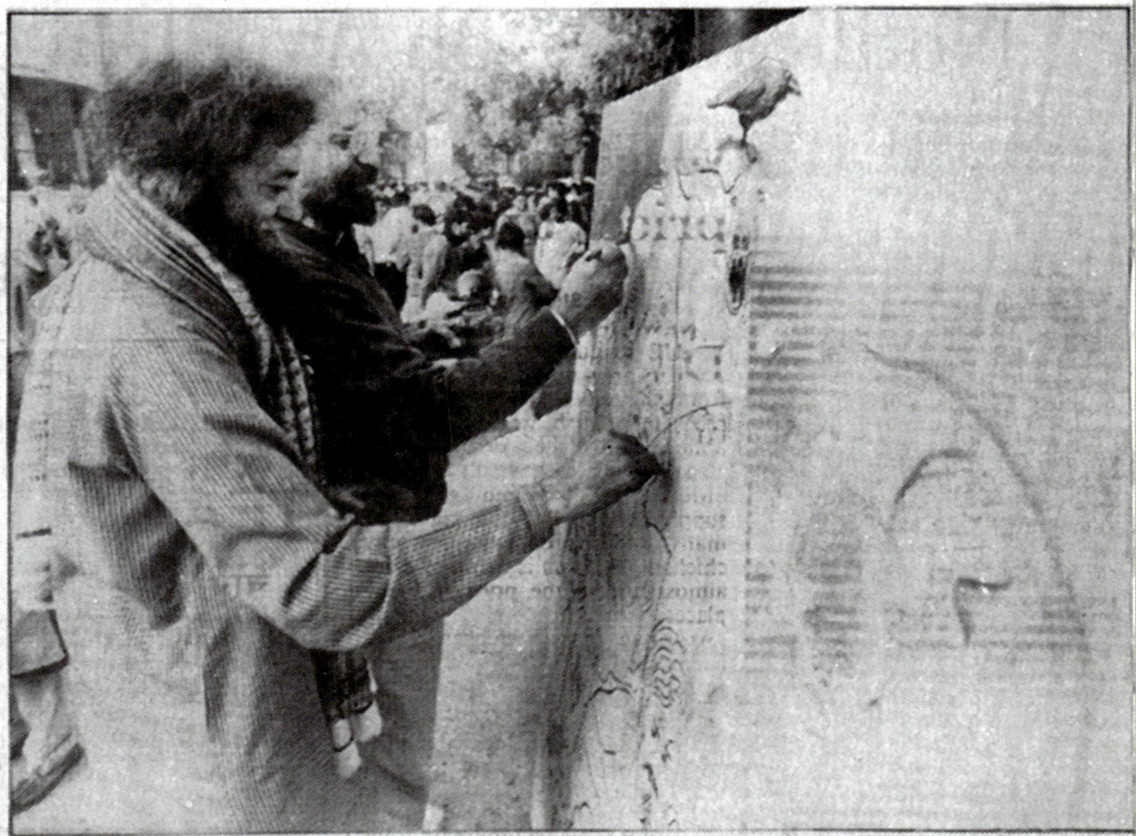

Painters Manjit Bawa and Paramjit Singh (in glasses) marking their 'protest' against the Ayodhya events at a meet in the Capital on Friday. — TOI

"Artists hold protest," *The Times of India*, December 12, 1992.

RAM RAHMAN

One of the key episodes in Sahmat's history links into a key episode in India's modern history—the destruction of the Babri Mosque in the city of Ayodhya in the central plains of northern India. The whole movement to destroy that mosque was led by extreme right-wing Hindu groups who held that the mosque had been built by the invading Mughals in the sixteenth century on the site of a temple that marked the birthplace of Rama, which they had destroyed and then appropriated as a mosque. That claim was much debated, particularly among historians and archeologists in India. The name of the town Ayodhya goes back to mythology to the *Ramayana* epic, which is a couple of thousand years old and is part of an oral tradition of epic poetry in India. There are no historical records indicating that the town now known as Ayodhya is actually the Ayodhya of the *Ramayana*.

Two years prior to December 6, 1992, L. K. Advani of the Bharatiya Janata Party (BJP) had led a *Rath yatra*, which is essentially a chariot procession, from the state of Gujarat to Ayodhya in Uttar Pradesh, whipping up sentiments over setting right the supposed wrong imposed by the Muslim invaders on the Hindu majority. This was a highly contentious kind of history to bring forth in a very public political action because it was extremely divisive and released very dangerous emotions. Those travels across India led to a rise in the communal temperature, which coincided with the formation of Sahmat. Despite all kinds of contrary promises to the government, however, the right-wing groups mobilized thousands of people to destroy the mosque, on December 6, 1992.

VEER MUNSHI

My active participation in Sahmat's activities began after the Babri Masjid demolition in 1992 and subsequently on many such issues that were important for Sahmat to take a stand on: the violence against Muslims in Gujarat after the Godhra incident in 2002, and the persecution campaign against Husain.

Sahmat has affected my work, absolutely. Politics and its repercussions became the subject of my art practice primarily because of my personal catharsis while being a part of protests—the Babri Masjid demolition, the fall of Saddam Hussein, the post-Godhra violence in Gujarat, etc. Sahmat changed my political perception. I became more and more analytical rather than reactive in my work, and issues became larger than just merely personal.

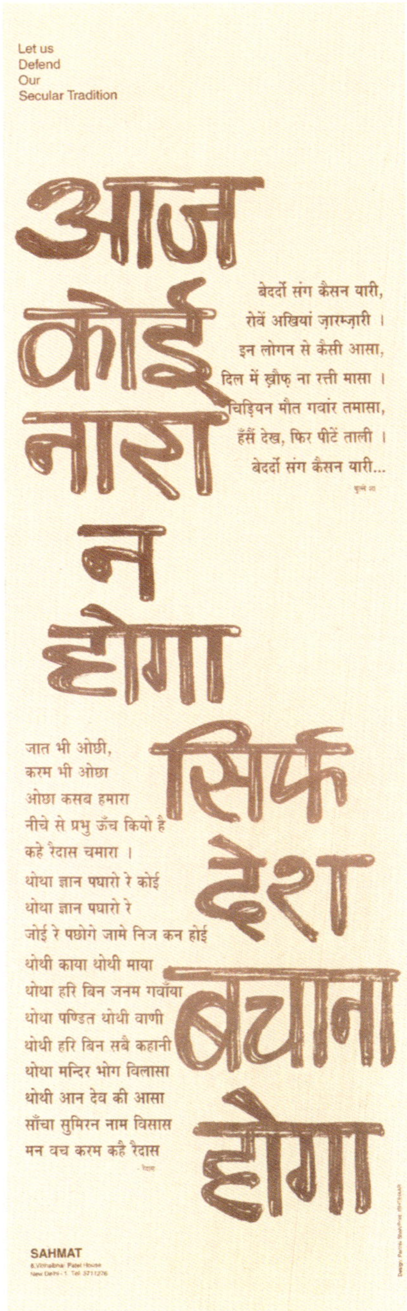

PARTHIV SHAH

Of all the posters I've done for Sahmat, perhaps those I made for *Anhad Garje* are closest to my heart. Most of my designs were created keeping in mind the resources we had at Sahmat, and so they were visually bold but not created on expensive paper or printed in the best printing press. For the poster that I designed, I divided the usual size (23 x 36 inches) lengthwise into two, to create an elongated vertical poster. The poster was printed on newsprint and in a single color with bold typography in Hindi to create the visual effect. Even now when I travel to different parts of India I see that poster framed and mounted on the wall in a village library or school; interestingly, I saw it also in the office of the chief minister in Madhya Pradesh! And, given that the poster was about using text cleverly, the message was deceptively simple: *Aaj koi naara na hoga, sirf desh bachaana hoga* (There shall be no slogans today, our only task is to save the nation).

Aaj koi naara na hoga, sirf desh bachaana hoga (There shall be no slogans today, our only task is to save the nation), poster, December 8, 1992, 36 x 11½ inches. Design: Parthiv Shah.

Right-Wing Communal Mobilization: From Ayodhya to Gujarat

Sukumar Muralidharan

Struggles for reclaiming the primordial identity of the "Hindu nation" were raging in India in the late 1980s, as Sahmat took shape as both a platform and a campaign. The very first year of Sahmat's existence witnessed widespread mobilization by the Hindutva combine (of majoritarian religious forces) in various parts of the country, riding the waves of a virulent tide of communal antagonism.

Violence reached a still higher pitch the following year as the Hindutva forces launched a motorized procession from Somnath (where a supposed historical injustice had been remedied by the restoration of a temple) to Ayodhya, site of a grievance, not yet redressed, of the "Hindu nation." All who thought that things were already as bad as they could be were quickly proved wrong with the demolition of the Babri Masjid at Ayodhya that December day.

The mosque had been erased, but the Hindutva combine's pursuit of political power required that the "alien other" be kept alive and active, for the insecurities it nurtured. The combine also needed to consolidate and build on the momentary triumphalism of December 6. The deeper social schisms that Ayodhya pointed to, such as the denial of authentic rights within the "nation" of an entire historical and cultural presence, continued to surface at regular intervals. Aggression from the Right—and the timidity of the political center—resulted in the conquest of new political frontiers by Hindutva.

Maharashtra, particularly the city of Bombay (now Mumbai)—site of some of the most horrific violence since the events at Ayodhya—was among the new territories that fell under the sway of the Hindutva combine in the mid-1990s.

So too, Gujarat.

There were worries about the possible consequences when a Bharatiya Janata Party–led government assumed power at the center. There were also suggestions that the responsibilities of holding elected office would induce a sense of pragmatic restraint on people who had been on an irrational quest for vengeance.

By 2002, in the post-9/11 world, Ayodhya had been supplanted—in the communal lobby's calculations—by "Islamic terror" as the issue that could best stir up popular anxieties for political gain. In February that year, the Hindutva combine played its last card in the Ayodhya maneuver, sending out unnamed, unidentified volunteers for a cause as yet unknown to them.

Those who were handling the volunteers did, however, proclaim their cause—the final and unequivocal occupation of the spot where the Babri Masjid had stood. The demolition of December 6 had evidently been an incomplete triumph. Hindutva's final victory proclamation had to wait till the hallowed spot was retrieved from a limbo of executive inaction and judicial restraint.

A train returning to Gujarat carrying volunteers who had participated in this project was attacked in Godhra in February 2002, and fifty-eight people were killed. For the next two months, Gujarat raged with communal fury.

Sahmat was a platform, among others, for shocked and horrified citizens to gather to denounce the pogrom that was let loose in Gujarat by the Hindutva hordes. In addition to the loss of life, there was a conscious effort by Hindutva to efface the cultural patrimony of the Muslim community, to deny the very legitimacy of its identity within the vast cultural expanse that is India.

Hindutva has sought, since then, to move the project of historical revanchism on to a plane of reason. These efforts have included some dubious inferences from archeology that have disregarded the procedural norms of the discipline.

1993

Anhad Garje

Before the Babri Masjid was destroyed, Sahmat had planned a program of Sufi-Bhakti performances for January 1, 1993, titled *Anhad Garje* (a phrase used by the medieval saint-poet Kabir that roughly translates to "the silence reverberates"). In the immediate aftermath of the demolition, the seventeen-hour stretch of performances took on an additional resonance by promoting communal harmony and serving as a reminder of the power of performance to voice resistance. As Sahmat explained in a pamphlet: "*Anhad Garje* was conceived and performed as a challenge to those who would reconstruct the identity of the people within the meanest parameters possible. [The Sufi-Bhakti tradition] is a humanized spirituality that demands opposition to tyranny in all its forms." Building on the strong response to this event, Sahmat took the program of music, dance, lectures, and plays to Bombay, Lucknow, Surat, Valod, Baroda, and Ahmedabad—all cities that had witnessed terrible communal riots.

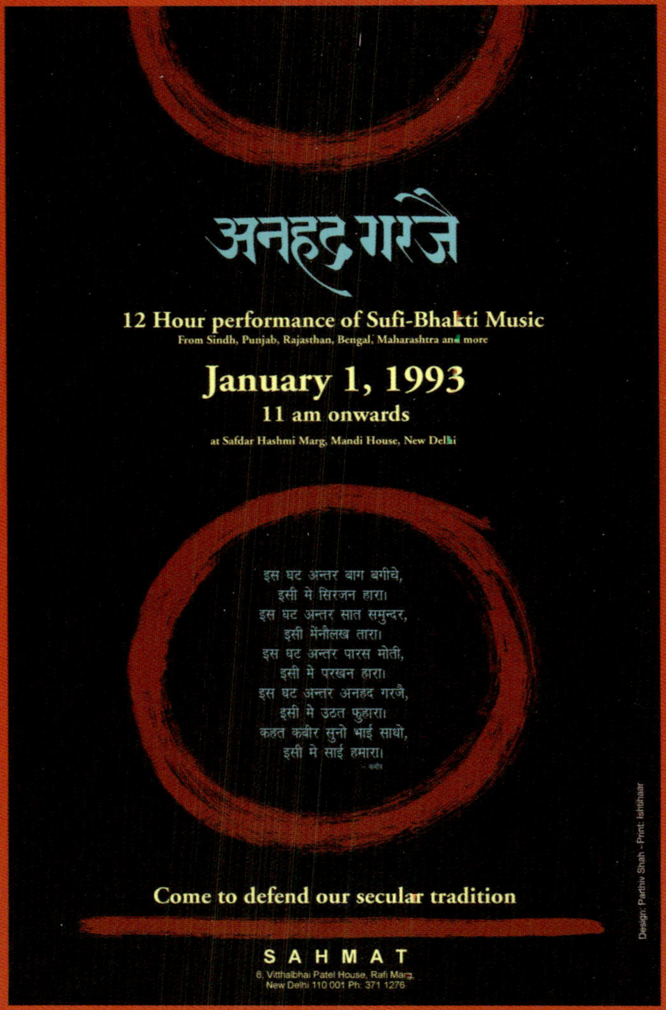

Anhad Garje poster, 1993, silkscreen, 36 x 23 inches.
Design: Parthiv Shah.

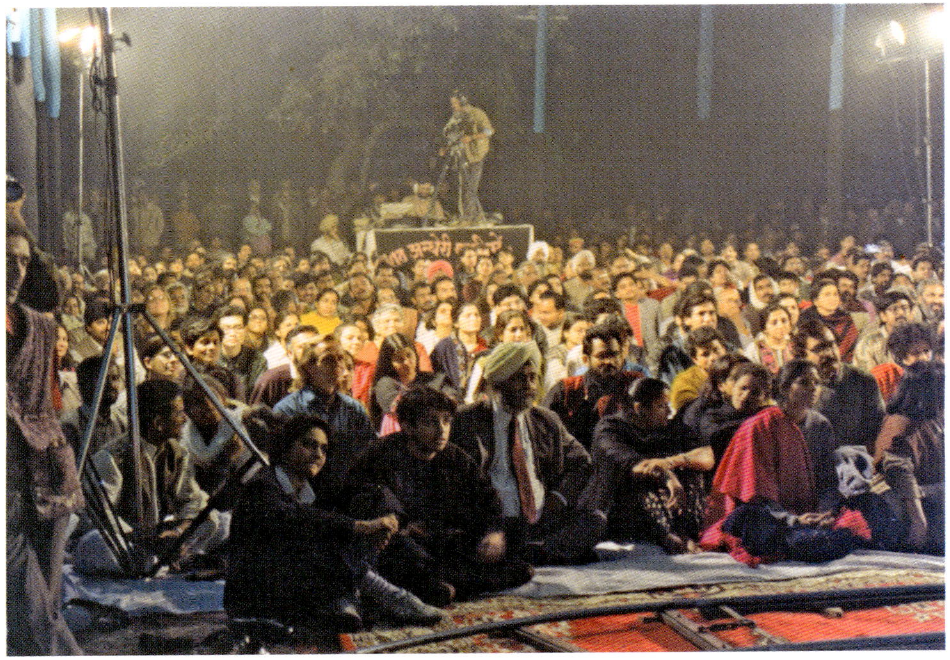

A view of the packed audience at the seventeen-hour-long *Anhad Garje* program in Delhi, January 1, 1993.

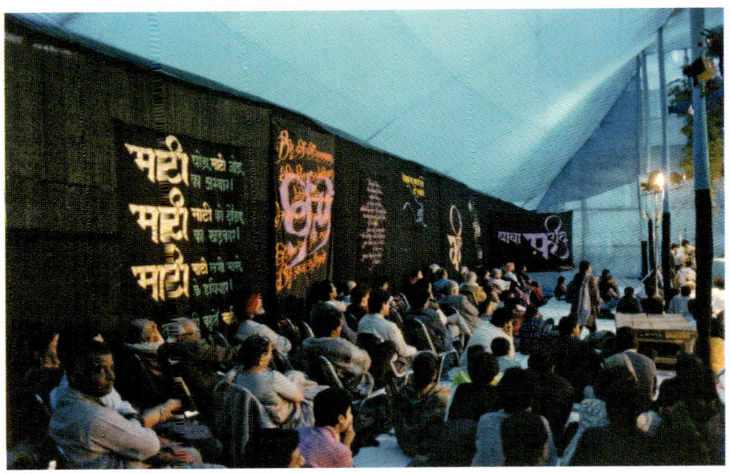

Anhad Garje tent, Delhi, January 1, 1993. The black side walls are covered with banners of calligraphed poetry in five languages.

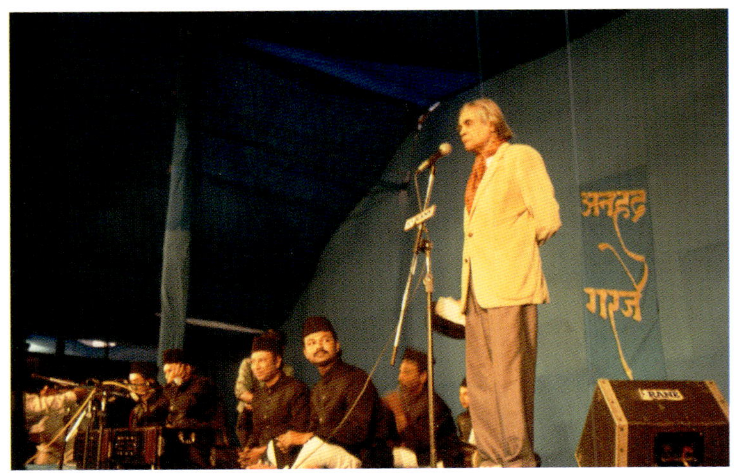

Poet Ali Sardar Jafri speaks before the performance by Qawwali singers Jafar Husain Khan. *Anhad Garje*, Mumbai, February 20, 1993.

ROMI KHOSLA

Containing Creative Energy for a Moment

For many of us who gather for the daylong performances on the first of January every year, the event has enormous significance. It reinforces our collective resistance to forgetting Safdar Hashmi's murder. Like Safdar's creative activities, the annual Sahmat event is conducted in public spaces and on the streets. This transient activity is not a passing show. On the contrary, the transience questions the boundaries and enclosures, the brick and mortar that conventional creative activities require. The Sahmat event of January 1 occurs in a temporary space, and demonstrates that it is possible to contain immense creative energies for a moment in time in a space that soon disappears.

The creation of such an impermanent space becomes important since it has to be able to contain the creative energies of a daylong event. The most memorable of these impermanent containers was created in 1993 for the series of *Anhad Garje* performances. The color of the fabric, the scale of the enclosure, its height and lighting, all contributed to poetical Sufi expressions of many of the performances. The tent became a magnificent spectacle that rose to over fifty feet covering the stage, at the center of which there was a tree. The platform under the tree became the performance space, and the sky-blue fabric that formed the backdrop recalled a clear blue sky. This translucency was enhanced by black fabric that covered the rest of the enclosure around the audience of maybe 1,000 people. For a person who entered the enclosure from outside, the experience of this enclosed impermanent space was magnificent. The entrance and the audience space was in pitch darkness while the stage looked as though it was suspended on the edge of space with foliage of a tree lit up against a translucent sky behind it. It seemed as if one were looking at a performer standing in some mythical open space.

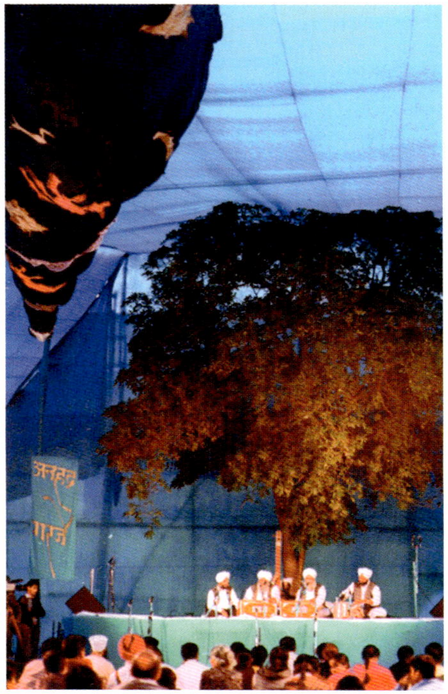

Ragi singers from Punjab perform under the tree in the tent designed by a team of artists led by architect Romi Khosla, as part of *Anhad Garje*, Delhi, January 1, 1993.

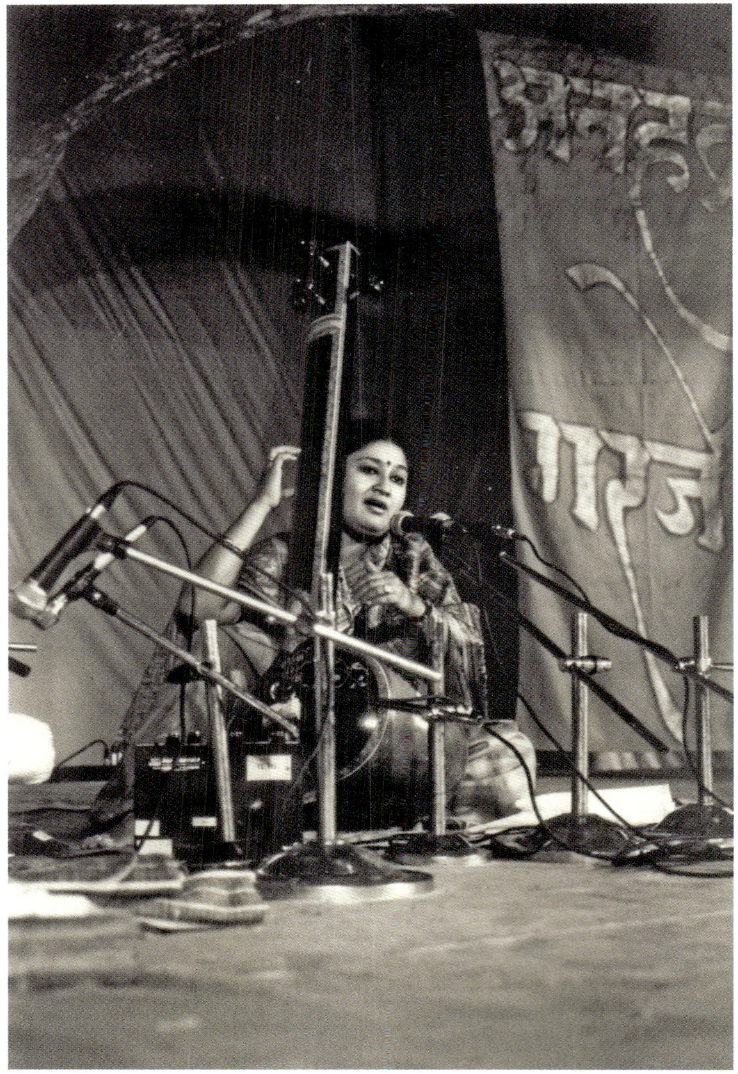

Shubha Mudgal sings at *Anhad Garje*, Lucknow, April 3, 1993.

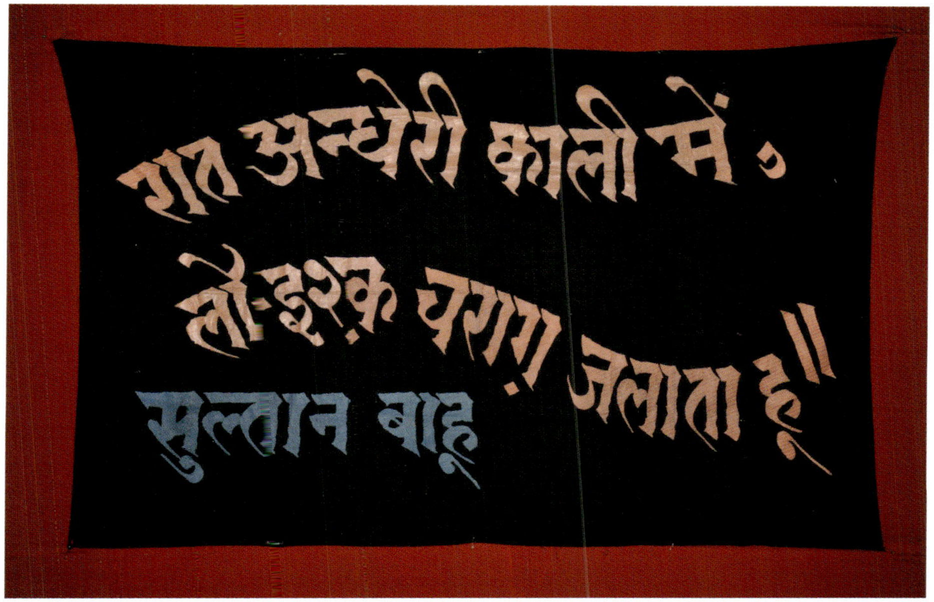

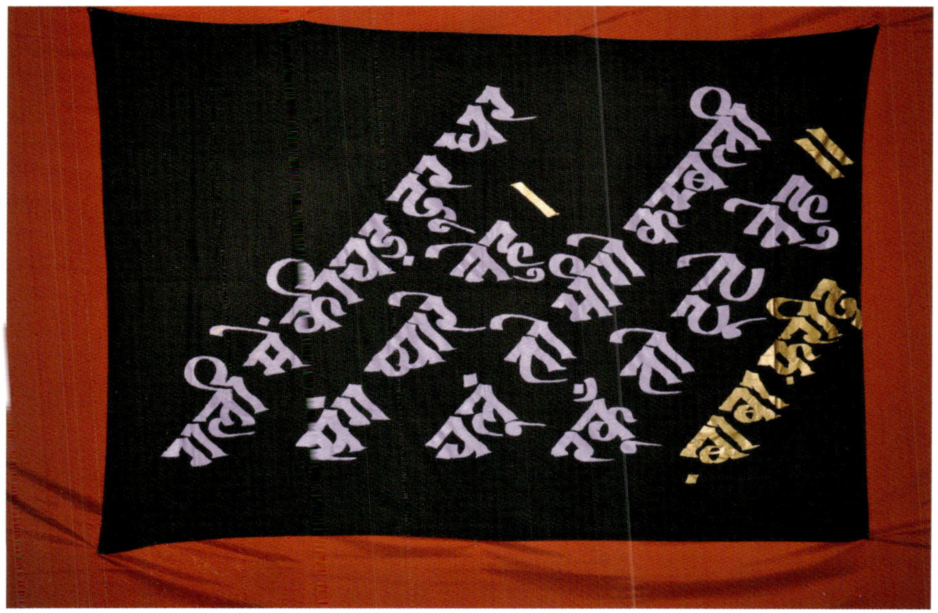

Examples of the banners with poetry in five languages that covered the side walls of the *Anhad Garje* tent in Delhi, January 1, 1993. Calligraphy: Sumant Jayakrishnan.

In the darkness of the desolate night,
I light the flame of love.
—Sultan Bahu

My beloved lives at the other end of this unclean path.
I sully my garment if I walk this way and lose my love if I don't.
—Baba Farid

RUMMANA HUSSAIN

Excerpt from "A statement for secularism," *The Independent*, February 19, 1993.

Historically, too, artists have always maintained the secular tradition. It's necessary to emerge from our insular shells, to come together and try and develop symbols of secularism. Moreover, a coming together of artists and viewers is a form of public participation, one that emphasizes the commonality of all—something which the Sufi-Bhakti tradition emphasizes.

SOHAIL HASHMI

Sahmat has been able to create spaces for cultural interventions, to reclaim spaces that were increasingly being denied to the democratic and pluralistic traditions of society, but most importantly, I think, the signal contribution of Sahmat is the foregrounding of the tolerant, pluralistic, and inclusive traditions of all creative processes—the underscoring of the continuity of the Sufi-Bhakti traditions, and the assertion that these ideas feed and nourish the contemporary secular discourse. By claiming the Sufi-Bhakti platform as part of our living heritage Sahmat also created conditions where these platforms were increasingly denied to forces that were bent upon distorting the inclusive agenda of the Sufi-Bhakti streams.

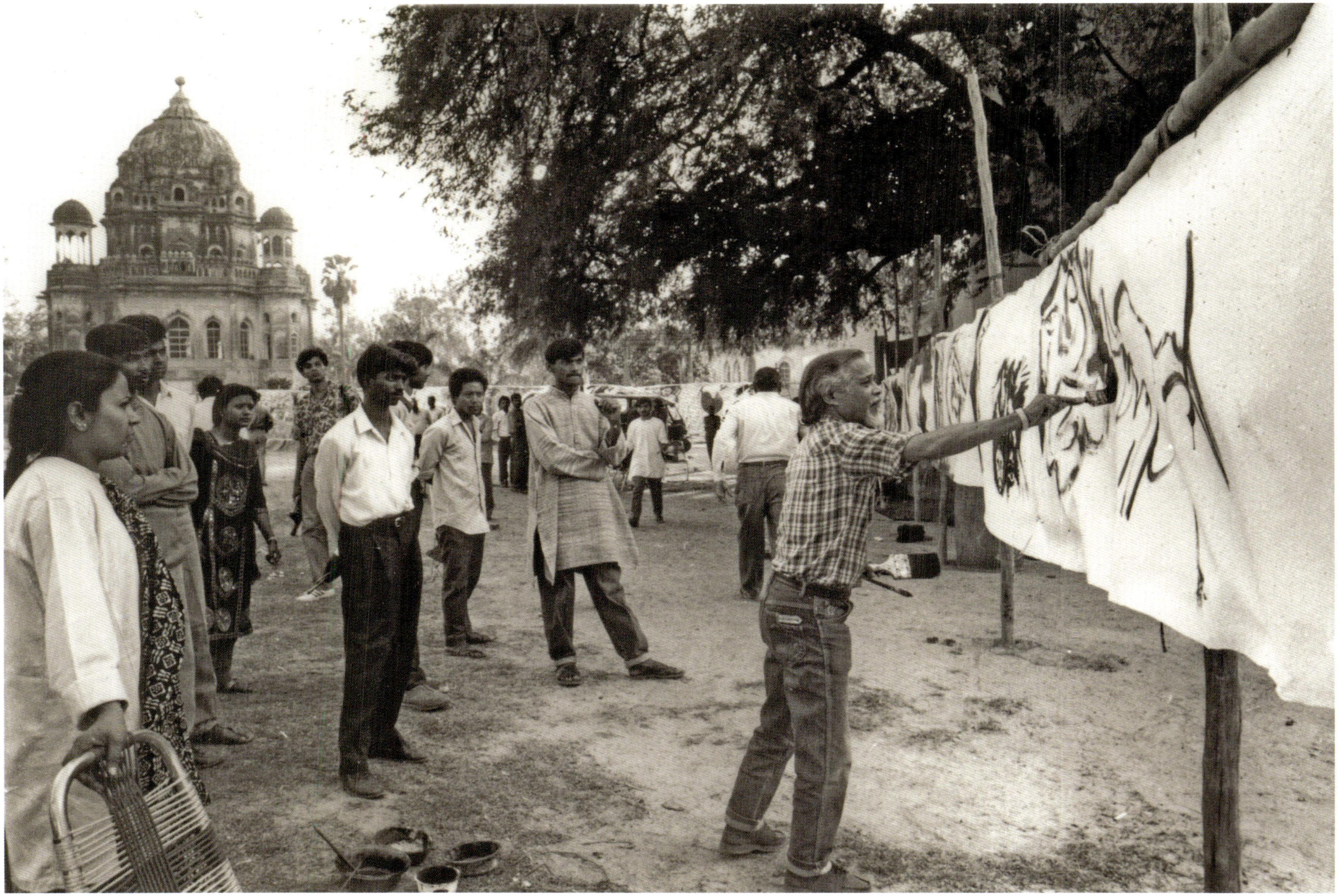

Artists paint a giant canvas at Hazrat Mahal Park during *Anhad Garje*, Lucknow, April 3, 1993.

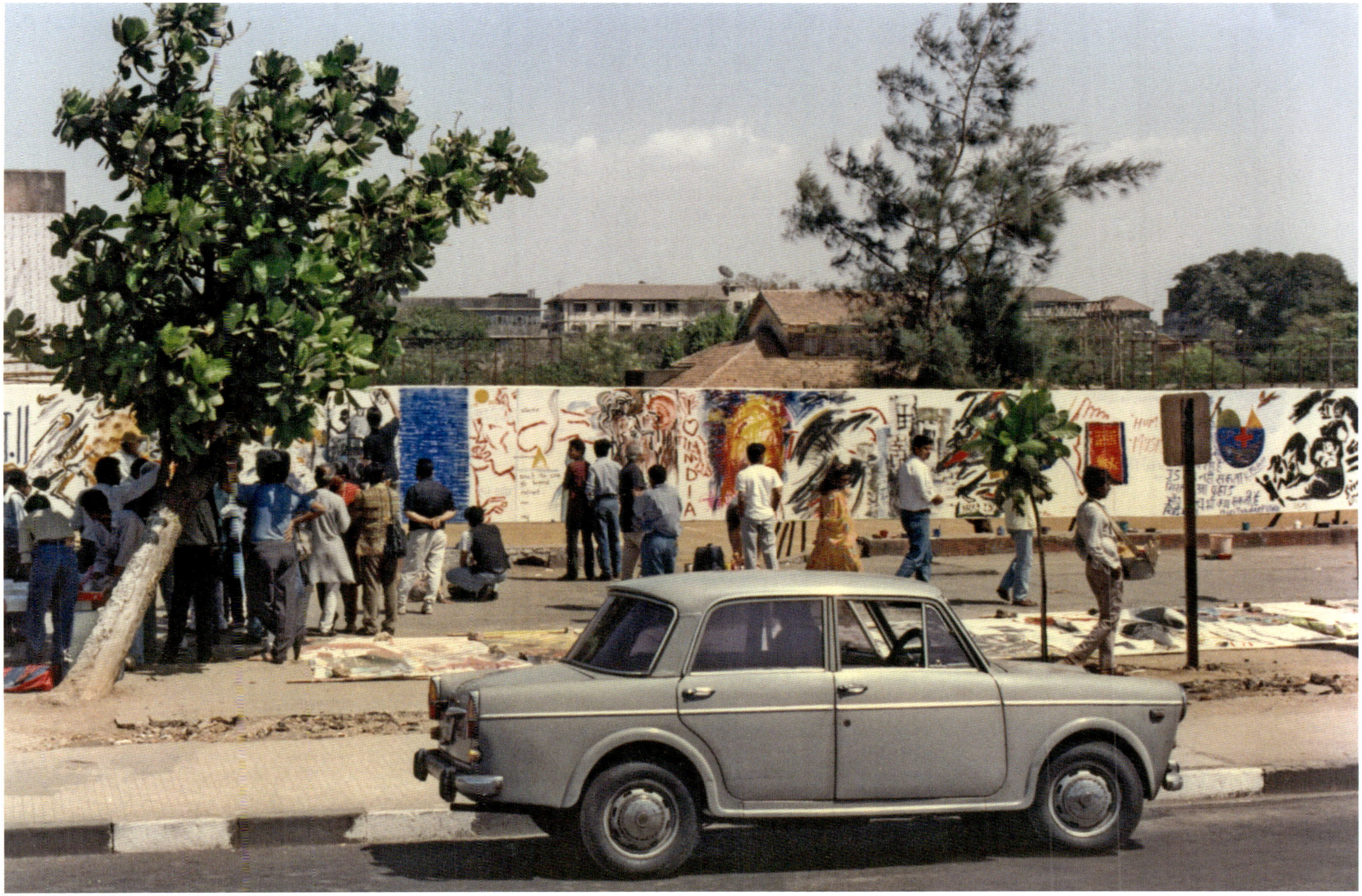

Artists paint a giant canvas on Marine Drive outside the performance venue during *Anhad Garje*, Bombay, February 20, 1993.

Pamphlet for *Anhad Garje* (New Delhi: Sahmat, 1993).

A Transcultural Reaching Out

Madan Gopal Singh

The Sufi experience within the Indian subcontinent may be described as a transcultural reaching out. One sees at its core a tremendous fluidity of emotion. At times, it passionately disavows the simple mystical oppositions of the I in perennial separation from the Other. In traditional Sufi poetry, even if there is a clamor for unmediated communion between the two, the Other is somehow always seen to command from a height. The subcontinental view develops in an altogether different direction. It unequivocally places the subject's substantiality at the center. No spiritual effect is possible without that. So there is no mystical transcendence at the expense of terrestrial experience. The unity of the I and the Other is above all the unity of the people. In this respect alone, the subcontinental Sufi experience may be seen as a radical and decisive move away from its largely ritual-ridden Persian antecedents. Its development, especially in the northern regions of the subcontinent, creates a pulsating edge against all forms of communal strife and discord. It throbs with mercurial energy and calls urgently for intervention. Its anxieties assume a highly irreverent voice and project a genuine self-criticality. In its anger and protest it spares no one, just as in its love it embraces all. Its subjects are here and now: the Hindus and the Muslims in a transcultural mix of creative joy. Their unity invariably spills out of religious boundaries. The dominant images and emotions come directly from the lived experience of the people. There is an almost tactile face to these images. This is the level where the people have become one without being the same. Leading Sufi poets such as Baba Farid, Shah Husain, Sultan Bahu, Bulle Shah, Shah Mohammad, and Shah Latif journey across the plurality of time—the days, weeks, months, etc.—or play with the essential structures of communion numbers, alphabets, words, phrases, etc. All these become not only the units of the poetical pulse—the beat in Sufi music being one of its most important aspects—but, more importantly, the carriers of the poet's longing for a carnivalesque unity of the people.

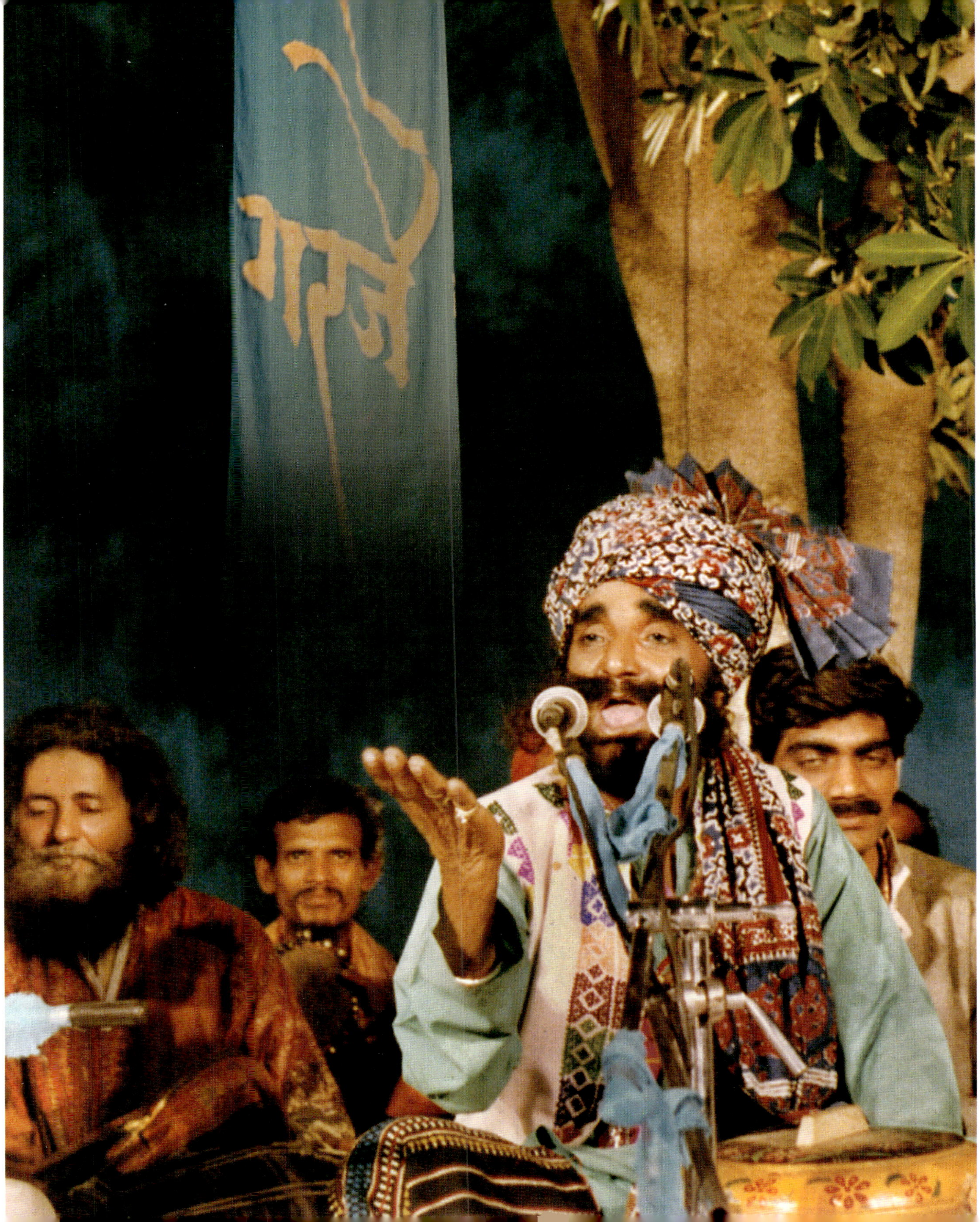

VIVAN SUNDARAM
Madan Gopal Singh is one of the people who initiated the bringing in of the Sufi-Bhakti tradition into contemporary art. Since then it has been accepted and promoted across the country. So if you ask what is one of Sahmat's biggest contributions to Indian culture, it lies in our recognizing the importance of the Sufi-Bhakti movement and foregrounding it in the present time, knowing that it would move out into the public domain, into the classical movement, into Bollywood, and become something that a large, liberal middle class would identify with. That could be named as a major strength of Sahmat in terms of cultural dissemination and influence.

Painter Manjit Bawa (on the left) plays the *dholak* (a percussion instrument) for the legendary Sindhi Sufi singer from Pakistan, Allan Faqir. *Anhad Garje*, Delhi, January 1, 1993.

1993

In Defense of Our Secular Tradition: Posters with Sufi-Bhakti Poetry and Contemporary Art

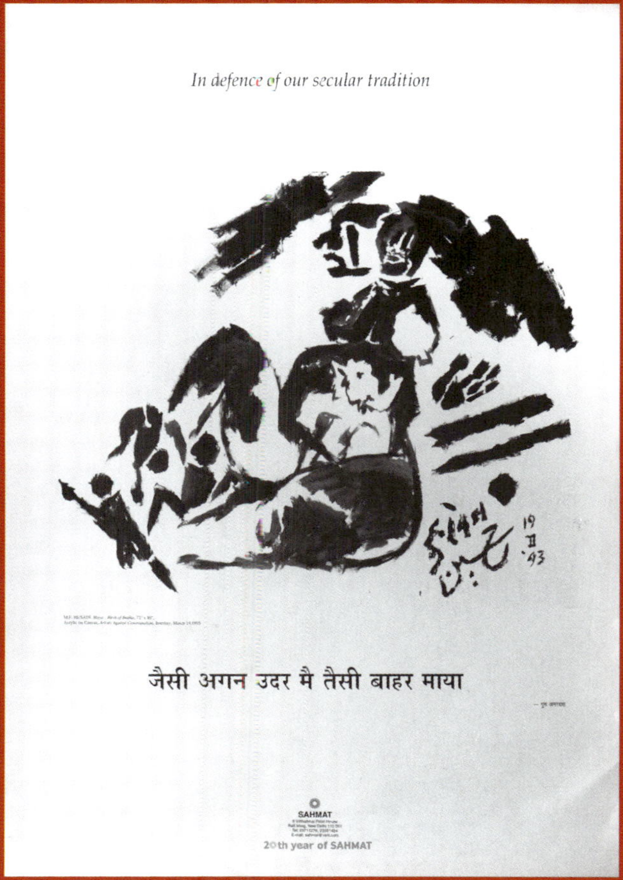

Sufi-Bhakti poster for *In Defense of Our Secular Tradition*, 1993, 27½ x 19 inches. Image: M. F. Husain's *Maya's Dream (The Birth of the Buddha)*. Design: Rajinder Arora.

Sahmat began producing posters that combined contemporary art images with medieval poetry texts as part of their Sufi-Bhakti program of *Anhad Garje* in 1993. Poetry from the Sufi-Bhakti traditions has been a key source of inspiration for Sahmat, as it embodies a tradition of resistance against orthodoxies and also reflects the truly secular fabric of Indian culture. Sahmat selected images by contemporary artists to accompany selected poetic verses from these traditions, and then these combinations were used to make a series of posters titled *In Defense of Our Secular Tradition*. Sahmat distributed thousands of copies of these posters among the general public and in universities and student organizations, with the hope of spreading their message of unity and introducing contemporary art to new audiences in an accessible format.

As is the fire in the womb, so indeed is the *maya* [appearance] in the world outside.
—Guru Amar Das (the third of the Sikh Gurus)

Artist M. F. Husain inaugurates the giant canvas placed outside the performance tent on Marine Drive, painted by artists during *Anhad Garje*, Bombay, February 20, 1993. Sahmat used Husain's painting *Maya's Dream (The Birth of the Buddha)*, on one of their posters in the series "In Defense of Our Secular Tradition" (left).

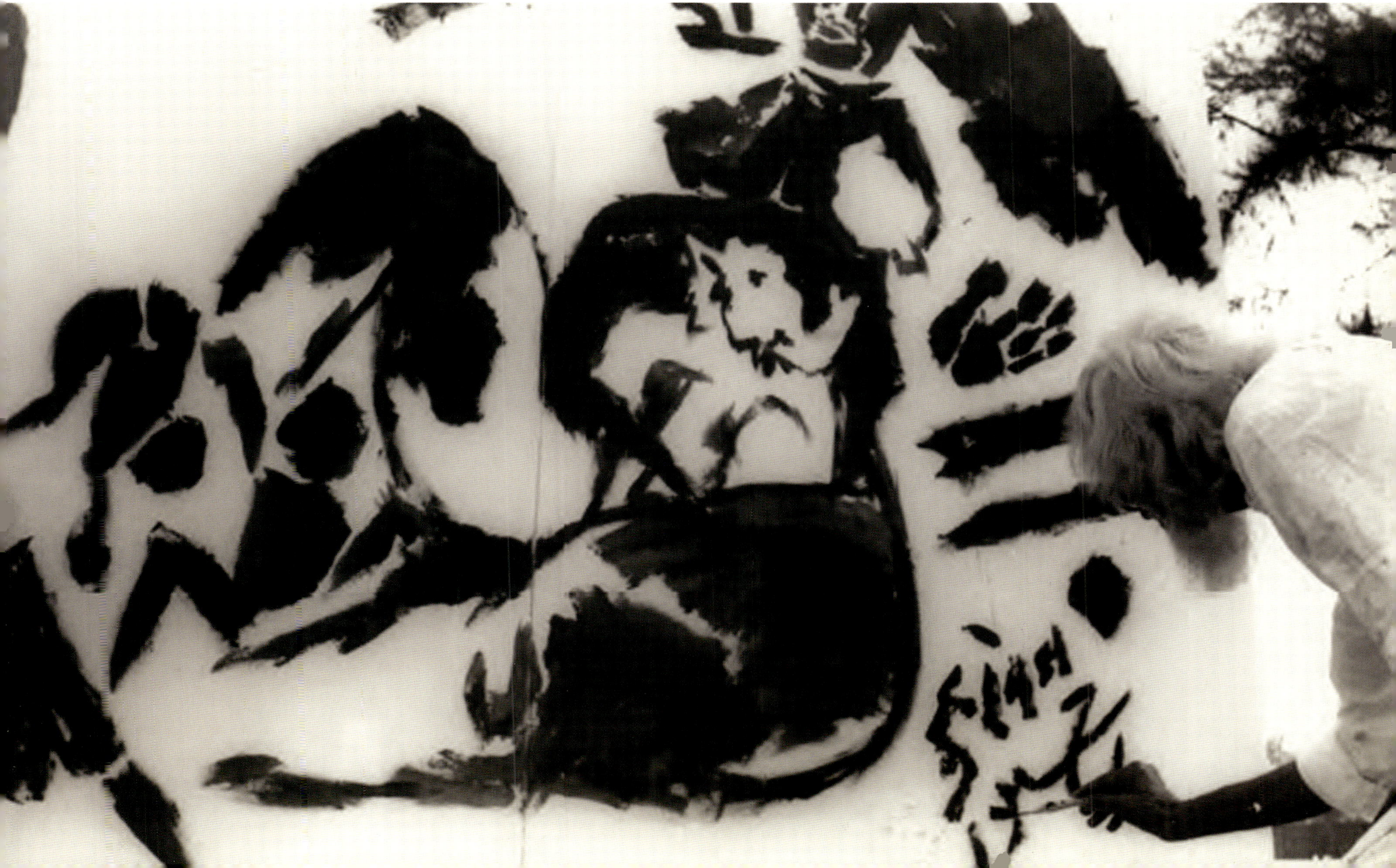

The sun sets,
the horizon turns red.
I bow before the one
who brings back the light.
—Bulle Shah
Image: Arpita Singh

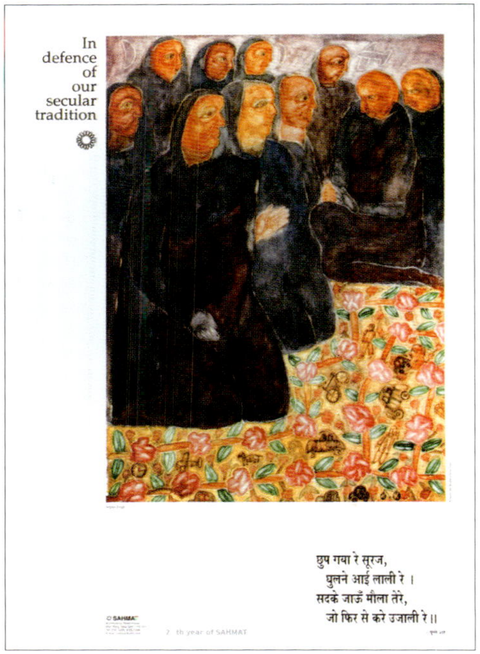

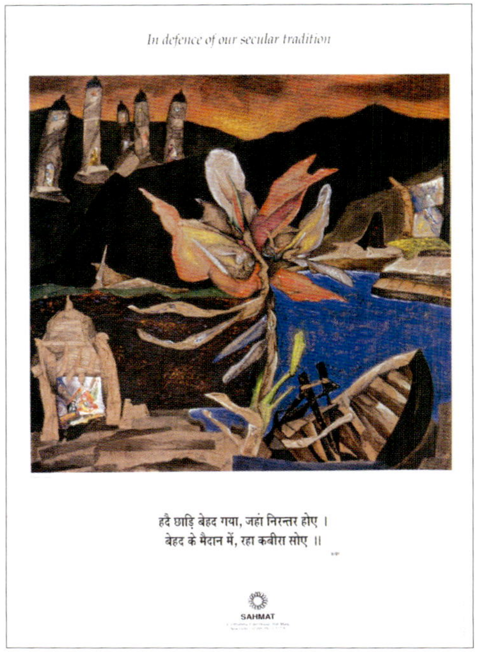

Discarding all confines he reaches
boundless land, land of the eternal.
In unbounded fields, "Kabir" now rests.
—Kabir
Image: Manu Parekh

One thread, a multitude of pearls,
The Creator brings them together.
Water waves and foam bubbles,
Forever inseparable from water.
—Namdev
Image: Haku Shah

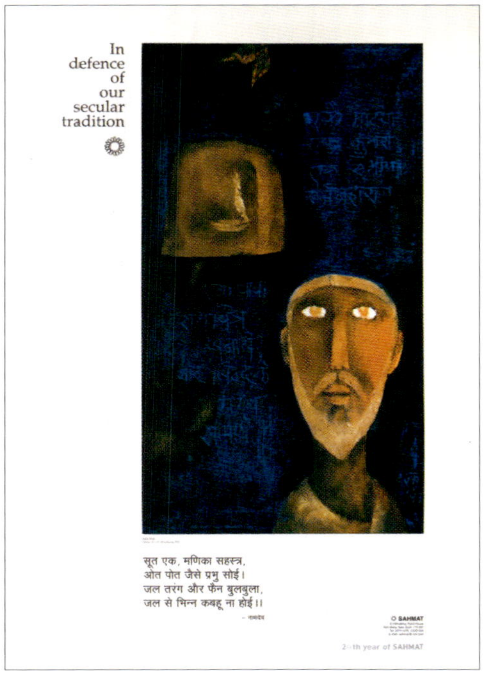

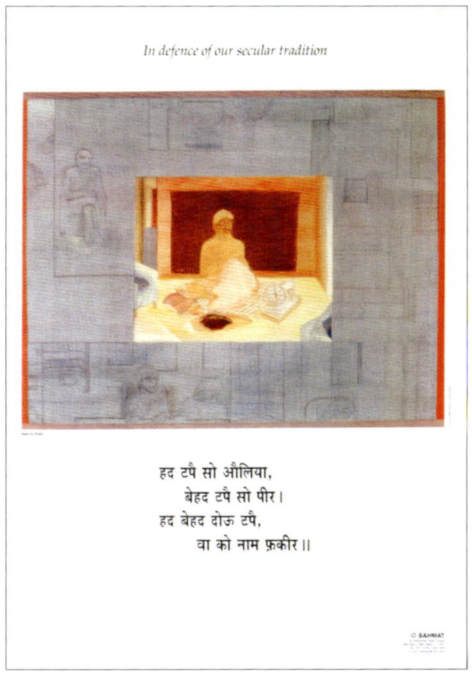

Those who transcend boundaries
are saints,
Those who transcend the
unbounded are seers.
And those who transcend both,
Limits and the limitless, are fakirs.
—Anonymous
Image: Nilima Sheikh

Sufi-Bhakti posters for *In Defence of Our Secular Tradition*, 1993, 27½ x 19 inches.
Design: Rajinder Arora.

Fire is better than "Bulle,"
for it cooks food.
Sufis and teachers gather around,
and come together as they eat.
—Bulle Shah
Image: Nalini Malani

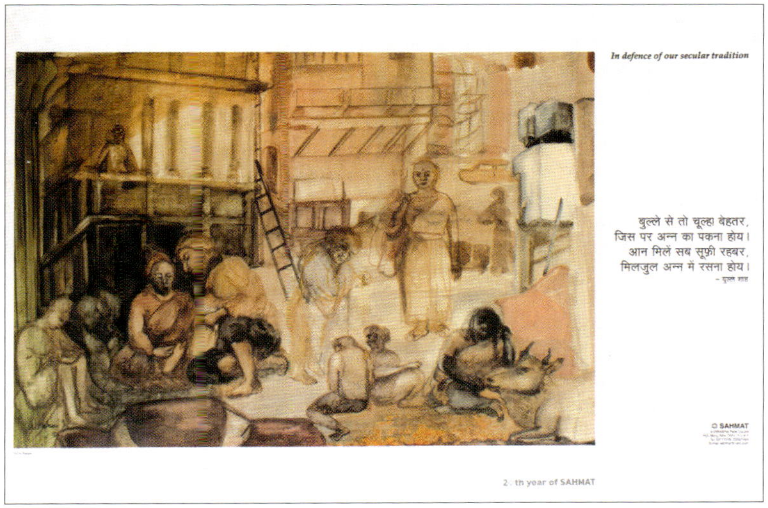

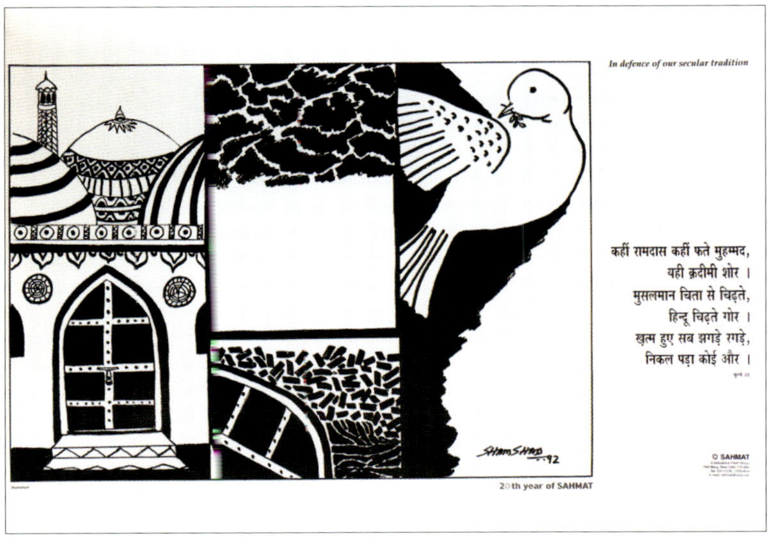

A Ramdas here, a Fateh Mohammad there,
The same old noise.
The Musalman hates the pyre,
The Hindu detests the grave.
All disputes end,
when one takes a new path.
—Bulle Shah
Image: Shamshad

Sufi-Bhakti posters for *In Defense of Our Secular Tradition*, 1993, 19 x 27½ x inches.
Design: Rajinder Arora.

RAJINDER ARORA

I have been associated with Sahmat, and participated in its sustained campaign on behalf of artists, almost since the collective's inception. We have worked against any attempt to thwart the creative expression of artists across the country, and made sincere efforts to assert the values of secularism and cultural pluralism.

These posters reflect a political commitment shared by all of us involved in Sahmat and protest any efforts to impose conformist beliefs that threaten the pluralist and secular culture of our country. The design points to a firm belief in the freedom of creative expression that Sahmat stands for and works to maintain.

As part of a movement that seeks to fuse the best of India's traditional and modern art forms, I worked seamlessly with artists from various streams, which made the process of designing these posters unique. Together, through the creation of the posters, we built solidarity.

I come from a graphic design background, and some of my works reflect the political role of a designer in communicating cultures and ideologies. As an agent of ideology, design also conveys one's commitment to larger collective interests. Aimed at communicating with people's subconscious perceptions, these posters use images and text to bring forth the social conflicts and difficult realities of our times in order to transcend violence. They reflect design as activism, as a cultural form of dissent, and as a vehicle of social change.

RAM RAHMAN

We started making these posters "In Defense of Our Secular Tradition" at the time we did *Anhad Garje*, right after the mosque demolition in Ayodhya. We had begun including contemporary art in many forms in our performance events through theatre, contemporary dance, even avant-garde cabaret acts. But we decided to use the poster format here with a double meaning. We used images by contemporary artists, many of whom were very well known, but whose work is relatively inaccessible to the general public, because we don't have a lot of art magazines or art books in India. We decided to combine the work of many of these artists, who had already been using themes of Sufism, in their work, with Sufi-Bhakti poems, which evoked the art and gave it a different layer of meaning. We found that for many average viewers, who were not used to seeing contemporary painting, the text helped them connect with the work. The contemporary art was reinforced by the medieval poetry, and we were hoping that the posters would have a resonance in the context of what was happening at the time with the communal temperature rising.

1993

Hum Sab Ayodhya

The members of Sahmat saw the demolition of the Babri Masjid as a fundamentally transformative assault on India's secular culture. Their intense debates and discussions on the event were reflected in the broadside (a large poster) *Ayodhya: What then are our invocations?*, which was printed and disseminated in the thousands. It depicted a conceptual mapping of ways to approach the fraught issues brought to the fore by the Ayodhya movement, particularly distortions of secular democracy, religion, and history.

This broadside provided a blueprint for further discussions with activists, artists, and students across India. In collaboration with a team of some of India's most prominent historians, including Irfan Habib, K. N. Panikkar, P. K. Shukla, Sushil Srivastava, Ravinder Kumar, Athar Ali, and Suvira Jaiswal, Sahmat then conceived the exhibition *Hum Sab Ayodhya* (We Are All Ayodhya), about the ancient city's rich historical and cultural antecedents and evolution. Reproductions of artworks, photographs, prints, and architectural drawings, accompanied by texts extracted from literary and historical sources, were displayed in configurations that brought out the layered and diverse traditions emerging from material documentation of the Ayodhya region.

The exhibition—which was conceived as a kit of portable panels—was presented in New Delhi's Nehru Memorial Museum and Library from August 9 to 21, 1993, and shown concurrently in seventeen other cities around the country. Two panels on multiple versions of the Rama myth (the *Ram Katha*) became the focus of an attack on the exhibition. The Bharatiya Janata Party (BJP) and right-wing groups campaigned successfully to have the panels banned and the Delhi police seized them. This attack on a secular, public space only clarified the battle for Sahmat. Calling attention to interpretations and misinterpretations of history, and the Right's steady efforts to bring communalism into the education system became a central focus of Sahmat's activities. Sahmat challenged the ban on the *Ram Katha* panels and, after an eight-year court battle, won a decisive legal victory. It became a landmark case for freedom of expression in India and a defining moment for Sahmat.

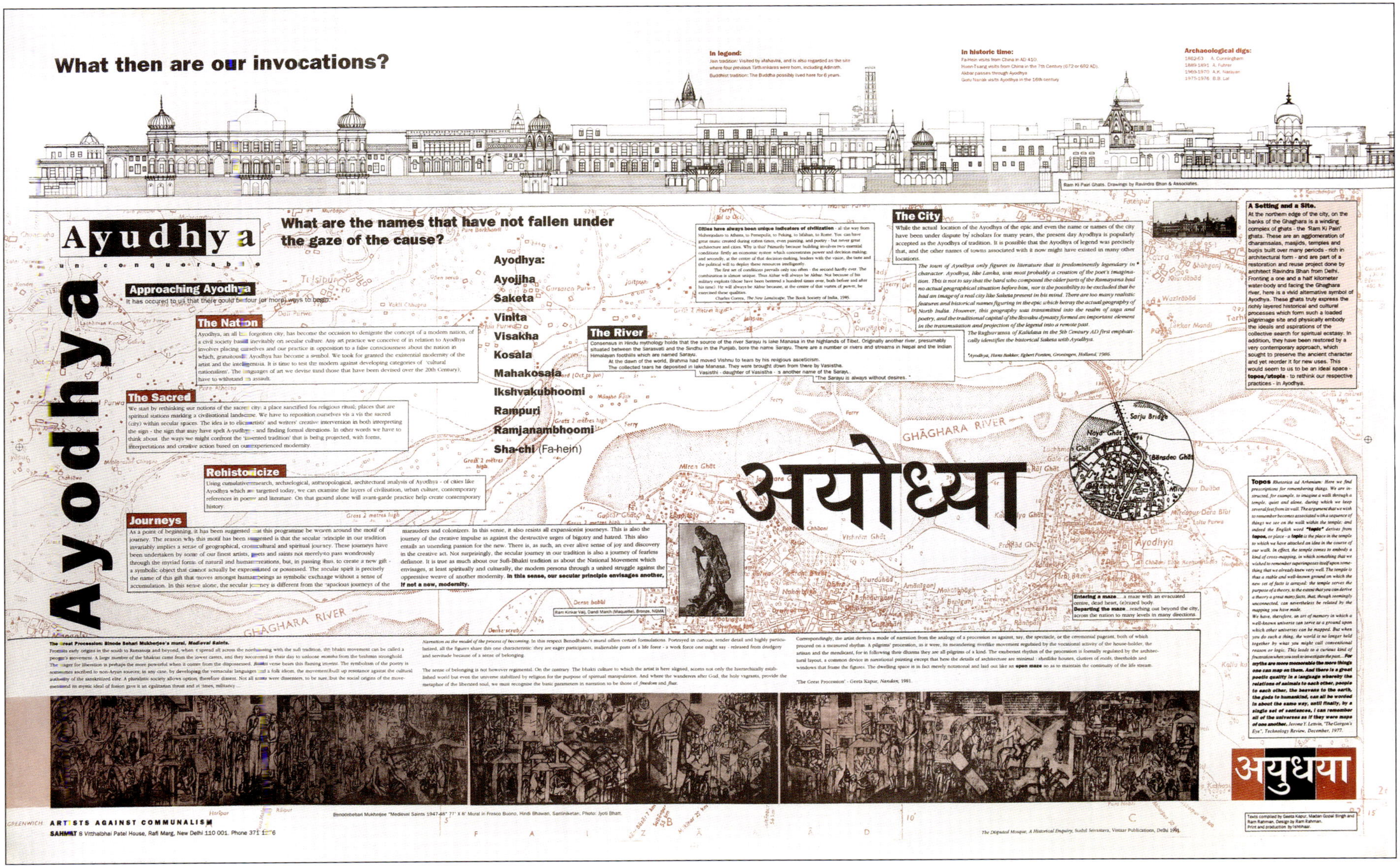

Ayodhya: What then are our invocations?, broadside, May 1993, 24 x 38 inches. Design: Ram Rahman. Texts: Charles Correa, Geeta Kapur, Madan Gopal Singh, and Ram Rahman, with contributions from Rajendra Prasad. Architectural drawings: Ravindra Bhan.

This broadside reflected the ideas that had come up at several Sahmat discussions on how to address the issue of Ayodhya, the site of the demolition of the Babri Masjid, in all its complexity. The *Hum Sab Ayodhya* exhibition and *Muktnaad* program in Ayodhya evolved after the broadside was mailed to cultural activists and student groups across India. Sahmat members traveled to several cities to hold discussions and workshops on how to approach the Ayodhya issue through a process of creative engagement. Historians, along with other academics, were an important and active part of the project to research and conceive *Hum Sab Ayodhya*.

RAM RAHMAN

Ayodhya: What then are our invocations? is a kind of mapping of several discussions we had in Sahmat in early 1993, while trying to come to grips with what the demolition of the Babri Masjid meant. The persons who primarily contributed to the broadside were Geeta Kapur, the art historian, Madan Gopal Singh, who essentially conceived the whole Sufi-Bhakti festival that we did that year, myself, and Rajendra Prasad, the guiding force of Sahmat, who is managing editor of the journal *Social Scientist.*

We had fairly different approaches to what had happened in Ayodhya. Geeta Kapur evoked a wall-mural of Sufi-Bhakti saints, painted by Binode Behari Mukherjee, a legendary artist of the early to middle twentieth century, at Visva Bharati in Santiniketan, West Bengal, the university founded by Rabindranath Tagore. Binode Behari's fresco was a key moment in modern Indian art that looked back at the Sufi-Bhakti poets in a contemporary interpretation. We printed an image of that huge fresco along with Geeta Kapur's text on that work, which talked about cultural modernity, but reaching back into tradition. Similarly, we included the image of a sculpture of Mahatma Gandhi done by Ram Kinkar Baij, also a legendary modern Indian artist from Santiniketan, which was a very radical, almost Cubist, interpretation of Gandhi, very different from the figurative statues of Gandhi that you normally see.

Madan Gopal Singh's text talked about journeys, a rich metaphor in the Sufi-Bhakti tradition. The journey is the physical journey of the mystic who travels the country, but it is also the journey of the individual reaching to the divine. We linked that idea of journey to the River Sarayu, on whose banks the city of Ayodhya stands, and I used a map of Ayodhya as a background.

Meanwhile, I had gone to Ayodhya and found, through one of the great drummers of north India, Pagal Das, who lived in the city, this site on the *ghats* (riverbank with steps) that had gone into decline. It was a great assemblage of medieval architecture. There were mosques, Sikh gurdwaras, temples, hostels for pilgrims to stay in—architecturally an amazingly rich ensemble, which had been restored by an architect from Delhi, Ravindra Bhan, who I happened to know. We printed his drawings as part of the project. Since the Babri mosque was a piece of architecture that had been desecrated and destroyed, we found his restoration work an example of something quite contrary. It celebrated the richness of a mixed tradition of architecture that had been restored for re-use, in stark contrast to the kind of destruction that had happened not far from this site.

Some conceptual texts were also included that came out of our discussions. There was a text by the contemporary architect Charles Correa, which was on the city and its meaning in history, and how it changed over time. There was a more abstract text by Jerry Lettvin, who had been my professor at MIT, which was on the meaning of topos and topic, related to site and city and circumambulation, how site was used as a device to register memory, and, getting a little more abstract, on the myth of earthly connections to cosmic events (both architectural and mythological).

So the broadside ended up having many complex layers. It was a kind of map that we printed in the thousands and sent to people all over India. The purpose was only to generate discussion and debate. We didn't have any other agenda in mind. We thought, okay, these are the kinds of discussions we've had here; let's put it out in some form, send it to people, and ask what we can do around these issues. From here evolved the large and sustained engagement that we had with Ayodhya, and the exhibition *Hum Sab Ayodhya*, which mapped some of the ideas we had projected in the broadside in greater detail.

Tale of a town

Anupa Mehta reports on 'Hum Sab Ayodhya', an exhibition organised by the Safdar Hashmi Memorial Trust and the National Museum, Delhi

SAHMAT (The Safdar Hashmi Memorial Trust), an organisation committed to promoting secularism through varied cultural activities, has from time to time in the course of its multi-pronged attempts at achieve its aims, come up with some unique artistic endeavors.

'Hum Sab Ayodhya', with its meticulously documented, well displayed assemblage of photographs, prints and architectural drawings which explore "the multi-faceted life of the people of Ayodhya in the context of the geographical, historical, social and cultural evolution of the town," is one such creative effort. (The last having been 'Anhad Garie', a programme of Sufi *bhakti* music).

The detailed historical perspectives, provided by the various folio prints and copies of old manuscripts, along with the many drawings, will give viewers an objective overview of the growth of Ayodhya

Presented in collaboration with the Nehru Memorial Museum, New Delhi, Hum Sab Ayodhya (August 9 to 15) also attempts, according to artist Rumanna Husain, to dispel popular (sometimes fabricated) propogandist notions about Ayodhya by affording the lay viewer a comprehensive glimpse into its complex history and rich cultural traditions.

Expected to culminate with the proposed 'Mukt Mad' in Ayodhya on the 15th of this month, this exhibition — meant primarily for Maharashtra — is also expected to be installed in various architechtural colleges and schools, as well in public places like the Prithvi Theatre so as to allow for maximum and diverse viewership.

The organisers hope that the detailed historical perspectives, provided by the various folio prints and copies of old manuscripts which are accompanied by concise copy, along with the many drawings, which highlight the hybrid architecture of the town, will give viewers an objective overview of the growth of Ayodhya.

Alongside, adding the human angle, are photographs of the denizens of Ayodhya, including a vintage snapshot of Begum Akhtar. Most of these, organisers reveal, have been shot by Ram Rahman and Samar Singh Jodha, while the drawings and other pieces in the exhibit have been researched and contributed by various leading artists, writers and art historians.

Indeed, this exhibition is important. For the Ayodhya seen here is a representative microcosm, a potent symbol of the pluralistic and composite traditions of India.

"Tale of a town," *Metropolis* Bombay, August 14–15, 1993.

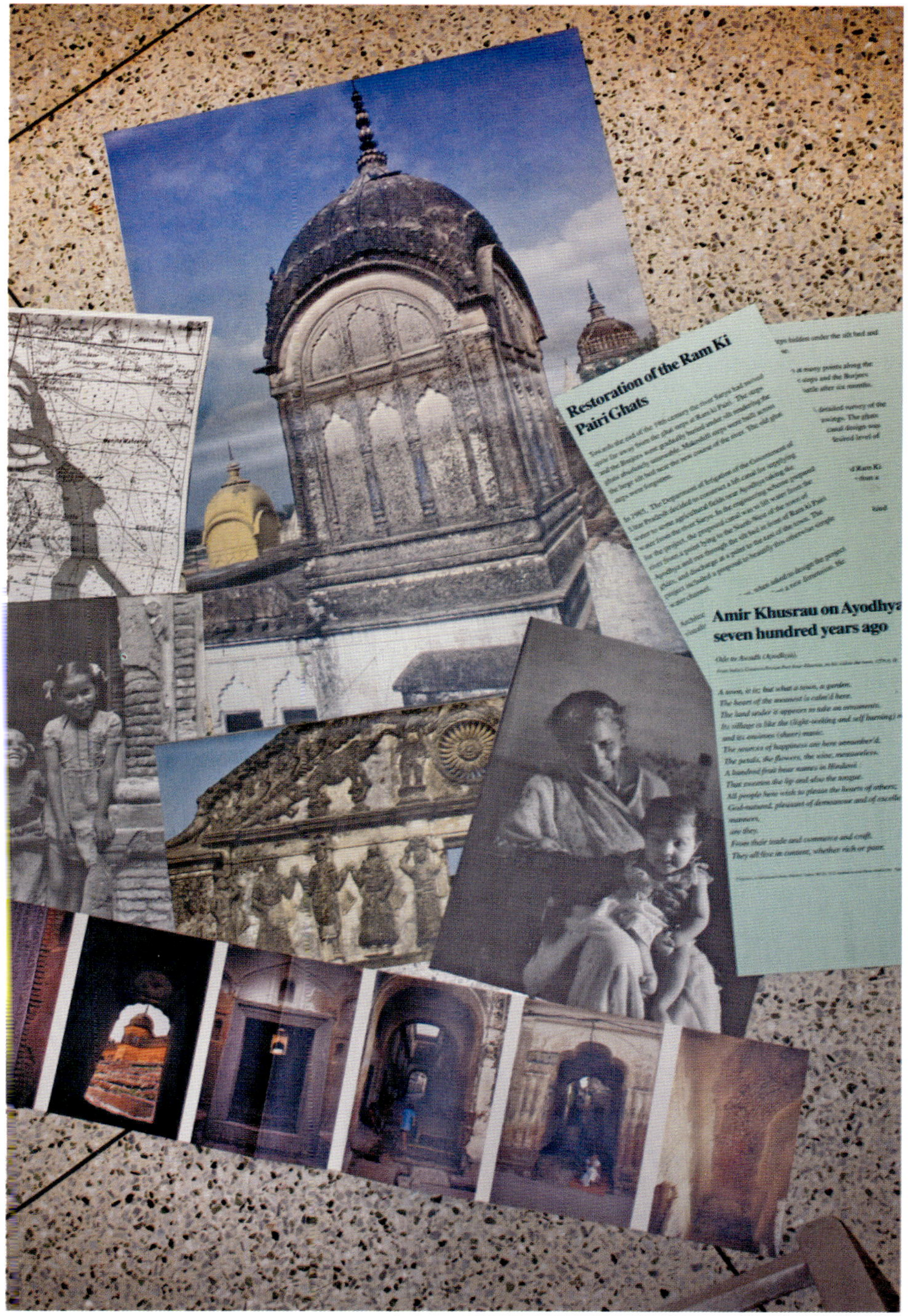

Hum Sab Ayodhya exhibition kit

Hum Sab Ayodhya **evolved as an exhibition kit. The urgency of the issue it sought to address meant that it was conceived, researched, designed, and produced within an extremely short period of time. Four hundred sets of the exhibition were prepared for wide circulation, comprising architectural and art historical images, drawings, maps, and plans, which were reproduced as offset colored prints. Texts to accompany the visuals were written by scholars or culled from historical and literary sources, which were then typeset, laser-printed, photocopied, and pasted on to complete the exhibition.**

RAM RAHMAN

After we had sent out the Ayodhya broadside, some of us traveled across the country in different groups, to meet academics and student and activist groups and discuss with them about how we could respond as cultural workers to the demolition of the mosque. That process evolved into two major events. One was the exhibition called *Hum Sab Ayodhya* (We are all Ayodhya), and the other a performance event called *Muktnaad* (Free Song), which would take place in the city of Ayodhya at the site of the restored *ghats*, which we had discovered while making the Ayodhya broadside.

Hum Sab Ayodhya was made over two months. We decided to launch the exhibition on August 9, the date of the launch of the Quit India Movement led by Gandhi during India's struggle for freedom. That was a major episode in the resistance against British colonial rule, which called for the freedom of all Indians, hence the term "Quit India"—"Leave India, this is not yours, it is ours'—and it was a people's movement. So we connected to that moment in our nationalist history through that date.

Hum Sab Ayodhya was a sort of pedagogical exercise on one level. The idea was to take that one city in which this terrible episode of the destruction of the mosque had happened, and to peel open the different layers of its history, contemporary, modern, and ancient. Ayodhya did have a very rich ancient history, and it was a great religious site; but we also looked at its political and economic histories. Because there were so many Marxist historians who participated in the project, it became a kind of exercise in Marxist historiography, but an exercise in popular/public culture at the same time, since we were producing it not as a book or a series of lectures, but as an exhibition. We took some of the quite complicated ideas and complex, little known histories, including archeology, early art history, and architectural history, and put them out in a form that could be seen and understood by the people at large. The idea was to take the microcosm of the city of Ayodhya as a representation of India's whole culture and civilization. It became an exercise in showing that if you unravel any site in India, you will find similar layers of complexity, and that there is no simple unitary identity or culture anywhere in South Asia. It is precisely those complex histories and complex cultures that comprise the richness of the living tradition of India.

Hum Sab Ayodhya ended up as a "kit" exhibition because even as we were making it—it was done in an insane frenzy—we were getting an incredible amount of textual information that we had to sift, classify, and incorporate into the panels in simple form. We decided to make it a very visual exhibition. So we had a lot of images of material that was actually from Ayodhya, including statues that had been found there or coins that had been excavated there. There were pieces of architecture, of course, from Ayodhya. There are references to Buddhism or Jainism having existed in Ayodhya, so we used art of the Buddhist and Jain traditions from other regions as equivalents to evoke that culture. And we defined it as such in the exhibition, so that everything that was from Ayodhya was clearly demarcated and designed as from that site or from that city, and the other visual references, which included paintings from the Mughal ateliers (depictions of the *Ramayana* and *Mahabharata* epics) were named separately. We showed paintings that had been made in the twin cities of Faizabad and Ayodhya both by late Mughal painters and by British painters like Tilly Kettle, who had painted in the eighteenth century simultaneously with the Indian miniature painters. Of course, we didn't have access to the original works—so we reproduced them from books. Our contribution was to make the connections between these images and place them together for the first time, in a sense, and certainly for the first time in a public forum.

The reason the exhibition became a kit was also because we were producing it in such a hurry; we had decided that we would make multiple copies and send them all across India. The exhibition eventually opened simultaneously in seventeen cities on August 9, 1993. I realized the only way to reproduce so many copies of the rich visual material we had was to use offset printing—we couldn't make photographic prints because they would have been vastly expensive, and photocopying wouldn't do justice to the quality of some of the material we had. In Sahmat we have this culture that even the wildest idea is not shot down, and the minute I said let's make it in offset, Rajen said, why make only seventeen copies then? Why not make *four hundred copies*—in offset that's very easy to do. So there we were, collating and designing the visual material and literally sending it out to different presses to get printed—and the

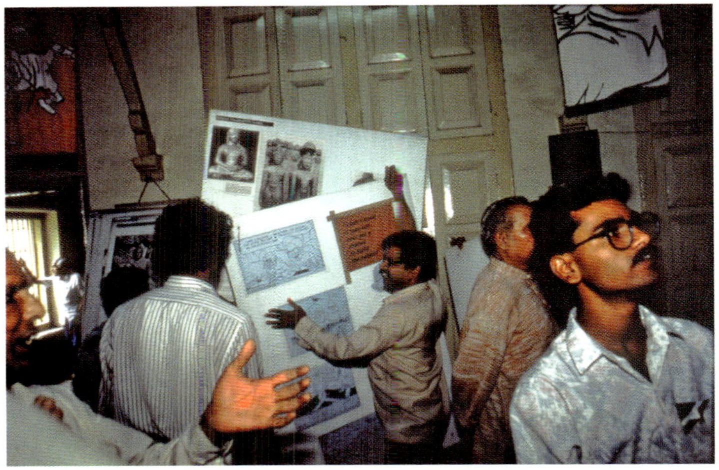

Activists from right-wing Hindu group RSS (Rashtriya Swayamsevak Sangh) attack and dismantle *Hum Sab Ayodhya* Pune, 1994.

text was being simultaneously written and edited and collated, so we couldn't manage to put the text and the images together before sending the panels of images to press. That was something we hadn't planned, but it ended up being a very practical solution because the panels of images became a kit and the text, which was photocopied separately, became a complementary kit. The advantage of doing it this way was that the texts could then be translated locally into the different Indian languages, and even handwritten, and the exhibition could be assembled according to the resources available to the local person(s). It could either be very informally mounted with pins or clips, or pasted on card, or it could be elaborately mounted and assembled.

The exhibition was an enormous success. It had a huge impact, especially because all the presentations opened simultaneously. The Hindu Right, and the right-wing groups that had led the movement to destroy the mosque got very agitated because of the content of the exhibition. It went against everything they stood for. Their definition of Ayodhya was that it was a Hindu site that needed to be reclaimed by the Hindu majoritarian community, and that others should be excluded. So the exhibition was a challenge to them even on a conceptual level. They tried to pick holes in it to destroy Sahmat's credibility. First, because we had the plans of the original Babri Masjid and photographs of the mosque as part of the exhibition, they spread rumors among the people of Faizabad and Ayodhya that we were going there to rebuild the mosque, and that the drawings in the exhibition were a map to rebuild the mosque. This proved ineffective.

Then, they picked on a text by the reputed historian Romila Thapar, included in the exhibition, on the multiple traditions and streams of the

Schoolchildren visit the exhibition *Hum Sab Ayodhya* in Pune a day after it was attacked, 1994.

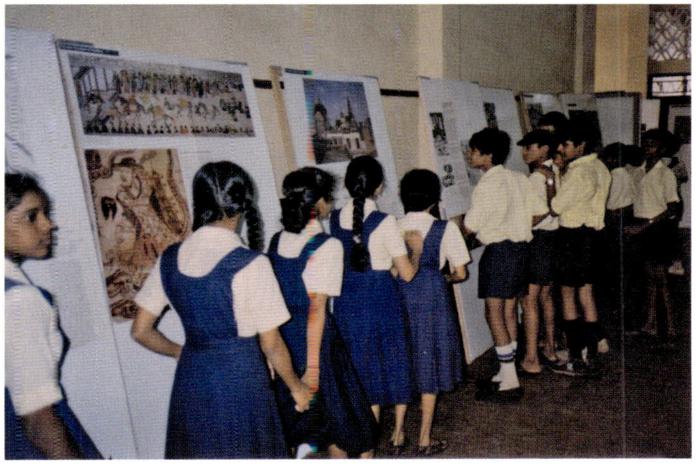

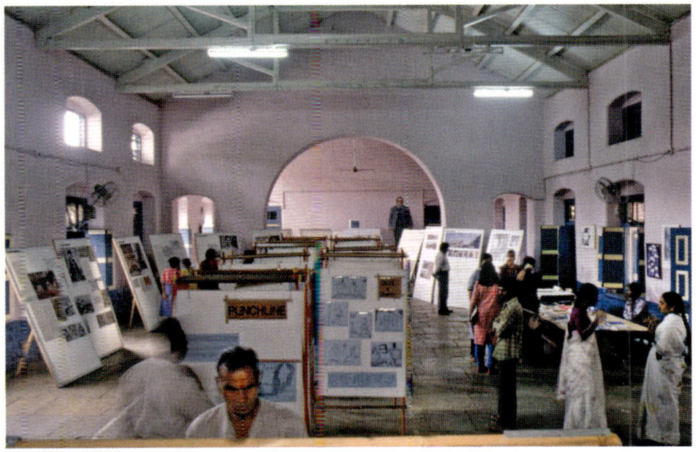

The exhibitions *Hum Sab Ayodhya* and *Punchline: Cartoons Against Communalism*, on display in Pune, 1994.

Ramayana and of stories of the god Rama—whose birthplace had been supposedly desecrated and whose temple destroyed, to build the mosque that in turn had just been destroyed. Now, the stories about Rama have multiple versions all across India and South Asia, and even Southeast and Central Asia. One of the earliest iterations of the story of Rama is a Buddhist version called the *Dasharatha Jataka*. In that story Rama and Sita, the king and the queen, and Lakshmana, are all siblings. It is a story of a jealous queen who exiles the children of another queen to the forest because she wants her son to rule. So there is the theme of exile, but there is no kidnapping of Sita, there is no Ravana, and there is no battle between Rama and Ravana. Rama and Sita do come back from exile and the text states that they ruled as king and queen for 16,000 years. The BJP and right-wing groups picked on that, saying that we were committing blasphemy by implying that Rama and Sita were brother and sister. They chose to ignore the fact that this is a version that exists in an ancient text that the Buddhist community regards very highly. The *Jatakas* are believed to be tales and stories told by the Buddha himself.

Sahmat was attacked for including this text in the *Hum Sab Ayodhya* exhibition, and the attack was very vicious, very coordinated. The exhibition was attacked physically first in Faizabad, and we were accused of religious blasphemy. The issue was then debated in the Indian Parliament for three whole days, with nobody having seen the exhibition or read the texts in it. This, despite the fact that the exhibition was mounted not very far from the Parliament in Delhi, at the Nehru Memorial Museum and Library, which is the former home of Prime Minister Jawaharlal Nehru and now a highly respected research institution that had actually coproduced the exhibition with us. We finally managed to get some parliamentarians late one evening to come and see the exhibition. We asked them, why are you debating this without actually seeing the material that is there? You are being subjected to misinformation. But it was too late, for the rumor machine of the Hindu Right, which is extremely effective, had planted the seed of doubt in everyone's mind that we had committed a terrible blasphemy. They even conjured up a nonexistent image of Rama and Sita, and we just did not have the means to counter that scale of rumor-mongering.

The exhibition was seized from the Nehru Memorial Museum and Library by the Delhi police under very serious charges in the Indian legal code, including criminal conspiracy against the state, and deliberate malicious use of material to cause communal disharmony. We all thought we were going to get arrested. In the event, however, the arrests never happened.

We decided to challenge the seizure of the exhibition, and the effective ban on it following the seizure, in court. Senior lawyers from the Supreme Court of India volunteered their time and effort to fight the case, and it became a major case on the freedom of expression in India. The reason I traveled with the exhibition through the United States was primarily because of the ban. American academics working on South Asia were shocked that a text from the *Dasharatha Jataka*, which was thousands of years old, could effectively be banned like this. So Columbia University invited me to mount the exhibition on the first anniversary of the destruction of the Babri Mosque. And I also took it to Berkeley, to Los Angeles, to MIT, and to Amherst in those years. In India too we continued traveling with the exhibition, having blacked out the paragraphs for which the exhibition had been seized. But we still had copies of books that had that text in them and the books had not been banned. So we showed the blacked-out texts in the books and that became part of the resistance.

After eight years, Sahmat won the case in court with a very strong judgment against the initial seizure and strong berating of the government. The judgment has since become a key verdict in debates around freedom of expression in the Indian legal system. Again, this was not something we had intended; it was something that happened to us due to circumstances that were way beyond our control. But it was a key episode in Sahmat's history that led to our sustained engagement, in subsequent years, with issues related to the rewriting of history and historical pedagogy, and with the system of education and knowledge production in general.

TRAVELERS ACCOUNTS OF AYODHYA

A Mad Man
"He related that there was a mad man (diwana) in the town of *Avadh*. A theologian Maulana Kamaluddin was an eminent religious divine. He saw in a dream that the mad man was narrating the Prophet's praise from the sermon-stand, and angels were present listen to him. When it was day he went to the bazaar. He saw the mad man sitting at the shop of a cooked-lamb seller (barrapuz). As the cooked-lamb seller put the meat in the cauldron, he pulled it out, hot as it was, from the cauldron and ate it. When the Maulana saw him, he said in wonderment 'What does he do at night, and what in daytime!?' "

Meeting the Sultan's Minister
"The Shaikh recalled that Qazi Hamiduddin, the Chief Merchant (Malik-u't Tujjar) and Alauddin Khalji's minister for religious affairs and land-grants, came about that time (Alauddin Khalji's reign, 1296–1316) to *Avadh*. He held a reception and invited me (among others). When most people had left, some of us remained sitting together with him. The minister narrated how he saw Sultan Alauddin sitting in a small place, head bowed."

Nasiruddin Mahmud in *Avadh*
"Shaikh Nasiruddin Mahmud was born in the town of *Avadh*. His father died when he was nine, and he was brought up by his mother. ... He was forty-two years old when he left Avadh for the capital city of Delhi, where he sought and obtained the discipleship of Shaikh Nizamuddin Muhammad Badauni. At that time his mother lived in the town of Avadh. Shaikh Nasiruddin returned to *Avadh* to be in attendance upon her. After her death, he stayed a few months in the town of *Avadh* by way of mourning. His mother's grave is behind the idgah."

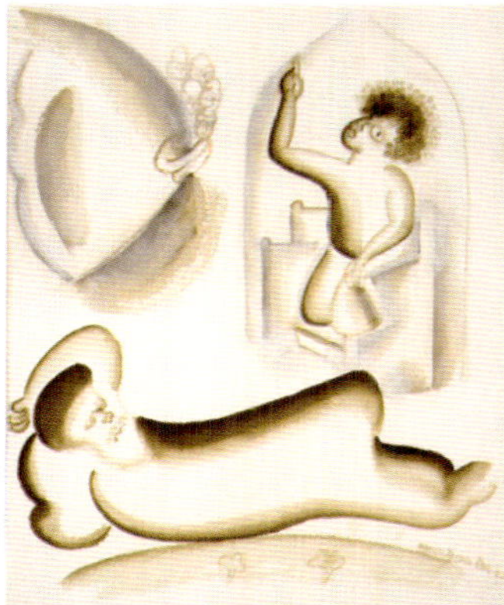

Gulammohammed Sheikh, *Dreaming and the Mad Man* 1995

16 Hum Sab Ayodhya

LEFT AND RIGHT
Panels from the *Hum Sab Ayodhya* exhibition.

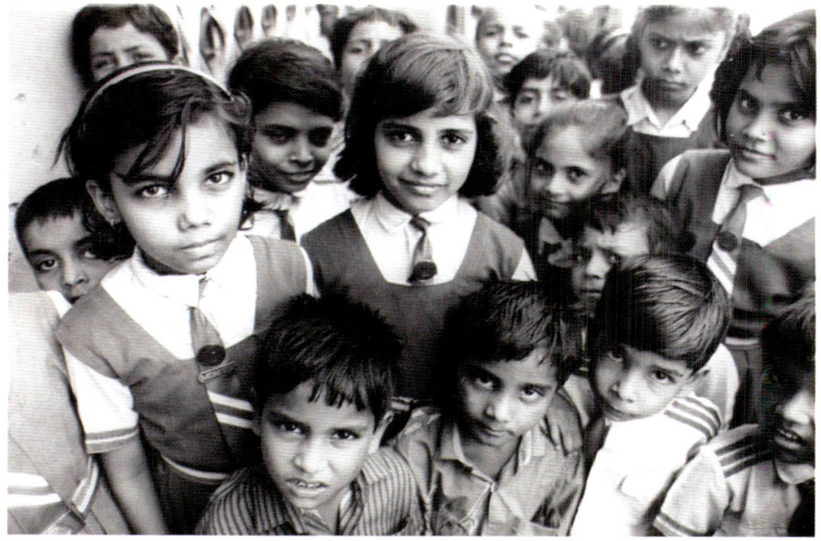

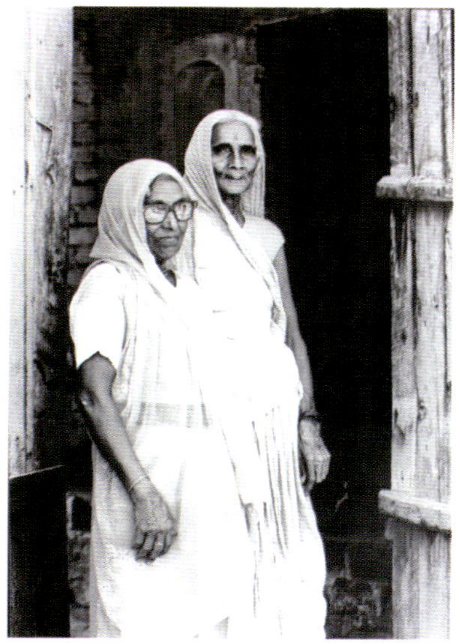

Images in the Exhibition

This exhibition presents a narrative of the site and city of Ayodhya with contemporary photographs, maps, and art historical examples of sculptures and paintings. The art historical references are in some instances directly from the region of Ayodhya and are marked as such.

A large number of these images are cross-referenced to enable viewers to visualize the life of the people in that region through material evidence, historical parallels and imaginative correspondence. The life of the people includes everyday artisanal and trading activity, as well as reverential relationships to mythic and iconic images.

The images in the exhibition should be seen as visual configurations that bring out the layered and diverse traditions emerging from material evidence of the Ayodhya region, as of all regions of India. They recall a composite civilization from ancient times to the present.

The exhibition ends with the skyline of Ayodhya, gracefully crowned by roofs, domes and shikharas, sheltering a population whose selected portraits as inscribed in this historical account add up to the title: Hum Sab Ayodhya.

7 Hum Sab Ayodhya

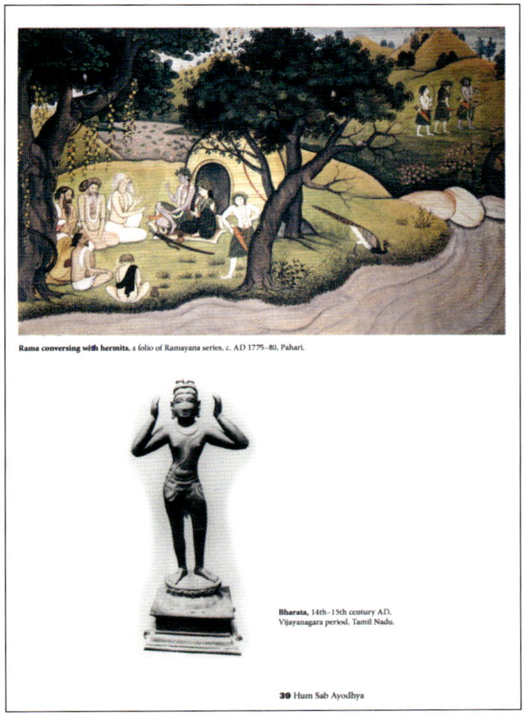
Rama conversing with hermits, a folio of Ramayana series, c. AD 1775–80, Pahari.

Bharata, 14th–15th century AD,
Vijayanagara period, Tamil Nadu.

39 Hum Sab Ayodhya

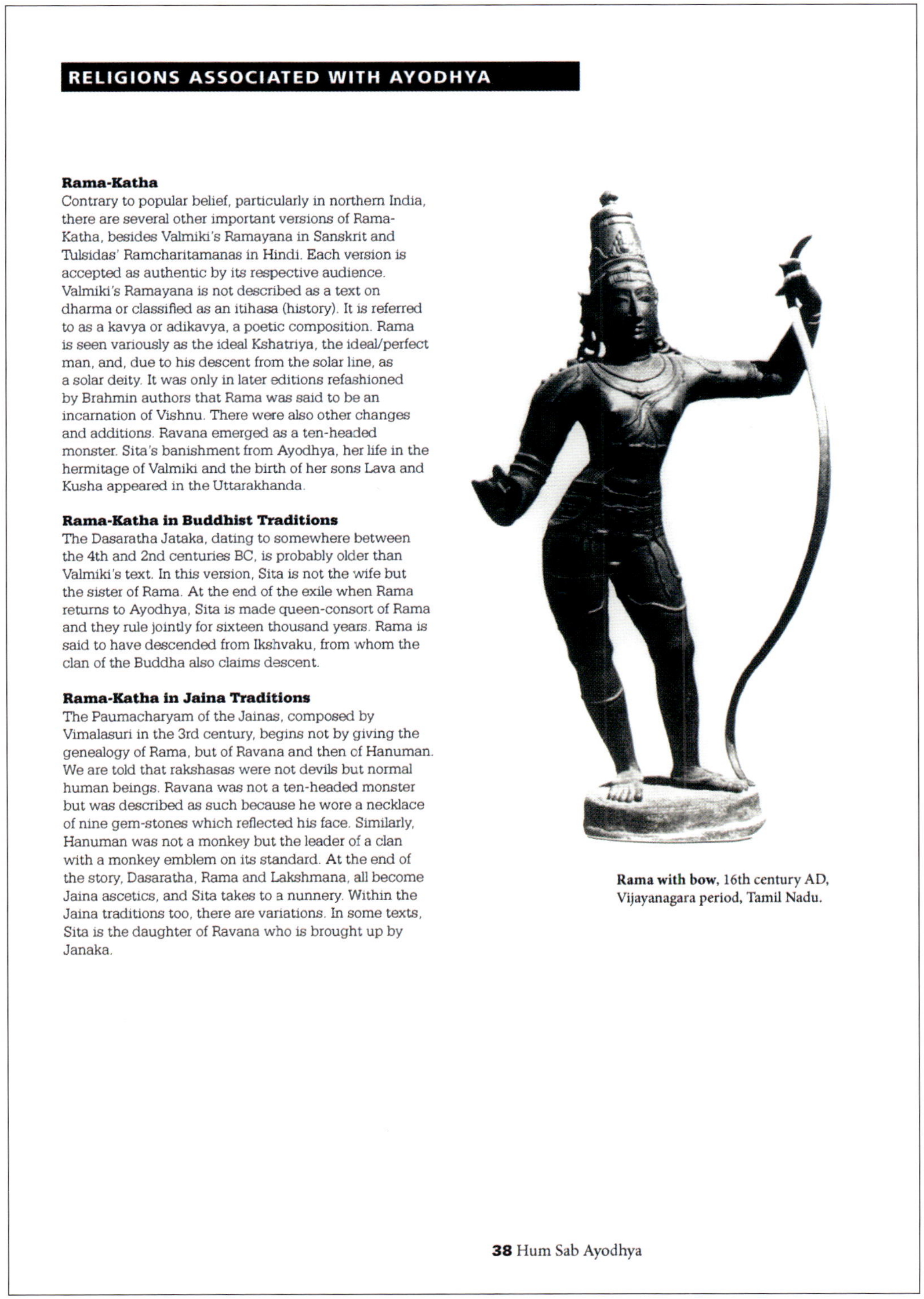
RELIGIONS ASSOCIATED WITH AYODHYA

Rama-Katha
Contrary to popular belief, particularly in northern India, there are several other important versions of Rama-Katha, besides Valmiki's Ramayana in Sanskrit and Tulsidas' Ramcharitamanas in Hindi. Each version is accepted as authentic by its respective audience. Valmiki's Ramayana is not described as a text on dharma or classified as an itihasa (history). It is referred to as a kavya or adikavya, a poetic composition. Rama is seen variously as the ideal Kshatriya, the ideal/perfect man, and, due to his descent from the solar line, as a solar deity. It was only in later editions refashioned by Brahmin authors that Rama was said to be an incarnation of Vishnu. There were also other changes and additions. Ravana emerged as a ten-headed monster. Sita's banishment from Ayodhya, her life in the hermitage of Valmiki and the birth of her sons Lava and Kusha appeared in the Uttarakhanda.

Rama-Katha in Buddhist Traditions
The Dasaratha Jataka, dating to somewhere between the 4th and 2nd centuries BC, is probably older than Valmiki's text. In this version, Sita is not the wife but the sister of Rama. At the end of the exile when Rama returns to Ayodhya, Sita is made queen-consort of Rama and they rule jointly for sixteen thousand years. Rama is said to have descended from Ikshvaku, from whom the clan of the Buddha also claims descent.

Rama-Katha in Jaina Traditions
The Paumacharyam of the Jainas, composed by Vimalasuri in the 3rd century, begins not by giving the genealogy of Rama, but of Ravana and then of Hanuman. We are told that rakshasas were not devils but normal human beings. Ravana was not a ten-headed monster but was described as such because he wore a necklace of nine gem-stones which reflected his face. Similarly, Hanuman was not a monkey but the leader of a clan with a monkey emblem on its standard. At the end of the story, Dasaratha, Rama and Lakshmana, all become Jaina ascetics, and Sita takes to a nunnery. Within the Jaina traditions too, there are variations. In some texts, Sita is the daughter of Ravana who is brought up by Janaka.

Rama with bow, 16th century AD,
Vijayanagara period, Tamil Nadu.

38 Hum Sab Ayodhya

LEFT AND RIGHT
Panels from the *Hum Sab Ayodhya* exhibition that were the focus of the attack.

These panels on multiple versions of the Rama myth became the focus of the attack on *Hum Sab Ayodhya* and the campaign of misinformation launched by the BJP and right-wing groups. While both the Buddhist and Jain versions of the myth drew their ire, the Buddhist *Dasharatha Jataka*, in which Rama, Sita, and Lakshmana are characterized as siblings (and not as king-husband, chaste wife, and devoted brother, respectively, as in accepted popular versions) became the specific target of attack. The quotations cited on these panels are all from ancient texts regarded as sacred by the Buddhists and Jains.

The canard spread by Hindu right-wing groups that Sahmat had made a "poster" depicting incest led the government to seize these panels from the exhibition, and to arraign Sahmat with a slew of serious legal cases. Sahmat's challenge of the confiscation of the panels and of the charges brought against it in court became a landmark for upholding the constitutional provisions for free speech and freedom of expression in India.

Sahmat show sparks protest in Los Angeles

By Ramesh Gune

LOS ANGELES, Jan 23

A PICTORIAL exhibition and a documentary on 'Ayodhya -1993', put up by Sahmat, sparked vociferous protests by Hindu groups here, who claimed it amounted to blasphemy, reports IANS.

More than 150 men, women and children voiced their anger at the January 18 opening of the display 'Hum sub Ayodhya' in the city of Buena Park. The exhibition also had a panel discussion on the aspects of secularism. About 60 people attended.

"Sahmat go back" shouted the protesters, who said that the " Show organisers were a bunch of communists who have scant regard for our gods and faith".

But organiser, Ram Rahman denied the charge saying, the show was simply a reflection of Ayodhya's cultural history which we want to project in the right prespective.

An exhibit that troubled Hindus refers to the story of Ram in the Buddhist tradition.' The Dasaratha Jataka',as the narration is called dates back to somewhere between the fourth and the second century. The panel said, it is probably older than the one written by Valmiki. In this version, Sita is not the wife but sister of Ram. It said at the end of his exile, the story continues, when Ram returns to Ayodhya, Sita is made the queen consort of Ram and they ruled jointly for 16,000 years. Ram is said to have descended from Ishaku, from whom the clan of Buddha claims descent.

The protesters said that 'this Ram story'amounted to blasphemy and asked the organisers if they would put up such a show against the Muslims,"Would you honour what Salman Rushdie has said in his Satanic Verses?", asked Chander Mittal, an activist of the Federation of Hindu Association, an umberalla organisation of various cultural and religious bodies which spearheaded the protests. "Why do you want to hurt the feelings of Hindus, your intentions is malicious", he told the organisers.

The exhibition displayed the location of Ayodhya, supplemented by scores of travellers' description of the city and a passage from a Sufi saint's reminiscence of Ayodhya. It also told the story of Ayodhya under the rule of the Mughal Emperor Akbar.

A display on the Babri Masjid declares it was built by Mir Baqi, under the orders from Emperor Babar, after pulling down a temple at a place where Lord Ram was born. The exhibit does not mention the controversy.

But Ved Vatuk, one of the organiser said, that the passage that has offended Hindus was indentical to the one published in an RSS publication, that commemorated the centenary of Swami Vivekananda. The description in the Jatak Ramayana of Ram and Sita as brother and sister, Vatuk said was written in an article by a ranking RSS leader Eknath Ranade.

The Federation of Hindu Associations recently urged Hindus in a newspaper advertisment to 'Please wake up to safeguard your rights and religion.'

"Sahmat show sparks protest in Los Angeles," January 23, 1994.

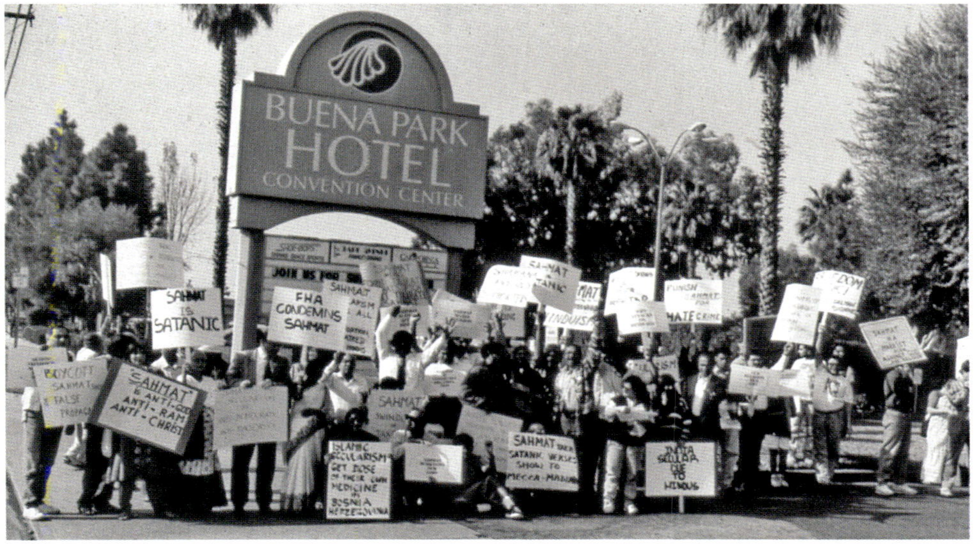

Supporters of the Bharatiya Janata Party protest *Hum Sab Ayodhya* in Los Angeles, January 1994.

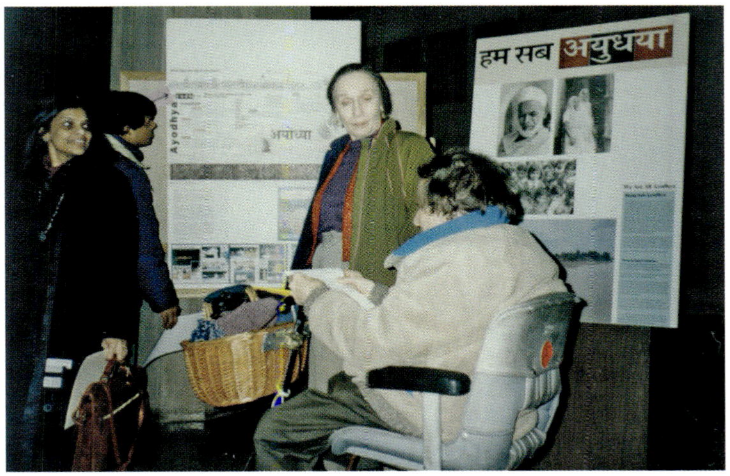

Physicist Philip Morrison (in wheelchair) and Phyllis Morrison view the exhibition *Hum Sab Ayodhya* at the Massachusetts Institute of Technology, Cambridge, January 1994.

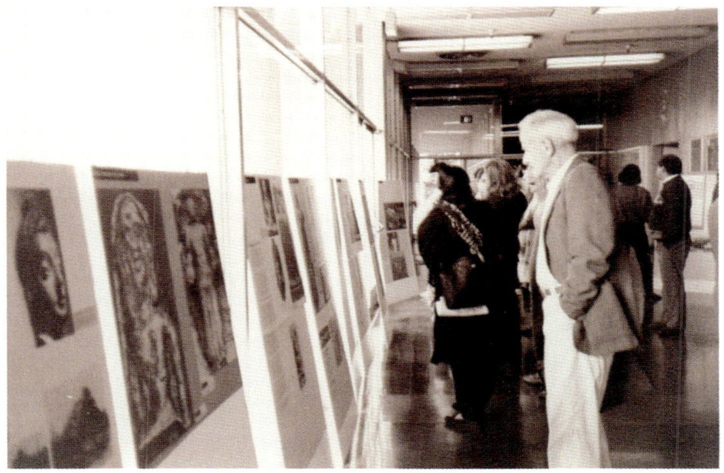

Sanskrit scholar Fritz Staal views the exhibition in Berkeley, California, January 1994.

Hum Sam Ayodhya **has traveled widely within and outside India, and it continues to be shown even today, since the Ayodhya issue remains critical to the definition of India as a secular republic two decades after the demolition of the Babri Masjid—as mirrored in the archaeological debates and divides the criminal charges against the demolition that are still in court, and the various court rulings on the title to the site, which is yet to be settled. Sahmat has played a central role in many of these continuing debates and developments not only through the exhibition, but also through other interventions such as symposia and publications.**

On the Exhibition *Hum Sab Ayodhya*

Geeta Kapur

Excerpt from *Muktnaad/Hum Sab Ayodhya*: a selection of reports, editorials, discussions, and comments from the press (New Delhi: Sahmat, 1994).

A lot has appeared in the media about *Hum Sab Ayodhya*. Now it is urgently necessary that we take stock of the situation. The exhibition was held simultaneously between August 9 and August 15, 1993, in sixteen cities other than Faizabad. It went off without a single unhappy incident. Sahmat has received supportive reports and requests for taking the exhibition to other venues. However on the twelfth of August there was an attack in the one city of Faizabad, where a band of about fifteen people, identified as members of the Sangh Parivar ("family" of right-wing Hindu nationalist organizations), came and tore down the exhibition alleging that two references in the text panel titled *Ram Katha* were objectionable.

Subsequently, the Bharatiya Janata Party (BJP) leadership launched a campaign of lies where they dropped the context of the entire exhibition and spread the word that Sahmat had issued a "poster" in Faizabad/Ayodhya "depicting" Rama and Sita as brother and sister. The exhibition had eighty-three display units with extensive text, and cross-referenced archaeological, art historical, and photographic examples on the history of the city and the people of Ayodhya from ancient times to the present. The *Ram Katha* was one text unit and the reference in question consisted of a few words under the subheading of "Buddhist and Jaina versions."

The issue was precipitated in the Parliament for a week, leading to a statement by the Speaker on August 20 which convinced Sahmat that BJP's vicious slander had, for the moment, shaken the faith—that there was not, perhaps for obvious reasons of political discretion (and expediency?), the will and the desire to resist the BJP—even among the Left, liberal, and secular parliamentarians.

On this account, Sahmat announced on August 21 its decision to withdraw the exhibition from the Nehru Memorial Museum, New Delhi, the only venue where it was scheduled to continue to run. The same afternoon the police, on behalf of the lieutenant governor of Delhi, came and confiscated the text panel on *Ram Katha* under Section 95 of the Criminal Procedure Code. Just days before Sahmat had already been charged in Faizabad under Section 153 (wantonly giving provocation with intent to cause riot); Section 153-A (promoting enmity between different groups on account of religion, etc., and doing acts prejudicial to maintenance of harmony); Section 295-A (deliberate and malicious acts intended to raise religious feelings of any class by insulting its religion or religious beliefs); Section 298 (uttering words, etc., with deliberate intent to wound religious feelings); Section 505 (statements conducing to public mischief); and Section 120B (criminal conspiracy). The cases were filed on August 16.

Thus Sahmat is legally designated as a criminal organization, and its identifiable members and those who helped with the exhibition—artists and designers, eminent historians from Jawaharlal Nehru University, New Delhi, Aligarh Muslim University, Allahabad University, and the Indian Council of Historical Research in Delhi—are liable for arrest if the state wishes to use its draconian powers. *Hum Sab Ayodhya* has not only been vandalized by the Sangh Parivar, but also misrepresented by state action, in fact and in the conscience of the public.

All along Sahmat had made a strenuous effort to give the facts, provide the original text of the *Dasharatha Jataka* in Pali and in English, and invite Members of Parliament (MPs) and the press to see the exhibition. But propaganda is contagious, and many simply assumed that there must have been a poster with some sort of an image, and that this was flyposted in Ayodhya clandestinely by fools or mischief-makers from Sahmat. At first even the disinterested intelligentsia believed this version, even those who should know the cunning of the Sangh Parivar.

Just before the exhibition closed Sahmat succeeded in getting about ten MPs, representatives of secular political parties, to come and see it. They were aghast at the way the disinformation had been allowed to mislead the Parliament and it was then that the MPs Somnath Chatterjee, Bhogendra Jha, and Ram Vilas Paswan took up the cause, the latter in eloquent defense and direct confrontation.

A few important points: the text panel on *Ram Katha* was based on the recently published book, *Anatomy of a Confrontation*, edited by Professor S. Gopal, with a contribution on the *Ram Katha* by Professor Romila Thapar. It referred back to the sources available to ancient Indian historians of all ideological persuasions. Taking Valmiki's *Ramayana* and Tulsidas's *Ramacharitamanas* as standard versions, or at any rate the most popular and best known, it mentioned variations of the Rama story to suggest how, as a generative legend of ancient times, it adapts itself to different characterizations, to different moral and ethical purposes, and indeed to different norms of iconography. It proliferates into different stories of kinship, lineage, and kingship with or without divine descent. In referring to the Buddhists' *Dasharatha Jataka*, possibly one of the oldest versions of the Rama story, the sibling relationship of the couple that ruled for "sixteen thousand years" establishes the symbolic purity of the royal line within that particular tradition. The same tradition holds that Rama is a Bodhisattva, belonging to the same lineage from which the Buddha is descended, hardly a denigration of the divine personage in that tradition! Similarly the Jain version was mentioned, and it has yet another genealogy. Major regional versions like the *Kamba Ramayana* in Tamil, the Bengali *Krittibasa Ramayana*, and Eknath's Marathi version were mentioned, as well as Southeast Asian versions. Nonreligious but richly characterized poetic references, for example in Sanskrit drama beginning with Kalidasa, were also mentioned.

The criticism of the panel would rather be the fact that it was too sketchy, that it merely signposted, in a brief line or two, the fact of affinity and transformation of mythic material within the long narrative stretch of this legend. The criticism would also come from the fact that this brief text implied that there can be no hegemonic discourse on the subject. Both of these criticisms are, to my mind, valid. There was a desire to release the narrative into its several layers of symbolic meaning that become, each in its own tradition, a source of pedagogy for people of all faiths, and for the aesthetic contemplation of atheists as well. If this is considered culpable, then one admits to it, while defying the criminality that has been imposed suddenly, and virtually for the first time in India, on such a transparently secular position.

But this secular position is precisely what has come in for mockery. Almost everyone was recommending to Sahmat (in hindsight, let it be said) a dose of pragmatism on the ground of realpolitik and occasionally also on the plea of public sentiment. Both these issues need to be debated at length. Let me only say that if there is a question involved it is of principle, that in India we must fight to maintain the freedom to transmit knowledge as a foundation of that more controversial issue of the freedom of expression.

In the long battle ahead, where every post in the intellectual and imaginative space opened up by modern India will have to be defended against the motivated bigotry coming from fundamentalist versions—fascist versions—of culture, it is not through spurning liberal intelligence, nor through declaring the modern artist redundant, that the strength to fight will be gained.

We are all asking, now that we have been embroiled in a national debate and criminal proceedings, what is our course of action? There is of course the court of law, and this will be moved by some eminent lawyers who have stood against bigotry and the compromise of the state before. There is the enlightened section of the press, which, as you will have already seen in finely balanced and sometimes bold editorials, is beginning to understand the dangerous implications of allowing BJP triumphalism to work in the field of culture as it has in politics, and they have chastised the state for its open partisanship with communal forces. There are, finally and not least, academics who have come forth in the appeal signed within the space of one morning by scores of scholars, writers, and journalists. Major figures in the intellectual field have addressed press conferences and student gatherings in the most passionate and fearless terms, stating that this case affects the free transmission of knowledge, and that they would want to participate in the act of taking the battle further afield through their teaching activity. Some of those who have spoken out are the academics Veena Das, Irfan Habib, Suvira Jaiswal, Rajni Kothari, Ashok Mitra, Gyan Pandey, K. N. Panikkar, Prabhat Patnaik, K. M. Shrimali, and Romila Thapar, and the constitutional lawyer Rajiv Dhavan.

As follow-up action, they have offered that together with Sahmat, they would like to help make people participants in the political and legal battle forced upon Sahmat, thus making a chain of supporters alert to the progress of fascist pressures of which we shall all be victims sooner or later if we do not resist now. We should remember that defeat begins with equivocation, and then the fascist victory is as if inevitable. It is for supporters of Sahmat, who have participated in its activities and hold faith with its principles, to suggest what might be our course of cultural action given the current climate and circumstance. Sahmat is not a monolith, it is persons and groups who join in and take its activities across different parts of the country. Before all else the concrete activity of resistance, which has taken on the irreversible movement called Artists Against Communalism, has to continue in the smallest gesture as in large collectives.

We are, I think, well advised to read the writing on the wall and to recall, with far greater urgency, the first injunction we placed on ourselves when Sahmat was formed: Artists Alert!

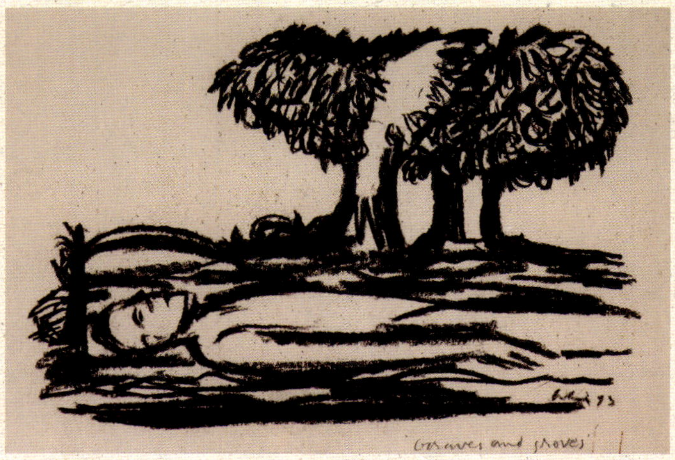

ALEX MATHEW
Graves and Groves, 1993, charcoal on paper, 7 x 10 inches.

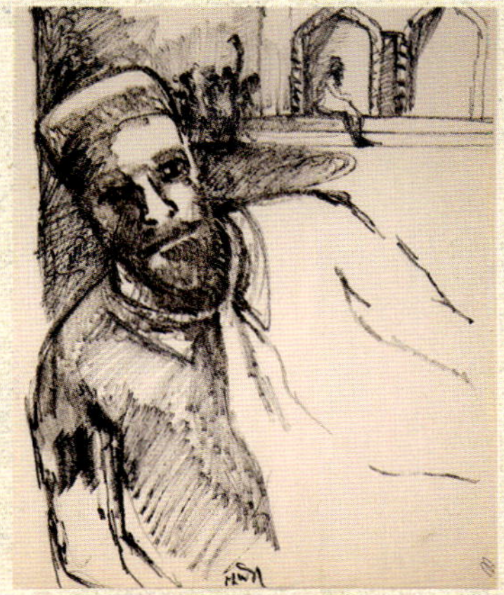

BHUPEN KHAKHAR
Untitled, 1993,
ink on paper, 11½ x 8½ inches.

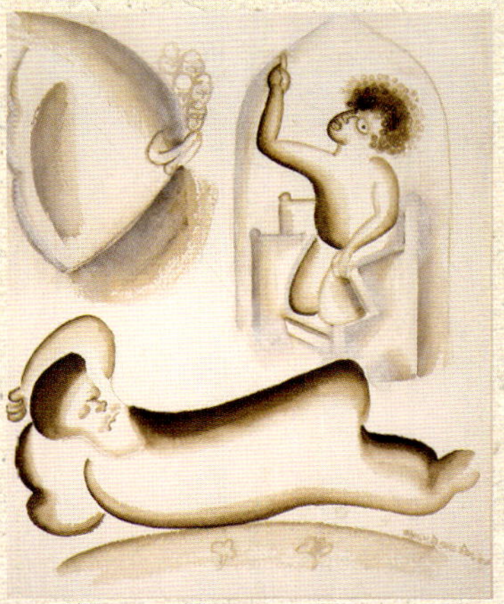

GULAMMOHAMMED SHEIKH
Dreams and Dreaming, 1993,
watercolor on paper, 11 x 9 inches.

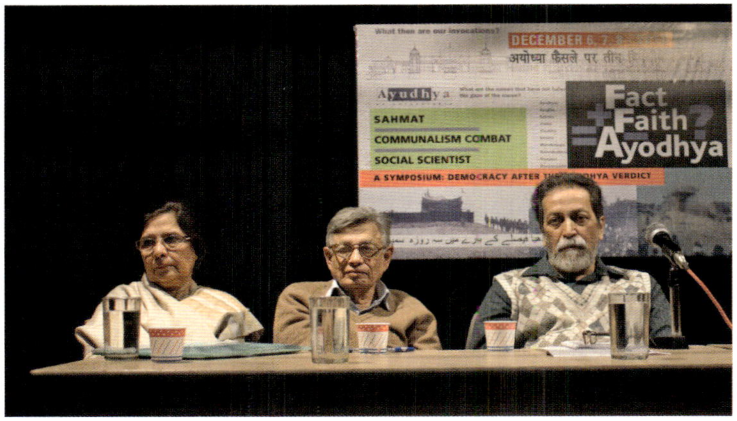

Historians Shireen Moosvi and Irfan Habib, and economist Prabhat Patnaik, at the Sahmat symposium "Fact and Faith: Democracy after the Ayodhya Verdict," held on December 6–8, 2010, after the Allahabad High Court verdict on the Babri Masjid issue.

The Ayodhya Verdict, 2010

The Allahabad High Court's three-judge Bench on Ayodhya Matters, Lucknow, gave its judgment on the Ramjanmabhoomi–Babri Masjid dispute on September 30, 2010. The judgment raised several major points on issues related to history and archaeology. These are issues on which Sahmat has, over the years, pointed out the erroneous and retrogressive positions adopted by various government and quasi-government agencies, and by earlier court orders and verdicts. Sahmat organized a three-day symposium, "Fact and Faith: Democracy after the Ayodhya Verdict," from December 6 to 8, 2010, to analyze the political implications of the Allahabad High Court's judgment, and to examine the veracity of the historical and archeological assumptions underlying it. The participants in the symposium included historians and archaeologists, other academics, lawyers, retired judges, journalists, and citizens' activist groups.

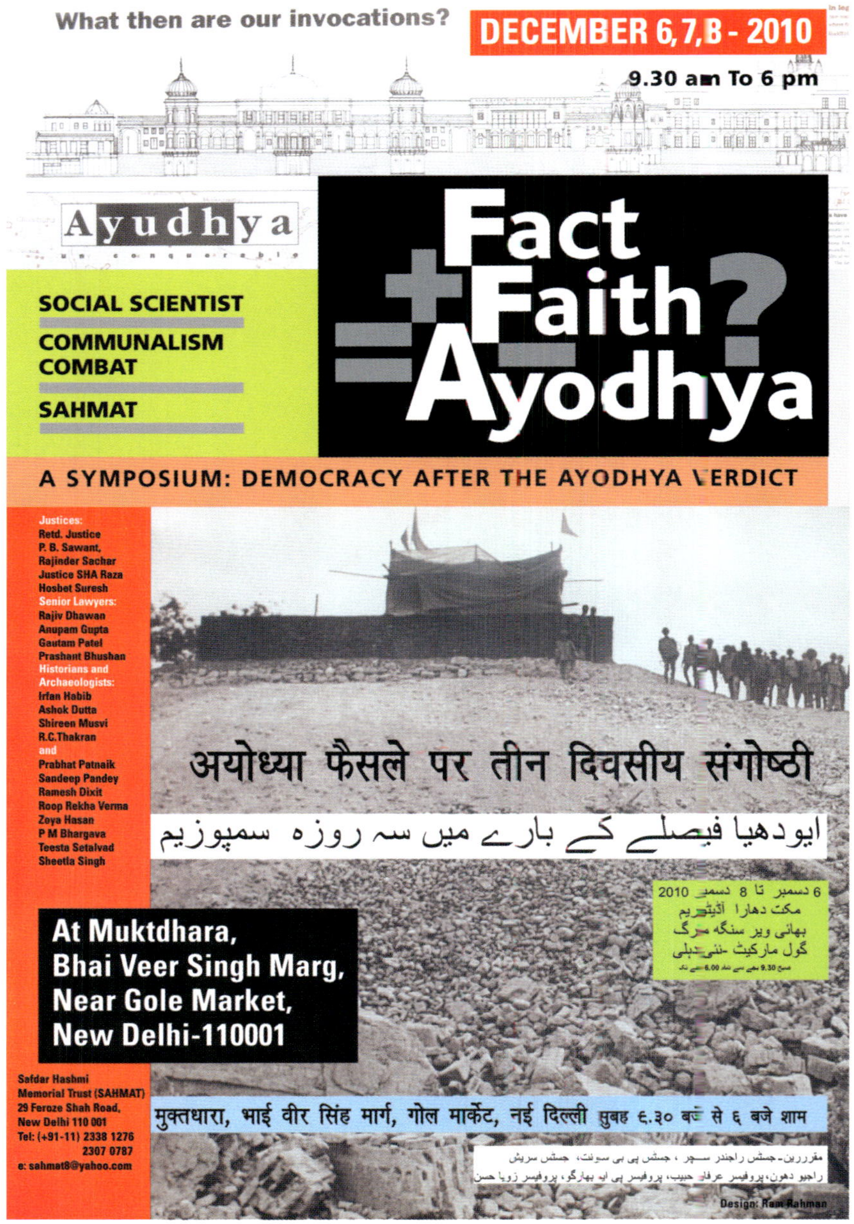

Fact and Faith poster, December 2010, 17 x 14 inches. Design: Ram Rahman.

Against Cultural Hegemonism

Sukumar Muralidharan

Excerpt from article published in *Frontline*, August 4, 2001.

A ruling by the Delhi High Court last fortnight showed how perilously close the country was to having a part of its historical tradition excised from the collective memory. On July 16, a three-judge bench of the Delhi High Court struck down a notification issued by the lieutenant governor of Delhi in August 1993 banning the exhibition of a panel depicting the different traditions of the Ramayana legend. Couched in extremely broad terms, the notification had held the exhibition, which depicted the Buddhist and Jain traditions of the Ram Katha, as insulting to the religious beliefs of a "particular community." Invoking Section 95 of the Code of Criminal Procedure, the lieutenant governor proceeded to declare "every copy" of the exhibition and any other material with the "above said objectionable" contents, forfeited to the government.

Most public-spirited citizens, including scholars and historians, were appalled at the implications of this broad power of seizure and censorship that the Delhi administration had assigned to itself. In the months following the Ayodhya demolition of December 1992, this was a stark illustration of the manner in which administrative will had been bent and subverted to suit the purposes of an aggressive communal mobilization. The High Court ruling striking down this recourse to draconian fiat was in this sense celebrated by most observers as a welcome return to sanity.

Mounted in August 1993 by the cultural organization Sahmat (the Safdar Hashmi Memorial Trust), the exhibition titled *Hum Sab Ayodhya* was one element in a campaign designed to neutralize the image of vandalism and intolerance that had begun to be associated with Ayodhya since the preceding December. It opened in seventeen cities across the country on August 9, timed symbolically to coincide with the anniversary of the Quit India movement. At Faizabad near Ayodhya, *Hum Sab Ayodhya* was intended to be the prelude to a major gathering of performing artists on the banks of the Sarayu on August 15. Titled *Muktnaad*, the cultural event was more than an expression of syncretism, tolerance, and diversity. It was also a conscious effort to recapture the space of Ayodhya that had been under occupation by the Hindutva forces.

As the momentum of public participation in the event began to gather, the Vishwa Hindu Parishad (VHP) and its affiliate, the Bajrang Dal, floated the rumor that *Muktnaad* was part of a covert operation by Muslim communal organizations to infiltrate Ayodhya and reconstruct the Babri Masjid. On August 12, some activists went on the rampage through the exhibition space, tearing up every panel that was on display. The vast simulation of rage had apparently been provoked by a panel depicting the Buddhist and Jain traditions of the Ram Katha.

Suffused with righteous indignation, members belonging to the Bharatiya Janata Party (BJP) raised the matter of wounded religious sensibility in Parliament. The Speaker of the Lok Sabha, displaying the paralysis of political will that seemed a contagious affliction, issued his own statements deprecating the exhibition and demanding administrative action. Cowering before the threatening posture of the Hindutva forces, the administration in Delhi showed a curious alacrity in cracking down on the popular challenge to majority communalism.

On August 21, the Delhi Police arrived in force at the premises of Teen Murti Bhavan where *Hum Sab Ayodhya* was on display. The exhibition was ordered closed and the panels depicting the different traditions of the Ram Katha were confiscated. One of the targets of the Delhi administration's action was the Buddhist narration of the Ram Katha, which large numbers revere and generations of historians have endorsed as being part of authentic Indian tradition. In the panel put up by Sahmat, the narration ran as follows: "The Dasharatha Jataka, dating back to somewhere between the fourth and second century BC, is probably older than the one by Valmiki. In this version, Sita is not the wife but the sister of Rama. At the end of the exile when Rama returns to Ayodhya, Sita is made queen-consort of Rama and they rule jointly for sixteen thousand years."

There is, as most historians have pointed out, little that is perceived as taboo in this version either by the expert reader or the lay audience. Rather, the depiction is only meant to emphasize the undiluted royal bloodline of the ruling dynasties of antiquity. The subtleties, however, were beyond the comprehension of Hindutva.

A similar outpouring of rage surrounded the narration of the Jain tradition, where rakshasas were depicted not as demons but as ordinary human beings. In some interpretations within the Jain tradition, as *Hum Sab Ayodhya* pointed out with rigorous attention to historical texts, "Sita is the daughter of Ravana who is brought up by Janaka."

In striking down the Delhi administration's seizure of this material, the High Court has held that there has been no proof of "deliberate or malicious intent." The communication sent by Delhi Police to the Union Home Ministry and subsequently to the lieutenant governor does not specify any grounds for invoking the draconian power of censorship and seizure. Indeed, as Chief Justice Arijit Pasayat and Justices D. K. Jain and C. K. Mahajan have observed, it shows a singular lack of "application of mind" by the authorities concerned. July 20 saw a gathering in Delhi to commemorate a long overdue triumph in the battle against cultural hegemonism of the Hindutva kind. The singer Shubha Mudgal rendered some of her compositions, including several composed specifically for Sahmat events.

1993 Muktnaad

The exhibition *Hum Sab Ayodhya* preceded a major gathering of performing artists on the banks of the Sarayu River in Ayodhya, on August 14–15. At this nightlong program of music and dance, titled *Muktnaad* (Free Song/Sound Liberated), some of India's most celebrated musicians, dancers, and theatre artists performed for an audience of over a thousand people from across India. The performances began at midnight on August 14, and continued until ten in the morning of August 15, India's Independence Day. As one newspaper reporter described it, "There were no speeches, no political appeal, no confrontation. But the message was there all the same. The rich heritage of music and dance of this country, steeped in religious tradition, was offered by the artists as homage to the temple town" (*The Hindu*, August 16, 1993).

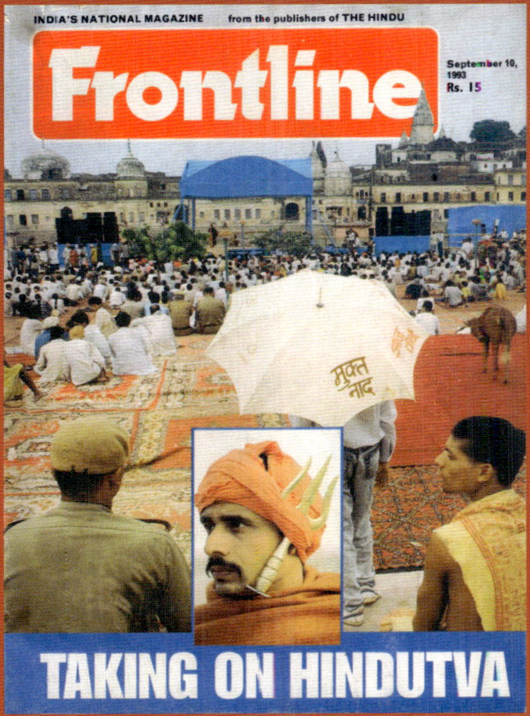

Cover of the *Frontline* issue on *Muktnaad*, September 1993.

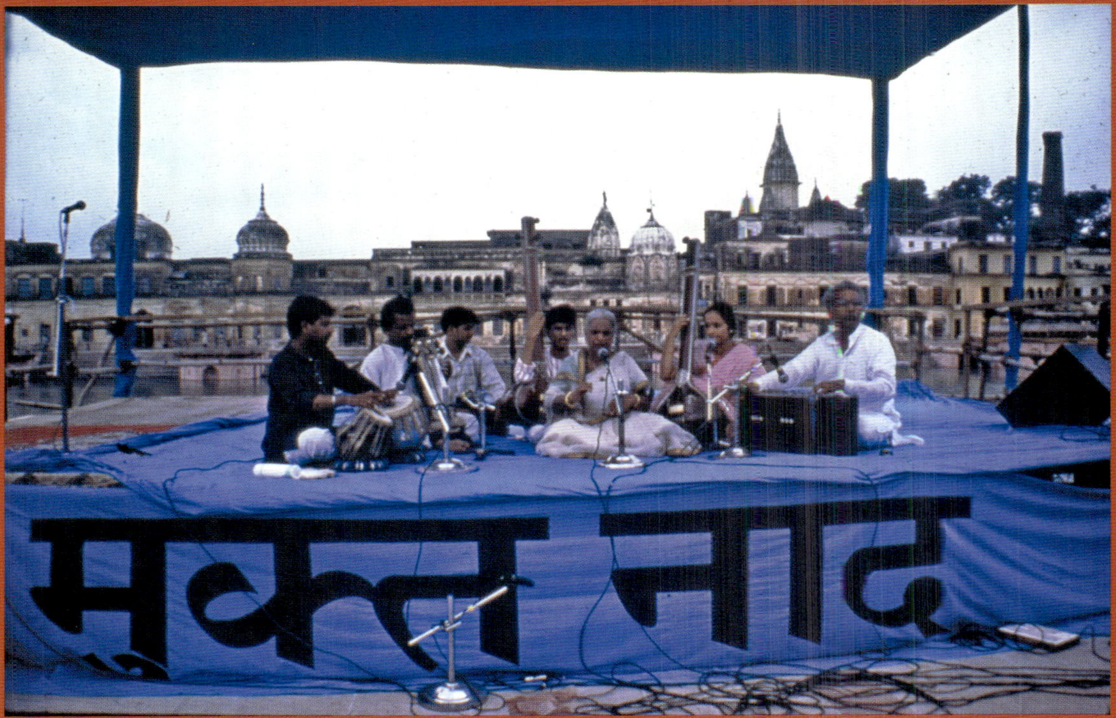

Girija Devi sings at dawn, *Muktnaad*, Ayodhya, August 15, 1993.

SOHAIL HASHMI

Muktnaad was truly heroic, almost audacious both in its conception and execution. The idea was to go to Ayodhya, the site of the demolition of the mosque on December 6, 1992—to go to a city that had virtually been taken over by Hindutva fascist organizations. All kinds of Hindu communal outfits had given calls to boycott the program. But the local administration soon realized that their threats had not worked, that the artists who were arriving could not be trifled with, and that there would be a national or even international scandal if any harm came to any of them. They then decided to so sanitize the performance area that no one would be able to reach the venue. Meanwhile the Hindu communal outfits issued directives to all the temples to conduct nonstop congregational prayers to keep the local audience away from *Muktnaad*, and also to drown the sounds of the performances at *Muktnaad* through music blaring from temple loudspeakers. Power supply at the venue was cut off, and the local generator operator had been scared away by threats of dire consequences.

None of this worked, however. Two of us set off in search of the generator operator. I had a foot in plaster and was hobbling about on a crutch. We found a cab, rushed to the town of Faizabad, and finally traced the generator operator to his shop. By midnight everything was in place and *Muktnaad* began with all the artists present floating small earthenware lamps on the river, and the famous Independence Day speech made by first prime minister of free India, Pandit Jawaharlal Nehru, on August 15, 1947, reverberating through all of Ayodhya on the hi-tech sound system that had traveled from Delhi. *MUKTNAAD*, "Sound Liberated," had prevailed.

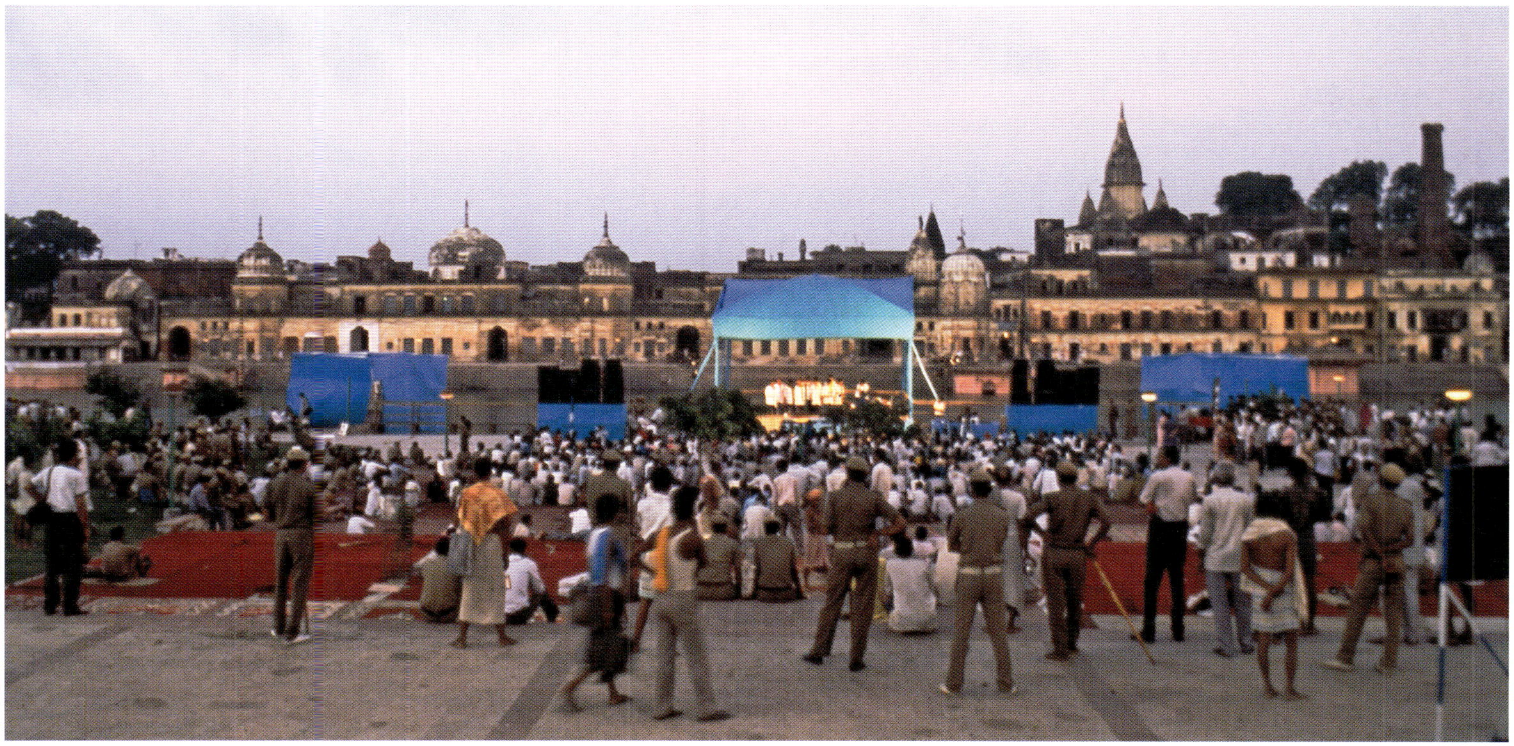

On a visit to Ayodhya after the mosque had been destroyed, members of Sahmat discovered that the landscape architect Ravindra Bhan had recently done a major restoration of the medieval riverfront. He collaborated with Sahmat on this project and the restored site became the setting for *Muktnaad* in August 1993, at the suggestion of Swami Pagal Das, the famous *pakhawaj* (Indian drum) exponent from Ayodhya.

Muktnaad at the Ram ki Pairi *ghats*, Sarayu River, Ayodhya, August 15, 1993.

12 GALLERY THE ECONOMIC TIMES NEW DELHI SUNDAY 29 AUGUST 1993

Photographs by K. K. LASHKARI

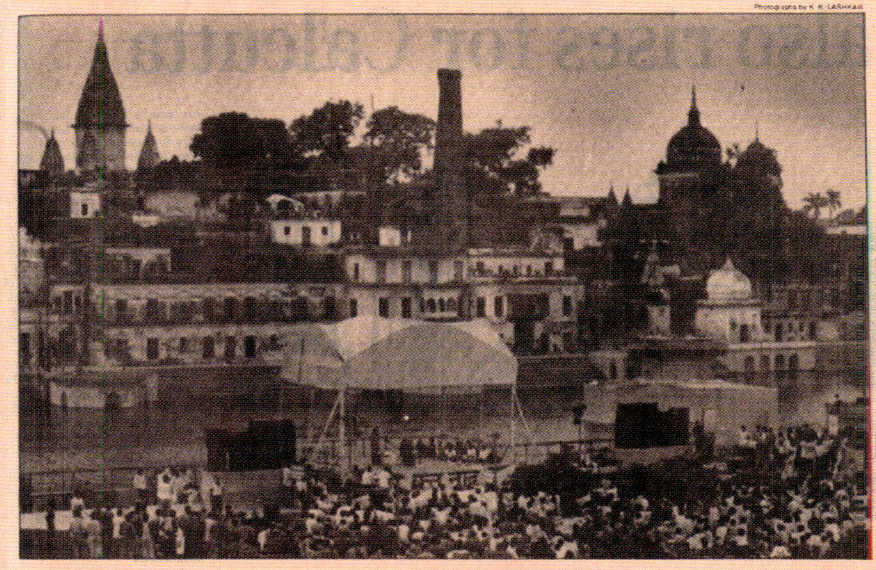

Battering Ram

The BJP may have got its tail in a cleft wedge and SAHMAT might still have the last laugh on the polemic around the several versions of the Ramayana, writes **Sadanand Menon** *analysing the cultural questions the debate needs to tackle.*

PITY THE BJP and its thump tank. With the mischief they triggered around the activities of the Safdar Hashmi Memorial Trust (SAHMAT)—first in Faizabad by vandalising the *Hum Sub Ayudhya* exhibition on August 12, and then carrying the battle on to Delhi and setting up a din over a text panel in the exhibition which describes scores of versions of the Ramayana prevalent in India (and South East Asia) over the last 2,500 years—they have inadvertently trod on something sticky which is bound to get their ankles soiled.

'Hum Sahmat se a-sahmat hain', droned a blase Atal Behari Vajpayee, as he justified the attack on the exhibition accusing it of featuring an aspect of the Ramayana myth (the 4th century BC version of the *Dasharatha Jataka* which has Rama and Sita as siblings) not certified by the BJP's theological Goebbels'. Of course, for a party for which history is mere mythology and which has no hesitation sanctifying mythology as history, dates and chronologies and 'historic facts' are merely symbols of a weak attitude to life.

Bajrang Dal chieftain Vinay Katiyar went a step further and valiantly announced he and his party would accept no version of the Ramayana other than the Valmiki or the Tulsi version. If ever any set of politicians have put their foot in their mouths so effectively, this must be it. Instead of all the mock battles for delinking religion from politics, the government might have a more productive debate on hand by mooting a bill for delinking idiocy from politics.

For our BJP worthies, in their haste to fashion Hinduism to resemble some sort an ultra-modern, corporate-ised, highly organic and internally consistent enterprise—a Japanisation of *hindutva*, if you please—are only succeeding in promoting it as a mono-cultural and pestilential weed, which makes mockery of current ecological mantras like diversity and heterogeneity. And a politics divorced from healthy ecological concerns is treading on thin ground indeed.

What the BJP and its pen-pushers are out to create in a rush is a form of organised mysticism whose main danger—and therefore its greatest weakness—is the the manner in which it will set about quantifying, itemising and labelling the cultural shelf without realising the ease with which they are pinning themselves into a corner.

Culture is not what is prescribed in law books. It is the grey areas of 'illegality' that constitute the spine of cultural formations. For every civilisational leap, there is a concomitant wild and untamed area of human expression that lurks around the corner for the first opportunity to set the wheels moving in reverse gear. For every vanity of 'normality', we have counterpoints that challenge the pathology of such 'normality'. A mere assertion of 'authority' has never been the criteria of 'truth'. This is a hard lesson our historically outdated right-wingers will have to learn first.

What really is behind all this *chi-chi* sentiments the BJP is trying to generate around sibling marriage. Are they really some kind of 19th century social reformers in safforn disguise out to lay Hindu society on the Procrustean bed of Western social mores and sanitise it of all its burps and hiccups or are they seriously out to challenge the largely endogamous nature of our culture? Half of Indian society is married to extremely close family relations. In my own Nair community, first cousins from the mothers side hitch up without batting an eyelid. Does the BJP have a value judgement on it? If so, lets hear them. These first cousin marriages are merely extensions of more intimate endogamies of the past which have been superseded in the civilisational march. But because of that will these sanitary inspectors of culture refuse to acknowledge a process in history?

What then will they do with the fact that King Dasharatha had four wives? What will they do with the Multani *Ramleelas* which are performed in public and are about as earthy as you can get on kinship relationships? What will they do with popular ditties like the one I heard the first time I was in Ayodhya some twenty-five years ago, which went:

Ram, Ram sab kahey
Dashrath kahey na koyi
Gar Dashrath kasrat na karey
Toh Ram kahan se hoy?

(Everyone takes the name Ram; no one utters the name Dashrath; but if Dashrath had not done his *kasrat* (exercise), then pray from where could have Ram come?)

OUR HUMOURLESS pseudo-Hindus would not ever concede that, for centuries, along with veneration and adoration, irreverence too has been the cornerstone of our devotional practice. What, may one ask, will they do with something like *ninda-stuti*—the practice of veneration through profanation that any casual visitor to the Puri *rath-yatra* festival must have experienced. What will they do with the *Krishna Karnamrutham* and the *Gita Govinda*?

Of course, we do not need to go very far for answers. Over fifty years ago, Wilhelm Reich had warned us that, "Mystical contagion is the most important psychological pre-condition for assimilation of fascist ideology." It is this 'mystical contagion' that our communal ideologues are trying to spread. But in the execution of this agenda, our comrades are displaying poor grasp of the lay of the land.

One could sympathise with the Vinay Katiyars were he to be denouncing something like the *Keemayanam*—Dravida firebrand E.V. Ramaswami Naicker's lampoon of the Ramayana. That surely was a gauntlet thrown before bramminical hegemony and, to the eternal credit of the tolerant nature of Indian society, it did not provoke any riots in the forties and fifties when it was performed from every street corner in Tamil Nadu. But for Mr Katiyar to be so rude and dismissive of something as grand as the *Kamba Ramayanam* is surely an indicator of where the *hindutva* bandwagon is going to meet its Waterloo.

The surprise in all this is how fickle our polemics is. It is a surprise how easily SAHMAT and its work has got isolated and sidelined as if it counts for nothing and as if the attack on them both from the BJP as well as self-righteous elements of other parties is merely their problem. It is even more surprising to see mainline newspapers editorialising: "It would have been advisable if... Sahmat had confined itself mainly to conventional programmes including musical sessions, plays and so on." This is most precious. 'Stay "conventional" and you will meet no opposition!' Dear sirs, even Sri Rama did not stay "conventional" and did some pretty unconventional things for a decendant of Raghuvamsha. If conventionality is the measure of normality, we would not have been debating this clash of tradition and modernity today.

It is poor sociology that defines culture as mere 'affirmation'. Culture is also 'negativity', otherness, abnormality. This negativity is a powerful social mechanism as it helps pose before society—positively—the image of its own underside as wel as its creative potential. Negativity is the social mechanism that provides us an occasion for the suspension of ordinary rules of behaviour and an entry into the realm of the sexual and the irrational—a largely repressed side of our society's consciousness which we can deny only at our peril and which returns with fixed regularity to haunt established culture with all it does not wish to acknowledge about itself.

SAHMAT may yet have the last laugh. ■

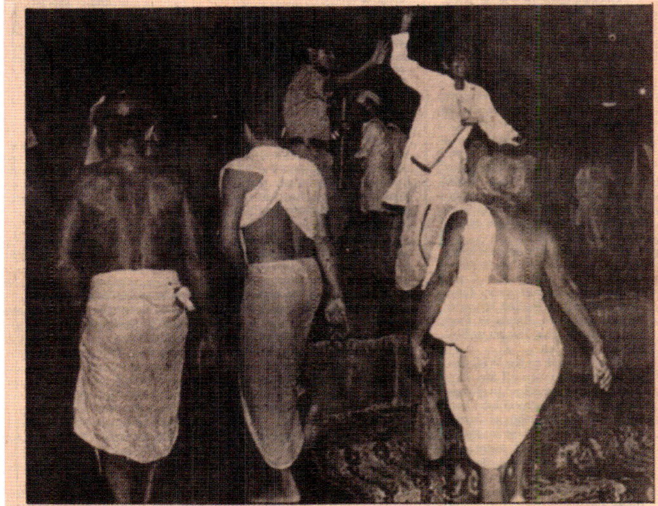

Police grappling with VHP-Bajrang Dal supporters who tried to disrupt the commencement of 'Muktnaad'

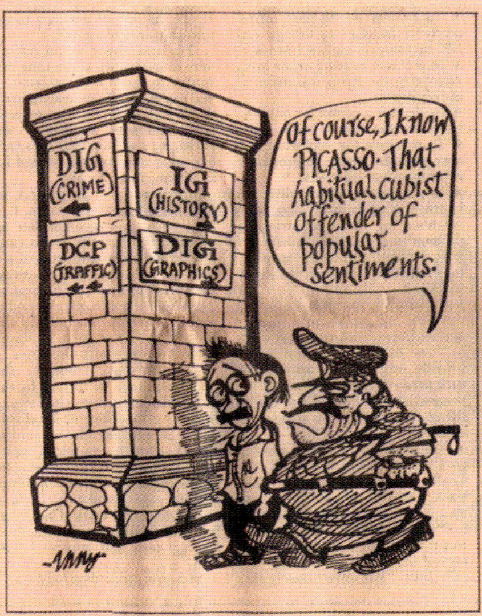

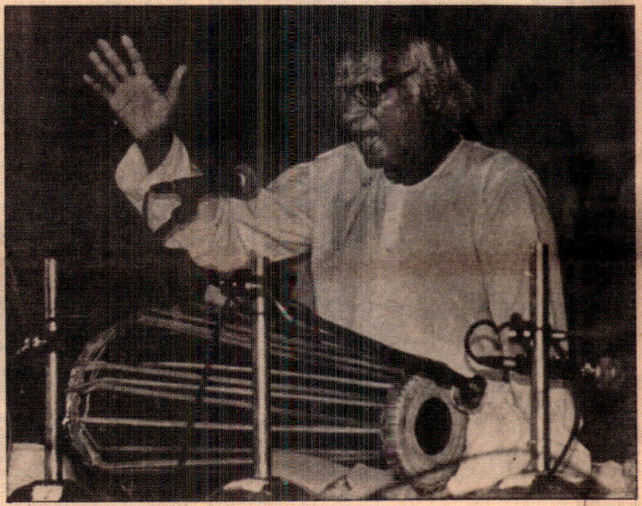

Pakhawaj player Swami Pagal Das, a resident of Ayodhya, regaling the audience at Ram ki Pairi ghat

"Battering Ram," *The Economic Times*, New Delhi, August 29, 1993.

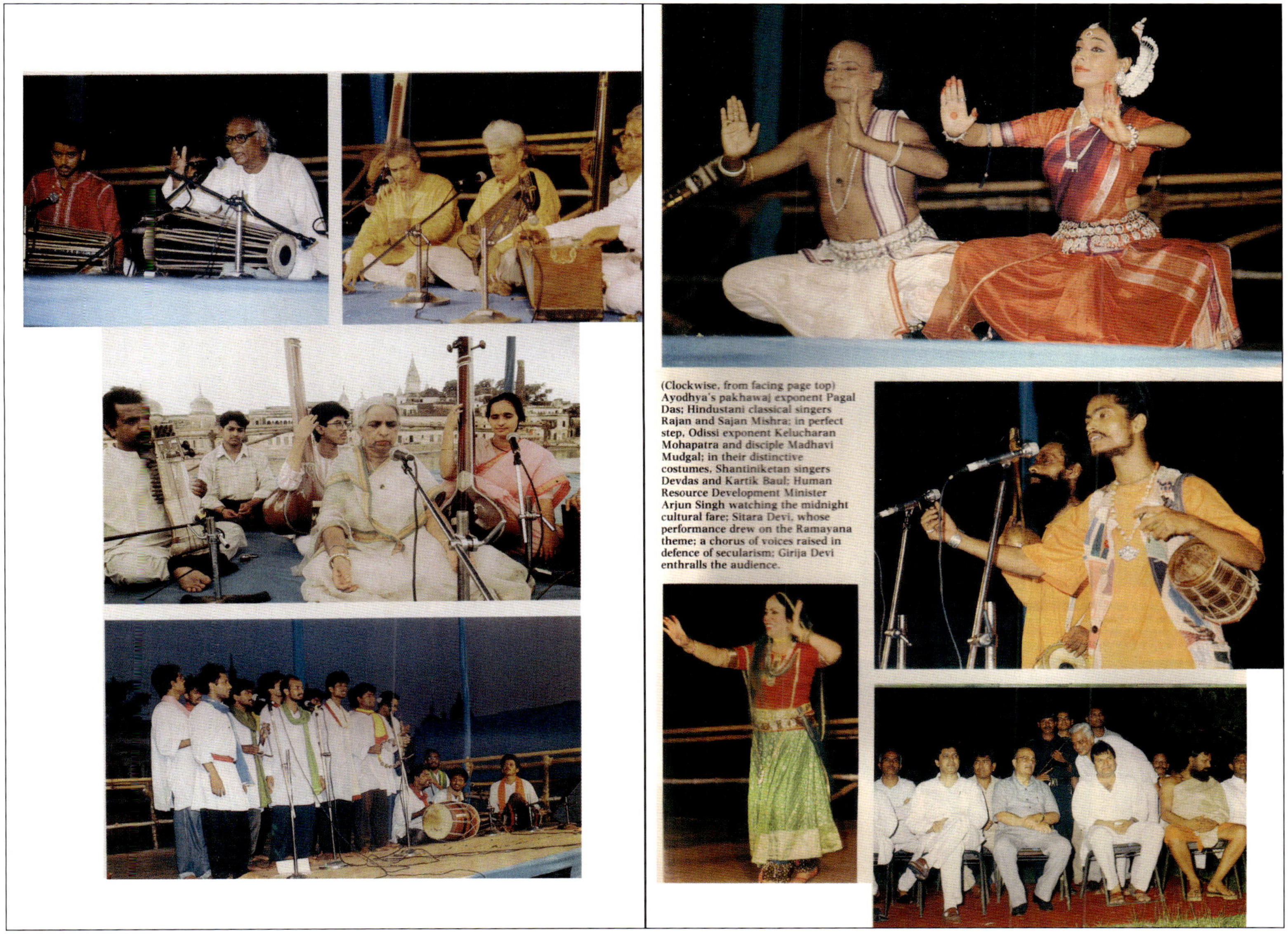

(Clockwise, from facing page top) Ayodhya's pakhawaj exponent Pagal Das; Hindustani classical singers Rajan and Sajan Mishra; in perfect step, Odissi exponent Kelucharan Mohapatra and disciple Madhavi Mudgal; in their distinctive costumes, Shantiniketan singers Devdas and Kartik Baul; Human Resource Development Minister Arjun Singh watching the midnight cultural fare; Sitara Devi, whose performance drew on the Ramayana theme; a chorus of voices raised in defence of secularism; Girija Devi enthralls the audience.

Double spread in *Frontline* issue on *Muktnaad*, September 1993.

M. K. RAINA

The high point of my involvement with Sahmat has been the breaking of the siege on Ayodhya after the demolition of the Babri Masjid. Over a thousand artists, intellectuals, actors, dancers, politicians, social workers, students, and teachers arrived in Ayodhya for an all-night cultural sit-in on August 14–15, 1993. The sit-in (*Muktnaad*) had an element of irony, because it opened with Jawaharlal Nehru's famous "Tryst with Destiny" speech of August 15, 1947, followed by music, dance, plays, poetry, etc. A message was sent out to the world by the creative community of India, cutting across class, caste, and religious faith, that Ayodhya belongs to us all and not to any particular community.

This event was debated in both Houses of Parliament and in the media. It unleashed a poignant debate about what was happening in the country. I personally believe that it was a turning point in the fight against the Hindutva forces, which gained momentum as time passed. It was a happening with implications for the entire nation.

1994–2005

Tribute to Gandhi

During 1994 and 1995, Sahmat commemorated the 125th anniversary of Mahatma Gandhi's birth with a yearlong series of events that promoted religious amity. The program was intended to invoke Gandhi's passionate quest for a secular India, as part of his pursuit for a sovereign nation and universal compassion.

Sahmat conceived and developed the program in its usual fashion, through discussions at an initial workshop held in Delhi in November 1994 at the Gandhi Darshan Samiti. The workshop participants included B. N. Pandey (director of the Gandhi Smriti and Darshan Samiti), historians Ravinder Kumar and K. N. Panikkar, art historian and critic Geeta Kapur, and artists Bhupen Khakhar, Madhvi Parekh, Ram Rahman, Parthiv Shah, Haku Shah, Shamshad, Gulammohammed Sheikh, and Vivan Sundaram.

Signaling the start of Sahmat's Gandhi program, Professor Irfan Habib lectured on "Gandhi and the National Movement," in Delhi on December 30, 1994, and then in Calcutta on January 22, 1995. Sahmat's annual *Safdar Hashmi Memorial* in Delhi on January 1, 1995, paid tribute to Gandhi. This program, titled *Manas Bana* (Weave of Humanity), included performances by musicians, dancers, and theatre artists. From January 22 to 27, 1995, the Oxford Bookstore and Gallery in Calcutta hosted the program "Remembering Gandhi," which included a painting workshop attended by schoolchildren from across the city, the launch of artist-designed posters, and the release of three children's books on Gandhi illustrated by artists Madhavi Parekh, Haku Shah, and Shamshad.

These activities, and others that followed, formed a context for reconsidering and re-evaluating Gandhi and the national movement. Sahmat conceived these events from a conviction that multiple, sometimes alternative and radical streams of political, social, and cultural practice were a part of India's nationwide struggle for independence.

As the members of Sahmat saw Indian politics move away from the modern, secular, and socialist legacy of the national movement, they felt compelled to defend the nation's cultural space against the imposition of a monolithic, Hindu-based identity. Believing the notion of a singular national identity to be at odds with the complex mosaic of ethnic, racial, religious, and philosophical traditions of South Asia, Sahmat wanted the cross-fertilizations within India's vibrant culture to remain in view.

Cover of *Bapu ka Aitihasik Mukadma* (Bapu's Historic Trial) by Mulk Raj Anand, illustrated by Shamshad, 1995.

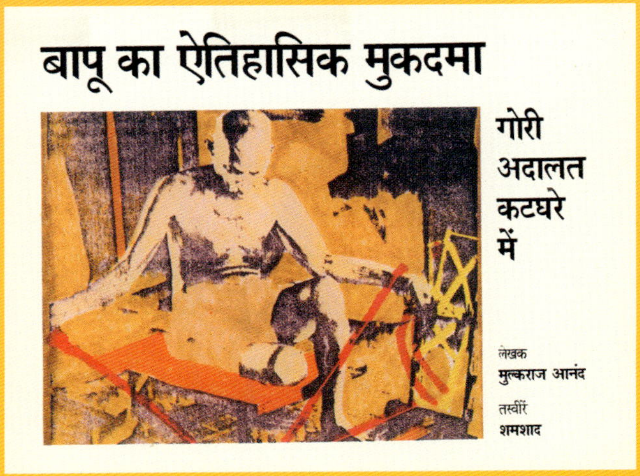

MADHVI PAREKH

I loved the Gandhi children's book project. Initially I was tense about it, but ultimately I really enjoyed it. Also, the umbrella painting workshop in Calcutta when the book was launched was absolutely wonderful. Senior artists and schoolchildren all painting together in public was so inspiring. It's important to work with children. They are so open, and when they grow up and have their own children, they will have been made more sensitive by experiences like this and can expose their own kids to the arts.

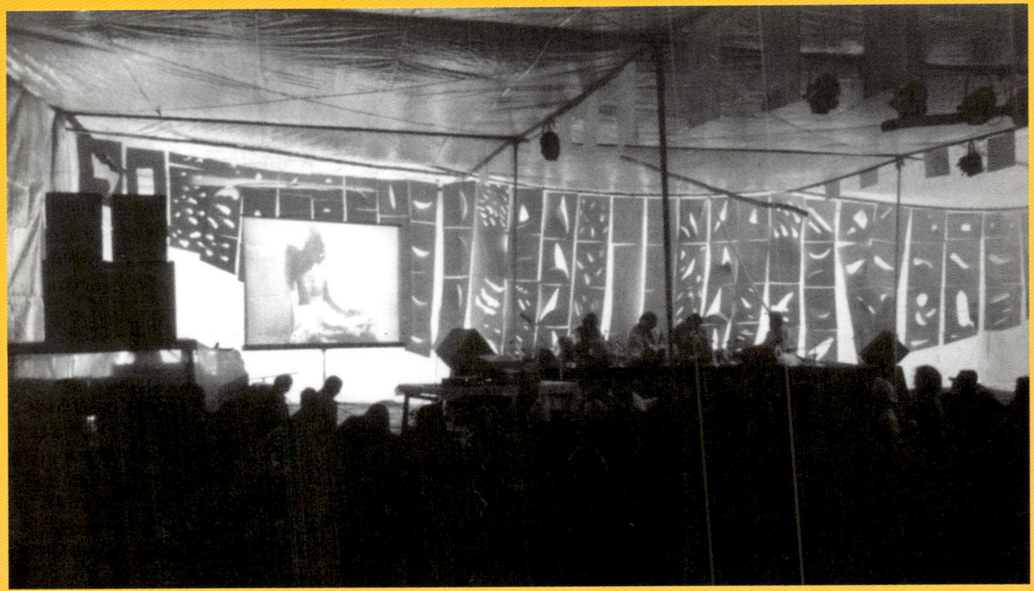

Manas Bana stage and tent, Safdar Hashmi Marg, New Delhi, January 1, 1995. Design collective: Vivan Sundaram, Ram Rahman, and Shamshad. Zakir Husain, Vikku Vinayakram, Selva Ganesh, and Bhawani Prasad perform with their percussion ensemble, with archival film footage of Gandhi's Dandi March (Salt March) projected behind.

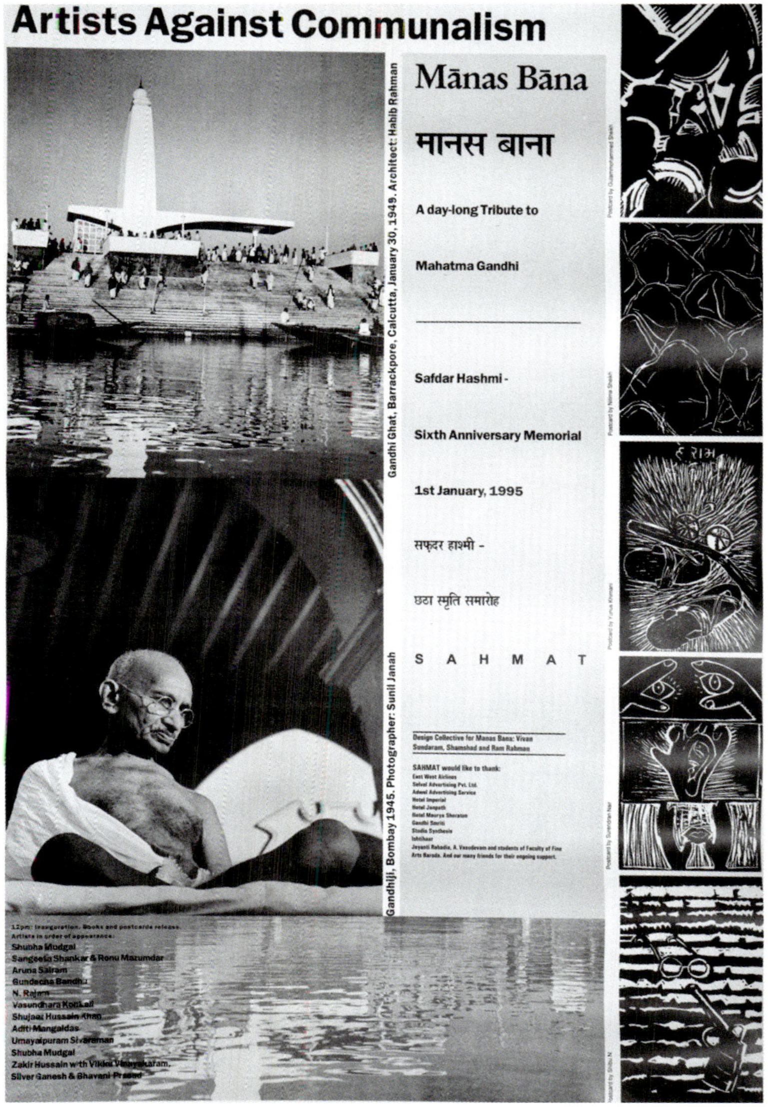

Manas Bana poster, January 1, 1995, 30 x 20 inches. Design: Ram Rahman. Photos by (from top to bottom): Habib Rahman and Sunil Janah. Postcards by (from top to bottom): Gulammohammed Sheikh, Nilima Sheikh, Yunus Khimani, Surendran Nair, and Shibu N.

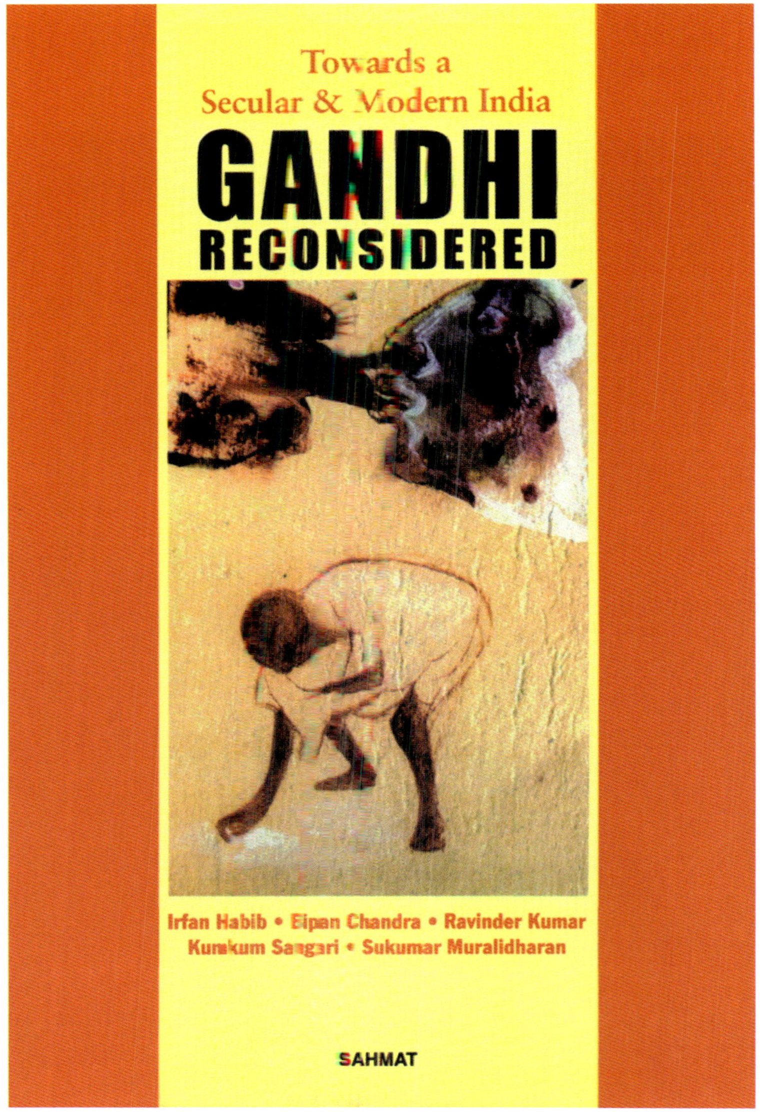

Book cover, *Towards a Secular & Modern India: Gandhi Reconsidered*, 2004. Design: Rajinder Arora. Image: Nilima Sheikh from *Postcards for Gandhi.*

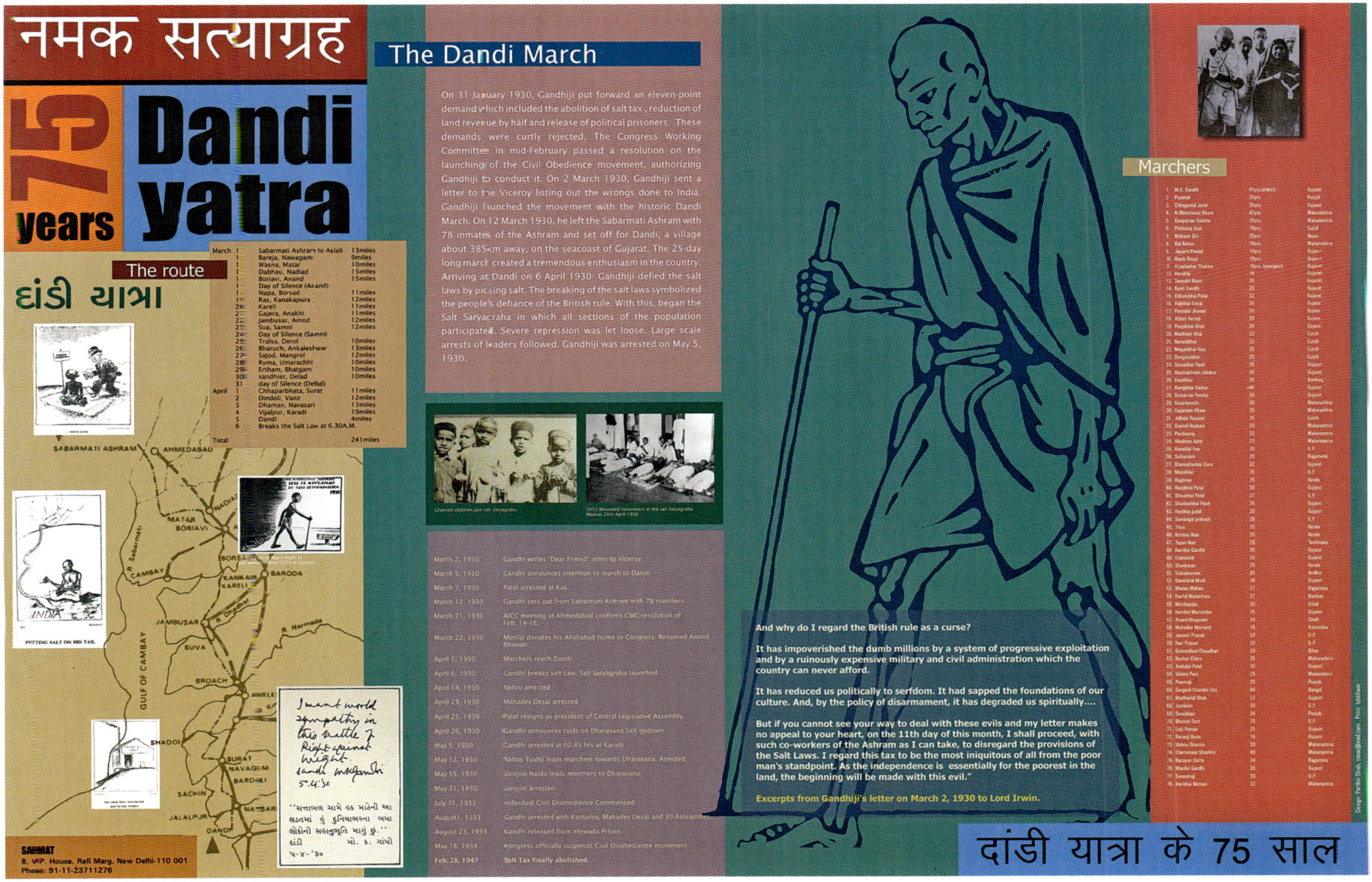

Poster to commemorate seventy-fifth anniversary of Gandhi's Salt March, 2005, 19 x 31 inches. Design: Parthiv Shah.

SHAMSHAD

Illustration for *Bapu ka Aitihasik Mukadma* (Bapu's Historic Trial) by Mulk Raj Anand, 1995, pen, ink, and watercolor on paper, 7½ x 8½ inches.

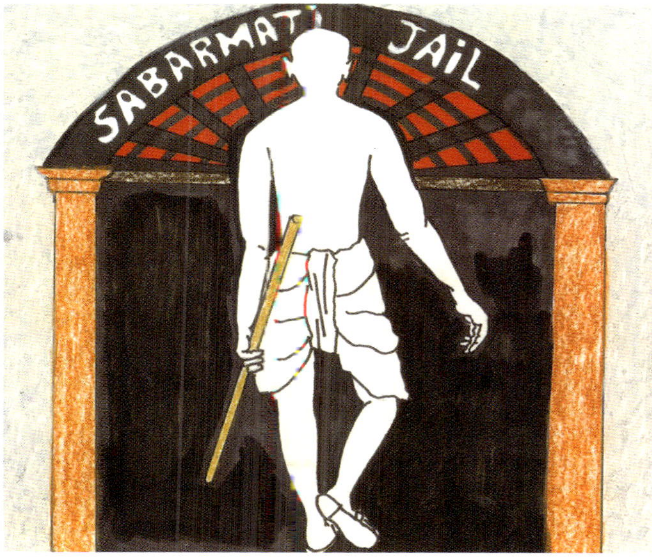

SHAMSHAD

Illustration for *Bapu ka Aitihasik Mukadma* (Bapu's Historic Trial) by Mulk Raj Anand, 1995, pen, ink, and watercolor on paper, 7½ x 8½ inches.

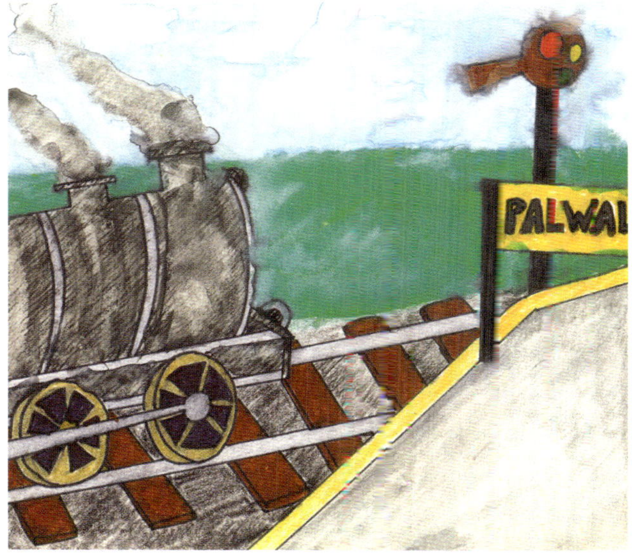

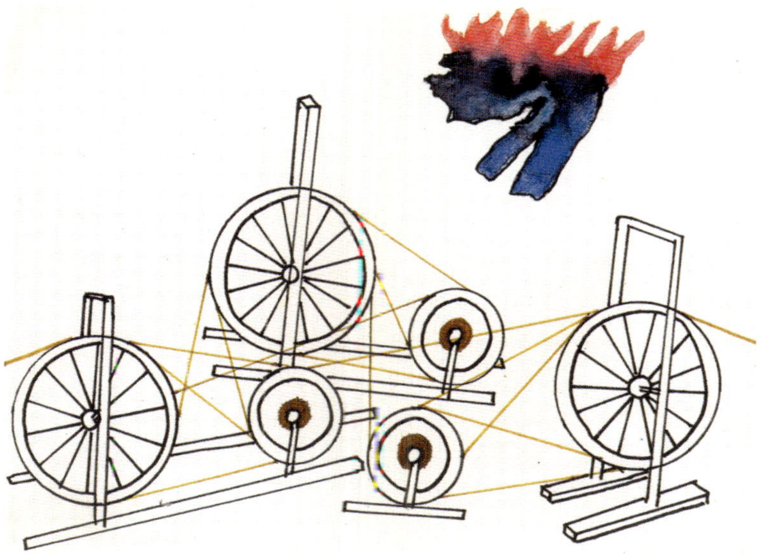

SHAMSHAD

Illustration for *Bapu ka Aitihasik Mukadma* (Bapu's Historic Trial) by Mulk Raj Anand, 1995, pen, ink, and watercolor on paper, 7½ x 8½ inches.

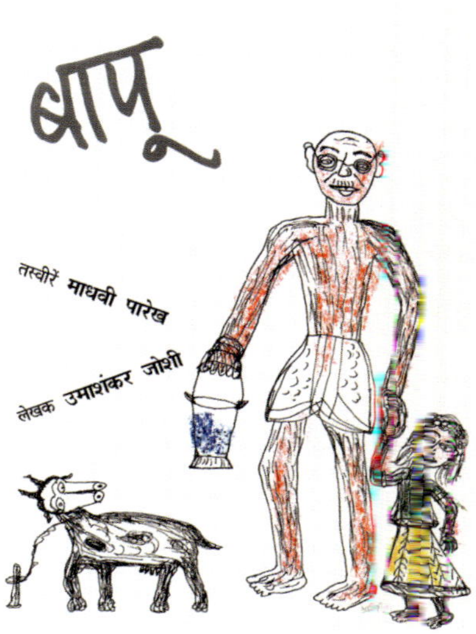

Cover of *Bapu* by Uma Shankar Joshi, illustrated by Madhvi Parekh, 1995.

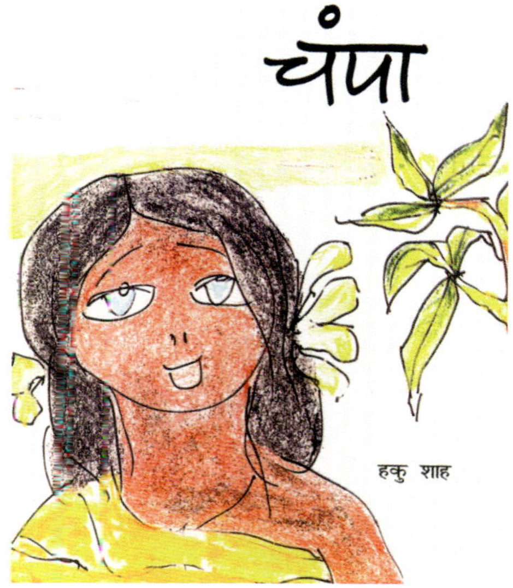

Cover of *Champa* by Haku Shah, illustrated by Haku Shah, 1995.

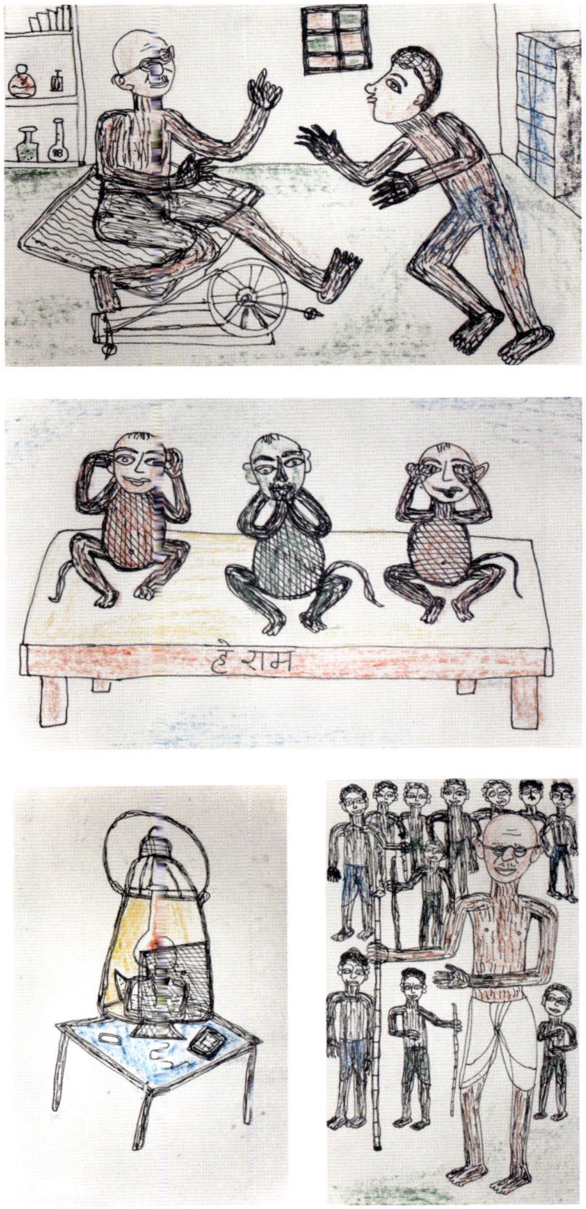

MADHVI PAREKH
Illustrations for *Bapu* by Uma Shankar Joshi, 1995, pen, ink, and crayon on paper, (top) 6½ x 10½ and (bottom) 10½ x 6½ inches each.

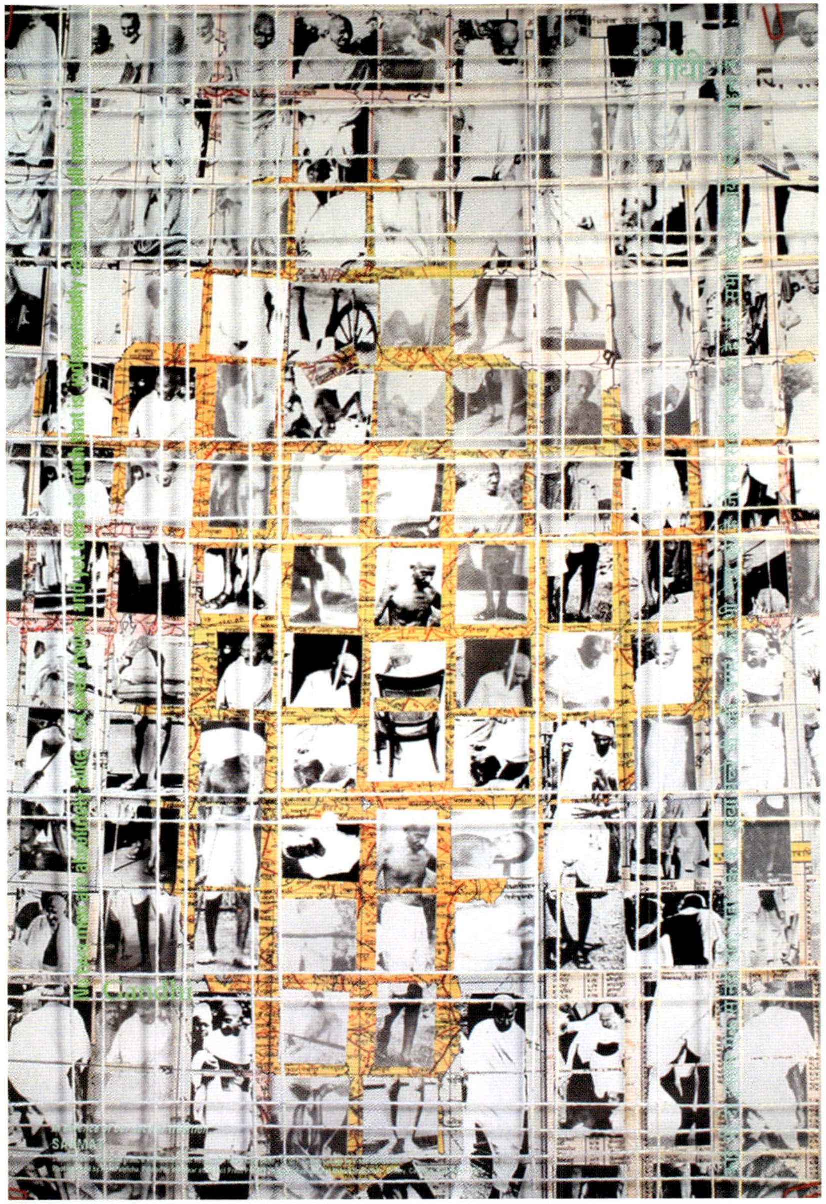

Poster depicting Gandhi's journeys, 1995, 27 x 18 inches. Design: Vivan Sundaram.

1994–
1995

Postcards for Gandhi

Sahmat's *Postcards for Gandhi* project was based on Mahatma Gandhi's famous practice of using inexpensive postcards to communicate with vast numbers of people. First, artists led by Gulammohammed Sheikh organized a lino-print workshop at the M. S. University of Baroda. Expanding on the idea, Vivan Sundaram, Ram Rahman, and Shamshad invited one hundred artists from across India to each make six different postcard-sized works that reflected their understanding of Gandhi's political leadership, philosophy, and relevance to contemporary India.

Postcards for Gandhi was one of Sahmat's first projects to engage a large group of artists around a single theme. The works contributed by artists were shown in exhibitions in six cities, all opening on October 2, Gandhi's birthday. Each presentation included one original work by each of the participating artists, making six different exhibitions. All the works were available for purchase at a uniform price of Rs 1,000 (less than $20) with proceeds benefitting Sahmat. A hundred thousand copies of the works were also printed as postcards. These strategies of simultaneous exhibition and low-priced artworks, no matter the artist's stature, reflected Gandhi's egalitarian ethos. One work from each artist was reproduced in the book *Addressing Gandhi*, designed by Sumant Jayakrishnan. The book, which a Sahmat delegation presented to President Shankar Dayal Sharma, also included commissioned texts by historians, social scientists, art historians, and artists that presented new scholarship on Gandhi's life and work.

The demolition of the Babri Masjid (Babur's Mosque) in December 1992 and the violent sectarian politics it unleashed had revived the memory of Gandhi, and his moral and ethical concepts. Sahmat saw the demolition as a betrayal of the values that had formed the basis of the national movement—values that Gandhi had struggled to develop into a moral political force. His strong advocacy of nonviolence and communal harmony acquired a resurgent meaning in the early 1990s, which was reflected and extended by artists.

The Sahmat collective noted that since his assassination, Gandhi had been remembered or commemorated primarily by public statuary. The significance of *Postcards for Gandhi* lay in artists engaging with the concepts and symbols that Gandhi used to marshal leadership of the national movement—the *charkha* (a spinning wheel, used for cotton), and *swadeshi* (encouraging domestic production while boycotting foreign goods), for instance. The evocative works made strong artistic statements against the right-wing politics of the time. As a thematically unified exhibition that opened simultaneously across India, it not only gave artists a platform to express their protest or anguish through their art, it also enabled them to draw on the timeless inspiration provided by Gandhi's life and work.

The text below, written by the historian Ravinder Kumar (1933–2001), was sent to the artists along with the *Postcards for Gandhi* project proposal. Professor Ravinder Kumar was the director of the Nehru Memorial Museum and Library, Delhi, for many years.

There were two great challenges which confronted Mahatma Gandhi: the task of drawing an ancient civilization into modern nationhood, and that of stimulating the energies of the common people in liberating his country from British rule. He faced these two challenges on the basis of *ahimsa*, or non-violence, which he equated with truth and God.

The Mahatma passionately believed that non-violence would arm the people of India with the strength to forge themselves into a modern nation, at the same time as they liberated themselves from alien rule. Yet Gandhi's notion of liberation was not confined to the exterior landscape of man's social existence. He believed that the ability of human beings to rid themselves of ignoble passion and selfishness was much more important than the formal trappings of freedom. The pursuit of non-violence as the basis of social action ensured several things. It ensured a firm link between ends and means; it enabled the actor to hold on to righteousness in the heat of the struggle; and finally, it transformed the oppressor through touching his conscience, at the same time as it ennobled the oppressed and equipped them with the courage to conduct their struggle with a self-confidence born out of the truthfulness of their cause.

GULAMMOHAMMED SHEIKH

I find Gandhi to be one of the most inspiring human beings in history, but I had not tried to visualize any aspect of his life or ideas until the *Postcards for Gandhi* project was launched. The idea of using postcards unleashed an unanswered desire. It was fascinating to use a regular postcard with its original color to draw upon. The innovative projects Sahmat initiated, like *Postcards for Gandhi* and *Gift for India*, enabled me to find forms that I may not have otherwise explored. Answering such demands enabled me to try different formats that I incorporated later in other works.

VIJAY BAGODI

This project took place in 1994–95. We were young and had just started our teaching career in the Faculty of Fine Arts, M. S. University. We were enthusiastic and energetic. In fact, the project had not much to do with the faculty—it was mainly mobilized by Sheikh Bhai [Gulammohammed Sheikh] with Suresh B. V., Sashidharan Nair, Jayanti Bhai Rabadia, and myself.

I took the responsibility of executing and printing the project in linocut medium in postcard size. Well, first of all, the project, as the name *Postcards for Gandhi* suggests, was about Gandhiji. This in itself inspired everyone to contribute collectively, to voluntarily extend their hands. Then, the chosen medium, linocut, was extremely suitable. Printmaking and linocut allow for working in a conducive, community-like atmosphere. It is almost Gandhian in that sense!

Everyone was excited and working together. For instance, I remember Bhupen Bhai [Bhupen Khakhar] sitting on a chair and cutting his lino, and infecting all of us with his enthusiasm and surprise at the unexpected result of the print! Sheikh Bhai formed the backbone of the project. He got us all going. Everyone helped to make the project a success—so someone would be printing while another would be spreading out the prints to dry, and yet another person would be putting together a set of dried, completed prints.

The collective effort put across a clear message—"pass it round" and remember Mahatma Gandhi.

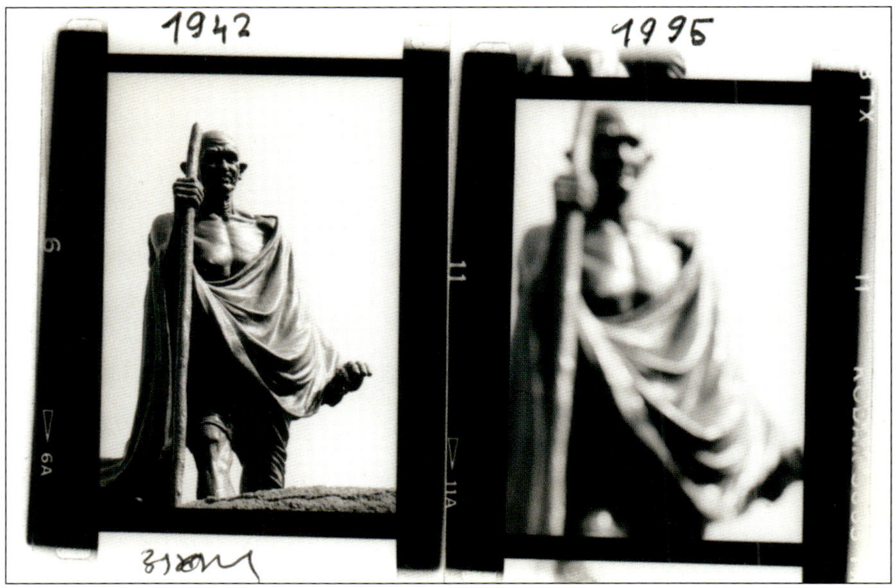

AMLAN PALIWAL

Untitled, 1995, photographs, 5¾ x 3½ inches.

Tapati Guha-Thakurta

Excerpt from "Locating Gandhi in Indian Art History: Nandalal and Ramkinkar," in *Addressing Gandhi* (New Delhi: Sahmat, 1995).

I would like at this point to slightly expand the focus from Ramkinkar and Santiniketan to the figure of Gandhi, with which I had begun the essay. If Ramkinkar was disappointed with the Debiprasad sculpture, it was primarily for the way it had been emptied of the spirit and personality of Gandhi: a spirit which many like Ramkinkar had seen as signaling a crucial alternative for Indian nationalism and modernity. The question I want to raise here would be: can one identify something like a Gandhian agenda in the history of modern Indian art? If so, how and where within this agenda does one situate an artist like Ramkinkar and the broader patterns of alternative art practice in Santiniketan that emerged since the 1920s? To address this question, the threads, I would argue, need to be drawn back from Ramkinkar to a prior conjuncture in Indian art history, to the more institutionally authoritative figure of his "mastar-mashay," Nandalal Bose. For, it was Nandalal Bose who would best exemplify the Santiniketan phenomenon in art, and in the process, carry through the Gandhian imperative of creating "a new national art for the people."

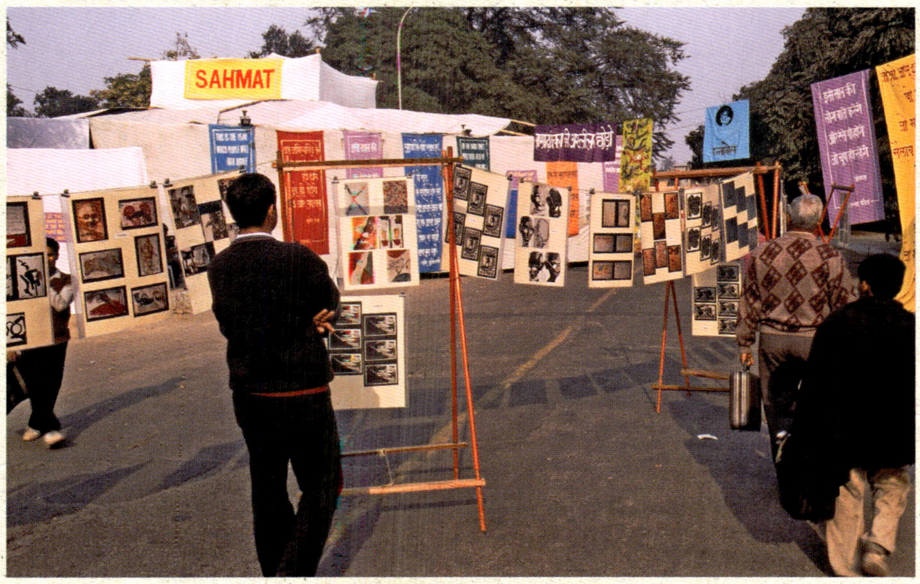

Street display of photographic copies of all 600 cards included in *Postcards for Gandhi*, Safdar Hashmi Marg, Delhi, January 1, 1996.

Is it possible, then, to talk of a Gandhian "moment of maneuver" in modern Indian art; a moment when, like nationalism, the category of "national art" tried to consolidate itself through a strategic denial of western modernity and an appropriation of rural, popular resources? In art, as in politics, the fundamental urge was that of representing the "national–popular." My point is not so much to suggest any direct links or programmatic collusions between the "artistic" and the "political"—for, ever since Abanindranath Tagore's Swadeshi art movement, the "political" had articulated itself in art only through a negation of its traces, allowing art to remove itself to the high ground of a distanced "aesthetic" sphere. My point, rather, is to show the way Nandalal's art and the Santiniketan experiment, within their self-anointed "aesthetic" spheres, found a prominent place in Gandhi's agenda—and the way that agenda itself shaped a particular construct of "Indian" theme and tradition in art.

There are a number of ways of locating Gandhi in the Indian art history of the period. One could refigure him as a special charismatic motif in art—compile an inventory of artists' images since the 1920s and 30s, and work out the lineaments of an iconography where the "artistic" would consciously separate itself from the "public" and "popular." Or, one can see Gandhi as signifying certain ideological thrusts and motivations in nationalisms that would play themselves out in the recasting of visual form, and in redefining the very notions of "art" and "Indian-ness." Taking up the latter line, attempting a selective enmeshing of images and agendas, let us see how Nandalal Bose, in the 1930s, comes to fulfill the Gandhian criteria of a "national" and a "people's" artist. Let us work out the paradigms of a new national public art from his iconic lino-cut image of Gandhi (*Bapuji*, April 12, 1930) to his well-known panels for the Haripura Congress pavilion of 1938. For it is only through mapping the contours of what came to be the mainstream nationalist project that one can suggest the spaces and positions that would prevail outside its demarcated frame. It is only in the context of Nandalal's singular success and national eminence that one can confront the issue of Ramkinkar's dissent and difference in the same period.

NALINI MALANI

Untitled, 1994, linocut, 3½ x 5¾ inches.

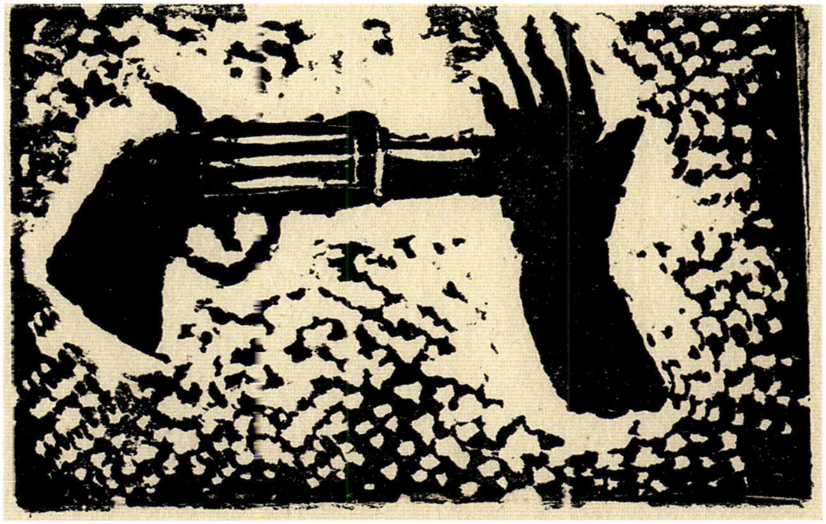

SURENDRAN NAIR

Untitled, 1995, watercolor on paper, 3½ x 5¾ inches. Collection: Vivan Sundaram.

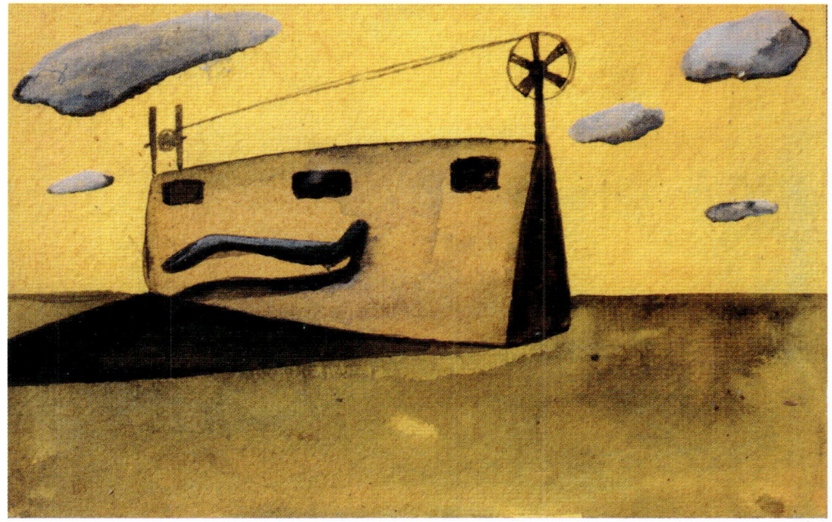

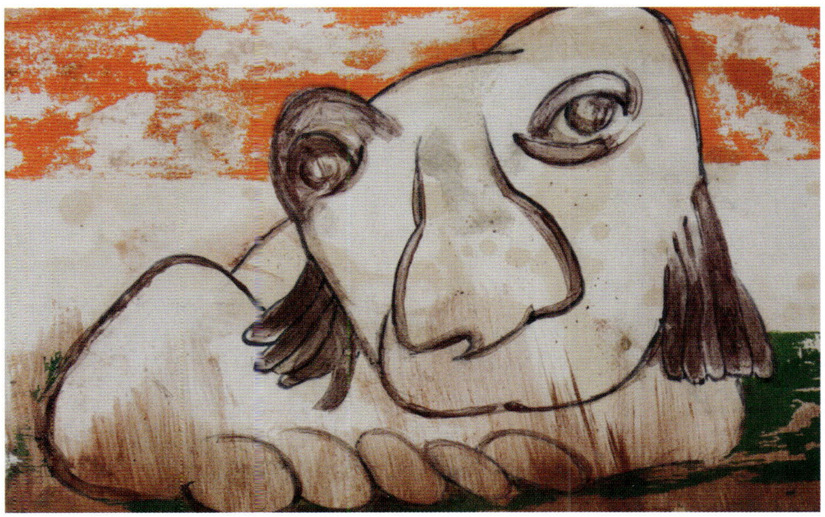

DEEPAK SHINDE

Untitled, 1995, watercolor on paper, 3½ x 5¾ inches. Collection: Lalit Nirula.

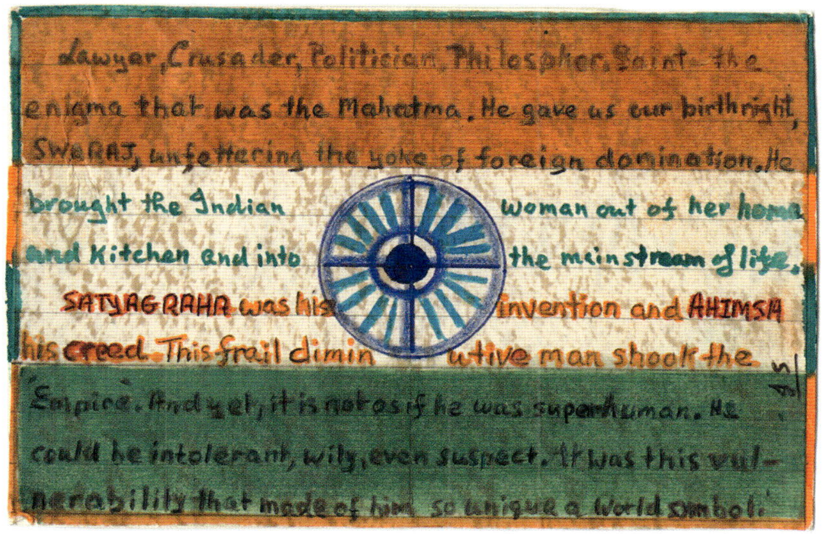

JEHANGIR SABAVALA

Untitled, 1995, ink and watercolor on paper, 3½ x 5¾ inches.

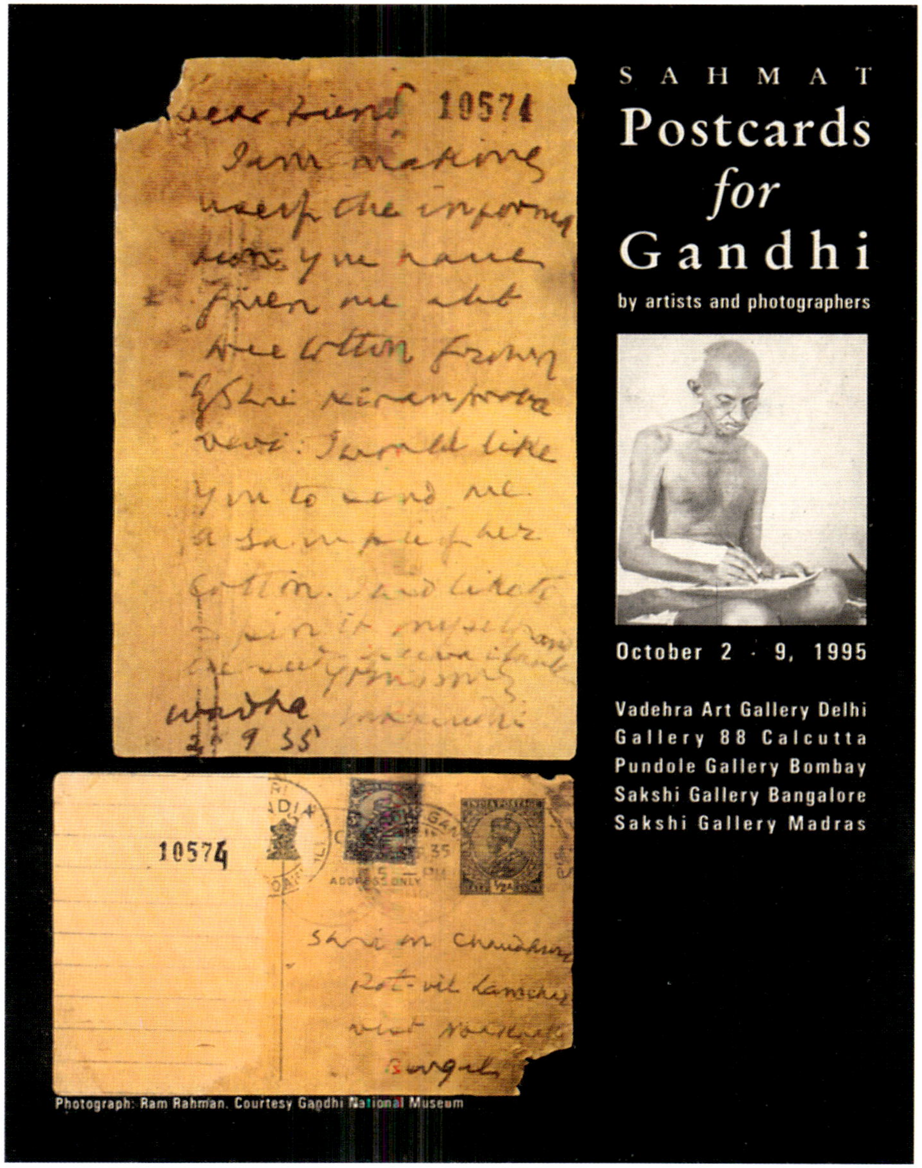

Flyer for *Postcards for Gandhi*, 1995. Design: Ram Rahman.

SURENDRAN NAIR
Untitled, 1995, watercolor on paper, 5 ¾ x 3 ½ inches. Collection: Lalit Nirula.

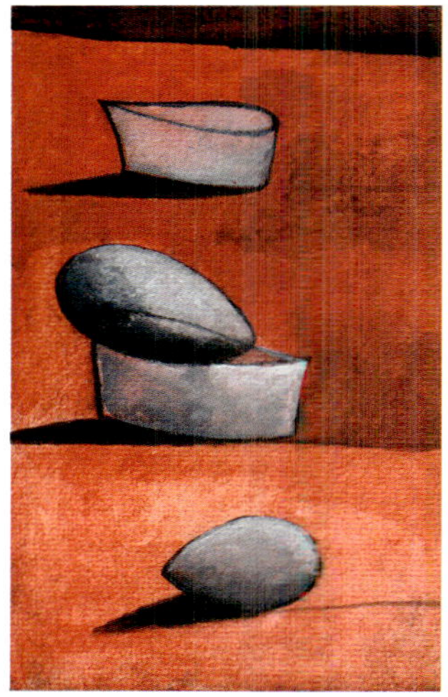

SANJIV SINHA
Untitled, 1995, watercolor on paper, 5 ¾ x 3 ½ inches. Collection: Lalit Nirula.

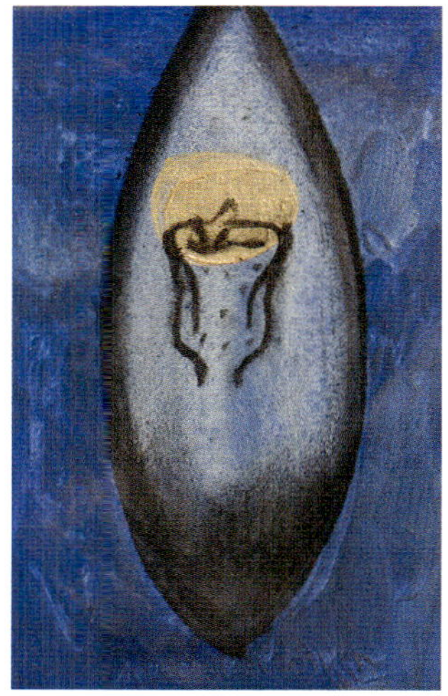

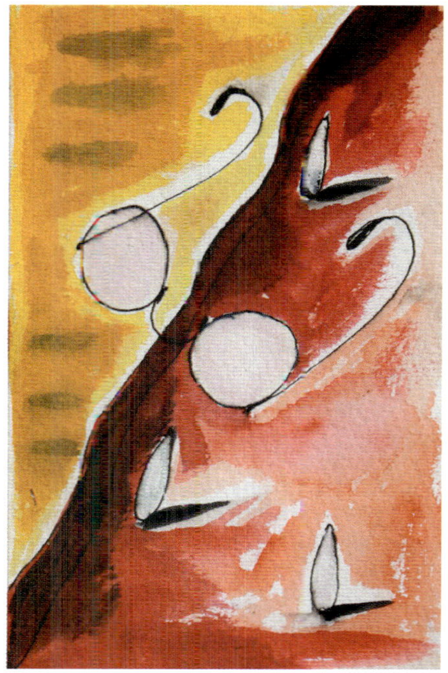

REKHA RODWITTIYA
Untitled, 1995, watercolor on paper, 5 ¾ x 3 ½ inches. Collection: Lalit Nirula.

K. G. Subramanyan

Excerpt from "Remembering Mahatma Gandhi," in *Addressing Gandhi* (New Delhi: Sahmat, 1995).

For a man like me Gandhi means many things. When I was young I knew him as one who gave this nation a backbone; and put fight and a sense of dignity into a large number of people.

A little later I knew him as one who tried to give a conscience to each activist, bringing home to him that he was fighting injustice and inhumanity, not a group of individuals; his real success lay in winning over the enemy, not wiping them out.

Further on, he gave a new focus to political action; its means had to be as unexceptionable as its ends; for it was not enough to gain one's ends, one had also to become, in the process, a better human being; otherwise the action will be self-defeating in the final count. In this he saw each small issue in the light of a larger one, as the terms he used imply; to him Swaraj was not just freedom from colonial rule and wielding the reins of power, it was also self-regulation in the interest of common good; Satyagraha was not just a strategy of unarmed resistance but also a way to persuade the adversary to see the truth of things. When more than half a century ago H. G. Wells enunciated the rights of man, and this was widely discussed all over the world, he was the one person to insist that, side by side with this, one had to enunciate the duties of man as well.

Gandhi was probably one of the first among the leaders of a nation to have a truly global perspective; he was keenly aware of the inter-dependence of the human individual, the human society and the environment, and insisted that no growth plan should lose sight of this; disbalanced growth could do incalculable harm. For him culture was not cosmetic; it was the outgrowth of the healthy interaction of these three factors. He considered the world as the common inheritance of all its peoples, not any group's fiefdom; they were its common trustees; and in the light of this all their disputes should be settled in a spirit of accommodation, not confrontation. This perhaps sounded archaic and retrograde to people sold out to the notion of class war and confrontational politics at one time. But pushed against the wall, this notion is probably changing and there is evidence of serious rethinking.

Gandhi had his contradictions like every man, great or small, is bound to have. But his perspectives were always large and elevating. And he had the courage to stand up for them, come what may. It is this depth of perspective and courage that make him exceptional. And for that reason exemplary. So, it is no surprise that a scientist-rationalist like Albert Einstein said at one time that a hundred years hence we will recall with wonder that such a man walked on this earth.

Ravinder Kumar

Excerpt from "Gandhi and India's Transition to Bourgeois Modernity," in *Addressing Gandhi* (New Delhi: Sahmat, 1995).

If we explore Gandhi's world-view as he set it out in *Hind Swaraj*, an essay written in the first decade of the twentieth century, it is obvious that he was already thinking of concepts like "appropriate technology" and "sustainable development" (his language was different and more innocent) at a time when such concepts were wholly unknown. So far as Indian society was concerned, in particular, Gandhi was clear that the relationship between available resources and the very substantial population to be sustained meant that the mechanical application of the European experience would lead to unmitigated disaster.

Last, but not least, I shall dwell upon modernity in culture, using the term in its most comprehensive sense. Gandhi, if we make allowances for his distinctive idiom, was deeply concerned with questions of popular and folk culture and the survival of popular and folk aesthetic traditions in the transition to modernity. In focusing upon the artisan in society, in focusing also upon the fusion of the aesthetic and the functional in the artifacts created by the artisan, Gandhi touched upon some of the basic issues relating to gainful employment and to the aesthetic quality of consumer goods produced in industrial society. His solution to the problems posed by industrialization lay in advocating labor-intensive economic activity in India. This is a suggestion which needs to be kept in view as India moves in the direction of a higher level of marketization.

When we touch upon culture, we are concerned not only with aesthetic creativity but also with the temper of social relations between individuals, social classes and religious communities within Indian society. There is a wide consensus among scholars and political actors that the cultural diversity of India is without a peer in the contemporary world. When Gandhi talked of culture, therefore, he was above all concerned with the question of creative coexistence between different social classes and cultural traditions in a plural society. The mechanisms of such coexistence are understood only partially by historians of India. Yet, there is reason to believe that different communities not only had a high level of cultural porosity in their interfaces, but their members also acted on the assumption that such diversity was a source of enrichment rather than of impoverishment.

Finally, we should recognize that the cultural diversity of India was drawn into the life-cycle of a highly disaggregated agrarian economy in which individuals, social classes and religious communities did not interact with one another very frequently or with any great momentum. It is necessary to highlight this because when we have done so, it becomes clear why the quickening of the pulse of economy, brought about through economic modernization, not only increases the production and exchange of material values, but also generates in the process intense social conflict. Indeed, the modernization of the economy is a dialectical process. At one level, it binds individuals and social classes together in the processes of production and exchange. Simultaneously, it generates intense social conflict between such individuals and social classes.

Cover of *Addressing Gandhi*, 1995.
Design: Sumant Jayakrishnan.

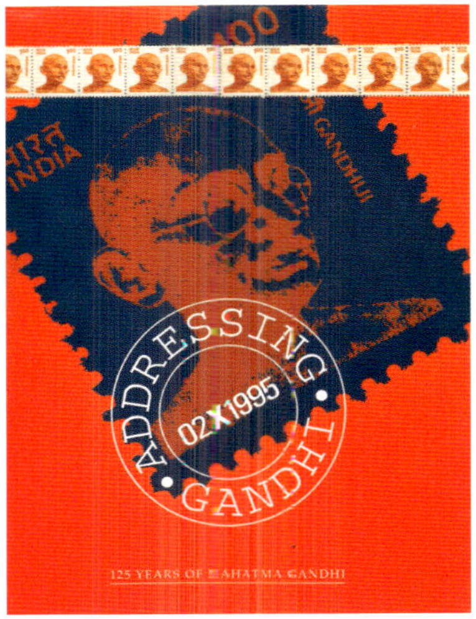

DEEPAK SHINDE
Untitled, 1995, watercolor on paper, 3½ x 5¾ inches. Collection: Lalit Nirula.

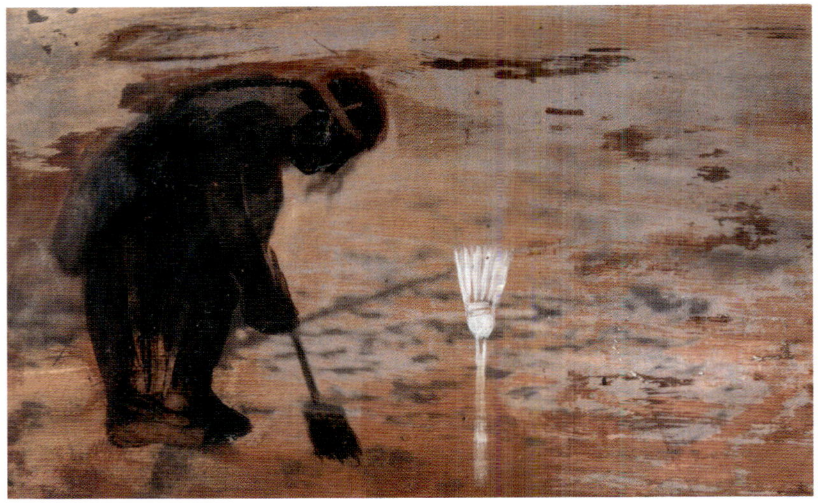

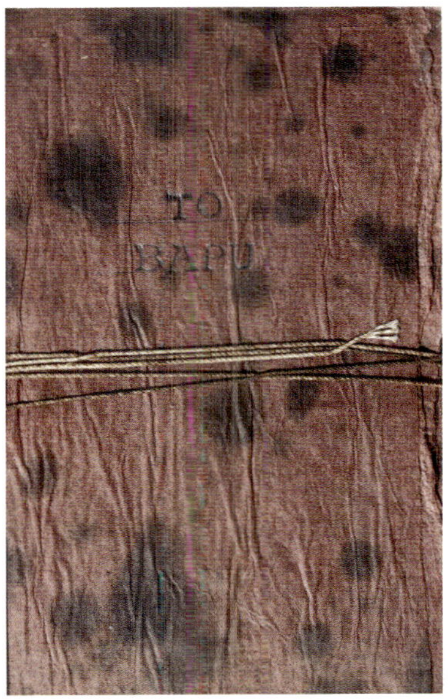

PUSHPAMALA N.
Untitled, 1995,
mixed media, 5¾ x 3½ inches.
Collection: Vivan Sundaram.

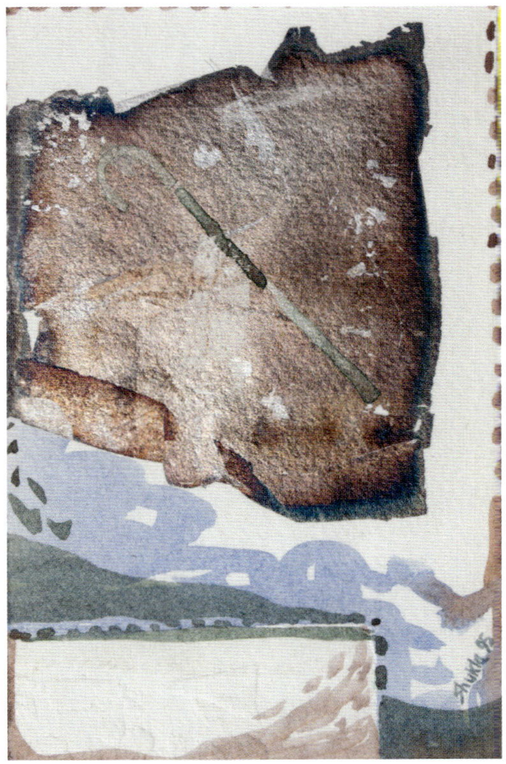

SHUKLA SAWANT
Salt of the Earth, 1995,
mixed media, 5¾ x 3½ inches.
Collection: Lalit Nirula.

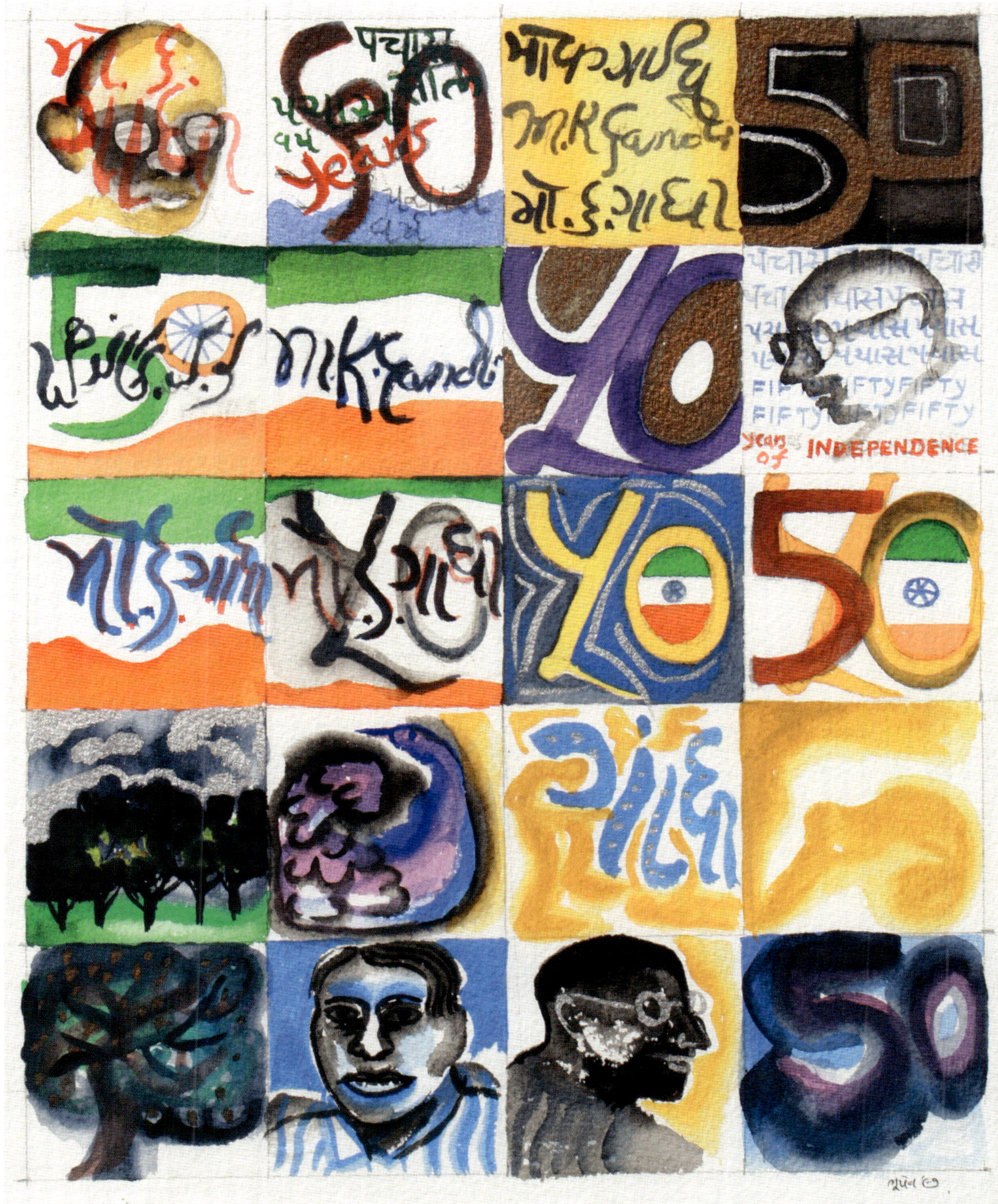

BHUPEN KHAKHAR

50 Years of Independence and Gandhi postage stamps, 1997, watercolor on paper, 12 x 10 inches. Collection: Anil Chandra.

1997

Gift for India

For this project, nearly two hundred artists from all over the world contributed an artwork, each in the form of a five-inch cube—a gift box—to commemorate fifty years of India's independence. Proposed by Vivan Sundaram, the project was coordinated for Sahmat by Sundaram, along with Shamshad and Ram Rahman. The works were exhibited at Rabindra Bhavan in New Delhi from September 11 to 20, and in Mumbai from November 27 to 30, 1997, where they were ultimately auctioned. The international scope of the project made it a distinctive one for Sahmat. Constructed of diverse materials and presented in different media, the gift boxes ranged from painted cubes to sculptural, fabricated objects. While this variety of materials and the use of text in many of the works clearly reflected the diversity of artists contributing to the project, the "gifts" attested to their common participation in paying tribute to India.

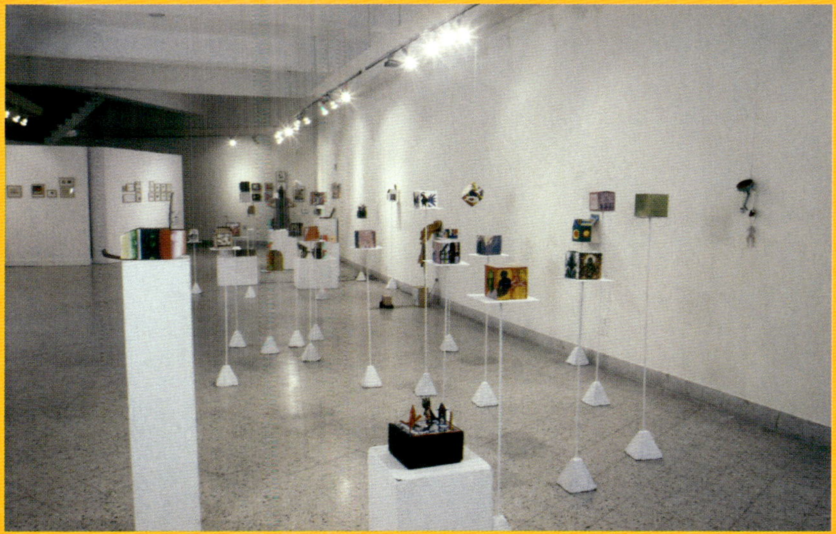

Gift for India, exhibition view, Lalit Kala Akademi Galleries, Rabindra Bhavan, Delhi, 1997.

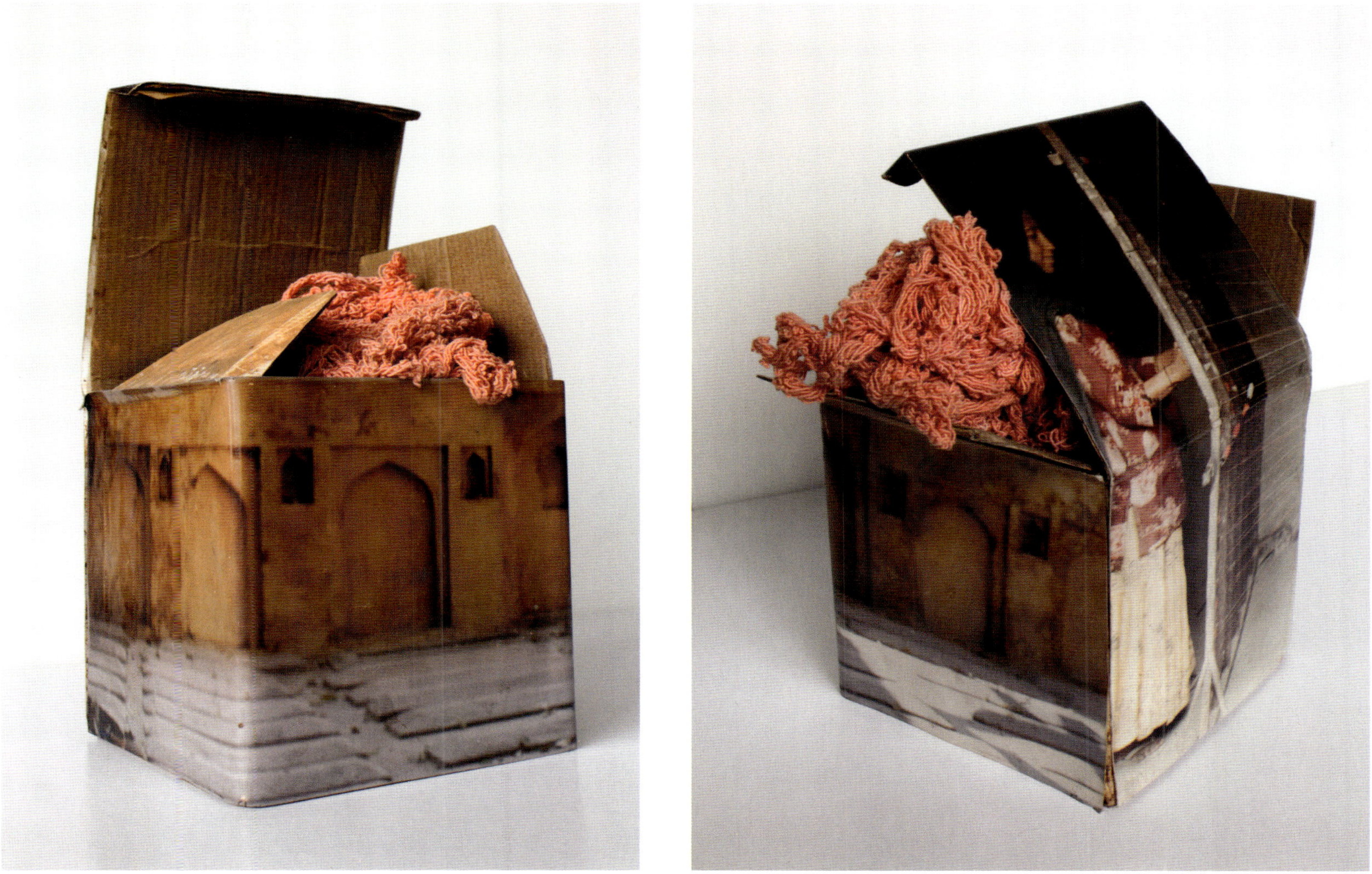

RUMMANA HUSSAIN (India)
Untitled, 1997, photograph and yarn on cardboard box, 5 x 5 x 5 inches. Collection: Peter Nagy.

A Gift among Friends

Vivan Sundaram

"The early pioneers of mail art were determined to show that art was a gift among friends. . . . Art was more than a commodity or an investment. It was an open structure that allowed for varied and full participation."[1]

Excerpt from *Gift for India* exhibition catalogue (New Delhi: Sahmat, 1997).

The 1960s mark the beginning of an era of freer movement across the globe, an informal hitch-hike trail across borders. The contemporary art movement called Fluxus, which generated art in non-institutional spaces, outside museum and gallery contexts, comes into existence around this time. Some decades later "mail art" becomes a political means to participate and transgress where borders are closed due to censorship. An exhibition shown in the 1989 Havana Biennial referred to Paraguay and brought together artists protesting against dictatorships in Latin America. One of the artists in this movement who stands out in ambition and scale is the Chilean Eugenio Dittborn. He calls his project *Airmail Paintings*, but he makes almost mural-scale works with photographs and folded sheets of paper.

"Envelopes contain Airmail Paintings like pregnant mothers contain their *unborn* children in amniotic fluid, like tombs contain *not-yet-dead* white bones."[2]

In the last decade we have witnessed a wide range of curatorial interventions in mail art projects: light-hearted requests, as in a project called *Doris Balls* where an English curator called for gifts for an imaginary wedding; a provocative statement by Shozo Shimamoto titled *Book Burning Edict* of 1992 for the exhibition *Essence* organized by the Australian Neil Degney, who called the space of such worldwide participation "Netland." Exhibitions of mail art have also been organized on a massive scale such as by John Held Jr. in Havana's Museo Nacional de Bellas Artes in 1995, where 900 artists from forty-four countries participated. In 1996, a project was conceived by Philippe Mouilon of France who got 125 artists from twenty countries to contribute images to be projected on a 150-metre-long eighteenth-century aqueduct, Arcos da Lapa, in Rio de Janeiro. The list of such exhibitions would be as long as it would be surprising. . . .

When Neil Degney from Brisbane asked me, in early 1995, to participate in *Essence*, I wrote a short statement which said:

"Mail art and the international networking is an 'invisible' journey connecting through alternative circuits. In these margins float fragments and voices; small packages with 'grand ideas'; foldouts which map politics and shift borders; envelopes with personal texts and drawings which are sent to known and unknown persons who become involved in the reception of art with very different paradigms from what mainstream art usually proposes."[3]

Whether it is a spontaneous response or one that is articulated in a complex manner, mail art is an affirmation of someone else's initiative, it breaks the taboo of the artist's privacy. In response to a letter from afar, the artist parcels his/her creative idea in an envelope or box, which arrives in the post, delivered by the familiar postman. In this journey there is still some of the romance of objects/ships sent out in bottles to sea that come afloat at unknown destinations across the globe. For ages past and well into the twentieth century, letters, mementos, and parcels have come by sea and land. These carry the evidence of time and long passage in their frank-marks, worn bulging covers and the enigmatic thing inside. . . .

"Airmail Paintings which function like boats—folding, compartmentalized life-rafts—inside which can be seen stirring different species, signs, substances, shapes resolutely determined to cross the *disaster* they are plunged into."[4]

"The journey implies a fixed point from which the person or object originated, and a destination. It implies locality, habitation, domestication, stratification, sedimentation. . . . On the other hand, motion, travelling, carrying, vagabondage is also a sort of primordial state. The Airmail Painting, as Dittborn himself points out, is only an extension of the first bag (and, beyond that, of the kangaroo's pouch, or the womb). And it is only the "work" that travels."[5]

As an artist/curator of mail art one can, with very little means and a small organization, realize a diversity of ideas, and bring together artists' works from all over the country and abroad. Creative expression, rather than being hampered, often opens out to the artist a new possibility of response and mutual recognition . . . Sahmat's visual art interventions have involved painters, sculptors, graphic artists and photographers, who have been invited to contribute their creative ideas on a number of themes. Each time an attempt has been made to propose a different format which opens up a dialogue between artists and persons from various other disciplines. . . .

As part of the celebrations for fifty years of India's independence, I proposed this *Gift for India* mail art project to the Sahmat collective. All celebrations have gifts as a part of their ritual exchange. These have some kind of a container, covers and packaging for the presentation of the gift, so it seemed appropriate to think of a box as a format. A five-inch white cube is the format we asked artists to work on. . . .

The fiftieth year of Indian independence will be celebrated throughout the year in many different ways. The Indian art scene has developed a peculiar tendency for extravagant showcasing of assorted works where the state and private dealers make an easy go of it in the name of the

1. John Held Jr., "Networker Essence," *Essence: International Networking Culture*, exh. cat. (Brisbane: Griffith University, 1995).

2. "Eugenio Dittborn: Correcaminos—Roadrunner," *Transcontinental: An Investigation of Reality* (London/New York: Verso, 1990).

3. Vivan Sundaram's statement, *Essence: International Networking Culture*.

4. "Eugenio Dittborn: Correcaminos—Roadrunner."

5. Guy Brett, "Eugenio Dittborn: Correcaminos—Roadrunner."

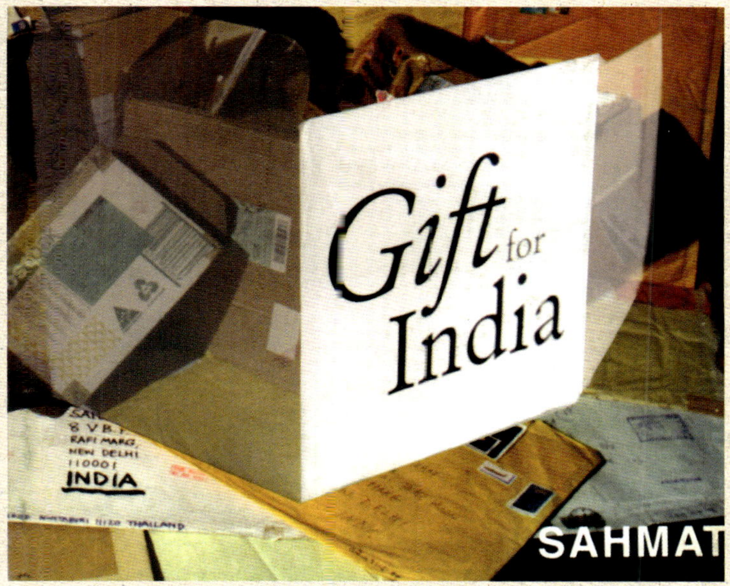

Cover of *Gift for India* catalogue (New Delhi: Sahmat, 1997).

national. There is an increasing need for non-institutional, democratic, informal initiatives that chip at this emerging monolith.

By its very nature Sahmat works as an alternative space to mainstream politics and commerce. *Gift for India* is part of a series of exhibitions marking historical moments in the life of the nation, but it works like something of a gesture. We send out a participatory signal and receive a response in the same spirit.

We invited artists from all over the world to send a gift box and the response, despite the short time, was overwhelming. Almost 200 artists' gift boxes constitute the exhibition. This spontaneous response makes up a sub-text which says that in a world of commodification, artists of considerable international reputation are happy to join with peers, strangers, young artists, to extend themselves creatively, and generously. The care with which some of our foreign participants have conceived and crafted this small sculptural project is gratifying. The messages that have come with the boxes endorsing the idea, Sahmat's existence and artists' solidarity on a common imaginative ground, make the project truly *a gift among friends*.

The Gift Box

The gift is in most cases a 5-inch cube:
the gift box is made of cardboard, wood, plastic, bronze, cement, steel, leather, copper, aluminium

the gift box has in it mud, water, clay, stone, salt, tea-leaves, feathers, fur, hair, seeds, egg-shells, sea-shells, ceramic, paraffin wax, glass, mirrors, straw mats, cloth

the gift box makes references to the **Buddha**, the **Bible** and **Gandhi**

the gift box has images of history, freedom, politics, **violence**, imprisonment

the gift box has salt and a knife **wound** to recall a march

the gift box is locked, has **nails** pierced, is **black**

the gift box is filled with **earth** from across the globe and **barbed wire** as a reminder of the exiled/missing

the gift box is a **speaking** box, a speaking **tree** with an excess of leaves, images, hidden messages, roots to the **past**

the gift box is a fragment of a **house**, hut, cage, and **heart**

the gift box is a space for **women**, struggles, symbolic objects, children's clothes

the gift box has the mirrored faces of **man** and the world he occupies

the gift box is a landscape, **map**, the planet earth, for **ecological** well-being

the gift box is a **bridge** that connects nature culture people

the gift box is an **object** for contemplation, is

white
the gift box is **celebration**, pleasure, play

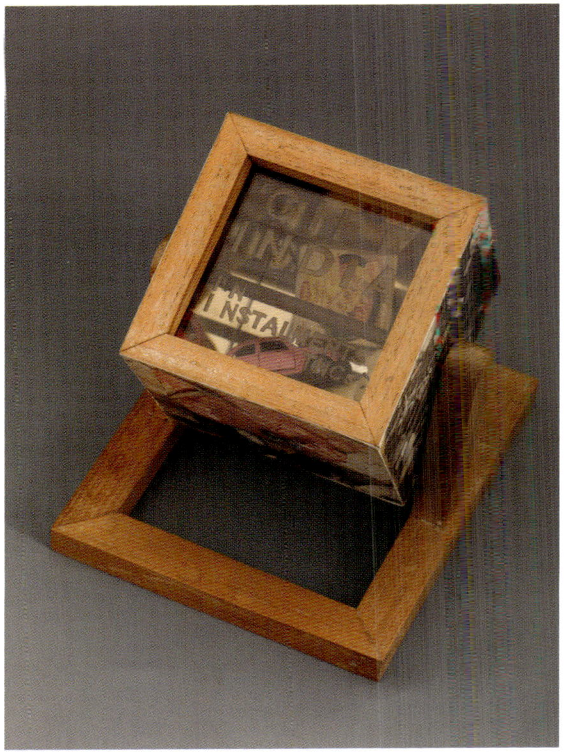

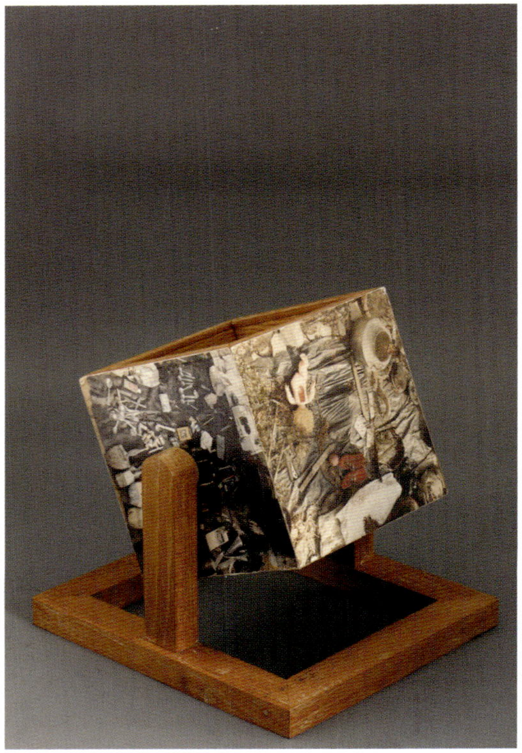

VIVAN SUNDARAM (India)
Gift India in Installments, 1997, wood, mirror, toys, photographs, and glass, 5 x 5 x 5 inches. Collection: Tasneem Zakaria Mehta.

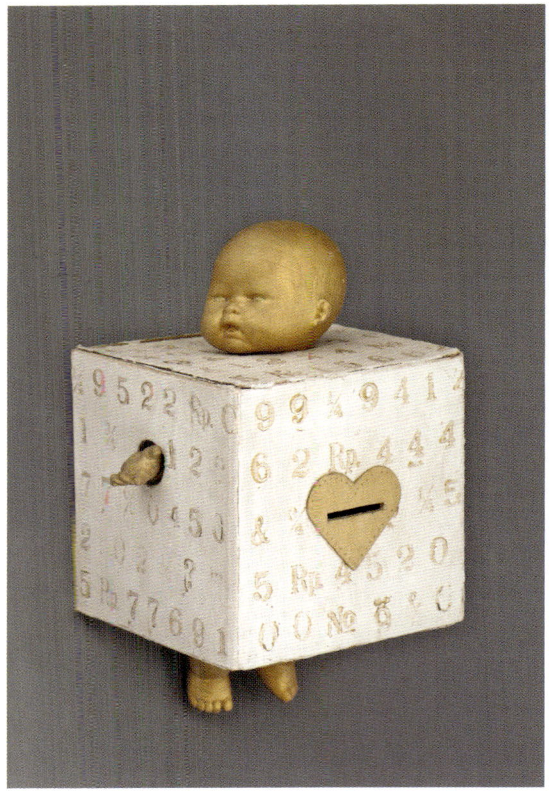

AUGUS SUWAGE (Indonesia)
Mohon Doa Restu and Little Bit of Love (Begging for prayer and blessing), 1997, plastic doll, gold paint, and wood on cardboard box, 5 x 5 x 5 inches. Collection: Tasneem Zakaria Mehta.

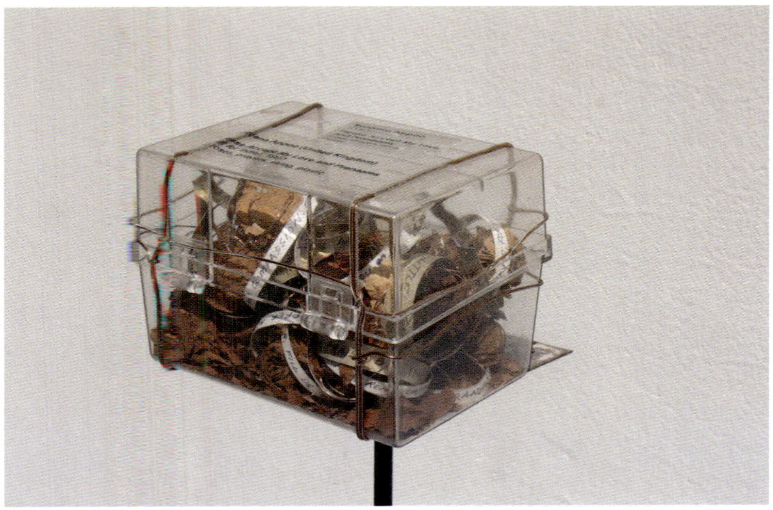

RANJANA APPOO (United Kingdom)
Please Accept My Love and Pranams, 1997, twenty-one roses, prayers, string, and plastic, 5 x 5 x 5 inches.

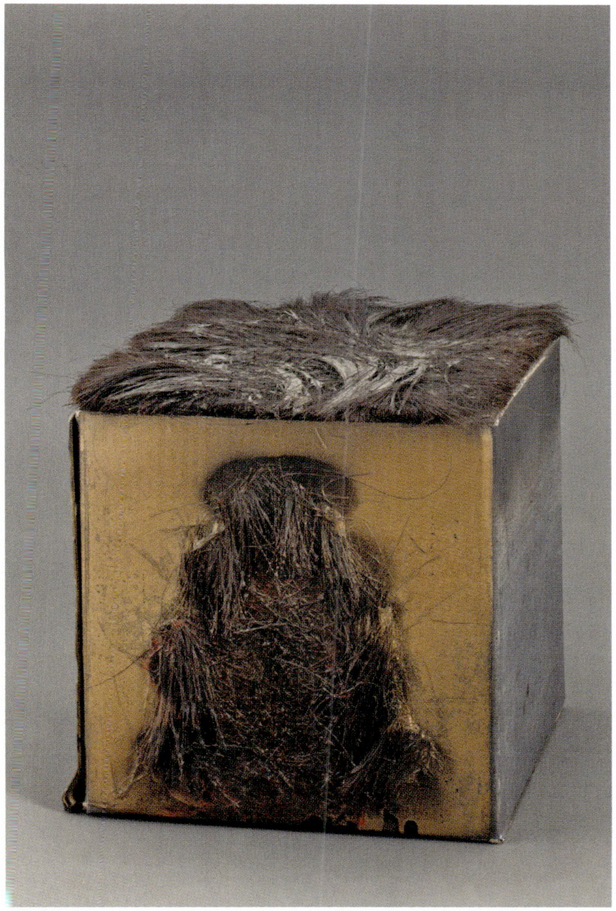

NINDITYO ADIPURNOMO (Indonesia)
Who has ever thought of using the body as art, 1997, hair, gold paint, and glue on cardboard box, 5 x 5 x 5 inches. Collection: Tasneem Zakaria Mehta.

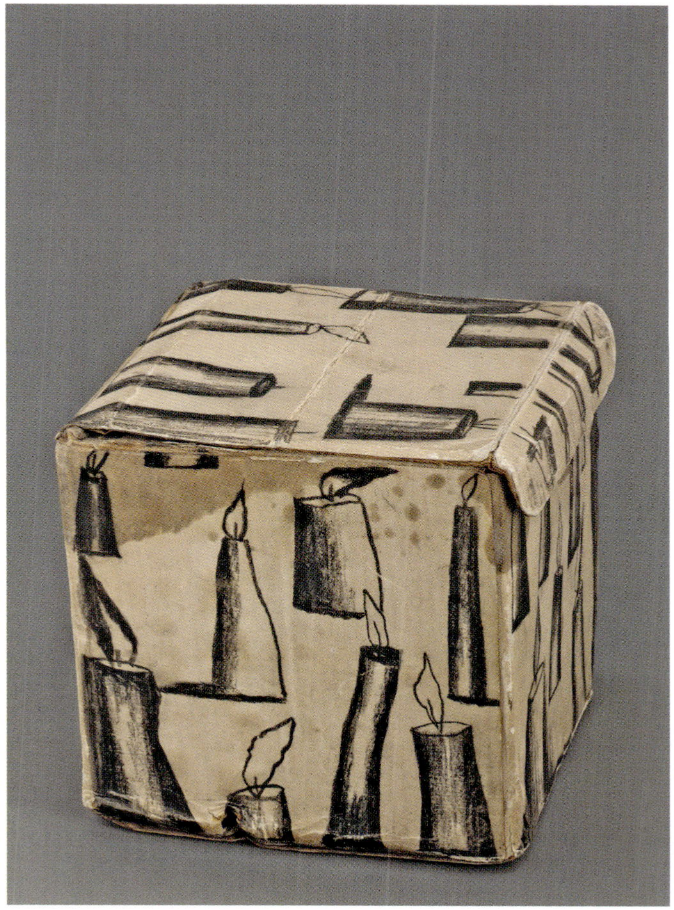

RIMZON N. N. (India)
Candle made in India, 1997, wax and charcoal on cardboard box, 5 x 5 x 5 inches. Collection: Tasneem Zakaria Mehta.

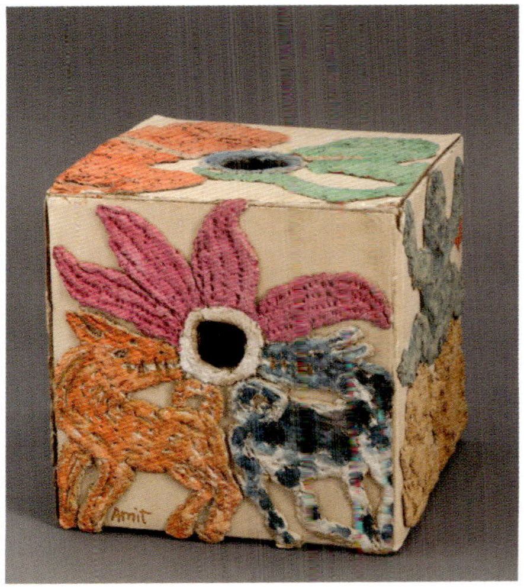

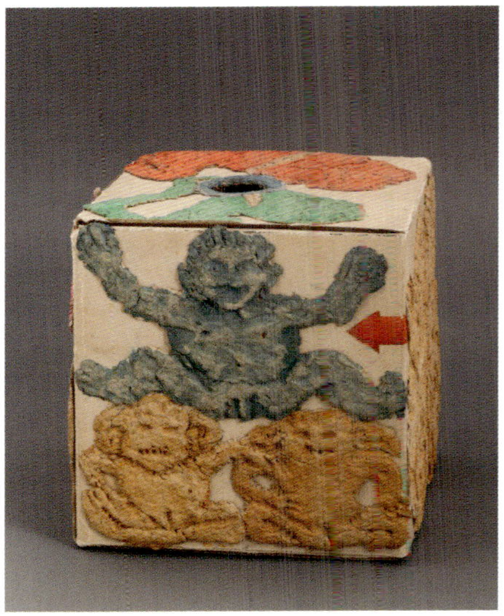

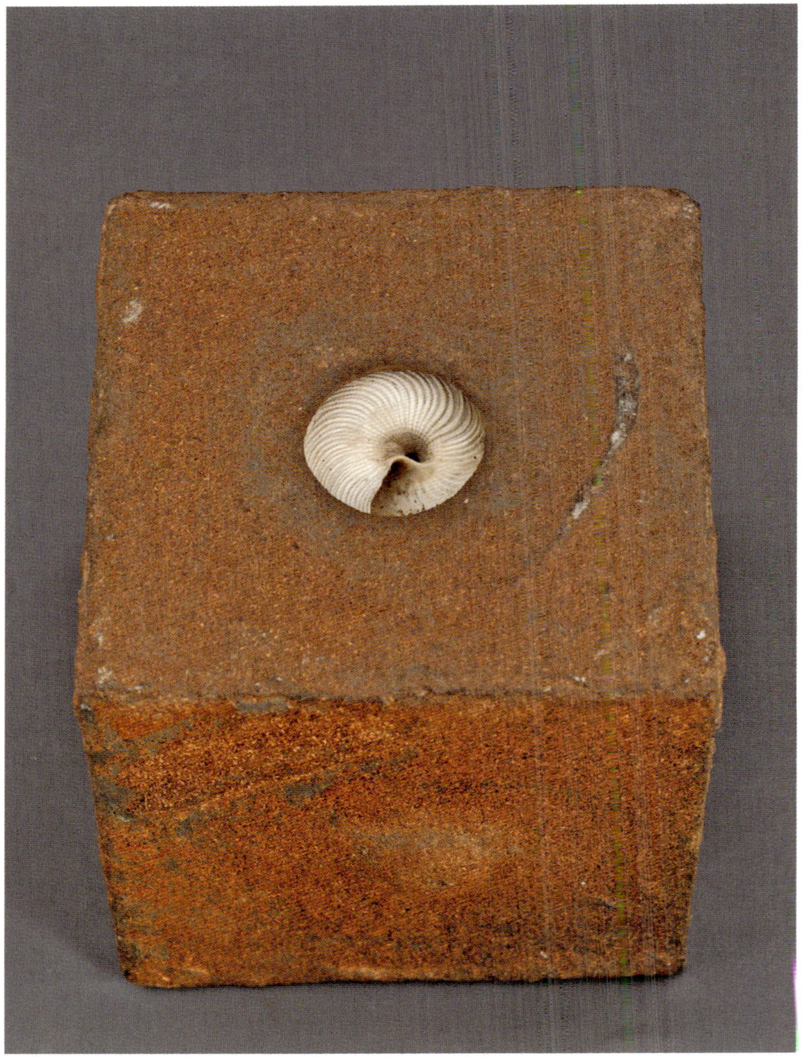

AMIT AMBALAL (India)
Untitled, 1997, papier-mâché on cardboard box, 5 x 5 x 5 inches. Collection: Tasneem Zakaria Mehta.

GARGI RAINA (India)
Untitled, 1997, shell and colored sand on cardboard box, 5 x 5 x 5 inches. Collection: Tasneem Zakaria Mehta.

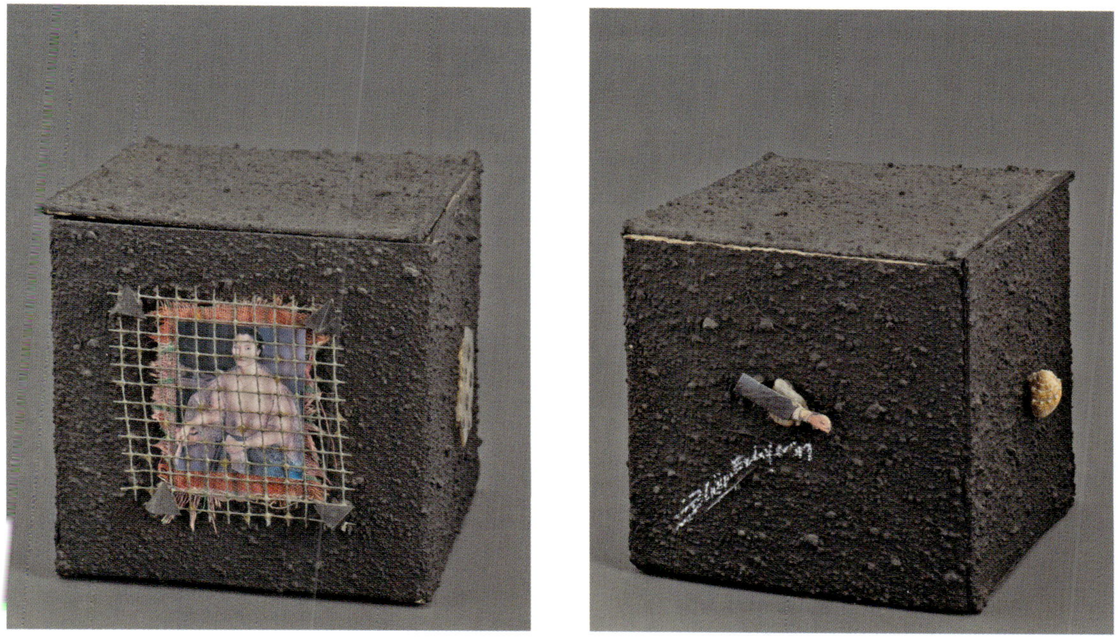

IMELDA CAJIPE ENDAYA (Philippines)
Theodora's Box, 1997, cloth, metal wire, and photograph on cardboard box, 5 x 5 x 5 inches. Collection: Tasneem Zakaria Mehta.

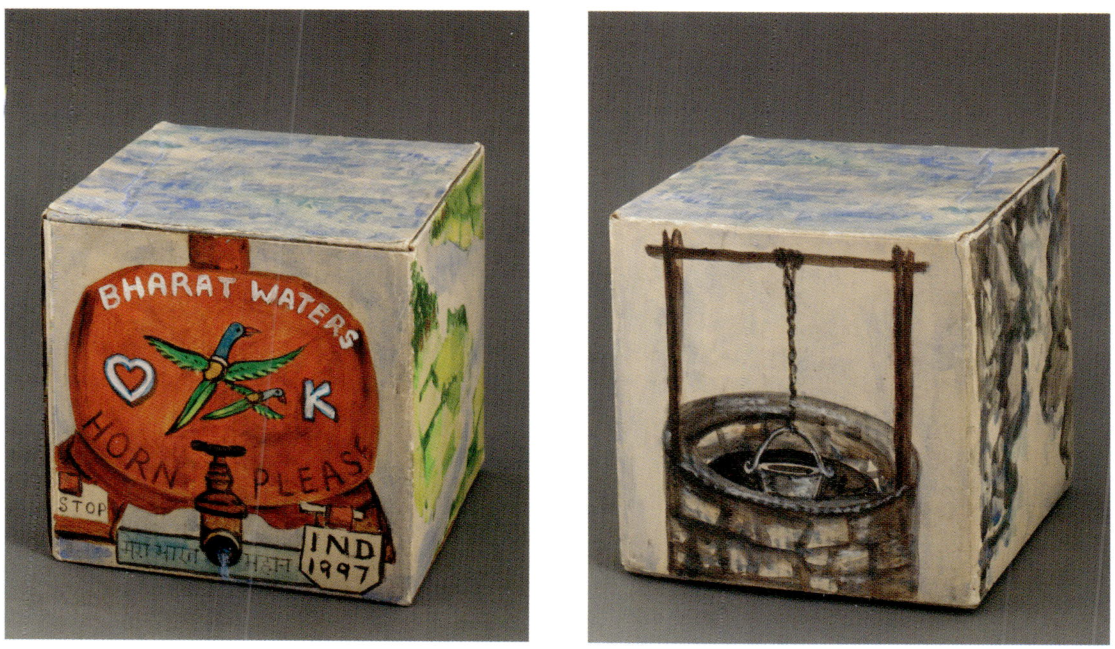

MEERA DEVIDAYAL (India)
Water, 1997, watercolor on cardboard box, 5 x 5 x 5 inches. Collection: Tasneem Zakaria Mehta.

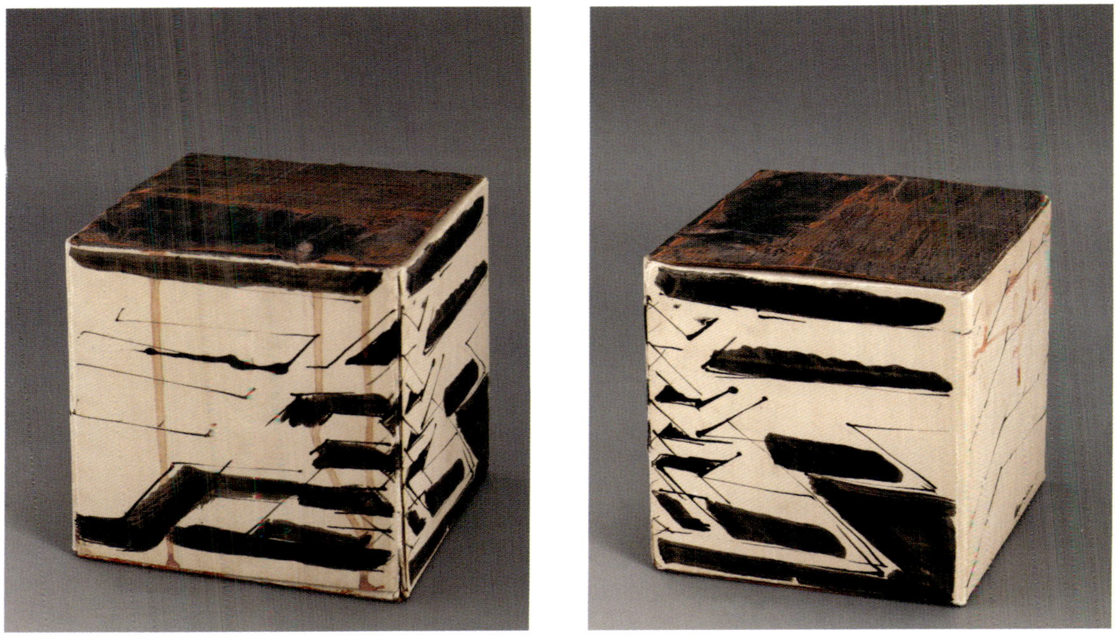

VISWANADHAN (France)
Untitled, 1997, watercolor on cardboard box, 5 x 5 x 5 inches. Collection: Tasneem Zakaria Mehta.

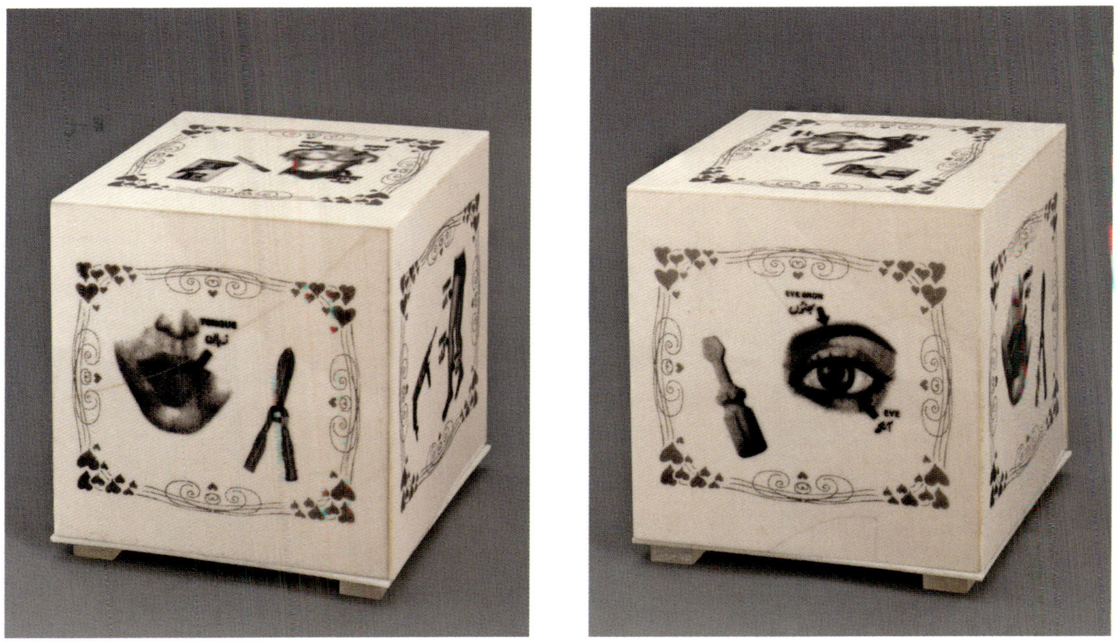

IFTIKHAR AND ELIZABETH DADI (Pakistan)
Untitled, 1997, print on plastic, 5 x 5 x 5 inches. Collection: Tasneem Zakaria Mehta.

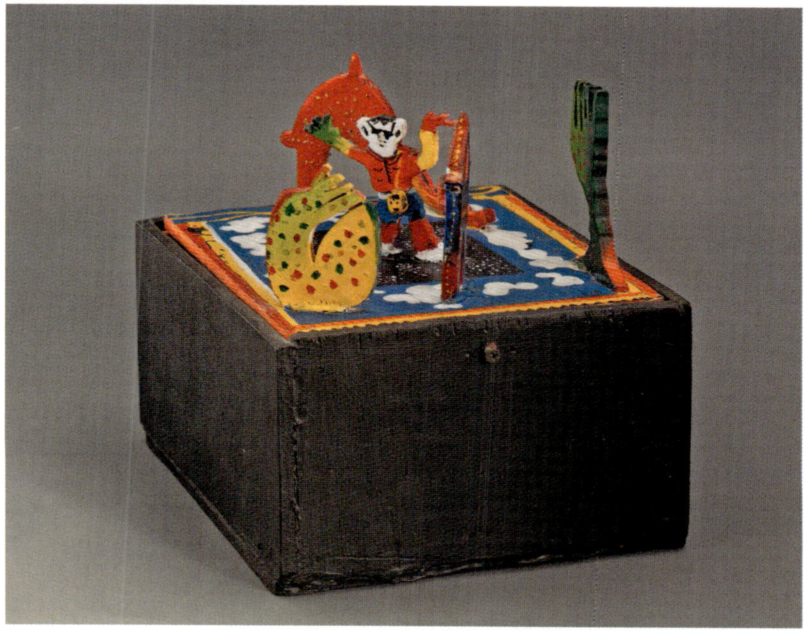

AZYZ SHARAFY (United States)
Cosmic Confusion (Layout for a walk-in installation), 1997, acrylic on wood, approximately 5 x 5 x 5 inches. Collection: Tasneem Zakaria Mehta.

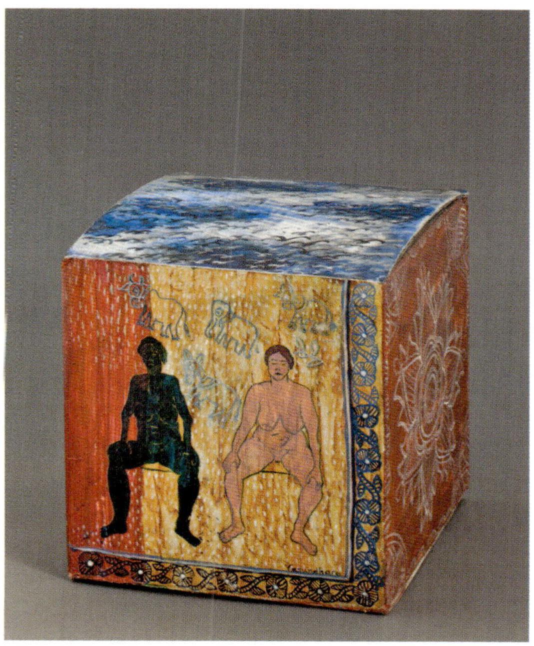

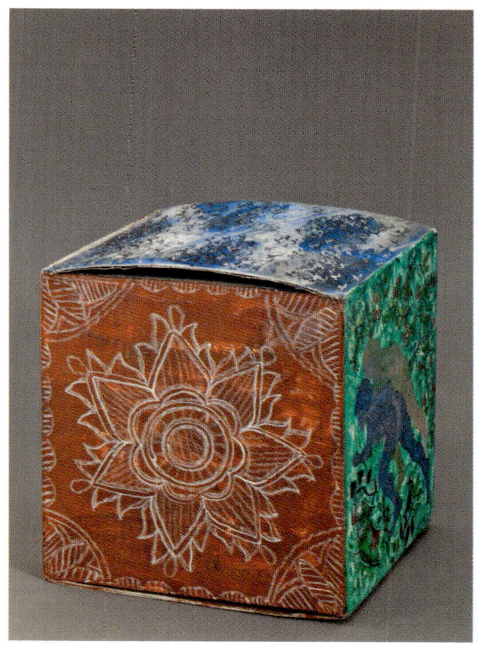

VASUNDHARA TEWARI (India)
Untitled, 1997, watercolor on cardboard box, 5 x 5 x 5 inches. Collection: Tasneem Zakaria Mehta.

2001 *Art on the Move*

Especially rapid changes to India's capital city, which includes the areas known as Delhi, New Delhi, and "New" New Delhi, are evident in its dynamic visual culture. Artists, through various modes of expression, engage with the explosion of images and other visual elements that characterize the city and its streets. The breaking down of established conventions of traditional, popular, and contemporary art has resulted in a fluid crossing of borders. For *Art on the Move*, Sahmat invited young artists to conceive mobile works that would take cues from modes of transport used by laborers, street vendors, and rickshaw pullers—namely, bicycles, pushcarts, and hand/cycle rickshaws. Building on a ready-made base of such humble vehicles, the artists erected iconic, architectural, circus-like, and ritual forms, and then demonstrated their viability by riding, pushing, and pulling them out before the spectators and on to the road. In an imaginative rendering of three key terms—art, mobility, and public space—Sahmat's *Art on the Move* was among the group's earliest projects seeking a wider engagement among artists, the city, and its people.

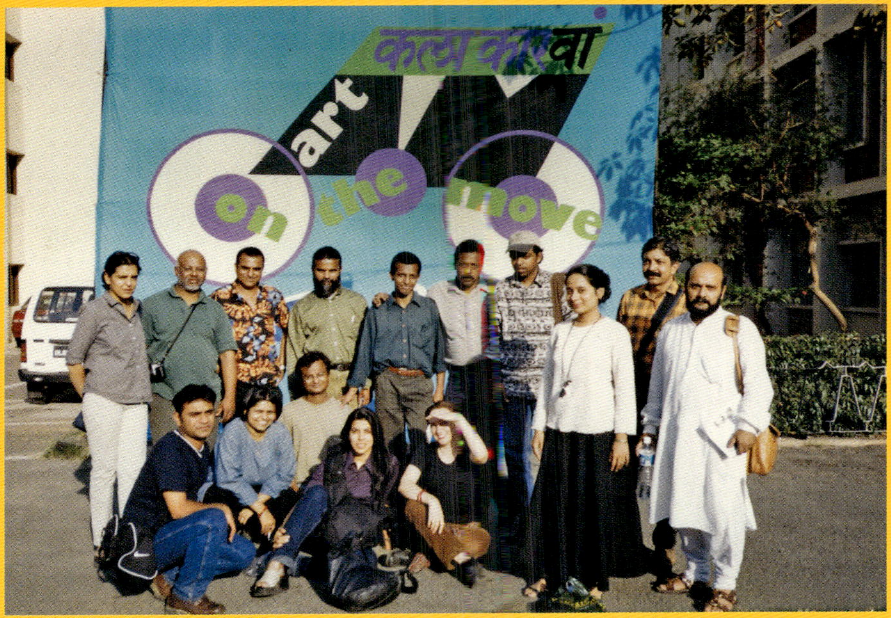

Art on the Move, participating artists, Delhi, 2001. Standing (from left to right): Bharti Kher, Subba Ghosh, Jehangir Jani, M. J. Enas, L. N. Tallur, Alex Mathew, M. Sovan Kumar, Eleena Banik, Prasanta Mukherjee, Veer Munshi. Sitting (from left to right): Manjunath Kamath, Ma[illegible] Ray, Kausik Mukhopadhyay, Reena Saini Kallat, Nicola Durvasula.

The project, conceived by Vivan Sundaram, differed in scale and format from earlier projects. Sahmat received sixty proposals from artists; sixteen were chosen by the selection committee

(Rajeev Sethi, K. T. Ravindran, Amit Mukhopadhyay, Vivan Sundaram, Shamshad, and Ram Rahman). The selected artists developed their works in their respective studios and then brought them to a weeklong workshop at Aya Nagar in Delhi, where they fabricated the artworks on wheels.

Artists responded to these suggested themes:

The city: a site and space for collective identity. The democratic citizen is under assault by forces that are breaking secular congregations, dividing society along communal lines.

Imaging shelter/home in the metropolis. The right to live and work in the city is a privilege not only of the elite. With its informal settlements of migrant labor, the big city is a vast human resource that develops its own infrastructure.

Goods and globalization. India is now open to an uninterrupted flow of goods from across the world produced and traded by multinational corporations, which satisfy the needs of a growing consumerist middle class. Indigenously produced goods move along other routes, fulfilling the needs of the majority of the people.

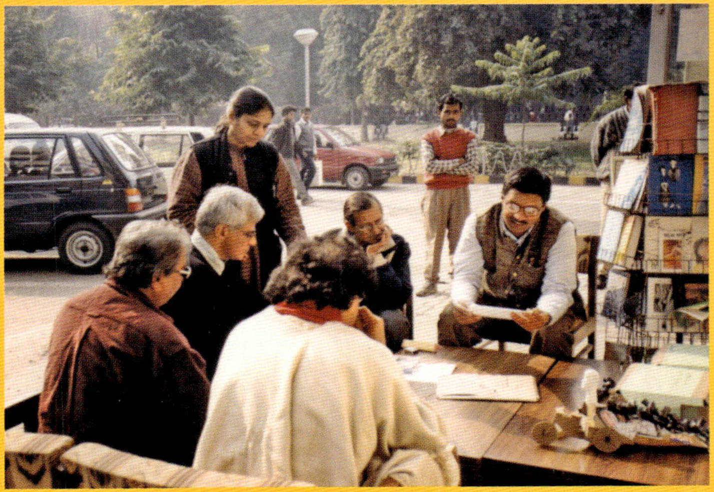

Meeting of the selection committee for *Art on the Move*, Delhi, 2001. (Clockwise from bottom): Rajeev Sethi (back to camera), Shamshad, Vivan Sundaram, Ashok Kumari (standing), Amit Mukhopadhyay, Ram Rahman.

NICOLA DURVASULA
Discussing Politics, Part III, 2001, painted wood.

Politics here is the politics of everything in life, both big and small. The politics within a thought, a word, an action . . . within the mind, the house, the world. It can include the politics of art. In the realization of the idea of the cutout, the placing of a paintbrush in my hand establishes the possibility that I am in some way related to the visual arts. I feel that the paintbrush is still the most identifiable tool of the trade. It represents what I am, an artist. There can be many associations with the paintbrush, at all levels. For example, "paint the town red" indulge in riotous fun. Or, on a more serious note, the brush could be seen as weapon-like. For example Picasso, on the completion of his masterpiece *Guernica*, spoke of "painting [being] . . . an instrument of war." Using paint and paintbrush, he portrayed the absolute horror and tragedy of war. There is an irony of sorts in the fact that I have not painted this cutout myself. It is by K. Basava Krishna Prasad, a cinema hoarding painter based in Hyderabad. Prasad comes from a community of board painters and has been painting film stars, politicians, and religious leaders (ranging from ten feet to eighty feet tall). In realizing this project at the workshop, I have adapted the bamboo scaffolding to suit the structure of the pushcart on which the cutout is placed. A ladder extends midway up to the back of the head of the cutout. This structure could be seen as a space/a site in itself. —N. D.

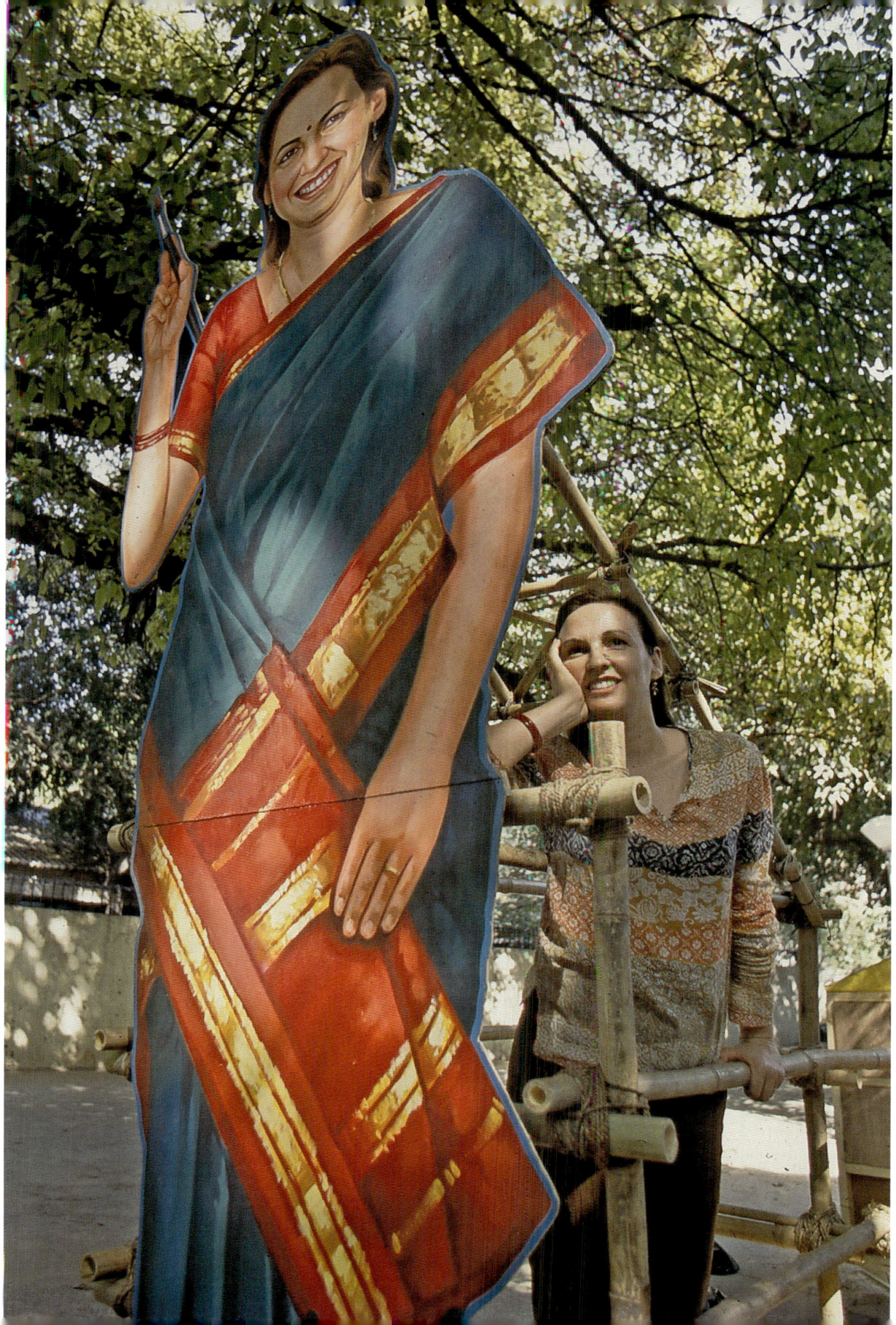

The visual that I have created is a manifestation of the survival needs of the global human, using of course the middle-class paradigm. A bedroom with an attached toilet is the prerequisite. So this comes together on the pedestal of the pushcart. An appliqued canopy (crafted traditionally in Orissa) becomes the manual sky hoisted above the pedestal on four bamboos. A mattress is spread on the wooden base of the cart and two plump pillows rest on it, creating an ambience of leisure and comfort. The standard sleeping package for the middle class is complete. No, wait. There is something else that cannot be missed. An Indian-style toilet has been installed right there in the middle of the bed.

With the stage set, the second part of the project began. Twenty transparent bags were given to twenty middle-class homes in the neighborhood and the people were asked to put their used or consumed goods inside the bags within the camp period of seven days. The bags were opened on the last day and all that was in them is displayed on the cart. —M. S. K.

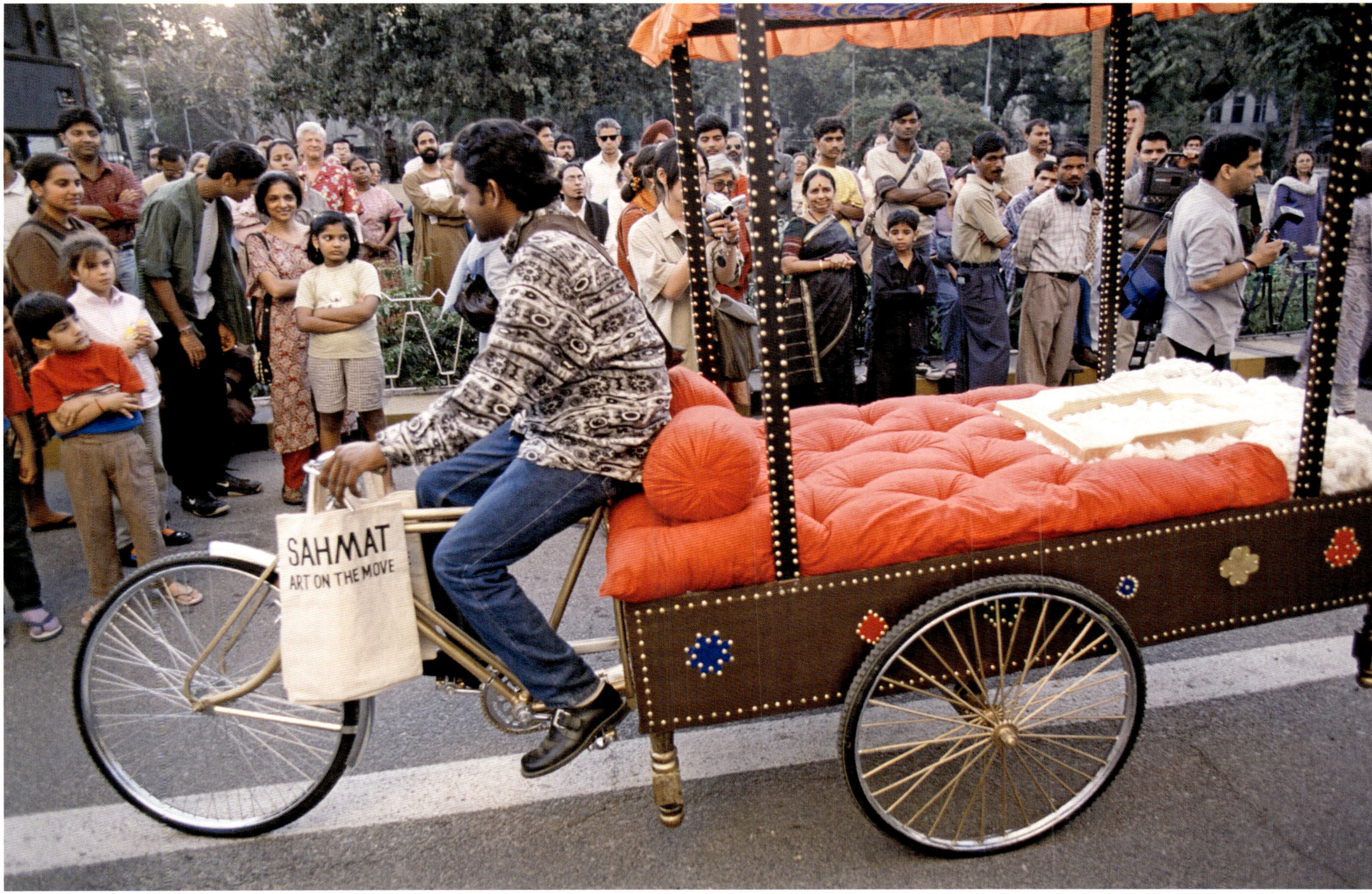

M. SOVAN KUMAR
bicycling his work *Mobile Shelter* at the opening event for *Art on the Move*, Delhi, March 18, 2001.

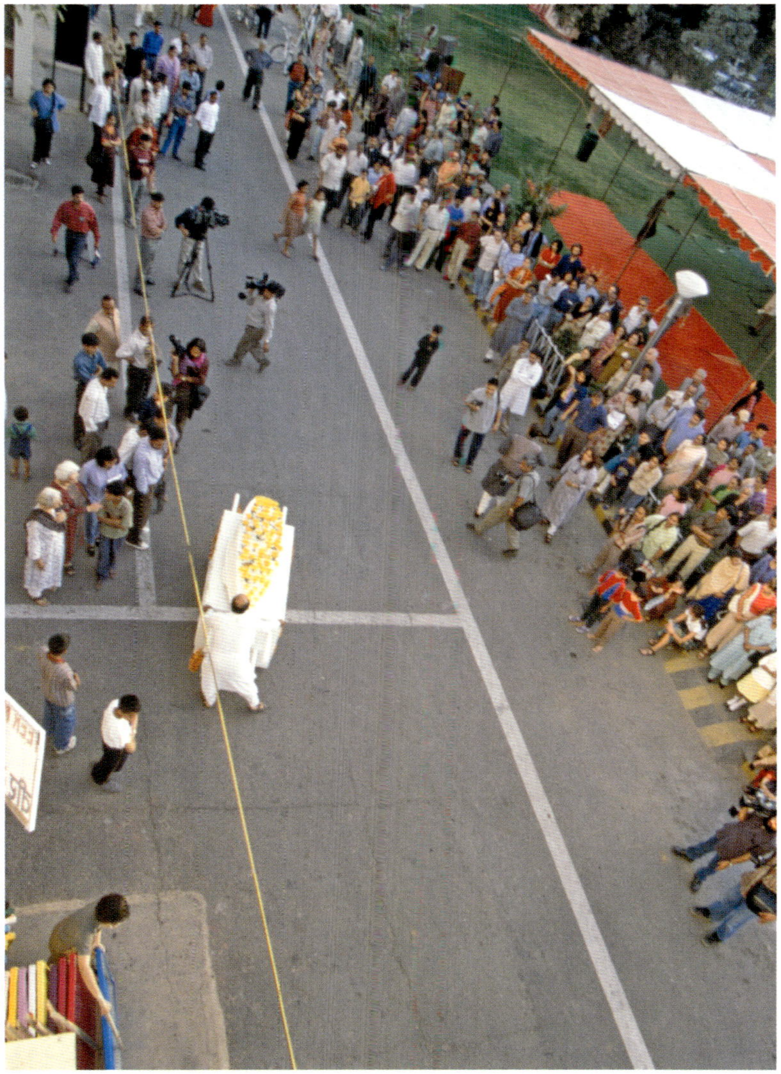

Veer Munshi pushing *Burial* at the opening event for *Art on the Move*, Vitthalbhai Patel House, New Delhi, March 18, 2001.

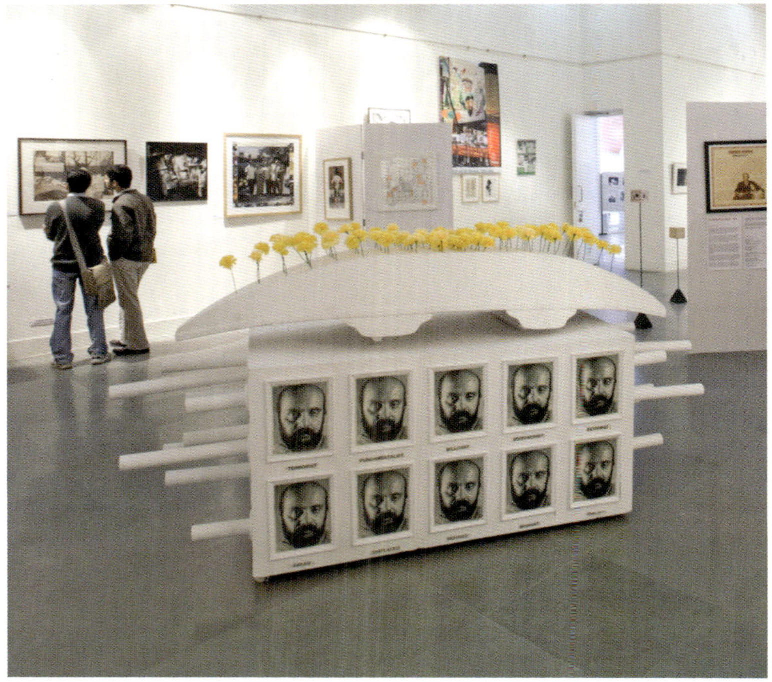

VEER MUNSHI
Burial, installation view of *Image, Music, Text: 20 Years of Sahmat*, M. F. Husain Gallery, Jamia Millia Islamia University, Delhi, 2009.

The boat, which was once an invitation to the happy valley of Jammu and Kashmir, no longer floats on the still waters of Dal Lake. The laughing girls do not place in it their bouquets of fresh flowers to be sold to the tourists. The boat is inverted and placed on a cart and plastic flowers rest on it. On the oars are fresh flower garlands that the viewers can take and hang on the picture, which repeats itself frame after frame from 1991 to 2000, symbolizing a decade of violence. This installation sees present-day human creatures in the grip of irrational and vicious violence. The content involved not only the political degradation but also the tension and the lull between victims and tormentors. The horrendous happenings have reduced the status of a common Kashmiri to a "label": SECESSIONIST, EXTREMIST, FUNDAMENTALIST, or, for that matter, DISPLACED, MIGRANT, EXILED, REFUGEE. These words are in common use in the media and they point to a collective insanity. In this episode, the boatman and I stand together to seek Refuge/Shelter. Or is it a Burial? —V. M.

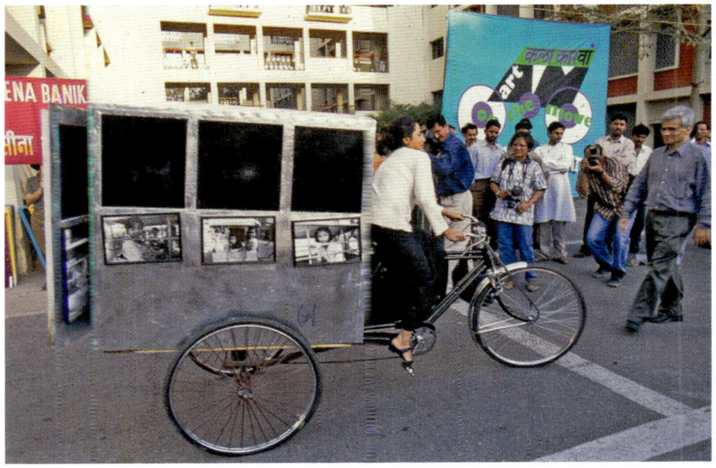

ELEENA BANIK
pulling her work *Mum, Please Don't Tell Me to Go to School*, at the opening event for *Art on the Move*, Vitthalbhai Patel House, New Delhi, March 18, 2001.

The logo for *Art on the Move*.
Design: Ram Rahman.

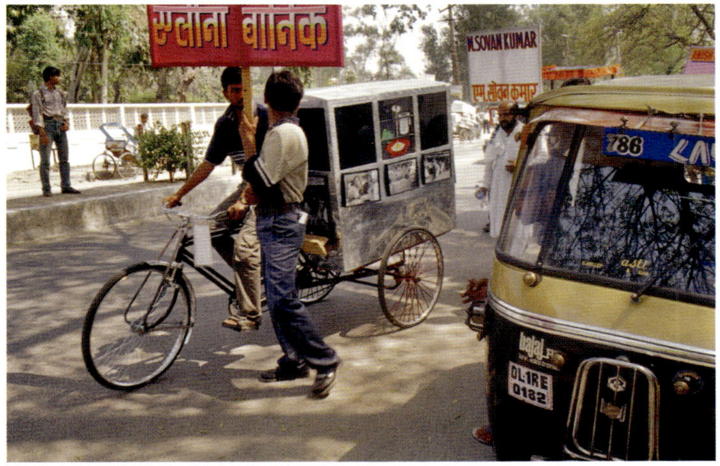

Eleena Banik's *Mum, Please Don't Tell Me to Go to School*, at Jamia Nagar, New Delhi, 2001.

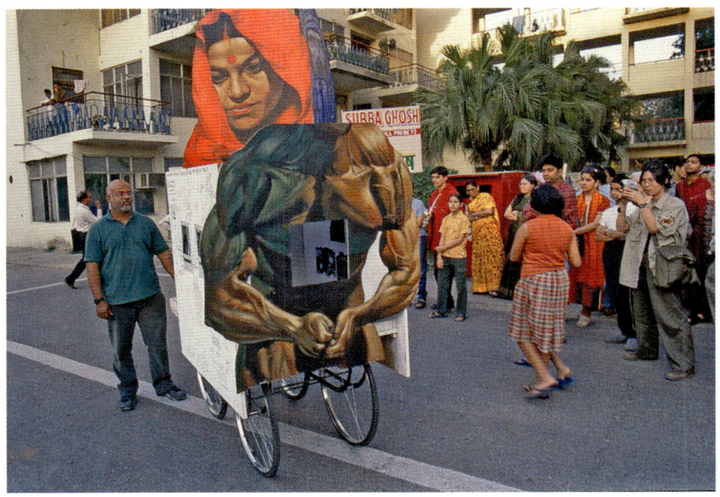

SUBBA GHOSH
with his work *What Will You Be*, at the opening event for *Art on the Move*, Vitthalbhai Patel House, New Delhi, March 18, 2001.

VIVAN SUNDARAM
In a sense, *Art on the Move* for me was Sahmat's most innovative project as a form of public art. Especially the format of the artwork—I think the fact that it was erected on a moveable pedestal, a platform on wheels, was the most interesting thing. This form of transport with four wheels and a flat platform is used by street vendors for selling goods, vegetables, anything at all . . . they move to a particular spot or through the streets selling their wares. Also, we made it at a workshop, in a lively studio atmosphere. The pedestals, in a sense, were all the same, and while the artworks were actually being assembled, each artist developed it to expand from that basic platform using a whole range of materials. This was the most stimulating and exciting aspect of the work.

For the opening, artists took their works in a kind of procession, going down crowded streets among the public. Suddenly people would see these quite unusual objects and think: what are these items and are they really for sale? People would come up and view them as if it was an exhibition, and stop and ask questions. So, in a way, it was also the most interactive of all the art projects.

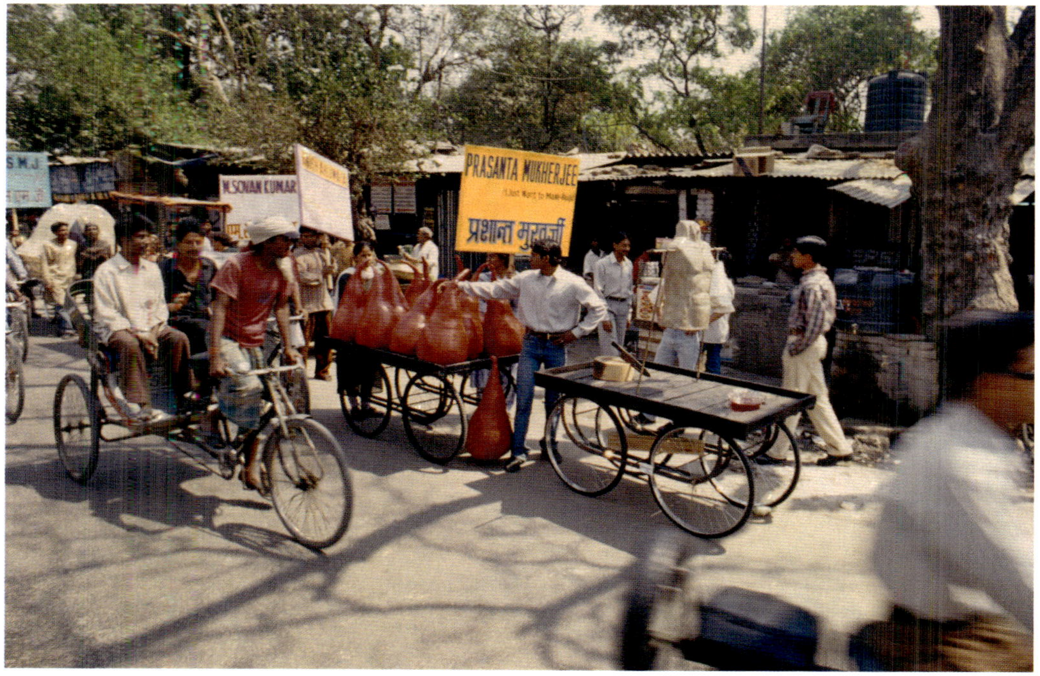

Street scene, *Art on the Move*, at Jamia Nagar, New Delhi, 2001.

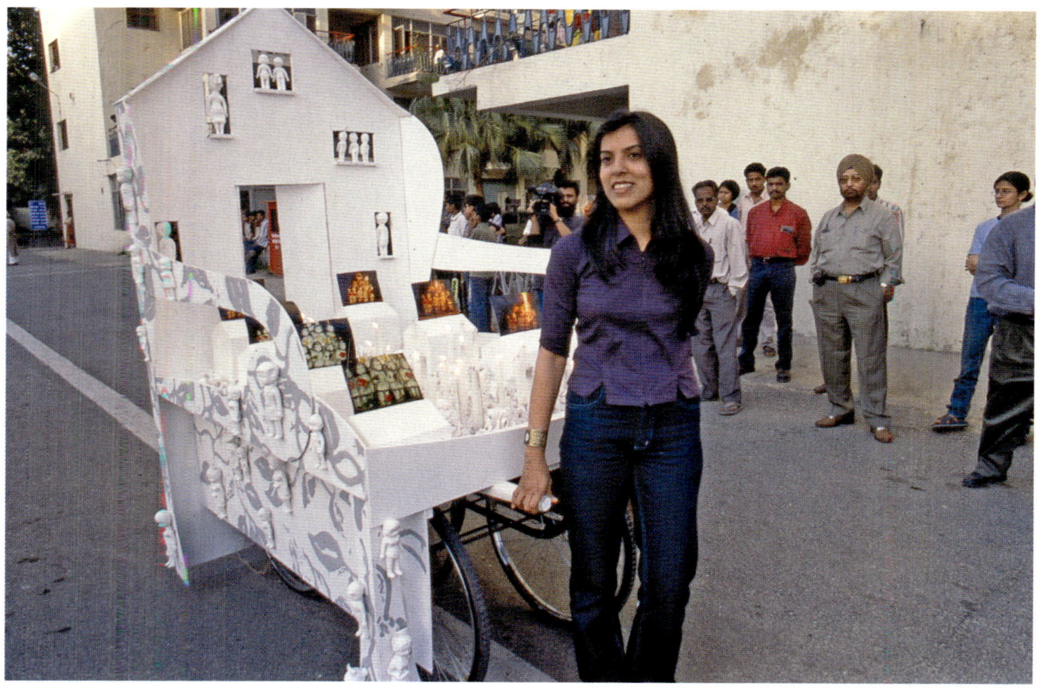

REENA SAINI KALLAT with her work *Heal Anthem*, at the opening event for *Art on the Move*, Vitthalbhai Patel House, New Delhi, March 18, 2001.

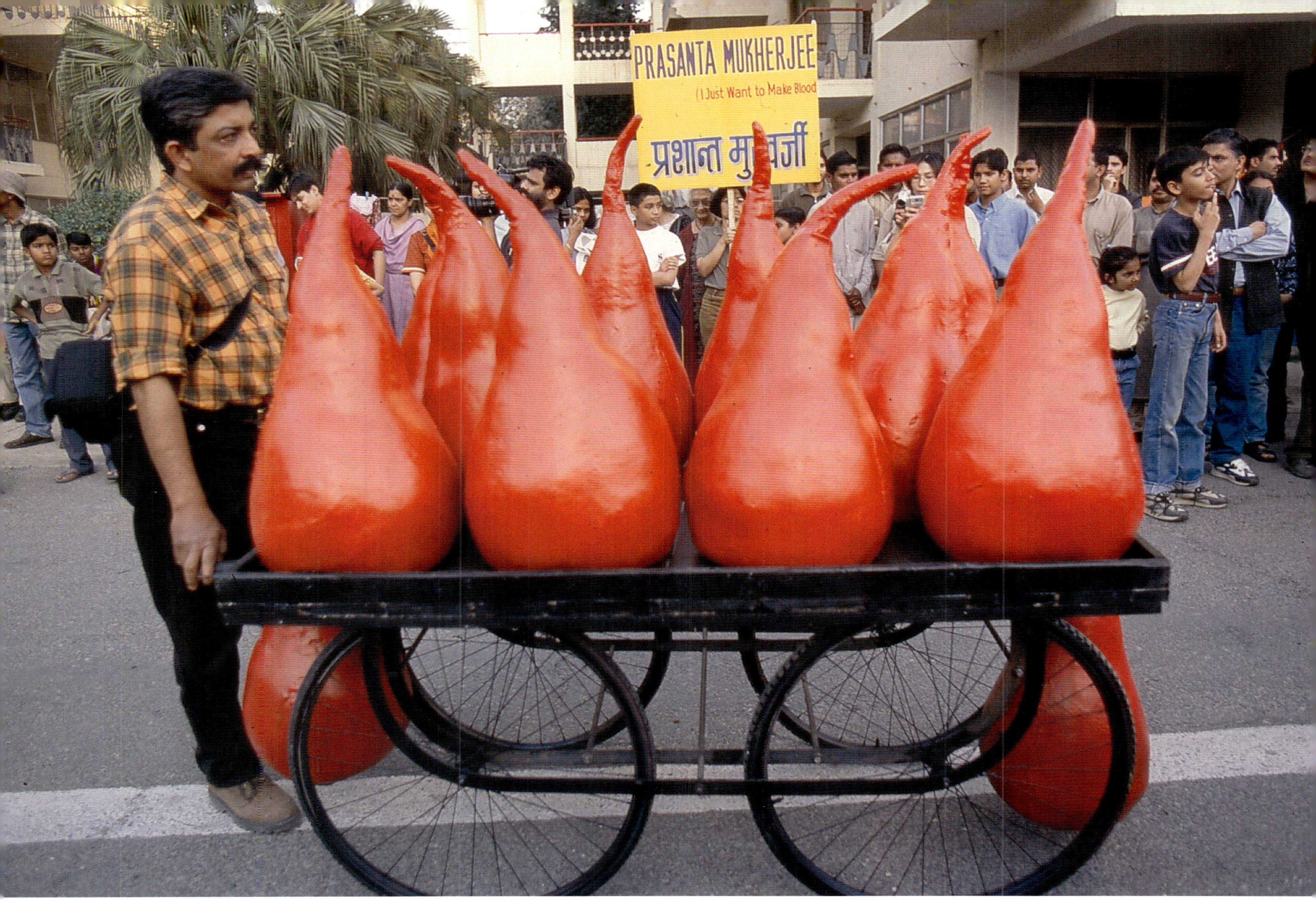

PRASANTA MUKHERJEE
pushing his work, *Aftermath*, at the opening event for *Art on the Move*, Vitthalbhai Patel House, New Delhi, March 18, 2001.

2002–
2003

Ways of Resisting

Sahmat's exhibition *Ways of Resisting* (December 23, 2002–January 4, 2003) spotlighted Indian artistic production during a volatile political decade of sectarian and communal violence, in the years between the demolition of the Babri Masjid (Babur's Mosque) in Ayodhya in December 1992 and the massacre in Gujarat in February 2002. Curator Vivan Sundaram chose existing works from the decade that were for the most part emotionally charged and ambitious in scale, while also introducing new strategies of contemporary art-making to Indian audiences. Featuring modes of opposing political and social forces of religious fundamentalism through installations, videos, paintings, photographs, and archival material, one of the curatorial aims of *Ways of Resisting* was to examine Sahmat's role as a shared platform and its influence on the artists who worked with the group. Many of the assembled artists had been activists since the 1990s, and they sought to develop a critical language that reflected and critiqued their historical situation as they saw it: the distortion of democratic and secular values, and the parodying of these values by the then ruling coalition led by the Bharatiya Janata Party.

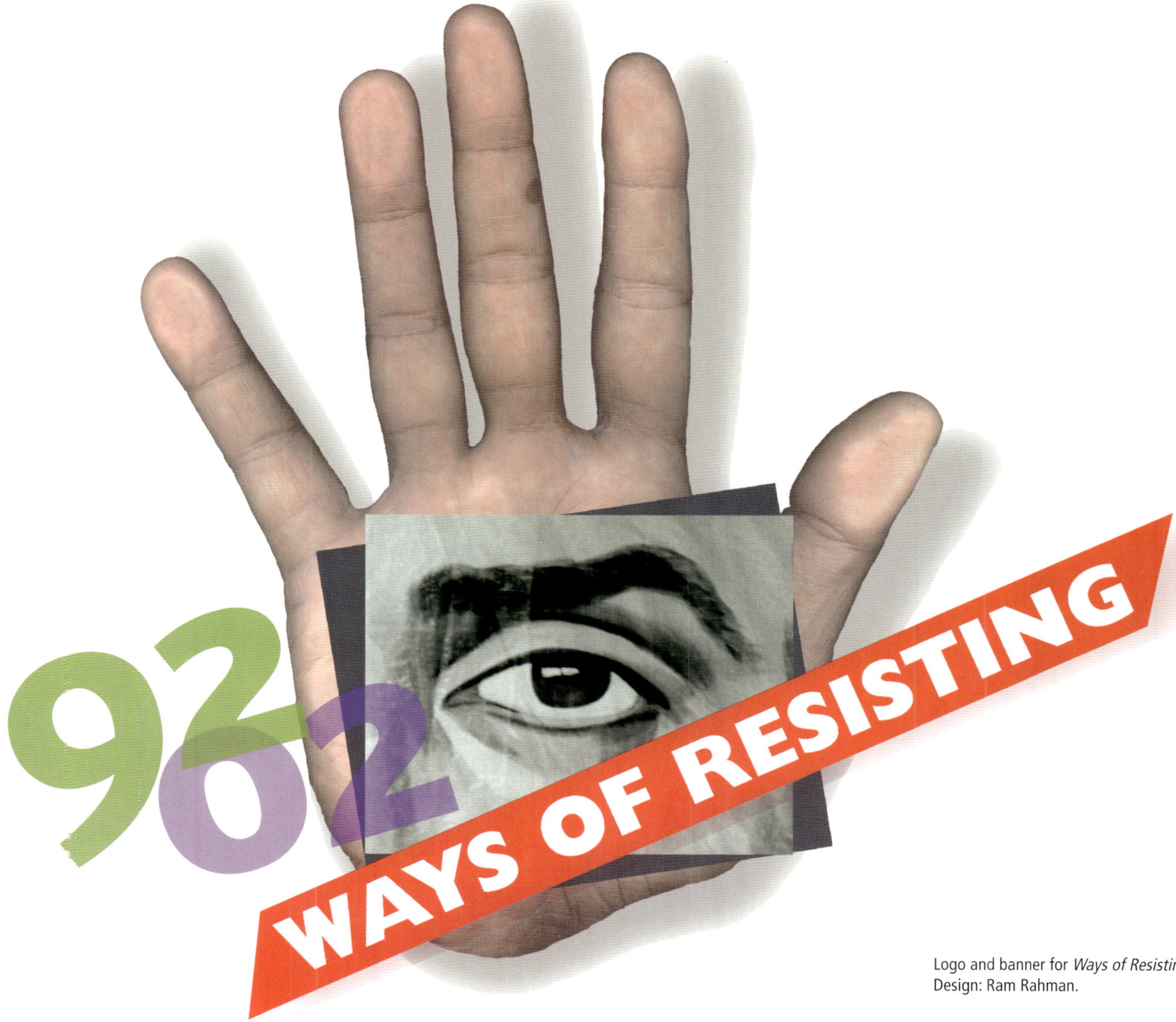

Logo and banner for *Ways of Resisting*, 2002.
Design: Ram Rahman.

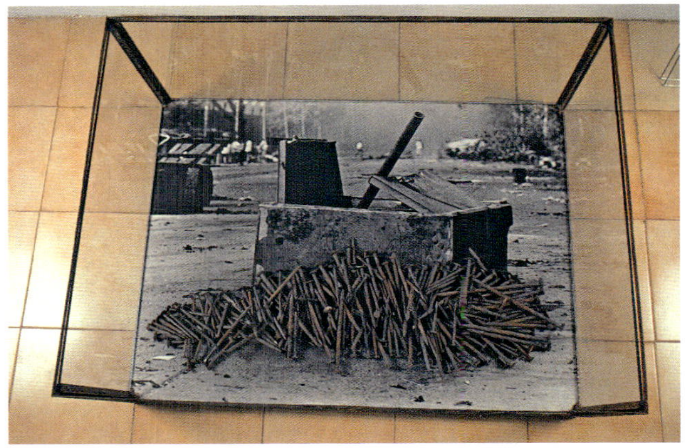

Memorial: Burial 1, 1993, iron and glass vitrine, iron nails, and black-and-white photograph (by Hoshi Jal, *Times of India*, Bombay, February 23, 1993), 19 x 24 x 12 inches.

Memorial: Burial 2, 1993, iron and glass vitrine, iron nails, and black-and-white photograph (by Hoshi Jal, *Times of India*, Bombay, February 23, 1993), 19 x 24 x 12 inches.

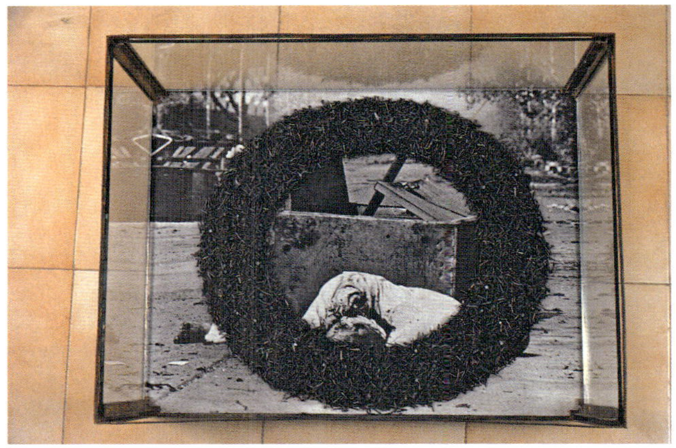

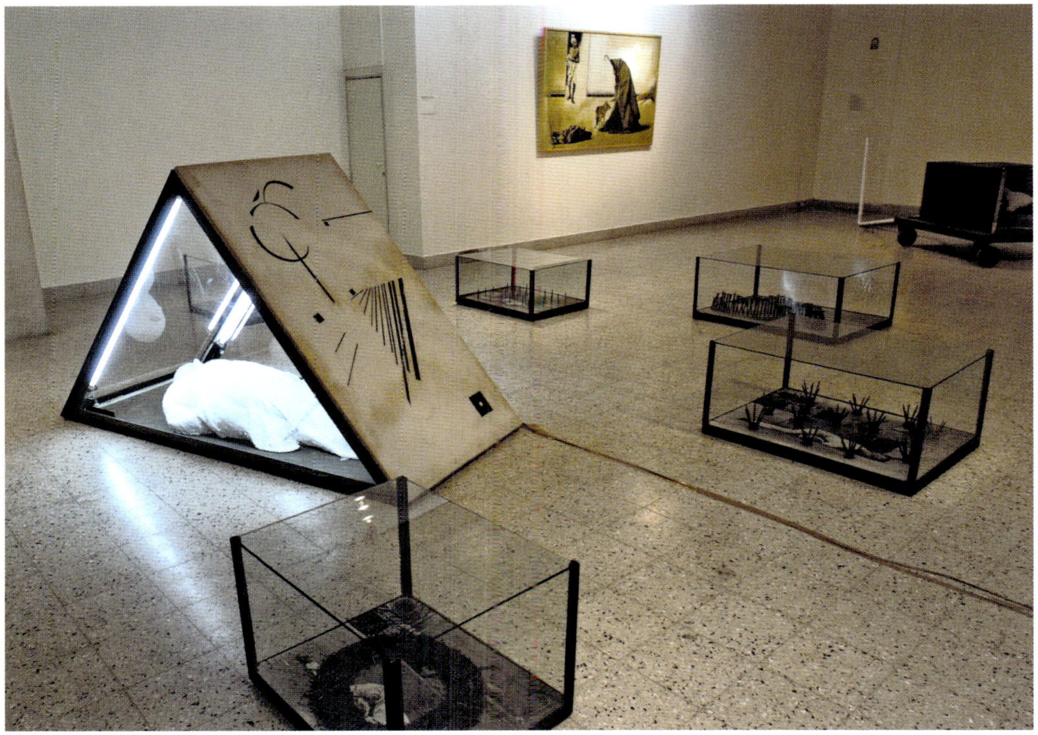

VIVAN SUNDARAM
Memorial: Mausoleum, 1993, installation of steel, glass, neon light, white inlaid marble, and plaster cast of live body, 54 x 76 x 36 inches. Collection: the artist.

In his conceptually structured installations, Vivan Sundaram proposes that the political remains unrepresented in most of the representational conventions used in Indian art. His sculptural installation *Memorial*, based on a newspaper photograph taken during the communal riots in Mumbai by the photographer Hoshi Jal, positions the dead man on the street as an icon of political shame. In an elegiac act the artist gives the man a mantle of nails, places the iron coffin on a gun carriage, and buries him on behalf of the state—an attempt to retrieve a political ethic through an acknowledgement of public death. **—Geeta Kapur**

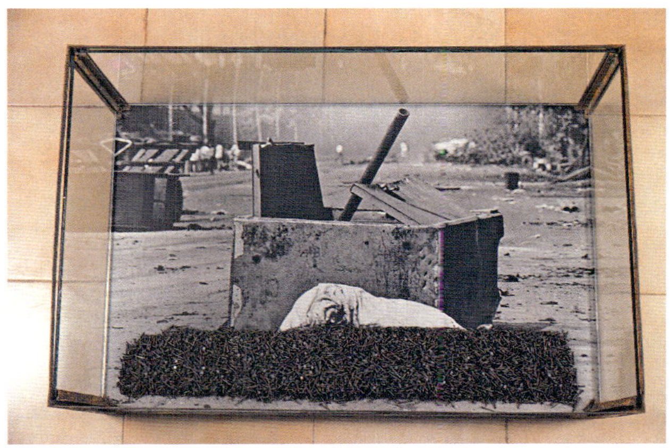

Memorial: Iron Pyre, 1993, black-and-white photograph (by Hoshi Jal, *Times of India*, Bombay, February 23, 1993) with nails in vitrine, 29 x 40 x 15 inches.

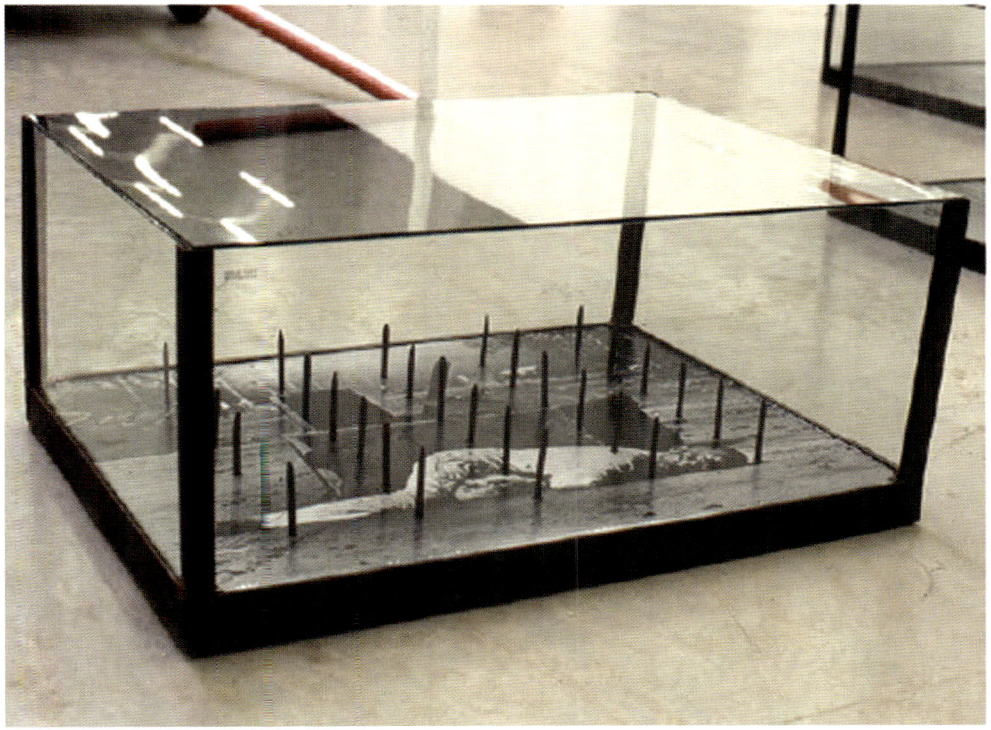

VIVAN SUNDARAM
Memorial: Burial 6, 1993, black-and-white photograph (by Hoshi Jal, *Times of India*, Bombay, February 23, 1993), 19 x 24 x 12 inches.

Looking back, I would call *Ways of Resisting* and *Art on the Move* my favorite Sahmat projects. *Ways of Resisting* was a museum-level show and it could definitely have been bigger. If a catalogue had been published it could have included many other references, so you could have had a much larger, impressive, and consolidated picture of how artists did not look the other way—they were working quietly, in resistance. The show came together with thirty-five artists but it could have included many more, and that's a loss.

The Sahmat Collective will feature some of the work from *Ways of Resisting*, including a fragment of my work *Memorial*. Done a year after the demolition of the Babri Masjid, it is considered to be one of the first examples of installation art in India. What was important for me was that it signaled, one, the presence of photography and how artists use photography—the photograph used in this work was already in the public domain. And two, the relationship between photography and sculpture—how different materials, like nails or iron, become an integral part of the work, which has a photographic image as the base. It is a moving and disturbing work, but it speaks of the moment. I was interested in an interface—what I would call an intervention in terms of the form of minimalism, say of Carl Andre or Donald Judd—positioning/filling an empty container from one's own perspective. Artists the world over have introduced content of different kinds into such forms or containers. So here was a very topical, very poignant, very painful political image, which could be addressed by forms that American minimalists proposed from the 1960s onward. —V. S.

Rummana Hussain lived a very short and tragic life, but in a very exceptional, intuitive way she was able to bring very new strategies into her art-making. She used a range of materials in a very fluid manner and was able to integrate an emotional, personal register into the social and the historical, and *Home/Nation* is about that. So she could use cloth, photographs, wood, and make an installation. Her work actually belongs to that moment in the early 1990s which signals the shift from conventional painting and sculpture to more radical political content and form.
—**Vivan Sundaram**

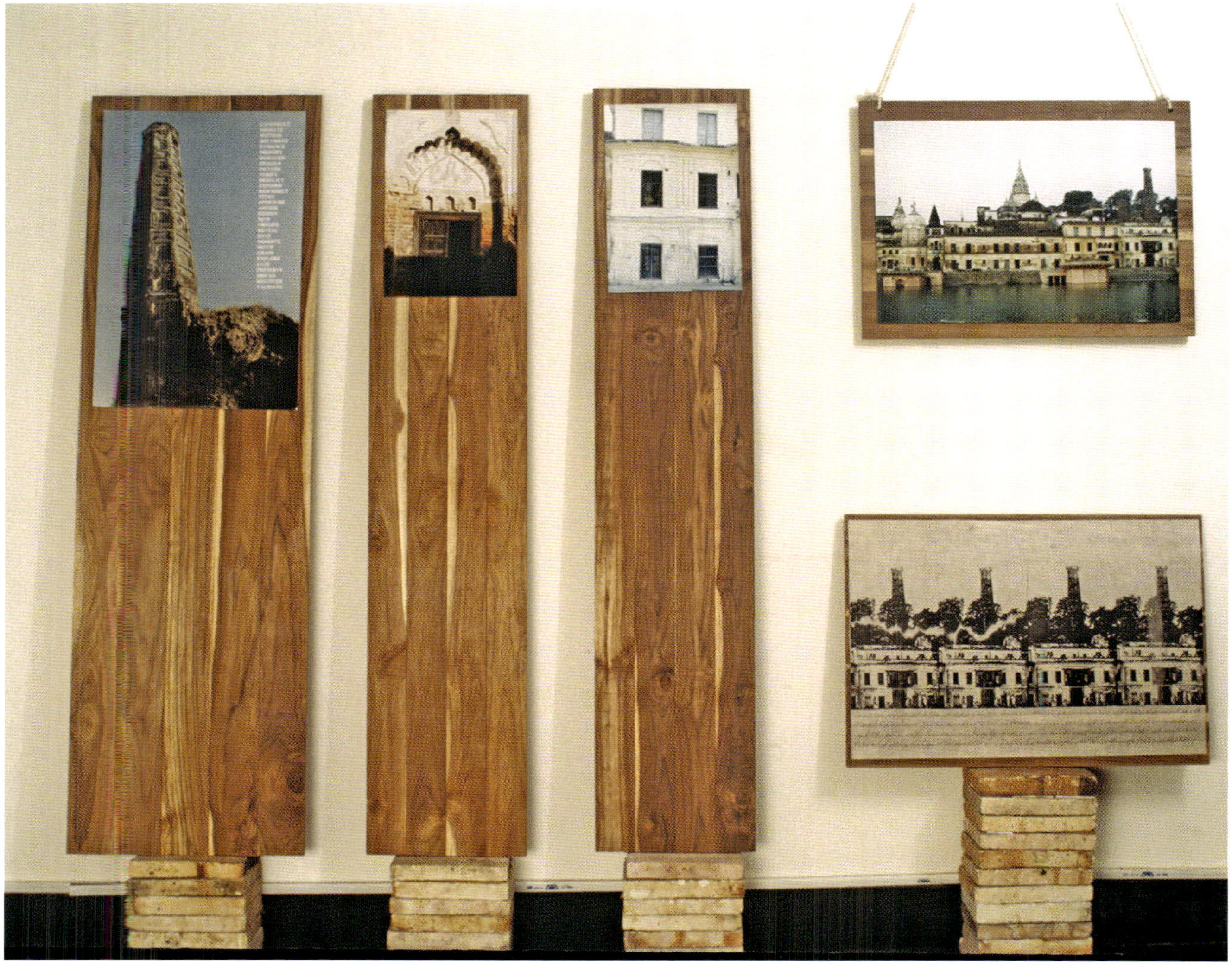

RUMMANA HUSSAIN
Home/Nation, 1996, installation of photographs, cloth, glass bottles, and found objects, dimensions variable. Courtesy Talwar Gallery, New York.

RUMMANA HUSSAIN

Home/Nation, 1996, installation of photographs, cloth, glass bottles, and found objects, dimensions variable. Courtesy Talwar Gallery, New York.

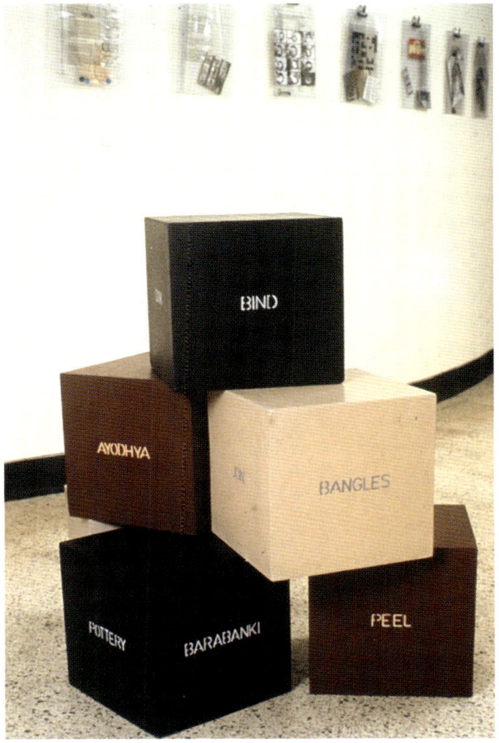

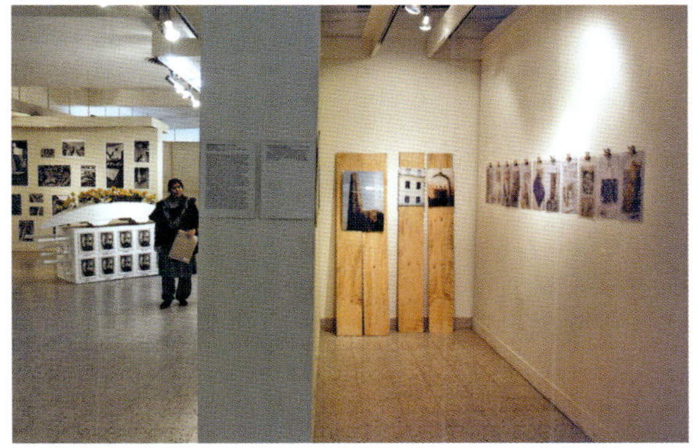

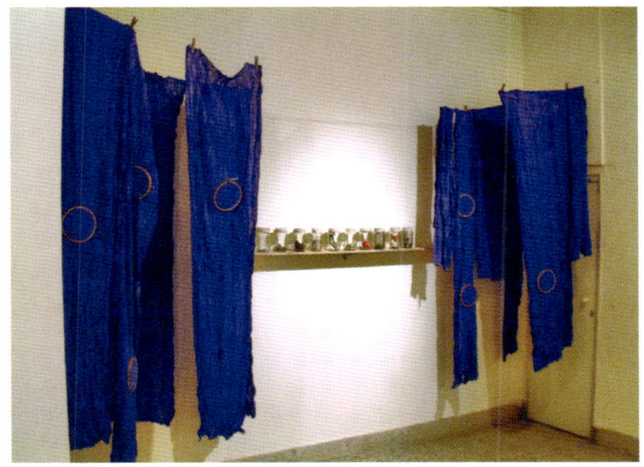

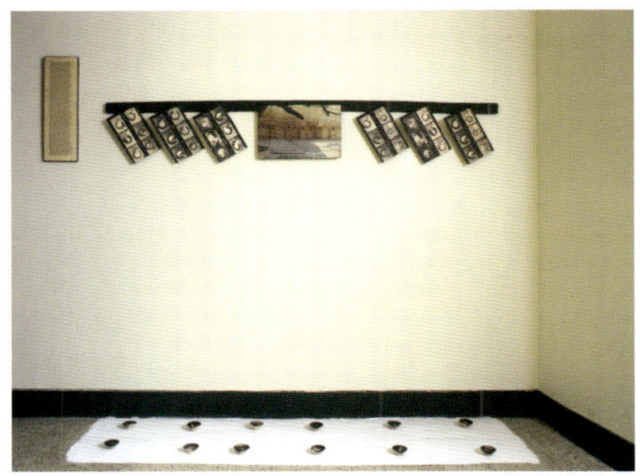

Rummana Hussain's *Home/Nation* evolved directly from her Sahmat activism. Rummana and her family had to flee their flat and remove their nameplate in an elite area of Mumbai during the riots that followed the demolition of the Babri Masjid in 1992. A violent national tragedy finding its way into her personal space deeply shocked the artist. The communal riots in Mumbai suddenly thrust her "Muslimness" in her face in a way she had never imagined. A short while earlier, the discovery that the sores in her maid's mouth were probably a manifestation of a thrush infection caused by HIV, and that she had hidden it in desperation from her employer, also caused great anguish for Rummana (the maid died soon after from AIDS). It was around the same time that Rummana was diagnosed with breast cancer, to which she succumbed in 1999. This combination of events collapsed personal and national conflicts into a searing struggle in her person, which led Rummana to abandon her earlier expressionist figurative painting to search for other formal means as an artistic language.

Home/Nation with its photographs of women's open mouths, the maid rolling *chapattis* (Indian flatbread) in the kitchen, architectural doorways and arches, objects in bottles defining a so-called Muslim cultural identity from her roots in Lucknow, and defined the maturing language of assemblage that transformed Rummana's work. The architectural elements came directly from her installation of Sahmat's *Hum Sab Ayodhya* in Mumbai and subsequent travel to Ayodhya for *Muktnaad.* This work exemplifies the complete transformation of an art practice due to the events of that decade, something that occurred among many artists in India at the time.

—Ram Rahman

ATUL DODIYA
B for Bapu, 2001.
Exterior: oil and enamel paint on grilled metal roller shutter; interior: acrylic and varnish on canvas with thread and lock, 108 x 72 inches. Collection: Lekha and Anupam Poddar, Delhi.

The inclinations and obsessions have moved. As my notions of security and beauty have changed, a deluge of images has hit me. Living in a nation steeped in poverty, maybe it is unavoidable. Death, decay, corruption, compromise, struggle are not distant metaphors of the fall of man. These are real, right here, lived with. Metallic omnipresence. Metal as a roller shutter guard to a shop. Opening/closing it is a symbol of the daily grind. . . . Constant contradiction is the truth. Imagine the earth shifting beneath one's feet perpetually. Gandhi's absence manifests itself in the different mounds of ruin—the political mess, the hypocrisy and deceit of the individual in the national playground where we are all sliding down. As an armless, helpless individual I have made an archive of our citizens' sleeves. Crafting wings from chopped arms is the prerogative of a despairing artist-citizen. —A. D.

Atul Dodiya's series of paintings with roller shutters pitches the activity of painting against the mindless commerce of the marketplace and the pervading politics of today. *B for Bapu* shows, on canvas, Gandhi weakened, as if he has engaged in one of his long protest fasts. The fast seems to have just ended, and we see him taking a sip of some liquid food, perhaps honey-and-water, as was his practice. There are some honeybees on the case of the shutter, but they look too monstrous to be bringers of honey. The roller-shutter here has a grill surface and when shut, looks like a prison door over Gandhi. Gandhi taught his followers the importance of physical labor and demanded active involvement from them in the struggle for freedom. Perhaps Gandhi is nourishing himself for action, and the viewer is expected to open the prison gate of the grilled shutter enclosing him.
—Sitanshu Yashaschandra

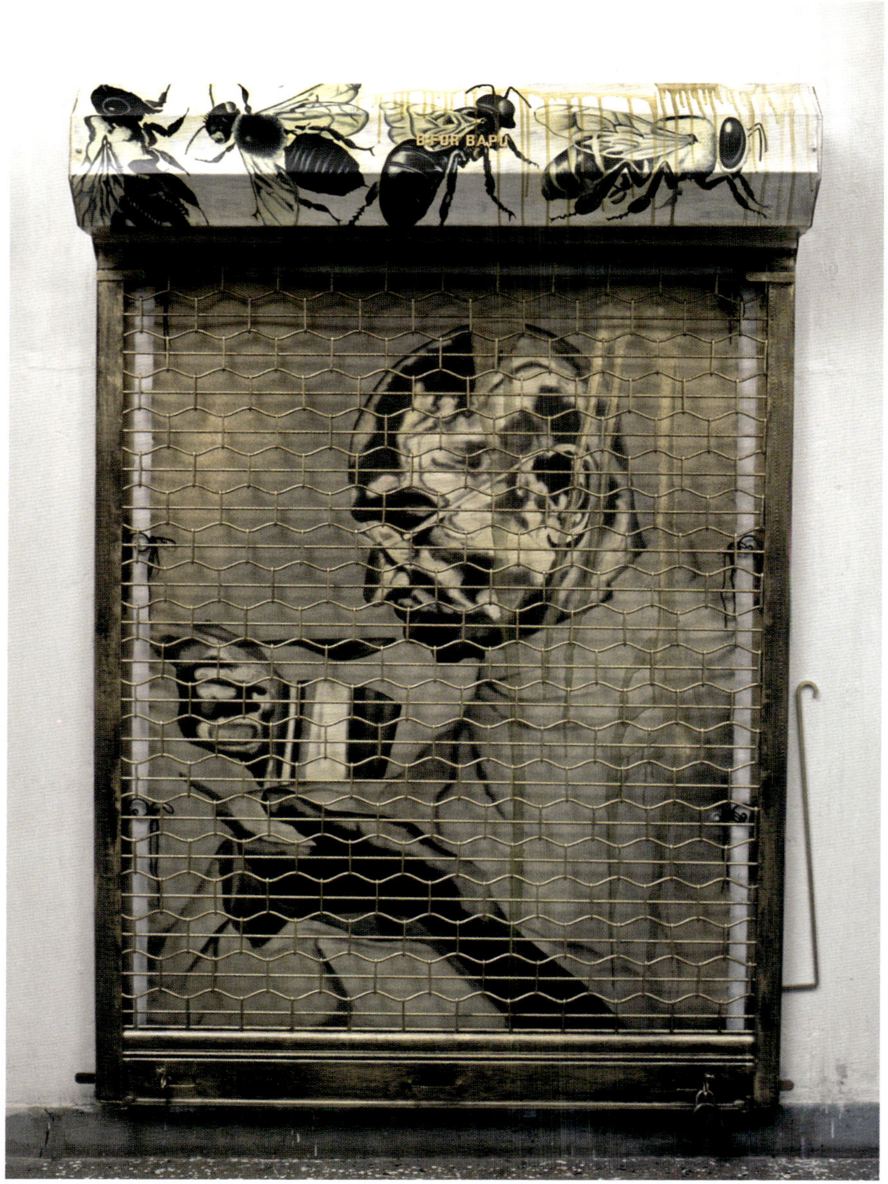

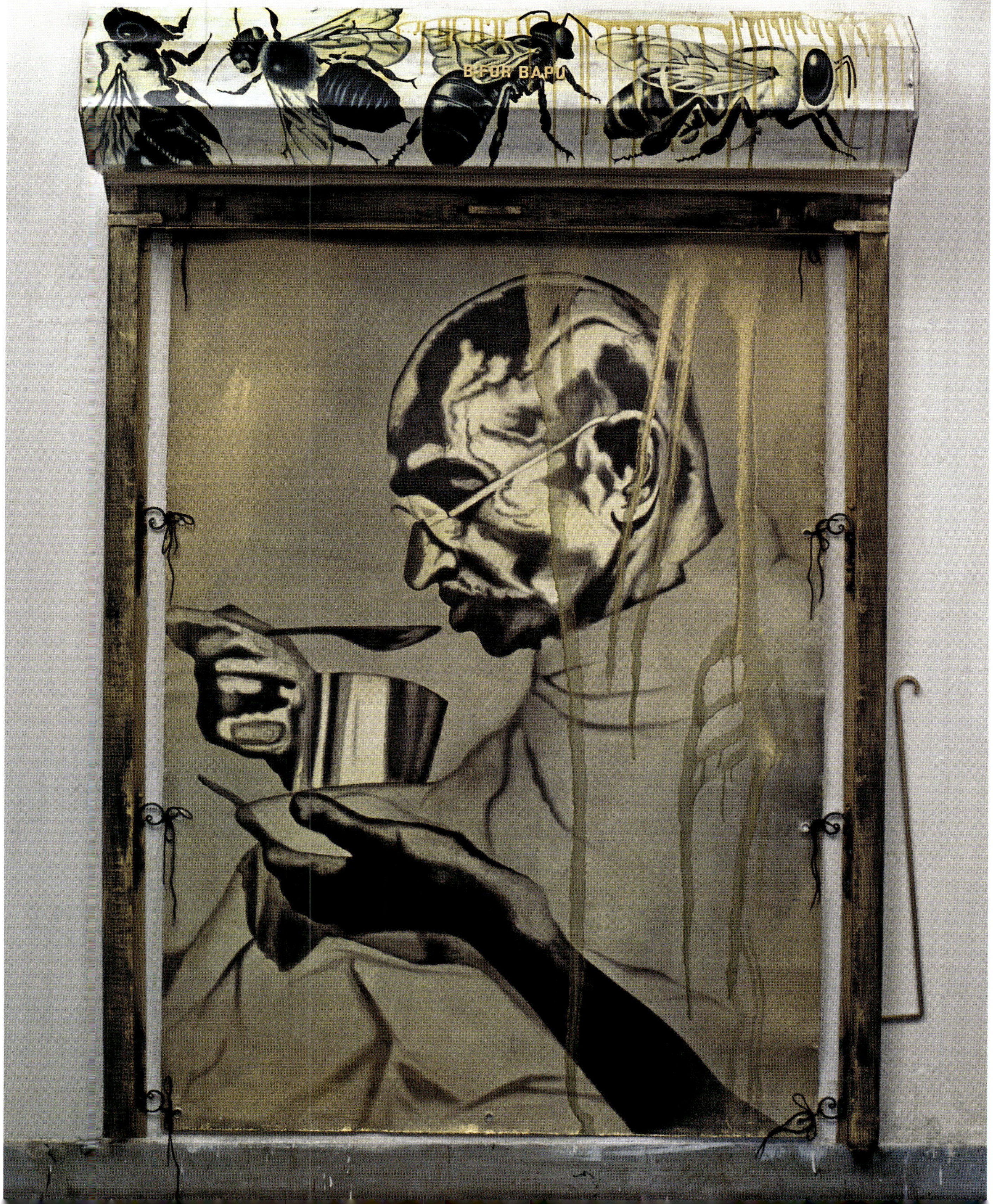
B FOR BAPU

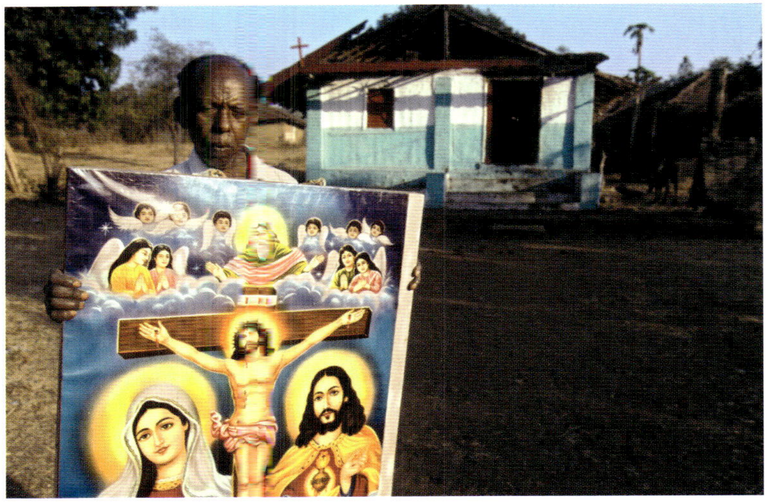

PABLO BARTHOLOMEW

A picture of Christ recovered from the wrecked church in the village of Mulchond in the Dang area of Gujarat, 1998, digital photographic print. Collection: the artist.

Pablo Bartholomew's photo-reportage has documented many important events across India. This photograph reported the wave of organized attacks against the minority Christian community in Gujarat by right-wing Hindu vigilante groups that had the apparent support of the BJP (Bharatiya Janata Party). These attacks had reached serious proportions in the late 1990s in many parts of India. The minority Muslim community had been the target of these groups for many years, but in the 1990s their campaign of violence expanded to include the Christian community. **—Ram Rahman**

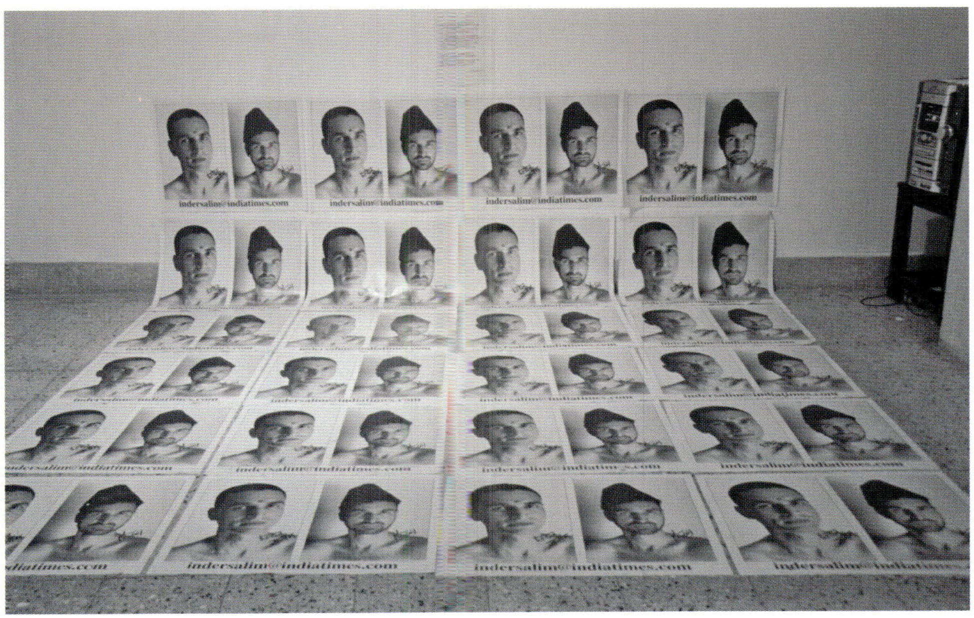

INDER SALIM

Indersalim@indiatimes.com, 2002, poster installation. Collection: the artist.

Inder Salim both straddles the boundaries between mediums and resists the transformation of his art into commodity. Much of his work is performance-based, generating documents and photographs for wide distribution. He uses decidedly low-brow and cheap materials so that his work can be available free to the public, effectively transgressing the commercial and institutional gallery structures and reaching out to an audience that does not normally come in contact with radical art practices. Among his favorite mediums is the cheap offset printed poster, which he both gives away and puts up in public places. Inder Salim addresses the difficulties of being a Kashmiri, caught between the rigid structuring of identities that his native place seems to require and his ambivalence towards belonging to either of these two communities (Hindu/Muslim), constructed solely on the basis of religious affiliation.
—Peter Nagy

The year 2002 brought difficult times for Muslims to assert their constitutional right to be equal citizens of India. My *INDER-SALIM* poster was a simple gesture to emphasize the inherent coexistential nature of these two communities: Hindus and Muslims, who have a unique history of love, music, poetry, food, and festivals. —I. S.

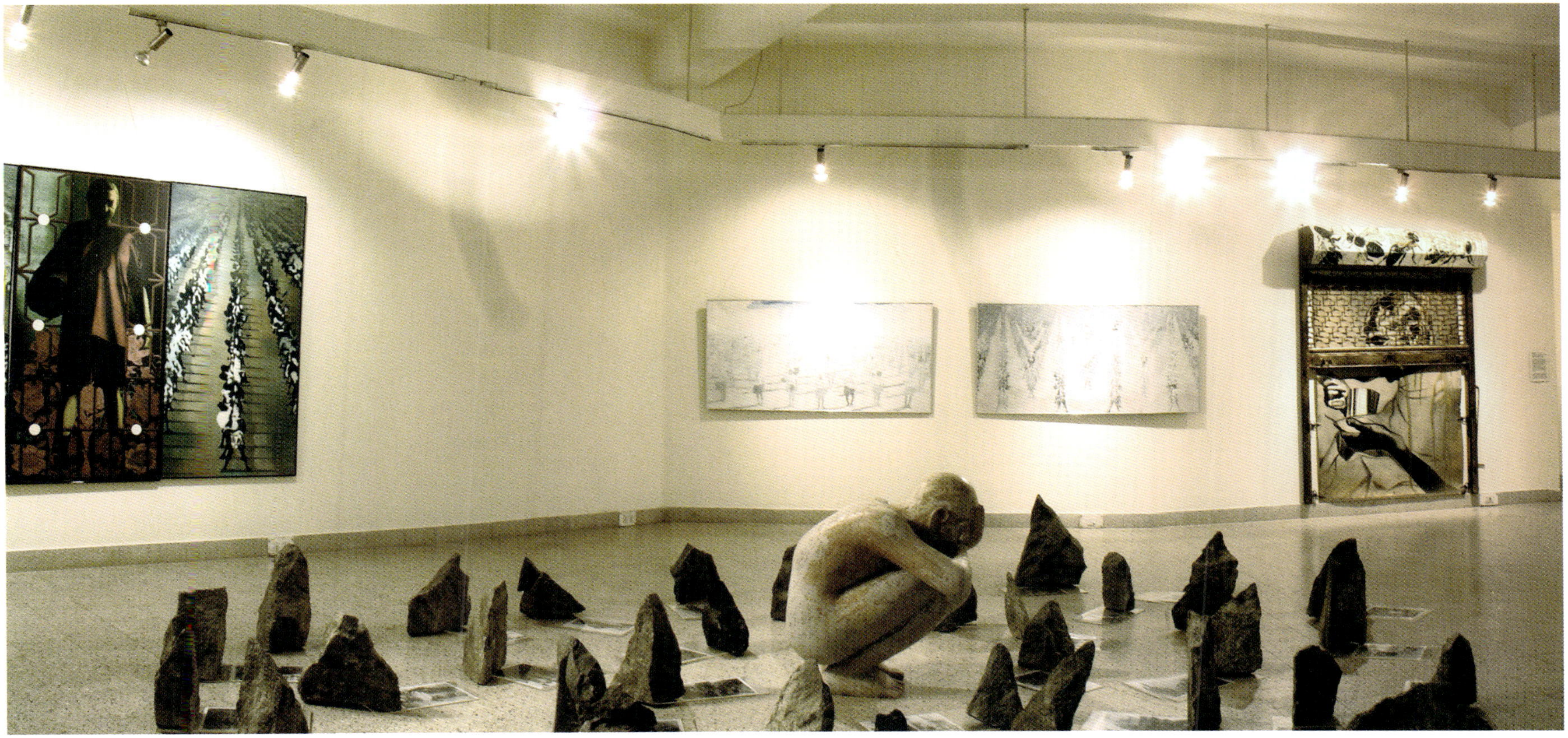

ON WALL, LEFT

NATARAJ SHARMA

The Footballer/RSS Parade (or How My Game Is Being Spoiled), 2002, triptych, mixed media on board. Private collection.

ON WALL, CENTER

Bad Dreams: A Hole in the Sky, 2002, mixed media on board. Collection: the artist.
Bad Dreams: The Garland, 2002, mixed media on board. Collection: the artist.

In recent years Nataraj Sharma's work has shifted from a meditation on transformation at the edge of an Indian city, to a more overt engagement with contemporary politics and culture. Among other subjects, the artist has reflected on the nuclearization of subcontinental strife and sexual mores in a repressive culture. His most recent work, produced at a time of genocide in his adoptive home in Gujarat, draws upon photographic imagery to place the artist's persona amid manifestations of right-wing mobilization. An RSS [Rashtriya Swayamsevak Sangh, a right-wing organization that is the controlling parent of the Bharatiya Janata Party] parade is transmuted into garlands/spikes on either side of a self-portrait, the blurred contours of the imagery abstracting and enlarging Sharma's individual position as citizen amid a ghostly gray muster of fundamentalist cadres. **—Chaitanya Sambrani**

ON FLOOR

N. N. RIMZON

Speaking Stones, 1998, installation of photographs, stone, fiberglass, and marbledust, dimensions variable. Collection: the artist.

A seated figure bends forward in a semi-fetal position—the classical stance of the thinker. Here, however, he hides his face and shrinks into mourning. Acknowledging and repudiating the violence of the social order, the figure is surrounded by a full circle of photographic images reporting the ethnic and religious violence that has been raging in the Indian nation from the moment of independence in 1947, also the moment of its partition. Drawn to the nonviolence of the great heterodox religions of India (Buddhist and Jain) and to Gandhi (the intrepid Mahatma of the twentieth century), one might extrapolate that Rimzon would likewise conduct the ethical work of mourning to expiate the guilt for an ignominious nationalism demonstrated by the new nuclear ambitions of India.
—Geeta Kapur

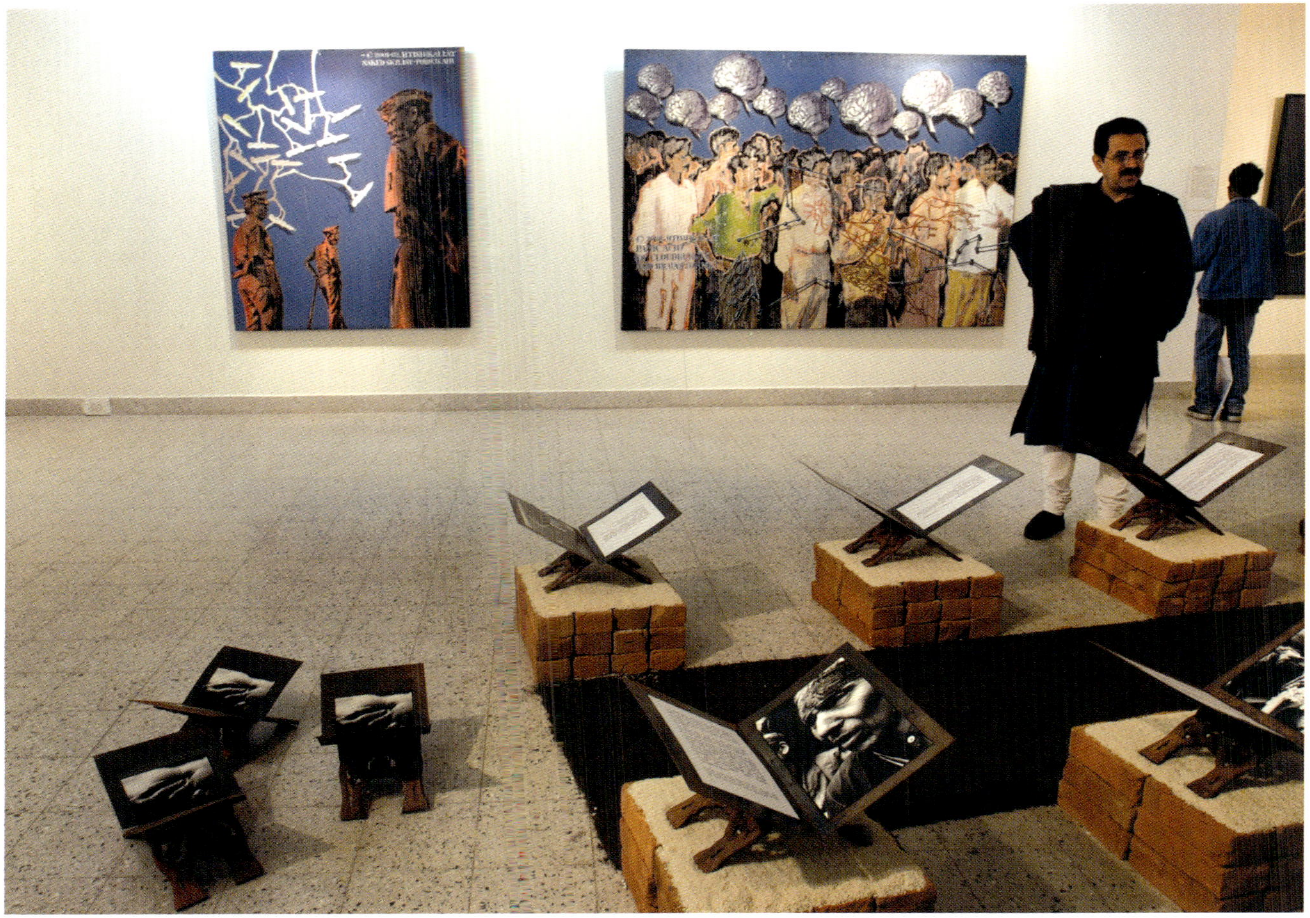

ON WALLS, LEFT AND RIGHT

JITISH KALLAT

Naked Skyline—Porous Air, 2001–02, mixed media on canvas. Collection: the artist.

Panic Acid (or Cloudbursts and Brainstorms), 2001, mixed media on canvas. Collection: Rajshree Pathy, Delhi.

ON FLOOR

SHEBA CHHACHHI AND SONIA JABBAR

"When the gun is raised, dialogue stops . . .": Kashmiri women speak (detail), 2000, photo-text installation, wooden rihals [book holders or stands], bricks, rice, soil, rusted sheets of iron, black-and-white photographs, and text, dimensions variable.

Jitish Kallat remains preoccupied with the urban environment of Mumbai. By synecdoche, never by illustration, he invokes its atmosphere of sprawl and menace . . . the frayed, ugly edges and manic pace of the postcolonial metropolis inform the jaggedness and pulsating distortions of Kallat's figures. The big city is a theatre of conflict that is unregulated, unpredictable, and unrefereed. Its asymmetries of attainment, its scarcities and pressures, breed pathologies of violence. The recurrent nightmares of Indian collective life—famine, drought, displacement of tribal populations, politically directed pogroms, the deaths of thousands of infants from malnutrition—inform Kallat's paintings profoundly. Kallat's engagement in the metropolis—the manner in which the city throws people together into the anonymity of the crowd, yet also allows the pursuit of individual life unrestricted by codes of community—offers up estranged individuals atomized by a mechanized society that has little time or use for the comforts of solidarity. One of Kallat's key protagonists is the survivor, the mutant, the victim—the secular martyr-hero of an urban iconography. **—Ranjit Hoskote**

Over the last ten years images of violence have dominated the media coverage of Kashmir, with armed mujahideen, soldiers, bomb blasts, and killings shaping the way we see Kashmir. These perceptions are only reinforced by the hardline statements made by the government, the army, the Pakistani establishment, the Hurriyat, the United Jihad Council, the RSS, and the VHP. But what about the ordinary Kashmiri? What happens to the Kashmiri woman who struggles to survive, to maintain life, sanity, ordinary human values, in the midst of war? We believe that the solution to political problems cannot be found through military means. India's security does not lie in bigger defense budgets or more soldiers in the Valley. The war in Kashmir has already lasted well over a decade—it threatens a terrifying permanency.

This photo-installation endeavors to give space to the women of Kashmir whose voices have been obscured by the clamor of war and contention all these years. The statements presented in the work, culled from interviews and testimonies gathered over a period of seven years, voice reason, compassion, and hope. Perhaps they can provide the seeds for a solution to the present crisis. **—Sonia Jabbar**

Ways of Resisting

Geeta Kapur

The following description of *Ways of Resisting* was originally written as wal text for the exhibition and later revisec for the 2009 exhibition *Image, Music, Text: 20 Years of Sahmat*, presented in New Delhi at M. F. Husain Gallery, Jamia Millia Islamia University.

In December 2002 Sahmat mounted a major exhibition, *Ways of Resisting*, at the Lalit Kala Akademi Galleries, Rabindra Bhavan, New Delhi. Curated by Vivan Sundaram, the exhibition included works by thirty-five artists, three artists' groups, and several documentary filmmakers—paintings and installations, photographs, videos, and related archival material.

The exhibition offered retrospective evidence on the decade of violence—from the demolition of the Babri Masjid in 1992 to the Gujarat carnage in 2002—instigated by the Sangh Parivar. Throughout this decade Sahmat had worked to sustain secular values within a public sphere that was under a right-wing siege. In the year 2002, the majoritarian ideology of Hindutva culminated with the BJP (Narendra Modi's) government in Gujarat openly supporting the genocide of Muslims in the state. Within the year, Sahmat's *Ways of Resisting* attempted to place a frame of understanding on this unprecedented violence by bringing to view artists' critical reflections on the conditions of survival at such a moment in history. Considering the artist as witness, the curated exhibition articulated questions about the self, citizenship, and exile within an already fraught polity torn apart by hate.

Several artworks in *Ways of Resisting* demonstrated that the violence of social coercion and its reprisal in hate should be addressed by the full protocol of mourning. The artists revealed that social suffering (as caused by communal carnage in India) requires a practice where reparation for injury is acted out in the public gaze. To memorialize encounters with oppressive regimes is the necessary task of historical recall conducted by courageous artists of all genres, at all times. *Ways of Resisting* had a preponderance of artworks that dealt with traumatic event and constructed memory, mourning, and memorials.

A number of artworks of this period deal with the distortion of symbols (traditional and contemporary), and the exploitation of religion and mythology by right-wing "culturalists." Keeping the secular as the transforming element in the social contract, Indian artists have sought to redevelop an iconography that draws on tradition's redemptive strains. The most generative source is, quite predictably, the syncretic Sufi-Bhakti traditions of medieval India insofar as they dismantle religious institutions and produce a new heterodox spirituality and an agnostic intercommunity exchange. In an inspired imitation of the eccentrics who belong to these traditions, contemporary artists have learned to hold in tension a sensibility for the *sacred* with a full play of profanation—and to offer an aesthetics of inversion necessary for social transformation.

If a generosity of spirit brings truth and compassion, faith and irony into social praxis, then it is not coincidental that the figure of Gandhi repeatedly figures as norm, icon, and enigma in the work of Indian artists (as well as in art projects staged by Sahmat, and in the revised discourse at the national level by leftist intellectuals). With their unconventional imaging of Gandhi, Indian artists have explored the possibility of an imaginative rendering of egalitarian ethics.

Yet another set of works in the exhibition attempted to pry away the question of the citizen-subject from that of the nation and the state, and to re-place it within civil society and its tattered borders. Attending to new subjectivities formed in the interstices of the city-fabric, these artists identify with confrontational positions inherent within subaltern—dalit, working-class, and peasant—consciousness. Several artists also offer provocative stances in relation to gender. Such forms of dissent invite interrogation of civic sloth and political crime, and it remains for critical discourse to inscribe the artwork in an exhibition such as *Ways of Resisting* within the public sphere.

1994– Ongoing

Reasserting Secularism

History and Culture

The roots of India's modernity are as complex as the disparate cultures that make up the subcontinent. Sahmat has initiated various projects as ways of examining both these beginnings and the making of a modern India by looking to various moments in India's cultural history as touchstones. One such moment was the medieval Sufi-Bhakti movement, based on Islamic and Hindu traditions that foregrounded an egalitarian order and framed individual agency as an important aspect of spiritual thinking and social practice. The 1857 Revolt of Indian sepoys against the British rulers, also referred to as the First War of Independence, was a widespread uprising that united and mobilized people of different classes and religions. The national movement for independence of the late nineteenth and early twentieth centuries, from which Mahatma Gandhi emerged as an iconic and inspiring leader, carried forward the task of uniting people across boundaries of religion, caste, and class, against colonial rule. From the 1930s onward India's Communist movement formed an important strand of revolutionary politics within the national struggle for freedom. The activist forms of cultural practice initiated by the Communist Party through the founding of the Progressive Writers' Association (PWA) in 1936 and the Indian People's Theatre Association (IPTA) in 1943 have been another important example for Sahmat. The PWA and IPTA have had a great impact on practices in literature, cinema, theatre, and visual arts of the time. Both Bhisham Sahni and Habib Tanvir, important guiding figures for Sahmat, came from that lineage.

Through the projects *The Making of India* (2004) and *Making History Our Own* (2007), Sahmat sought to actively engage artists in rethinking the country's cultural and political histories in their practices. These exhibitions were accompanied by symposia on different aspects of recent history with presentations by some of the most respected historians and social scientists of the country. Sahmat has since published collections of these papers in both English and Hindi. Thus these projects can be seen as part of an ongoing endeavor to understand Indian modernity through the histories and cultures that exist within it.

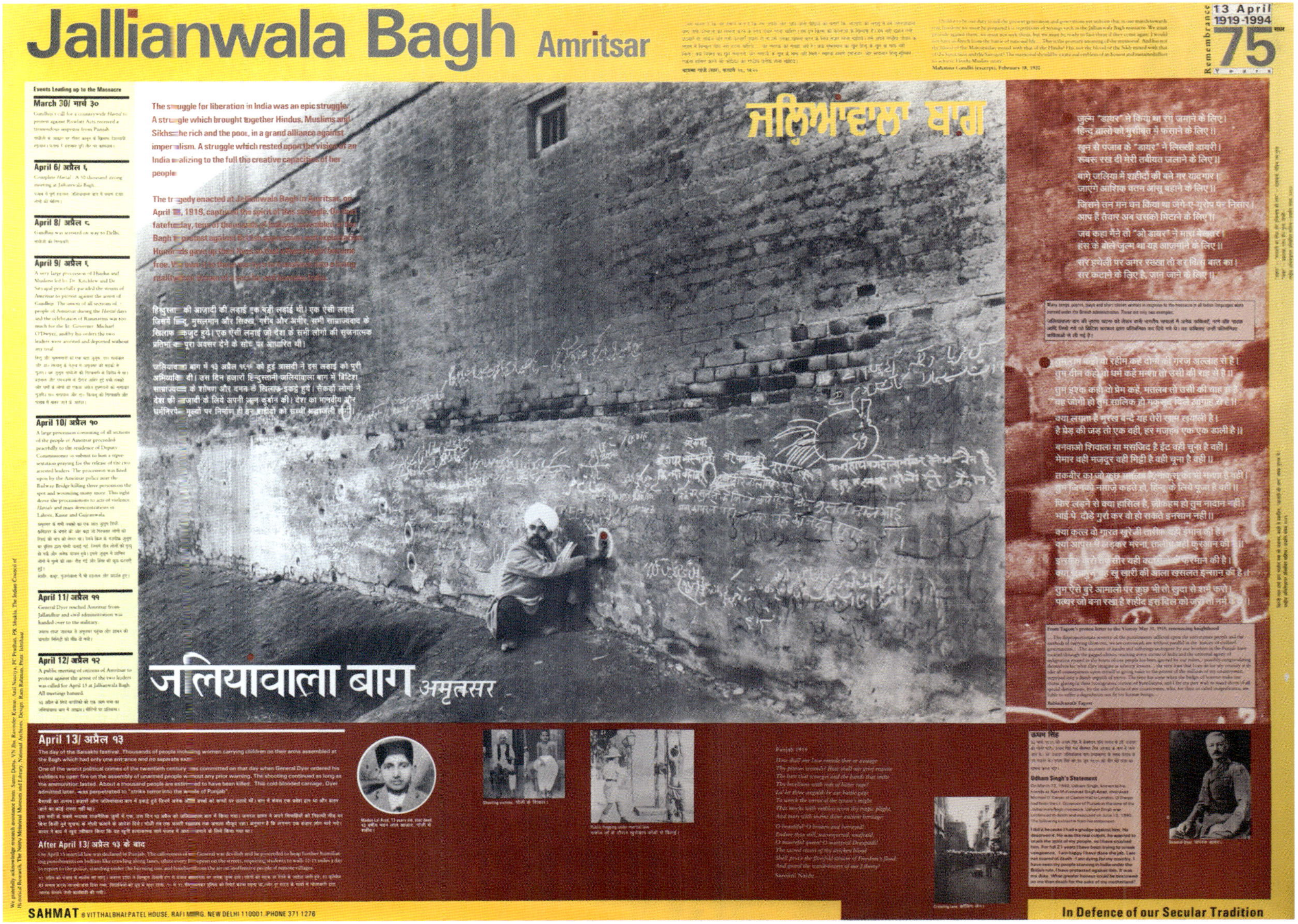

Jallianwala Bagh, 1994, broadside, 27 x 37 inches. Design: Ram Rahman.

Produced by Sahmat in commemoration of the seventy-fifth anniversary of the Jallianwala Bagh Massacre, this broadside was released by Captain Lakshmi Sehgal, an activist who led the women's regiment of Subhas Chandra Bose's Indian National Army against the British Army in the jungles of Burma during the 1940s. The broadside focuses on the British massacre of thousands of citizens who had gathered for a peaceful meeting at Jallianwala Bagh in Amritsar in 1919, a turning point in India's struggle for independence. It reproduces a letter by poet Rabindranath Tagore renouncing his knighthood, written after the incident, as well as fragments of poems and plays about the massacre—texts that had been banned by the British rulers and were discovered in the National Archive of India by Sahmat. In addition to the broadside, Sahmat's commemorative event on April 13, 1994, in Delhi, included readings by veteran actor Zohra Segal, film director Saeed Mirza, theatre director Ramgopal Bajaj, and Professor Malini Bhattacharya, as well as a performance of the play *Baghe Jallian* (once banned by the British), directed by M. K. Raina and performed by schoolchildren.

RAM RAHMAN

After 1993 when we made the exhibition Hum Sab Ayodhya, recontextualizing our present in terms of important moments in the past that contributed to the making of modern India, became a key part of Sahmat's activities and philosophy. It happened on many levels.

The year 1857 was regarded as a key moment in the struggle against British rule (before the British crown had taken over control of India). It was the East India Company then, essentially the first great multinational corporation, ruling much of India in the middle of the nineteenth century. There was a massive revolt led by the local army troops and the peasantry in north and east India against the British. The 1857 Revolt also happened to be the biggest single uprising anywhere in the world against colonial rule up to that time, and it really shook the British to their core.

The significance of the 1857 rebellion was that it was a unified front of Hindus and Muslims coming together to fight the common enemy (the British). It was a secular rebellion, and avowedly so. When we started looking at the poems, the texts, and the proclamations that had been issued at that time, which were not publicly known, and which we were able to access through our connections with the historians who were working with Sahmat, we saw that it was no different than what happened in the national movement in the 1940s. That whole idea of unity and diversity goes right back to that revolt. And that is a cultural tradition, or a political tradition, that the Hindu Right cannot claim, because the Hindu Right had a communal outlook and had actually collaborated with the British rulers in their communal policy of "Divide and Rule."

Much of this history had not been seen through the prism of culture. There are popular songs, poems, and plays written about the revolt that kept alive its memory in the public sphere that were not known to scholars, or musicians, or artists. There are other less known histories, or less extolled histories, as well. The Congress movement, and Gandhi, of course, were very well known as the major forces that led to India's freedom. But there were other resistance movements, some of which were militant: the rebellion in Chittagong in Bengal in the 1930s; Amritsar in Punjab, which became a hotbed of militant rebellion with Udham Singh and Bhagat Singh, both of whom were executed by the British. Our project was to revive those histories through visual means, through their cultural manifestations, in poetry, popular cinema, and popular iconography. History had become key to the "culture wars" as they were being defined and fought in India by the Hindu Right. Sahmat became a public platform for historians outside their academic confines to debate and inform on these issues that were having a divisive impact on politics in India.

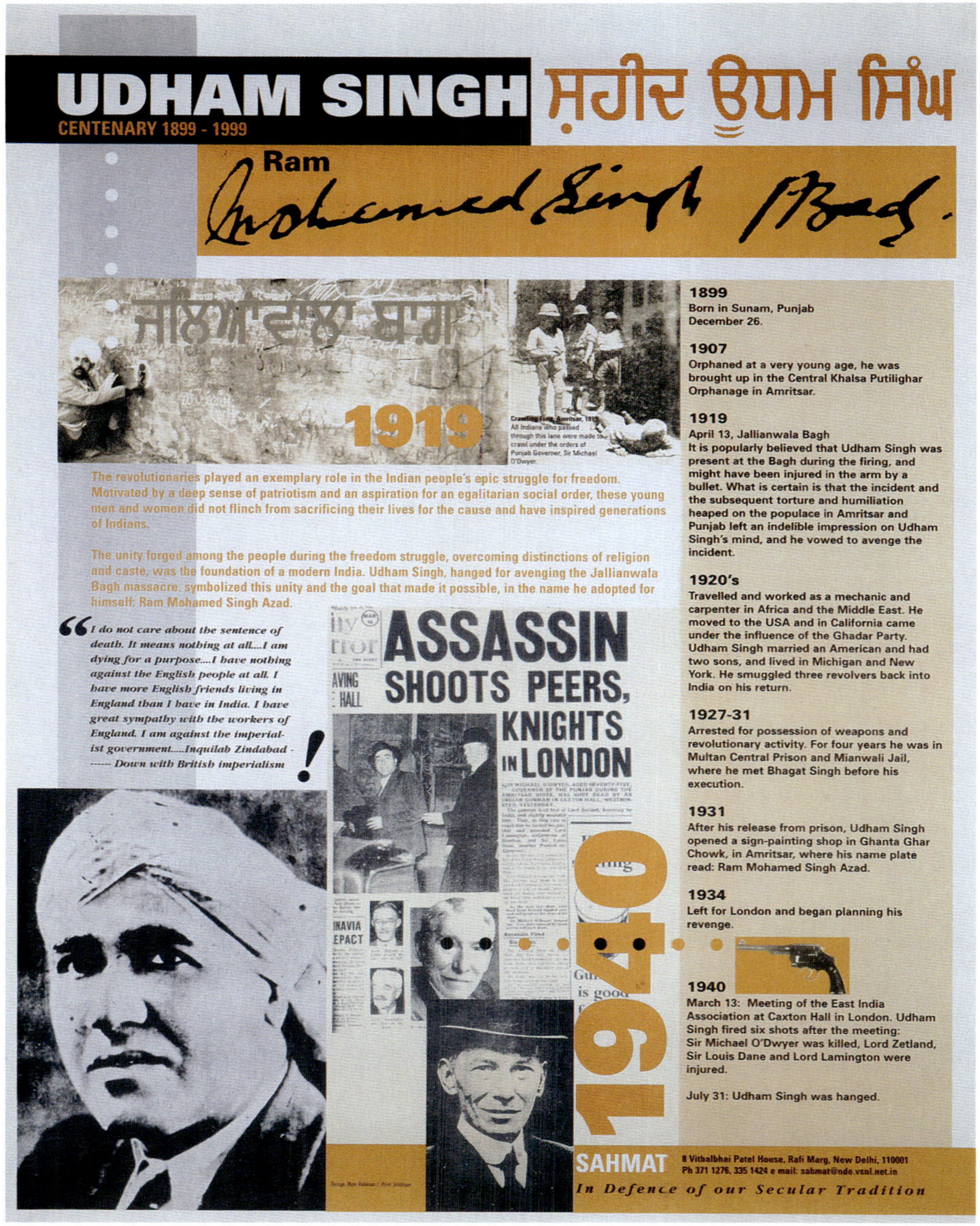

Udham Singh, 1999, broadside, 22 x 17 inches. Design: Ram Rahman.

◄
In commemoration of the centenary year of activist Udham Singh, Sahmat produced this broadside to be distributed at a lecture by Mohinder Singh, "The Freedom Movement in Punjab with Reference to Udham Singh," in New Delhi in 1999. In London in 1940, Singh assassinated the British governor of Punjab who had presided over the Jallianawala Bagh massacre; he was hanged later that year. Udham Singh is remembered across India for his belief that India's quest for freedom justified armed rebellion against British rule.

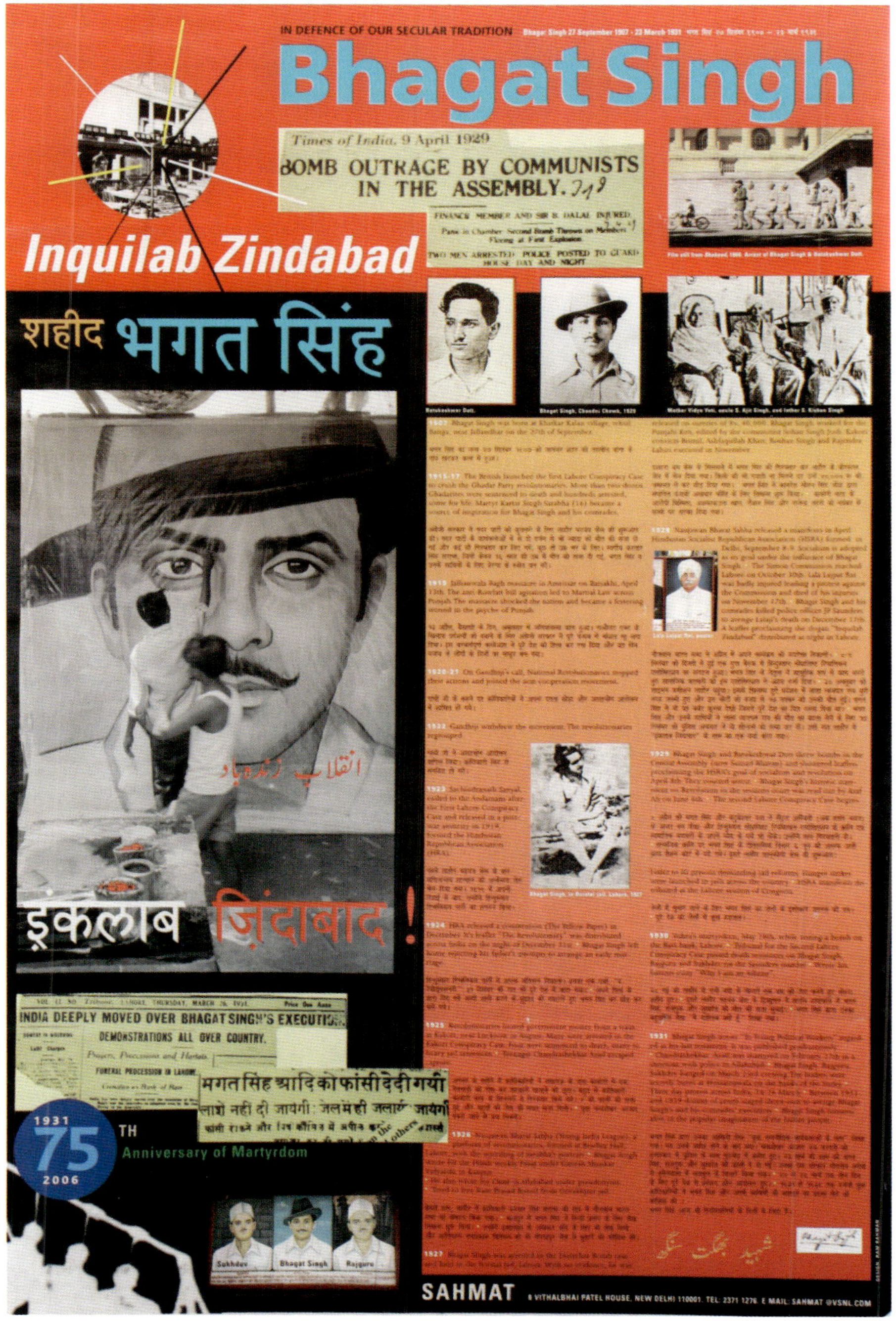

Bhagat Singh, 2006, broadside, 28 x 18½ inches. Design: Ram Rahman.

Released on March 23, 2006, this broadside commemorates the seventy-fifth anniversary of the death of militant revolutionary Bhagat Singh from Punjab. Bhagat Singh is a legendary figure in India's freedom struggle, who, like Udham Singh, was inspired by the Jallianawala Bagh massacre to turn to militant revolution. He was hanged by the British in 1931.

Commemoration of the 140th anniversary of the 1857 Revolt or First War of Independence, Red Fort, Delhi, May 11, 1997.

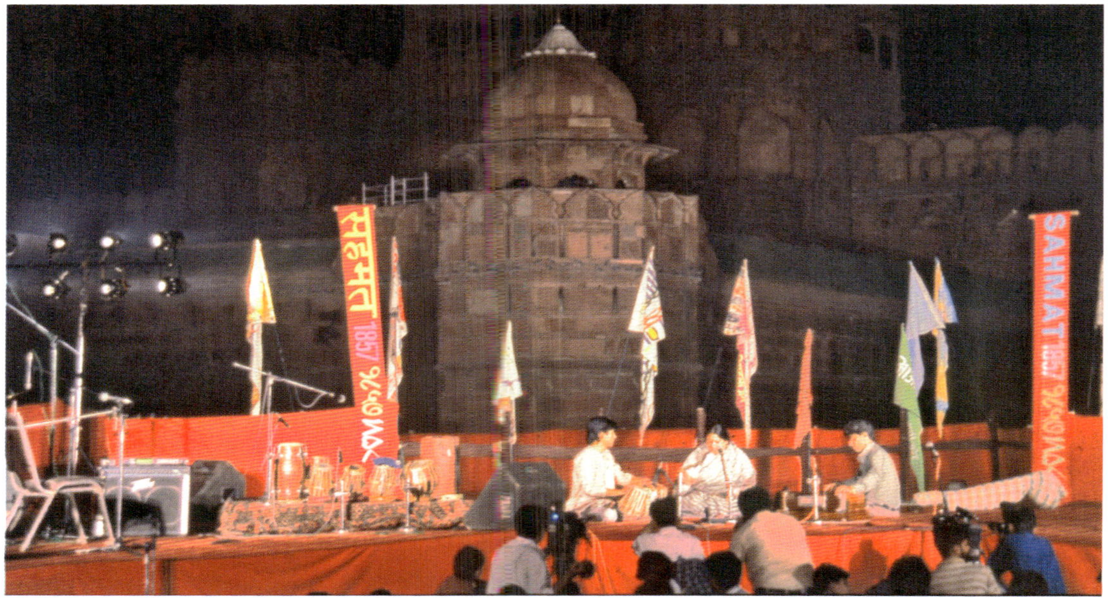

On May 11, 1997, Sahmat commemorated the 140th anniversary of the 1857 Revolt with a program at the Red Fort in Delhi. Participating artists included actor Zohra Sehgal, singers Shubha Mudgal, Vidya Shah, Harsh Deep, the rock band Indian Ocean, Ragini folk singers from Haryana, and the Indian Air Force Band. The program included an exhibition on the 1857 Revolt, *Red the Earth*, and the release of a booklet under the same title.

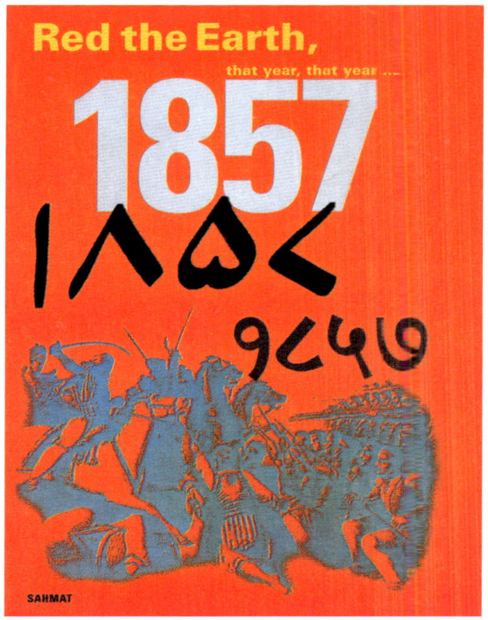

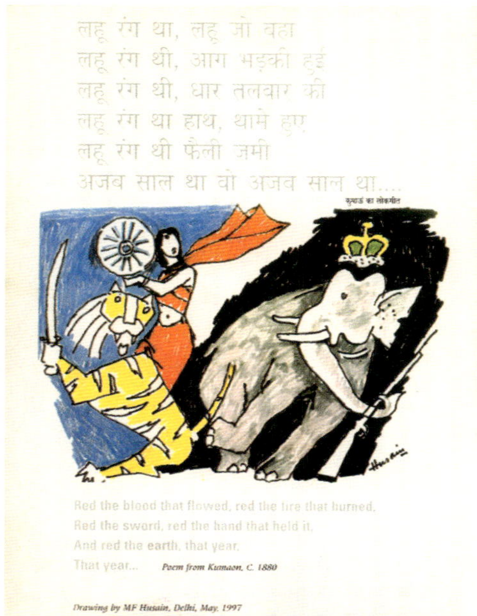

Cover of *Red the Earth*, 1997, booklet with frontispiece (right) by artist M. F. Husain.

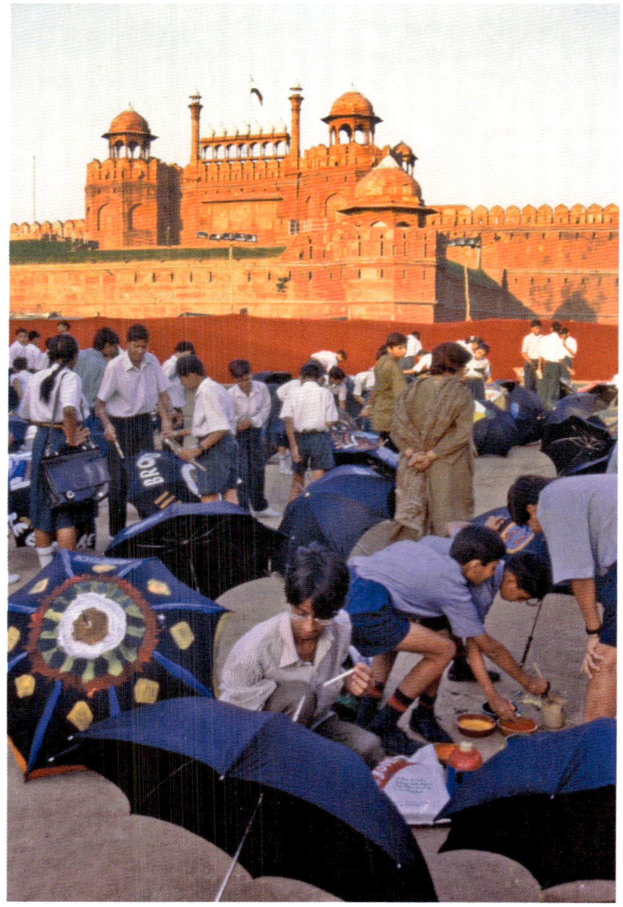

Schoolchildren paint umbrellas to commemorate the 140th anniversary of the 1857 Revolt, Red Fort, Delhi, May 11, 1997.

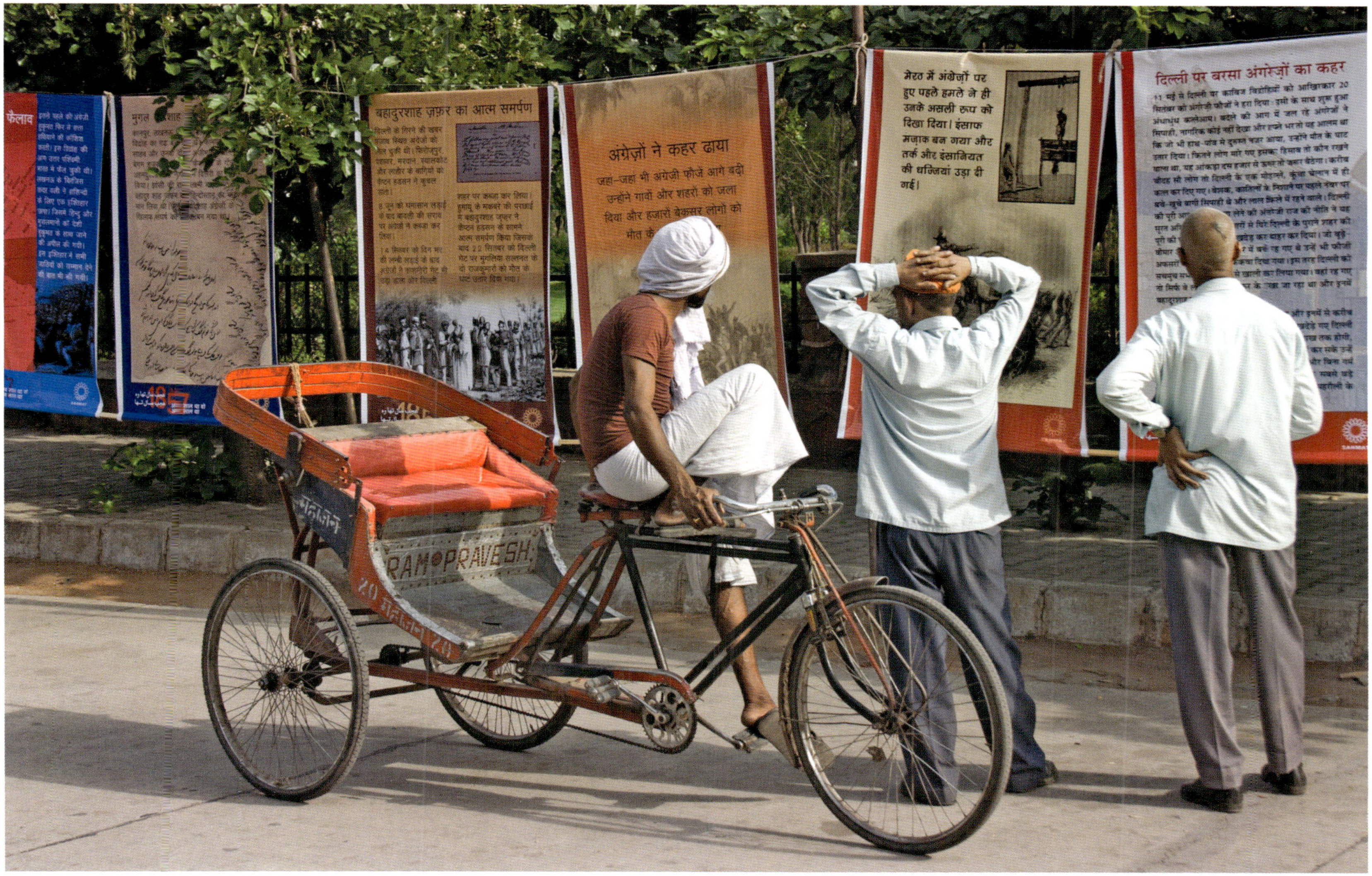

The exhibition *Red the Earth* on the 1857 Revolt, Delhi, 2007. Sahmat mounted the exhibition on the street at Khooni Darwaza (Gate of Blood) in Delhi, where the sons of Mughal Emperor Bahadur Shah Zafar were killed by the British.

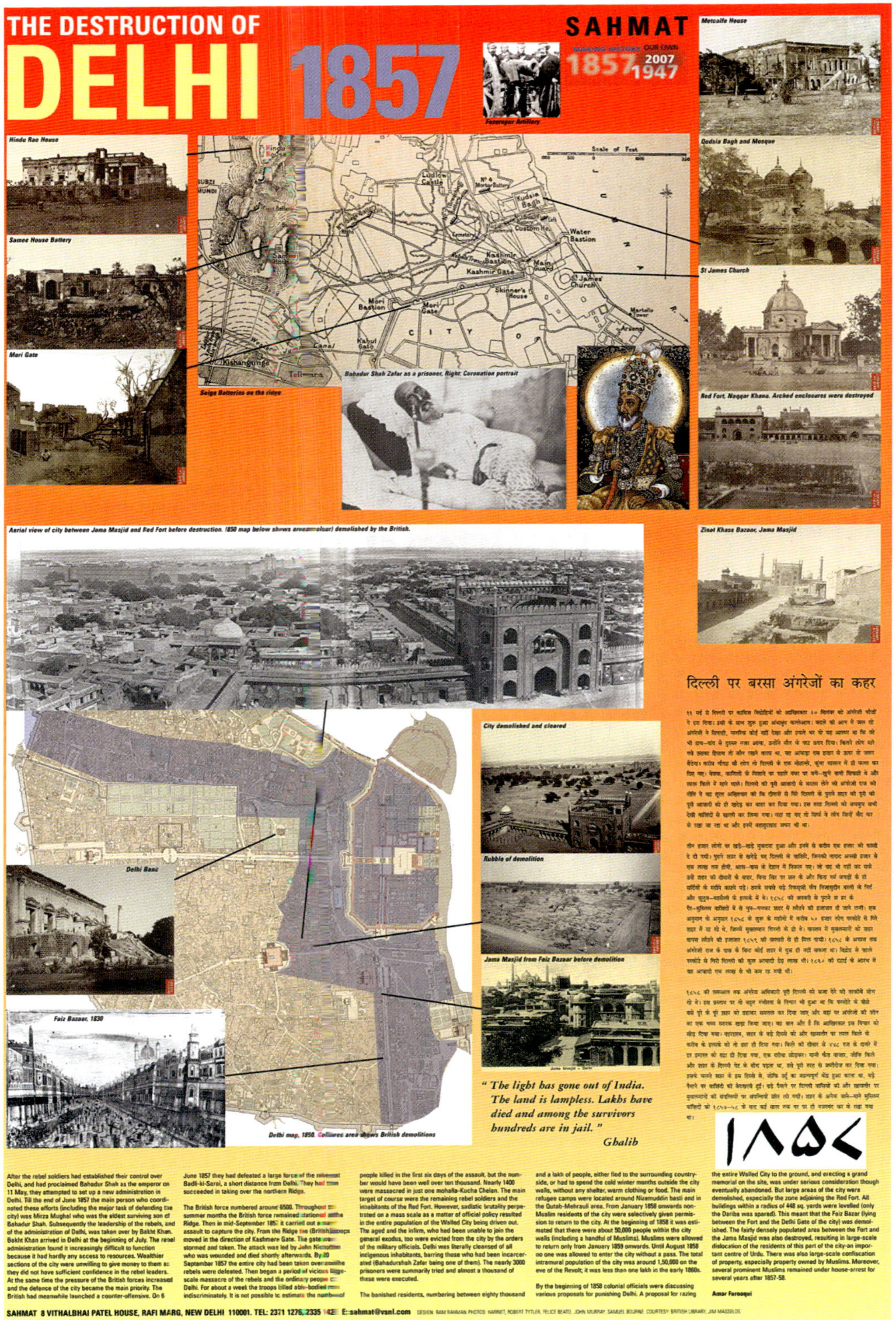

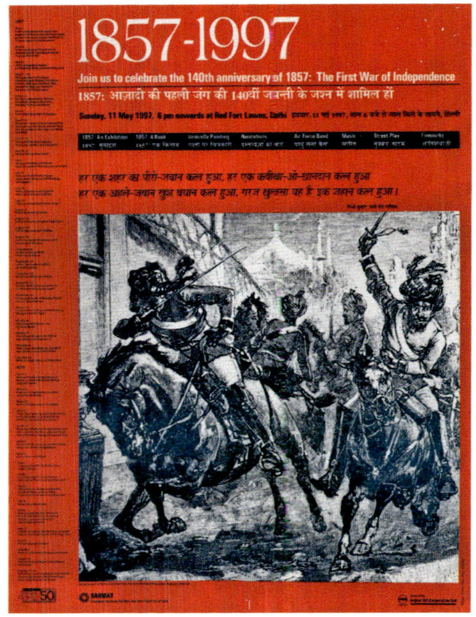

Poster for *1857–1997*, 1997, 30 x 22 inches. Design: Parthiv Shah.

The Destruction of Delhi 1857, 2007, broadside, 28 x 18½ inches. Design: Ram Rahman.

This broadside includes rare photographs from 1858 that show not only the physical devastation to the city of Delhi after the 1857 Revolt, but also the subsequent destruction by the British of the Mughal city and royal palace.

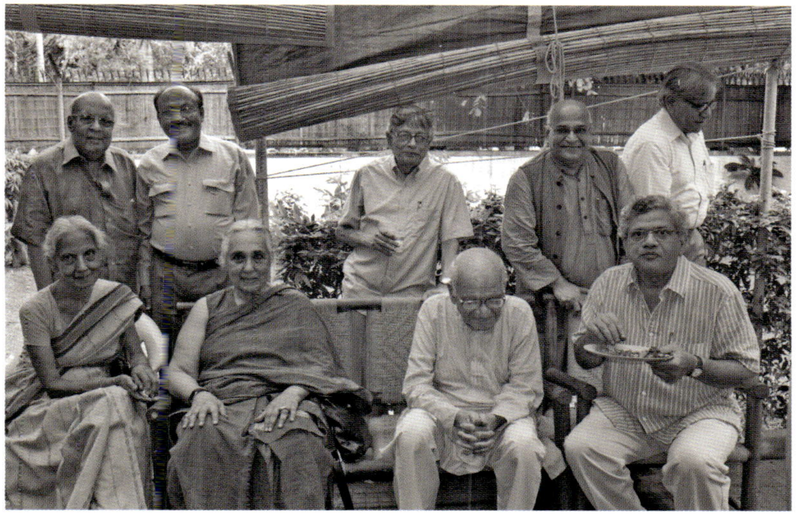

Back row (from left to right): Professor D. N. Jha, Dr. Ishrat Alam, Professor Irfan Habib, Professor K. M. Shrimali, Professor Arjun Dev. Front row (from left to right): Professor Saira Habib, Professor Romila Thapar, Professor Bipan Chandra, Sitaram Yechury, CPI(M) member of Parliament.

Sahmat organized a symposium, "Marxism Today," in Delhi on August 12, 2011, the eightieth birthday of the reputed historian and academic Professor Irfan Habib. Professor Habib has been an intellectual driving force and closely associated with Sahmat's campaigns against communal Hindutva forces, right from the Ayodhya project. Seen in the photograph above, with Professor Habib, are a number of fellow historians, senior academics, and scholars who attended the lunch hosted by Sahmat preceding the symposium.

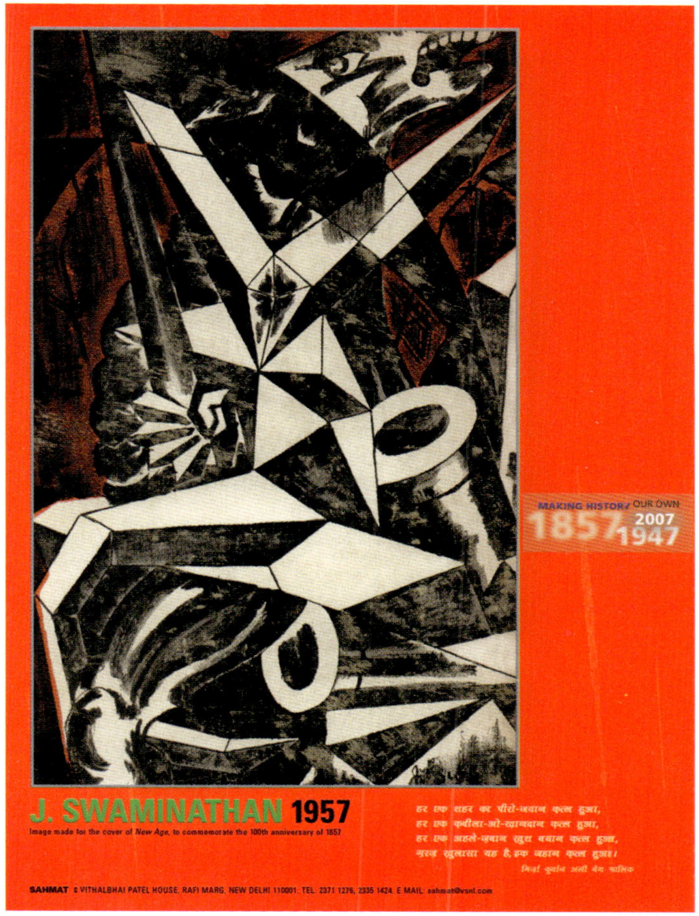

Poster, 2007, 19 x 14 inches.
Design: Ram Rahman.

This poster features a drawing made by J. Swaminathan in 1957 for the Communist Party of India's journal *New Age* to mark the centenary of the 1857 Revolt against British rule. Swaminathan made this drawing when he was a member of the Communist Party and it is an early example of his figurative art. He later became famous for his works of figurative abstraction.

2004

The Making of India

From the early 1990s, Indian politics witnessed the growth of a right-wing majoritarian view of India's civilization, history, and culture. In Irfan Habib's words, "The endeavor of the saffron [right-wing] forces to identify the Vedic [ancient] culture alone as the main, and even exclusive sources of Indian culture in the name of a so-called Cultural Nationalism stands in direct contradiction to the concept of Indian culture as a composite one."[1] Members of Sahmat believe that India, like every other major civilization in the world, has evolved through cross-fertilization of many traditions, beliefs, and practices. Sahmat's programs under the rubric *The Making of India* elaborated on this conviction.

In 2004, Sahmat planned *The Making of India* to mark both the completion of fifteen years of Sahmat's activities and the collective's ongoing celebration of India's plural and secular cultural histories. In September and October 2003, the collective approached artists and photographers, asking for ready-to-display works and providing a letter and concept notes prepared by Gulammohammed Sheikh, Irfan Habib, R. Champakalakshmi, and Aijaz Ahmad, detailing the project's themes and objectives. The artworks that Sahmat received were presented together in an exhibition and shown at three different venues in Delhi, from January to February 2004—at Rabindra Bhavan from January 6 to 12; at Vadhera Art Gallery from January 14 to 22; and at the School of Arts and Aesthetics, Jawaharlal Nehru University, from January 24 to February 10. In addition to the exhibition, Sahmat organized seminars and symposia and produced several publications to discuss the saffronization (communal distortion) of education and the "rewriting" of history in state-prescribed, school-level textbooks.

1. Irfan Habib, "The Making of Indian Culture," *The Making of India*, exh. cat. (New Delhi: Sahmat, 2002).

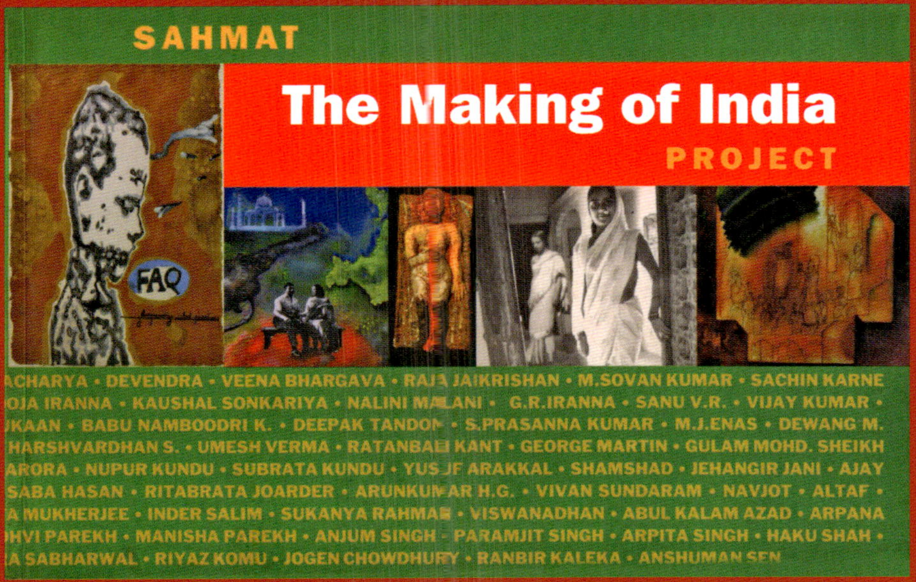

Catalogue cover, *The Making of India*, 2004. Design: Rajinder Arora.

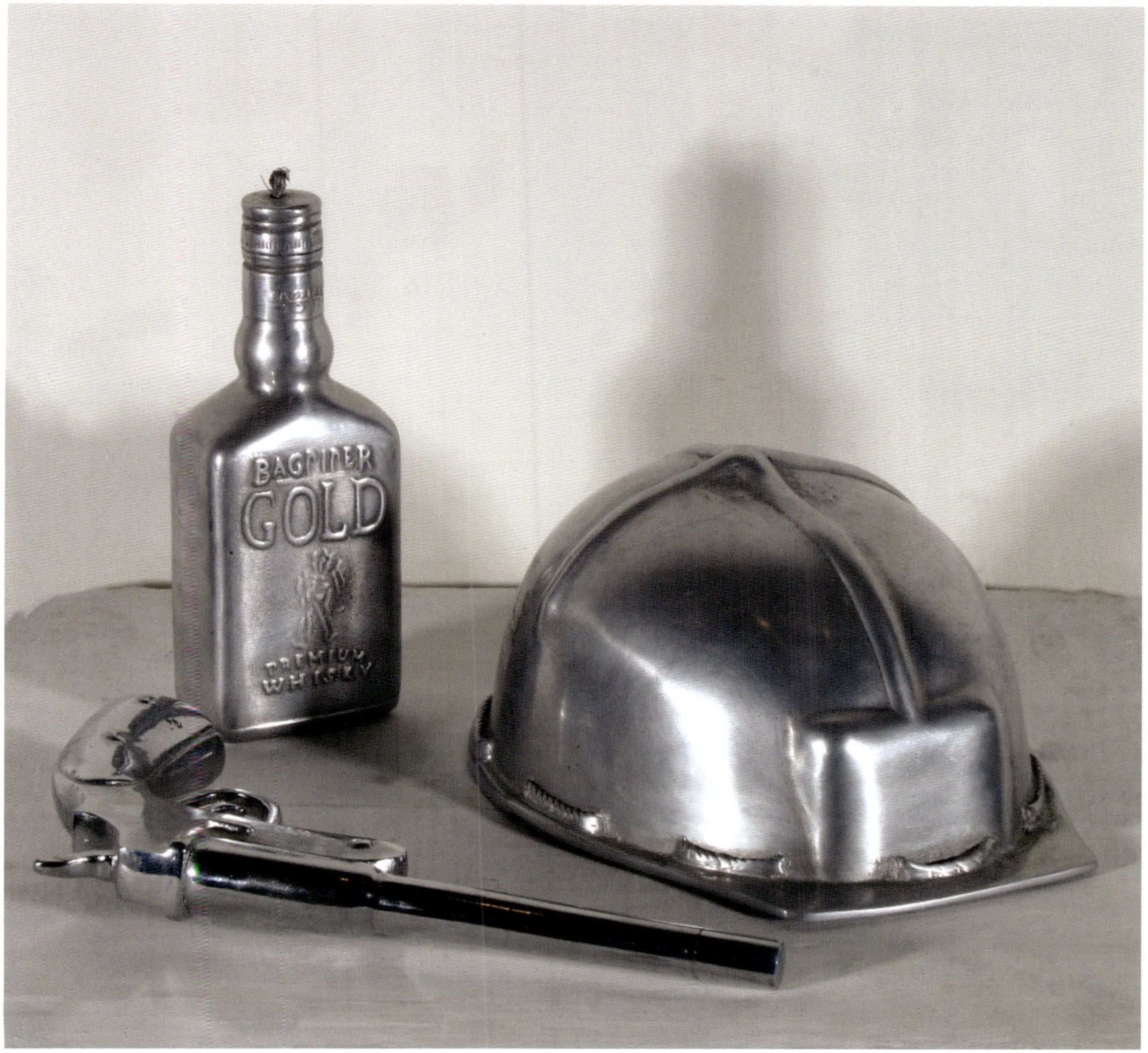

SUBODH GUPTA
Ab Bakri Ki Mimyane Ki Awaz Nahi Aati (Now one doesn't hear the sound of the goat bleating), 2004, cast aluminum, 20 x 20 x 15 inches. Collection: Priya Paul.

The title of this work is inspired by Ghalib's poetry. This work is very close to me and is one of my most important works. The complexity in it emotes the tension and drama in the life of an Indian laborer. Back in the days I would notice that after coming back from a day's hard work the laborers would unwind themselves by sitting around the fire, drinking and singing folk songs. This peaceful atmosphere is a rare scene nowadays. As survival is becoming increasingly difficult, the lack of opportunities and daily struggle for basics has filled that same man with angst. Where one could once hear music and laughter, now the ears are deafened by the cries of fighting men and gunshots in the dark night. Hence, the *dibri*, *katta*, and helmet signify that lost peace and tranquility in the life of a laborer. In this case, the *katta*, a country-made revolver, is not just a symbol of aggression but of self-defense in the face of danger and the laborer's fight to claim his basic rights. —S. G.

Note by Gulammohammed Sheikh sent to artists as part of the invitation to participate in the exhibition.

Is there an "idea" of India? Unity in diversity? A construct of contrasts and contradictions? A patchwork? Or a Speaking Tree with multiple voices?

Where does the "real" India exist? In its villages or its cities? In its past, ancient or medieval? Or in its modernity?

Is there an "Indian" sense of time? Is it about reclaiming an imagined timelessness or about forging a unilinear progression? Is it possible to live in multiple times?

What is an Indian sense of history? What space does it give to mythology? Is that different from the way others read history?

Is it possible to define the idea of India?

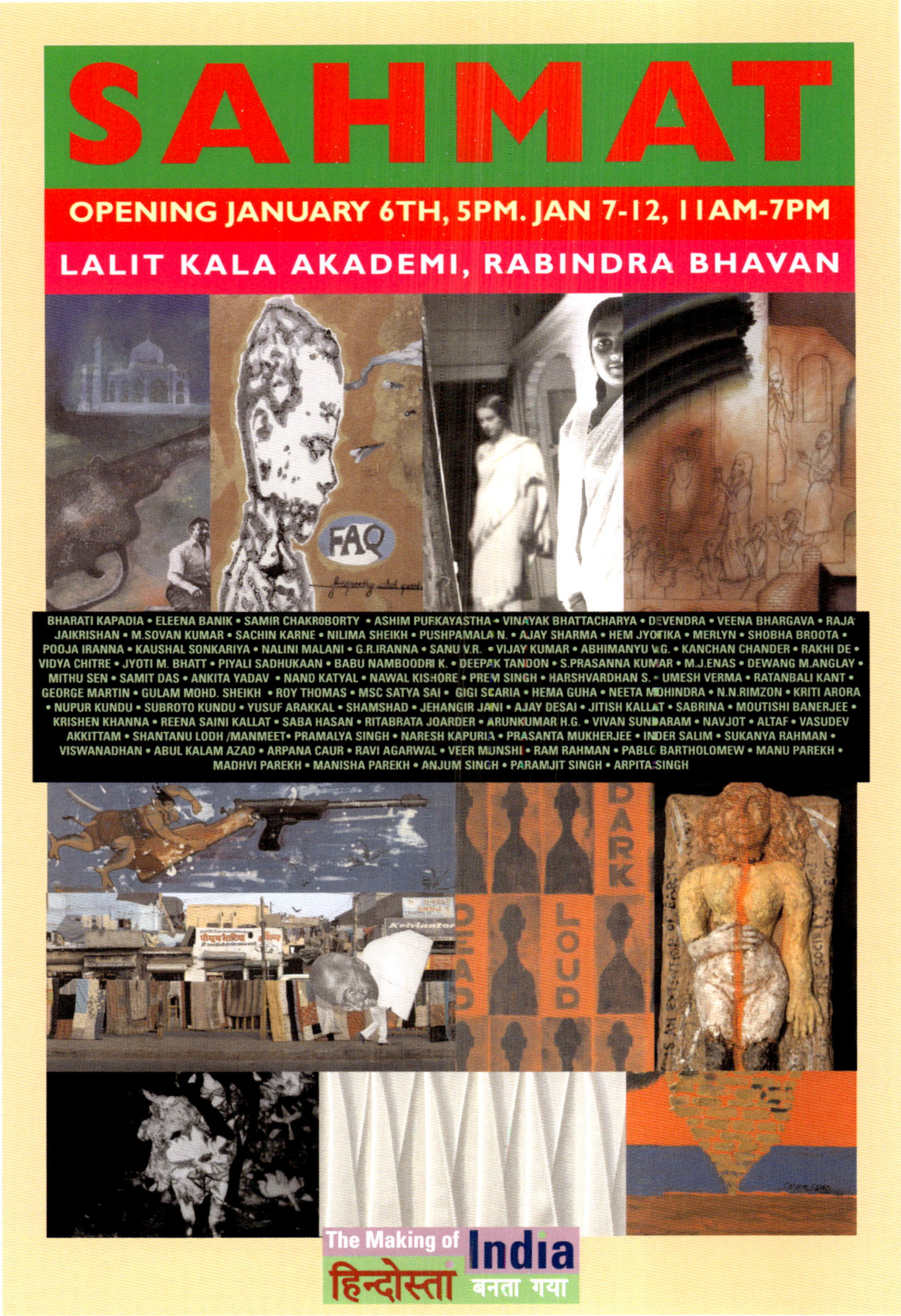

Poster for *The Making of India*, 2004, 17 x 14 inches. Design: Ram Rahman.

RAM RAHMAN

As part of the exercise of rehistoricizing, we involved artists and evolved exhibitions where we asked artists to explore ideas of nationalism, national histories, and personal histories. One was *The Making of India*, and another was *Making History Our Own*. The idea behind these projects was to engage art practice with a kind of historical pedagogy, but in a creative manner. We thought while national historical events are being celebrated, let's make an artistic historiography. It could be very personal because each one of us has a personal history that is actually a part of the national history. And if you really look at the personal history, this whole notion of unity and diversity comes alive, because each person has such a complicated individual history. We sent out fairly conceptual texts to many of the artists, because some of them hadn't read much history. That's been part of our objective actually—to give the community of artists a certain level of information from scholars that they would never get otherwise, either by attending a symposium or by getting a text as a proposal for making a work. In a way, this practice evolved from the idea of the Ayodhya broadside: that text, history, information, can actually spark ideas in an artist's mind. We can use them as a creative tool.

The letter sent to artists in 2004 soliciting works to include in the exhibition:

Safdar Hashmi was fatally attacked fifteen years ago, on 1 January 1989. Formed immediately thereafter, Sahmat (Safdar Hashmi Memorial Trust) marks its 15th anniversary this year.

Artists have been a core of Sahmat right from its formation. The historic *Artists Alert* exhibition and auction at Rabindra Bhavan in 1989 raised the initial funding corpus of Sahmat, which enabled us to survive and create projects over many years. Some of the subsequent collective artists' projects include *Images and Words, Postcards for Gandhi*, and *Art on the Move*.

As a nation, we have confronted huge challenges to accepted notions of identity, culture and nationalism, and a massive communal political mobilization which has led to violence, death and an atmosphere of fear and terror amongst many communities. The creative community itself has faced aggressive assaults as never before, in the attempt on the part of rightwing communal forces to stifle voices and project a narrowly defined notion of a "national" culture.

As part of Sahmat's 15th-year project, we are developing a poster exhibition on the theme of *The Making of India*, to celebrate the "complementary diversity" of our culture. In our landmark exhibition *Hum Sab Ayodhya* in 1993, we had looked at the multiple layers of culture, mythology, social development, and history associated with a single site. Here, we will expand the frame of our enquiry to encompass the subcontinent, and instead of a linear historical presentation, we will examine ideas, sites, cultural traditions, artefacts, architecture and social transformation through history.

We are proposing an art project that will be complementary to this project. The idea is for artists to make a work each, which is their vision of "who we are now." By the very nature of its content and the differences in approach, we hope that this exhibit will be a display of the multiplicities of contemporary art language which make up our cultural mosaic—a "snapshot," if you like, of our visual culture now.

We are leaving the theme and format fairly open-ended, but the work should be small in size (say, twelve by twelve inches) and sent in a ready-to-display manner. It should be framed or laminated, depending on the medium. The medium can be anything the artist wants to work with: painting, photography, construction, digital media, etc. We propose to show the work in both formal and informal settings. As in our previous projects, we will try and sell the work to cover costs and raise funds for further activities.

Please send us your work to the address given below, suitably packed to avoid breakage or damage. We are enclosing some concept notes and excerpts from papers written for *The Making of India* project for your reference.

—Ram Rahman, Shamshad, Vivan Sundaram

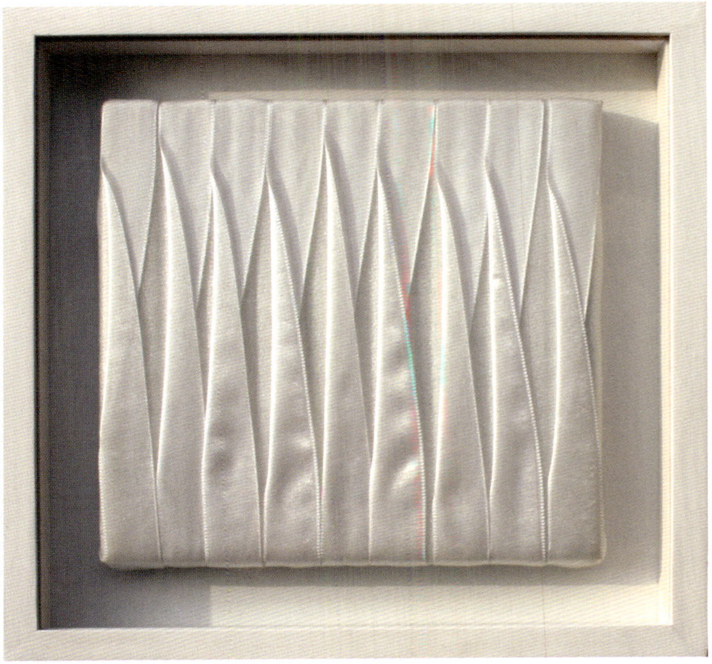

SHOBHA BROOTA
The Twist, 2004, fabric, 12 x 12 inches.

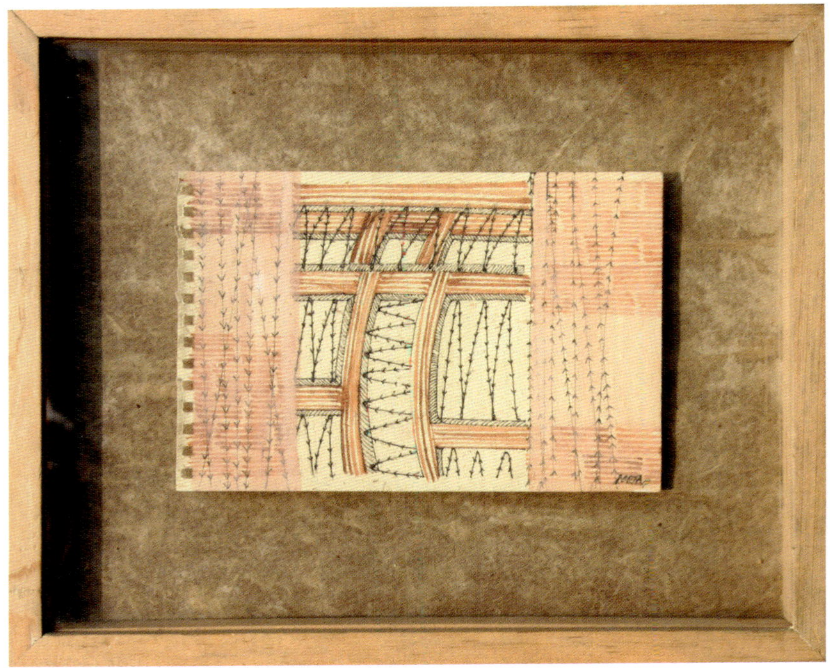

POOJA IRANNA
Untitled, 2004, ink and pencil on paper, 12 x 10 inches.

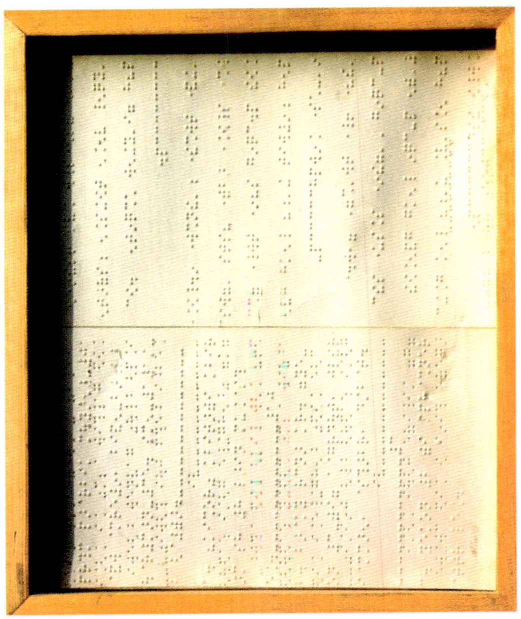

MITHU SEN
Blind Fold, 1994, Braille paper, 14 x 12 inches.

It's a very old work of mine, made in 1994, while working in a little school for blind students in my native town in Bengal. It's from a primary school where blind children get to know a new language to express themselves through touch. . . . When we see it, it is visual but for them it is a touch-feeling . . . what they remember, and they make their own literature through it. I liked that perspective on how we both (those who can see and those who can't) use our different senses to achieve a language, an understanding. It's the same thing but a different way of viewing, making, and understanding. The way Sahmat works in our contemporary life, the relation is similar. Therefore I choose to give the work to them. —M. S.

SONIA KHURANA
A true Hindu patriot, 2002, wood and paper, 4 x 8 x 5 inches.

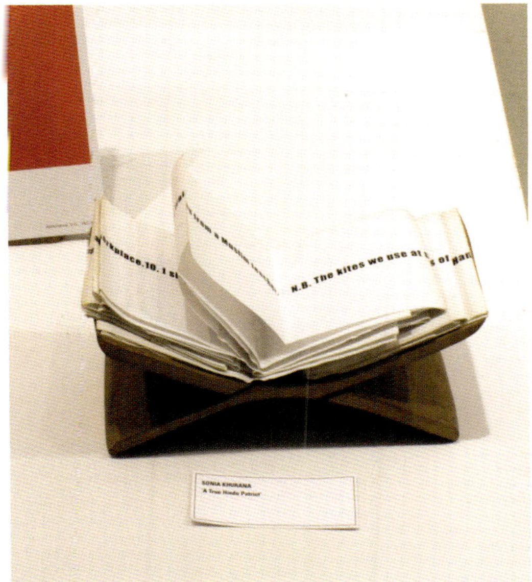

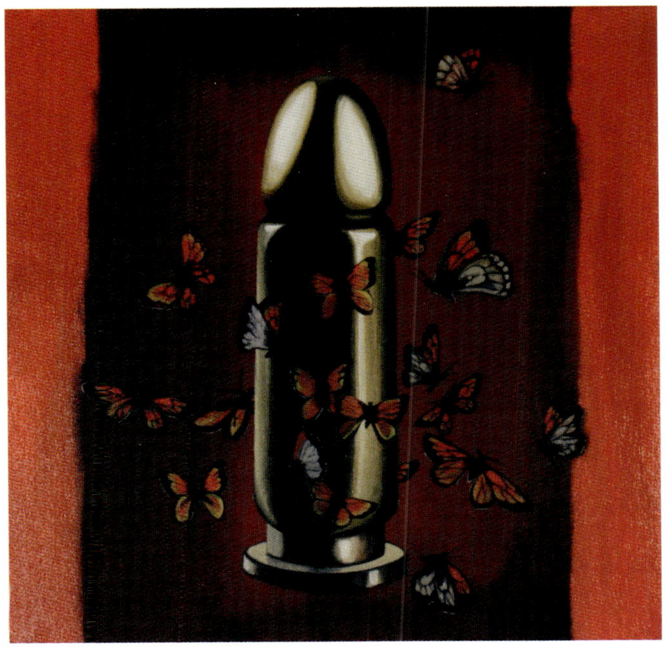

SACHIN KARNE
Study for Butterflies in the Stomach, 2004, acrylic and oil on canvas, 18 x 18 inches.

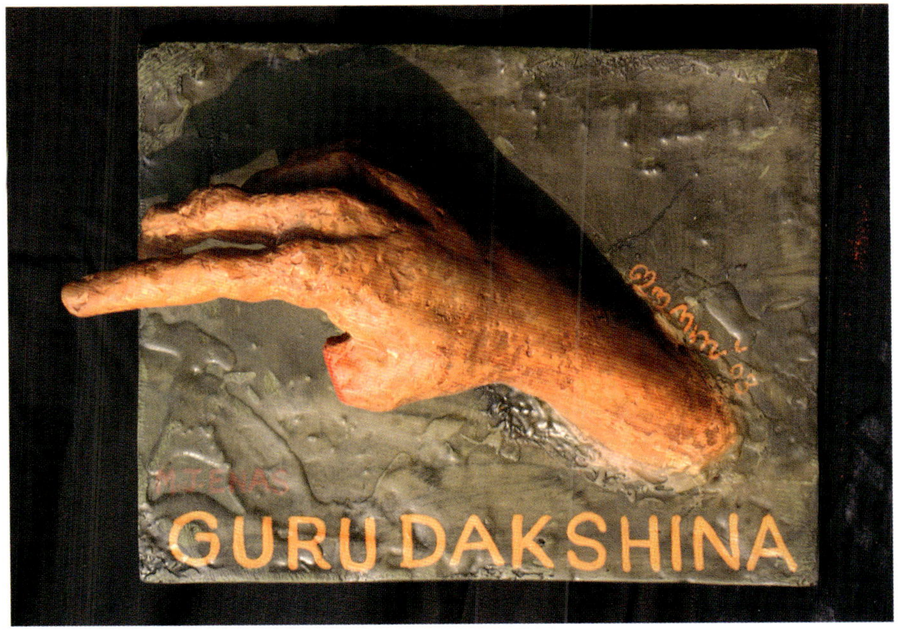

M. J. ENAS
Guru Dakshina (Gift to the Guru), 2004, painted plaster, 11½ x 13 x 6 inches.

This sculpture refers to a famous episode in the epic *The Mahabharata*. The great archer Dronacharya cannot teach archery to the low-caste Ekalavya. Yet Ekalavya teaches himself archery with an image of Dronacharya as inspiration. When Dronacharya hears of this and sees his skill, he asks for his thumb as *guru dakshina*, thus rendering him impotent as an archer. The story has great resonance for the lower castes in India who are still struggling for acceptance.

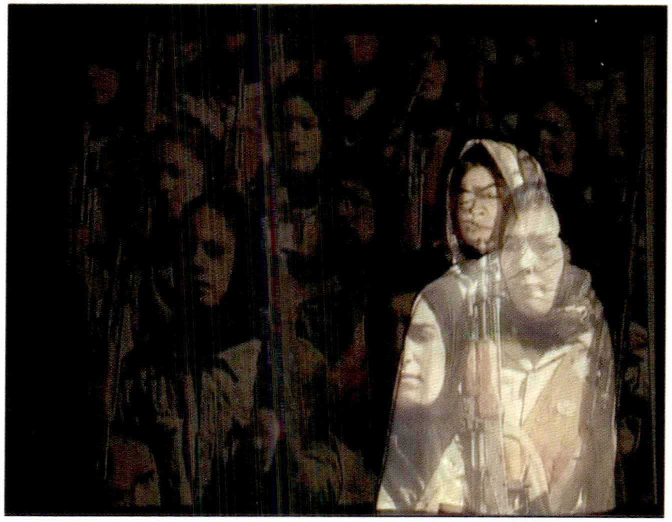

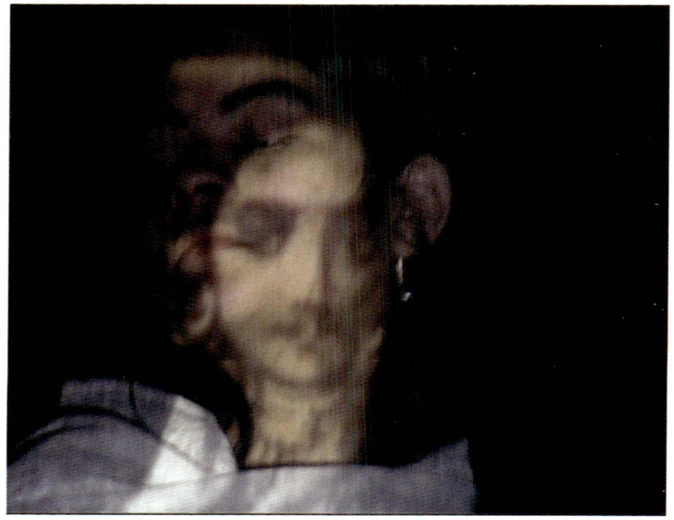

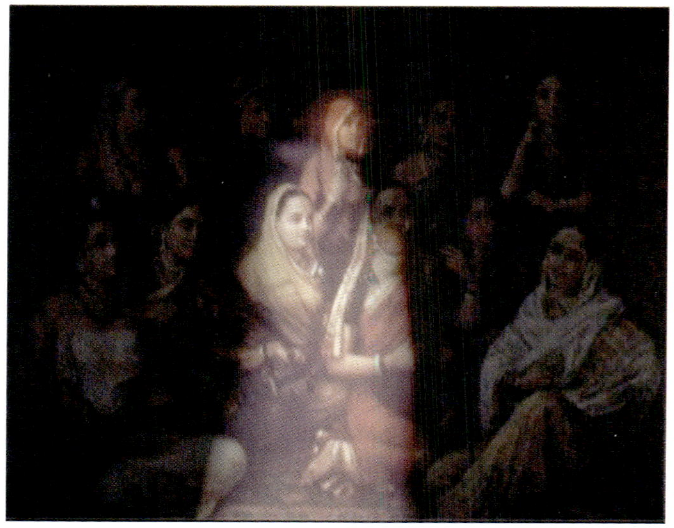

Malani's video *Unity in Diversity* (2003) was made in response to the Gujarat riots of February–March 2002, and makes reference to two well-known factors in modern Indian culture. "Unity in diversity" is the primary motto of cultural policy in a post-independence India. It is one of the foundational myths of the modern, secular democracy that was mobilized to support the creation of a sovereign state out of the disparate remnants of British colonialism. An early visualization of this ideal was Ravi Varma's *Galaxy of Musicians* (1893), which presents an orchestral arrangement of richly bedecked Indian women from identifiably diverse cultural and ethnic backgrounds, typical representations of Indian womanhood in its diverse guises assembled in a single symphony.

Malani has worked on this painting earlier, in her 1989 watercolor *Re-thinking Raja Ravi Varma,* where quoted figures from the *Galaxy* were presented as being pushed into the margin by the massively articulated form of a female nude that represents an animated conversation with normative notions of Indian womanhood.

Unity in Diversity speaks specifically, and with brutal clarity, of the atrocities committed against the Muslim minority in Gujarat, in collusion with state bureaucracy and law enforcement agencies. In the video, the fragile fabric of the national ideal is quite literally stretched, torn apart. The spectacle of bejewelled women from Ravi Varma disintegrates into the incomprehensible horrors of contemporary political violence. Using quotations from Ravi Varma juxtaposed with her own drawn animation based on his figures, Malani's work presents a vision of apocalyptic proportions compressed into an eight-minute single-channel video. **—Chaitanya Sambrani**

Excerpt from "Apocalypse recalled: the recent work of Nalini Malani," in *Nalini Malani: Stories Retold*, exhibition catalogue, Bose Pacia Gallery, 2004; reproduced with permission of the author.

NALINI MALANI
Unity in Diversity, 2003, video, 7 minutes, 30 seconds.
Collection: Walsh Gallery archives.

Nalini Malani

As for the selected artwork *Unity in Diversity* for this exhibition in Chicago I can say the following. Educated as a painter I was probably the first artist in India in the early 1990s to use the medium of video to reach a wider audience. The years of 1992–93 were a national disaster with Muslims being killed on the streets of Bombay. How could the frozen image of a painting in an upper strata gallery make meaning? I therefore started to use the moving image and to project images in alternative spaces, much along the line as we worked in Sahmat. *Unity in Diversity* was made as a reaction to a second wave of religious fundamentalism that caused an ethnic genocide in Gujarat in 2002. After growing up with ideas from a Nehruvian period where the slogan had been "Unity in Diversity," that now seemed further away than ever. This video play starts with an image of my painterly interpretation of the famous work *Galaxy of Musicians* by the nineteenth-century Indian artist Ravi Varma. He had painted a group of female musicians, each dressed in a regional costume, as an example of how this diverse group can play in harmony. But at the end of the twentieth century all this had changed for the worse situation ever, with atrocities that one could not even imagine. With text by Heiner Mueller, the painting in my video comes alive and shows in different layers the cruel history that India has gone through, and how with the rise of religious fundamentalism, everything, especially the position of women, deteriorates. The video ends with the quote of a female eyewitness who says in Hindi, "They poured petrol into the mouth of a six year old boy and threw in a lit match—he blew up like a bomb."

The other reason why I proposed to show *Unity in Diversity* in Chicago is a very specific one. Ravi Varma's painting was shown in Chicago during the World Congress of Religions in 1893. One of the speakers was the Indian philosopher Swami Vivekananda, who addressed the danger of orthodoxy in religion.*

Usually this video play is shown not as a single channel work but as an installation that represents a middle-class sitting room, with chairs, and photographs of Gandhi and Nehru on the wall, and a large ornamental painting frame in which the video is projected.

> *Sectarianism, bigotry, and its horrible descendant, fanaticism, have long possessed this beautiful Earth. They have filled the earth with violence, drenched it often and often with human blood, destroyed civilization, and sent whole nations to despair. Had it not been for these horrible demons, human society would be far more advanced than it is now. —Swami Vivekananda at the World Congress of Religions, Chicago 1893 —N. M.

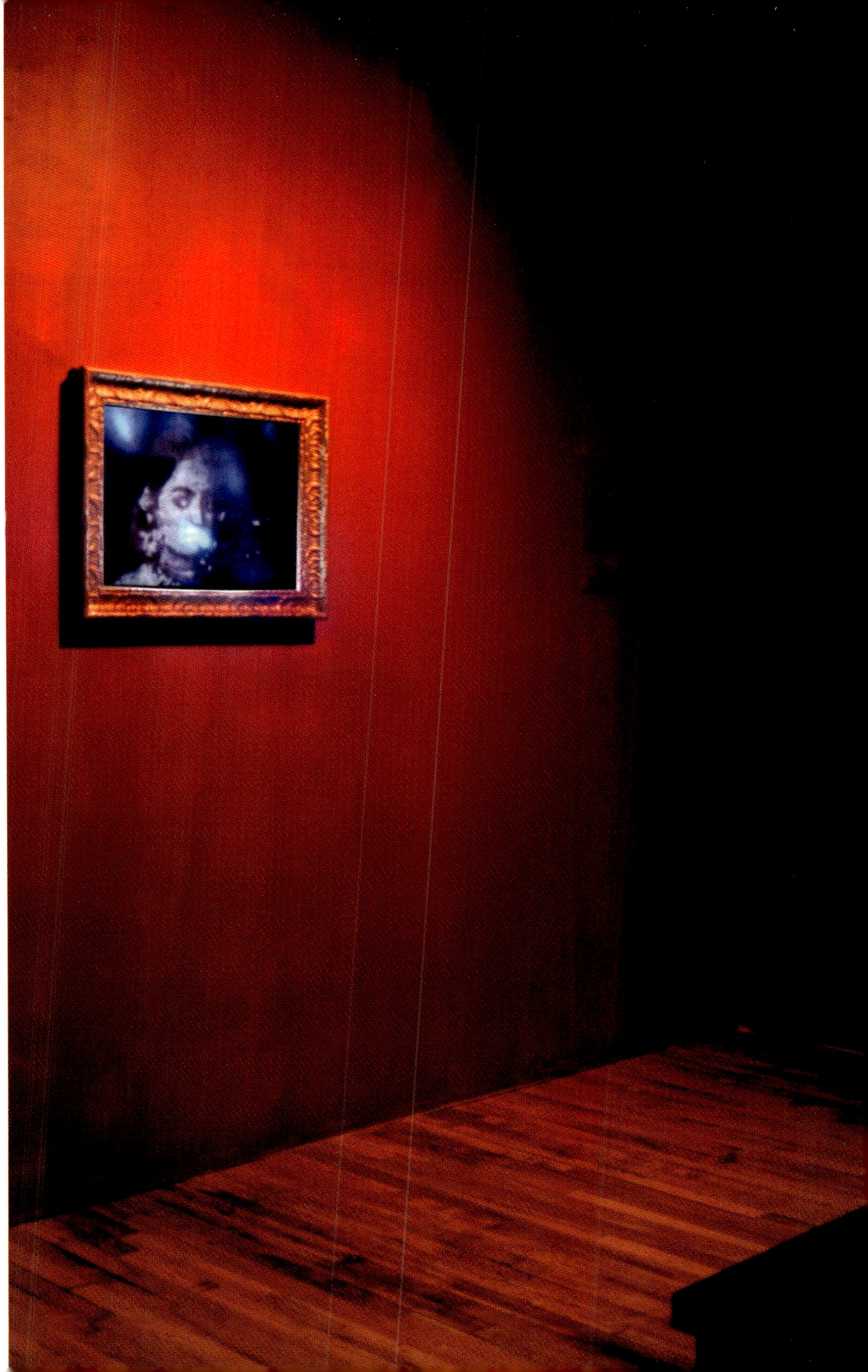

Nalini Malani, *Unity in Diversity*, installation view, 2007, Walsh Gallery.

The Making of Indian Culture

Irfan Habib

From the catalogue *Making of India* (New Delhi: Sahmat, 2004).

The culture of every country has to be seen in the context of the presence of certain universal values. That several ethical principles are shared by people wherever they live has been recognized since very early times. Elements of knowledge, especially sciences, overcame all boundaries, territorial or cultural, as they diffused from various centres in the ancient and medieval times. Ethics tend also to change with social development. Modern times have brought forth a whole set of social, economic and political values, such as equality (including gender equality), universal education, welfare state, socialism, and secularism, which are today in varying degrees regarded as necessary appendages to modern societies. The supremacy of reason and sciences is the vital ingredient of what may be called the modern civilization, which seeks to embrace every country of the world; and the culture of each country tends now to be seen as one complementing, not contradicting, this universal civilization.

The universality of civilisational values does not bar them, however, from co-existing with individual cultural traditions. Language, geography, history, social customs, art styles, and transmitted beliefs, are, perhaps, the main determining factors in creating such regional or national cultures. But such cultures too are subject to the laws of evolution: they have formed, developed, and, almost in all cases, changed fundamentally over periods of time.

India is a large country. Its culture has originated out of the intermingling of several regional streams and different traditions which have been interacting with each other, resulting over time in various common cultural features. It is surely incorrect to look for a single fountainhead of Indian culture, whether Austro-asiatic, Harappan (Indus), Dravidian or Vedic.

Several streams, both of indigenous and external origins, have continuously contributed to the enrichment of Indian culture; and, indeed, the framers of our Constitution (Article 5A) too, in referring to "the rich heritage of our composite culture," cannot but have had this process in mind. The endeavour of the saffron forces to identify the Vedic culture alone as the main, and even exclusive, source of Indian culture in the name of a so-called "cultural nationalism" stands in direct contradiction to the concept of Indian culture as a composite one. But this is not its only implication. As the new NCERT textbooks have shown, every conceivable philosophical and scientific achievement is being credited to the Vedas: the Upanishads contained the true elements of all later philosophies (including Jainism and Buddhism), the Vedic people knew already of zero, decimal position of numerals, helio-centric astronomy, geometry, etc. It has to be inferred from this that after the time of the Vedas the Indian people steadily lost all capacity for further growth, and, indeed, if the enthusiasts of the saffron brigade are to be believed, forgot a number of outstanding scientific discoveries that their Vedic ancestors had been able to make. Such a claim made to glorify Indian culture actually succeeds only in presenting it as stagnant and declining over the longer period of its life! Quite on the contrary, the true historic evolution of Indian culture has to be seen as a succession of advance and achievements, in thought, art, literature, etc. Another implication of the saffronised view of Indian culture is that it is free of all external influences. It had, we are assured, nothing to learn from the Mesopotamians or the Greeks in mathematics, astronomy, science and technology. It is obvious that a culture which remains closed to external influences, forgoes a very important factor of progress. Indian culture would have, indeed, been much poorer without such external infusions. It is true that, though present in all great cultures, the capacity to interact has not been equally strong in every historical phase. Alberuni (ca. 1035) noted in his work *Kitab al-Hind* in an oft-quoted passage, that while contemporaneously Indian culture was sought to be insulated from foreign influences, this was not the case in earlier times. This raises an interesting question: when did at least some Indians realise that there were common elements that made up their own culture, as against that of the outsiders, being non-Indians who lived differently. A saying attributed to the Buddha was that there were no castes among the Greeks, but only masters and slaves; here the caste system seemingly furnished one very distinguished element of Indian culture. When Ashoka referred to the absence of Shramanas (Buddhist, Jain and Ajiviks monks) and Brahmanas among the Greeks, the cultural difference assumes a religious light. In *Manusmriti* it assumed the aspect of territoriality as well, when the "twice-born" were forbidden from living outside Aryavarta (Northern India) and the outsiders (mlechchhas) were declared unclean and unworthy. Gradually, we see an Indian cultural self-consciousness taking shape, within the elite classes to begin with. The self-consciousness partly involved prejudice and narrowness towards outsiders, and this generated the kind of insularity against which Alberuni was led to protest.

The distinct features of Indian culture came to be identified with special emphasis when there was a considerable infusion of external cultural traits accompanying Islam, with its own composite background with Hellenistic and Iranian traditions. Viewing India from a Greco-Arab point of view, Alberuni in the eleventh century delineated the elements of Higher Indian culture in his *Kitab al-Hind*, while Amir Khusrau could similarly identify the major features of Indian popular culture in his *Nuh Sipihr*, in the fourteenth century.

This kind of material provides us with a picture of the achievements and characteristics of Indian culture as these appeared to persons familiar with an external culture. In other words, where intercultural comparison becomes possible, the individual cultures themselves can be better studied. But the very co-existence of external and internal traditions implied a process of mutual accommodation and interpenetration of customs and fashions. One tends to see it most obviously in the realms of fine arts, notably architecture, music, painting; and religion. In the religion, Ibn 'Arabi and Shankaracharya's Vedanta suggested common grasps of "truths" that could be "proved" merely by coincidental terminations of independent quests. At the same time an acceptance of the common essentials of the two faiths meant that parts which were not shared, notably, Islamic and Hindu ritual and, above all, that landmark of Indian culture, the caste system, must be rejected. The lowly origins of the main spokesmen of such rejection, e.g., Kabir, Sain, Ravidas, are a remarkable phenomenon; and if the Sikh gurus were not lowly in rank, their denunciations of caste too grew sharper with time.

There were other levels of interaction too, which come under the depiction of composite culture, but one is not sure whether they were always of positive consequences. Hindu women did not benefit from the larger shares on inheritance prescribed in Muslim law, but possibly fell under larger constraints, as women's seclusion among Hindus became as much a status symbol as among Muslims. Widow remarriage, on the other hand, tended to become less common among Indian Muslims, as a response to higher caste Hindu abhorrence of the custom. "Composite" cultures must, therefore, be as critically studied as insular cultures, though one need not doubt that generally such mixtures play a positive part in the evolution of cultures, as in biology. It is now fashionable (as in Said's *Orientalism*) to criticize Marx's thesis of destructive and regenerative consequences of colonialism, that was put forward by him initially in respect of India. The destruction of the old social order, and older crafts, necessarily constrained and distorted the older cultural traditions. But at the same time colonialism inevitable quickened the diffusion of radical social and political ideas from Europe. These had received their most powerful impetus from the French Revolution (1789–94), of whose principles Ram Mohan Roy was such an enthusiastic admirer. The Bengal Renaissance and the Indian Social Reform Movement of the 19th century owed their inspiration to West European thought, and it would be unhistorical and inaccurate to trace their ideological sources to the Upanishads or Vedas. In so far as these movements laid stress on science and modern education, on the transfer of modern thought into vernaculars on women's rights, and on opposition to caste-disabilities, they marked a notable stage of progress of Indian culture. Ram Mohan Roy, Keshav Chandra Sen, Jotiba Phule and Syed Ahmad Khan, among others, in varying degrees represented this effort at modernization and the reform of certain age-old features of our modes of thought. Its legacy is a precious element of our culture today.

The concept of India as a country was certainly established as early as the Mauryan Empire, which for the first time gave political shape to Jambudvipa—the name of India then in use. Political unity secured under the Delhi Sultanate and, then, the Mughal Empire, undoubtedly popularised further the notion of 'Hindustan' as a country. But India was not yet a nation: many divisive elements in our culture, notable caste (as Ram Mohan Roy pointed out in 1830), and religious divisions precluded its growth into a nation. The social reform movement, therefore, prepared the ground for this momentous change; but it was the need for a united opposition to colonial rule that created the momentum. It is in this sense that the genesis of India as a nation is owed to the Freedom Movement, and Gandhiji is the Father of the Nation. India's transformation into a nation was accompanied by the growth of two major elements in India culture, without which such a transformation was not possible: democracy and secularism. There were efforts to trace these two elements in the shape of the Village Community and mutual tolerance in our old culture (as in Gandhiji's *Hind Swaraj*), but their diffusion owed to both the national liberation movements the world over and the need of mass mobilisation and national unity for a successful anti-colonial struggle.

The Karachi Resolution on Fundamental Rights of the Congress, 1931, represents not only a major programmatic statement on the part of the Freedom Movement, but it is also an important reflection of the new cultural outlook of the Indian nation.

As against this powerful trend may be set Hindu "cultural nationalism" and Muslim separatism. Both, projecting a two-nation theory, are based on the identification of each "nation's" culture with a specific religious tradition. Though despite the Partition of 1947, Independent India affirmed the principles of secularism and a composite national culture, there is no doubt that this affirmation has been greatly compromised by the growing strength of the Hindutva forces during the last two decades. There is all the more reason today, therefore, to stress the fact that Indian culture cannot be seen as a static entity, or as a phenomenon of original perfection. It needs to be viewed critically, so that its capacities for creative effort and assimilation of new values and traits, and for internal reform and improvement, are made the special object of study. Its strengths and weaknesses have to be understood alike. Two aspects of Indian culture need to be particularly borne in mind. First, we have here a unity in diversity. The diversity is not surprising, given the size of the country; but that the unifying factors are strong, at levels of both Higher culture and folk culture is especially noteworthy. We thus need to have a perception of an Indian culture coexisting with cultures attached to its various component parts. Secondly, there is the necessity of seeing how far Indian culture assimilates universal values which, of course, are not themselves stationery, and are often mutually contradictory. "Free-market" values, and socialism, for example, are in conflict today all over the world, including India. It will be too trite to say that Indian culture needs to be universalist in content while historically specific in form. But certainly, one cannot view Indian culture in isolation from the winds of change in ideas and circumstances that blow over the world all the time.

The Making of India

Aijaz Ahmad

From "The Making of India," presented at the seminar "The Making of India," on November 2, 2003, at Asian College of Journalism, Chennai.

We could reflect in different ways on "The Making of India" into a modern nation. The British—administrators as well as scholars—claimed that it was only the Raj itself that had unified India for the first time in its history, which was otherwise an exasperating mosaic of conflicting communities, religions, sects, and races. We would argue, instead, that it was the anti-colonial movement, rather than the fact of colonial occupation, which put into motion the process through which a pre-modern civilization could make a transition to modern nationhood. As we look back upon even the earliest phase in the embryonic development of the national movement, from the 1880s onwards, when it was far from being a movement for national independence and was still very much an upper-class phenomenon, two features stand out.

One is struck, first, by an early and abiding concern that the national movement, in order to be truly national, had to be as inclusive as possible, taking into its fold people from different religions, regions and linguistic backgrounds—i.e., a unified national movement which was nevertheless internally accommodative and heterogeneous. Secularism was an inherent tendency in this nationalism, even when commitment to it was not clearly articulated as an ideological position, precisely because the society that was sought to be transformed into a modern nation was religiously and denominationally so very heterogeneous. One of the very many ill effects of the Partition of India is that one forgets that Muslims in pre-Partition India constituted roughly a quarter of the population and were the majority in India's two largest provinces, namely Bengal and Punjab. The ideology of secularism, or at least multi-denominational tolerance, arose in India as an intrinsic part of the ideology of nationalism itself; and the idea of secularism arose also as a mechanism of fundamental defense against varieties of communalism within society itself, as well as against the imperialist policies of "Divide and Rule." This was an objective requirement, independent of any particular leader's personal predilections, be it the agnostic and "socialistic" Mr. Nehru, or the Sanatani Mahatma Gandhi, or the pietistic Maulana Azad, or the rightwing Sardar Patel whose personal political culture was not far from that of Hindu communalism. So, between the founding of the national movement toward the end of the 19th century and (let us say) the 1970s when decline of the Indian National Congress begins, ideas of secularism and inter-faith toleration became more and more a constituent element in the ideology of Indian nationalism. I do not at all mean that bourgeois nationalism in India was always true to these ideas or that the main nationalist organizations, such as the Congress, were free of communal elements even among its leaders. I actually think that the main reason why the national movement failed to prevent the Partition and the creation of Pakistan was that it had within its own ranks a very substantial rightwing which was itself much too implicated in the politics of Hindu communalism, and was so perceived by large sections of the politically active Muslims. What I do mean, however, is that the leading core of the national movement always thought of secularism as a necessary ingredient in the making of a modern nationhood for India, and that this core perceived the lack of secularism among many of its own ranks as a weakness and a deficit in the power and legitimacy of the movement as a whole.

The multilingual and multiregional character of the national movement likewise arose out of the objectively perceptible historical and civilizational character of India. Unlike Africa or the Arab world, which colonialism had chopped up into numerous states, India had been integrated into a vast colony that spoke in numerous tongues. Most provinces of British India were larger than most countries of Europe. Speakers of Bengali in pre-Partition India were as numerous as speakers of French in Europe, and they understood as little of Tamil as the French might have understood of Serbo-Croatian, while Tamil was older—by far—than any of the modern European languages, including English and French. This multiplicity of consolidated languages, hence of cultural attributes that grow alongside each particular language, was intrinsic to the very nature of Indian society long before colonialism ever arrived on our shores, so that, in this concrete historical context, a modern Indian nation had to be fundamentally different, internally much more diversified, than the kind of monolingual, mono-cultural nation which is so typical of Europe and of advanced capitalism in general. The upshot was that English undoubtedly became a link language among the literate sections of the various regions, and there were of course moments of unbearable zeal and stupidity when Hindi was sought to be imposed as a "national language"—the so-called *rashtrabhasha*—upon all the peoples of India, but retreat from that latter position was also quick and there was, most of the time, a perfect recognition of the obvious fact that the

"Indian nation" whose unity was so ardently sought shall continue to speak in a couple of dozen tongues in its larger units, and many more tongues, in fact, beyond the larger ones.

This recognition surely corresponded to an objective fact, but the wide acceptance of this fact was owed, I believe, to the much older civilizational fact that we had been speaking a large number of languages through all those pre-national centuries in which something resembling a civilizational unity had come into being. This easy acceptance of a multilingual nationhood was remarkable enough. What was even more remarkable, considering that ethnicity and language has been so central in the history of the great majority of nationalisms, especially in Europe, is that India has displayed an astonishing lack of ethno-linguistic nationalisms. At no point in the course of the anti-colonial nationalism did there develop in India a powerful linguistically based separatist movement, on the model, say, of the communally based separatist movement that led to the creation of Pakistan. Instead, we have seen a large number of movements for the creation of linguistically based states within the Union. Multiplicity of languages, hence cultural diversity, is something that is simply taken for granted. This fact does not seem very remarkable to us only because we have grown up in a social milieu and a civilizational space that has given rise to this fact. We could, however, compare this situation with a country like the United States, the most resourceful in the world, where the citizenry consists of migrants (and children of former slaves) who originally belonged to some two hundred different linguistic groups but who are then required to forget those languages and are subjected to the monolingual dictatorship of the English language, which refuses to concede any constitutional status to any other language in the life of that uniglot nation. . . .

It is quite remarkable how uneasy the reformist and nationalist consciences were on the question of caste, and how sharp the perception that a society so profoundly divided on the question of caste can hardly call itself a nation, which presumes at least a horizontal social equality among members of a nation. Witness Vivekananda's famous quip that a Hinduism that could observe caste distinctions was, as he put it, merely a "kitchen religion." Or Tagore's observation, in his *Lectures on Nationalism*, that where people are free neither to dine together nor marry freely into each other's families can hardly be called a nation. Or Gandhi's declaration, on the eve of his Poona Pact with Ambedkar, that he would rather wish that Hinduism dies than that caste may live.

The centrality of caste among the countless projects of reform during the colonial period is undeniable. Why so? The first reason of course is that the question of caste has been the great unresolved question—but also the irrepressible question—in the history of Indian civilization and society since the grand confrontation between Brahminism and the Buddha. That the question has never been resolved, despite struggles ranging over millennia, testifies to the force of the Brahminical order and the systems of power and property associated with that order. But that the question has been irrepressible across millennia and constantly erupts into great social crises, testifies to the fact that regardless of the brute power of the dominant order, broad popular acceptance of that order breaks down constantly, so that the repressed returns punctually, refusing to be repressed, and the finest, the most progressive elements in our society have kept that question alive. My own sense is that the Bhakti-Sufi tradition, with its ideology of anti-caste social egalitarianism spreading over virtually every region and language in India, has contributed a great deal to aggravating that crisis of belief in the dominant social order and its justifications for itself. This past—with its history of oppression, but also its history of protest and opposition—weighed on the conscience of the principal reformers within the national movement, quite in addition to their perception that a really unified nation cannot possibly arise out of a caste-based society. But what made caste so central in the politics of the age was neither the inheritance of the traditions of protest nor the guilty conscience of the nationalist leadership, but the actual fact of the rise of anti-caste movements of the modern type, which arose much before the "national movement" (Jotiba Phule's Satyashodhak Samaj was established in 1873, virtually a generation before the founding of the Indian National Congress in 1885). The nationalist simply could not evade this question.

As the national movement became truly a mass movement from 1919 onward and gradually transformed itself into a clear-cut anti-imperialist movement over the next decade or so, both those emphases—that the national movement be culturally composite and denominationally inclusive; and that virtually every aspect of Indian society needed to be reformed in pursuit of a more unified and egalitarian India—were to be greatly strengthened. This essentially liberal make-up of the national movement of course provoked a rightwing backlash, notably from such organizations as the RSS and the Hindu Mahasabha, but this rightwing remained a very marginal element in Indian society throughout the anti-colonial struggle. Far more significant was increase in working-class militancy and the rise of the communist movement, from the 1920s onwards. Whereas the RSS etc. were known for their fascist sympathies and collaborated actively with the colonial authorities, the notable feature of the communist movement in India was that it attracted many militant sections of Indian society which were disillusioned by the limitations of liberal nationalism, and that it arose in the perspective of a world-wide anti-fascist struggle as well as a rising anti-colonial movement within the country of which it remained an intrinsic part. This accounts for the fact that whereas the far right remained utterly isolated in Indian politics in the early decades of the Republic after Independence, the communist left was widely perceived as the main ideological alternative to liberal bourgeois nationalism at that time, even though the communist left and the Nehruvian state shared the secular and democratic values of the Indian Constitution.

2007

Making History Our Own

Sahmat's projects often invite a shared moment of reflection. With *Making History Our Own* (2007), the collective chose to reflect on the sixtieth year of India's independence and the 150th anniversary of the 1857 uprising, as well as to mark the birth centenaries of important figures in India's history. As a supplement to the national celebrations, Sahmat sought to emphasize the complex cultural antecedents of the individuals and historical events being commemorated, and to personalize these cultural complexities through the differing visions of artists who drew upon their own lineages and inspirations to create works included in the exhibition. Sahmat operates from a basic conviction that there are multilayered influences on each individual's cultural identity—a unique amalgamation of religion, language, class, and race that derives from both traditional and contemporary cultural practices in the subcontinent—and that the expression of those varied influences produces the clearest resistance against a simplistic, homogeneous, majoritarian identity.

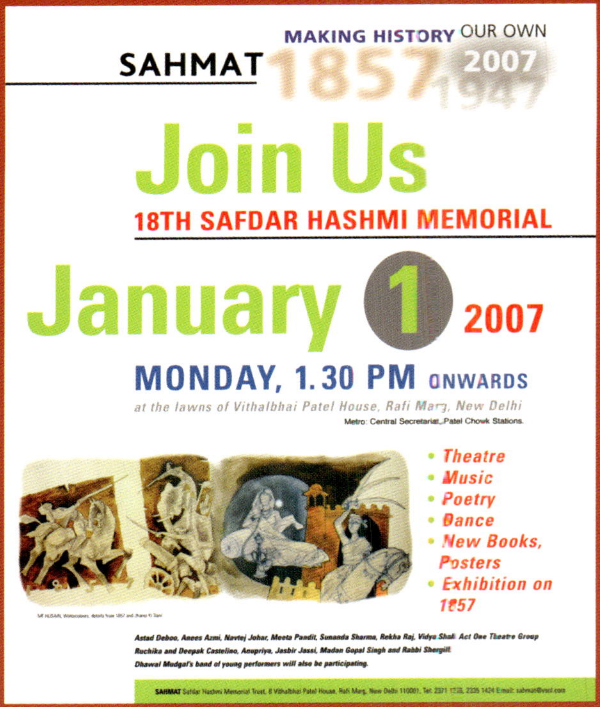

Poster for *18th Safdar Hashmi Memorial*, 2007, 17 x 14 inches.
Design: Ram Rahman.

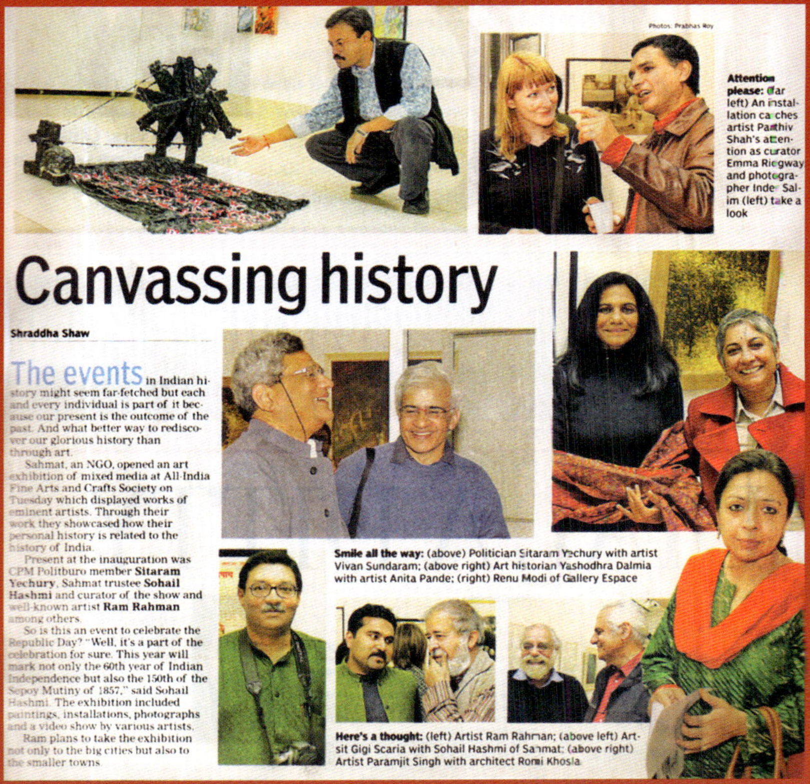

Canvassing history

Shraddha Shaw

The events in Indian history might seem far-fetched but each and every individual is part of it because our present is the outcome of the past. And what better way to rediscover our glorious history than through art.

Sahmat, an NGO, opened an art exhibition of mixed media at All-India Fine Arts and Crafts Society on Tuesday which displayed works of eminent artists. Through their work they showcased how their personal history is related to the history of India.

Present at the inauguration was CPM Politburo member **Sitaram Yechury**, Sahmat trustee **Sohail Hashmi** and curator of the show and well-known artist **Ram Rahman** among others.

So is this an event to celebrate the Republic Day? "Well, it's a part of the celebration for sure. This year will mark not only the 60th year of Indian Independence but also the 150th of the Sepoy Mutiny of 1857," said Sohail Hashmi. The exhibition included paintings, installations, photographs and a video show by various artists.

Ram plans to take the exhibition not only to the big cities but also to the smaller towns.

Attention please: (far left) An installation catches artist Parthiv Shah's attention as curator Emma Ridgway and photographer Inder Salim (left) take a look

Smile all the way: (above) Politician Sitaram Yechury with artist Vivan Sundaram; (above right) Art historian Yashodhra Dalmia with artist Anita Pande; (right) Renu Modi of Gallery Espace

Here's a thought: (left) Artist Ram Rahman; (above left) Artsit Gigi Scaria with Sohail Hashmi of Sahmat; (above right) Artist Paramjit Singh with architect Romi Khosla

"Canvassing History," *Hindustan Times*, New Delhi, 2007.

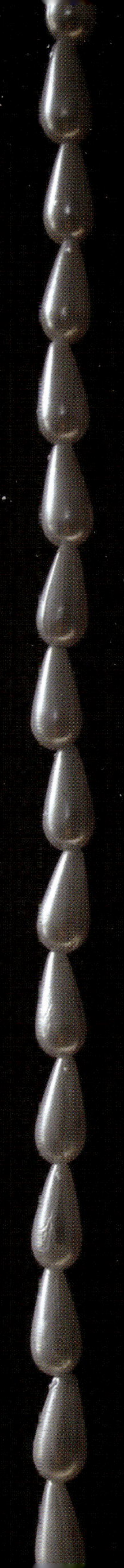

ZARINA HASHMI
River of Tears (detail),
2007, faux pearls on string
12 feet long, installed dimensions
variable. Courtesy Gallery Espace,
New Delhi.

Zarina Hashmi's faux-pearl beads are strung together to look like teardrops running down a thread. The string of beads is typical of the spare, powerful imagery Zarina has developed in her wood-block prints and cast paper sculpture. After leaving her native Aligarh, she lived a nomadic life as an artist in many parts of the world before settling in New York. Her subject has been this life of exile, and this work attests to the pain of the 1947 partition of the subcontinent on religious lines. Coming from a secular Muslim family that was divided across the two countries of India and Pakistan, Zarina expresses the loss of cultural roots in her *River of Tears* with its two shores close and yet so far apart—the river, which is like a tear across the wearer's heart, delineates the geographic border that separates the two countries.

Regarding River of Tears, for Sahmat's show *Making History Our Own*, they asked me what the Partition of India meant to me, and I said it was like a river of tears for millions of people who had to leave their homes and settle in a new place. —Z. H.

The year 2007 marked a number of anniversaries of events and individuals that form significant milestones in the journey of modern Indian politics and culture. Many of these had already been addressed by Sahmat's projects in the past, but the coincidence of the birth centenaries of radical participants in India's struggle for independence with anniversaries of events in the national movement against British rule provided an occasion to reassert Sahmat's core ideals and values.

• Centenary of the **launch of the Satyagraha movement** in South Africa by Mahatma Gandhi

• **60th anniversary** of India's independence from British rule

• 150th anniversary of the **1857 Revolt** against the British. Sahmat had commemorated the 140th anniversary in 1997 with a huge public program at one of the sites of the revolt outside the Red Fort in Delhi.

The centenaries of:

• **Bhagat Singh (1907–1931)**, from Punjab in the northern plains. Singh was a young revolutionary who figured prominently in the militant resistance to British rule, a strand that stood apart from Gandhi's call for passive resistance and was influenced by Communist ideology. The British executed Bhagat Singh by hanging when he was just twenty-three, causing a huge emotional upsurge across India. Bhagat Singh continues to be a powerful symbol of resistance to imperialism.

• **P. C. Joshi (1907–1980)**, the first general secretary of the Communist Party of India, between 1935 and 1947. Joshi's leadership emphasized the inclusion of artists, poets, writers, and actors as active members of the party or the cultural fronts formed during his tenure—the Progressive Writers' Association (PWA, 1936) and the Indian People's Theatre Association (IPTA, 1942). Writer Bhisham Sahni and theatre director Habib Tanvir, the first two inspirational chairpersons of the Safdar Hashmi Memorial Trust who held that post in succession, were members and products of both these organizations.

• **Ramkinkar Baij (1906–1980)**, a painter and sculptor from Visva Bharati in Santiniketan, Bengal, the university founded by the poet Rabindranath Tagore. A maverick and radical figure, Ramkinkar made art inspired by both cubist and futurist work from Europe, as well as by his rural roots in Bengal. His modernist work stands apart from the revivalist school then prevalent in Santiniketan, which had exerted a significant influence across India.

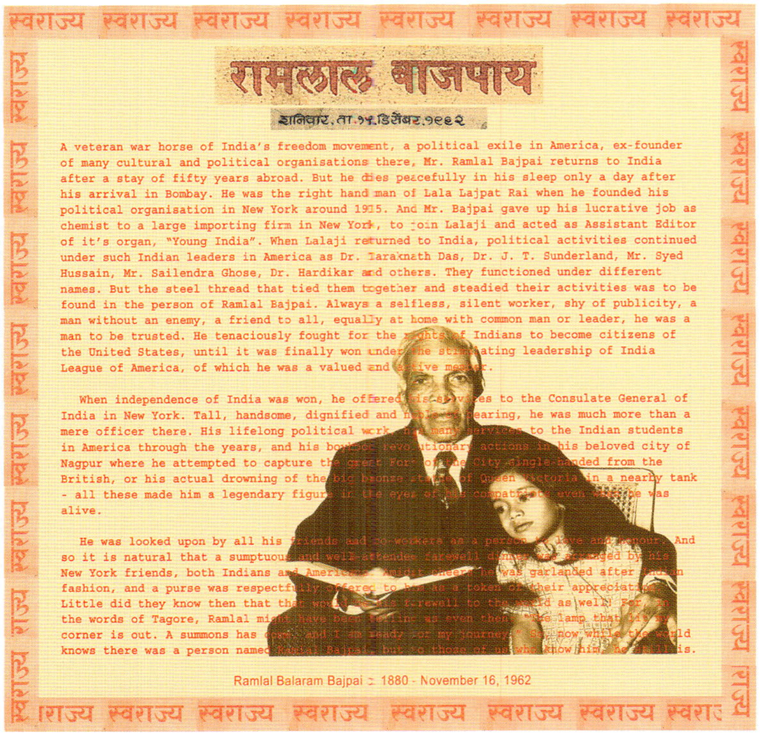

SUKANYA RAHMAN
Nagpur ke Nana, 2007, digital print, 20 x 20 inches.

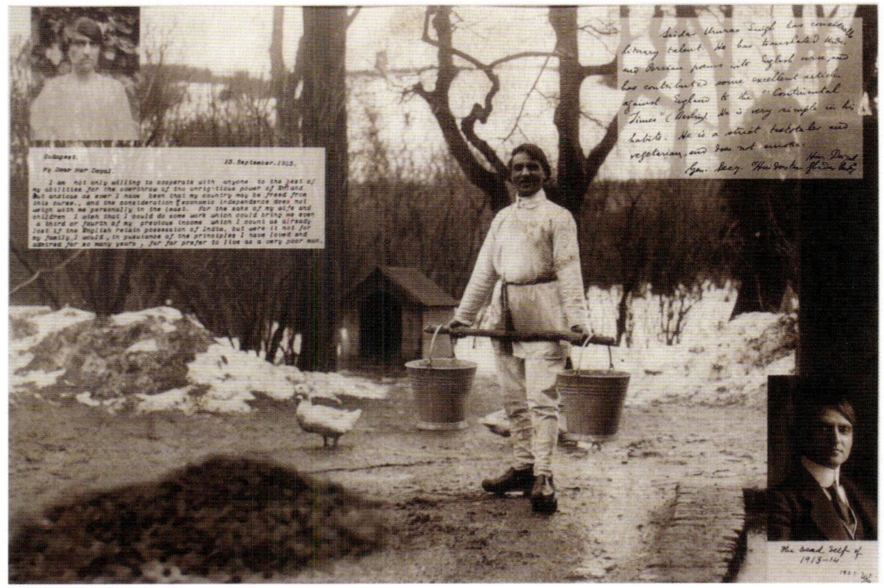

VIVAN SUNDARAM
Working for a Cause, 2007, digital print, 26 x 33 inches.

Both Sukanya Rahman and Vivan Sundaram unpack their family archives and the revolutionary histories of their respective grandfathers who connect across continents.

Sundaram's digital photo-collage from his family album depicts his landed Punjabi grandfather, Umrao Singh Sher-Gil, dressed as a Hungarian peasant. (Umrao Singh had married a Hungarian.) The name of the revolutionary Har Dayal in the typed letter from Umrao Singh to Har Dayal, and in Har Dayal's handwritten note extolling Sher-Gil's commitment to struggle against British rule in India, is inscribed as "General Secretary of the Hindustan Ghadar Party." In the early part of the twentieth century Indian political exiles from British India formed the Ghadar Party in the United States.

Sukanya Rahman's digital collage is based on the obituary of her grandfather, Ramlal Bajpai, who was a political exile in America associated with the Ghadar Party there. These two figures who fought for India's freedom across continents are remembered by two artists who are their direct descendants.

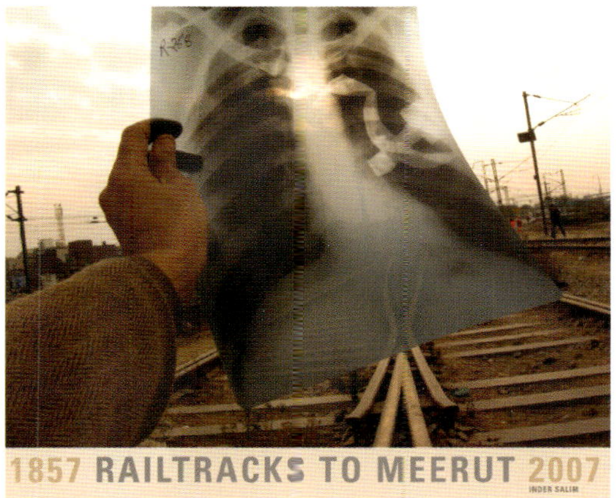

INDER SALIM
Railtracks to Meerut, 2007, digital print, 17 x 20 inches.

Ram Rahman gave the title *Railtracks to Meerut* to the image I shot on dead railway tracks in Delhi. These are tracks that once led to Meerut, the site of the first uprising during the Revolt of 1857. Railways in the pre-independence era in India were a vital link between politically sensitive areas. Meerut is particularly important in this context, since the first uprising against the British Empire happened here and these railway tracks were functional in those days, following the revolt. —I. S.

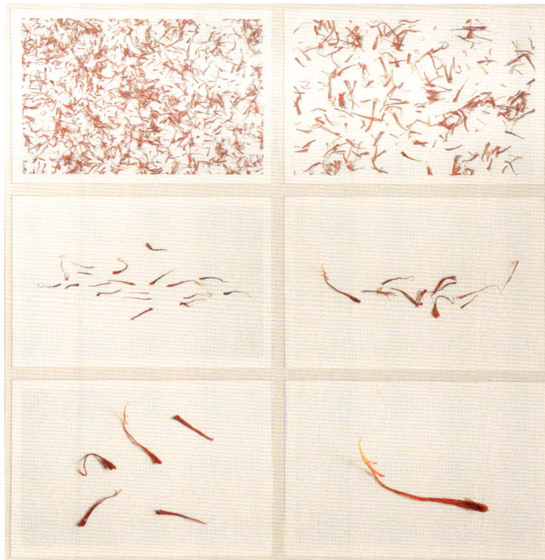

GARGI RAINA
The Scattering (Zafran), 2007, blood on archival print, six prints, 10 x 7½ inches each.

The Scattering (Zafran) **is Gargi Raina's ode to her predicament as a Kashmiri Pandit. When the separatist movement exploded in Kashmir in 1987, there was an attempt to make it a communal issue. Kashmiri Pandits (Hindus) were forced into exile to the plains, in fear of their lives. Here Gargi uses the metaphor of** ***zafran*** **(saffron, the famed spice of Kashmir) and its drying and scattering to evoke the fate of her family and community. In the very last frame, the yellow stain of saffron merges into a streak of blood. The multireligious culture of the Kashmir Valley has been torn asunder by political insurgency, leading to thousands of deaths over the last two decades.**

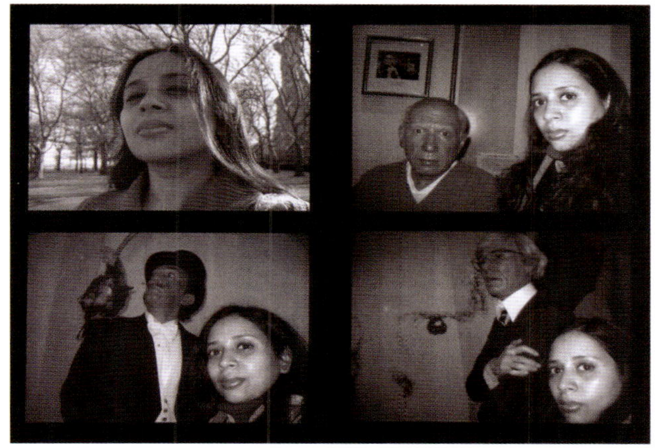

MAHULA GHOSH
Self-Portrait with Inspiration/ Still Life, 2007, digital print, 14 x 18 inches.

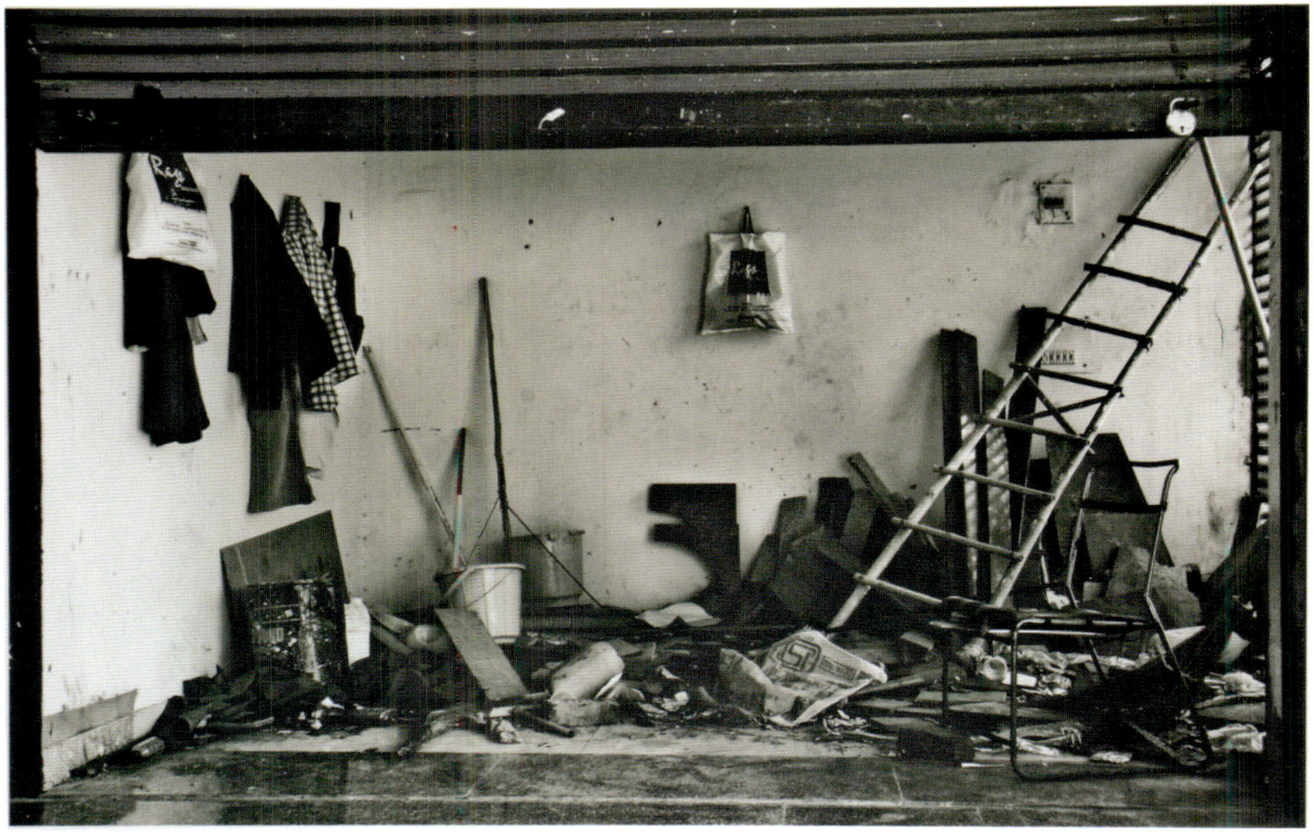

GIGI SCARIA
Details of a Personal History, 2007, digital print, 20 x 30 inches.

Making History Our Own was organized in memory of the 1857 Revolt, which was the first uprising against the British rule in India. This is where Indians identified themselves with a national movement for independence. Within that context, Sahmat asked the artists to think about their personal history and how that forms a part of a larger history. During this period, I was traveling through the city of Delhi observing drastic changes in the form of new constructions and architectural interventions. In one particular mall, I found the personal belongings of workers in a showroom space that was under construction. That was when I felt that personal history also leaves marks that will never be traced back by the ones who made them. —G. S.

PUSHPAMALA N.

My Mother as Jhansi ki Rani, 2007, digital print, 20 x 20 inches.

Pushpamala N.'s photographic self-portraiture is part-parody, part-performance, inspired by the traditions of the photo studio as well as those of the cinema and folk performances. This image from her family photo album falls into an entirely different category, however. It shows her mother dressed up as the Rani of Jhansi. Rani Lakshmibai (Queen of Jhansi in central India, ca. 1835–1858) is a legendary figure of the 1857 Revolt against the British. After leading her troops into battle on horseback, she died fighting. Pushpamala's mother dressed up as the Rani of Jhansi in a home pageant or tableau, and photographed in a heroic posture, is a startlingly similar precursor to Pushpamala's own practice of self-portraiture, which developed after she switched her medium from sculpture. Through this photograph, she is acknowledging multiple histories and inspirations.

The work is from a family photograph of my mother who was an amateur actress. She used to organize pageants and tableaux for her Ladies Club functions, and a popular one was called "Great Women of India." It was a pageant usually done for Independence Day or Republic Day events. "Jhansi ki Rani" (Queen of Jhansi) is a national icon of the 1857 War of Independence. The nationalist pageant, a popular form in India, is also presented in schools and colleges. I am also working on a large ongoing project on "Mother India." I thought this was apt for the show. —P. N.

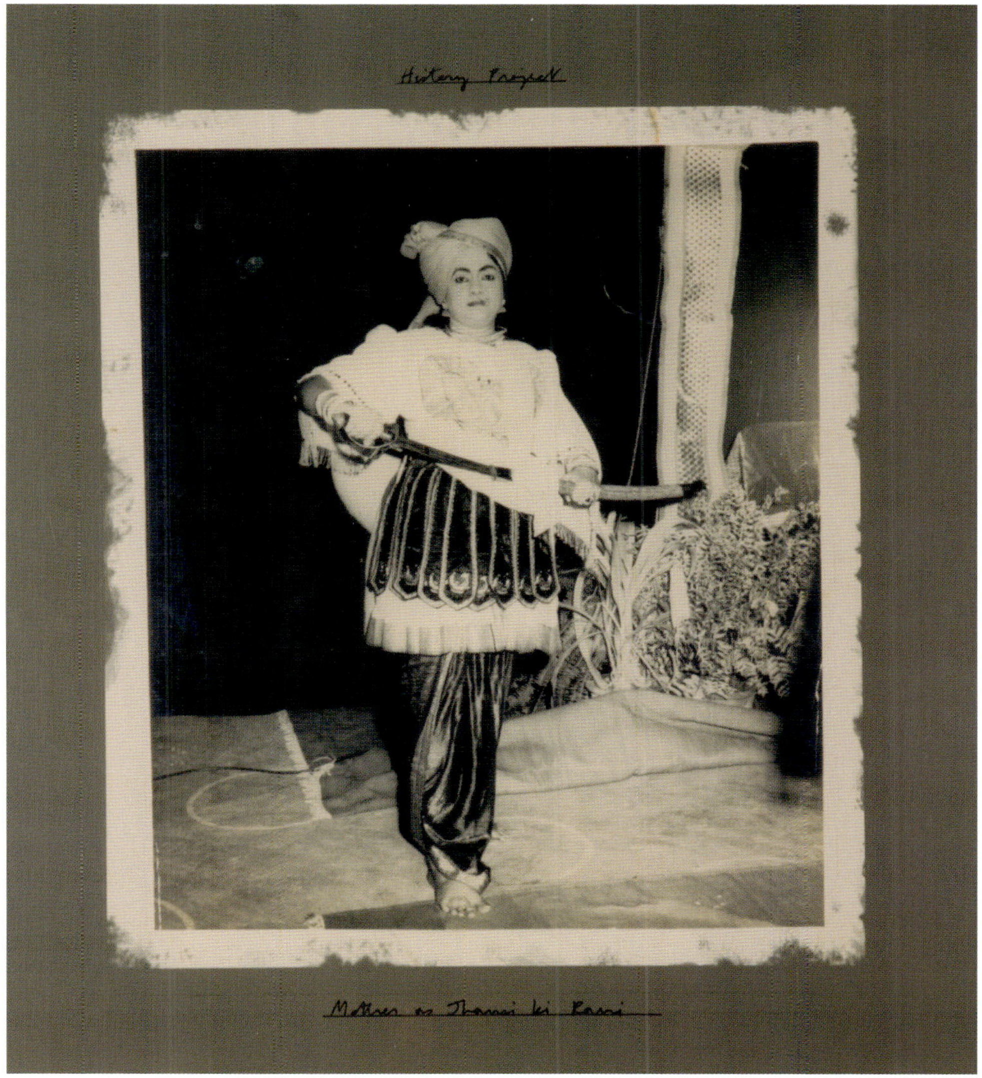

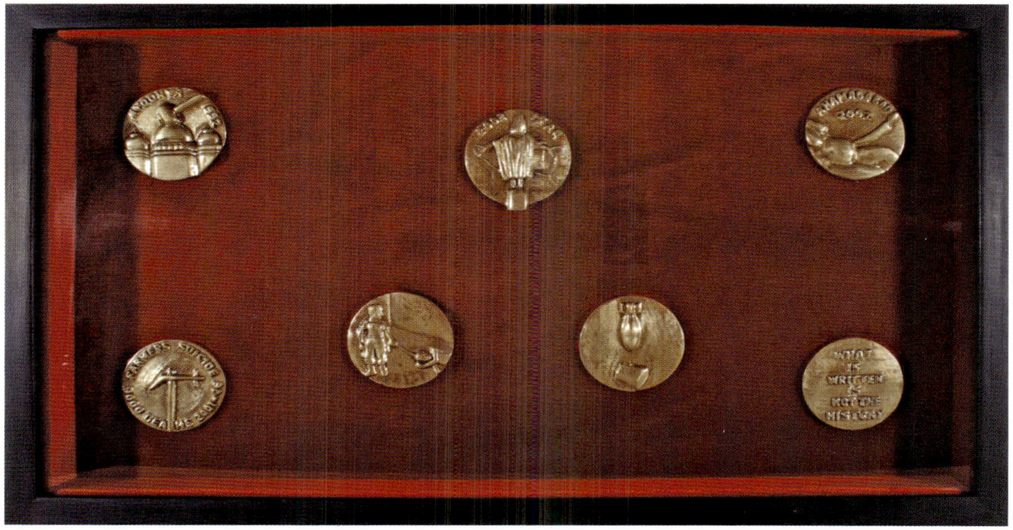

ARUNKUMAR H. G.
The Other Side, 2007, mixed media, 14 x 26 inches.

The Other Side is a work based on the idea of the official issue of coins. I thought of using the tradition of release of coins by the government to showcase its achievements and establish a particular history in people's minds, and doing a take on it. Then what happens to the other serious wrongdoings that are committed by governments or states? How are these grave incidents recorded in the history? Obviously these will not be on the coins. —A. H. G.

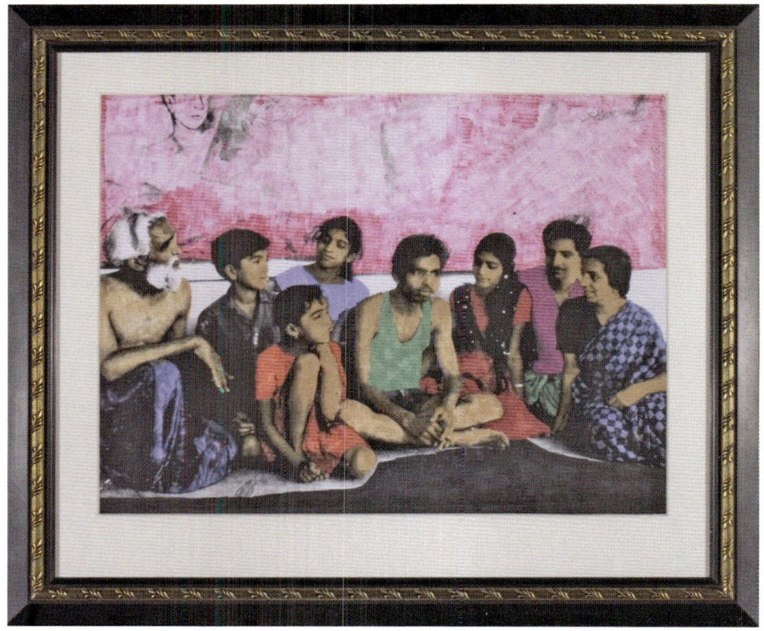

SHAMSHAD HUSAIN
Untitled, 2007, watercolor on photograph, 11 x 15 inches.

This hand-colored photocopy of an image is from the family album of the artist, Shamshad Husain (fourth from right). Shamshad's father, the painter M. F. Husain (1915–2011), on the far left, was one of modern India's best known artists—he was the patriarch of his own family, and a father-figure to artists in India's post-independence period as well as to the extended Sahmat family. The casual hand-coloring by Shamshad is a tribute to the street photographers of the bazaar, and to the artistic roots of M. F. Husain, whose art journey began in the bazaars of Indian towns and cities.

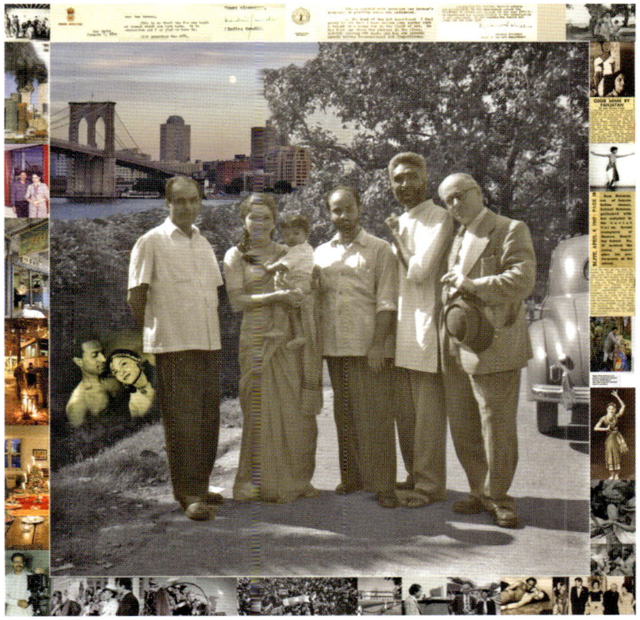

RAM RAHMAN
Family Photo, 2007, archival digital print, 28 x 28 inches.

Ram Rahman's *Family Photo* also salutes personal artistic lineage. Originally taken in 1957, the photograph documents a gathering of people who were vital to the making of Indian modernity in the 1950s. The politician Inder Gujral, on the left, became prime minister of India in 1997. The infant Ram is in the arms of his mother Indrani, who was a key figure in the revival of India's classical dance traditions after independence. Artist Satish Gujral, brother of Inder, stands next to the artist M. F. Husain. Also pictured is the Hungarian Buddhist art critic Charles Fabri, an important member of the 1950s art world.

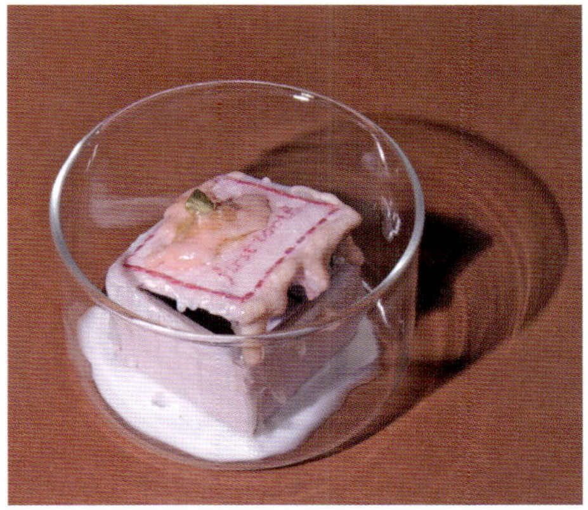

MITHU SEN
First tooth, 2007, mixed media,
5 inches high x 5 inches diameter.

In many places it is a ritual to save the first tooth of a child. It is a trophy of childhood and innocence. But if you look carefully, you will see that it is a grown-up person's tooth . . . it is ambiguous. It speaks for either immaturity or for early growth of an innocent. —M. S.

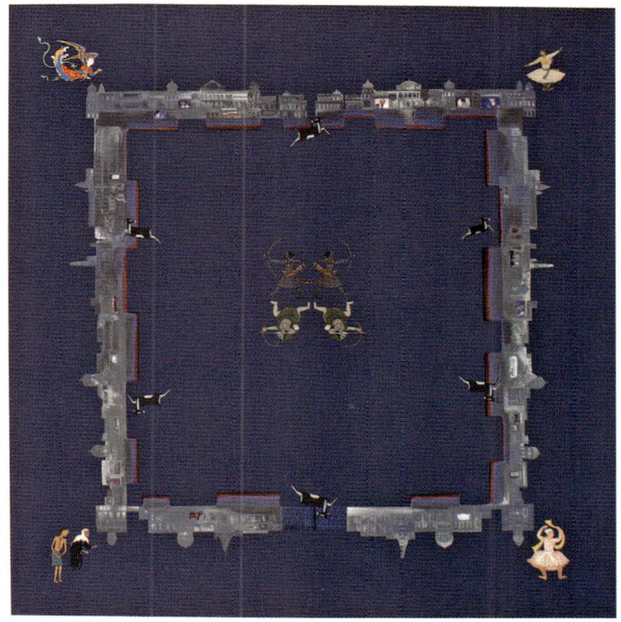

GULAMMOHAMMED SHEIKH
Requiem for a Ghost City: Ayodhya, edition of 10, 2007, digital print, 10 x 10 inches.

Gulammohammed Sheikh's digital print incorporates the architectural drawings of the Ayodhya riverfront by Ravindra Bhan, which were a part of the 1993 Sahmat exhibition *Hum Sab Ayodhya*. Sheikh's recent digital collage works quote from Mughal, Pahari, and Persian painting traditions. In this work there are references to the story of Rama hunting the magical deer in the jungle from the *Ramayana*, as well as to Sufi mystics and dervishes. The formal geometry evokes the mystical mandalas of the Hindu, Buddhist, and Jain faiths.

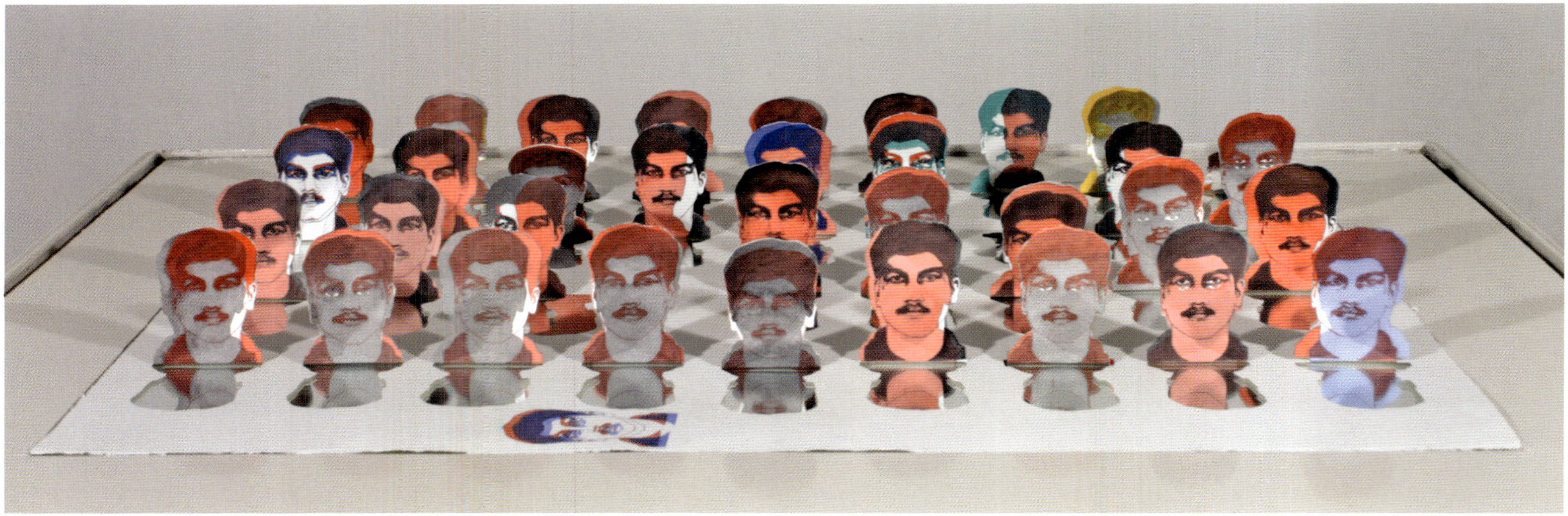

ASHIM PURKAYASTHA
Moy, Self, Me, I, Ami, Hom, 2007, ink on paper with mirror, 30 x 44 x 5 inches.

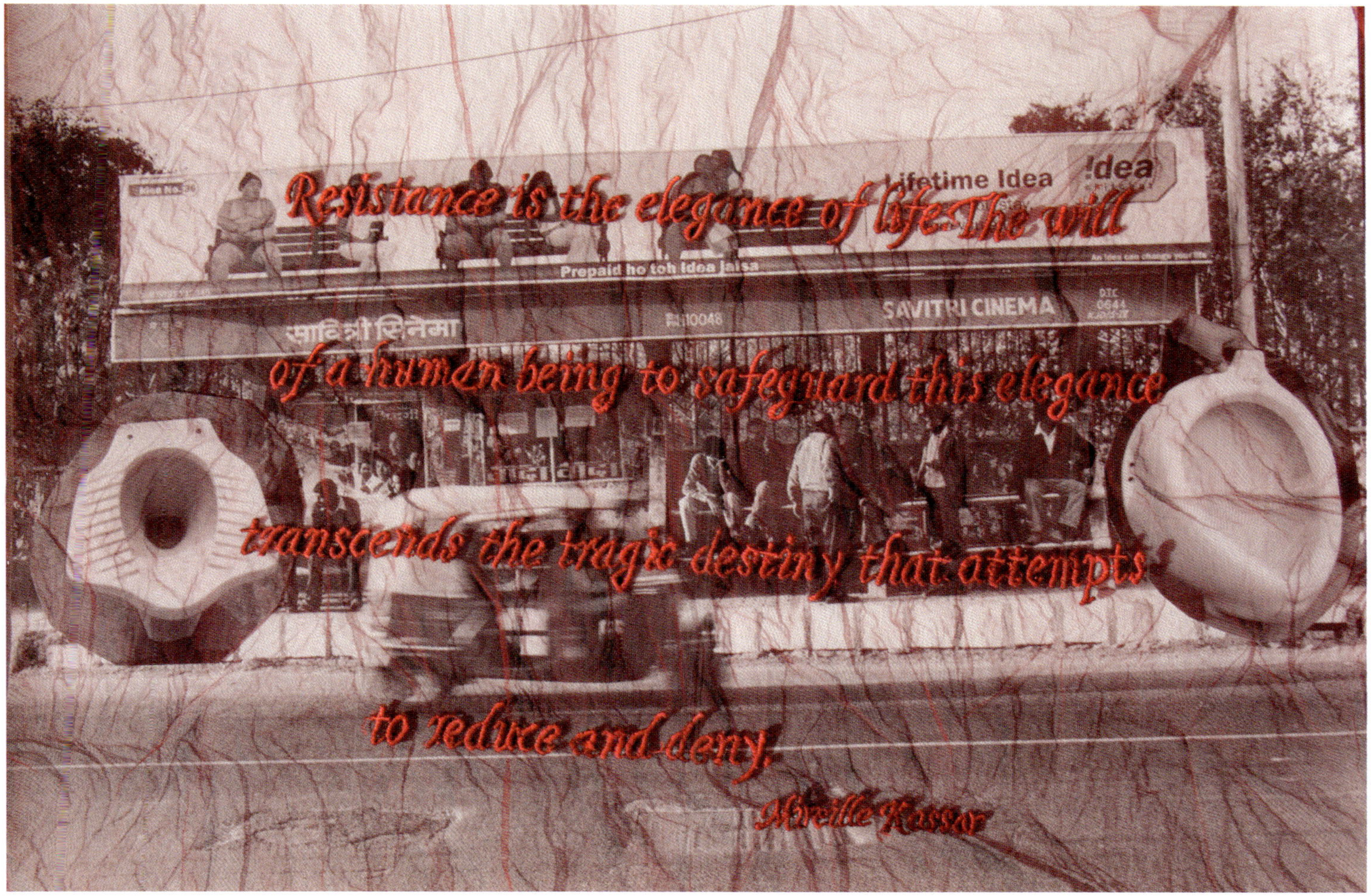

ANITA DUBE
A Toilet at Every Bus Stop, 2007, photograph with netting and embroidered text, 16 x 20 inches.

History in Education

Historians associated with Sahmat regarded the political projection of distorted history that was used to justify the destruction of the Babri Masjid (Babur's Mosque) in Ayodhya in 1992 as a dangerous development. When the National Democratic Alliance (NDA) government led by the Bharatiya Janata Party came to power in 1998, one of its immediate actions was to revamp the curricular frameworks of school and university education, and to begin rewriting history and social-science textbooks to propagate communal versions of history in classrooms. Senior academics and educationists in India regarded these curricular changes to be not only unscientific history but also highly divisive, and Sahmat became a forum where these voices of dissent could alert the public to their implications.

In addition to initiating a publication program of books and pamphlets, Sahmat organized a number of symposia and conferences to counter these interventions in education. Its first initiative to this end was to organize a major national convention in August 2001 in New Delhi that brought together education ministers from all the non-NDA ruled states with historians, economists, scientists, educationists, vice chancellors of universities, representatives of teachers' associations, artists, and cultural activists, to debate the issues of the new textbooks and the related changes to education in India. This convention marked the beginning of a sustained campaign by Sahmat, over the next four years, to counter the attempts at a communal interpretation of India's history and polity through the issue of new textbooks and the framing of new policy guidelines and curricula in education. Sahmat held press conferences on these issues with dissenting historians and academics, and organized six further conventions—in November 2001, December 2002, June 2004, May 2005, August 2005, and September 2005.

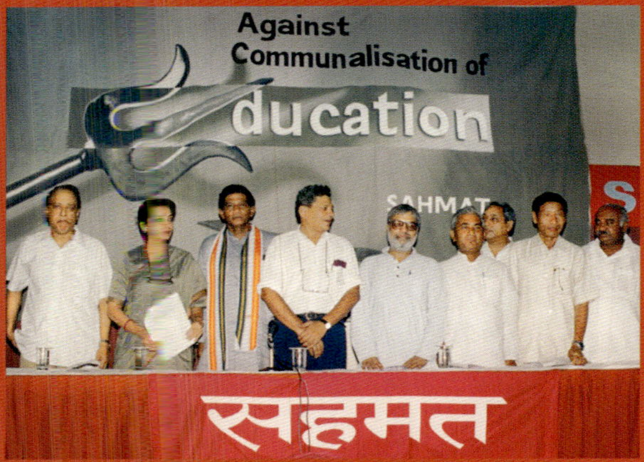

National Convention Against Communalisation of Education, August 4–6, 2001. From left to right: Eduardo Faleiro (member of Parliament, Congress Party), Shabana Azmi (actor and social activist), Ajit Jogi (chief minister, Chhattisgarh), Sitaram Yechuri (member, Polit Bureau, Communist Party of India [Marxist]), C. P. Joshi (education minister, Rajasthan), Satyanarayan Sharma (education minister, Chhattisgarh), Ramchandra Purwe (education minister, Bihar), Chuba Chang (education minister, Nagaland), H. Vishvanathan (education minister, Karnataka).

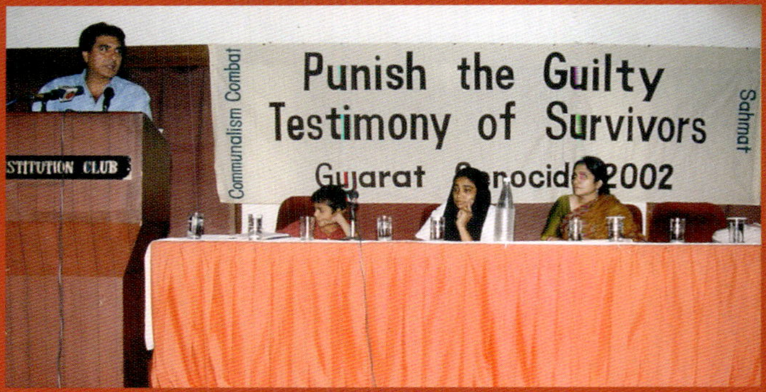

"Punish the Guilty: Testimony of Survivors," April 2002. Actor Raj Babbar at the podium, two survivors, Teesta Setalvad, activist and editor of *Communalism Combat.* The two-day public testimony was held at the Constitution Club in Delhi and co-organized by Sahmat and *Communalism Combat.*

Prabhat Patnaik

Excerpts from "Introduction," *Against Communalisation of Education* (New Delhi: Sahmat and Sabrang, 2002).

History in education had become a very controversial subject when the Bharatiya Janata Party (BJP) was in power. State academic institutions were staffed by right-wing ideologues, and school and university textbooks—particularly history textbooks—were being rewritten to bolster communal ideology. . . .

The most concentrated expression, and the most palpably sinister manifestation, of the assault on rational discourse is the promotion of the communal outlook. The starting point of the communal discourse is not real, concrete people in their mundane daily existence, but idealized totalities, "the Hindus," "the Muslims," and so on. When the reality is seen to differ from this idealized universe, this divergence is attributed to "conspiracies": "Marxist conspiracies," "conspiracies of the Muslims," "conspiracies of the Christians." Paranoia replaces argumentation. Excluding viewpoints other than one's own rather than engaging with them becomes the dominant obsession. Filling offices in the sphere of education with still more hacks, replacing less loyal hacks with more loyal hacks, is seen as the solution to end these myriad "conspiracies." The attenuation of rational discourse thus acquires a ruthless and spontaneous dialectic.

But while the propagation of the communal outlook is the concentrated expression of the assault on rational discourse, it does not constitute the entirety of this assault. Or, looking at it differently, in terms of the real counterpart of these ideas, the attack on the secular foundations of the State is not merely a phenomenon in itself, but is an integral part of the social counter-revolution I talked of earlier. Combating communalism, preserving the secular foundations of the State, are urgent tasks that have to be undertaken not merely in the interests of the minorities; they are not even tasks whose urgency arises merely because one cannot be free as long as someone else is oppressed; their urgency lies in the fact that communalism is integral to counter-revolution.

Combating the communal outlook that is sought to be spread through the education system under the BJP dispensation is integral to the preservation of the rational discourse, which is why this effort, whose overall rubric is the communalization of education, is concerned with the entire gamut of policies aimed at snuffing out rational discourse. I referred earlier to the dialectic inherent in the process of attenuation of rational discourse; this dialectic has to be arrested and reversed. To be sure, doing so is not a matter confined to the sphere of education and educationists alone. But the task has to begin somewhere. The present effort is just a beginning.

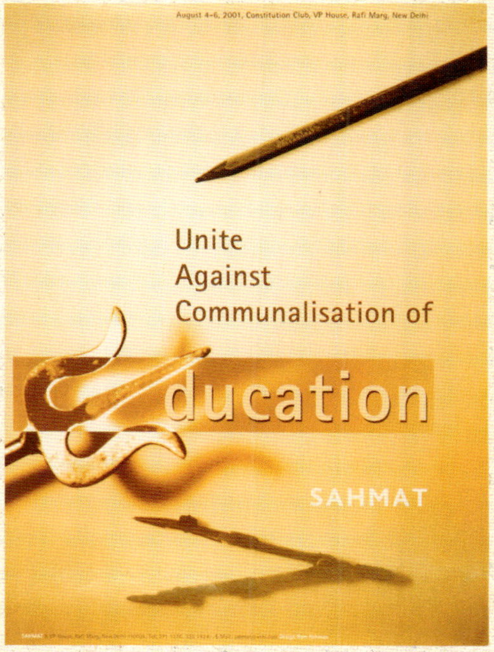

Cover of *Unite Against Communalisation of Education*, Sahmat and Sabrang.com, Delhi, 2002. Design: Ram Rahman.

Excerpts from "Introduction," *Saffronised and Substandard: A Critique of the New NCERT Textbooks* (New Delhi: Sahmat, 2002).

Ever since the publication of the "new" NCERT textbooks in 2002, scholars, schoolteachers and parents have pointed out the communal bias in these books as well as factual errors, most of which are deliberate and motivated by the ideological predelictions of the Sangh Parivar. All those who challenged the communal, chauvinist and irrational view of India's society were dubbed "leftists" and described as "intellectual terrorists" who were as dangerous (if not more) as terrorists from across the border, by the Minister of Human Resources Development [of the BJP-led NDA government] late last year. . . .

A communal revision of history has been central to the agenda of the BJP and its allies. As early as 1939, the RSS mentor Golwalkar had exhorted his followers to "[re]write our history ourselves." In a text which outlines the RSS philosophy, *We or Our Nationhood Defined*, he wrote: "But obsessed with the idea that Aryans came to Hindustan from somewhere near the Caspian Sea or the Arctic region or some such place, and invaded this land in bands of marauders, that later, they settled down first in the Punjab and gradually spread eastward along the Ganga, forming kingdoms at various places, at Ayodhya among them, the historian feels it an anachronism that the kingdom of Ayodhya in the Ramayana should be older than the more western Pandava empire in Hastinapur. And he, with pedantic ignorance, teaches us that the story of the Mahabharat is the older. Unfortunately such misconceptions are stuffed into the brains of our young ones through textbooks appointed by various universities in the country. *It is high time that we studied, understood and wrote our history ourselves, and discarded such designed or undesigned distortions*" [emphasis added].

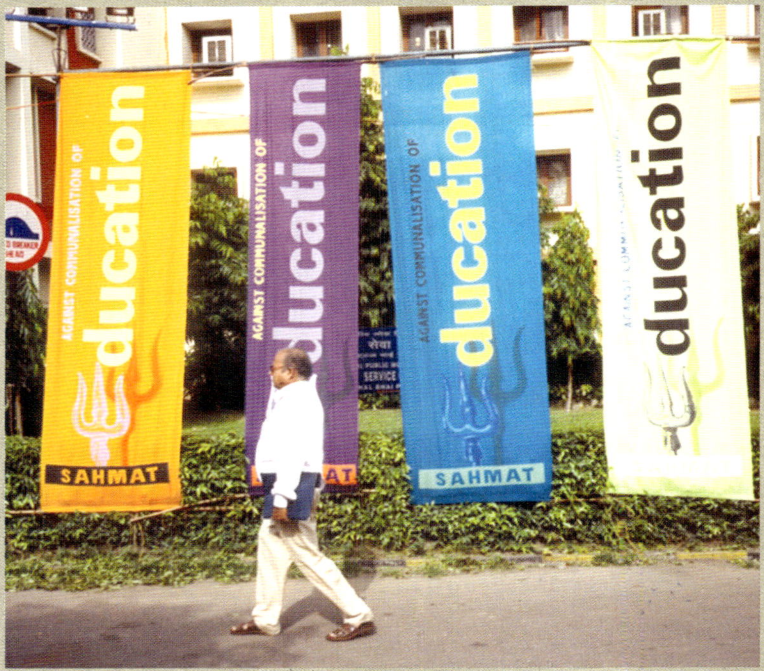

Banners, National Symposium on Education, August 2001, Delhi.

Teesta Setalvad

Assaults on body and soul, physical attacks aimed to maim, humiliate and kill, fueled by hate and distorted and manipulated narratives of the past, especially of history and culture, are the overt manifestations of the ideology of division and Othering. Uniquely, South Asia has recognized and suffered this politics, defining it as communalism since the mid-nineteenth century. Having surfaced as a vicious byproduct of the struggle against colonial rule, it has taken a life and shape of its own beyond the bloody vivisection of the subcontinent in 1947. Regional variations have not affected its ability to influence sections of state and society alike, vitally altering the quality of public discourse within India that is today laced with underpinnings of a widely accepted majoritarianism. The failure of governance structures to tackle issues of institutionalized discrimination has helped to bring to the fore latent strains of othering within minorities, leading to minority communalism and even radicalization.

The mid-1980s gave a fresh fillip to this politics, leading us at Sabrang to concentrate our energies and expertise in combating the politics of communalism and its manifestations, first informally (in mid-1986) and thereafter in a more organized fashion through the launch of *Communalism Combat* (1993) and KHOJ (education for a plural India program). If the first attempt, through a monthly publication, endeavors to deconstruct the politics of hate and division, the latter makes curricular interventions in primary and secondary schools through the creative application of history and social studies teaching. The Sahmat collective has been a fellow traveler on this journey, with a specific emphasis on public art and academic interventions. Sahmat's creative forms of protest and publications have inspired *ways of seeing*, the very aspect of secular activity that the fascist agenda of communal politics means to prevent.

The first trial by fire for us was the anti-Muslim pogrom in Bombay after the Babri Masjid demolition, which was made possible by the partisan conduct of the police in siding with the Shiv Sena–led mobs. For the first time, the issue of bias within the police force became an issue to be reflected upon and debated. For Sahmat, the lead- up to the demolition of the Babri Masjid in 1992 was both a challenge and its finest hour. The years 1998 and 1999 saw the launch of a dangerous experiment to overtly hegemonize mind-sets, by the BJP-led NDA government's Human Resources Development Ministry (under Murli Manohar Joshi). In October 1998, at the conference of state education ministers, an attempt was made to introduce an obscurantist education policy. This was followed by the issue of the New Curricular Framework for Value Education (December 2000), a coercive introduction of courses like astrology and Vedic mathematics. 1998 was also the year when a spate of attacks on Christians all over the country culminated on a Christmas day attack on churches in Dangs (tribal south Gujarat) and thereafter the burning alive, in January 1999, of an Australian missionary, Graham Staines, and his two young sons, in Orissa. The politics of majoritarian communalism was visibly making an assault on the republic created by the Constitution of India.

Consistent work in the areas of the rule of law and education and culture, inspired by a worldview and methodology that activism and protests need to recover fast-diminishing public spaces, made Sahmat and Sabrang come together institutionally for the first time in a three-day Convention against the Communalization of Education (August 4–6, 2001). The convention was the first of its kind as it drew in many from the political class concerned with or in charge of education. More than anything else, it created the basis for a sustained understanding of the issue of communalism in general and its manifestations in particular. A researched paper presented by Sabrang at the convention argued how the uncontested misuse of educational curriculae had shaped and manipulated young minds and cadres. Nowhere were the connections between control and manipulation of education, culture and the assault on life and dignity (assault on body and soul) so starkly visible as in Gujarat, the land that gave us Gandhi.

The genocidal killings in Gujarat of 2002 and the ten years since has cemented this organic relationship between Sabrang and Sahmat. *Communalism Combat's* special issue of March–April 2002 (Genocide Gujarat 2002) was released by Sahmat at the Press Club in Delhi. Before this, on March 3, 2002, a press conference was organized on the lawns outside Sahmat's office where some of us spoke in detail about the massacre of 2,500 Muslims in reprisal violence in Gujarat, stage managed by the man at the helm, which set the tone for the national discourse on the issue. The Public Hearing of Victim Survivors of Gujarat in April 2002, attended by three former Indian prime ministers, was arguably the first time that survivors spoke in their own voices.

The ten years since have seen many such collaborative programs, reflecting shared and complex visions, and linked to people's left movements across the country. In 2009, *Communalism Combat* published a special edition commemorating in print Sahmat's twenty-odd years' journey. In December 2010, the dismay and anger at the judgment of the Allahabad High Court on the Babri Masjid issue (of September 2010) moved us yet again into collaborative action, to hold a three-day conference in Delhi on "Fact vs. Faith." The academic grounding to the conference provided by Prabhat Patnaik, Irfan Habib, and Shireen Moosvi was complemented by presentations on the communalization of the law and order machinery and the majoritarian shift of the judiciary, by Justices P. B. Sawant, Sikri, and Hosbet Suresh, advocate Anupam Gupta, senior journalist Manoj Mitta, and Teesta Setalvad. Members of activist groups from Faizabad-Ayodhya, Gorakhpur, Hubli, Mangalore, Malegaon and Lucknow gave insights into the growth of communalism on the ground.

On February 27, 2012, Sahmat collaborated with Sabrang and Citizens for Justice and Peace (CJP) in organizing a memorial, with live webcast, to mark ten years of the killings at the Gulberg Society in Ahmedabad during the Gujarat carnage. From the conceptualization of the event—which featured photographs by Binita Desai, Ram Rahman and Kanishka Prasad, writings by Shiv Visvanathan, music by Shubha Mudgal, Sudhir Nayak, and Aneesh Prasad—to its culmination, Sabrang, CJP, and Sahmat stood as one. Anti-communal groups in Faizabad-Ayodhya, Madurai, Malegaon, Mumbai and Delhi viewed the moving and magical moments at Gulberg Society as they held their own commemorations. Thousands from all over Gujarat made their way to Gulberg Society that day. In those moments of grief and celebration of a collective journey, spaces were opened up for future battles.

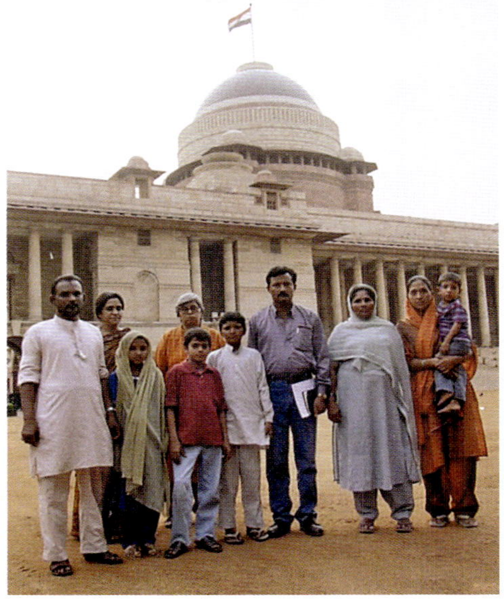

Eight Gujarat survivors outside Rashtrapati Bhavan, the residence of the president after their meeting with him. Teesta Setalvad and Shabnam Hashmi are in the back.

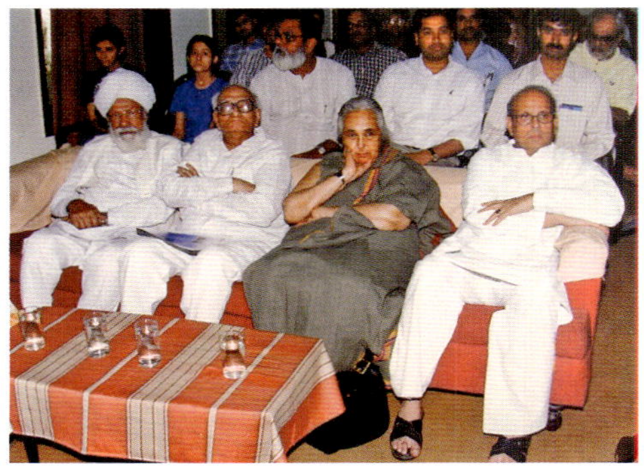

"Punish the Guilty: Testimony of Survivors," April 2002. Harkishan Singh Surjeet, general secretary of the Communist Party of India (Marxist), Socialist leader Madhu Dandavate, historian Romila Thapar, and former Prime Minister V. P. Singh at the testimony.

Gujarat 2002

In 2002, ten years after the demolition of the Babri Masjid, Sahmat once again became a platform, among other secular platforms, for shocked and horrified citizens to denounce the violence unleashed in Gujarat by the forces of Hindutva. As an immediate response, Sahmat organized a fact-finding team to visit Gujarat in March 2002, and the team's preliminary findings were published soon after under the title "Ethnic Cleansing in Gujarat." On April 26–27, 2002, Sahmat collaborated with Teesta Setalvad of *Communalism Combat* and Citizens for Justice and Peace (CJP), who have been in the forefront of the campaign for justice in Gujarat, to organize a public testimony in Delhi of survivors of the Gujarat violence. This event, "Punish the Guilty: Testimony of Survivors," at which forty survivors from relief camps in Gujarat gave firsthand accounts of the attacks on their homes and families and the lack of assistance from the state government, was attended by leaders of all the major political parties (except the BJP), as well as the press, artists, and activists. Sahmat presented an exhibition of photographs from Gujarat by Sahir Raza, *Listen to the Survivors: Genocide in Gujarat 2002*, on the occasion, and on April 28, a delegation of Gujarat survivors, Teesta Setalvad, and Sahmat members met with Indian President K. R. Narayanan.

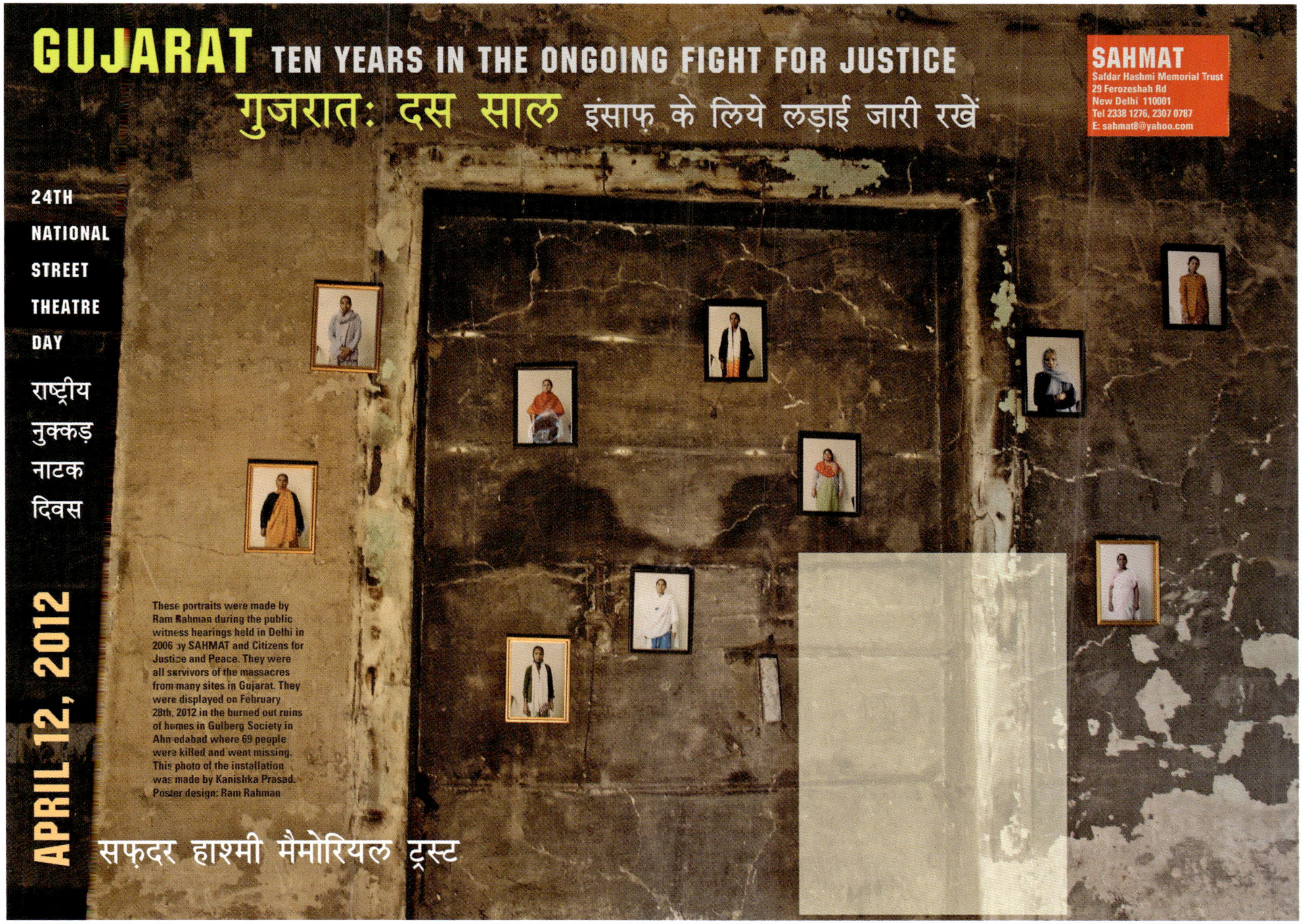

National Street Theatre Day poster, April 12, 2012, 14 x 19 inches. Design: Ram Rahman.

Sahmat released this poster on National Street Theatre Day, 2012, to mark ten years of the fight for justice in Gujarat. Portraits of the survivors who had testified at the Sahmat/*Communalism Combat* hearings in Delhi in 2002 were exhibited in the burned-down ruins of the Gulberg Society building in Ahmedabad, Gujarat, in February 2012. This was the site of one of the worst massacres in the violence of 2002. A historic judgment was delivered by the Gujarat High Court in August 2012, convicting a former minister of the Gujarat government, Dr Mayaben Kodnani, to life imprisonment along with thirty-one others, in one of the cases in which these survivors provided crucial testimony. Teesta Setalvad, editor of *Communalsim Combat*, and her colleagues in the legal team of the Committee for Justice and Peace (CJP) were an important part of the investigations leading to the convictions.

1994–Ongoing

Free Speech and Defending Husain

For Free Speech

The fight for the freedom of expression and the defense of free speech has been central to Sahmat's mission. Over the last two decades Sahmat perceived that attacks on free speech in India were increasing in intensity and frequency as weapons in the arsenal of regressive political parties and fundamentalist groups. Safdar Hashmi's murder in 1989 was a particularly chilling manifestation of the rising political intolerance that was becoming endemic across India.

Sahmat's campaigns against attacks on artists, writers, theatre persons, filmmakers, activists, and journalists have taken many different forms. There have been street marches, protests, press conferences, and statements issued in the press. Sahmat has also attempted to evolve more novel and creative modes of protest: When an unstated ban (a customs' restriction on the import of the book) was imposed on Salman Rushdie's novel *The Moor's Last Sigh* in December 1995, the group held a public reading from the book at Safdar Hashmi Marg in Delhi. The writers, artists, lawyers, and actors who participated, read in front of a blown-up portrait of Rushdie by the painter Bhupen Khakhar, and in symbolic resistance to the ban, Sahmat sold photocopies of the novel.

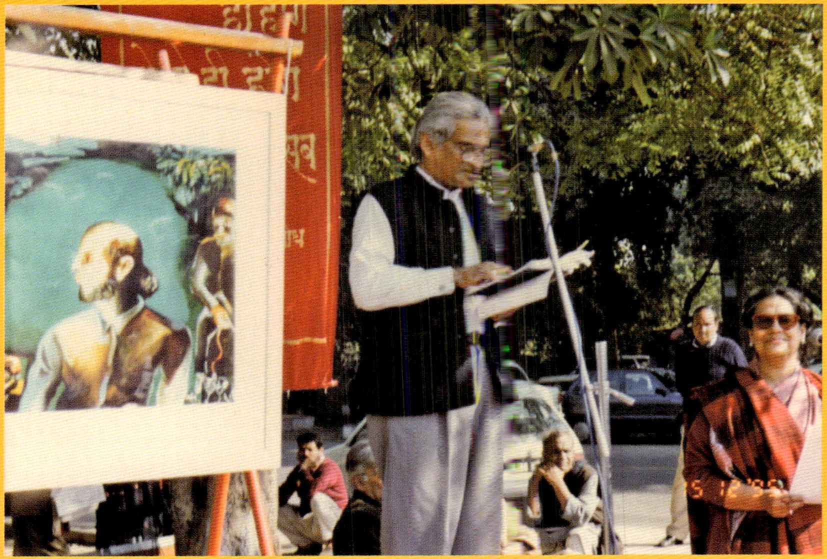

Meeting to protest the customs' ban on Salman Rushdie's novel *The Moor's Last Sigh*, Safdar Hashmi Marg, Delhi, December 15, 1995. Supreme Court lawyer Rajiv Dhavan reads from the book as he stands in front of a portrait of Rushdie by artist Bhupen Khakhar. Geeta Kapur is on the right.

Sahmat's poster project *Harvest of Hatred* (1999) evolved from observing the frequency of such anti-Muslim, anti-Christian attacks on actors, writers, and artists across India. Madhu Prasad from Sahmat culled reports from the press and replicated them as a series of thirty-eight posters designed by Rajinder Arora. The collective then sent the posters to student groups, activists, and labor unions across the country. By refiguring text and image produced by the press, the project boldly called attention to the growing threat to freedom of expression.

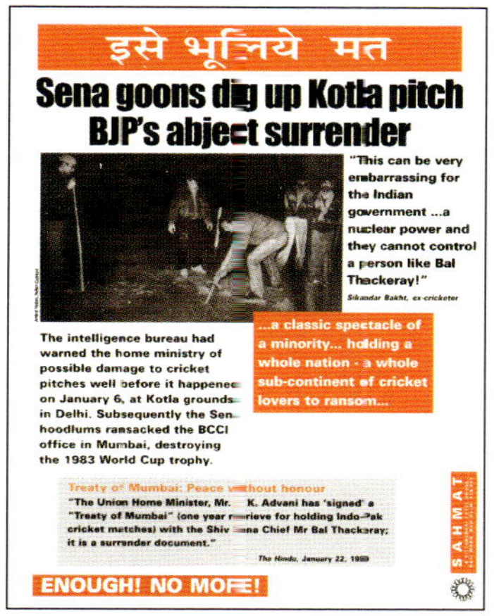

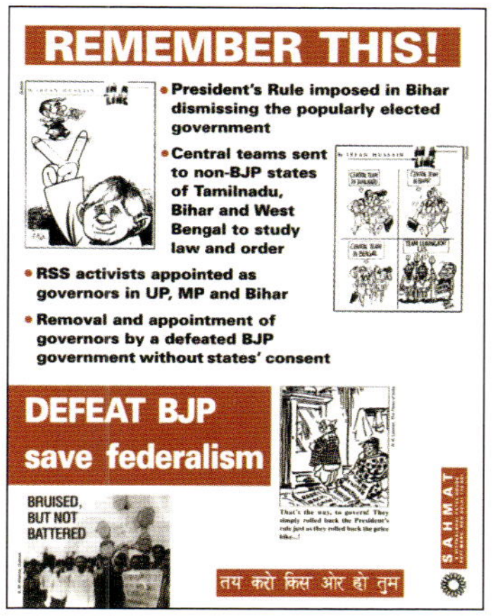

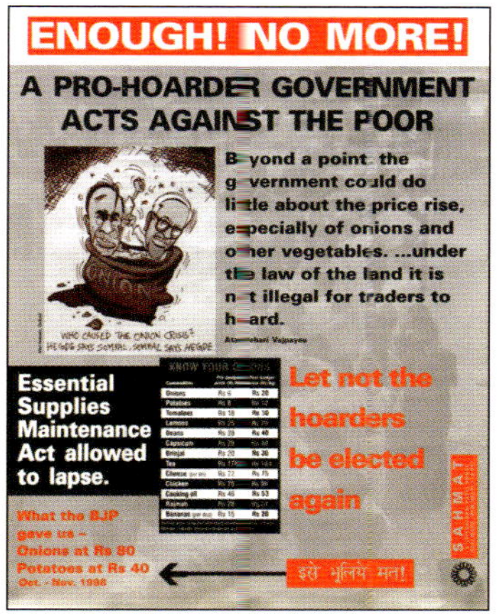

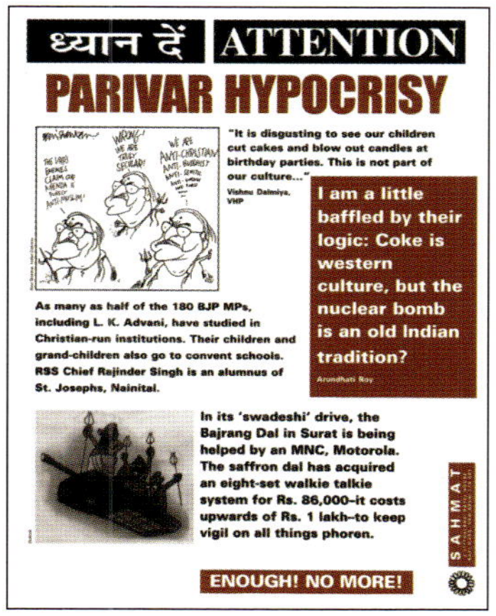

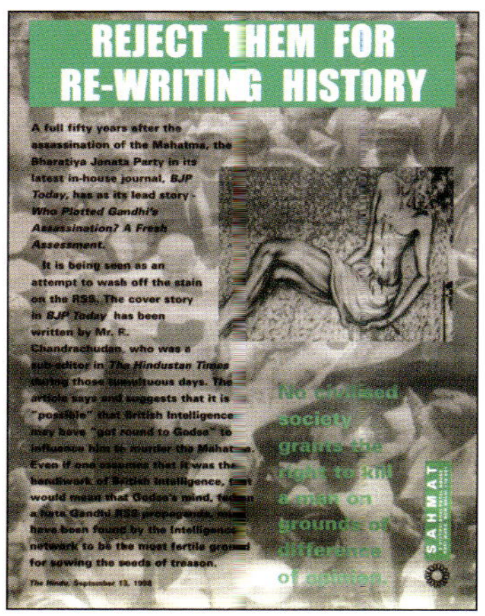

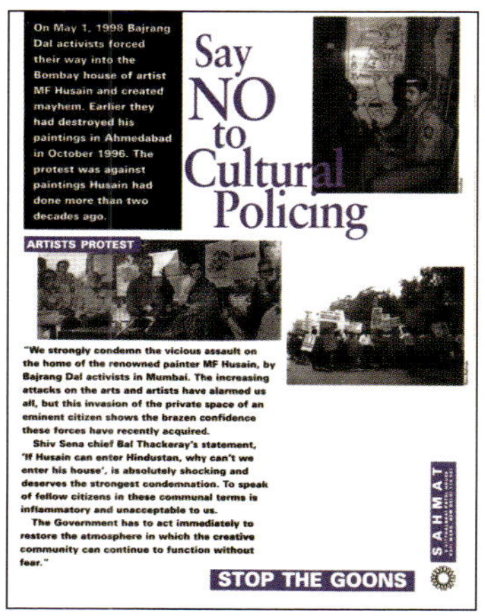

Harvest of Hatred, 1999, posters. 21 x 16 inches each. Design: Rajinder Arora.

Views of *Harvest of Hatred* exhibition at different venues.

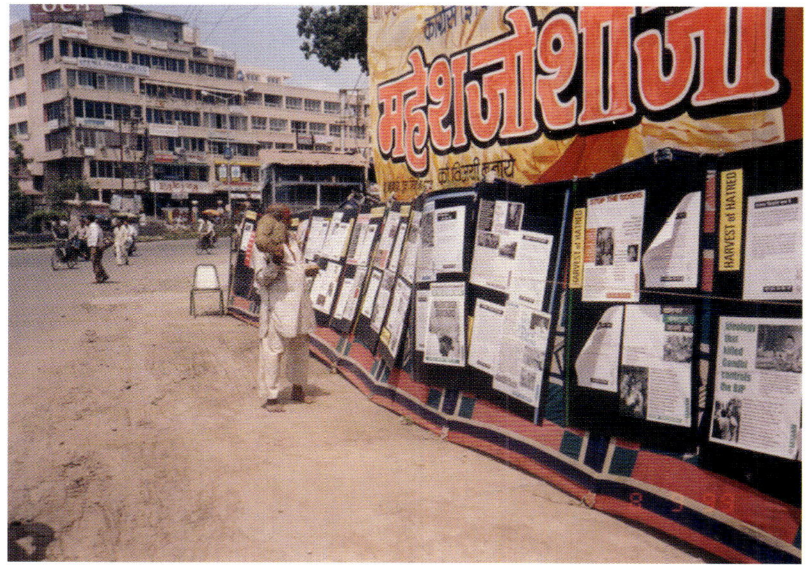

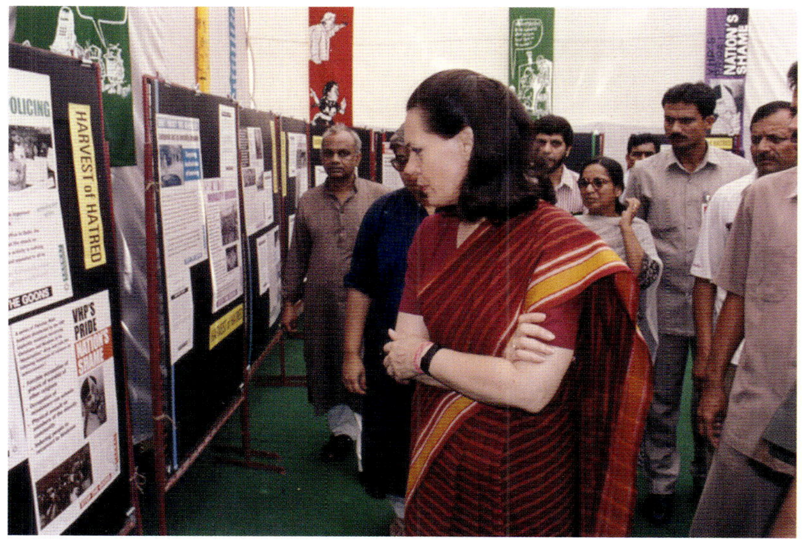

Sonia Gandhi, president of the Congress Party, views the *Harvest of Hatred* exhibition, Delhi, August 1999. Rajendra Prasad, Shabnam Hashmi (partially hidden), Rajinder Arora, and Madhu Prasad are in the photograph, in addition to Mrs. Gandhi's security detail.

Some key events in Sahmat's fight for free speech

July 8, 1994
Protest against fundamentalists' attack on writer Taslima Nasreen.

December 16, 1995
Protest meeting against ban on Salman Rushdie's novel *Moor's Last Sigh* at Safdar Hashmi Marg, New Delhi. Readings of excerpts from the book by Mulk Raj Anand, Krishen Khanna, Alok Rai, Roshan Seth, Dilip Padgaonkar, Rajiv Dhavan, Habib Tanvir, Veena Das, Malini Bhattacharya, and Geeta Kapur.

October 18, 1996
March in support of M. F. Husain, from National Gallery of Modern Art to Rabindra Bhavan, New Delhi.

May 4, 1998
Press conference to condemn attack, two days earlier, on M. F. Husain's Mumbai residence. Participants in the press conference include artists Manu Parekh, Anjolie Ela Menon, and Vivan Sundaram.

May 20, 1998
A delegation of artists and gallerists meets with President of India K. R. Narayanan to submit a memorandum on the issue of the attacks on M. F. Husain; afterward the delegation holds a press conference.

December 12, 1998
Candlelight protest meeting against the attack on actor Dilip Kumar's Mumbai residence, at Home Minister L. K. Advani's house in New Delhi.

August 16–23, 1999
Harvest of Hatred—an exhibition of thirty-eight panel posters documenting the attacks on civil society, minorities, and cultural freedom by communal forces. Inaugurated by political leaders Sunil Dutt, Manmohan Singh, and Sitaram Yechury.

August–September 1999
Harvest of Hatred and *Teen Terah ka Chakkar* (street play by Sahmat Rangmanch) at Nagpur, Jhansi, Bhopal, Kanpur, Delhi, Sihore.

September 24–October 1, 1999
Hunger strike by Shabnam Hashmi at Gandhi Maidan, Lucknow, to protest attack on Sahmat's street theatre group Sahmat Rangmanch.

September 1 and October 9, 2003
Protest meetings against attacks on Habib Tanvir and Naya Theatre. Staging of plays by Janam and Act One.

January 31, 2004
Protest meeting in Delhi against destruction by members of the Hindu organization Vishwa Hindu Parishad (VHP) and its youth group, Bajrang Dal, of paintings by M. F. Husain and Chitrabanu Majumdar in Golden Art Gallery of Art and Textiles, Surat.

February 21, 2004
Protest meeting against attacks on culture (with Janvadi Lekhak Sangh). Speakers: Sudhir Chandra, Githa Hariharan, Ashok Mitra, Prabhat Patnaik, and Namwar Singh.
Poster and book release: *Barbarians at the Gate.*

September 5, 2006
Symposium on "Rewriting Art History," in support of M. F. Husain. Speakers: Rajiv Dhavan, Sudhir Chandra, Geeta Kapur, Tapati Guha Thakurta, Parul Dave Mukherji, Naman Ahuja, Akhil Sibal, Geetanjali Shree, Mihir Bhattacharya, and Ram Rahman.
Book release: *Iconography Now.*

May 9, 2007
Press conference in support of M. F. Husain.

May 14, 2007
Protest meeting at Rabindra Bhavan lawns, New Delhi, against the attack on Shivaji Panikkar and others at Faculty of Fine Arts, M.S. University of Baroda, Vadodara.

May 30, 2007
Press conference in support of freedom of expression and against the attack on Shivaji Panikkar and others in the Faculty of Fine Arts, M.S. University of Baroda, Vadodara.

May 19, 2008
Meeting on Husain judgment by the Delhi High Court.
Speakers: Akhil Sibal, Rajiv Dhavan, Geeta Kapur, and K. Bikram Singh.
Book release: *Maqbool Fida Husain . . . Petitioner.*

August 22–25, 2008
Exhibition of reproductions of M. F. Husain's works, and photographs of Husain by Madan Mahatta and Parthiv Shah, at Vitthalbhai Patel lawns, Rafi Marg, New Delhi, presented in protest against Husain's absence from the *India Art Summit*. The exhibition is vandalized on August 24, and following a protest meeting, Sahmat extends the exhibition.

August 26–September 2, 2008
Husain exhibition is moved to a second venue at Jamia Millia Islamia University.

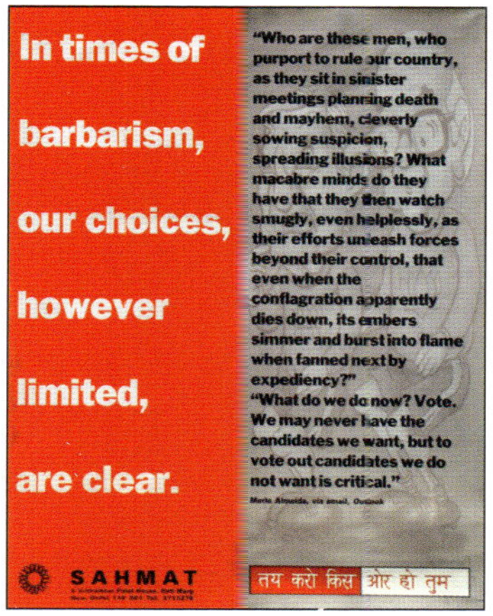

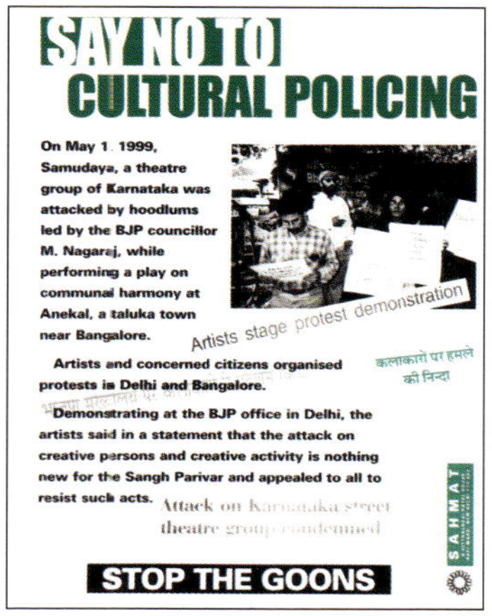

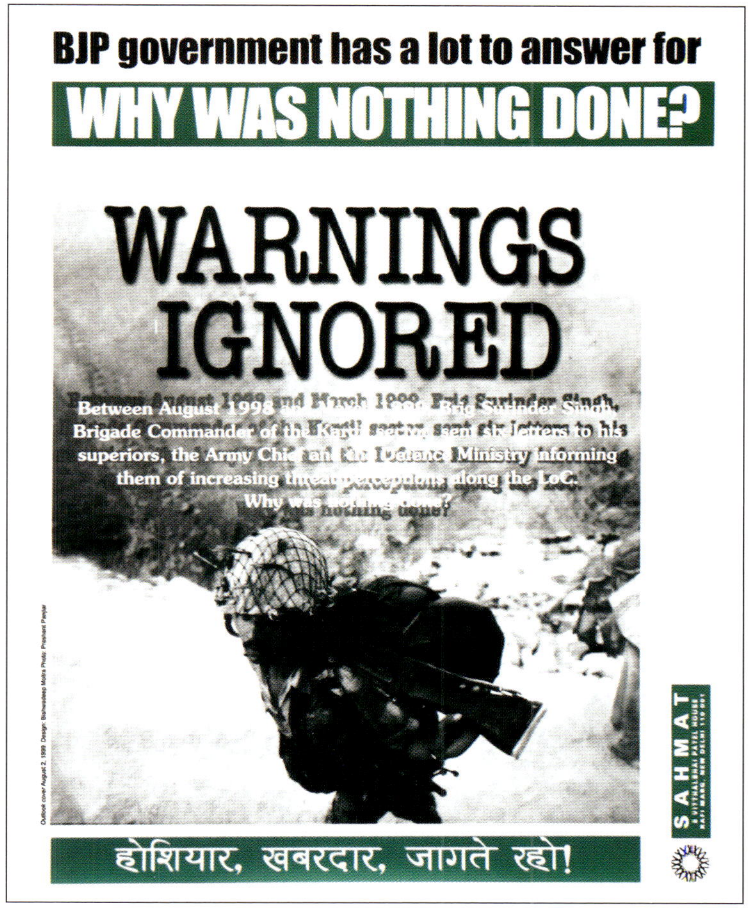

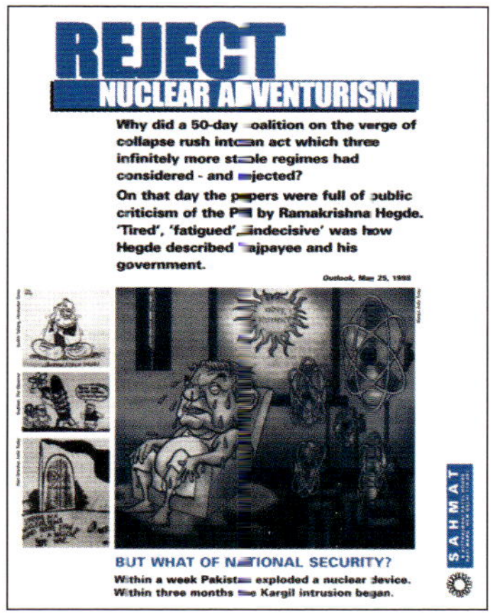

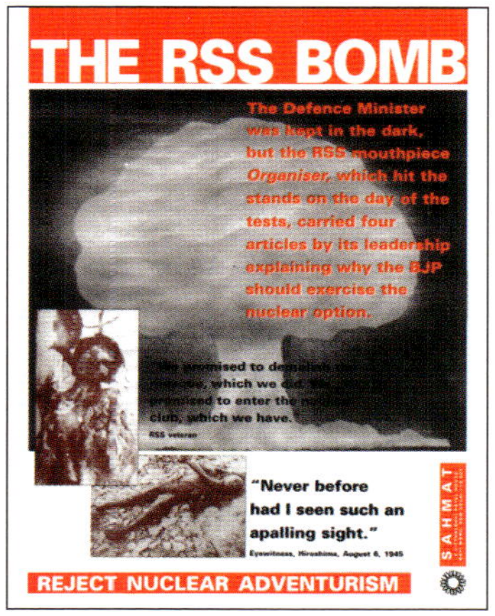

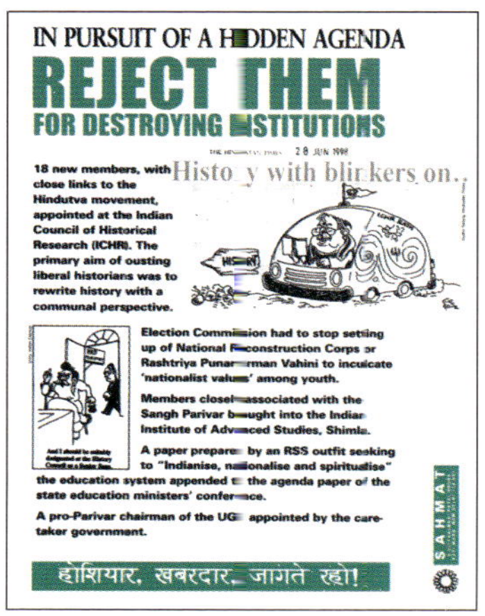

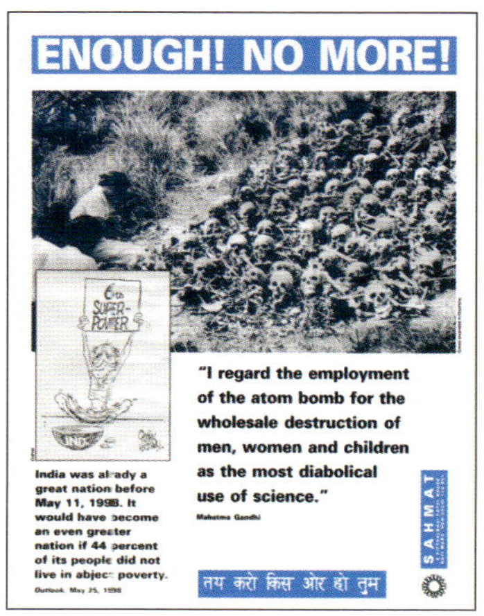

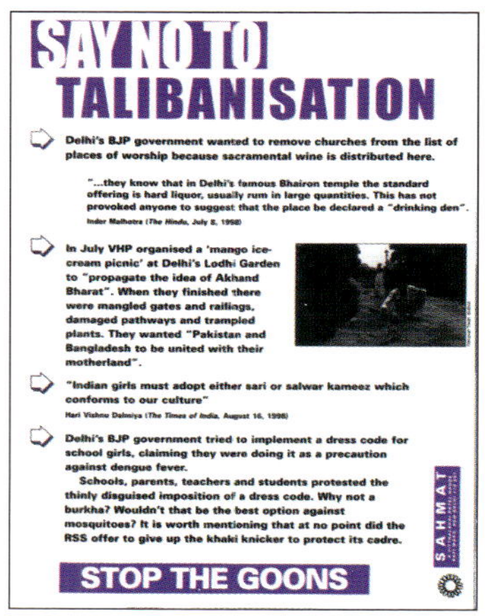

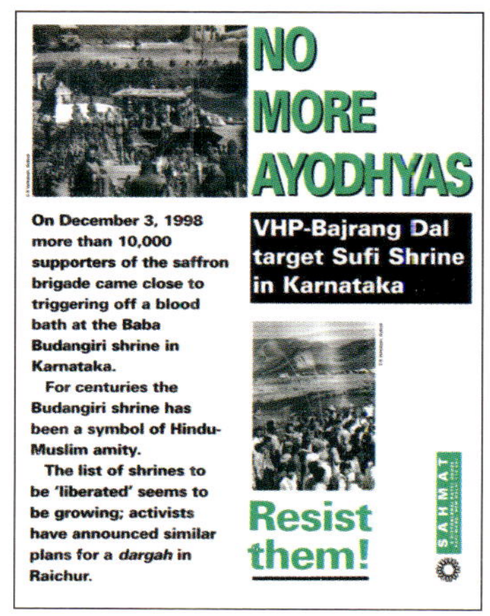

Harvest of Hatred, 1999, posters, 21 x 16 inches each. Design: Rajinder Arora.

Artists protest vandalism in varsity

Madhur Tankha

NEW DELHI: Describing the attack on a student of M. S. University in Vadodara as the latest instance of bludgeoning of the public right of expression, a number of artists, politicians and civil rights activists on Monday pledged their support to all the beleaguered artists who have so far been attacked by members of the Sangh Parivar.

Gathered under the banner of Sahmat, people from different walks of life stood outside Rabindra Bhawan here protesting against senior artists such as M. F. Husain being made targets of violence and innumerable law suits "whose intent is to browbeat and intimidate freedom of expression".

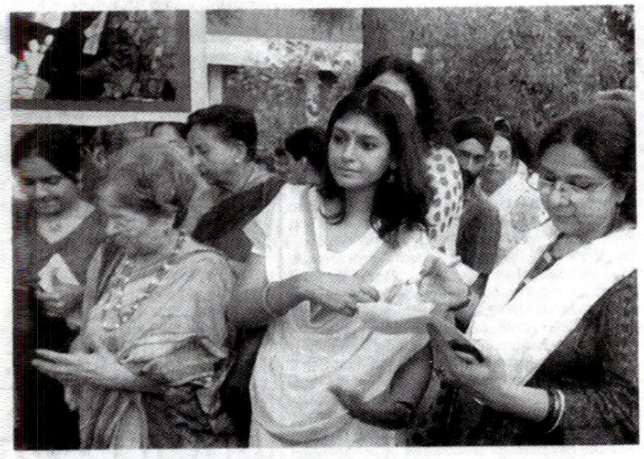

"WE PROTEST": *Film actress Nandita Das along with other artists at the protest rally in New Delhi on Monday.* - PHOTO: S. SUBRAMANIAM.

Referring to the latest incident at M. S. University, artist Ram Rahman said it was done with full State collusion.

"On May 10, Neeraj Jain, a known BJP activist, along with a group of Vishwa Hindu Parishad members, entered the premises of the Fine Arts Faculty where students' art works were on display as part of the process of annual student evaluation. They used violence against Chandramohan, a Master's candidate, and the police arrested him. The charge levelled against him is that of hurting religious sentiments. He was released from jail on bail only today."

Condemning the attack by Sangh Parivar members, Communist Party of India (Marxist) Polit Bureau member Sitaram Yechury said the unique diversity of the country needs to be celebrated.

"We should see the attack in the larger context. Such attacks that reflect personal intolerance and vendetta cannot be tolerated. We need to strengthen the bond of commonality," he said, adding that he had moved a notice in the Rajya Sabha two days ago for a discussion on the issue.

Describing the attacks on artists as "distressing happenings", Communist Party of India secretary D. Raja said the latest incident was nothing but "a fascist attack on our culture and freedom of expression": "It is an attack on our institution. The CPI and mass organisations will collectively take up the fight against these fascist forces. Gujarat is the place where all these things are happening. We cannot allow fascist dictatorship to target writings, literature and artists works."

Veteran painter Anjolie Ela Menon said, "The police have been behaving as lackeys and poodles of the goons. The Vadodara incident was a preconceived attack."

Memorandum

Earlier, a memorandum signed by eminent people was issued appealing to all secular parties, organisations and individuals to raise their voice against misuse of the police, judicial system and State machinery to "muzzle the freedom of expression through coercion and intimidation".

Among those who attended the protest meeting were noted writer Arundhati Roy, painter Vivan Sundaram, poet Ashok Vajpeyi, artist Jatin Das, actress Nandita Das and photographer Raghu Rai.

See also Page 12

"Artists protest vandalism in varsity," *The Hindu*, New Delhi, May 15, 2007.

RAJINDER ARORA

"Heart is a good fertile ground. Anything planted there—Love, Hate, Fear, Hope will surely grow and bear fruits. It is for us to decide what to plant and harvest."

The *Harvest of Hatred* series of posters were conceptualized collectively by Madhu Prasad, Dr. Rajendra Prasad, and myself and published by Sahmat to bring forth the ugly face of Hindu nationalist and right-wing fundamentalist campaigns and their violent attacks—not only on Muslim, Christian, and Sikh minorities in India, but also attacks on artists, media houses, sports activities, and their Taliban-like dictates on education curricula, social events, and dress code, etc., during the Bharatiya Janata Party (BJP)-led NDA government rule in India in 1998–2000.

Depicting the serious social schisms that emerged in the country during these times, these posters urged all democratic people to stand up and act against the insidious designs of the Hindu communalists who have been out to subvert the secular foundations of our polity. In times of barbarism, our choices, however limited, are clear, hence the centrality of the message in these posters was STOP THE GOONS who were spreading hatred, unleashing violence, and corrupting innocent minds.

During this painful period the country saw churches being vandalized and burned, nuns being raped, the gruesome killings of missionary Graham Staines and his two children, who were burned alive in a van, and the burning of Bibles across many states. The Gujarat state governments' counsel Fali Nariman resigned in protest against the inaction of the state and central government. The idea of a Hindu nation was being built through:

- Targeted attacks by Shiv Sena goons on sportsmen and digging up of sports grounds and pitches
- Attack on media with stern warning of dire consequences against reputed national publications like *Indian Express* and *Outlook*
- Attacks on members of Sahmat and on its exhibitions at various centers
- Forced inclusion of divisive ideology of Hindutva in text books
- Publication and blatant distribution of a series of booklets by Hindu right-wing group that explicitly mentioned terrorizing Christians and Muslims in its drive to force Hinduism on the country and listing the following as its achievements:

> Forcible occupation of places of worship of other religions
> Occupations of missionary schools
> Assaults on members of minority communities
> Inducing people to reconvert to Hinduism

These horrendous attacks were also an effort to dismantle the fundamental rights and personal freedoms guaranteed by the Constitution of India, as illustrated in these posters.

Sahmat has always upheld the right to freedom of expression and unfailingly protested any attack on this fundamental right. The *Harvest of Hatred* posters were a part of this ongoing protest. These posters were displayed and distributed throughout the country as an independent exhibition and also mass distributed through various organizations.

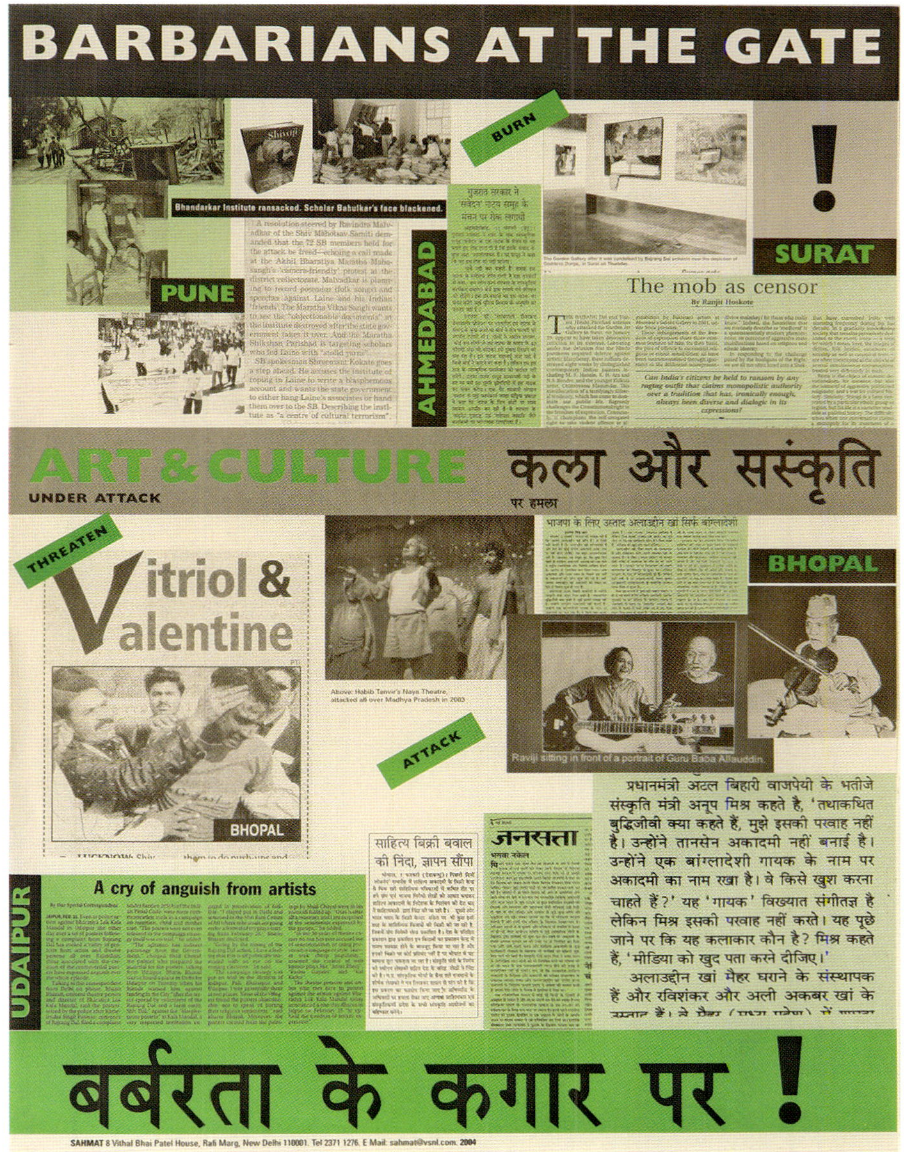

Barbarians at the Gate, poster released at protest meeting against attacks on culture (with Janvadi Lekhak Sangh), February 21, 2004, 22 x 16½ inches. Design: Ram Rahman.

In Defense of M. F. Husain

M. F. Husain (1915–2011) was India's best known and most highly regarded modern artist. A flamboyant figure who rose to super-stardom from extremely humble origins, the barefoot artist became a national icon. The only artist recognized by the poorest worker and the globetrotting industrialist alike, Husain had actively cultivated an almost Sufi-like persona. Throughout his career, his subject had been the narrative of India's journey to modernity, through its popular culture, folk traditions, and the rich mythology of its many religions. As a Muslim artist who had freely painted Hindu icons for decades (often bare-breasted, like their classical depictions), Husain became the perfect and most prominent target for the "culture wars" launched by the Bharatiya Janata Party (BJP) and the Hindu right wing (the Sangh Parivar) a few years after their successful demolition of the Babri Masjid (Babur's Mosque) in Ayodhya, as they took offense to Husain's renderings of the icons.

The attacks on Husain took many forms—beginning with the publication of an article against the artist in a right-wing magazine in 1996. His gallery in Ahmedabad, Gujarat, was targeted in October 1996 and some of his work was destroyed. There were attacks on exhibitions of his work in Delhi (1998) and on his home in Mumbai (1998), as well as protests all over the country against any of his work being exhibited or his films being screened. There was also a new strategy in play: magistrates across India accepted cases of religious blasphemy filed against the artist in an attempt to enmesh him in mandatory personal appearances at court hearings in cities all across the country.

Sahmat met the orchestrated attacks on Husain with a long and sustained defense. In a well-attended march from the National Gallery of Modern Art to Rabindra Bhavan, Lalit Kala Akademi in New Delhi, participants—including prominent politicians—carried images of classical sculpture, emphasizing the fact that all the goddesses in these traditions have always been bare-breasted and that nudity in Indian art had never been regarded as obscene. Sahmat took up Husain's cause in many public forums presented by artists and scholars, and organized academic symposia to discuss the issues exposed by these attacks. Sahmat also led delegations to the president of India, the president of the Congress Party, and the home minister. Through Sahmat, the artists' community expressed a vocal and visible solidarity in defense of the artist and his art.

Sahmat's defense of Husain was based on the understanding that the accusations and attacks were politically motivated and managed, having nothing to do with the so-called public sentiment cited as justification. From Sahmat's point of view, the issue went beyond the individual. Indian society was allowing groups to cynically use religious sentiment as a political weapon, allowing them to set the discourse of cultural and artistic practice. The attacks on Husain forced him into voluntary exile in Dubai, shocking the art community. In the face of pressure from the BJP and right-wing groups, the government did not provide Husain protection to return to his homeland. The artist died in exile in June 2011.

PARTHIV SHAH

I met Husain at my home in Ahmedabad when I was a small boy. He knew my father who is also an artist. In 1993 the National Gallery of Modern Art (NGMA) held a first major exhibition of works by M. F. Husain called *Let history cut across me without me*. I was assigned to photograph the show and opening by a private gallery that collaborated with NGMA. I got to know later that they had hired me on Husain's insistence. At that point, for me as a young photographer, it was really very exciting—to get to know the man, his creative approaches, and to engage photographically with him. During this period, when the show was on, I kept meeting him and when the show was about to finish I asked him to spend some time with me as a favor. He readily obliged me, and I created a series where I made him interact with his paintings. And I interact with this dynamic as a photographer and the viewer becomes an extension of this conversation among him, his work, and my photographs. The people who vandalized my work did not vandalize his paintings. There was absolutely nothing objectionable in those photographs, except that they were portraits of Husain. The vandals were actually attacking the artist Husain as portrayed in these photographs. That is why it is important to show those vandalized images, to reiterate the senselessness of acts with creative works.

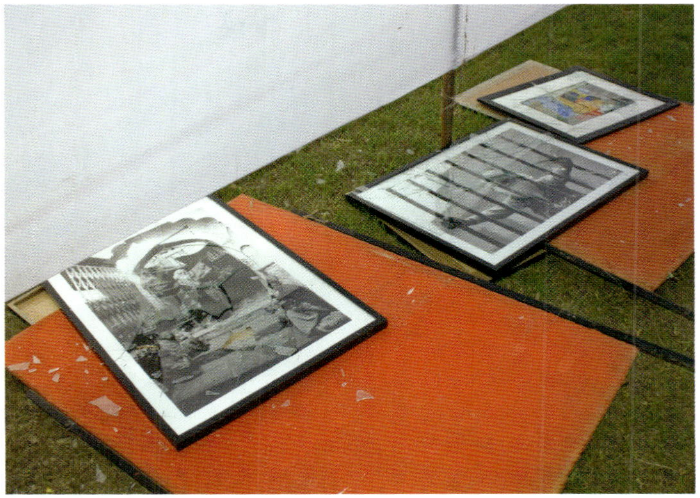

Photographic portraits of Husain by Parthiv Shah vandalized by the Shri Ram Sena during their attack on the Husain exhibition outside the Sahmat office, Vitthalbhai Patel House lawns, Rafi Marg, New Delhi, August 2009.

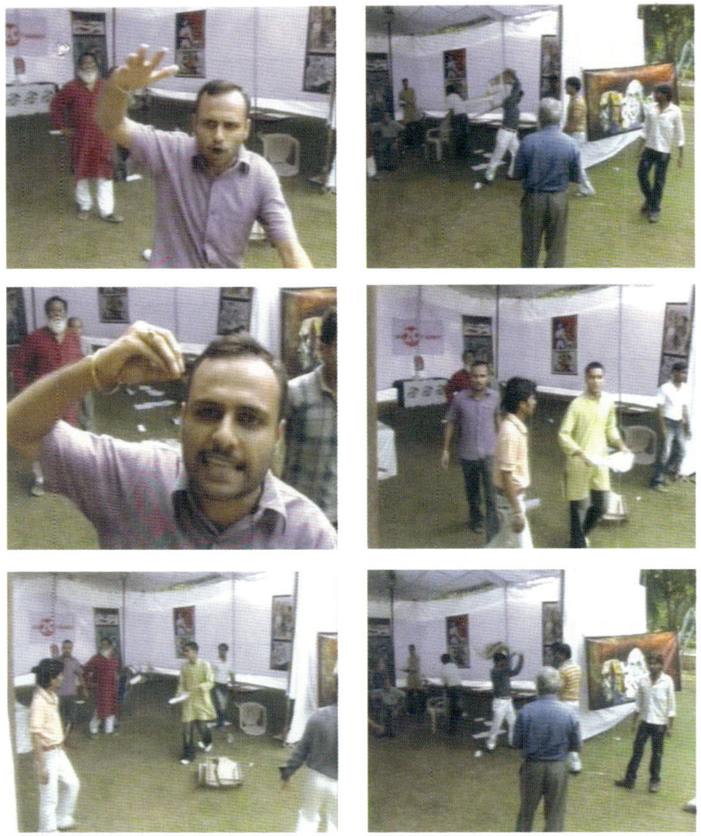

Video grabs of the Shri Ram Sena attack on Sahmat's Husain exhibition, August 2009.

A viewer looks at a photographic portrait of Husain by Madan Mahatta, vandalized by the Shri Ram Sena when they attacked Sahmat's Husain exhibition outside the Sahmat office in New Delhi, in August 2009.

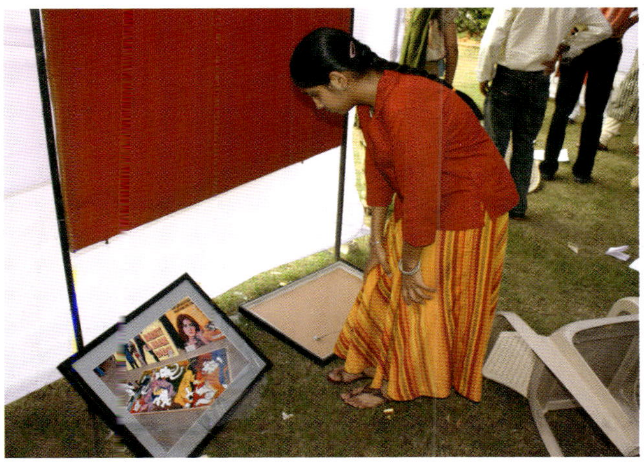

Letter to the President of India on M. F. Husain

Reprint from *Sahmat 20 Years, 1989–2009: A Document of Activities and Statements* (New Delhi: Sahmat, 2009).

We, the undersigned, write to you to suggest that the arts and the nation would be made proud if the contribution of the distinguished artist, Maqbool Fida Husain, is recognized in the form of the highest award of the land: India's Bharat Ratna.

M.F. Husain has received national and international recognition in abundance; it remains for him to join the constellation of Bharat Ratna awardees—Satyajit Ray, M.S. Subbulakshmi, Ravi Shankar, Bismillah Khan, Lata Mangeshkar—to become one the most treasured artists of this country. A large number of artists, art historians and critics, as well as spectators in the general public, believe that M.F. Husain, the 91-year-old painter and filmmaker, most fully belongs in this constellation.

The Indian civilization, in all its diversity, has been Husain's basic inspirational project. Since the year of Independence, through the Nehruvian decades and thereon, cognizant of all the challenges involved in nation-building, Husain has been steadfast in maintaining a most affirmative relationship with the Indian people's consciousness of their national identity. Through him, we have learned to address a whole gamut of issues pertaining to the interactive dynamic of modernity with the country's many-layered art and culture. We believe that he has made a signal contribution in reworking the aesthetic traditions of India including especially the tradition of iconographic innovation. He is among those few modern artists who have focused on mythological and epic narratives, and, for over half a century, he has painted themes from the epics in literally thousands of paintings and drawings.

This alone speaks of his passion for these narratives and, further, of his understanding that their literary, performing and visual form has changed through the centuries, and therefore carries the mandate for new articulations within the contemporary. Equally important, these series of Husain paintings have been shown in urban and rural sites through unique modes of public dissemination. And it speaks of the generous comprehension of this project by viewers all over India, viewers who cut across barriers of class and culture, that they have been received with the affectionate regard and playful participation they require. Posterity will certainly name Husain as one of the most prominent post-Independence artists to shape the contemporary in the spirit of a living and changing tradition. More than any other modern artist in India, he has understood how a syncretic civilization and the dynamics of a multi-ethnic, multi-religious nation have together prompted these interpretations and empowered the community of artists to evolve a uniquely modern language consistent with the complexity of these civilizational narratives. Indeed, Husain is such an iconic figure that we could use the very iconography of Maqbool Fida Husain, of the person himself, to forward ideas about Indian visual culture in the framework of a dynamic public sphere. Already, his life and work are beginning to serve as an allegory for the changing modalities of the secular in modern India–and the challenges that the narrative of the nation holds for many of us.

This is the opportune, and crucial, time to honor him for his dedication and courage to the cultural renaissance of his beloved country.

Signed by:

Vivan Sundaram, Ashok Vajpeyi, Gulammohammed Sheikh, Krishen Khanna, Ram Rahman, M. K. Raina, Geeta Kapur, Arpita Singh, A. Ramachandaran, Aditi De, Akbar Padamsee, Alaknanda Patel, Amit Judge, Amiya Bagchi, Aneesh Pradhan, Anil Chandra, Anuradha Kapur, Arun Vadhera, Ashutosh Gowarikar, Astad Deboo, Atul Bhalla, Atul Tiwari, Aziz Mirza, Bal Chabda, Balkrishan Doshi, Bharati Kher, Bhaskar Chandavarkar, C.P. Chandrasekhar, D.N. Jha, Dadi Pudumjee, Dadiba Pundole, Dolly Narang, E. Alkazi, Gayatri Sinha, Geeta Mehra, Gitanjali Shree, Indira Chandrasekhar, Indra Pramit Roy, Irfan Habib, Javeed Alam, Jayati Ghosh, Jitish Kallat, Jogen Chowdhury, Jyotindra Jain, K. Bikram Singh, K.G. Subramanyan, K.T. Ravindran, Kedar Nath Singh, Kekoo Gandhy, Khorsheed Gandhy, Krishen Baldev Vaid, Kumar Shahani, Kundan Shah, Laxma Gaud, Madangopal Singh, Madhu Prasad, Madhukar Upadhyaya, Malini Bhattacharya, Mani Kaul, Maya Rao, Mira Nair, Mihir Bhattacharya, Mrinalini Mukherjee, Muzaffar Ali, Nadira Babbar, Nagji Patel, Nalini Malani, Namwar Singh, Navjot Altaf, Neelam Man Singh, Nilima Sheikh, Paramjit Singh, Paritosh Sen, Parthiv Shah, Prabhat Patnaik, Prasanna, Pushpamala N., Rafeeq Elias, Raj Babbar, Raj Rewal, Rajeev Bhargava, Rajendra Yadav, Rajinder Arora, Rajiv Sethi, Ram Kumar, Ramgopal Bajaj, Ranbir Kaleka, Reene Saini

Kallat, Renu Modi, Saeed Mirza, Sangita Jindal, Sashi Kumar, Sasidharan Nair M., Shashi Tharoor, Sheba Chhachhi, Shireen Gandhi, Shireen Moosvi, Shubha Mudgal, Shyam Benegal, Sohail Hashmi, Subodh Gupta, Sudhir Chandra, Sudhir Mishra, Sudhir Patwardhan, Sukumar Muralidharan, Suresh B. V., Teesta Setalvad, Tyeb Mehta, U. R. Ananthamurthy, Veer Munshi, Vidya Shah, Vijay Bagodi, Virendra Saini, Zarina Hashmi

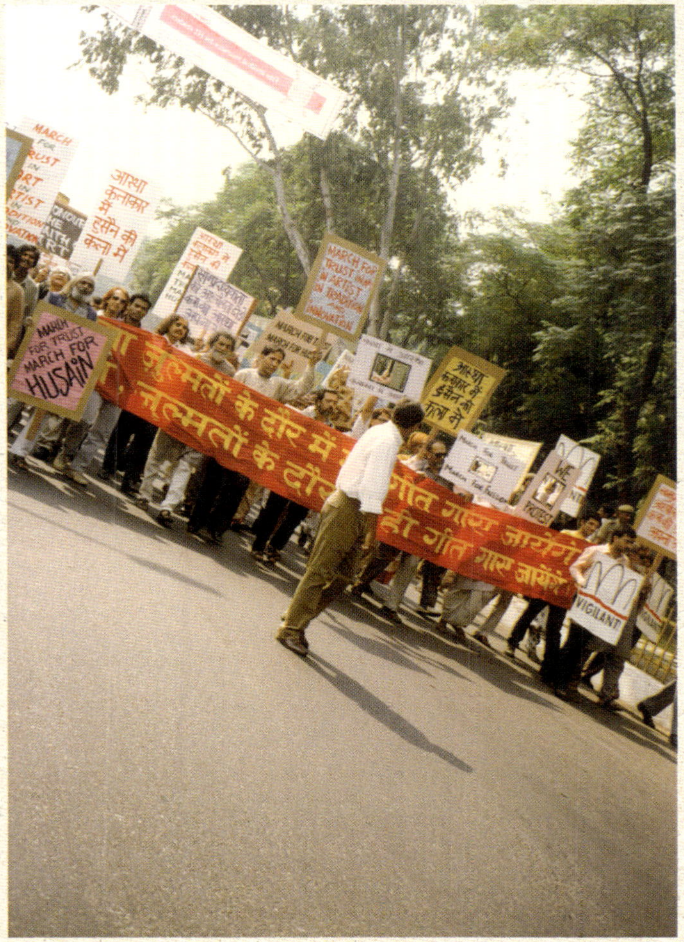

March in defense of Husain led by artists from the National Gallery of Modern Art to Rabindra Bhavan, Delhi, October 1996.

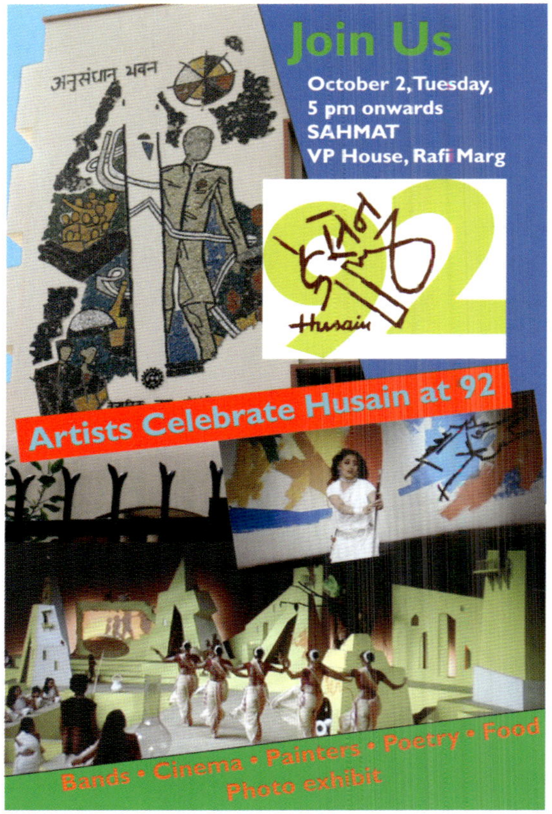

Artists Celebrate Husain at 92, poster, 2007, 17 x 14 inches. Design: Ram Rahman.

Actor Shabana Azmi joins film billboard painter Abbas and his team in painting a billboard with images from Husain's autobiography, *Artists Celebrate Husain at 92*, Delhi, October 2, 2007.

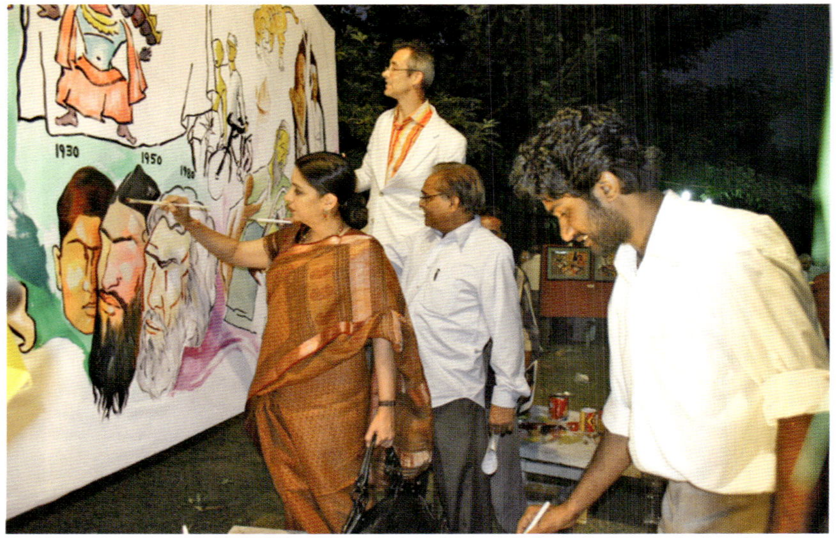

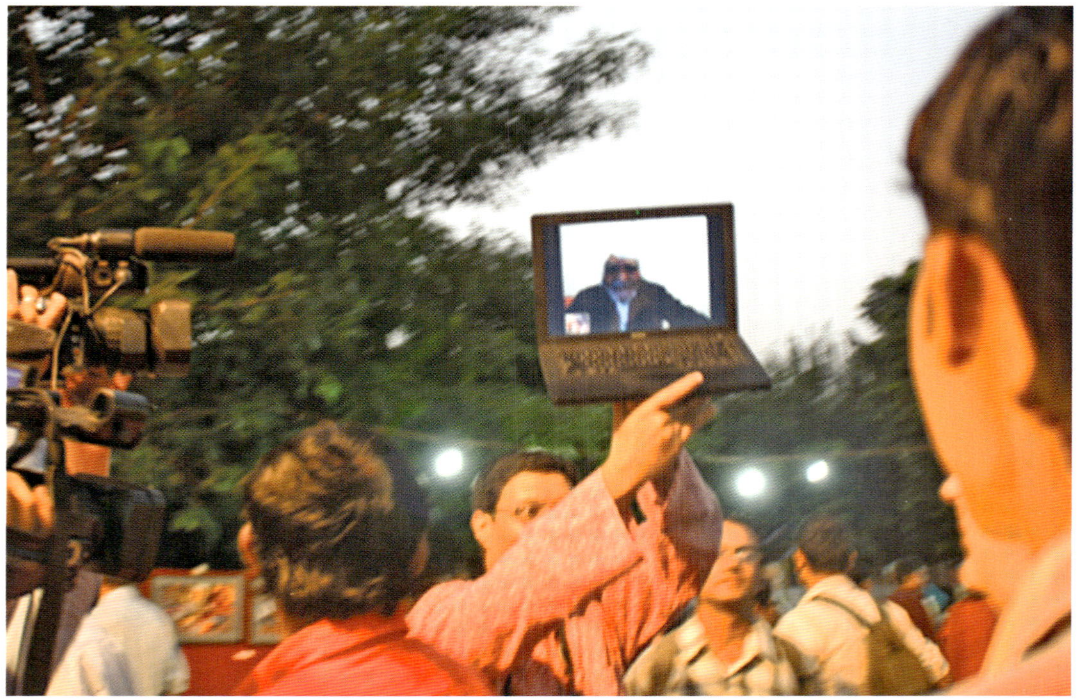

M. F. Husain on Skype from London, witnessing his birthday festival in Delhi, *Artists Celebrate Husain at 92*, October 2, 2007.

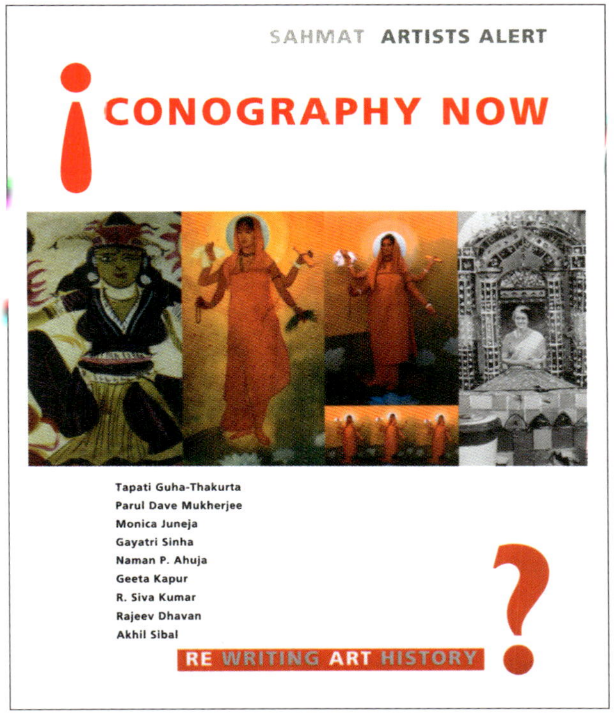

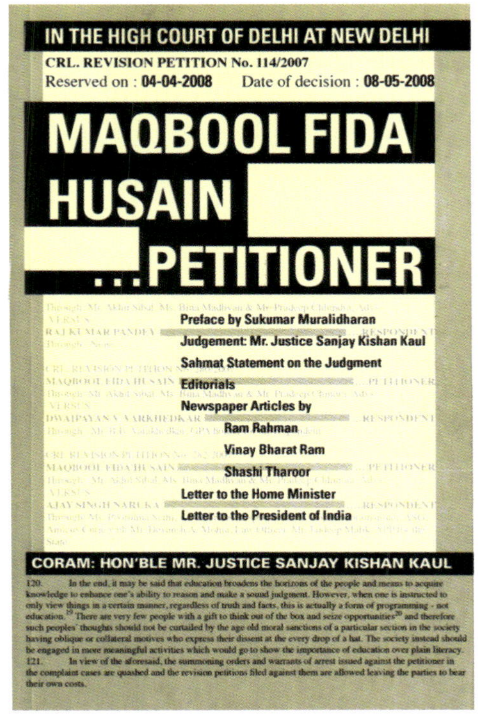

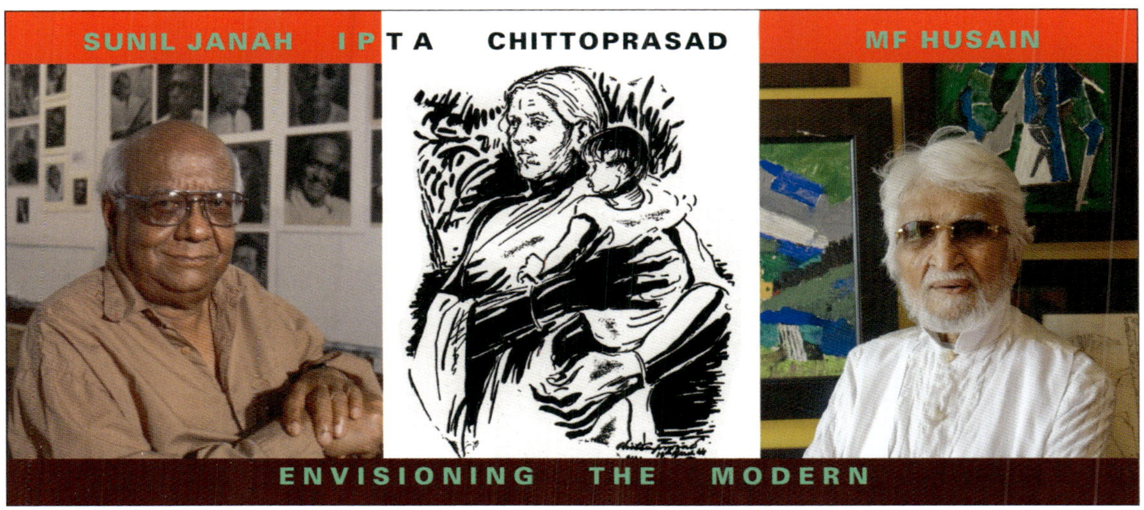

CLOCKWISE FROM LEFT

Book cover: *Iconography Now: Rewriting Art History?* Collection of papers presented at the symposium in Delhi, 2006. Design: Ram Rahman.

Book cover: *Maqbool Fida Husain . . . Petitioner,* 2008. Design: Ram Rahman.

Invitation card for *Envisioning the Modern, Safdar Hashmi Memorial,* January 1, 2008.

2009

For Husain at 94

On Husain's ninety-fourth birthday in 2009, over eighty artists came together in both tribute and protest. Through works made in the artist's honor—in many cases using the iconography for which he was forced into exile—they demonstrated their collective voice of resistance. The exhibition was organized for Sahmat by Parthiv Shah, Ram Rahman, and Vivan Sundaram and installed at the M. F. Husain Gallery at Jamia Millia Islamia University in Delhi. Small-scale works by some of India's most celebrated artists were presented as if wrapped in colorful gift boxes—both gestures of offering and potent symbols of the ongoing struggle for freedom of expression.

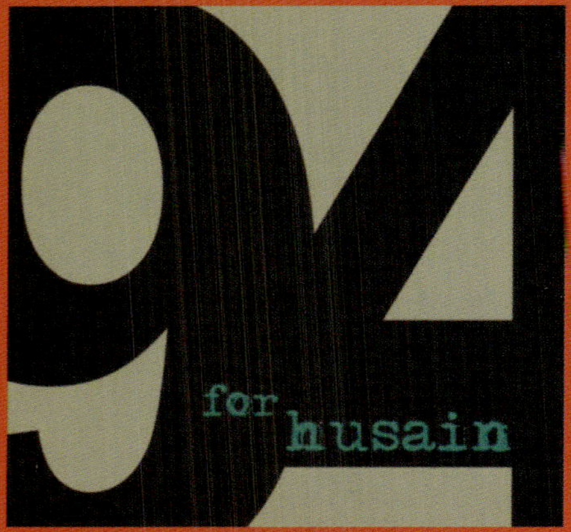

Catalogue cover for *For Husain at 94*. Design: Parthiv Shah.

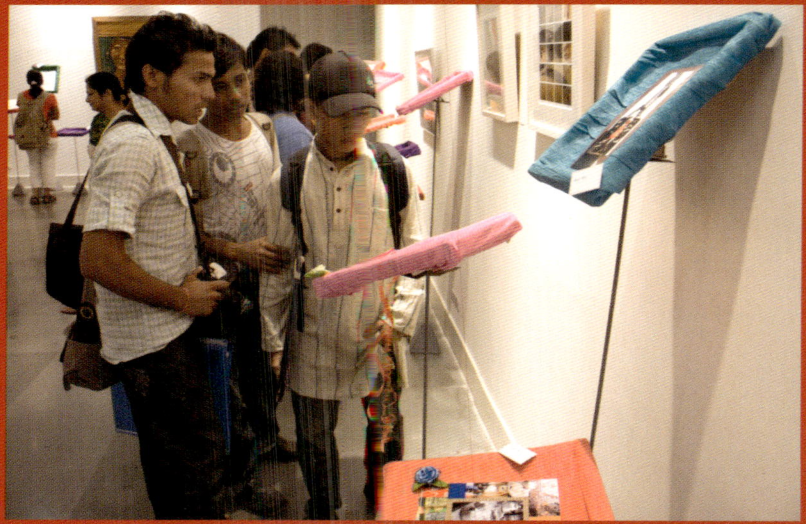

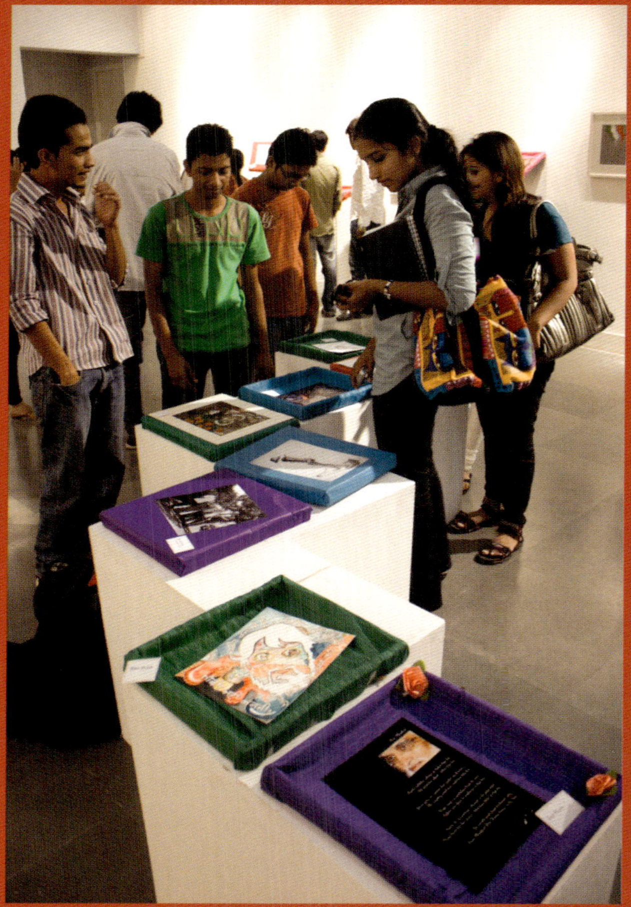

ABOVE AND RIGHT
For Husain at 94, exhibition at the M. F. Husain Gallery, Jamia Millia Islamia University, Delhi, September 17, 2009.

Ram Rahman

From *For Husain at 94* catalogue (New Delhi: Sahmat, 2009).

For the artists' community in India, the predicament that Maqbool Fida Husain finds himself in evokes many emotions: disbelief, anger, fear, puzzlement, and indignation. For a culture that venerates age, it is shocking that we have allowed this 94-year-old to be hounded out of his home and his *matrubhoomi* [motherland] Husain's forced exile is not just the case of an individual who has been falsely accused of religious blasphemy by right-wing groups and the Bharatiya Janata Party. It has serious implications for each of us as a citizen of the republic. The cynical stoking of religious hatred by political groups is not new to us. The experience of the partition is still raw and festering. Yet the Ayodhya mobilization in the 1990s opened a new wound on the body of the republic. Not without coincidence, the attacks on Husain started in 1996, on works by him that had been painted years before and which had been in the public realm.

The new tactic, with repercussions for us as a nation, was to use the law as a means of attack and harassment. By filing cases against the artist across the country in a well-coordinated and strategically managed campaign, the right-wing enmeshed him in a legalistic nightmare. Experts made us realize that this perverse use of the legal framework could be directed at any one of us, and Husain was perhaps its first, most prominent victim.

Since 1996, Sahmat has mobilized the artists' community on numerous occasions, and in various forms, in defending Husain. Protest marches, letter campaigns, meetings with the President of India, the Congress Party president, Home Ministers and lawyers, and a petition to award Husain the *Bharat Ratna* [India's highest civilian award] are some of these. In 2007, when we realized the futility of all these efforts, we decided to honour Husain on his 92nd birthday in a truly "Husain" manner—with a birthday *mela* [street festival]. The gathering at the Vitthalbhai Patel House lawns in New Delhi was memorable, with Husain joining us on live webcam from London.

Now, when he turns 94, artists are coming together in this project to make or contribute an artwork as their gift to Husain. This is, in a way, a creative protest against those who blaspheme Husain's art. It is also a celebration—of his work, ideals, history, and of the man himself. This little book, presented to Husain from all of us, is a reminder that the artists' community holds him in reverence and affection, and no cynical politics can ever change that.

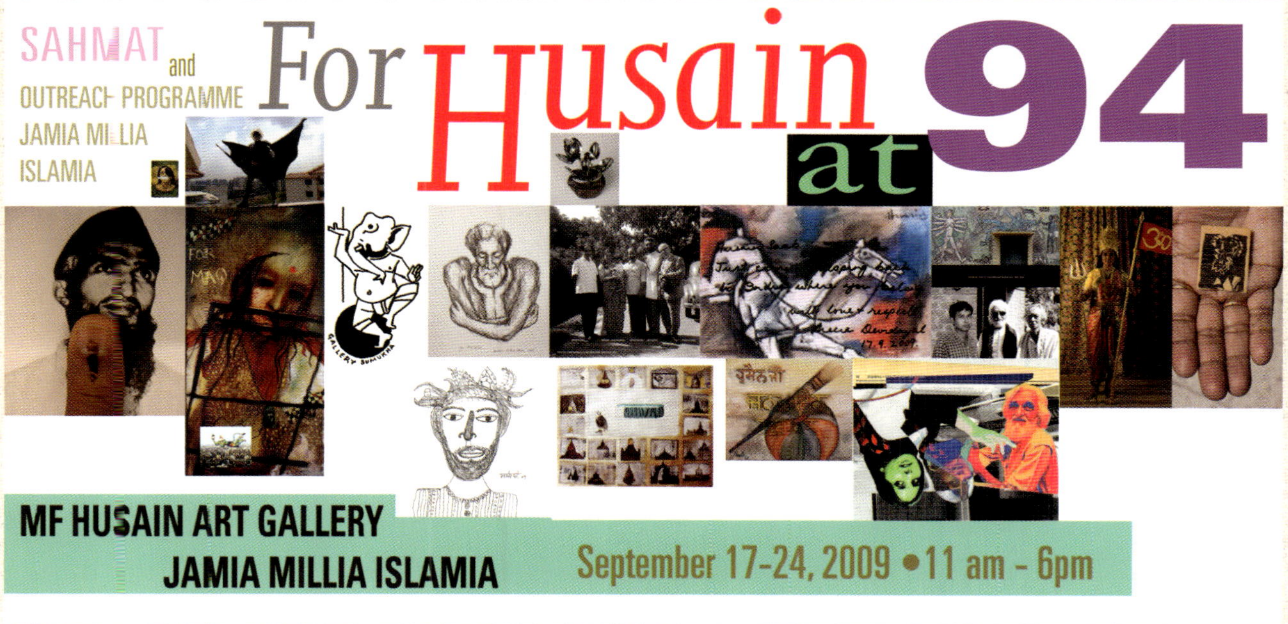

Banner, *For Husain at 94*, September 2009. Design: Ram Rahman.

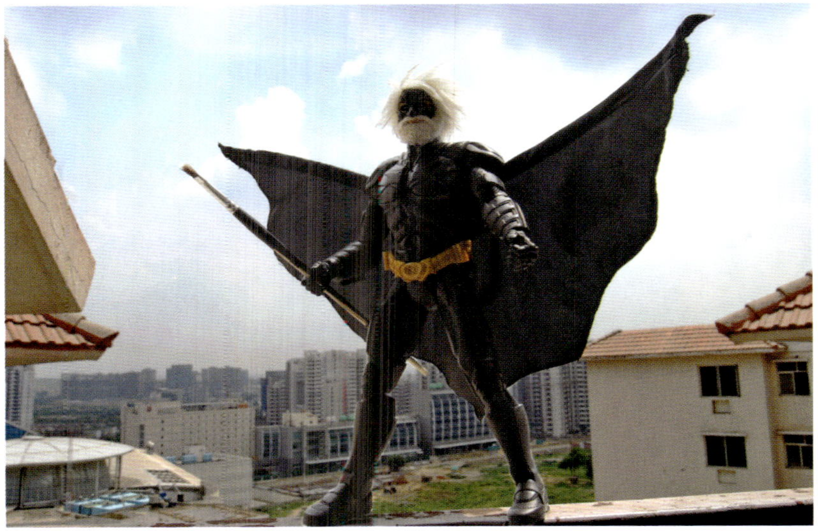

ARUNKUMAR H. G.
Untitled, 2009, digital print, dimensions variable.

There is no title to this work. For me Husain and his life are like a fairy tale: I have been hearing a lot of tales about Husain since my childhood. He has left behind a much larger life in history and the minds of people. He was everywhere as if he had wings like Batman or some such character. He is to be faster than the time. One very famous classical singer dies in Chennai and he was there the next day with a painting to pay tribute to the singer. I couldn't have thought of anything else than this in a lighter vein. I take the example of his life to explain the meaning of youthfulness.

I made this work especially for this show, to demonstrate solidarity with the great man who had to be in another country at that age. Sahmat was one of the very few groups of people who stood in support of Husain in his situation. We saw defending Husain as defending the freedom of expression in the country. —A. H. G.

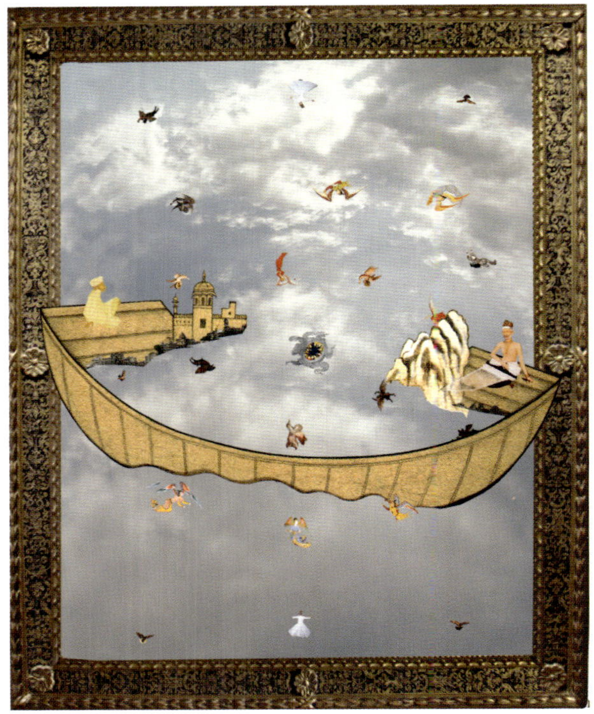

GULAMMOHAMMED SHEIKH
Untitled, 2009, digital print, dimensions variable.

The work was meant to bring in the plight of the artist set in a sky full of angels and demons with the gift of a boat to sail with Gandhi and Kabir. It was important to stand in solidarity with an artist who was and continues to be a living symbol of the inclusive plurality we all cherish. As an artist, I believed it was important to stand by him to fight the radicalism in our country. —G. S.

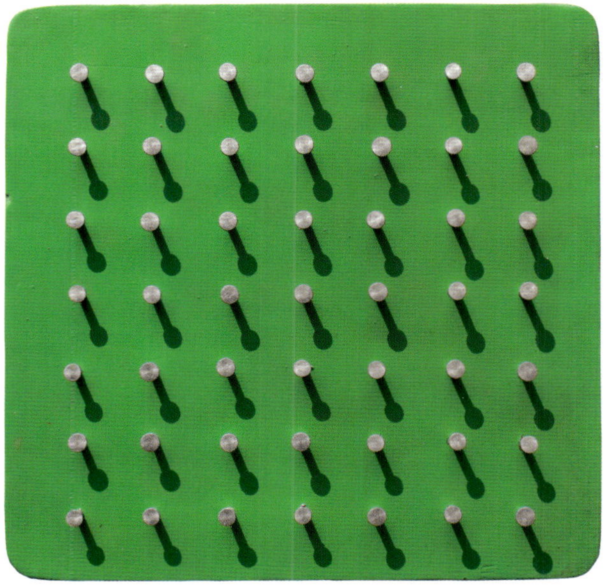

MONA RAI
Untitled, 2009, digital print, dimensions variable.

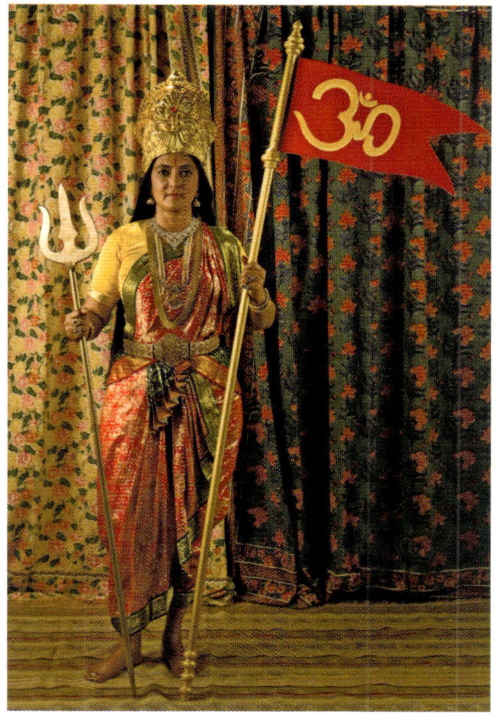

PUSHPAMALA N.
Motherland with Om Flag and Trishul, 2009, digital print, dimensions variable.

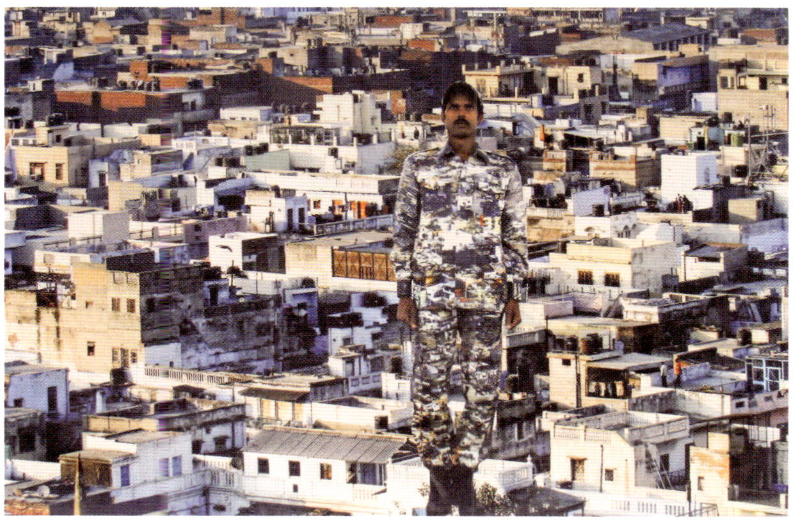

VIBHA GALHOTRA
Neo-Camouflage, 2009, digital print, dimensions variable.

M. F. Husain has been consistently and violently attacked by the Hindu Right (and the Muslim Right!) since the 1990s for using Hindu iconography in his work. Artists of all religions have used these archetypal icons and symbols, but Husain was cynically targeted as the preeminent painter for political reasons to gain mileage, though his work was innocuous. The most recent Husain controversy was about his using a nude Mother India figure in one of his works, which was incidentally painted decades before. Husain's use of Hindu or national iconography is celebratory and hardly critical or insulting. But identity politics here has become hypersensitive, which was not the case in an earlier, secular India. So my work comments on this, and shows me dressed as the figure of the Hindu national goddess used popularly in Hindu political party events, holding militant symbols like the Om sign and Siva's weapon, the Trishul. The whole thing is a staged tableau recalling a bazaar photo studio set-up, referring to the cynical "staging" of the new nationalism.

M. F. Husain was targeted as anti-national and had to flee the country and finally died in exile in London. (By the way, it was a mob censorship and not government censorship that went after Husain, though the Indian government did not take a stand about his persecution.) Sahmat's strong support of Husain is very significant, as it is a very vocal and visible force, upholding simultaneously the ideal of a secular India and the right to freedom of expression. —P. N.

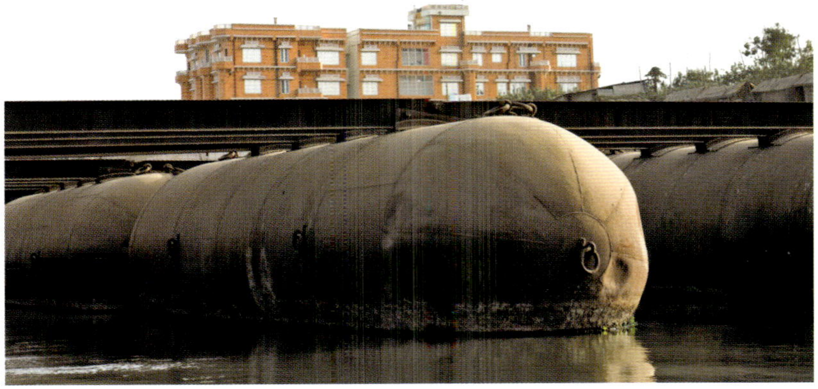

GIGI SCARIA
Between the Devil and the Sea, 2009, digital print, dimensions variable.

Sahmat has always been a catalyst for freedom of expression and its rightful use within the political context of our country. During the time of the "Husain controversy" Sahmat conducted many meetings and seminars to deeply consider the judicial aspects in the context of freedom of expression and works of art. In addition to artists and cultural theorists, lawyers were invited to take part in the discussions. Many of these discussions were an eye-opener for me. I also understood the limitations we face, in the field of visual art, when it comes to freedom of expression.

Between the Devil and the Sea was actually a gift to Husain, who by that time was an artist in exile. The title had come to me as an understanding of Husain's state of being in another country, without being able to come back to his homeland at the age of 94. The title was given especially keeping in mind Husain's mental as well as physical state. —G. S.

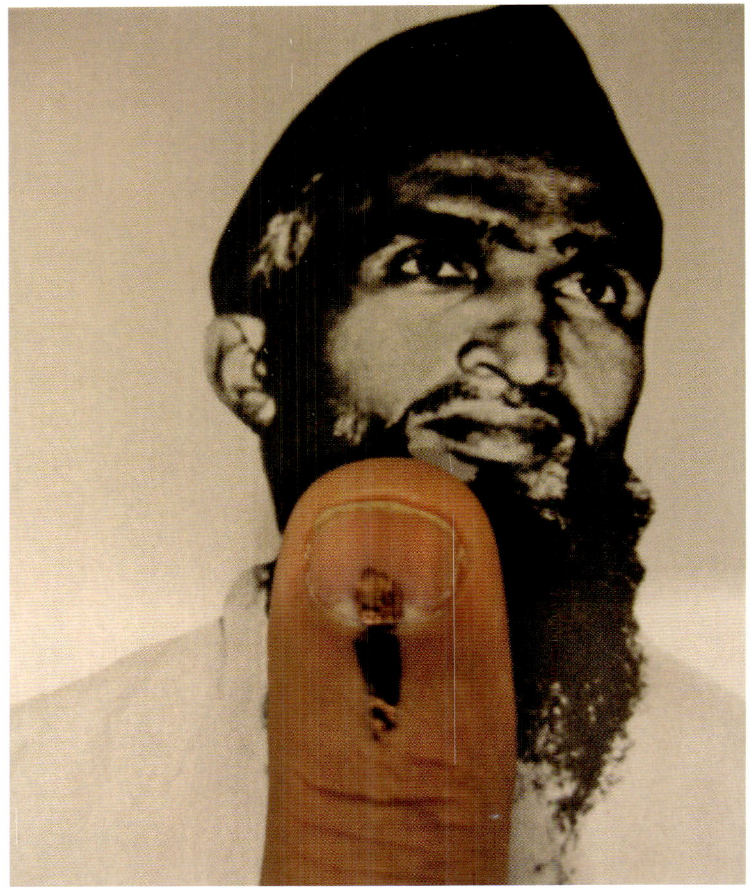

ATUL DODIYA
Untitled, 2009, digital print, dimensions variable.

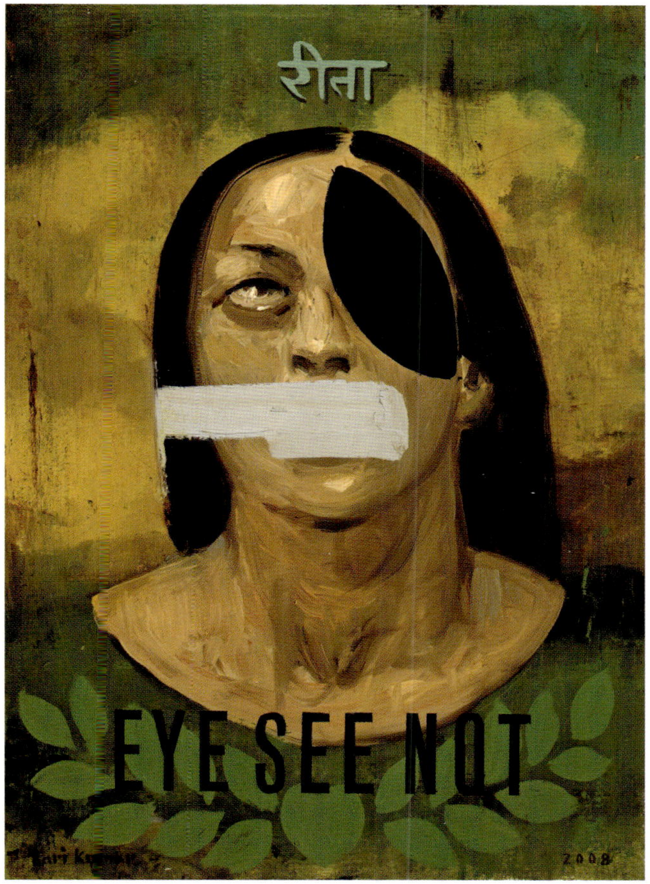

BARI KUMAR
Eye See Not, 2009, digital print, dimensions variable.

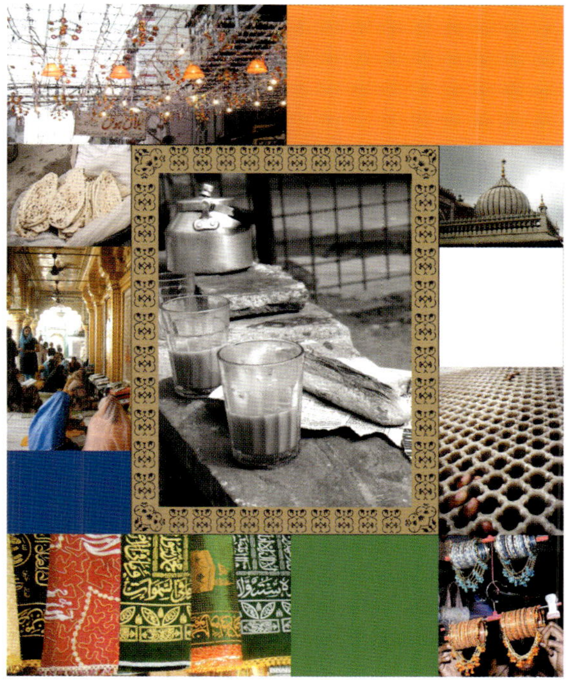

PARTHIV SHAH
Untitled, 2009, digital print, dimensions variable.

One of the places M. F. Husain would invite me to join him was the Nizamuddin in Delhi, where he loved to eat and drink tea. He knew many people in that area including tea shop owners, cooks at restaurants, car mechanics, and so on.

When he was exiled from India, he missed India, his friends, food, smells, people, and places of India. I wanted to give him a "Nizamuddin experience," which was very dear to him. The artwork that was created became a montage of photographs containing typical teacups and architecture of that area.

In many ways the Husain scenario epitomizes the lack of tolerance that people haplessly get into. When we conceived *For Husain at 94* at Sahmat, we invited artists to create a special artwork to give to Husain on his ninety-fourth birthday. One of the ideas was to convey to Husain that the creative community in India is with him and they all love and miss him. The other was to provide a platform and an event to artists who wanted to show their solidarity with Husain. The third was to convey to the fascist forces that Husain is not alone, and we will express whatever we believe in without any fear. —P. S.

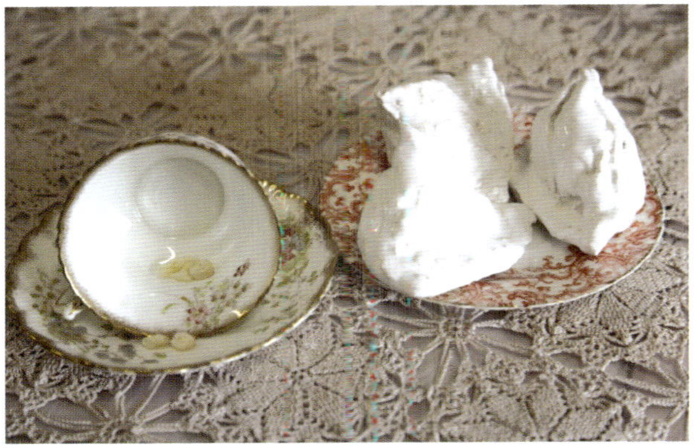

BHARTI KHER
Untitled, 2009, ceramic and lace doily, 12 x 12 x 10 inches.

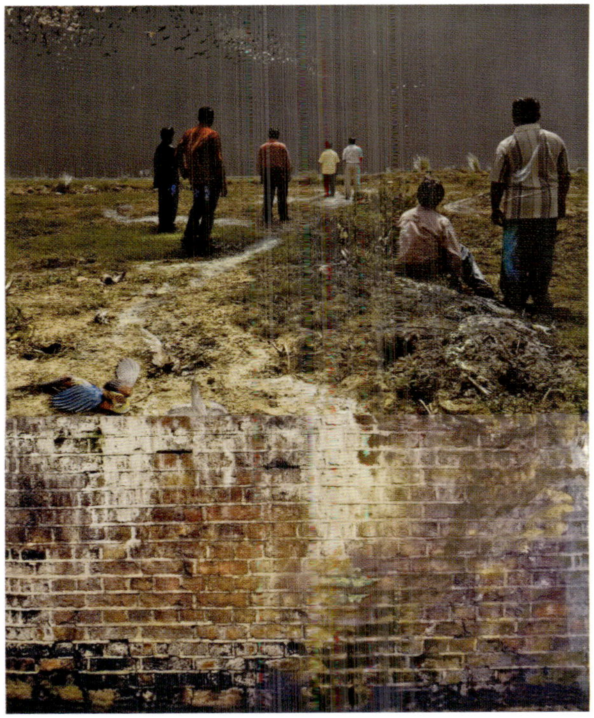

RANBIR KALEKA
Contested Desires, 2009, digital print, dimensions variable.

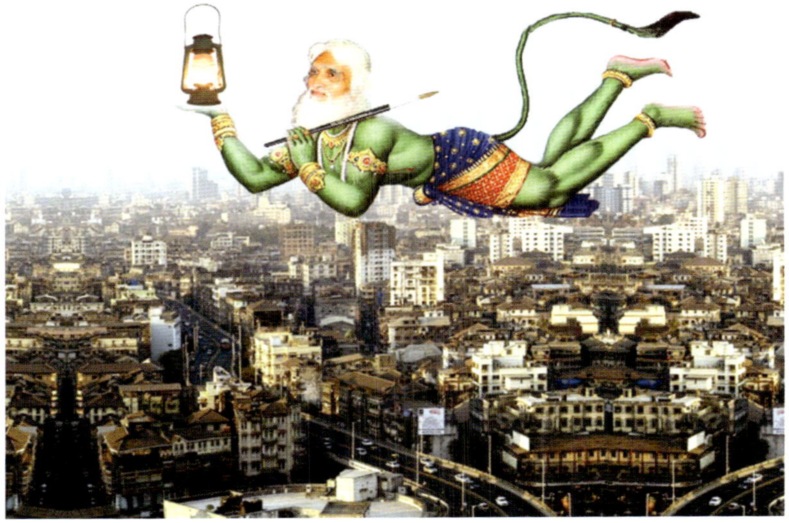

VEER MUNSHI
Hamara Hanuman, (Our Hanuman), 2009, digital print, dimensions variable.

Hamara Hanuman was part of *For Husain at 94*, organized by Sahmat. It was more a tribute to Husain, who I felt was like a Hanuman of the art fraternity, victimized by the right wing and denied space in his own country, yet carrying a lantern (light) like an athlete to wherever he was destined to go.

I think denying Husain his right to India was a challenge to the freedom of expression. As an artist, I believed it was important to stand by him to fight the radicalism in our country.

Sahmat structured the show in an unconventional way and thus gave artists the democratic freedom to participate in whatever medium, whatever language one chose to express a sociopolitical comment in front of an audience, especially for upcoming generations to seek the answers. *Hamara Hanuman* shows Husain flying above the urban city of Mumbai with a light to evoke the consciousness for freedom of expression. —V. M.

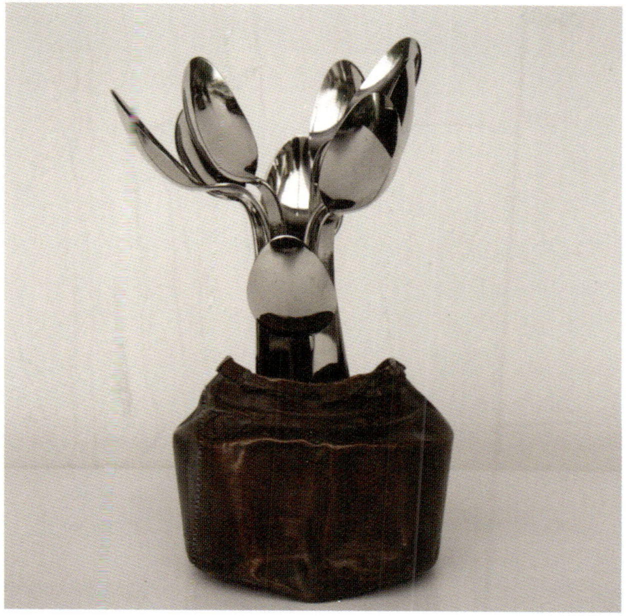

SUBODH GUPTA
Untitled, 2009, stainless steel and brass, 10 x 10 x 12 inches.

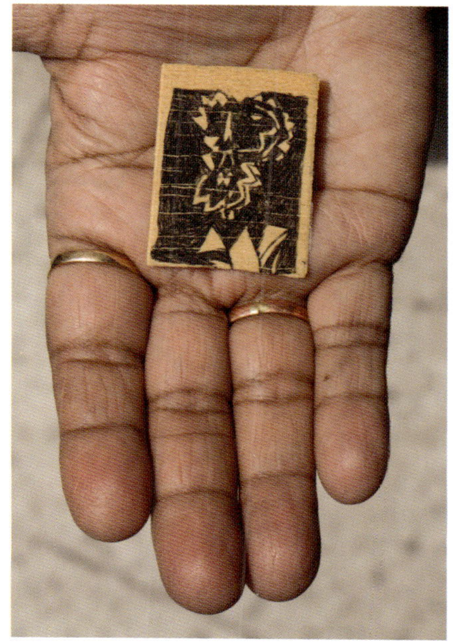

AMITAVA DAS
Untitled, 2009, digital print, dimensions variable.

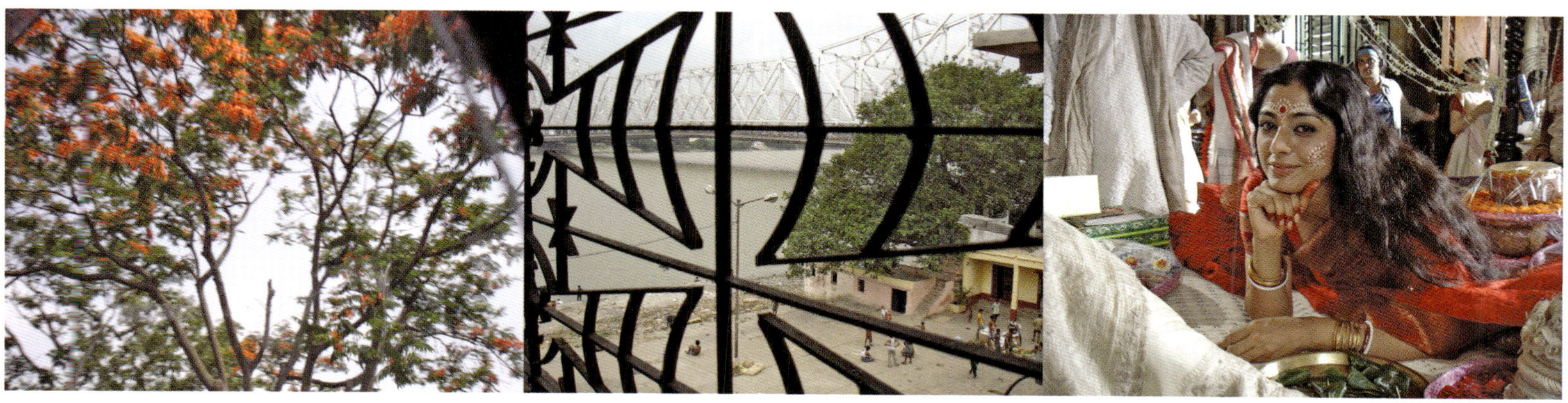

MIRA NAIR
Untitled, 2009, digital print, dimensions variable.

2010

Husain @ 95

M. F. Husain was the artist most connected to and most inspired by both popular and street culture in India. In earlier events celebrating Husain, Sahmat had street wedding bands, cinema billboard painters, and street food. On the artist's ninety-fifth birthday, the art students of Jamia Millia Islamia University had a one-day art-making workshop inspired by the work of the artist. Ram Rahman created an M. F. Husain photo booth using a portrait he had made of Husain in Dubai as a digital cutout, dressed in Arab robes that Rahman had bought with Husain in the Dubai souk. It seemed fitting, as Husain had been intimately connected to the cinema in Bombay and had started his career painting cinema billboards. In a poignant tribute, artists and art students posed with the cutout of the missing artist. The students made imaginative use of the robe by moving the arms and making videos of the animated figure. Seeing the images later in Doha, Husain chuckled at his animated figure blessing rows of students who bent down to touch his feet in respect!

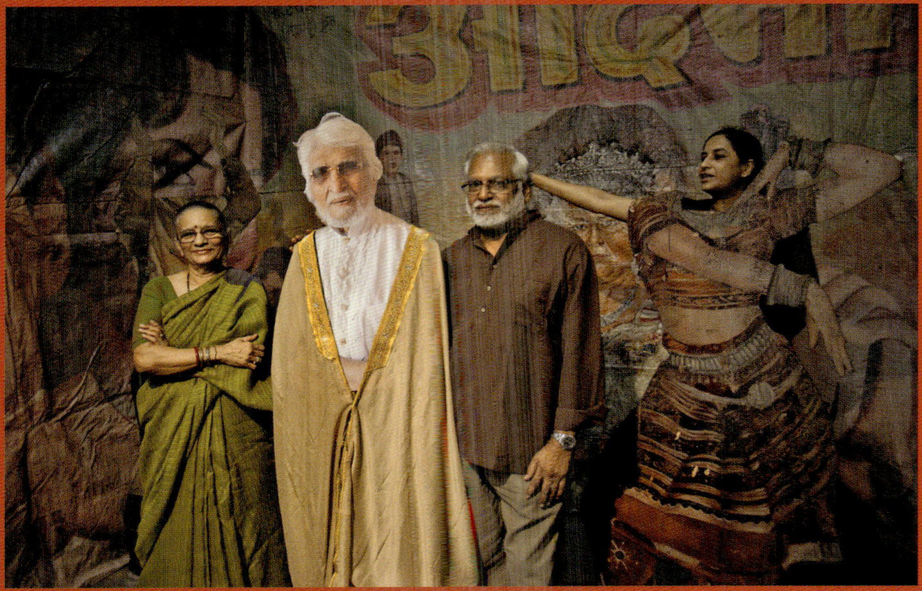

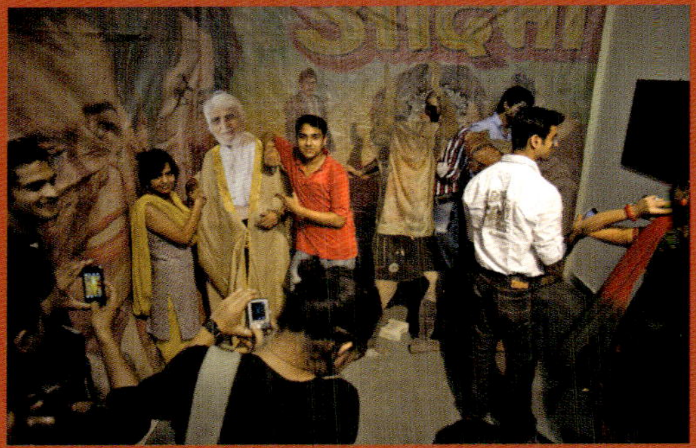

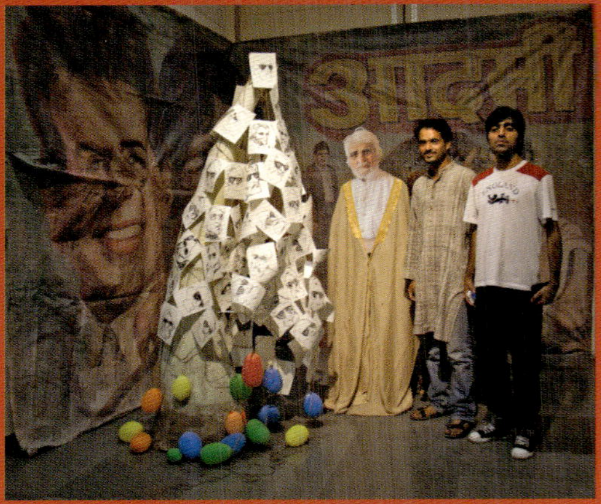

ABOVE
Artists Madhvi Parekh, Manu Parekh, and Manisha Parekh in the M. F. Husain photo booth, *Husain @ 95*, Jamia Millia Islamia University, Delhi, September 17, 2010.

RIGHT TOP
Students in the M. F. Husain photo booth, *Husain @ 95*, Jamia Millia Islamia University, Delhi, September 17, 2010.

RIGHT BOTTOM
Husain installation by students, *Husain @ 95*, Jamia Millia Islamia University, Delhi, September 17, 2010.

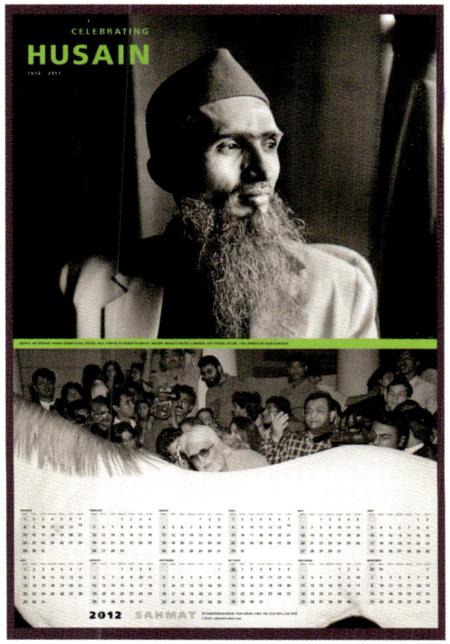

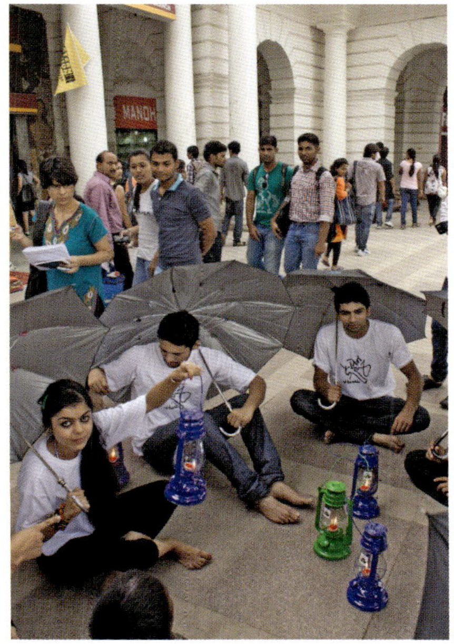

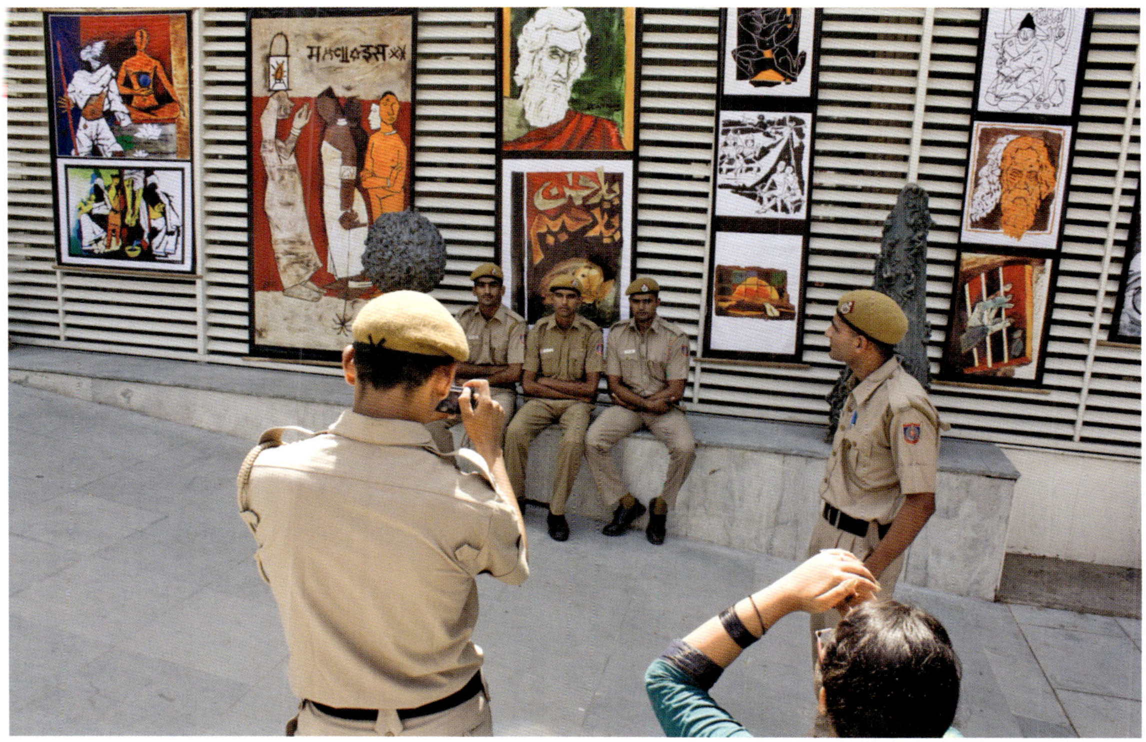

CLOCKWISE FROM LEFT

Sahmat's Husain memorial calendar for 2012. Design: Ram Rahman.

Actors from Act One in a street performance with umbrellas and lanterns, Husain's favorite motifs, in front of his mural at Dhoomimal Gallery at Connaught Place. Husain memorial, Delhi, July 2011.

Delhi police on guard photograph each other in front of paintings by M. F. Husain. *Husain @ 95*, Jamia Millia Islamia University, September 17, 2010.

1989–
Ongoing

Publications, Design, and Graphics

Publications

From its inception, Sahmat has made publications a key component of its activities, both as an integral part of the collective's projects and as a means to record and disseminate information about those projects. Sahmat's publications also underscore the collective's evolving design aesthetic, which brings together graphics, visuals, and text in inventive formats. Through a range of forms—from scholarly texts to children's books, posters to audio, video, and digital recordings—Sahmat has pursued a varied and intensive publishing program in order to reach large numbers of people in different parts of the country and over time, something not possible through event-oriented projects. Publication proceeds also generate sizeable revenue, which helps to subsidize the group's operating costs and to support other Sahmat activities.

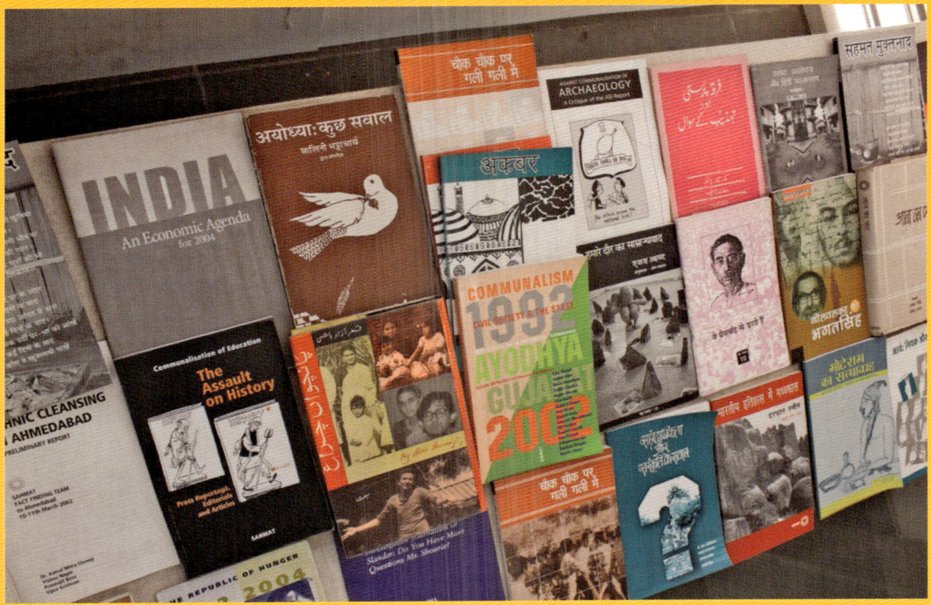

A selection of books published by Sahmat on display at *Image, Music, Text: 20 Years of Sahmat*, Jamia Millia Islamia University, Delhi, 2009.

Within a few months of its formation in 1989, Sahmat produced twelve publications—books, catalogues, and brochures. A number of them document the depth and spread of actions protesting Safdar Hashmi's murder, and the involvement of artists, writers, media persons, and cultural activists in those activities. In addition to the books for children illustrated by artists, Sahmat published a collection of Safdar Hashmi's critical writings and interviews titled *Right to Perform*, as well as *Chowk Chowk Par Gali Gali Mein* (At the Crossroads and on the Streets), a two-volume selection of scripts from Hashmi's street theatre group Jana Natya Manch.

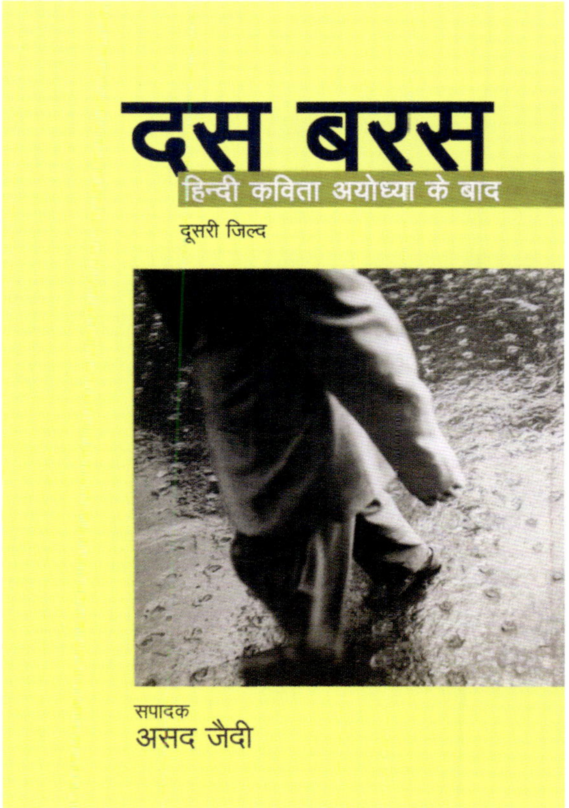

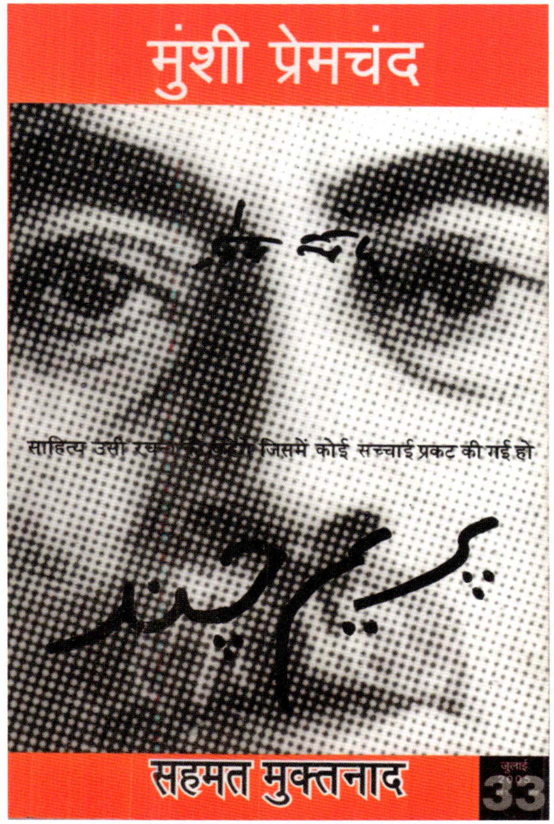

LEFT TO RIGHT

Cover of *Dus Baras* (Hindi Poetry after Ayodhya), 2002. Image: Tarun Bhartiya. Design: Rajinder Arora.

Cover of the Munshi Premchand special issue of *Muktnaad*, Sahmat's Hindi journal, edited by Rajendra Sharma, 2005.

Sahmat has published a number of anthologies of poems and stories in Hindi that underline how poets and writers have contributed to Sahmat's efforts to oppose communalism in the field of literature. These volumes include an anthology of short stories by contemporary writers, *Aaj ka Path* (Today's Path, 1994), and three books of popular songs and poems that promote secular and democratic values: *Apni Zuban* (In One's Own Tongue, 1994), *Yeh Aisa Samay* (Such Times as These, 1994), and *Soorat Badalni Chahiye* (A Change of Face Is Needed, 2008). The half-yearly journal in Hindi *Muktnaad* has been regularly published for over a decade, and Sahmat publishes at least two new books in Hindi every year. The journal and several other Hindi publications are edited and translated/authored by Rajendra Sharma for Sahmat.

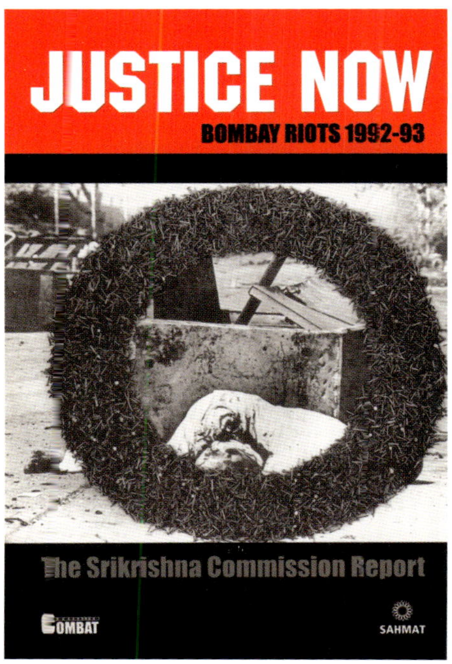

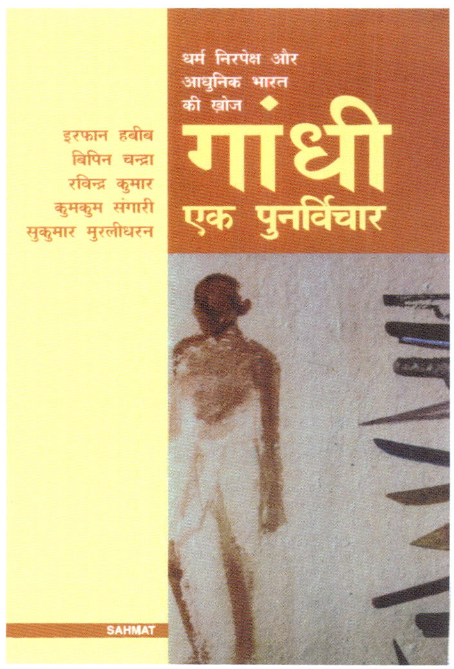

LEFT TO RIGHT

Cover of *Justice Now: Bombay Riots 1992–93*, 2007. Image: Vivan Sundaram. Design: Rajinder Arora, 2007.

Cover of *Gandhi: Ek Punarvichar* (Gandhi Reconsidered), 2004. Image: Nilima Sheikh. Design: Rajinder Arora.

Over time, with the growing involvement of historians, economists, and other social scientists in Sahmat's activities, Sahmat began to make key texts on specific themes of political and social relevance more widely available. They commissioned Hindi translations and published them as series. For instance, the ongoing series *Yeh Samay* (These Times/The Present Moment, 1993–2006) features booklets authored by Irfan Habib, Romila Thapar, K. N. Panikkar, Ravinder Kumar, Aijaz Ahmad, Prabhat Patnaik, C. P. Chandrasekhar, and others.

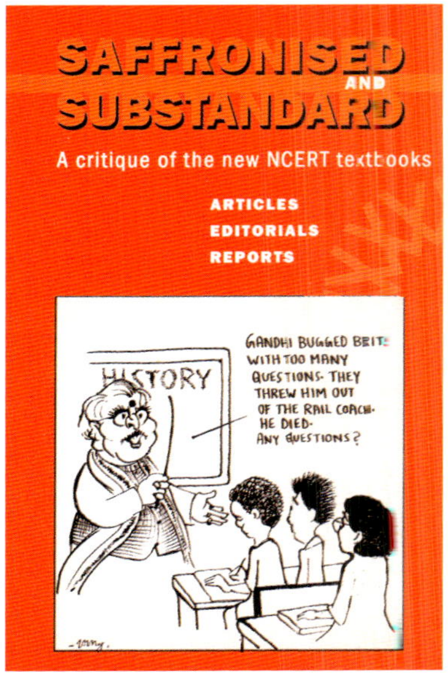

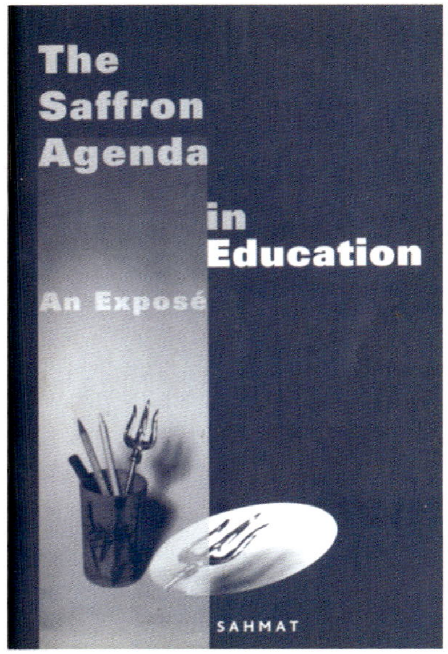

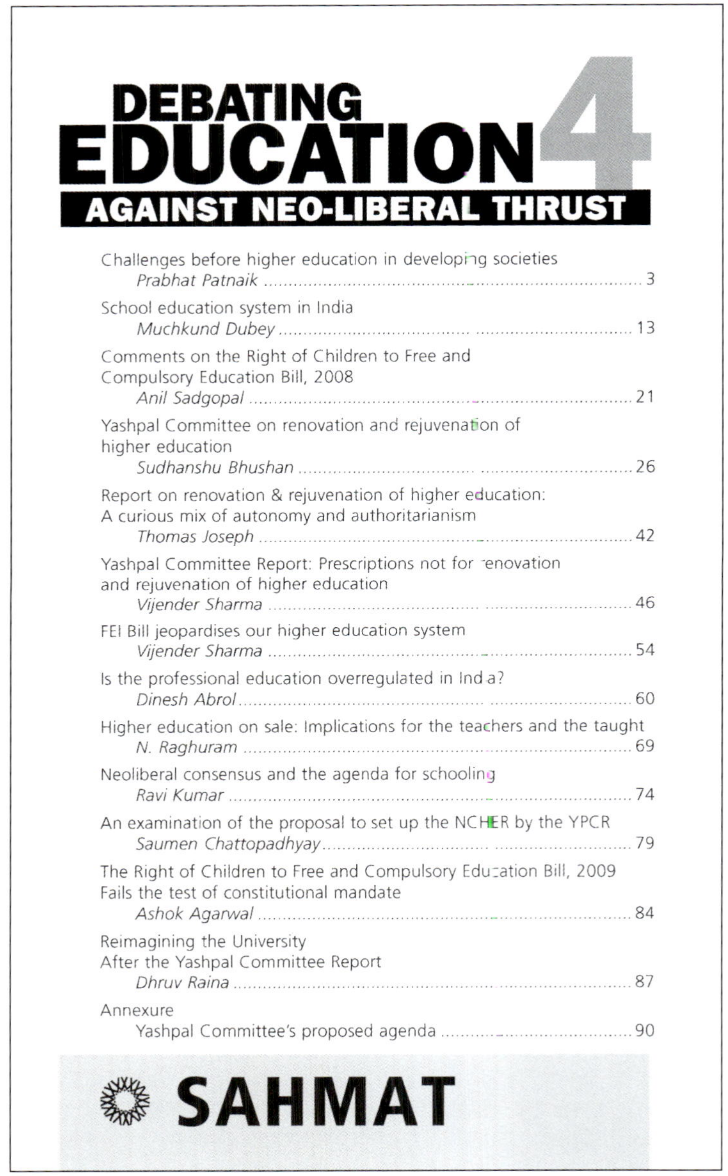

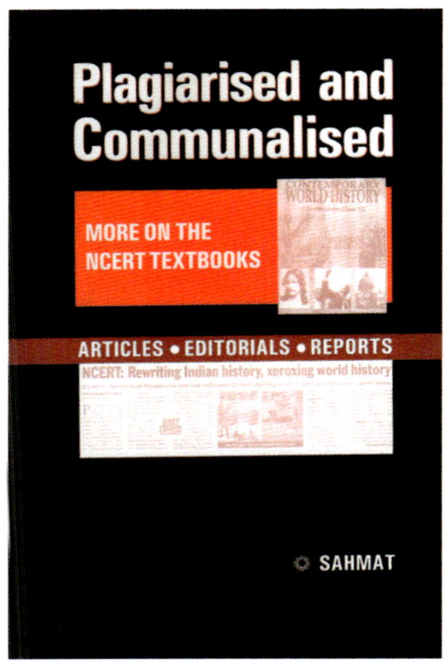

CLOCKWISE FROM TOP LEFT

Cover of *Saffronised and Substandard, A critique of the new NCERT textbooks*, 2002. Cartoon: Unny. Design: Rajinder Arora.

Cover of *The Saffron Agenda in Education*, 2001. Design: Ram Rahman.

Cover of *Debating Education 4–Against Neo-Liberal Thrust*, 2009. Design: Rajinder Arora.

Cover of *Plagiarised and Communalised: More on the NCERT Textbooks*, 2003. Design: Rajinder Arora.

Sahmat has also published books that relate to the wide arena of communalization of society and assert the ideology of secularism. These titles include *Essays on the National Movement* (1999), *Republic Besmirched* (2002), *Communalism, Civil Society and the State* (2002), *Gandhi Reconsidered: Towards a Secular and Modern India* (2004), *The Savarkar Controversy* (2004), *After Ayodhya* (2009), and *The Ayodhya Judgment* (2011), among others. A related series focuses more precisely on the impact of these issues in the arena of education. In order to combat the rewriting of school textbooks by the BJP-led NDA government (1999–2004) in ways that Sahmat viewed as distortions of history, Sahmat published a series of books of collected essays against the communalization of education: *Against Communalisation of Education* (2001), *Saffronised and Substandard* (2002), *Assault on History* (2002), and *Plagiarized and Communalised* (2003). Other issues related to education such as privatization, commercialization, and affirmative action through reservations (meaning the reservation of seats for disprivileged social groups through a quota system) are addressed in the *Debating Education* series (2005–09).

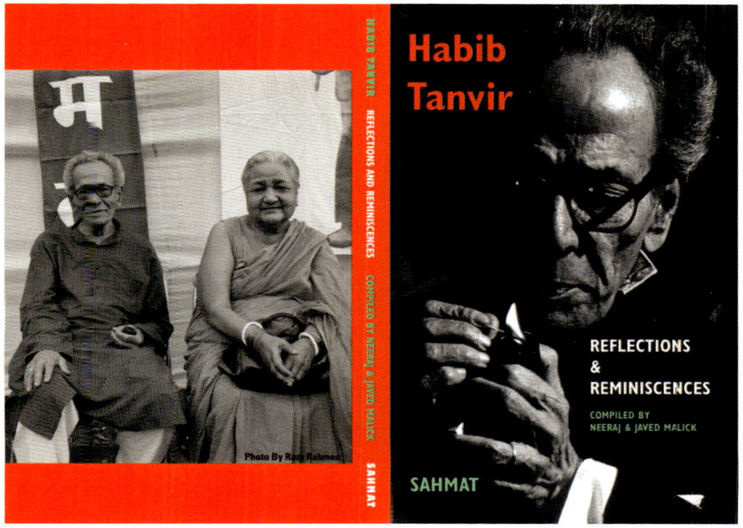

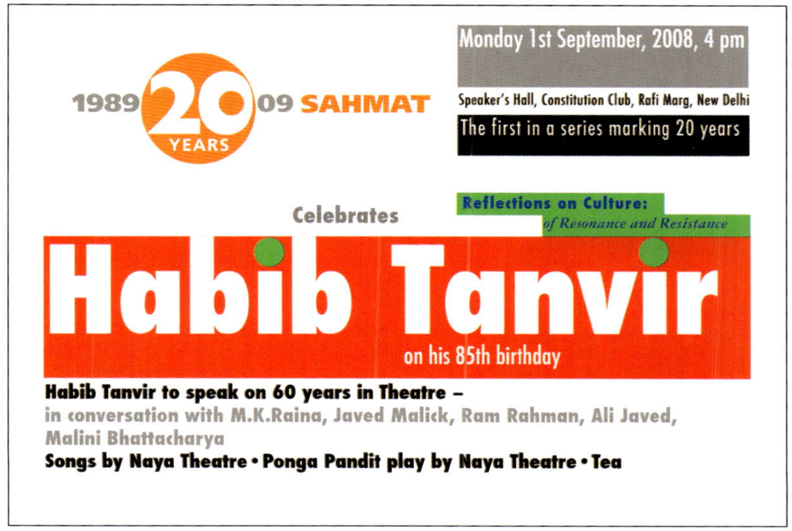

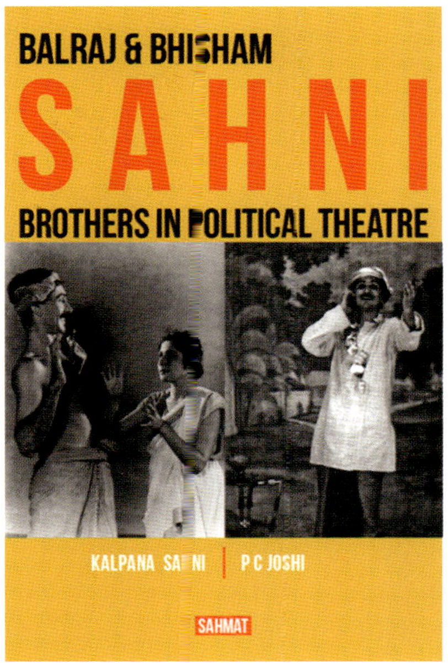

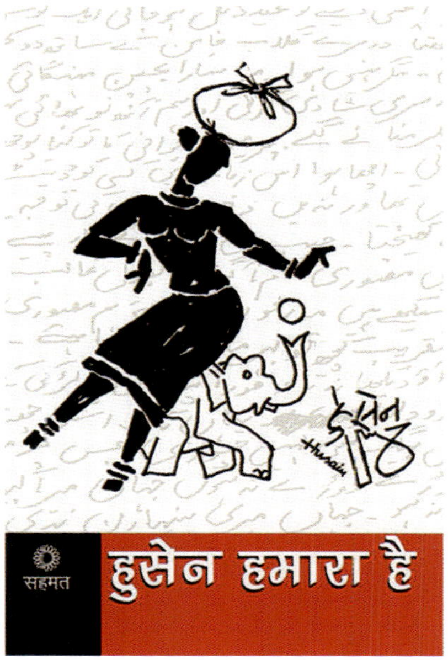

CLOCKWISE FROM TOP LEFT

Cover of *Habib Tanvir: Reflections & Reminiscences*, compiled by Neeraj and Javed Malick, 2010. Design: Ram Rahman.

Invitation card, 2009. Design: Ram Rahman.

Cover of *Husain Hamara Hai* (Husain Belongs to Us), 2011. Image: M. F. Husain. Design: Rajinder Arora.

Cover of *Balraj and Bhisham Sahni: Brothers in Political Theatre*, essays by Kalpana Sahni and P. C. Joshi, 2012. Design: Ram Rahman and Raghuvir Khare.

Sahmat has published several books defending renowned artist M. F. Husain against political opposition to his work and his forced exile, and on the High Court verdict in his favor: *Iconography Now* (2006), *Harassing Husain* (2007), *Maqbool Fida Husain . . . Petitioner* (2008), *Husain Hamara Hain* (Husain Belongs to Us, 2011). Sahmat has also published books celebrating the life and work of progressive thinkers of modern India, like the writer Premchand, historian D. D. Kosambi, political leader Jyoti Basu, playwright Habib Tanvir, poet Makhdoom, and the actor-writer brothers Balraj and Bhisham Sahmi.

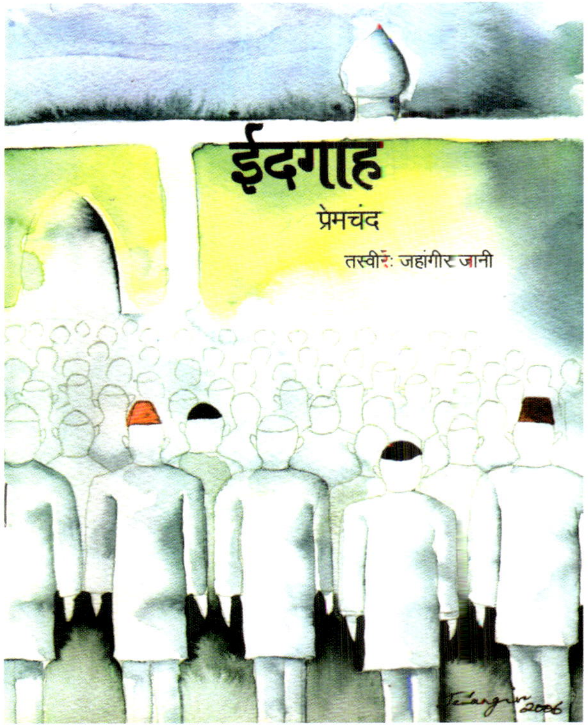

Cover of *Idgah* by Munshi Premchand, illustrated by Jehangir Jani, 2005. Design: Rajinder Arora.

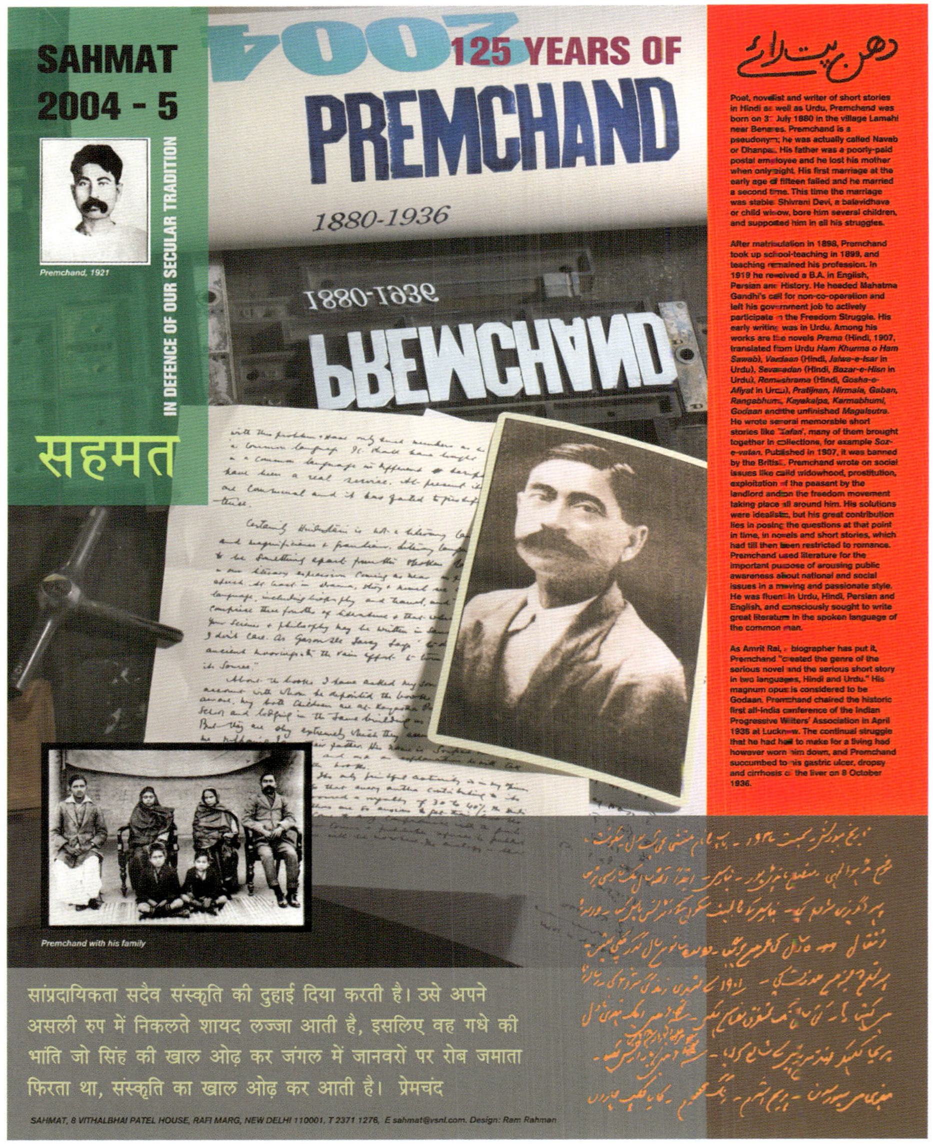

Poster for *125 Years of Premchand*, 2005. Design: Ram Rahman.

The *Safdar Hashmi Memorial* on January 1, 2005, commemorated the125th anniversary of the birth of Munshi Premchand, a renowned progressive writer in Hindi and Urdu. Besides readings from Premchand and the staging of plays based on his stories, the event included an exhibition of works made by eighteen artists in tribute to Premchand, and the release of a set of twenty-five postcards and a calendar with reproductions of these images. Sahmat also released a children's book based on Premchand's story *Idgah* (Place of Worship), illustrated by artist Jehangir Jani.

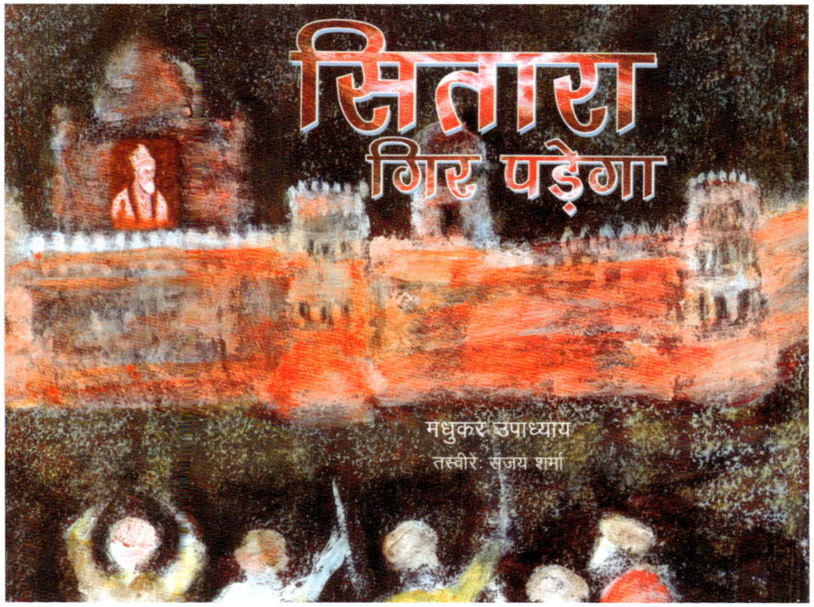

Cover of *Sitara Gir Padega* (A Star Will Fall) by Madhuker Upadhyay, illustrated by Sanjay Sharma, 2007. Design: Rajinder Arora.

***Sitara Gir Padega*, published in 2007, the 150th anniversary of the 1857 Revolt, tells a story of the first Indian War of Independence.**

In 2012, Sahmat commemorated the 150th anniversary of the birth of Nobel Laureate, philosopher, and writer Rabindranath Tagore with *Tagore Tells and the Patua Paints*. The project produced Hindi, English, and Bengali versions of three children's texts by Tagore, illustrated by traditional visual artists of rural Bengal, known as *patuas*. The selected Tagore texts were *Tota Kahani* (The Story of the Parrot), a tale in prose; *Bir Purush* (The Brave Little Man), a boy's fantasy adventure in verse; and *Brishti Pare Tapar Tupur* (Daylight Is Fading), a poem describing a rainy sunset. Eleven *patuas*, young and old, participated in a workshop in Kolkata from May 11 to 18. They created thirty-two works, which became illustrations for the books and also were exhibited in Delhi. The project was conceived and coordinated by Malini Bhattacharya for Sahmat.

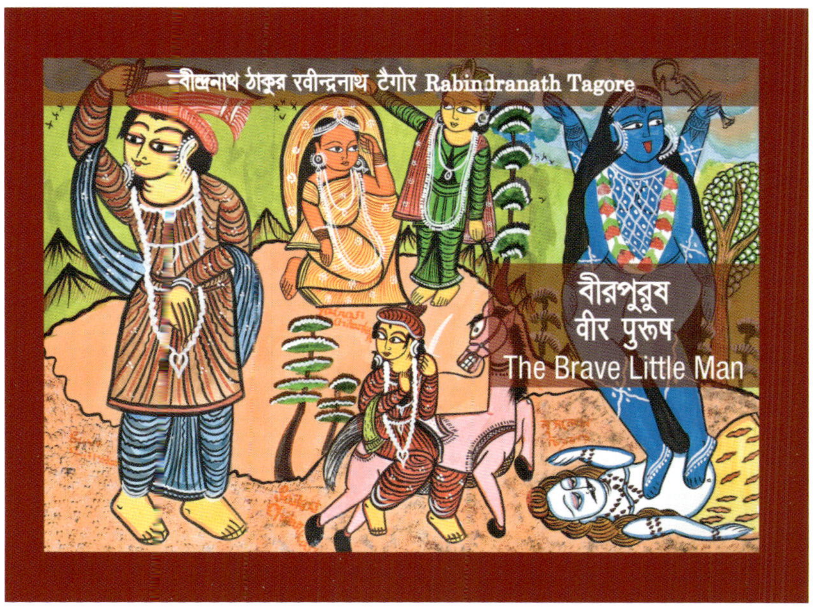

Cover of *The Brave Little Man* by Rabindranath Tagore, illustrated by *patuas* from Bengal, 2012.

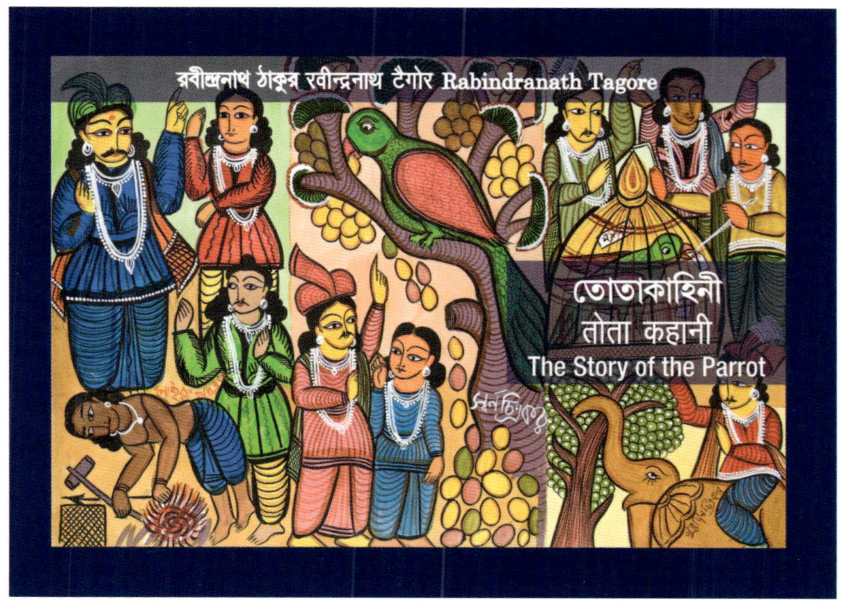

Cover of *The Story of the Parrot* by Rabindranath Tagore, illustrated by *patuas* from Bengal, 2012.

Besides books, Sahmat has released several audio-video cassettes of its music and dance performances. The most popular of these is a recording of the Sufi-Bhakti music presented at *Anhad Garje*. It has been in circulation for the last twenty years and is available in a set of four CDs. Other recordings include *Safdar*, a film made by Sashi Kumar soon after Safdar Hashmi's murder, *Jung-e-Azadi* (music, 1997), *20 Years of Sahmat* (music, 2009), and *Ways of Resisting* (exhibition, 2009).

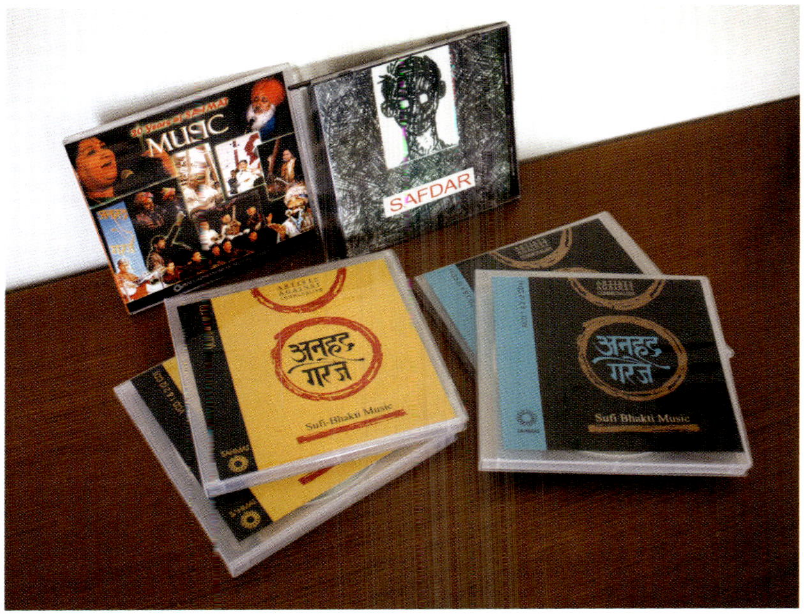

Sahmat produces posters, annual thematic calendars, and postcards with artists' images on a regular basis—and they are very much in demand. Sets of *100 Postcards for Gandhi*, 25 Premchand cards, and 50 artists' cards from *Making History Our Own* have been in circulation for a number of years.

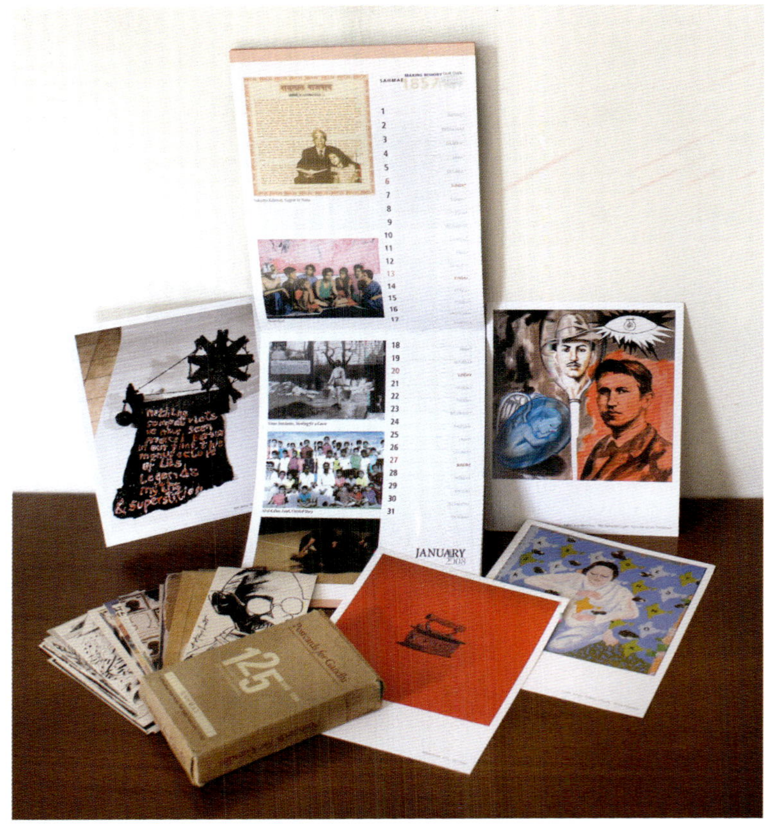

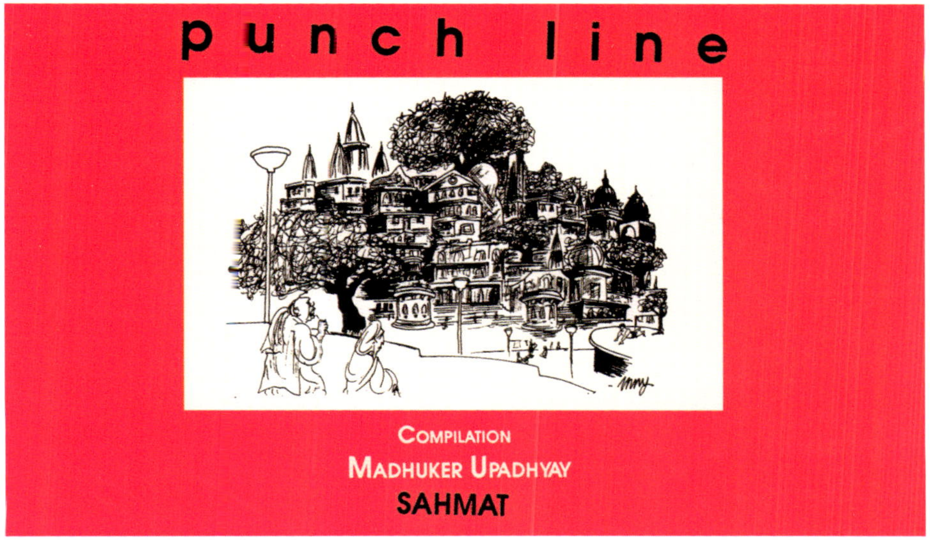

Cover of *Punchline: Cartoons Against Communalism,* compiled by Madhuker Upadhyay, 1994. Design: Parthiv Shah.

Laxman . . . define[s] cartooning as "the art of disapproval and complaint. It treats men and matters with a certain healthy scepticism and good-humoured ridicule, but never malice. A cartoon attempts to preserve the sense of humour of the community which is so essential for survival in day-to-day existence." Laxman's point is unexceptionable and the cartoon can at last be said to have come of age in the Indian print media. The preceding year, 1993, can definitely be categorized as the "Year of the Cartoonist," as the purveyors of the genre—junior and senior—en bloc extended the frontiers of the form in a manner unprecedented in our times, by succeeding in making political and social points far more effectively and radically than even the editorial writers in the press. What was most striking was the way in which they took communal politics head on and laid bare the hollow claims of politicians seeking to ride piggyback on the religious sentiments of people.

Excerpt from the essay by Sadanand Menon in *Punchline: Cartoons Against Communalism*, compiled by Madhuker Upadhyay (New Delhi: Sahmat, 1994).

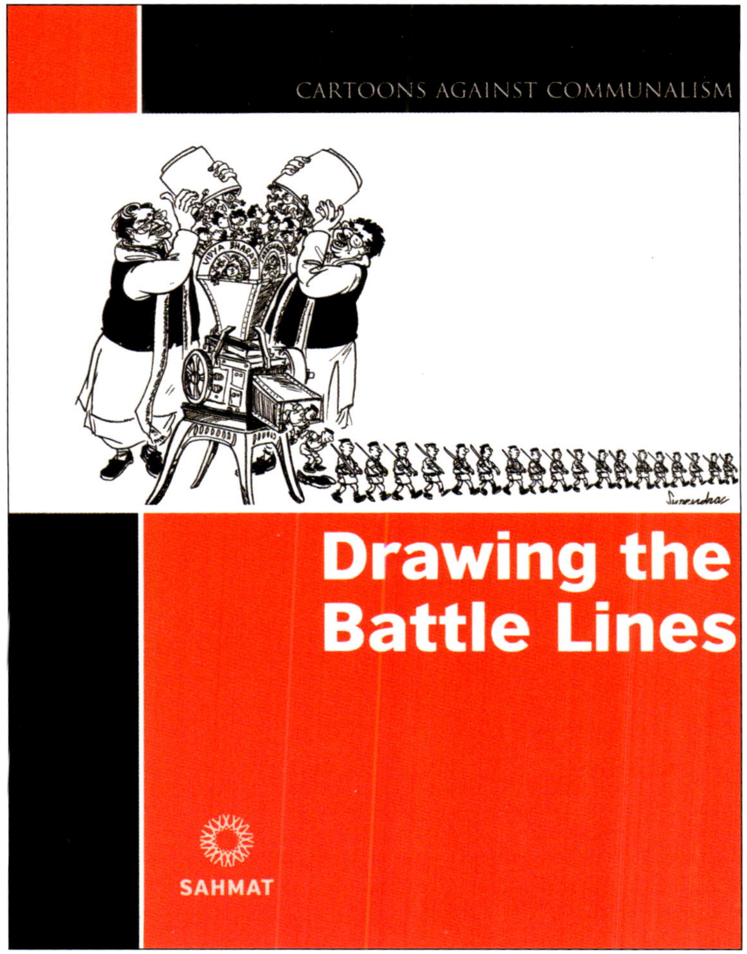

Cover of *Drawing the Battle Lines,* 2002. Cartoon: Surendra. Design: Rajinder Arora.

Sahmat presented *Punchline*, an exhibition of cartoons culled from many of the different language publications across India, curated by Madhuker Upadhyaya in 1994. One of the first compilations to include the work of cartoonists from these publications, it provided an overview of cartoonists' responses to the communal politics witnessed in the previous few years. A symposium was held in Delhi with some of the foremost cartoonists of the country, including Abu Abraham, R. K. Laxman, Sudhir Dhar, Sudhir Tailang, Irfan, Ponnappa, Maya Kamath, Roopam, and Unny, and journalists Sadanand Menon, Santo Dutta, and Darryl D'Monte. The exhibition traveled across India for many years and the book was a landmark in collecting cartoons on a single theme. It was followed by another compilation of cartoons, *Drawing the Battle Lines*, in 2002, after the Gujarat riots, which presented updated responses to the increased communalization of the following years.

Design and Graphics

Many of the founding members of Sahmat are artists and graphic designers, so from the beginning it was important to convey a distinctive visual identity for all the print material produced by the collective. This attention to graphic design expanded to cover the group's art projects, performance spaces, and street actions. Sahmat's emphasis on bold and color-filled typographic design intentionally diverged from the dominant look of political graphics in India in the 1980s and 1990s. Many earlier political posters in India were hand-designed and printed as lithographs. During the Ayodhya movement starting in the mid-1980s, the Hindu Right developed a visual iconography for their campaign based on popular "calendar art" styles of depicting mythological figures, particularly the god Rama. In contrast, the visual culture of protest and resistance launched by Sahmat had roots in Soviet constructivism and the German Left of the 1920s.

Guided by this overall aesthetic, the visual character and materiality of each publication project was carefully considered by the group. All forms of design technology—high and low—were marshaled as needed, from photocopying, silkscreen, and stencils to the fax machine and computer layout programs as they became more available in the Indian market. Despite the expense, the members of Sahmat decided to sometimes use offset color printing on good paper, especially when reproducing art and photography, but the collective has also turned to more traditional single-color printing on newsprint or cheaper paper for mass campaigns that called for print runs in the hundreds of thousands. An example of the latter is the Ayodhya broadside *What then are our invocations?* (1993), one of a characteristic series of posters that mingle historical text and imagery within a visually dense design style to bring a contemporary urgency to past events.

The group's interest in graphic style extends beyond its publications: for instance in the boldly lettered, hand-painted banners—often produced in a creative collaboration with billboard painters—that fill the performance tents and stage that are constructed every January for the Safdar Hashmi memorials. Professional designers, artists, and architects volunteer their skills both in design and research to Sahmat's projects. Sahmat has also developed an in-house design team, led by Lalit Narain (Bunty), to collaborate with the professional designers. Over the years, Sahmat has thus become a platform for experimental design—a vital part of its larger goal to disseminate progressive information and ideas in compelling and lasting ways.

Invitation card for *Safdar Hashmi Memorial*, 2010—an example of the typical graphic style developed for printed material produced by Sahmat.

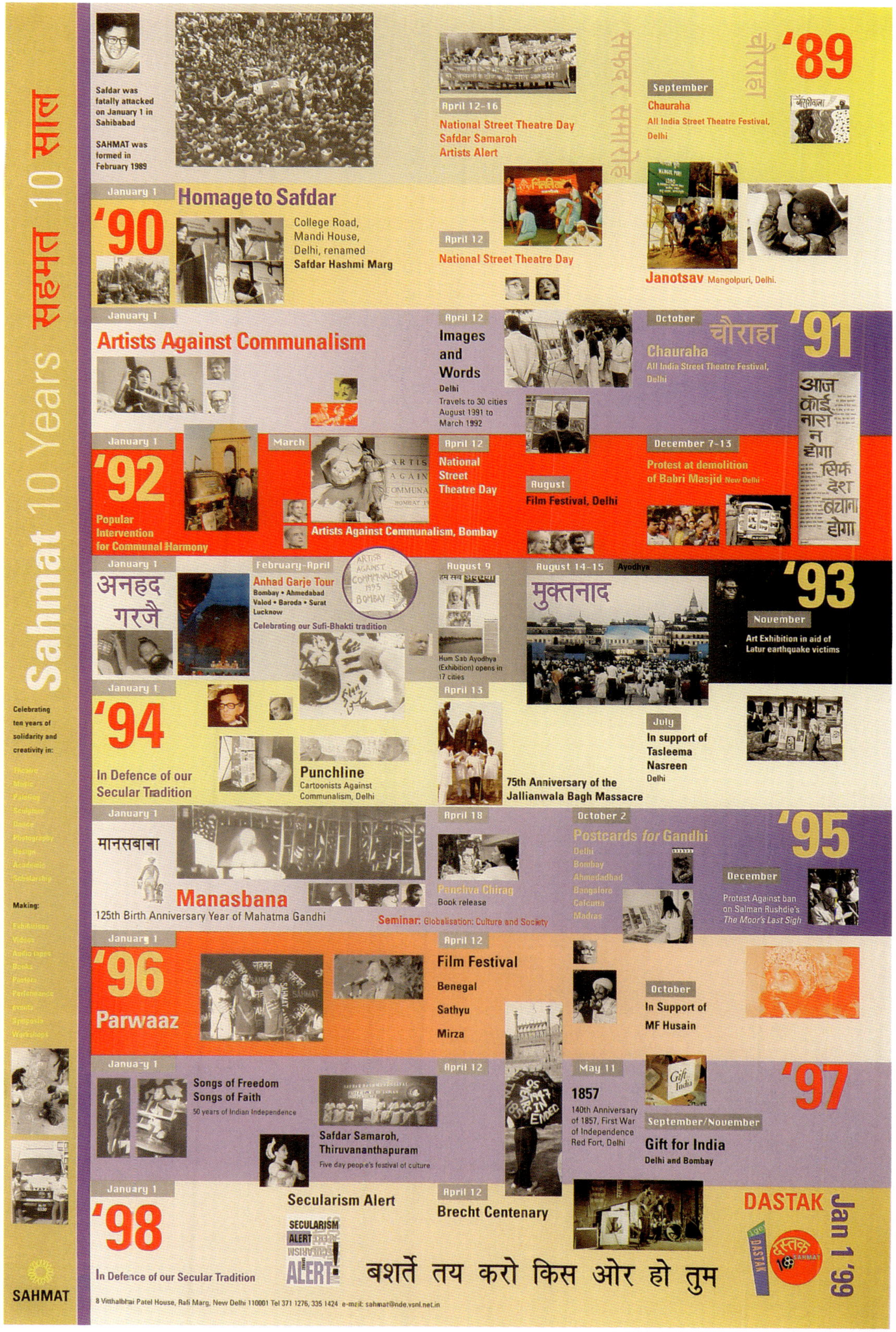

Poster for *Sahmat 10 Years*, 1999,
27 x 17 inches. Design: Ram Rahman.

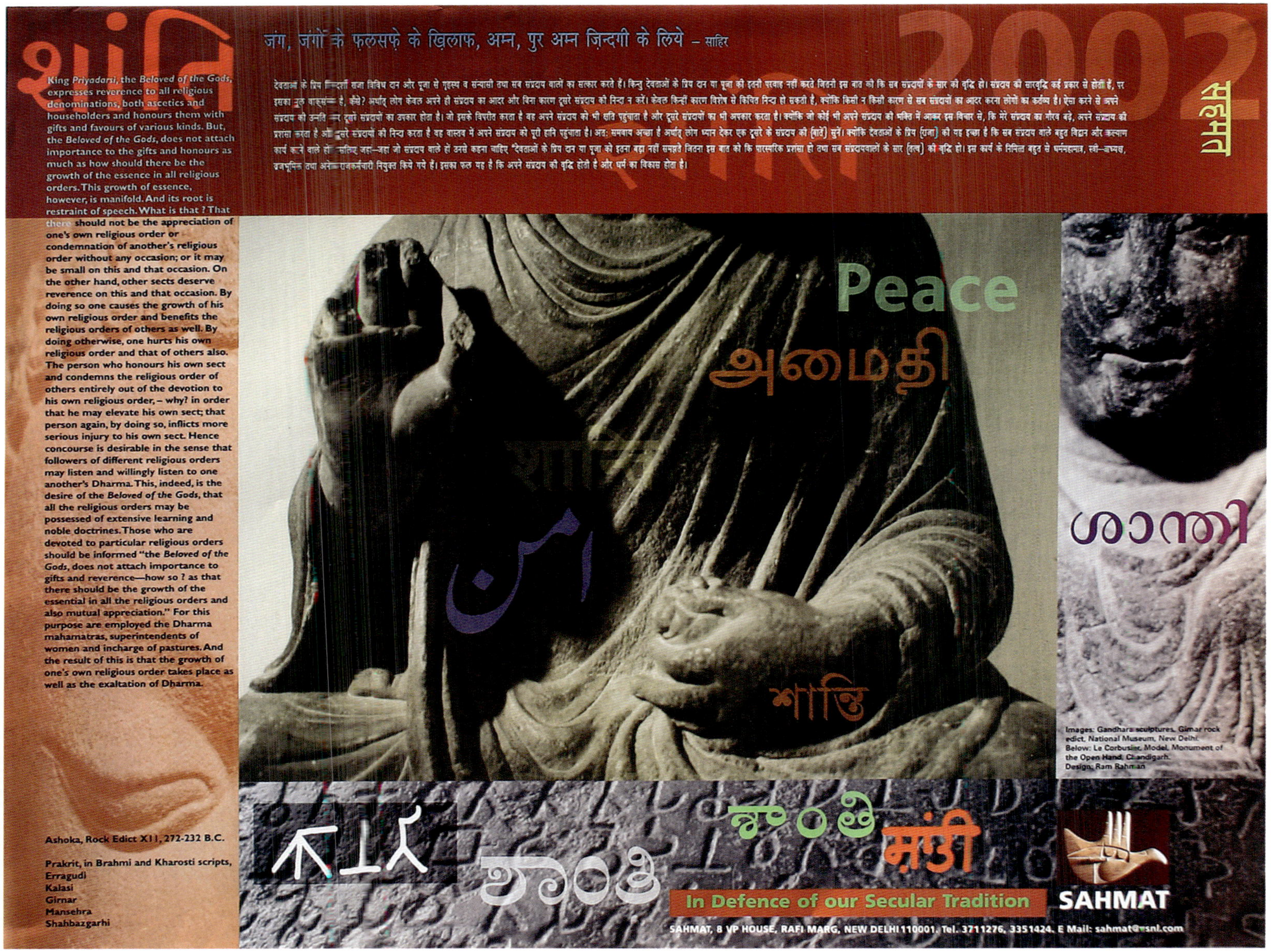

Peace, 2002, poster, 17½ x 22½ inches. Design: Ram Rahman.

This poster was a response to the destruction by the Taliban of the Bamiyan Buddha statues in Afghanistan in 2001. It uses texts from the rock edicts of the Mauryn Emperor Ashoka (ca. 272–232 BC), some of which are in Afghanistan. The edicts call for a just rule for all people to live in peace, regardless of individual religious beliefs.

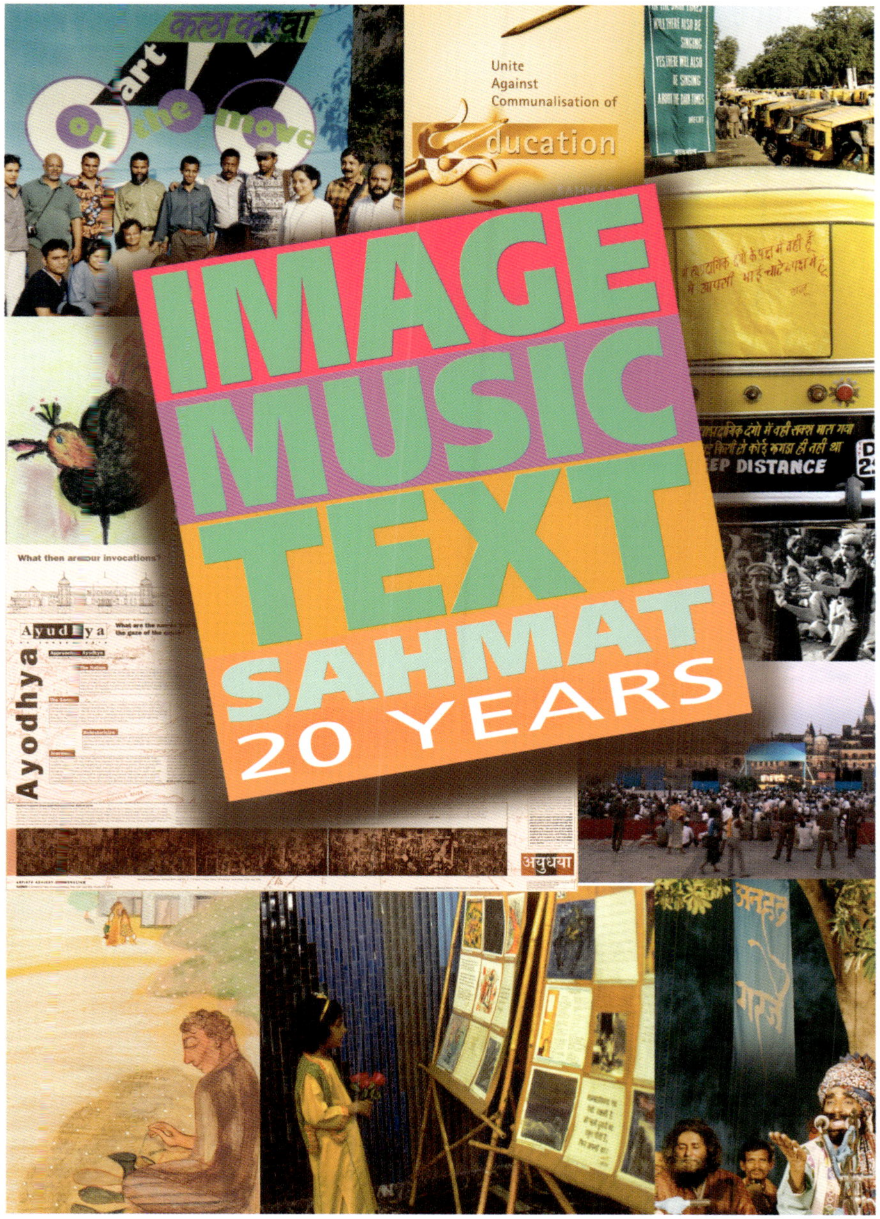

Poster for *Image, Music, Text: Sahmat 20 Years*, 2009, 17 x 14 inches. Design: Ram Rahman.

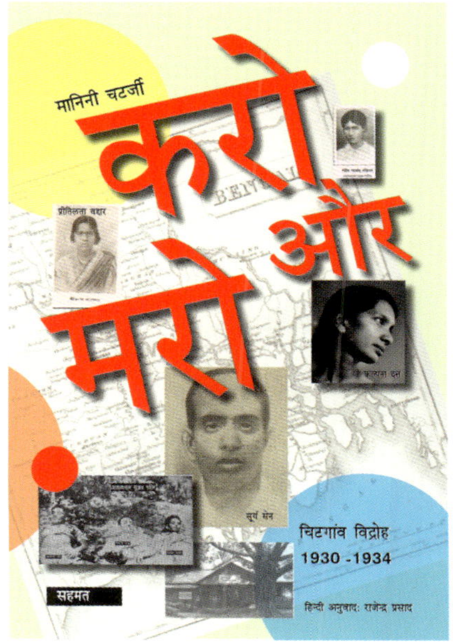

Book cover for *Karo aur Maro* (the Hindi translation of *Do and Die*) by Manini Chatterjee, on the Chittagong uprising against the British 1930–1934, 2010. Design: Ram Rahman.

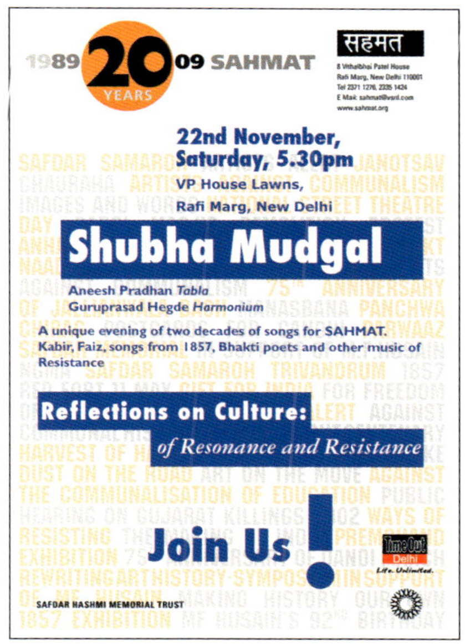

Poster for concert by Shubha Mudgal, 2009, 11½ x 8½ inches. Design: Ram Rahman.

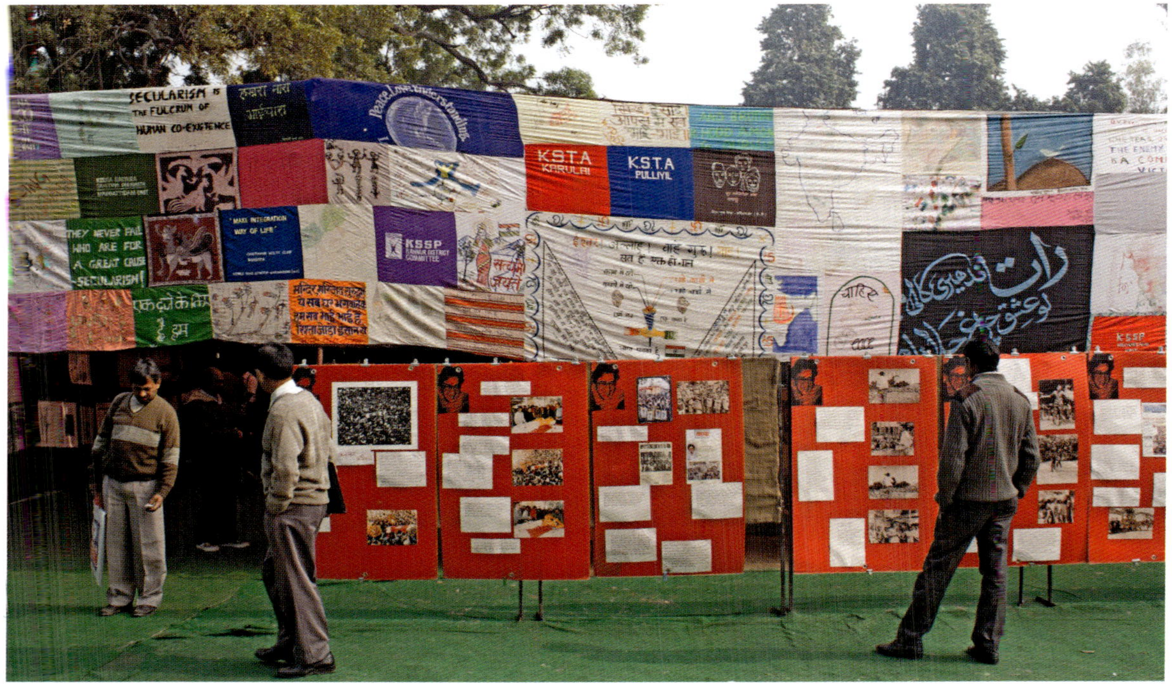

Exterior of tent, *Safdar Hashmi Memorial*, January 1, 2009.

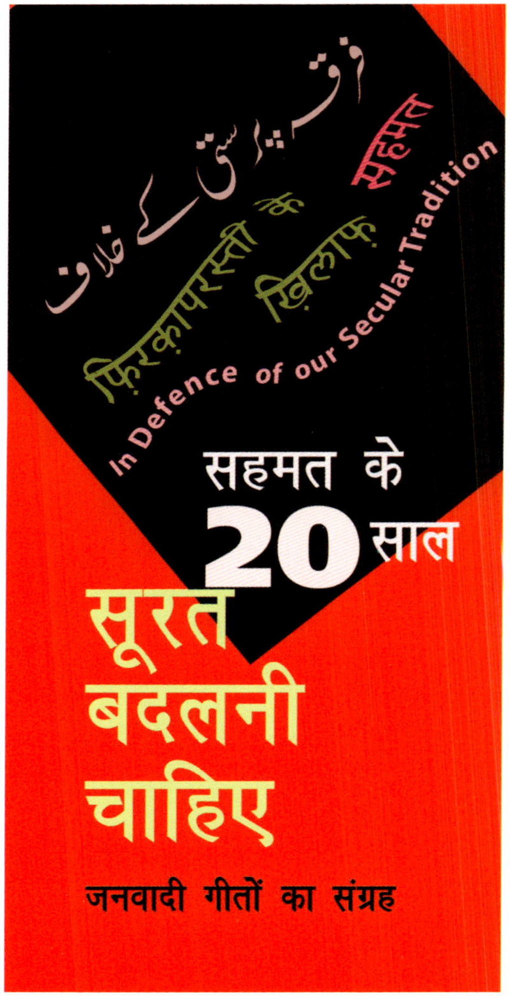

Book cover for *Soorat Badalni Chahiye*, 2009, a collection of popular protest songs. Design: Ram Rahman.

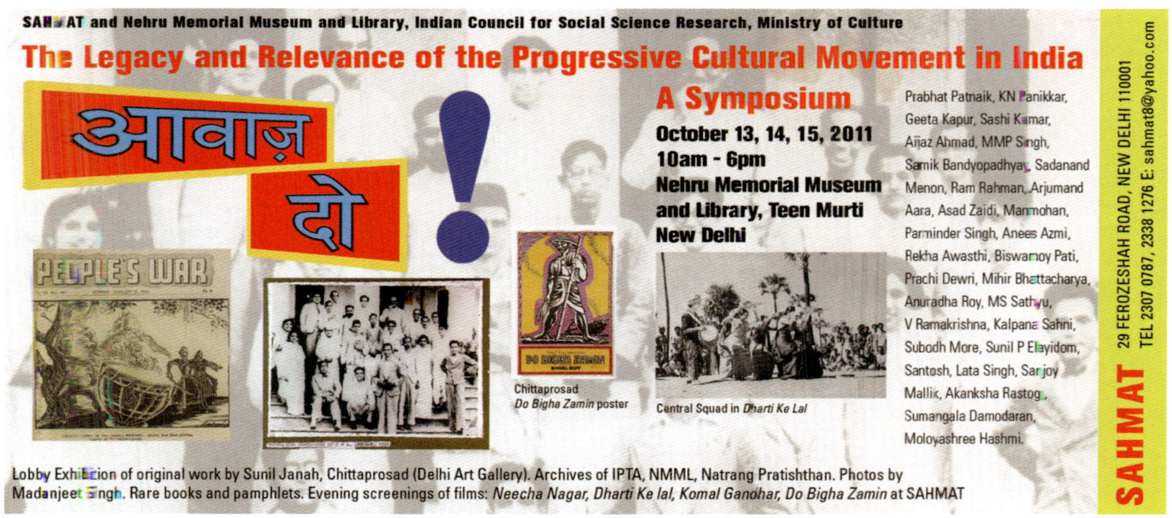

Invitation card for *Avaaz Do!*, October 13–15, 2011.

Avaaz Do! **(Raise Your Voice!) was a three-day symposium organized by Sahmat on the legacy of the progressive movement of the 1940s and its lasting impact on literature, cinema, theatre, and the visual arts in India today.**

Interior of performance tent, *Safdar Hashmi Memorial, The Making of India*, January 1, 2004.

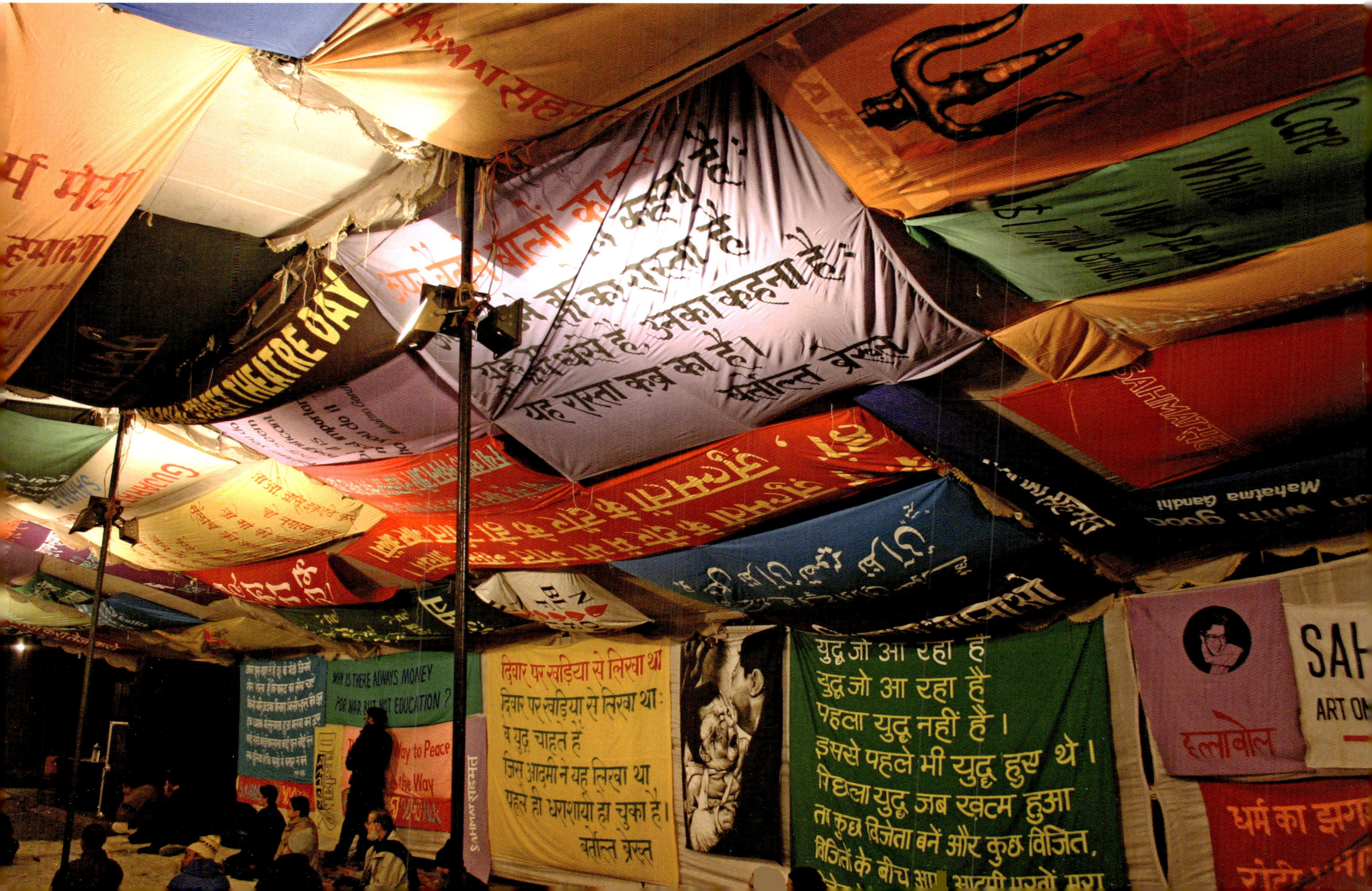

Essays

Prabhat Patnaik

An Experiment with Political Theory

I

Sahmat is a complex, elusive, and changing entity. The political role it plays while intervening in the realm of culture, to me, is the most fascinating aspect of Sahmat, so that is what I propose to write about here. Sahmat exhibits different forms at different times. If I were writing this article about Sahmat not this morning but tomorrow morning, then I would perhaps be writing a different article altogether. But it is this morning, so here I go.

To say that Sahmat has been in the forefront of the struggle against communalism is to state the obvious. But that fight, though the cause of its luster, does not constitute its specificity. There are other civil society organizations in India that are also bringing together artists and intellectuals to fight communalism and authoritarianism, and they have been as active and energetic. Sahmat's location in the heart of the nation's capital makes greater demands upon it and also brings it greater attention. But the reason it is sui generis lies elsewhere. Even while carrying out the struggles for which it is justly renowned, Sahmat remains a part of the Left and linked to the Communist Party of India (Marxist)—CPI(M)—but in a unique way that constitutes its specificity.

Sahmat is not like the usual civil society organizations because its leading personnel are unashamedly political; they belong to the Left and many of them to the CPI(M). At the same time, it also differs from civil society organizations set up by activists of the CPI(M) itself. There are many leading functionaries of the party, in West Bengal, for instance, who have set up organizations of their own with the avowed objective of rendering social service, but such organizations, despite being set up by political activists, are not themselves political. Sahmat, by contrast, is political.

At the same time, even while many of its leading personnel belong to the CPI(M), Sahmat is not a front organization of the party, and it has consciously and consistently avoided any party control or direction. It functions autonomously of the party and has always done so. And it eschews any attempt on its own part to project or promote the party. Everybody knows the loyalty of several activists of Sahmat to the party, yet nobody even for a moment would suspect them of carrying out some hidden party agenda, whether dictated to them by the party itself or arrived at on their own. So Sahmat remains an organization that enjoys the trust of people who are distant from the party (though they may differ from it *intellectually*), but its leading activists are themselves not distant from the party. *The dialectics of this relationship between Sahmat and the party constitutes its specificity*. This dialectics was never consciously worked out; it simply evolved over time, and constitutes an experiment in political theory—an experiment that nobody designed, nobody even consciously wanted, and whose setting up was a process fraught with irritation, even occasional animosity, on both sides.

What is so special about this relationship? There are broadly three different groups of intellectuals that Communist parties traditionally have had a relationship with (and here I am not talking about intellectuals who are hostile to them ab ovo): (1) those inside the party who are accepted and trusted, but run the risk over time of losing their independence of thought and simply mouthing the party's position even when they know it to be at variance with reality; (2) those who are celebrities among intellectuals and who occasionally take positions sympathetic to the party without actually belonging to it (and who for that reason tend to get lionized by the party); and (3) those who come to differ from the party on particular issues over time, despite not being hostile to it to start with, who tend to get castigated by it. A situation where intellectuals who differ from the party nonetheless have a relationship with it, without being castigated for those differences and without, therefore, moving further and further away from the party, has been rare. (The old Communist Party of Great Britain may be cited as a counterexample, since many of its leading intellectuals left in 1956 over Hungary but did not develop any antagonistic relationship with the party, but it must be remembered that the party was small while the intellectuals, like Christopher Hill, were outstanding. The British case therefore does not exactly fall into our third category.)

The case of Jean Paul Sartre may also be cited as a counterexample, but Sartre too has to be classified in the second group and not the third; his abiding, but complex and critical relationship with the French Communist Party does not negate the proposition that intellectuals who drift away from the party tend to drift further and further away from it. They are castigated by intellectuals belonging to the party and by its front organizations. This leads to their becoming isolated and dispirited, and hence they move further away from the party until they eventually lapse either into political inactivity or absorption into the "establishment." *An organization like Sahmat plays the role of arresting that drift.*

If you have opposed the West Bengal Left Front government's action in Nandigram and had tiffs with the party on that score, then you would be uncomfortable participating in a demonstration organized by one of the front organizations of the party against, say, an attack on an M. F. Husain exhibition—but you will have no such discomfort participating in a Sahmat demonstration on the same issue. Sahmat provides a location where artists and intellectuals who are not anti-Left but who may not be enthused by the party, as well as those who for some reason have parted company with the party, can join others who are closer to the party in the praxis of resistance.

One can go even further. An organization like Sahmat serves even to keep alive the praxis of resistance for artists and intellectuals within the penumbra of the Left. The party, for a variety of reasons, is not always quick off the mark in raising protests, getting signature campaigns going on particular issues, or issuing statements. It has an inevitable inertia. The party's cultural front organizations move slowly too, since, being front organizations, they have to be sensitive to the party's positions on all these issues, which take time to discuss and formulate. Such delays tend to be galling to artists and intellectuals angered by particular turns of events. An organization like Sahmat, which does not have to check the party position on issues before resorting to protest, has a galvanizing effect in this context. It keeps resistance alive. It can act like a band of guerrilla fighters that moves ahead and launches attacks even as the big, massed armies at the back are in the process of organizing.

II

There are at least two occasions that readily come to my mind when Sahmat has played the role of a band of intellectual guerrilla fighters. The first of course was in the immediate aftermath of the demolition of the Babri Masjid in Ayodhya. The demolition was completed by the late afternoon of December 6, 1992. Everyone watched incredulous and dumbstruck at that most brazen and premeditated attack on the rule of law in our country, on the Constitution, and on the foundations of our nationhood. Most were dismayed; many were angry. The anger among artists and intellectuals was palpable, and the desire to express it carried them spontaneously in large numbers to the Sahmat office that evening, as well as the next morning. On the morning of December 7, a small delegation went to meet Shankar Dayal Sharma, President of India, who appeared equally shell-shocked and anguished that everything his generation had fought for during the freedom struggle was being reduced to ruin.

And from those spontaneous gatherings began Sahmat's epic ideological-cultural campaign against communalism all over the country, which included events like *Anhad Garje* and *Hum Sab Ayodhya*. At that time one could hardly think of a single artist or intellectual of note and mettle who did not participate in one or the other activity organized by Sahmat, from Pandit Jasraj to Guru Kelucharan Mahapatra to Pandits Rajan and Sajan Mishra, not to mention the long-standing friends and "family" of Sahmat (whose names I need not selectively list). What was particularly gratifying at the time was the singular absence of any artistic or intellectual luminosity among the votaries of "Hindutva," which remains the case to this day, despite their ascent to power in the interim.

The political formations of the Left moved more slowly and, typically, more politically. They moved ultimately to great effect, however. A good deal of the credit for the decisive defeat of the Hindutva-led coalition in the 2004 election, from which it has still not recovered (though the "neoliberalism" of the current UPA-II government may yet resurrect it), goes to the Left, which strategized this defeat with great meticulousness. But for me and scores of others like me, our fury on December 6 would have remained impotent and bred only cynicism if Sahmat had not been there.

The second, more unobtrusive but no less significant intervention of Sahmat, an instance when it acted in advance of any political formation, was its resolute defense of secular education. When the Hindutva-led NDA government scrapped the use of school textbooks written by some of the most eminent historians of the country, when it stalled the "Towards Freedom" research and publication project, and when it sought to insinuate its own ideological outlook into school curricula, Sahmat carried out an indefatigable campaign against it. Again, one can hardly think of a single prominent intellectual in the country who did not enlist, one way or another, in that campaign.

The project of the Hindutva forces to insinuate their odious ideology into school curricula ended with their electoral defeat in 2004, but Sahmat's campaign for a democratic education system continues, since the successor government, under thrall to neoliberalism, has been hell-bent on making education a commodity, removing all creativity and independence of thought from it, and setting up a system where students will be proficient only at parroting whatever is sanctified as "knowledge" by the educational "establishments" in the centers of imperialism. In this sphere, as elsewhere, Sahmat's activities have been informed by an acute awareness of the dialectics between neoliberalism and communal fascism. And its activities have been of immense help in drawing the attention of political forces, especially of the Left, to these issues.

Sahmat thus contributes in various ways to the strengthening and consolidation of the Left even while combating communal–fascist and authoritarian tendencies in society at large, and in the world of art, letters, culture, and education in particular. It provides opportunities for activism to artists and intellectuals, including those close to the party and even those belonging to its front organizations; it prevents their impatience from remaining barren or being stifled in unproductive forms of protest—and in doing so it not only avoids damage to the Left, but indeed strengthens the Left in the broad sense.

The innovation of such an organization with its dialectical relationship with the CPI(M) and the Left is of great significance. The point is often made that protest in the contemporary period is spearheaded not by traditional Communist parties or even by their front organizations, but by civil society organizations that have nothing to do with the Left. Sahmat represents an overcoming of this dichotomy. It is a civil society organization spearheading protests that has *something* to do with the party and the Left.

Of course no such organization, including Sahmat, can ever take the place of the party: they are not, by their very nature, designed to be system-transcending organizations. But an entity like Sahmat keeps alive the tradition of continuous Left intervention, in a situation where the larger Left itself is structurally handicapped to do so.

III

The creation of Sahmat in its dialectical relationship with the party attests to the vigor of the Indian Left. The credit for the innovation that characterizes Sahmat must of course go to its founder-members. But the innovation would have been impossible had the party stuck to its old ways and insisted that party members working in other organizations be subject to party direction. The fact that it did not do so reflects innovativeness on its part. Sahmat, in short, demonstrates a degree of innovativeness all around, the scope for which was created in the post-Soviet world when all the rigidities stemming from earlier certainties of the Communist position disappeared; but the fact that this scope was realized is significant and testifies to the robust nature of the Indian Left.

There were other factors that were conducive to this process of innovation. One was Sahmat's location in Delhi. If it had been based in one of the strong Left states (West Bengal, Kerala, or Tripura), then it would have either been swamped by the party or developed an antagonistic relationship with it. Sahmat would not have enjoyed the position it has today: autonomous, yet dialectically linked to the party. If Sahmat had been located in one of the weak states of the Left, then it might have dominated the party to the detriment of both. Sahmat's activism would have become a substitute for party activism, distorting the development of each. Its location in Delhi has prevented both these potential outcomes.

The second conducive factor is more basic and points to a fundamental characteristic of Sahmat, namely, that it is not given to any frenetic activism. Days go by when its activism remains quiet and unobtrusive. This relative calm can be off-putting for newcomers who come to its office hoping to see a place abuzz with activity, but find instead a couple of Sahmat regulars, together with stray visitors, quietly sipping tea and exchanging gossip on various issues of the day. They miss a critical point about Sahmat, which is that its rationale lies in its very being, not in the pace of its activity. It is not a project set up to do things; it is a project set up above all to be—a group of people committed to certain ideas who simply meet. When they feel the need for doing something, they do, but there is no compulsion about this feeling. Sahmat's implicit, underlying philosophy: *to be* is itself *action*.

In this sense Sahmat is like an ashram. In Richard Attenborough's film *Gandhi* there is a scene where national leaders descend on Gandhi's ashram, and Gandhi insists on continuing with his mundane activity of feeding the goats, despite the presence of these luminaries and the supposedly momentous issues that have brought them there. The ashram is not just a venue where people gather to manifest their urge for activism. It is, on the contrary, a way of life, and immanent in that way of life is an activism that is more quiet and less frenetic, yet more robust and implacable.

The Gandhian ashram was physically removed from the centers of power and political activity. Sahmat, though not physically removed, is nonetheless epistemologically removed from such centers, engaged in a discourse of its own in surroundings that speak of Kabir, Munshi Premchand, and M. F. Husain. Books on the Indian People's Theatre Association (IPTA), on the Progressive Writers' Association (PWA), on India's freedom struggle, breathe down on you, as if instead of the historical time in which we are all placed, Sahmat's time descends directly from the Sufi-Bhakti movement, via the freedom struggle, to that tiny room where assorted individuals partake of *masala dosa* at lunch time.

This sense of relative calm is in sharp contrast to almost all other organizations of protest. Reminiscent of Regis Debray's statement that the "revolution revolutionizes the counter-revolution," that is, that any movement leaves its stamp even on its opponents, we find these days that the frenetic pace of the neoliberal world, though devoted to self-promotion and self-aggrandizement, also infects those who are opposed to such self-promotion and self-aggrandizement. Sahmat however exists in a category apart. Its struggle against the neoliberal world, and its communal-fascist fallout, takes the form not of its jumping into the fray but of stepping back from that world.

This is not to suggest that Sahmat is some sort of a back-alley club for the elderly and the retired. Everybody knows this is not so; everybody knows its glorious record of struggle. In fact an outlook that sees *being* as action contributes to far more resolute action than one that sees action in purely instrumental terms. The clearest example, and also the most exhilarating moment in my long association with Sahmat, was the nightlong festival of music and dance organized by Sahmat on the banks of the Sarayu River in Ayodhya on the night of August 14, 1993, within a stone's throw of the demolished Babri Masjid. The local member of Parliament, a prominent Hindutva activist, had vowed that Sahmat would not be able to get away with the event, and prudent tactics on Sahmat's part would have dictated that it cancel the event rather than risk a confrontation between a mob of fanatics and some of the finest artists and intellectuals of the country. But the being-as-action outlook produces a kind of intransigence—some may even call it "mulishness"—that turns its back upon such tactical niceties. Almost

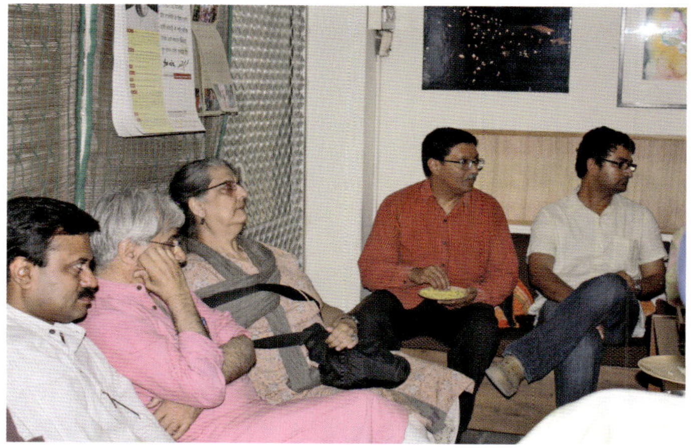

Thursday meeting at Sahmat. (From left) Parthiv Shah, Vivan Sundaram, Geeta Kapur, Ram Rahman, and Shankar Chandra, 2008.

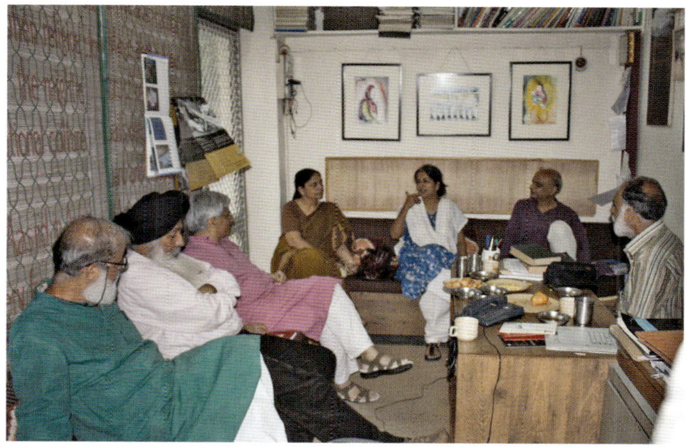

Thursday meeting at Sahmat. (From left) Sohail Hashmi, Madan Gopal Singh, Vivan Sundaram, Ashok Kumari, Indira Chandrasekhar, Rajendra Prasad, and M. K. Raina, 2009.

everybody gathered on that memorable evening was infected by this mulishness—*this is my country and I am free to go anywhere I like; no gang of toughs can take away my right to do so.* It was a sheer existential issue, nothing to do with strategy or tactics: if we give in on this, then there is no end to our giving in.

As the program was about to begin the tension in the air was palpable. My son had also gone to the event. He was seventeen, an age at which one guilelessly expresses one's opinion to all and sundry, and engages in arguments without circumspection. As he drifted off into the darkness arguing against the demolition with a group of strangers, my personal tension could be cut with a knife. And yet as the evening progressed, the charm of the setting, the beauty of the music, and the camaraderie gradually took over, and as the sun rose and Jawaharlal Nehru's midnight speech was played on the air, almost everyone present had an indescribable sense of elation, a sense of triumph at the sheer assertion of *being*.

Neither a negation nor a downgrading of action, being-as-action is action more resolute, struggle not for the sake of struggle but struggle as expression of one's being. It is not just that Sahmat carries out struggles, but also that the ambience associated with its struggles is different. This ambience is intrinsic to Sahmat. I have seen people that the world calls celebrities—from Politburo members of the party to ex-foreign secretaries of the country to famous film stars—come into the Sahmat office, and once there, they too sit around sipping tea, browsing through Irfan Habib's books, and imbibing the aura of Kabir, Premchand, and Husain. In Sahmat's reckoning, being part of this aura is action too.

The Saturday lunches at Sahmat express this outlook. Sahmat of course is not unique in this respect. Paul Sweezy and Harry Magdoff's *Monthly Review* used to have the culture of Wednesday lunches. Lots of people belonging to the Left and passing through New York would make it a point to drop in at the *Monthly Review* office to meet one another, and be sure of meeting Sweezy and Magdoff. At Sahmat of course one can be sure of meeting its leading personnel any day at lunch. Saturday provides the additional bonanza of meeting a wider assortment of individuals. The Saturday lunch meeting is not specifically designed to plan action, but discussions occur on a range of topics, from Karl Marx's *On the Jewish Question* to the latest shenanigans of some political ragamuffin. And out of such discussions, plans of action emerge. Sahmat thus transcends the duality of *being* and *acting*.

This very absence of frenetic activity has smoothed the way for the development of a dialectical relationship between the party and Sahmat. Sahmat is not high profile, and Sahmat personnel are not seeking office anywhere. Sahmat is a low-key organization that does a number of things that the party would not necessarily get around to doing otherwise. True, its famous January 1 get-together with its sumptuous feast of music and performances may recall the *l'Humanité* fete in the suburbs of Paris that the French Communist party's newspaper used to organize once a year. But in India there has been no such Communist event anyway. So Sahmat's doing so does not tread on anyone's toes. The bemused tolerance with which Sahmat's apparently old-world ambience is accepted, is undoubtedly a factor contributing to the development of the dialectics between Sahmat and the party.

There is an additional conducive factor here that I would list as the third one that supports the development of the party–Sahmat dialectics, which has to do with the internal organization of Sahmat. Its mode of activism is different, yes, but its internal organization is different as well. In tune with its specific mode of activism, Sahmat's organization does not replicate that of the party or the party's front organizations; there is no chain of command within it, no clear center, and hence no enforcement of any discipline. Work is not parceled out from the "top." Rather, different people take the initiative to organize different events. There is consultation within the collective about how one should go about doing something and about who does what, but no "leader" enforcing discipline. Discipline comes from within oneself, from a sense of responsibility to the collective to which one belongs, and from one's commitment to the specific event that one is engaged in organizing. There is therefore a flourishing "libertarianism," but within a collective; there is an entity that functions, but without an all-powerful center; there is an absence of enforcement of discipline, but without anarchy.

Artists, as creative individuals with a distrust of being "directed," find such an organizational arrangement congenial. At the same time, the fact that the Sahmat organization is a loose one with little interest in replicating the party or its front organizations contributes to a sort of modus vivendi with the party, which enables the dialectical relationship to develop.

To say all this is not to suggest that Sahmat represents the ideal organization for cultural activism, and I do not mean to imply that other organizations, like the party's own front organizations in the realm of culture, insofar as they are structurally different from Sahmat, are incapable of playing a significant role. That would be an absurd claim. Different organizations have different roles to play. Their diversity allows them to play these different roles, which is why there is room for diverse organizations. Sahmat, for instance, is an essentially metropolitan phenomenon. It has made no attempt to set up branches or chapters in the interior of the country; indeed, given its philosophy of being-as-action, it would never even think of doing so. The artists and intellectuals who gather around it are mostly metropolitan practitioners who have little contact with the hinterland of the country. Sahmat takes up larger causes, not causes related to the conditions of the artists themselves, except with regard to artistic freedom. If other organizations modeled themselves after Sahmat, then an entire field of artistic mobilization and artistic struggle will simply be liquidated, and this is quite apart from the fact that other organizations modeling themselves successfully after Sahmat would be a logical impossibility.

So is Sahmat then just a one-instance wonder, a unique, nonreplicable phenomenon? Certainly Sahmat itself is nonreplicable, but at this juncture we do need organizations like it, not just in the realm of cultural activism but in other spheres too—organizations that embody innovativeness within themselves and also have an innovative dialectical relationship with the Left and the Party. They cannot supplant other existing organizations in their respective fields, just as Sahmat cannot supplant other existing organizations of cultural activism. Sahmat cannot even be a model for other existing organizations of cultural activism. But among the different organizations there must be innovative ones like Sahmat as well, and not only one but many. The emphasis here must be on *innovations*, not on developing *clones*, which is impossible anyway.

IV

But why do we need more such organizations? Does the development of organizations with such a dialectical relationship with the party have a place in the larger scheme of things? I believe it does. Lenin visualized the Communist Party as constituting a self-correcting vanguard. For such self-correction to happen, however, the leadership requires inputs, especially of information. The inputs it obtains from the party channels, even assuming that these are not tainted by the desire to please the leadership (that is, by the desire to tell the leadership what the leadership would like to hear), are only one source. In the contemporary world the leadership needs to obtain (and does obtain) its information from a variety of sources, and the source it typically turns to is the bourgeois media. In fact, the more it feels that the information filtering through from party sources is infected by wishful thinking or by a desire to tell the leadership what it is assumed the leadership wants to hear, the greater its reliance on the bourgeois media. But that reliance can derail the process of self-correction, since the information from the bourgeois media comes enmeshed with bourgeois ideas, and it is not always easy to detach the two. An obvious example is the bourgeois media's adulation for so-called development, something at which Chief Minister Narendra Modi is supposed to have excelled!

One obvious way that such derailment can be prevented is if the party functions within a wider culture of resistance that is not reducible to the party itself and also encompasses several groups and organizations, but at the same time has an oppositional role vis-à-vis the ruling classes. The party of course must not become merely subservient to this culture of resistance; it must separate wheat from chaff in all the inputs it receives, including those from non-party elements belonging to this broader culture of resistance. But to the extent that non-party elements belonging to this broader culture of resistance are also engaged in the task of separating wheat from chaff, the party can benefit from their efforts.

For these benefits to come into play, however, this broader culture of resistance must exist to start with, and the party must function within it and learn from its inputs in the process of its self-correction. An organization like Sahmat has played a pioneering role in effecting the creation of a broader culture of resistance. Many more such organizations are needed, which, by not only having a dialectical relationship with the party and the Left generally, but also by creating the broader culture of resistance from which the party can benefit, can forestall in India the kind of fate that has overtaken Third International parties elsewhere in the world.

Since such a fate overtaking Communist parties works only to the advantage of international finance capital, anyone who believes in the project of human emancipation cannot but wish that Communist parties will manage to refashion themselves to cope with the present, rather than becoming marginalized in the new epoch. Anyone who believes in the project of human emancipation therefore cannot but wish for more instances of the kind of innovativeness, on all sides, that has produced Sahmat.

Prabhat Patnaik studied at Oxford University on a Rhodes Scholarship, obtaining his D. Phil. in economics. He has taught at Cambridge University, UK, and at Jawaharlal Nehru University (JNU), New Delhi. He retired from the Sukhamoy Chakravarty Chair at JNU in 2010 and is currently writing a book on capitalism as a UGC Emeritus Fellow at JNU. He has been associated with Sahmat from its inception.

Madan Gopal Singh

Song of the Unvanquished

Beginning(s) and Continuities of Sahmat: A Brief Personal History

Sahmat took off long before it did. Its beginnings are variously spread out.

I look back with nostalgic fondness and see four friends at their youthful zenith. I find myself in the midst of their pulsating interactions. There was Safdar Hashmi himself—the indefatigable theatre artist and political activist after whom Sahmat was named. There was Manjit Bawa—then emerging as a frontline painter who was more into cooking, storytelling, and singing than direct cultural interventions; M. K. Raina—a relentlessly questioning maverick, and by then already a highly fêted theatre person and film actor; and N. K. Sharma—a comrade in arms with Safdar who had the sharpness of an unusually charged thinker. Amid these four energetic minds, I happened to trespass as a nowhere man. I recall some very beautiful evenings when the four would meet over food ever so delectably conjured up by the magician chef Manjit. There was something about their coming together that reminded one of the congregations of *faqirs*. The bonds of camaraderie over shared food and song, interspersed with heated discussion, deepened as the evenings matured.

I am sure there were many such beginnings happening elsewhere in which artists would spontaneously converge in acts of coming together. All such acts seemed rooted in creative joy and abandon, although not infrequently triggered by happenings around us. But I have always felt, somewhat narcissistically, that there was something special in the beginning of which I was a small part.

Barring me, the other four were distinguished artists in their respective fields. I was quite simply an occasional crooner, a reluctant theatre person, and an obscure film theorist—a mere hanger-on. Over a period, I have somewhat immodestly convinced myself of the utility of this non-professional who merely "hangs on." Though peripheral, such hangers-on often act as a crucial alloy to the formation of *tolis* or loosely knit groups.

We would meet regularly. Mostly, these unplanned meetings were marked by friendly joy and mirth, but there were occasions when we met in deep anxiety over the rapidly evolving communal miasma that was beginning to engulf much of India in the 1980s. Punjab stood seriously ravaged by religious fundamentalism. There was eerie disquiet in Kashmir. The Ram *sevaks* of the Sangh Parivar were getting mobilized to unleash their bloody communal experiment on the highways and backstreets of India. This was the beginning of dark times and we had to devise ways of "singing of the dark times"—to resist, as it were.

Safdar's little office above the West Bengal crafts emporium in New Delhi was fast emerging as a cultural hub. With writers, filmmakers, musicians, theatre persons, cultural activists, students, there was always a sense of exciting flux about his office which, before we realized, began to look like a performance space. Safdar, by then, seemed obsessed with the idea of developing a blueprint for an endless celebration of the people's culture. This was his ideological response to the fetishized official festivals of India in which completely ahistorical ideas of the great civilizational continuity were projected across the world with patronizing hubris.

We also met quite regularly at artist Ranbir Kaleka's bedroom-cum-studio in Jangpura, where we immersed ourselves in slightly more relaxed discussions about what was going on in the fields of cinema, art, and music. Late into the night, Manjit and I would sing forgotten love-legends of Punjab, trying perhaps to exorcise the real demons we could sense all around us, ruthlessly "othering" large chunks of the Indian people in the name of cultural nationalism.

There was never any dearth of serious, irreverent discussions. We were living through critical times. The scourge of communalism and identity politics was moving menacingly closer to the center space. The wheels of the communal juggernaut were beginning to take over our public spaces—trains, buses, highways, and even *addas*. The virus of intolerance was eating into our resonant plurality and inclusive diversity. We seemed to be in a state of demise. The challenge thrown by the communal forces was far more structured and therefore far more lethal. It had emerged from its invidious lurk and was now beginning to overwhelm the public domain. Now our little meetings had an increasing sense of urgency. More than ever, we felt a need to forge links with the larger communities of artists, intellectuals, and cultural activists from across India and even, perhaps, South Asia. This was the time when we were opening up self-reflexively to other histories, traditions, and modes of radical cultural resistance. More than ever before, there was a need to critically reassess our creative strength.

And then, on the first day of 1989, we heard of the fatal attack on Safdar while he was in the midst of a street theatre performance on the outskirts of Delhi.

Solidarity and the Search for Invocations

There was an unprecedented convergence of people and practitioners cutting across beliefs and disciplines at Safdar's funeral procession. This was a loose and spontaneous unity of people, but it was quite clearly held together by a firm resolve to resist all those who sought to stifle creative freedom, to defy all those who were out to obstruct them from being part of a joyous carnival of compassion and inclusion. We were reminded of Safdar's favorite sequence from Sergei Eisenstein's film *Battleship Potemkin* where innocent people are shot on the Odessa steps followed by the counter-roar of the lion rising from slumber. It was important to convert the profundity of emotion stirred by Safdar's assassination into effective and meaningful resistance through cultural self-renewals. It was important to be in a state of artistic preparedness. Such indeed was the intensity of the challenge.

Sahmat took off almost immediately after Safdar's assassination. Its formation was an act of solidarity that had to move beyond the first spurt of spontaneous emotions, albeit with all their intensity. It was a coming together of people, intellectuals and artists, from a broad spectrum of life. There were certain shared beliefs but never ever any mandated agenda of art practice. This posed a primary question: what then are our invocations?

The Word and Its Voices

Given the alarming rise of communalism, the question had gained an utmost edge. It was a question that had been uppermost in the minds of quite a few of us. In search of an answer, we had to engage our present in a critical dialogue with past negotiations and thereby intuit possibilities of our own future creative practices. For some of us, at least, the modern had to speak with the lure of contra-modernities that formed a complex and playful maze within the grid of our cultural resonance. The word and its textual and oral lures seemed irresistibly vital leads to follow. We had to pry open the magic casements of language at the very outset.

The word was simultaneously free and rigorous, precise and excessive, abstemious and seductive. And it was, for a whole lot of us, a great way to resist. The word in its style, speech, song, and visuality appeared as a political universe all by itself and a powerful cry of the unvanquished. Such an invocation appeared to us an act of poignant reclamation. In our ceaseless search for the secular self, we would reach out to narratives, discourses, and histories that had been subjected to relentless attacks by the openly mocking ideologues of strident communal identities. The word was a weapon and the song a stake.

I do not know if we realized the implication of such an engagement in its fullness, but a new music was almost instantaneously beginning to appear on the anvil.

We opened with a remarkable campaign. "Artists Against Communalism" was the name we gave it. It saw an overwhelming consolidation of artists. In an ennobling gesture, they came together to paint, perform, sing, shoot . . . to occasionally speak and to seminar. They came together to express solidarity, to say that they would resist and not let this menace pass unchallenged. I remember moving like an excited child into our first illustrated tent installed as a performative space. Black and rusted brown, it had rich calligraphy in shining silver gray. There were enormous signs of hope in this womblike darkness. It had the feel of a studio where images surface through watery trays. The "walls" on both sides had calligraphic verses from the eighth-century Sufi poet Rabia al-Basri to the twentieth-century radical poet Faiz Ahmad Faiz. The podium had a huge banyan tree rising from the middle and going right through the roof.

Kabir and Artists Against Communalism

And then, in the midst of it all, Shubha Mudgal's magical voice rose with fearless intensity:

Is ghat andar baag bageeche
Isi mein sirjan haara
(Within this earthen vessel are bowers and groves
And within it is the Creator)

These fifteenth-century verses by the Bhakti poet Kabir became Sahmat's clarion call. The commoners and the cognoscenti, the masses and the maestros, were struck by the sheer power of Shubha's melodic assertion. Something was astir.

Kabir was among our primary invocations.

Born a Hindu and brought up as a Muslim, Kabir was a seminal figure in our cultural history. Within the popular accounts of his life, the "high" and the "low" converged in a critical dialogue. The ambiguity about his caste and religion was as if an aperture were opening with an eegy urgency on a social landscape that was riven with divisions, exclusions, superstitions, and various grades of isolation. This new attention to Kabir was the much-needed ballast for our thinking and practice. In one giant step, we could see an entire space of poetic self-belief opening up. It brought together the metaphysics of a homespun philosopher and the material engagement, through song, of an artisan with his heirloom, within the same creative flourish. His birth shrouded in mystery, he was like a child of destiny found abandoned beside the river of life awaiting a mother. There was the image of a home denied and that of the home recovered, both rooted in the idea of a profoundly secular and often irreverent journey. Through his songs, Kabir defiantly put humankind at the playful center of his cosmos, nudging God equally playfully to the periphery. His was a poetic proclamation of a new, inclusive legitimacy. This was the peak of *our* renaissance—a fearless act of reconfiguring humankind. There could not have been a better invocation than this, and there could not have been a more intense exponent than Shubha to carry it across.

Artists Against Communalism drew musicians from all over India to participate in the campaign. There were those who came and performed, those who came and addressed, and yet those who sent warm and touching messages of support. There was hardly an artist who did not take a profoundly involved view of our effort. The entire gamut of India's musical diversity—the classical, the urban and rural folk, and the tribal—emerged as a possible signpost through this campaign.

Kabir was, in a sense, the defile or aperture. Through him we could passionately reconstruct unwritten, unsung history/ies of our own cultural renaissance, for he was the one who fearlessly taught us what it was to resist. He cut across various strands and schools of beliefs and refused in the end to be identified with any one of them. He seemed to freely traverse in the past and to influence a whole lot of poets after him. We had the great Bhakti poets on one side and the Sufis on the other. Kabir was the threshold from where one could approach both.

The Holy *Granth*

We continued to invoke ancient and medieval texts of social and cultural connectivity through our songs. Books such as the sixteenth-century *Guru Granth* of the Sikhs now appeared quite concretely as a topography of compassion reaching across apparently unrelated communities. We could clearly visualize through this huge poetic volume how the "other" within spoke with the "other" without. In one musical tradition we had the entire South Asia put into a mode of spiritual, melodic dialogue. The Hindus were in communion with the Muslims, the Sufis with the Bhakti poets, the lower castes with the upper castes, classicism with folk, the artisans with the so-called artists.

The Sufis

Our search for invocations brought us almost instantly to the rich, transgressive, and defiant universe of the Indian Sufis. In the aftermath of the demonic demolition of the Babri Masjid in 1992, we had decided to hit the road in a reverse journey to symbolically reaffirm our solidarity with the wounded, and to proclaim that the syncretic ethos of inclusion, diversity, and plurality were more than ever alive and singing. Homeless, we moved from city to city and door to door—with the Warsi Brothers, *qawwals* from Hyderabad, singing the Urdu verses of poets Wali Dakhani and Hazrat Amir Khusrau from the thirteenth- to eighteenth-century poetic heritage of India. We also had with us the legendary Manganiar singer Bunger Khan from the sand dunes of Rajasthan who sang incredibly in five languages with equal ease and conviction. It was obviously impossible to draw a line in the sand. His voice wove mesmerizing soundscapes in the Rajasthani, Hindustani, Sindhi, Seraiki, and Punjabi dialects and languages. We were suddenly face to face with an individual's wonderment at being simultaneously part of a huge cosmic design and a wonderstruck beholder. We were also accompanied by Keshav Badge and his wife. The case of Badge was unique. He had begun as a percussionist with the legendary vocalist Pandit Bhimsen Joshi—among the best-known classical singers of our time. Somewhere along the line, he decided to become a simple bard of verses from the Bhakti poets of Maharashtra. He sang even as he played the tabla and freely interpolated the medieval texts with his own experience of the lived in a contemporary idiom.

We went around singing "what do I know of who I am" of the seventeenth–eighteenth-century Sufi poet of the intoxicated spirit, a maverick and a rebel, Baba Bulle Shah. The legendary Allan Faqir came from across the border to sing Shah Abul Bhitai's Sindhi Sufi verses. We had Eltaf Hussain of Afghanistan and Jaffar Hussain of Badaun singing Rumi, Hafiz, Chiragh Dehlavi, and Amir Khusrau. We had Vaishnav Bauls from the Bolpur region of Bengal singing nineteenth-century verses of Lalan Fakir and Hasan Raja. We heard poems where Muslim dervishes sang the Hindu *rang* or the festival of a riot of colors, and of love legends where the Hindu God Krishna and his companion Radha appeared as Heer and Ranjha. There was one particular performance in which close to thirty performers from across South Asia spontaneously joined Allan Faqir on stage. It was as unique an event as one ever experiences, and it has never left my memory. There is no previous history of such celebrative and radical eclecticism.

One recalls how, after the demolition of the Babri Masjid, an incredibly large cross-section of cultural activists and musicians alighted on the banks of the River Sarayu one evening to keep a night-long musical vigil to express solidarity with the people who had been hurt by that act of unprecedented vandalism, presided over and encouraged by the main opposition party at that time. One recalls with a sense of deep poignancy when, in the aftermath of the anti-minority pogrom in Gujarat in 2002, the same musicians went hoarse musically registering their protest. The invocations of medieval texts led to a further celebration of their poetic embedding in contemporary works of literature, poetry, music, and fine arts. The idea of radical cultural resistance is an unending work in progress that has been definitively underlined by the singing of the poetry of some of the recent poets of the subcontinent—among them Rabindranath Tagore, Kazi Nazrul Islam, Faiz Ahmad Faiz, Majaz, Baba Nagarjun . . .

The songs of *Artists Against Communalism* have continued to travel ever since—in vigilance, often without sleep but always dreaming. They have been heard, followed, and sung all over India and South Asia, as also across continents. They have led to the formation of small, independent groups in small towns and campuses. They have inspired important cultural productions in other fields. Ironical though it might seem, even the mainstream music industry had to sit back and take note of these cultural recoveries. It will not be vain to assert that the emergent popularity of the Sufi music in particular has not a little to do with some of our invocations. However, the world of music consumption and the space of cultural resistance are far too distinct to be conflated like this. Our songs have invariably remained more than just soft, soothing music. Our balladeers continue to sing these songs of the unvanquished and their undying resistance.

Madan Gopal Singh is a leading Sufi scholar, singer, lyricist, and composer in India. He is best known for his renditions of Punjabi Sufi texts and love legends and has translated a wide range of Sufi lyrics into Punjabi, Hindustani, and English. Madan Gopal Singh has also written screenplays, and composed and performed music for several films. He has written extensively on cinema, and has been a member of the editorial board of *Journal of Arts & Ideas* (founded in 1982).

William Mazzarella

Mind the Gap! Or, What Does Secularism Feel Like?

Even in Your Sleep

It is easy to feel exhausted by the endless debates about the exhaustion of Indian secularism. Time and again, we hear the same questions: What is secularism? How can one be secular? Is secularism foreign to India?

Given that the collective of artists, scholars, and activists known as Sahmat has largely defined itself by its commitment to secularism, we might be forgiven for thinking that our exhaustion in the face of these questions may be symptomatic of the exhaustion of Sahmat's project. Are we now taking stock, in an elegiac mode, of a movement whose time has passed? Many would argue that the very word *secularism* has become all but meaningless in the Indian context, a floating signifier opportunistically harnessed to every passing political project. And yet it lingers. As the late great Indian playwright Vijay Tendulkar put it in a 2004 conversation, "*Who* is secular? It's the word you hear—every minute. You cannot forget that word even in your sleep. The word doesn't mean anything. It has been dead years back."[1] If this word haunts dreams, then perhaps it still contains unresolved questions. Sahmat's distinctively aesthetic form of activism implies one such question, a question that is inseparable from its work and yet largely ignored: What does secularism *feel* like?

In posing the question this way, I follow Terry Eagleton and Susan Buck-Morss in retrieving the ancient meaning of aesthetics as that which pertains to sense experience.[2] For me, the question of the aesthetics of secularism is therefore not in the first instance a question about a secular politics of representation (excellently discussed elsewhere by Karin Zitzewitz[3]) but rather a question about the public life of the senses in modernity. Or to put it a bit differently: a question of public—and therefore political—affect.[4] So what *does* secularism feel like?

With all the fuss in recent decades around supposedly obscene pictures in Indian painting and film, it might seem as if secularism feels most of all like hurt feelings.[5] Starting in the mid-1990s, Sahmat staunchly helped to defend India's best-known modernist painter, M. F. Husain, against a torrent of defacement and harassment from Hindu chauvinists complaining of injured religious sentiments.[6] But secular feelings are also so vulnerable. After Sahmat's 1993 exhibition *Hum Sab Ayodhya*—a response to the destruction of the Babri Masjid (mosque) in Ayodhya the previous December—was itself vandalized by Hindu activists, Sahmat issued a statement claiming that the attacks had "dismayed and hurt the sentiments of all sensitive citizens."[7] Are there secular and nonsecular ways of being sensitive?

The emphasis on hurt feelings has, understandably, tended to direct our attention to the allegedly offending objects: pictures, writings, performances. Defenders of free expression have bemoaned the calculated ease with which the politically thin-skinned are allowed to cry injury, especially when they seem largely ignorant of the actual content of the works to which they object.[8] Art historians remind us of the many ways, secular and nonsecular, within and beyond India, that images have been credited with agency, efficacy, and life.[9] In cases of injured sentiment, an offending artwork is of course the proximate medium of hurt feelings. But our opinions about the meaning or validity of such injury depend not only on our beliefs about what should or should not be said or shown, but also on our more or less implicit assumptions about how and where public affect should move—and thus how and where it should move us.

This, then, is also what secularism feels like: a deep ambivalence about the life of public affect. The much-mooted "crisis of secularism" is often assumed to involve the breaching of a necessary boundary: the boundary between, on the one hand, a domain of coolly reasoned public discourse and, on the other, a realm of hot irrationality, typically associated with illegitimately politicized religious sentiments but more generally with what one might call loose affect—that is to say, affect unmoored from the temperance of liberal civic judgment. But the crisis is not just about public affect out of place. From the standpoint of secularists it is also, and perhaps paradoxically, about the affective deficit that seems to afflict the very idea of secularism.

Sahmat's career cannot be understood apart from the rise of the Hindu Right to national prominence in Indian politics and, especially, its ability to mobilize passionate engagement with a series of spectacular and sometimes violent acts of communal assertion. By contrast, by the late 1980s, the Congress Party, political heir to the nationalist struggle and long-standing herald of Indian secularism, seemed utterly lifeless. As one of my interlocutors put it, the power of the Hindu Right lay in the sustained passion of its hatred while the Congress Party was no longer even passionate about its greed. By the 1990s, the time of Sahmat's most energetic efforts, Indian public culture had arrived at the point where a voice captured in Anand Patwardhan's documentary *Father, Son and Holy War* (1995) could proudly declaim, "Impotent secularism is no match for potent Hinduism."

Bombardment

Any discussion of public affect implies an image of the public space in which that affect lives and moves. While the apparent medium of hurt feelings is often a picture or a text, it may be useful to remember Alexander Kluge's argument that the first and most important medium is that kinetic collective resource that feeds what we variously call public culture, public sphere, public domain, or simply "experience."[10] This collective resource has, consciously and consistently, been Sahmat's medium of intervention. In a press release announcing its 2001 project *Art on the Move*, Sahmat affirmed its ambition to make "public space and public domain coincide." Responding to an idea by Vivan Sundaram, artists designed works on wheels that could, on the humble vehicular base of a cart or a cycle-rickshaw, be driven around the streets of Delhi, thus allowing the movement of art to coincide with the ordinary circulations of the city.

Some have suggested that Sahmat's commitment to mobilizing everyday and ordinary forms, media, and spaces has bordered on anachronism—or at least on nostalgia—at a time when the meaning of the everyday and the ordinary in urban India has undergone such rapid change. In Sahmat's time, religious nationalism joined hands with consumerist liberalization.[11] The promise of globalizing markets took on a glossy, visceral appeal through a newly transnationalized style in advertising.[12] Any kind of public cultural activism had to find its feet and its energies in a profoundly transformed media-scape: "Today, the symbols of almost any movement have to compete with the visual bombardment of images on television."[13]

Between branding-driven corporate cultural enclosure and a variety of subaltern-populist claims on Indian public space, the old post-Independence compact between a "national intelligentsia" and the Indian state is under siege. In its place, we see a new "national-popular" symbolic domain in which aesthetic/political authority is an open question.[14] As Tapati Guha-Thakurta and others have noted in the context of the attacks on M. F. Husain, the cultural immunity enjoyed by Indian modernist artists is, for better or worse, no longer secure in a transitional era that juxtaposes cultural democratization with surging intolerance.[15]

This, then, is the highly contentious space in which Sahmat has tried to devise strategies of aesthetic intervention that are popular without surrendering to the pull of populism. It is also the space in which Sahmat's work has competed for public attention with the highly energetic antisecular publicity tactics of the Hindu Right, all the way from the *ramshilas* and *rath yatras* of the Bharatiya Janata Party/Rashtriya Swayamsevak Sangh/Vishwa Hindu Parishad combine, through the Shiv Sena's *maha-aartis* and Ganpati tableaux, to the mechanical lotus that delivered Gujarat Chief Minister Narendra Modi to a wildly enthusiastic Mumbai crowd in the very year that he presided over an anti-Muslim pogrom of shocking brutality.[16] Sahmat's challenge has been to devise public cultural interventions that can be heard against the roar of antisecular publicity while resisting the temptation to imitate the shortcut rhetorical amplification of its opponents' authoritarian theatrics.

So what distinguishes a secular "intervention" from antisecular "propaganda"? The question may at first sight seem idle. For is it not clear that Sahmat and its allies are trying to secure public space for a diversity of opinions, images, and positions while its opponents are trying, often violently, to shut them down? Is the difference not obvious between the "anti-imperialist, secular, and egalitarian values that were woven into the rich fabric of the nation's liberation struggle"[17] and the rigidly monocultural heterophobia of the cultural Right?

At this level, the struggle would seem to be obvious enough: liberal pluralism versus incipient fascism. We can understand several of the controversies in which Sahmat has engaged at a discursive level in this way—the textual aspects of a project like *Hum Sab Ayodhya* or the campaign against the "saffronization" of Indian history textbooks in the early 2000s.[18] But Sahmat is most distinctive as a collective of artist-activists, and in that capacity its projects are necessarily also struggles over the incitement and containment of public affect. The problem of how to bridge a conventional liberal-democratic language with an understanding of the dynamics of collective sentiment as something other than dangerous disturbance both defines and haunts Sahmat's work.

Pro-Vocation in the Secular Gap

Significantly, the story of Sahmat's birth already presents us with an opposition between cynically manipulated hatred and authentic moral outrage. It is common knowledge that Sahmat was formed in response to the shocking daylight murder, by politically sponsored thugs, of left-wing street theatre activist Safdar Hashmi in January 1989. Sahmat emerged from the germinal wave of mourning and anger that followed: a "spontaneous, nationwide wave of revulsion, grief and resistance."[19] In other words, a figure of unmediated, spontaneously emergent secular affect is foundational for Sahmat. That foundational figure establishes the idea that secular affect is natural and spontaneous and challenges the same claim on the antisecular side: when mass carnage erupted in Gujarat in 2002, Chief Minister Modi and his men insisted that the violence was a spontaneous (and therefore, from a populist standpoint, legitimate) reaction to injured Hindu pride.

Sahmat's position on antisecular affect is ambivalent across its writings. On the one hand, its enemies exhibit a bad, regressive spontaneity: "communal passions," "fundamentalist hysteria," "rabidly communal," "rule of the mob," and so on. Against such atavistically unregulated passions, Sahmat's communiqués tend to emphasize the tempering of liberal judgment, the mediation of reason. On the other hand, Sahmat damns the affective politics of antisecularism for not being spontaneous enough. For example, when performances by Habib Tanvir's Naya Theatre were disrupted by right-wing activists in Gwalior in the autumn of 2003, Sahmat commented: "The attacks . . . have been sustained, pinpointed and coordinated—proof, if any was required, that the attacks were not a spontaneous outburst of 'people's emotions.'"[20] Similarly, Sahmat founding member Ram Rahman argues that the attacks on M. F. Husain's work involved not "an upsurge of 'public sentiment' against Husain," not "a 'spontaneous' protest or reaction, no matter how hard the Pariva[21] tried to portray it as such," but rather a "cynical" action "led by political cadres."[22] In Sahmat's reading, nonsecular affect is at once hyper- and hypo-rational, a kind of disciplined indiscipline. Nowhere does this doubling appear more clearly than in a 2002 communiqué alerting readers to the massing at Ayodhya of "no less than 10–20 thousand zealots, *groomed in irrationality*."[23]

The contest over authentically spontaneous mass affect is important because, just as the forces of the cultural Right have always claimed that their injured sentiments are spontaneous, so has Sahmat consistently argued that, although secularism may be taking a beating today, India is nevertheless inherently, and in that sense spontaneously, secular. Indian secularism lives in a gap: it is both indigenous and incomplete, an attitude that is always already present but not yet fully achieved. This gap, again, is Sahmat's space of operation, a terrain in which it can pursue "the *recovery* of the *authentic* in Indian history and culture" and make it available for a contemporary "political and social engagement."[24]

The idea that Indians are naturally secular guarantees the authenticity of Sahmat's outreach to what it calls "the secular masses"[25] who enjoy a "rich tradition of cultural pluralism" and a natively "sophisticated critical outlook."[26] On one side of the gap is a "traditional" past whose resources may be mobilized for a "national revival" premised on unity-in-diversity. On the other side, a future that "depends on the activation of the hitherto largely untapped potential of the Indian people."[27] Ultimately, says Sahmat, Indian secularism, while powering a distinctively national unity, resonates with "the indivisible fabric of a universal cultural humanism."[28]

For all the talk of spontaneity and manipulation on both sides, then, one might say that Sahmat and its opponents have always been locked in a contest over what kind of strategic interventions can count as authentic awakenings of Indian collective experience. When Ram Rahman notes that the BJP failed to "grip the people's imagination" with a rumor that Sahmat was circulating architectural plans for a new mosque in Ayodhya,[29] he is not only pointing out that the Hindu Right does not enjoy infallible access to Indian public sentiment. He is also implicitly acknowledging that any attempt to mobilize public sentiment, whether by the "fundamentalists" or by Sahmat, amounts to a kind of semiotic wager: a gamble on what may be actualized out of the latent potentials of public culture. This is also the reason why even the most apparently cynical propaganda can only succeed by resonating with existing public potentials (which is by no means the same thing as existing public opinion, although all ideological discourse depends on making them appear isomorphic—"Acknowledging the present passions of people is not the same thing as accepting things as they are").[30]

One definition of what art does is to translate unconscious impulses into consciously available forms. One might also say that the work of publicity—the work that Sahmat shares with its antisecular rivals—consists in pro-vocation, literally *calling forth* and thus giving determinate form to the potentials that live in collective experience.

Bridge Across the Heat

If Indians are natively endowed with a "sophisticated critical outlook," then why do they fall prey to antisecular provocation? What else lives in the gap between the past and the future?

For one thing, the heat of a permanently agitated present—the kind of radiation that mutates the pathways by which latent collective resources may develop into tolerant forms of collective life: "The communal temperature and the communal discourse had become hugely heated."[31] Denatured by this heat during the 1990s, the allegedly deep DNA of Indian secularism apparently fell easy prey to propaganda strategies that were at once infernally cunning and shamefully simplistic. Writing in the torrid afterglow of the Babri mosque episode, leading art theorist and Sahmat associate Geeta Kapur lamented the devious skill with which the Hindu Right was able to deploy "symbols of discontent . . . launching them as inversions, blatantly insulting the intelligence of their audience and yet 'succeeding' in targeting truth, riddling it with lies."[32] In such a hothouse atmosphere, the contagious capacity that is so often attributed to crowds[33] seemed capable of generating its own.[34]

Habib Tanvir, whose plays had, as noted above, attracted the unwelcome attention of right-wing goons, claimed that the Hindu nationalists' strategies were all about whipping up affect in order to distract public attention away from the much more difficult (and implicitly, much more "real") problem of basic provision: "*roti* [bread, food] is very difficult to provide, shelter is very difficult to provide, but passion is very easy to provide."[35] But Kapur seemed to be suggesting something more like a *debasement* of public affect produced by the right wing's bad-faith populism, an appeal to "public sentiment" that amounted to a lowest-common-denominator version of what might count as "common ground" between the people and the political leadership. Here, it seemed, propagandistic simplification and outright lies were being used as short cuts between "fundamentalist" ideology and the vast, dynamic resource of collective experience. It was "as if the distortions of the communal and fundamentalist forces inspired by a desire for absolute control are the best means to get to the feeling structure within what is being called people's culture."[36]

But precisely how to understand this precious-yet-easily-manipulated "feeling structure" was the question that kept haunting Sahmat's liberal discourse. It was as if as soon as a bridge across could be imagined, the gap between past and future Indian secularisms reappeared as a gap between a substantialist localism emphasizing diverse Indian traditions, rich with grounded feeling, and a formalist conception of "the liberal ambience in which artists and scholars could work freely."[37] The major leitmotifs here were freedom of expression, democratic citizenship, and civil society. Diversity against singularity. "Rational discourse" against "fascism."[38] All well and good, of course, but in no way expressive of the specific challenges of *aesthetic* engagements with, and in, public culture.

To equate the freedom of artistic expression with the freedom of deliberative discourse may be strategically useful in an overheated public sphere, especially when artists are being attacked at every turn. But it is also in the long run a trap, because it buys a claim on tolerance at the cost of recognizing the specificity of what art can do. The problem is not just the one identified by cultural critic and dramaturge Rustom Bharucha, when he complains that modern secularist politics, for all that it may project its own sensibilities back onto "traditional" forms of life, is not equipped to acknowledge nonmodern forms of expression because "they are cast in languages that are not just verbal, but gestural, kinetic, expressive, farcical, and ritualistic."[39] The problem is that analogous nonverbal forms of expression are in fact *already* central to modern forms of mass public culture, where most of the time they operate in what William Connolly calls a visceral register: "There is always a sensibility moving below and within the argument."[40] This visceral register, which remains at best implicit in formalist understandings of liberal secularism, becomes explicit in the peculiar form of public address known as art. But not only there. It also infuses "lower" types of public artifact like propaganda, advertising, and commercial entertainment. The declining cultural immunity of modernism in 1990s India could at the same time be interpreted as a democratization of Indian public culture.[41] The new proximity of so-called high and low registers of cultural production was at once volatile and exciting. It made the affective politics of secularism exceptionally touchy and yet full of creative potential.

Pinching a Nerve

Sahmat was born in imperative urgency, has thrived in imperative urgency, and risks, perhaps, getting stuck in imperative urgency. The shamelessness of Safdar Hashmi's murder set things in rapid motion. Since then Sahmat has often, and deservedly, been praised for the alacrity of its response to situations that have left other progressive groups in the dust. When the Babri mosque came down in Ayodhya in December 1992, Sahmat had 200,000 posters printed up and nationally distributed within 48 hours. By the following month, hundreds of artists and performers were on the road under the banner of *Anhad Garje*. But the violence kept escalating, culminating in the Gujarat riots of 2002, in which some two thousand people, a majority of them Muslims, were brutally killed. The greater the violence, the more urgent the imperative to mobilize a forceful alternative. Through an ongoing labor of citizenship, Sahmat has, in an exemplary way, stood firm against what it calls, not unfairly, a politics of hate. But this stance of principled resistance has also exacted a price.

During Sahmat's lifetime, organized street violence has moved perilously close to becoming a form of statecraft in India. Aside from the damage that it inflicts on lives and bodies, this violence also insidiously debases progressive politics. There is always the understandable temptation, when faced with its numbing tautology (violence is irreducible, untranslatable, untransformable; ultimately violence = violence), to dismiss aesthetic considerations as either beside the point—"fiddling while Rome burns," for instance—or dangerously irrational. Bharucha, for example, mulls over the adequacy of carefully crafted exhibitions of India's intrinsic pluralism in the face of "the very real vandalistic attacks."[42]

Others have called into question the formal adequacy or aesthetic relevance of the artwork that has been produced under the Sahmat banner. That is not my concern here; I am not in any case convinced that aesthetic relevance is the same thing as being "up to date." Arindam Dutta offers the important observation that Sahmat has, over the course of its existence, allowed its political lobbying activities to reduce the scope and frequency of its artistic projects.[43] If this, too, is a symptom of operating in an overheated climate of imperative urgency, then the real cost to Sahmat's force as a public cultural intervention may not be just a gradual displacement of its art, but also the constant deferral of a real reckoning with the (problematic/productive) gap between the affective politics of its art practice and the liberal discourse that justifies it against the virulent intolerance of Sahmat's opponents.

As Geeta Kapur points out in one of Sahmat's inaugural statements, "Artists Alert," Safdar Hashmi's death, meaningless as it otherwise was, did remind his peers that "an artist is not so innocuous."[44] This, by the way, is one of the gifts a censor reliably, if unwittingly, offers us. But we, like Sahmat, too often oppose the censors with liberal invocations of free speech that, while designed to protect artistic freedom, make art innocuous again by reducing it to the terms of propositional discourse. On that question, Kapur notes: "the artist's right of expression is taken for granted in a democratic society both because this is a publicized feature of liberal culture and because artists are rendered innocuous anyway in that culture."[45]

One might say that the *potentiating* as opposed to the *representational* power of the aesthetic is where artworks can pinch a public nerve. This is the power that lives in the gap between a romanticized conception of cultural tradition (in which Indians are always already either secular or religious nationalists) and a formalist-procedural ideal of a liberal public sphere that does not know what to do with the kind of deep affective potentials that Kapur refers to as "feeling structure."

If Sahmat's career to date shows us anything, it is that the so-called crisis of secularism may also be an opportunity for something more open endedly creative than merely holding the line on a liberal public sphere. William Connolly reminds us of Alexis de Tocqueville's perspicacious point about American secular democracy in the nineteenth century: that it rested on an implicitly shared affective foundation of Christianity, a foundation one might indeed call a "feeling structure," that existed prior to the founding of the United States.[46] Conversely, as in many postcolonial "new nations," and despite the mobilizing power of the nationalist movement, the Indian nation state was established in the absence of any such taken-for-granted foundation.[47] The official hegemony of Nehruvian secularism during the first post-Independence phase only papered over these fault lines; in many ways, the shocks and upheavals of post-Independence Indian public culture have arisen from the constant friction between its tectonic plates. Too easily pathologized as languishing in a state of underdevelopment, insufficient modernity, or cultural regression, the public culture of post-Independence India is a vital, because unsettled, space of aesthetic potential, one that Sahmat will not allow us to ignore.

It might seem altogether perverse to invoke the deeply unfashionable value of aesthetic autonomy here, for does not everything in Sahmat's language point in the opposite direction? Is not Sahmat's agenda precisely about breaking down the walls between gallery and street, between aesthetics and politics, between refined taste and popular democracy? And from another standpoint, is any talk about aesthetic autonomy in the case of Sahmat not simply code for social privilege, an attempt to dignify its members' cosmopolitan class positions and undeniable proximity to (some would say complicity with) the Indian state?[48] In what sense could it possibly be useful to speak of autonomy here?

For one thing, we must surely resist reducing the potentials of an artwork either to the sociological location of its producer or to the social relations that make it possible. An artwork—whether someone calls it "activist" or not—activates and remediates its social context by exceeding it. Aesthetic autonomy is a value most often associated with the modernism that, in India as elsewhere, easily becomes a code word for out-of-touch elitism. Indeed, this is the ideological rod that the populist right wing routinely uses to bash the kind of secular-liberal intelligentsia that populates a group like Sahmat. In response, as we have seen, Sahmat and its allies have pushed back on two fronts by claiming that (1) India is traditionally and organically secular, and (2) that a liberal tolerance for diversity provides the best link between India's past and its future. By framing its claim this way, though, Sahmat's discourse risks preemptively and defensively repressing precisely that domain of mobile sensuous potential that, (in 1), appears under the stable sign of cultural tradition and, (in 2), disappears behind a discursive disguise. And as we have seen, the repressed visceral register returns as a pathological irrationality attributed to the Other—mob affect, whether wild and loose in street rampages or tightly regimented in fascist ranks.

This splitting between rational secularism and its irrational others is an understandable response to the imperative urgency imposed by a climate of violence. Twenty years ago, in the heat of the mosque demolition and its awful sequiturs, Geeta Kapur felt it necessary to oppose a universal "capacity for symbolic and abstract thought" against "the stuff of sentiment" with which the reactionary populists were apparently manipulating the masses.[49] But this kind of opposition also makes it harder to recognize a space of aesthetic potential that is autonomous in the specific sense of being deeply rooted in collective experience without being always already mediated by the symbolic orders of tradition or liberal civil society. And in fact in her essay for the present volume, Kapur reintroduces an invocation of aesthetic autonomy: "Perhaps, after all, an artwork remains always at one remove in its relayed, iterative and deferred meaning. If so, the issue is to what degree is the internal logic of an artwork—a formal equivalent of the structure of language and properly placed in realm of the symbolic—conditioned by and responsive to political circumstance?" Although Kapur's emphasis here is still on the symbolic, I choose to read the phrase "political circumstance" as referring not only to an objective "situation" that may be rendered in narrative terms but also to that inarticulately eloquent visceral register of collective experience that both potentiates and exceeds a language of (political, aesthetic) representation.

Perhaps we are now retrospectively ready to recognize this register in the span of Sahmat's work. Faced with hatred and brutality, we all want to move faster on the bridge across the heat, the leap from chaos to order. But perhaps this is one place where, after all, it makes sense to slow down? Perhaps this is also what secularism feels like: Letting go of the need to be assured about whether India really is or ever was "culturally" secular. Dropping all competing claims to spontaneity, origin, and injury. Minding—not racing across—the gap.

William Mazzarella is currently professor of anthropology at the University of Chicago. His engagement with Sahmat emerges out of a long-term concern with the political anthropology of mass publicity in India. He is the author of *Shoveling Smoke: Advertising and Globalization in Contemporary India* (2003) and *Censorium: Cinema and the Open Edge of Mass Publicity* (2013).

NOTES

1. Author's interview with Vijay Tendulkar, Mumbai, March 20, 2004.

2. Terry Eagleton, *The Ideology of the Aesthetic* (Oxford: Blackwell, 1990); Susan Buck-Morss, *Dreamworld and Catastrophe: The Passing of Mass Utopia in East and West* (Cambridge, MA: MIT Press, 2000).

3. Karin Zitzewitz, *The Aesthetics of Secularism: The Cultural Politics of Modernist Art in Contemporary India* (forthcoming), and her essay in the present volume.

4. My use of the term "affect" throughout this essay is meant to bring recent debates on the social life of affect—embodied feeling, sensuous intensity—into conversation with a conception of aesthetics that is rooted in sense experience. I also presume, as indexed by the term "public affect," that public life, not least in the domain of mass-mediated aesthetic experience, is profoundly conditioned by collective currents of sentiment. For background reading, see, e.g., Lauren Berlant, *Cruel Optimism* (Durham, NC: Duke University Press, 2011); Veena Das, "Of M. F. Husain and an Impossible Love," in Sumathi Ramaswamy, ed, *Barefoot Across the Nation: M. F. Husain and the Idea of India* (New York: Routledge, 2010); Melissa Gregg and Gregory Seigworth, eds., *The Affect Theory Reader* (Durham, NC: Duke University Press, 2010); William Mazzarella, "Affect: What is it Good For?," in Saurabh Dube, ed, *Enchantments of Modernity: Empire, Nation, Globalization* (New York: Routledge, 2010).

5. It is instructive to consider the extent to which the statutes at issue in these struggles organize their language around questions of public affect—not only injury to religious sentiments but also problems of public excitability.

6. Sumathi Ramaswamy, ed, *Barefoot Across the Nation: M. F. Husain and the Idea of India* (New York: Routledge, 2010).

7. Sahmat, *Sahmat 20 Years 1989–2009: A Document of Statements and Activities* (New Delhi: Sahmat, 2009): 73.

8. William Mazzarella, *Censorium: Cinema and the Open Edge of Mass Publicity* (Durham, NC: Duke University Press, 2013).

9. Richard Davis, *Lives of Indian Images* (Princeton, 1997); Kajri Jain, *Gods in the Bazaar: The Economies of Indian Calendar Art* (Durham, NC: Duke University Press, 2007).

10. Alexander Kluge, "On Film and the Public Sphere," *New German Critique* 24/25 (Autumn 1981–Winter 1982): 206–20.

11. Arvind Rajagopal, *Politics After Television: Hindu Nationalism and the Reshaping of the Public in India* (Cambridge: Cambridge University Press, 2001).

12. William Mazzarella, *Shoveling Smoke: Advertising and Globalization in Contemporary India* (Durham, NC: Duke University Press, 2003).

13. Rustom Bharucha, *In the Name of the Secular: Contemporary Cultural Activism in India* (New Delhi: Oxford, 1998): 63.

14. Arindam Dutta, "Sahmat, 1989–2004: Liberal Art Practice Against the Liberalized Public Sphere," *Cultural Dynamics* 17: 193–226 (2005); Kajri Jain, "Taking and Making Offence: Husain and the Politics of Desecration" in Sumathi Ramaswamy, ed, *Barefoot Across the Nation*; see also Geeta Kapur's essay in the present volume.

15. Tapati Guha-Thakurta, "Fault-Lines in a National Edifice: On the Rights and Offences of Contemporary Indian Art," in Ramaswamy, *Barefoot Across the Nation*, 172–98; Arvind Rajagopal, "The Gujarat Experiment and Hindu National Realism," in Anuradha Dingwaney Needham and Rajeswari Sunder Rajan, eds, *The Crisis of Secularism in India* (Durham, NC: Duke University Press, 2007).

16. The *ramshila* campaign of 1989 was part of the lead-up to the demolition of the Babri Mosque. Bricks were collected from all over India and brought to Ayodhya for the construction of a new Ram temple on the contested site of the mosque, allegedly the birthplace of the Hindu god-king Ram.

Rath yatra literally means "pilgrimage by chariot." The 1990 version was a massive publicity stunt/mobilization organized by the Hindu nationalist Bharatiya Janata Party (BJP) and its affiliate organizations, under the rubric Ram Rath Yatra (a *rath yatra* in the name of the Hindu god-king Ram). Riding a "chariot" (actually a modified truck), BJP President L. K. Advani intended to proceed, in a winding 10,000-kilometer itinerary from Somnath on India's west coast (the symbolically pregnant site of a Hindu temple destroyed by Islamic invaders in the eleventh century) to Ayodhya. In the event, and after much violence along the way, the *yatra* was cut short when Advani was arrested in Dhanbad in the state of Bihar on October 23, 1990.

In Mumbai, the aggressively nativist Shiv Sena proved particularly adept at developing a populist ritual idiom: its *maha aartis* were scaled-up public devotional ceremonies explicitly and provocatively designed to create a Hindu counterpart to Muslim Friday prayers. Its sponsorship of neighborhood tableaux during the annual Ganpati/Ganesh festival appropriated festively creative local energies for the party's assertively identitarian ideology. Gérard Heuzé, "Cultural Populism: The Appeal of the Shiv Sena," in Alice Thorner and Sujata Patel, eds, *Bombay: Metaphor for Modern India* (New Delhi: Oxford University Press, 1995), 213–47; Thomas Blom Hansen, *Wages of Violence: Naming and Identity in Postcolonial Bombay* (Princeton, NJ: Princeton University Press, 2001); Raminder Kaur, *Performative Politics and the Cultures of Hinduism: Public Uses of Religion in Western India* (London: Anthem, 2003).

17. Sahmat, "Safdar Hashmi: 12 April 1954–1 January 1989" (New Delhi: Sahmat, 1989).

18. This refers to the attempt, during the BJP-led national government

of 1998–2004, to rewrite Indian history textbooks according to an unapologetically partisan Hindu nationalist vision.

19. Sahmat, "Safdar Hashmi."

20. Sahmat, *Sahmat 20 Years*, 249.

21. The Sangh Parivar, or "Family of Associations," the umbrella term for the Hindu nationalist organizations whose national political face is the BJP.

22. Ram Rahman, "Defending Husain in the Public Sphere: The Sahmat Experience" in Ramaswamy, *Barefoot Across the Nation*, 166, 155, 149.

23. Sahmat, *Sahmat 20 Years*, 191, emphasis added.

24. Ibid., 11, emphasis added

25. Ibid., 252.

26. Ibid., 316.

27. Ibid., 88.

28. Ibid., 14.

29. Rahman, "Defending Husain," 153.

30. Stephen Duncombe, *Dream: Re-Imagining Progressive Politics in an Age of Fantasy* (New York: The New Press, 2007), 35.

31. Rahman, "Defending Husain," 151.

32. Geeta Kapur, "On the Exhibition *Hum Sab Ayodhya*," (New Delhi: Sahmat, 1993).

33. For an extended discussion of crowd contagion as a trope in social theory, see William Mazzarella, "The Myth of the Multitude, or, Who's Afraid of the Crowd?," *Critical Inquiry* 36 (Summer 2010): 697–727

34. For example, the claim that Sahmat was circulating a poster depicting Ram and Sita as incestuous siblings. "This was the result of decontextualizing and distorting a few words from a panel depicting Buddhist and Jain versions of the *Rama Katha*, in which the *Dasaratha Jataka* refers to Rama and Sita as brother and sister who ruled jointly in Ayodhya for 16,000 years" (Bharucha 1998: 56; cf Rahman 2011).

35. Neeraj Malick and Javed Malick, "The Drama of Confrontation," *Economic Times* July 20, 1993.

36. Kapur, "On the Exhibition *Hum Sab Ayodhya*."

37. Sahmat, *Sahmat 20 Years*, 126.

38. Ibid., 183.

39. Bharucha, *In the Name of the Secular*, 38.

40. William Connolly, *Why I Am Not a Secularist* (Minneapolis: University of Minnesota Press, 1999): 7.

41. Jain, "Taking and Making Offense."

42. Bharucha, *In the Name of the Secular*, 57.

43. Dutta, "Sahmat 1989–2004."

44. Geeta Kapur, "Artists Alert: 12–16 April 1989" (New Delhi: Sahmat, 1989), reprinted in the present volume.

45. Ibid.

46. Connolly, *Why I Am Not a Secularist*.

47. Rajagopal, "The Gujarat Experiment."

48. Bharucha, *In the Name of the Secular*; Arindam Dutta, "Sahmat 1989–2004."

49. Kapur, "On the Exhibition *Hum Sab Ayodhya*."

Geeta Kapur

Secular Artist, Citizen Artist

Framing Categories

The two terms I use to construct this argument—secular and citizen—annotate each other and suggest ways to connect contemporary art practices with a historical agenda. The secular is constructed on an agonistic principle that is particularly relevant to artists working in the public domain. Citizenship is a contestatory site involving struggles for civil rights and forms of political empowerment in relation to the state.

For all its worldliness, the term secular (meaning "of this world") could indicate, as with Edward Said, a sense of liminality: secularism is an oppositional critical practice whose meaning emerges in contrast to the practice of religious solidarity, nationalist movements, professionalism, and "organic" or class-aligned intellectualism.[1] Witness-in-exile is a favored trope of the twentieth century; it becomes an enabling form of internationalism that empowers intellectuals in the third world to dismantle and reshape metropolitan systems of authority. On the strength of Said it can be further argued that the secular is central to the very formation of modernity and artistic modernism, and that being secular is an integral part of being an artist in modern times.

To be secular implies participation in an abstract form of citizenship that approximates a universal condition and, hence, a dialectically understood (un)belonging. Vulnerabilities within the practice of secularism have been foregrounded in the global present by the paradoxical reemergence of specifically nationalist, ethnic, and religious communities. These vulnerabilities have brought into focus a more situational idea of citizenship, making it imperative that we acknowledge historical dilemmas of identity and advance specific instances of radical partisanship within the nation-state and outside it, within civil society and across the more volatile ground of the political.

A distinction made by the political theorist Partha Chatterjee between civil society, political society, and the state is relevant here. Chatterjee states: "The question that frames the debate over social transformation in the colonial period, is that of modernity. In political society of the post-colonial period, the framing question is that of democracy."[2] He argues that civil society comprises the realm of rule-governed negotiations in a legal framework that privilege certain citizens on account of class, caste, etc.; the political domain consists of a more chaotic process of negotiation in which different sections of the population fight—within a manifestly unequal society—for their democratic rights to benefits, public services, representation, and entitlements on behalf of a community or cause.[3]

Being a citizen within the terms of the nation-state rests on contractually conducted, ideologically overdetermined, and often *exclusionary* privileges. Global citizenship (necessitated by the logic of global capital and the contingent need for a mass movement of labor) frequently translates into a systematic process of *disenfranchisement*: the badge of alienation is worn by millions of migrants. Heavy with historical contradictions, an international civil society is postulated at an elevated (possibly utopian) level even as the discourse of citizenship is rhetorically renewed by asking how the citizenry—as a multitudinous force—comes to be redeemed within and outside state formations.

If what distinguishes political from civil society is that the discourse of citizens' rights must translate into a preemptive commitment to radical change, we need to reopen a familiar, intensely polemical question: *does the artist-as-citizen still have a role to play in translating political projects into a vanguard aesthetic?*

Progressive Movements in Indian Art

There is a recognized set of historical precedents exemplifying styles of political intervention in modern Indian art. These are the two left-initiated writers'-and-artists' movements in pre-independent India of the 1930s and 40s: the Progressive Writers' Association (PWA), formed in 1936 in the syncretic culture of the north Indian city of Lucknow, and the Indian Peoples' Theatre Association (IPTA), formed in 1943 amidst the great political ferment in Bengal.[4] IPTA remains the most valorized movement of "revolutionary" artists to this day. Most members of IPTA were communist sympathizers, and the organization served as a Communist Party Cultural Front.

Comprised largely of performing artists—actors, singers, dancers, pedagogues—these spirited troupes saw themselves as the cultural vanguard and formed virtual "brigades," going into the country to gain nationwide solidarity. IPTA's proclaimed task was to mobilize people into a performative mode in preparation for a revolution, tapping nationalist and revolutionary fervor alike. Indeed IPTA should be seen as a moment of culmination for a liberationist agenda when flanks of creative youth joined the national struggle and took on, in a concerted effort, the malaise of indigenous feudalism, British imperialism, and fascism. (Notwithstanding their ongoing struggle against imperial rule, Indians fought in willing collaboration with the Allies against fascism.)

Though named after Romain Rolland's idea of a "People's Theatre," IPTA was in fact part *narodnik* in style and part Soviet in ideology—referring especially to agitprop movements and artists' collectives in the early decades of the Soviet revolution. Thus, while it envisioned a mythos of the land and its people in a still largely peasant country by configuring indigenous radicalisms and extant folk forms, it drew equally on a hundred-year-long critical and creative dialogue in India on the *processes of modernity*. It was thus in a position to engage with Western radicalisms and to deploy advanced strategies of political persuasion. IPTA also became the fulcrum for new literature and new cinema, such as that of the great Marxist filmmaker Ritwik Ghatak, who gave a passionate turn to the politics of realist cinema (different in style and ideology from his more famous, more sedate peer, Satyajit Ray). Riding the last wave of India's anti-imperialist struggles, IPTA lasted beyond independence (1947) and through the 1950s, though on a diminished scale. In cultural lore it became the originary moment of "true" radicalism in the Indian arts as it cut across nationalist/communist and postcolonial/statist worldviews. Though the nationalist and communist movements were not always in consonance, they followed a rubric of radical change, and IPTA made a direct *political* intervention, combining the fervor of both and situating the working people at the fulcrum of India's liberation struggle.

There is another level at which Indian artists, as honorary members of the national elite in a postcolonial state, function. Occupying a relatively secure space in civil society, they do engage with the question of social and cultural transformation, but their voice is heard within a fairly discreet public sphere. It is useful here to refer to the concept of "passive revolution" advanced by Antonio Gramsci, and brought to bear on our understanding of the modalities of change in pre- and specifically post-independence India by Partha Chatterjee. Because the rubric of revolution becomes somewhat ironic by the use of the epithet "passive," Indian cultural practitioners foreground the term "progressive." This is a term taken over from leftist discourse and made more accommodating to a liberal disposition; it is, however, distinguished from the standard Western notion of liberalism in that a peculiarly charged, though somewhat abstracted, ideal of people's sovereignty is assumed to emerge in the aftermath of decolonization.

All through the national movement and up until the recent past, Indian artists represented, both euphorically and critically, the imagined community of the nation and the state. The new national state that came into its own under Jawaharlal Nehru looked to the intelligentsia, the intellectual and artist community, to stage an honorable transition from the feudal to a modern, democratic, secular, and moderate version of socialist society. Correspondingly, the cultural position of post-independence Indian artists has been largely "reformist" in relation to tradition and indigenist/communitarian formations. As members of the intelligentsia, artists can be seen to function not only within the terms of this new body politic, but in tune with the state's embodiment of an emancipatory agenda. They have "trusted" state initiatives in establishing its claims of a democratic and secular polity via constitutional norms and good governance. They have found forms of critical affiliation, devised genres, styles, and figural types, as well as aesthetic strategies for the purpose of addressing the *national*.[5] Indeed, for a period, artists in India can be seen to play a substantial mediatory role in the very site of those cultural institutions deemed progressive by the postcolonial state—and only occasionally has the project of modernization and the historical teleology set up on its premise been opened out for critical consideration. *Thus a peculiar coincidence occurs between the state's constitutional promise of democratic secularism and the secularizing logic of aesthetic modernism.*

The declarative stance of artists as modern, secular, progressive members of the national elite has led to the valorization of artists as "universal" moderns and, as such, citizen-subjects with an enhanced sovereignty. Significantly, these artists have exercised their special liberties in order to subvert religion, gender norms, and class in a language both eccentric and acute—as befits alternative embodiments of subjectivity in the modernist mode.[6] Indian artists, highly "accredited" members of the Indian Republic, have wielded power as bearers of the *national imaginary* with, through, and also, at times, outside the sanctioning institutions of the state. By way of introducing alternative readings, I argue further that several of these artists recognize the changing contours of Indian democracy and, faced with assertive aspects of state power, take political dissent beyond the protocol of civil society. Particularly since the late 1970s—thirty years after independence—the more political among these artists have faced the historicist bind of the nation-state and found the problematic of a plural culture, as handled by the centrist government and its state bureaucracy, inadequate. They have sought allegories or otherwise deconstructed signs of the national whereby they can be both inside the nation and outside the state in their interpretative rendering of the political.[7]

Consider some specific instances during the Indian Emergency declared by the supposedly left-liberal government of Indira Gandhi in 1975–77. As the state cracked down on all opposition and suspended the democratic process to combat what it called a situation of nationwide anarchy, a considerable number of Indian artists tested their courage and challenged the state's injunctions.[8] On another plane, since 1992 there has been a sustained opposition to the ascendant right-wing party (the Bharatiya Janata Party [BJP], which led a ruling coalition, the National Democratic Alliance [NDA], from 1998 to 2004). How artists responded when right-wing ideology and anti-secular/proto-fascist forces engineered riots and conducted a virtual massacre of the Muslims will be discussed later. Here I seek to establish that modern cultural history will see Indian artists not only as supporting the more progressive values of a democratic polity, but as positioning themselves in the public sphere to engage moderately but significantly with urgencies of the political moment.

Beyond this left-liberal response is the more intrepid position that rejects the (self-attributed) placement of the artist as member of the national elite, and demands that radical social intervention be predicated on a position that is exactly its opposite—the *subaltern* position. Two such contexts need to be established. There has been an explosive development in literature from the 1960s with group formations and collective movements taking on a forthrightly antagonistic role. Foregrounding their view from a *subaltern* locus, *dalit* (the lowest/"untouchable" members of the Hindu caste hierarchy who have assumed the term *dalit,* the oppressed, as a sign of their estrangement *and* defiance) writers challenge, defy, and mock the ideology of the ruling class and caste, the hegemony of the state, and the very legitimacy of the national. There is a generically different *dalit* literature (especially in Marathi and Tamil) that places unprecedented pressure on what a culturally validated modernist aesthetic could possibly mean or, rather, fail to mean, in the deeply divided social life as in the national-political formation of India itself.

Additionally, anti-state Maoist politics came into existence in the late 1960s and created a counter-culture prevailing in metropolitan India: an outright rejection of what was declared by the revolutionists to be hollow promises of the Indian Republic, and therefore a rejection of the constitutional and democratic structures of the nation-state. The Communist Party of India (CPI) split in 1964 and gave birth to the Communist Party of India (Marxist) or CPI(M), which split again in 1967 to found the Communist Party of India (Marxist-Leninist) or CPI(ML). This last formation, the CPI(ML), is also referred to as the Naxalite movement after the location of Naxalbari in Bengal; here, in 1967, the first call was given for armed capture of land by, and on behalf of, the deprived and landless peasantry. The CPI and the CPI(M) have participated in the democratic process, have held power in the states of Kerala, West Bengal, and Tripura for decades, and act as major players in the existing politics of India. Meanwhile, the field of operation of the CPI(ML), or the Naxalites, has been the predominantly tribal, peasant, and lower-caste regions—first Bengal, Kerala, and Andhra, then parts of Bihar and adjoining states. At its high point through the 1970s it had a committed following in urban India as well. The call for action directed against the class of landlords, but also against India's comprador bourgeoisie, the pro-landlord-capitalist state, and the urban middle classes with their flawed trust in parliamentary democracy, also attracted students and middle-class youth, as well as sections of the intelligentsia. Unlike the classical CPI with its legion of artist-affiliates (including IPTA) and the CPI(M) (of which I shall soon speak), artists' input in the Naxalite movement is more locally, though no less radically, configured through vernacular traditions of dissent. Fewer visual artists from the metropolis were involved in the movement, except during the late 1980s when a brief and brilliant intervention was made by The Radical Painters' and Sculptors' Association, largely comprised of young artists from the communist-ruled state of Kerala.[9] However, a broad flank of ultra-left writers, filmmakers, and theatre practitioners (and these few artists) have expressed their identification with subaltern movements and strengthened the subjectivities produced therein. The corresponding genre is either expressionist or documentary, and though each has a very different genealogy, they privilege a rhetorical style of address intended to expose the (un)truth of the state's democratic claims.

By the 1990s the socialist compact, such as it was in the early post-independence decades, was devolving into neoliberal strategies and leading on to India's induction into global capitalism. This soon became declared state policy. It was accompanied by right-wing ascendancy (not unexpectedly, perhaps, given a worldwide record of such a tendency), with cultural agendas antithetical to the modern, secular claim of the Indian Republic. The artist community tended to view this economic transformation as inevitable; India—as widely believed by a massive upwardly mobile middle class—had to accept the logic of the world economy. In fact, object/commodity-orientated visual artists found it more and more conducive as the art market expanded manifold and there was an unprecedented acceleration of Indian artists' participation in global art events. But the entire artist community—almost as a whole and across the entire nation—responded with alarm at the turn towards religious sectarianism in the political and cultural arenas. There has been a refusal of Hindutva ("being" Hindu or the Hindu way) and of the retrograde ideology of the BJP that came into power and formed a ruling coalition between 1998 and 2004.

A New Collective Agency in the Public Sphere: SAHMAT

SAHMAT (Safdar Hashmi Memorial Trust) is an artists' and intellectuals' forum formed in early 1989 in solidarity against the murder by goons of the ruling Congress Party of Safdar Hashmi, a young theatre activist and member of the CPI(M). A charismatic figure, Hashmi's funeral was attended by comrades and others in the thousands, and it became, in its outpouring of grief and rage, an unparalleled rallying point.[10] SAHMAT (henceforth referred to as Sahmat, since the acronym means agreement/compact) issued its first call with the slogan "Artists Alert!" Mobilizing artists, academics, journalists, and activists in Delhi and across the entire country, it provided a platform to articulate dissent in moments of crisis, when democratic rights of citizens are flouted. Almost in one stroke, Sahmat succeeded in placing the Indian artist at the center of a cultural juncture where civil society and the national state can be said to have entered an ongoing crisis (a crisis that decidedly dates back to the declaration in 1975 of the Indian Emergency). By energizing public debate on issues of art and citizenship, by activating a dialogue on the relevance of the arts within the sub/or proto-bourgeois public sphere in India, Sahmat succeeded in attributing a responsibility to the artist on behalf of an often-recalcitrant state. In that process, Sahmat faced and won battles against attacks by belligerent parliamentarians as well as state forces compromised by the pressure of a growing right wing within Indian political culture. Well understood to be broadly aligned with the left wing, Sahmat on occasion acts like a *de facto* cultural front of the CPI(M); on other occasions it privileges its artists' constituency and defies the party line, thus developing remarkable strategies of commitment and autonomy.

Well known to be especially proactive on issues of minorities, their rights and security within the national cultural space and Indian polity at large, Sahmat has functioned:

- within *civil society* as a conciliatory platform
- vis-à-vis the *state* through channels of government policy
- out in the *public sphere*, addressing issues of civil society, of governance and justice
- directly within the *political arena*, via confrontational debates in the Parliament, in the judicial courts, and in the media

Indeed, Sahmat's mediatic success in galvanizing opinion in the public sphere has been staggering, given that the media was overrun by a right-wing blitz from the 1990s through to 2004. Building opinion through directing media attention to issues of urgent public interest—via signature campaigns, petitions, widely reported press conferences, the staging of public rallies and protest meetings, and artist-designed posters as well as "direct action" at street level—Sahmat can be said to have proposed a *rhetorical form of public culture.*

> Sahmat's emergence in 1989 resulted in, numerically speaking, extraordinary participation by the entire breadth of India's artists, from academy-style painter to classical singer, from alternative filmmaker to community theatre enthusiast, from Communist Party griot to small-town photo-journalist. Sahmat's interventions quickly laid out a new mode of artistic operation in the Indian context, bringing on board waves of voluntary conscripts from the art world, the intelligentsia and "cultural workers" who embraced Sahmat as a national platform for anti-state and progressive dissent. By the time of its "Anhad Garje". . . [meaning unborn, boundless, raging sound] campaign of 1993—its quick-fire response to the Babri Masjid demolition, when all other elements of civil society and the state seemed paralysed—Sahmat was routinely pulling off tremendous logistical feats on a national scale, straddling events in several different cities (up to 30 at a time) with input and involvement from hundreds, even thousands, of artists. From certain standpoints, this made Sahmat into the largest-ever voluntary collective of artists coming together to share a single political platform.[11]

To elaborate on some of its activities, soon after Safdar Hashmi's death Sahmat declared his birthday, April 12, as National Street Theatre Day; 25,000 street plays based on democratic/leftist issues are believed to have been staged throughout the country on that day in 1989. From the early 1990s, the Hindu right wing began acting out its agenda for cultural, economic, and political majoritarianism, propagating an anti-Muslim (anti-minority) ideology of hate, and resorting to political vandalism (the demolition of the sixteenth-century Babri Mosque in December 1992), riots, and massacres (Mumbai, 1992–93). In 1991 Sahmat responded with a multiple-arts project, *Artists Against Communalism*, which brought together musical performances, lectures, films, and street theatre. This traveling project was staged in several cities.[12] After the demolition of the mosque, Sahmat composed, designed, printed, and distributed 20,000 protest posters across the country. On January 1, 1993, *Anhad Garje*, a stupendous musical program, turned into a caravan of classical, folk, and popular musicians, traveling from Delhi to six riot-torn cities, including the curfew-strapped cities of Gujarat. They also performed in burning Mumbai and in Lucknow near Ayodhya (where the mosque was razed to the ground). *Anhad Garje* turned the syncretic, *sufi-bhakti* traditions of music from a medieval genre into a contemporary one. Its rare dynamic, the way its subliminal dissent resounded against the vulgar demagogy of Hindutva ideology, marked a new stage in the very definition of how, and when, traditional art forms become (re)radicalized; how they acquire political iconicity and a fresh aura.[13] On the eve of Independence Day in 1993, within a year of the demolition of the mosque, *Muktnaad* (meaning "free note"), an all-night performance, was held on the banks of the River Sarayu in Ayodhya by a similar constellation of musicians, completing this paradoxical canonical/anti-canonical solidarity. An accompanying exhibition of text and image titled *Hum Sab Ayodhya* (meaning "we are all from the syncretic culture of Ayodhya") presented archival/historical resources about the contested site of Ayodhya, underscoring India's plural culture. Printed in an edition of 500 for pedagogic dissemination, this was shown in Faizabad/Ayodhya and in seventeen other cities simultaneously.

It is this kind of interventionist temper that has placed Sahmat in direct relation with the state. This is a complicated relationship, and in many ways a pragmatic one. Sahmat conducts negotiations with state authorities that are sympathetic to its cause, and for that reason it is sometimes called a *para-statist* organization. But if its confrontational aspects are considered, it becomes a *political player prodding the state to declare its hand.* Sahmat takes a critical/collaborative stance when there is a progressive potential at stake within state ideology, while it is boldly anti-statist at other junctures. Correspondingly, Sahmat has received state funds and permissions to launch its public projects, and it has also faced bans (and judicial cases amounting to criminal charges) against particular activities considered politically transgressive. *Muktnaad*, the all-night performance on the banks of the holy river in the assaulted city of Ayodhya, had full state support sanctioned by the ruling Congress government. But the historically researched exhibition *Hum Sab Ayodhya*, which illustrated the layered culture of India's civilizational sites to gain a mandate for modern secularism, was vandalized by right-wing goons in the adjoining city of Faizabad, and then banned and confiscated in Delhi on ludicrously framed criminal charges. This led Sahmat into a ferocious controversy in the media as well as the Parliament where the Congress Party, and even the otherwise sympathetic left parties, succumbed to the virulence of the anti-Sahmat campaigners. This small artist organization was forced to face criminal charges of communal offence (attempt to stir religious disaffection). It took the brilliant lawyer Rajiv Dhavan until 2001 to fight and win, on a truly triumphant note, at the Delhi High Court.

Sahmat believes that its fight on behalf of the secular principles of the Indian Constitution—an affirmative agenda—*can disentangle the undertow of several distorting tendencies within the classic sphere of ideology, that is to say, within culture, education, media, and the expressive arts.* Just as open-air performances of egalitarian and dissenting strains in classical and folk music (*Anhad Garje, Muktnaad*) have signaled a cultural mandate for secularism, contemporary poetry and street theatre in the rhetorical mode have given a political mandate to popular forms. Sahmat's programs and events have included what it calls "Alerts!" whenever there is a perceived threat by national and global forces to the constitutional rights of artists as citizens—in the matter of life, speech, and expression. Sahmat has provided a platform of solidarity and support for Salman Rushdie, for the communist theatre director Habib Tanvir, and, concertedly for fifteen years, for India's most famous modernist-artist Maqbool Fida Husain, who was in exile on account of life-threatening, criminal charges framed by Hindutva thugs (and their counterparts amongst Muslim fundamentalists).[14]

Sahmat has regularly staged thematic visual arts exhibitions that are pedagogic as well as experimental. These all elicit a collective refusal of narrow sectarianism and an opening out to the emancipatory cultural resource of the *national imaginary*. For instance, in the portable street exhibition *Images and Words*—a companion piece to the ongoing programs of *Artists Against Communalism*—artists and writers together addressed the thematic of the secular, and the exhibition traveled to thirty cities in 1991. As already mentioned, in 1993 *Hum Sab Ayodhya*, replete with a seminal court case based on the *realpolitik* of the state's farcical censorship laws, became a matter of parliamentary debate. Exhibitions of mail art produced on a shoestring budget, such as *Postcards for Gandhi*, opened in six cities in 1995, affirming the renewed evaluation of Gandhi's "truth" in the distorted heart of India's body politic during a strife-ridden decade. Alongside artists' reconstruction of the figure of Gandhi, Sahmat invited Marxist philosophers and social scientists to reflect on the political relevance of Gandhi, an exercise long neglected by the Indian Left. In 1999 Sahmat published and toured a poster exhibition titled *Harvest of Hate* that chronicled acts of harassment, moral policing, and violence pursued against all norms of a democratic society by the Hindutva brigades.[15]

Ways of Resisting

Of seminal importance is the exhibition *Ways of Resisting*, mounted by Sahmat in Delhi in 2002–03.[16] This was the period when a near-fascistic ideology, at once homogenizing and sectarian, reached its peak. In early 2002 the state of Gujarat instigated a genocide of Muslims on a scale of violence unprecedented in independent India. In the wake of these events—forms of "ethnic cleansing" conducted by Hindutva forces in the guise of spontaneous religious riots—Sahmat held, as I have already recounted, many different forms of protest. In the dire circumstances of Gujarat 2002, a succession of meetings were held—direct encounters with the victims of the pogrom who placed their horrific testimonies before the press and public in the capital city of Delhi—for the nation to witness. In continuation with this testimony, the exhibition *Ways of Resisting* placed the violent decade of 1992–2002 as a frame of reference to bring to attention artworks (of thirty or so artists) that articulated questions of self and society in a situation where an already fraught polity was suddenly torn apart.

Several of the issues discussed in the main body of this essay—self, citizenship, alterity, and exile, and those I have not discussed—pain, mourning, and death, found a language, or at least an enunciative mode, in and through this carefully curated exhibition. A number of artworks of this period dealt with the usurpation of *religion* and *mythology,* and the demagogic distortion of *symbols* (traditional and contemporary) by reactionary culturalists; the artists did this to forge an iconography that draws on the tradition yet spells alterity.[17] The aspiration of secular artists working within a transforming ethos of traditional societies is complex: they may be inclined to weave their way through philosophic (mystical) radicalism to reach the destination of political dissent; or they may

Navjot Altaf, *Links Destroyed and Rediscovered* (detail), 1994, installation with mixed media, dimensions variable.

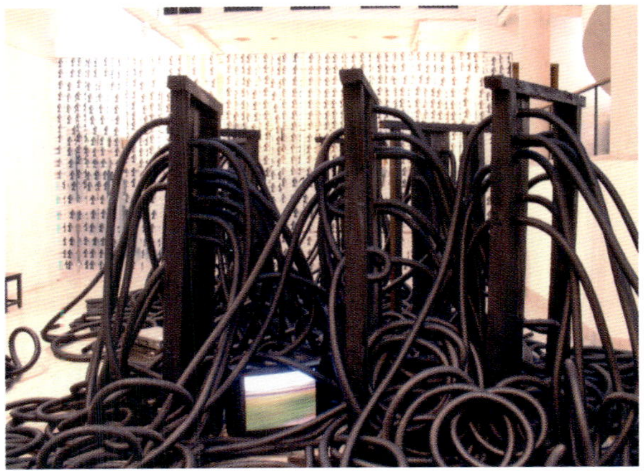

Sheba Chhachhi and Sonia Jabbar, *"When the gun is raised, dialogue stops . . .": Kashmiri women speak*, 2000, photo-text installation, wooden rihals [book holders or stands], bricks, rice, soil, rusted sheets of iron, black-and-white photographs, text, dimensions variable.

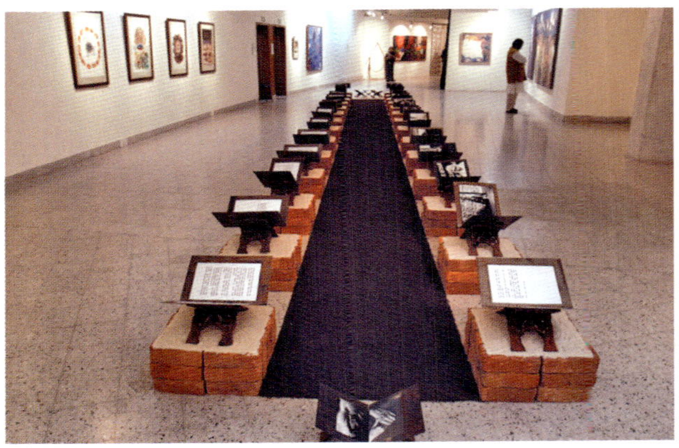

Surendran Nair, *The Unbearable Lightness of Being (Corollary Mythologies)*, 1998, oil on canvas, 70 x 47 inches.

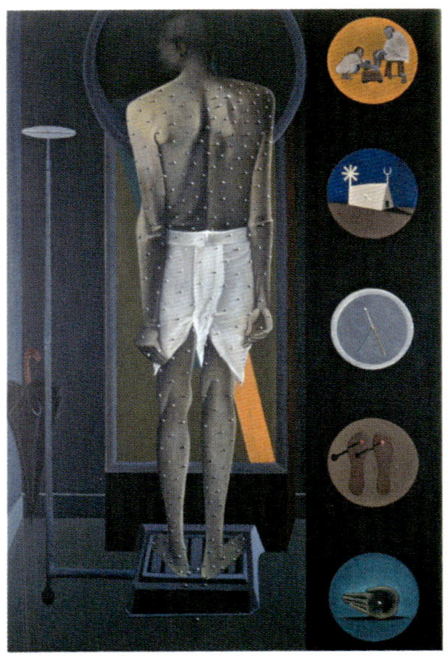

navigate a return from the other shore—from contemporary disenchantments, to the recognition of loss and thence to the historical task of ethical redress. In this two-way process, the most generative source Indian artists have tapped into, predictably perhaps, is the syncretic *sufi-bhakti* traditions of medieval India that produced a new heterodox spirituality and a dissenting, near-atheist autonomy aiming to dismantle religious institutions and nurture egalitarian, intra-community exchanges. In doing so, contemporary artists (not unlike their medieval counterparts) hold in tension a sensibility for the *sacred* along with a full play of *profanation*—what in aesthetics may be called the play of inversions—deemed necessary for every ethical enterprise.

Indeed artists have attempted to do what the Marxist political philosopher Akeel Bilgrami calls the "re-enchantment of the secular" within his exegesis on the "philosophy" of Gandhi.[18] Bilgrami considers it necessary that we, in our time, understand Gandhi's insistence on attributing a normative concern and irreducible value to nature and human society alike, whereby even rational thought must entail both doubt and its transcendence. If a generosity of spirit brings truth and compassion, faith and irony into social praxis, then it is not so coincidental that the figure of Gandhi should repeatedly figure as norm, icon, and enigma in Indian artists' work (as well as in art projects staged by Sahmat and in the revised discourse at the national level by left intellectuals).[19] Though seemingly literal, such figuration can offer the possibility of facing authoritarian command with an imaginative rendering of our everyday lives.

Several artworks in *Ways of Resisting* demonstrate that one of the ways of resisting both the violence of social coercion and its reprisal in hate is by conducting the full protocol of mourning.[20] This recalls Gandhian ethics of "remorse," as it does Western scriptural and psychoanalytical understanding. If politicality comes as much from agonistic reason as it comes from a recognition of affects, artworks make evident that social suffering (as caused by communal carnage in India) requires reparation for injury acted out, in the case of an artist's practice, in the public eye. To memorialize courageous encounters with coercive regimes is the necessary task of historical recall conducted by artists of all genres at all times. *Ways of Resisting* had a preponderance of artworks that dealt with traumatic event and constructed memory, mourning, and memorials.

Yet another set of works in the exhibition attempted to prise away the question of citizen subject from the national, conventional setting of civil society. By considering the question of new subjectivities formed outside in the interstices of the city fabric, these artists adopt confrontational positions pertaining to *dalit* and working-class identities; they also offer provocative stances in relation to gender questions.[21] Such forms of dissent invite punctual interrogation of civic sloth and political crimes; it remains for critical discourse to inscribe the artwork within the public sphere for a continued activation of their condensed and replete meaning.

The Present Moment

With the centrist, declaredly secular, pro-globalization Congress Party earning the election mandate in 2004 to form a coalition government (the United Progressive Alliance—UPA), what role was Sahmat able to play? Not surprisingly and indeed appropriately, Sahmat's position ran parallel, though on a relatively minor key, to the role played by Indian left parties when dealing with the alternating rule of the BJP and the Congress Party. The Communist parties of course are in direct confrontation with the BJP; they supported the ruling coalition led by the Congress Party from outside the government. The CPI(M), in particular, had a strong presence in three states and the elected parliament at the center; so together the Communists formed a large and articulate pressure group that offered critical collaboration as well as active resistance to the ruling ideology. It can be argued that Sahmat, too, launched a holding operation within what has always been defined as a progressive national—now perhaps just a liberal national—space. This involved activities of a more academic nature.

Since 2000–01 Sahmat has extended vigorous support for scientific history writing in a context where debates around the criteria of "truth," both at the advanced level of scholarship and at the level of textbooks for schoolchildren, were distorted by a communal government and its Hindutva ideology. A critical evaluation of the economic policy of not only the BJP, but also of the centrist, Congress-led government, has been sustained by economists on the Sahmat platform. Symposia have been held on the policy that the UPA government forged in consultation with its left allies in the form of a Common Minimum Programme (CMP), which included large-scale relief measures to ensure minimum wage and welfare provisions for the rural poor—a policy toward which the neoliberal elements within the government and outside it, among the "captains" of industry and the swelling middle class, show persistent disdain. This ideological critique now forms the fulcrum of the left agenda, and Sahmat, likewise, presses for greater recall of socialist antecedents in matters of economic and social justice while keeping a vigil on the correct rendering of election promises in education and culture. It hopes that by treating the *national as a continued site of struggle*, indeed by drawing on the largest, most inclusive legacy of democratic and anti-sectarian forces, it can engage with the changing discourse on modernization which now coalesces with agendas of economic liberalization that brazenly subsume people's rights within the hegemonic universe of global capital. It is necessary to recognize the ideologically overdetermined frame of the dream that India's ruling class is so eager to embrace: that of a global (super) power, with its economic and military strategies serving vested interests at home and in the West—emphatically the United States of America. It is precisely what the left alliance and the still substantially Marxist intellectuals in India are able to critique, and Sahmat has become one of the more public platforms for that purpose.

Does the Sahmat platform need to restructure itself?[22] Sahmat is criticized because earlier expectations of a *narodnik*-style populism, reminiscent of IPTA, were allowed to lapse. It has not become anything like a people's movement for an alternative culture hypothesized in terms of an alternative society with "revolutionary" caste and class politics. Though Sahmat determinedly exceeds the more conciliatory institutions and foreign-funded NGOs negotiating the norms of civil society—which sometimes operate as a ploy of the ruling class in a class-divided society—its own, more rigorous agendas may also be in need of a shake-up. The issues Sahmat tries to address are so fundamental as to be dealt with on several cultural and political sites. It now needs to be asked whether cultural politics in India must rely on the concept of the citizen within the terms of a national state that is itself facing an almost irretrievable contradiction: between democracy and the globalizing ambitions of a centrist government, between affluent India and the hugely turbulent polity with quite other political agendas on the ground. The issue is whether Sahmat's commitment to the modern nation state and to a left-wing nationalism can command unquestioned allegiance from a variously motivated, utterly volatile populace. The questions asked in theoretical support of these multiple sources of discontent are whether we must invest all energy into the "rights" discourse characterizing civil-society ethics, and whether there is not another form of politics that takes citizenship as problematic and interrogates the now unstable categories of nation and state. As much as its agendas are cultural, Sahmat may have to pitch its dynamic into an even more fraught public domain of politics where the terms of discourse and the possibilities of praxis are more conjectural and also more risky.

If Sahmat has to wedge itself into the burgeoning neoliberal economy of India (and its contingent, hugely flourishing art market), endowed with multiple subterfuges that undo class as well as nation and state, it must acknowledge that the historical reality on which a mandated left politics is sustained is not available in its classical form. We need to reconsider Sahmat's artistic practice considering that a younger, cosmopolitan artists' constituency rejects the nation-state and nationalism (even when these are offered by progressive forces) on the grounds that they must now deal with, participate in, and critique the irreversible process of globalization. By its very positioning, Sahmat has tried to sustain a minimum debate on the changing meaning of artistic radicalism and political commitment. In the process it has attempted to deploy strategies appropriate for art in the public domain, but its projects are mostly framed by known conventions and do not constitute an avant-garde within the terms of the practice itself—neither in language nor in terms of technologies. In fact, art as a social project on site—and such forms as mail art, agitprop poster campaigns, street expositions, as well as symposia and teach-ins—seems now to rest on a mediated exploration of aesthetics, discourse, and activism within the "norms" of *civil society*, and not of what stands as its dialectical pair: *political society*. This struggle with the contradiction between the radical in art and in politics cuts across the entire twentieth century, and Sahmat, it should be said, is not in command of any special aesthetic dispensation on these matters; it is even perhaps a little behind within the Indian context itself. How that context is evolving is another long and still speculative area of exploration that is not within the scope of this essay.[23]

I will, however, close this discussion with a related set of propositions. The Indian documentary and short film (in film/video/digital format) took a new and brave turn at the very time of the Naxalite movement, then again during the Emergency, and once more during the 1990s. Indeed one definition of the political "artist" of our time, at least in India, has become the radical documentarist, and the contradiction between the terms artist and documentarist may actually be the point from where to speak dialectically about the nature of art's radicality. For the moment I will name the best known among the 1980s' generation of Indian documentarists, Anand Patwardhan, whose work spans the period mentioned above.[24] His work proves the efficacy of (Brecht-like) pedagogy within the form of the documentary, addressed to large numbers of co-citizens with due rhetorical flamboyance and a pointed politics. It also exemplifies the role that such a figure plays in activating dormant debates on media, communication, and censorship within the public sphere, and, not least, in questioning state ideology and state policy on art, culture, and politics, thus catapulting civil-rights politics into direct political address.

Provoked by right-wing politics, documentarists from all over India have set up a platform (Vikalp, 2004) with more than 300 practitioners working to articulate and disseminate a critical relation to the nation and the state. It is also the documentary and independent/experimental video movement that suggests that the mode of critical address may now have to be differently devised. Amar Kanwar, India's most internationally celebrated documentarist today, is widely shown at public screenings and political forums; he is shown as widely in art spaces, including international museums and biennales, for his unique rendering of the moving image in documentary *and* avant-garde forms. Kanwar provides an advanced example of how a new criticality imbricates itself in what are also new subjectivities within the "abandoned" space of the national—as indeed, now, within the total dominion of global capital.[25]

When the national state, claiming custodianship of its people's economic interests, is handicapped and eventually even crippled by global capital, the widespread travail is accompanied by the emergence of fresh affiliations in the form of affirmative or, more properly, partisan action at the grassroots level. Some of this action is "documented" in the very process of formation by the filmmakers and videographers who are working independently, or with national and international NGOs. Covering the subterrain of a nation's neglected populace, this work looks towards human rights within renewed forms of normative discourse, and establishes the legitimacy of a micro-politics that promotes self-knowledge and empowerment for the subaltern subjects. However, grassroots activism may be quite circumspect and even compromised on account of easy international legitimacy and a corresponding, international-style humanitarian agenda that often substitutes the political for the ethnographic, and radicalism for sentimental forms of idealism. In this respect it is perhaps relevant to keep in focus the counter-reference—of a nationalist/statist engagement—such that Sahmat, now so frequently criticized, insists on maintaining.

The badge of secular artist—citizen artist, usefully defined within the terms of the nation-state, is now catapulted into a trans-subjective, "free zone" of democratic exchange which relies on an instant, quick-fire mode of communication at the global scale. Not surprisingly, younger artists tend to identify with these less "classical," more expansive realms of indeterminacy and often adapt a mediatic (expressly new media/cyberspace) version of the avant-garde, thereby sealing the rupture with all institutional associations of the *erstwhile* political. What the new political might be is being scripted, ironically, in fragments and within intensely discursive enclaves. It looks like it will be some time before it is able to make common cause with the idea and emergence of "multitudes," that putative "revolution" of the people who are now *on the move* as disenfranchised citizens, as migrant laborers in a deindustrialized era, as political refugees.[26] With the widespread conviction that the globe is now deterritorialized, the idea and very cause of this new politics (in India as elsewhere round the globe) is anarchist and virtual at once, and given the actual grip of global capital, it is euphorically pitched into a form of futurism.

Geeta Kapur is a Delhi-based art critic and curator. Her books include *Contemporary Indian Artists* (1978), *When Was Modernism: Essays on Contemporary Cultural Practice in India* (2000), and *Ends and Means: critical inscriptions in contemporary art* (forthcoming, 2013). One of the founder-editors of *Journal of Arts & Ideas*, she has participated in Sahmat's activities from the collective's inception. Her curatorial projects include the co-curated *Bombay/Mumbai* for *Century City: Art and Culture in the Modern Metropolis*, presented at Tate Modern, London, in 2001. A member of the Asian Art Council, Guggenheim Museum, she has served on the jury for the Venice Biennale, the Dakar Biennial, and the Sharjah Biennial. Her academic fellowships include the Institute of Advanced Study, Shimla; Nehru Memorial Museum and Library, Delhi; Clare Hall, University of Cambridge; Jawaharlal Nehru University, New Delhi; and University of Delhi, Delhi.

Geeta Kapur, "Secular Artist, Citizen Artist," in *Art and Social Change: A Critical Reader*, Will Bradley and Charles Esche, eds. (London: Tate Publishing in association with Afterall, 2007), 422–39. Reprinted with permission.

Notes

1. Reference here is to Edward Said's famous "Introduction: Secular Criticism," in his *The World, The Text and the Critic* (London: Vintage, 1991); and to his later monograph, *Representations of the Intellectual (The 1993 Reith Lectures)* (London: Vintage, 1994).

2. Partha Chatterjee, "Beyond the Nation? Or Within?," in Carolyn M. Elliott, ed., *Civil Society and Democracy: A Reader* (Delhi: Oxford University Press, 2003).

3. This includes, above all, the mass movement led during the 1940s by B.R. Ambedkar and his followers until the present day to claim an equitable space for the *dalits* in a modern Indian state; armed struggles by the Maoists/Naxalites to claim land rights for displaced peasants from the "landlord-capitalist" state; insurgencies by neglected/alienated "nationalities" and other minorities seeking autonomy from the space of the nation-state; forcible negotiations by disenfranchised labor and urban "slum" dwellers to secure their living rights.

4. See Sudhi Pradhan, ed., *Marxist Cultural Movement in India: Chronicles and Documents, Vol. III: 1943-64* (Calcutta: Mrs Pradhan [publisher], Pustak Bipani [distributor], 1985). See also Malini Bhattacharya, "The IPTA in Bengal," *Journal of Arts & Ideas*, no. 2, January-March 1983; and Rustom Bharucha, *Rehearsals for Revolution: Political Theatre in Bengal* (Calcutta: Seagull, 1983).

5. For example, two major post-independence artists—Maqbool Fida Husain and K. G. Subramanyan—can be said to have forged a painting vocabulary corresponding to what the Indian state, the intelligentsia, and an enlightened public would designate as national, modern, secular consciousness.

6. As an example I refer to the painter Francis Newton Souza (1924–2002), Goan-Catholic turned modernist, misogynist, universal antagonist—an *enfant terrible* of Indian art; and to Bhupen Khakhar (1934–2003), master subversionist who produced a remarkably unique iconography for gay sexuality. I also refer to feminist articulations by artists using a wide range of materials and strategies: for example, painters Arpita Singh and Nilima Sheikh; installation/video artists and photographers Nalini Malani, Rummana Hussain, Navjot Altaf, Sheela Gowda, Pushpamala N., Dayanita Singh, Anita Dube, Sheba Chhachhi, Sonia Khurana, Tejal Shah, and Shilpa Gupta. Together this output marks, quite literally, the full stretch of vanguard art practice in India.

7. I refer here to India's lofty tradition of *auteur*-based, modernist, and avant-garde cinema and, when we talk of testing the limits of sovereign-subjectivity, to filmmakers as diverse as Satyajit Ray, Ritwik Ghatak, Kumar Shahani, Mani Kaul, Mrinal Sen, and Adoor Gopalakrishnan.

8. During the Indian Emergency and later, between 1992–2004, when anti-secular/proto-fascist forces engineered riots and virtual genocide of the minorities in different parts of India, visual artists were able to articulate the rupture in the democratic equation between the state and the polity by changing the course of what until then was a largely classical/modernist art scene. Artists—foremost among them Vivan Sundaram, Nalini Malani, Rummana Hussain, and Navjot Altaf, followed by younger artists, especially the Mumbai-based Open Circle—incorporated documentary photography and switched over to sculptural and video installations, as well as public art interventions. By boldly changing their language-in-use, they also changed the subject-position of the artist, making it more unstable, more volatile, and more radical.

9 The Radical Painters' and Sculptors' Association (1987–89) was led by the dynamic K. P. Krishnakumar until his suicide in 1989. This brought a tragic closure to the youthful movement that questioned and refused all before them—in art and politics alike. See Anita Dube, *Questions and Dialogue*, exhibition catalog (Baroda: The Radical Painters' and Sculptors' Association, 1987), and Shivaji Panikkar, "Indian Radical Painters and Sculptors: Crisis of Political Art in Contemporary India," in Ratan Parimoo, ed., *Creative Arts in Modern India: Essays in Comparative Criticism*, Vol. II (Delhi: Books and Books, 1995). A strongly polemical handling of the issues is to be found in Ashish Rajadhyaksha, "The Last Decade," in Gulammohammed Sheikh, ed., *Contemporary Art in Baroda* (Delhi: Tulika Books, 1997).

10 Safdar Hashmi's street theatre group, Jana Natya Manch (People's Theatre Platform), run by his comrade-wife Moloyashree Hashmi and the group's ideologue, Sudhanva Deshande, sees itself inheriting some of its activist energies from IPTA; it also acts as a cultural front of the CPI(M). See, among their other publications, a special issue of their journal, *Nukkad Janam Samvad*, on "People's Art in the Twentieth Century: Theory and Practice," vol. II/III, nos. 4–8, July 1999–September 2000.

11. Arindam Dutta, "SAHMAT, 1989–2004: Liberal Art Practice against the Liberalized Public Sphere," *Cultural Dynamics* (London, Thousand Oaks, CA, and New Delhi: Sage Publications, 2005), 199. There are scores of very important publications produced by Sahmat that spell out its activities, its ideology, and its battles.

12. The term "communalism" has a negative meaning in Indian usage; the descriptive term—communal—is turned to mean religious and ethnic sectarianism, and those hostile forms of identity politics that generate inter-community violence.

13. The mystical strains in Islamic and Hindu religions merge from the twelfth century to generate a culture at once philosophic, popular and syncretic. *Sufi-bhakti*, a performative tradition, continues until the nineteenth century, producing remarkably beautiful, radical, and enlightened poetry and music. Musicologists/musicians Madan Gopal Singh and Shubha Mudgal, active members of Sahmat, initiated a virtually new movement in Indian performing arts by conceiving and choreographing Sahmat's musical caravans.

14. Habib Tanvir (1923–2009) was one of India's foremost theatre directors: active since the 1940s with the most radical art movements in northern India (PWA and IPTA), he trained at theatre schools in England (RADA and Bristol Old Vic), returned to India, and formed his repertory company Naya Theatre in the late 1950s. Pioneering a new relationship between the vernacular and the modern (between actors from rural and urban Indian contexts; between texts from Sanskrit and Renaissance traditions; between social realist, Brechtian, and popular forms), his theatre exemplified the most advanced form of democratic parity in the conception of contemporary arts in post-independence India. An inveterate atheist/iconoclast, Tanvir was born into a Muslim family, and has been heckled and attacked by conservative audiences, usually Hindu groups claiming to be offended by his handling of religion and caste.

The artist Maqbool Fida Husain (1915–2011) has been an icon for the national imagination and has moulded perceptions of modern art and visual culture in post-independence India. Hindu fundamentalists now declare Husain's portrayal of Indian iconography (drawn throughout his long career from the prodigious resource of Hindu mythology) to be offensive to Hindu sentiments. In the last decade or so of his life he had dozens of criminal cases pending against him in courts all over India and was forced into exile.

Tanvir performed for and was staunchly defended by Sahmat whenever he faced attacks. Husain, though not especially close to the left or to Sahmat, received support from Sahmat in the form of press statements, representations to the government, symposia, and publications. There was a sustained effort to persuade the public and the very state that honored him with the highest awards to safeguard his life and art.

15. At a more experimental level Vivan Sundaram (activist-artist and founder-trustee of Sahmat) has curated several exhibitions for Sahmat, such as an international exhibition of mail art, *Gift for India* (1997), followed (in 2001) by a playful public art project on the Delhi streets called *Art on the Move*. In 2004 and 2007 exhibitions on the diverse history of this nation have been curated by another Sahmat activist, the photographer-designer Ram Rahman.

16. Curated in 2002 by Vivan Sundaram, this large exhibition comprised of seminal works from the preceding decade. As always with Sahmat, it was organized on a shoestring budget with committed contributions from artists and Sahmat sympathizers. Openly critical of the belligerently anti-Sahmat, ruling right-wing government the exhibition showed 100-or-so artworks, including some very large installations, in a public space run by the State Academy of Fine Arts (Lalit Kala Akademi). It hosted films and discussions and involved large audiences including political leaders in a dialogue with artworks that dared to speak up against the onslaught of fascistic tendencies in the country.

17. I refer to the artists Gulammohammed Sheikh, Nilima Sheikh, and Arpana Caur.

18. See Akeel Bilgrami, "Secularism, Nationalism and Modernity," in Rajeev Bhargava, ed., *Secularism and Its Critics* (Delhi: Oxford University

Press, 1998); and "Gandhi, Newton and the Enlightenment," *Social Scientist*, vol. 34 nos. 5–6, May–June 2006.

19. I refer to the artists Akbar Padamsee, Surendran Nair, and Atul Dodiya.

20. Reference is to landmark installations by Vivan Sundaram, Rummana Hussain, Navjot Altaf, N. N. Rimzon, Pushpamala N., Sheba Chhachhi, and Tejal Shah, all made in the aftermath of communal riots. Reference is also to a growing body of critical iconography about violence by Arpita Singh, Sudhir Patwardhan, Nalini Malani, Nataraj Sharma, Gargi Raina, and Jitish Kallat. Also included in the exhibition were works and documentation of initiatives by artist-resistance groups in Baroda, Mumbai, and Bangalore who prepared image-text exhibitions in the midst of communal riots in their cities.

21. Artists Savi Savarkar, Suranjan Basu, Probir Gupta, Veer Munshi, Altaf Mohamedi, M. J. Enas, and Riyas Komu, working in different mediums, referred to the persistence of caste, class, ethnic, and religious conflict, as did photographers Ram Rahman, Parthiv Shah, Pablo Bartholomew, and Prashant Panjiar. Artists Jehangir Jani, Inder Salim, and Walter D'Souza referred to gender dilemmas.

22. Besides the more journalistic attacks, there are of course recurring critical evaluations of Sahmat. The oppositional polemic sustained by the cultural theorist Rustom Bharucha (see his *In the Name of the Secular: Contemporary Cultural Activism in India*, Delhi: Oxford University Press, 1998) is to be positioned within the terms of his larger interrogation of secularism and left politics. Arindam Dutta's critique ("SAHMAT, 1989–2004") is the most remarkably researched and argued text yet written on Sahmat. In an elegant if elegiac form of narration, Dutta marks the peaking of Sahmat's role in a direct adversarial mode against an aggressive right wing, and enumerates, regretfully, the reasons that Sahmat seems to have arrived at some form of closure.

23. Avant-gardist practices have emerged from other artist-run groups: the Raqs Media Collective, a trio located in the city of Delhi, have developed a theory and practice of documentary/video/new media art to generate extended allegories of subversion and site them punctually in cyber-*mohallas* (neighborhoods) and cosmopolitan expositions alike. Given their preferred tropes of migration/displacement and marginality/surveillance, they function across the transcultural zone of global art and bring a unique conceptual-discursive politics into the Indian art scene. Open Circle (Mumbai) is engaged in the activist genre of public art—on the streets of Mumbai protesting/"performing" along with people's resistance movements, or at sites such as the World Social Forum in Mumbai and other cities of the world. Youthful organizations that are not quite as political, such as Khoj (Delhi), break the ground with workshops and residencies hosting eccentric and transgressive artists from all over the world. New initiatives are also now being encouraged in the private sector where all art, even radical art, is subject (of course) to rapid commodification. What Sahmat might do in the face of a rampant art market boom that draws Indian artists into the vortex is another story altogether!

24. For an update on Patwardhan's films, see www.patwardhan.com. For a radical contextualization of his film practice, see Anand Patwardhan, "Waves of Revolution and Prisoners of Conscience: The Guerrilla Film, Underground and in Exile," M. A. Thesis, Department of Art History and Communications, McGill University, Autumn 1981. Patwardhan has seen himself, and has been seen by film theorists such as Paul Willemen (see Jim Pines and Paul Willeman, eds., *Questions of Third Cinema*, London: BFI Publishing, 1989), as continuing to contribute to the famous debate initiated by the critics and filmmakers Gettino and Solanas in a work titled *Towards a Third Cinema*. Other references to Patwardhan include: Sean Cubitt, "Interview with Anand Patwardhan," *Framework*, vol. 30/31, 1986; Robert Crusz and Priyath Liyanage, "Interview with Anand Patwardhan," *Framework*, vol. 38/39, 1992; Miriam Sharma, "Anand Patwardhan: Social Activist and Dedicated Filmmaker," *Critical Asian Studies*, vol. 34, no. 2, June 2002.

25. A selected filmography for Amar Kanwar includes: *A Season Outside*, 1998; *Matrubhoomi*, 2000; *The Many Faces of Madness*, 2000; *King of Dreams*, 2001; *A Night of Prophecy*, 2002; *To Remember*, 2003; *Somewhere in May*, 2005; and *The Face*, 2005 (the first pair from his ongoing project of four films on Burma). See Amar Kanwar, *Notes for A Night of Prophecy* (Chicago: The Renaissance Society, 2003); Anne Rutherford, "'Not firing arrows': Multiplicity, Heterogeneity and the Future of Documentary. An interview with Amar Kanwar," *Asian Cinema*, vol 16, no. 1, Spring 2005; Ida Kierulf, "Amar Kanwar—Portraits," exhibition catalog (Oslo: Fotogalleriet, 2005); Marit Paasche, "Strong Political Film Portraits," *Aftenposten*, October 2005; Jerry Saltz, "Worlds Apart—A Meditation on Separation: Amar Kanwar Walks the Border Between India and Pakistan," *Village Voice*, February 2004.

26. Michael Hardt and Antonio Negri, *Empire* (Cambridge, MA: Harvard University Press, 2000).

Karin Zitzewitz

Signature and the Secularity of Artistic Subjectivity

Sahmat has commanded the nearly unanimous support of the Indian art world. The country's most prestigious and best-known artists routinely participate in its activities. They sign petitions, demonstrate in the street, attend public events, and, perhaps most importantly, they donate performances and works of art to Sahmat's projects and exhibitions. As with all participatory politics, the visibility of the artists' actions is essential, but Sahmat's activities are rarely spectacular in the manner of mass movements. Sahmat-sponsored events are typically small in scale and immediate in address. The organization's geographical breadth and its ability to induce artist communities across India to act simultaneously are dazzling, however. In addition to events that attempt to engage a nonelite public, Sahmat also holds exhibitions in more exclusive art world spaces, encouraging artists to explore the character of the secular and its relationship to their artistic practice. These exhibitions posit a productive relationship between a political commitment to secularism and an artistic practice that is at once ethically rigorous and fundamentally critical.

As Geeta Kapur argues in this volume, all of Sahmat's actions rely upon the idea of the exemplary "artist-citizen." While this role for the artist may seem to be unusually bounded and instrumental, it also emphasizes the relationship between the knowledge practices of art, the constitution of artistic subjectivity, and practices of citizenship. The focus on ethical practice is central to Sahmat's anticommunal activities, which distinguish between Hindu nationalism as religion-as-ideology and religion-as-practice, as found in the devotional practices of *Bhakti* and Sufi Islam. Sahmat's actions in the aftermath of the 1992 mosque demolition in Ayodhya, including the 1993 *Anhad Garje* and *Muktnaad* concerts and the *Hum Sab Ayodhya* exhibition, hinge on that distinction. Collaborations of performing artists and historians, these events celebrated and provided evidence of what Sahmat typically describes as the "Bhakti-Sufi traditions," the syncretic devotional practices that, they argue, span the divisions between Hindus and Muslims in everyday life. Sahmat opposes a definition of secularism as the absence of religiosity, for that would needlessly deprive people of ethical resources and expressive pleasures. Instead, it finds secular ethics—especially the toleration of difference—in both the religious Bhakti and Sufi traditions and a broadly secular tradition of modern art.

Later projects with visual artists, particularly *Postcards for Gandhi* (1995) and a portion of the *Ways of Resisting* exhibition (2002–03), explicitly suggest commonalities between these embodied and aesthetically rich forms of religious practice and the secular practices of artistic creation. By calling what artists do "secular practice," I mean to mark as normatively secular the body of attitudes, sensibilities, and knowledge that underlie the production of art. But I also wish to compare secular practice to the more common categories of artistic practice, which comprises the range of critical and embodied techniques entailed in the production of art, and religious practice, which typically focuses on everyday rituals and bodily acts associated with religious faith. Indian art's secularity derives from the country's participation in a transnational history of modernism in the late colonial period. But it also stems from the conscious commitment of artists to the secular-nationalist project of nation building, a project that Sahmat sees itself as maintaining, if in an unusually critical manner. And so, through these exhibitions the organization has engaged in a thoughtful interrogation of this commitment, exploring the role that secularity plays in connecting everyday practice and ethical commitments to politics.

Sahmat's campaigns maintain the individuality of artistic practices—most Sahmat exhibitions do not encourage artists to work collectively, as such, but rather invite them to approach issues on their own terms—while giving them the opportunity to stretch their usual practice through the introduction of constraints or unusual media. That approach both facilitates the participation of commercially successful artists and, more significantly, links Sahmat's activities to the forms of art pedagogy developed in Santiniketan and Baroda (Vadodara), connecting the projects of the 1990s to a deeper history of modern Indian art. Those art pedagogies focused in part in developing the subjectivity of the artist as an exemplary figure, one whose work is at once expressive of culture and critical of it. That idea of the artist was later marshaled in the defense of M. F. Husain, in an enthusiastic campaign that hinged upon the idea that Husain's "life and work . . . [could] serve as an allegory for the changing modalities of the secular in modern India."[1]

Practice: Religious, Secular, Artistic

The distinction between a pernicious ideological form of religion and a more enriching domain of religious practice is most closely associated with Indian psychoanalyst and cultural critic Ashis Nandy's critique of secularism. Nandy adopted this framework in an essay published in 1990, although he used the word "faith" where I use "practice."[2] Nandy's definition of faith—"religion as a way of life, a tradition that is definitionally non-monolithic and operationally plural"[3]—emphasizes both eclecticism and the everyday, and appears as a reservoir of depth of feeling and complexity that counteracts the bounded categories of state secularism. Nandy excoriates secularism and those who defend it, writing that "secularism has little to say about cultures . . . and the orthodox secularists have no clue to the way a religion can link up different faiths or ways of life according to its own configurative principles."[4] Because secularism depends on religion-as-ideology, he writes, it is incapable of dealing with the more fluid conceptions of the self that are common in South Asian societies. That is a problem, because only those fluid conceptions of self can support the ethic of toleration prized by secularists.

Nandy was not the first to identify the distinction between ideology and faith/practice in religion. Taken slightly more generally, this distinction was crucial among the left-influenced, late-colonial primitivist, and post-independence modernist artists who privileged "the folk" as the most crucial subject of art.[5] In their images, practices that could be considered religious were typically understood as everyday forms of life.[6] But Nandy's essay reacts to a context in which the project of state secularism was acknowledged to be in crisis. In the decades after the publication of Nandy's influential essay, Sahmat has worked to answer its claims by not only criticizing culturally arid treatments of religion—including those that take easy recourse to a disenchanted category of "the folk"—but also insisting upon the importance of secularism's

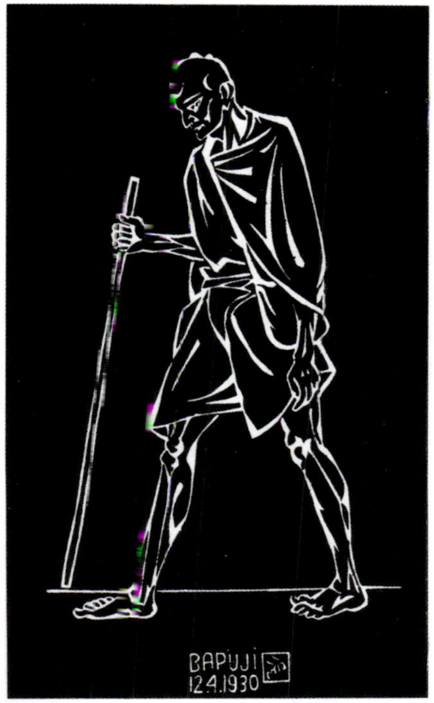

FIG. 1 Nandalal Bose, *Dandi March (Bapuji)*, 1930, linocut, 11½ x 6½ inches. Collection: National Gallery of Modern Art, New Delhi.

defense. Sahmat does so by drawing upon the rich set of discussions of artistic practice and pedagogy that developed over the twentieth century in two colleges of fine arts: Kala Bhavana of Visva-Bharati University, the Institute of Fine Arts, in Santiniketan, and the Faculty of Fine Arts of the Maharaja Sayajirao University in Baroda. Artists associated with those institutions articulated how the secular epistemologies of modernist art could be integrated into the wider field of Indian visual culture, and many of those artists later became active in Sahmat.

Santiniketan's Kala Bhavana, with Nandalal Bose as its head **(FIG. 1)** directly countered the colonial syllabus of art instruction, which had mimetic drawing as its foundation, by encouraging students to pursue multiple disciplines. Craftsmen were also invited to demonstrate their skills, and students sat alongside their professors to master popular art practices. The curriculum at M. S. University was fashioned in part by Santiniketan-trained artists, particularly in the period in which K. G. Subramanyan was dean. As Nilima Sheikh has written, Subramanyan paid unusual attention to the physical aspect of art-making, often prescribing a set of physical exercises to help students overcome problems of representation.[7] But he also

FIG. 3 Ram Rahman, *Gandhi March*, 1995, photograph, 5¾ x 3½ inches.

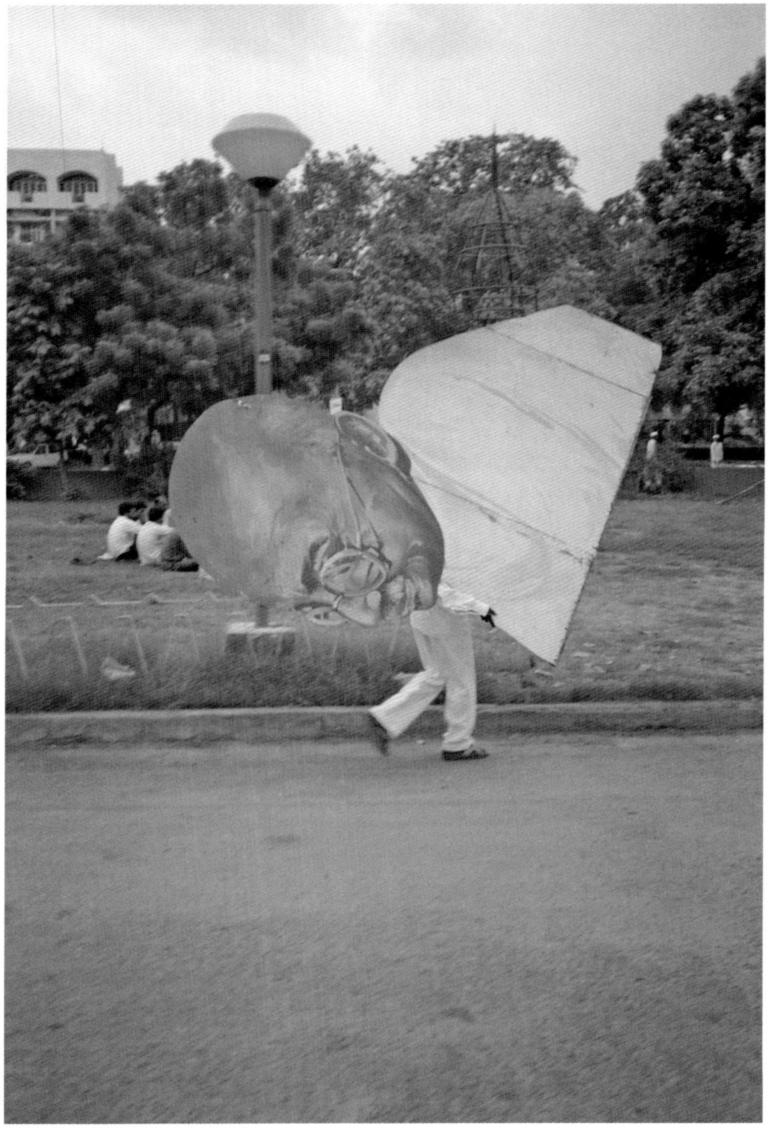

insisted that a critical attitude distinguished art from craft and he urged students to think carefully about translating their intentions into their work. The cross-medium approach begun at Santiniketan was continued in Baroda, most importantly during an annual Faculty of Fine Arts Fair, a time in which students worked collaboratively and in unfamiliar mediums to produce cheap works that would appeal to the public.

Baroda artists recalled that kind of practice as they worked together to produce a group of linocuts for the *Postcards for Gandhi* exhibition in 1995. They chose the medium used by Nandalal Bose in 1930 to produce an iconic image of Gandhi. The results are indifferent—none of the images come close to Bose's in strength—but together, they gesture toward the place of practice itself, including communal experimentation with new mediums, in artistic production.

Postcards for Gandhi: Ethics, Embodiment, Critique

Postcards for Gandhi opened on the 126th anniversary of Mahatma Gandhi's birth, October 2, 1995, in art galleries in the six largest cities in India: Ahmedabad, Bangalore, Bombay (Mumbai), Calcutta (Kolkata), Madras (Chennai), and New Delhi. Sahmat invited one hundred artists to produce six postcard-sized works, which were then divided among the venues. The postcard was Gandhi's favored form of communication, allowing him cheaply and efficiently to maintain correspondence with a wide array of people, both in India and internationally. It is therefore one item in Gandhi's extraordinarily recognizable iconography, which includes both objects that the leader used—sandals, glasses, walking stick—and his body itself.

Most of the artists worked with this repertoire of Gandhian signs. Many works were mournful, treating the objects as memento mori. But others were more pointedly ironic in tone. In one particularly effective work, *Atul Dodiya*, an artist known for both his skillful painting and his appropriation and reuse of popular images, submitted a charcoal drawing of the well-known photograph of Gandhi reaching down to harvest salt in Dandi, the culmination of a

1930 march resisting the colonial salt tax **(FIG. 2)**. Dodiya's drawing appears on a palimpsest of a sheet of one-rupee stamps, which have Gandhi's face, layering a dynamic image of noncooperation over a static image issued by the postcolonial state. Ram Rahman's photograph of a man carrying a huge billboard of Gandhi's head similarly, if more humorously, points to how absurdly the leader's memory has been coopted **(FIG. 3)**. Pushpamala N. makes a similar point simply by attaching to her postcard a small spindle of homespun thread and a toothpick flag sealed in tiny plastic bags **(FIG. 4)**. These works point to the failure of the Indian state to live up to Gandhi's aims and forms of discipline.

Other works represent the practices promoted by Gandhi as an alignment of ethics and politics while highlighting the bodily practices of art-making. Nilima Sheikh shows the barest of outlines of Gandhi spinning, in an extraordinary gestural but controlled watercolor **(FIG. 5)**. Sudhir Patwardhan submitted an exquisite pencil drawing reproducing a well-known 1899 image of Gandhi volunteering with the Indian Ambulance Corps during the Boer War in South Africa **(FIG. 6)**. In these works, such skill is evidence of training, of the embodied practices of art that constitute artistic self-discipline. For Gandhi, bodily discipline, cultivated through the craft of spinning, for instance, was both the prerequisite for political subjectivity and an operation of it.[8] Rummana Hussain's photograph straightforwardly makes that point **(FIG. 7)**. It shows a woman spinning thread in Saidanpur, in the Barabanki District of Uttar Pradesh, accompanied by the caption "Co-Existence. Self-Reliance. Interdependence. Mahatma Gandhi."

If *Postcards for Gandhi* challenged artists to work within unusual constraints, *Ways of Resisting*, curated by Vivan Sundaram in the wake of devastating pogroms in Gujarat in 2002, highlighted the manner in which artists had consistently worked against the atmosphere of violence of the decade before. The question of what ethical, political, and artistic meanings can emerge from practice, which was at the core of the Gandhi exhibition, drove one section of *Ways of Resisting*, which collected works that "questioned the easy appropriation of the Indian tradition . . . by the distorting

FIG. 4 Pushpamala N., *Untitled*, 1995, spindle and flag in plastic bags, 3½ x 5¾ inches.

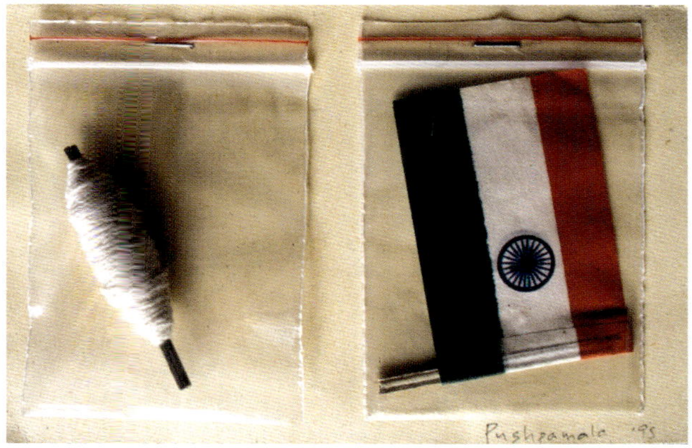

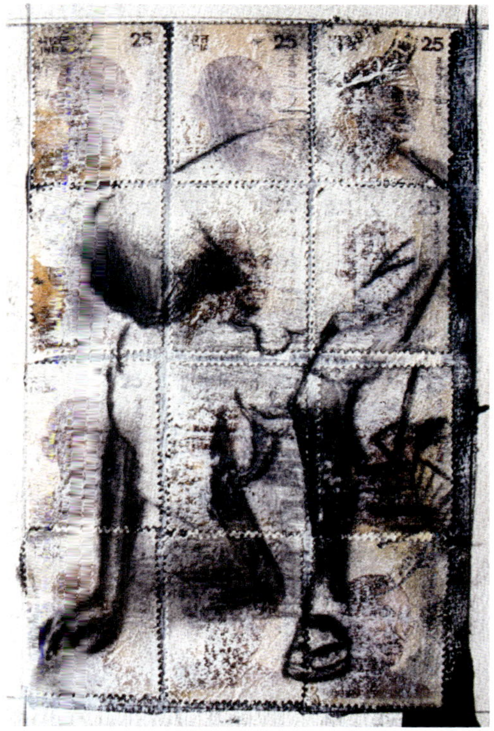

FIG. 2 Atul Dodiya, *Bapu IV*, 1995, mixed media, 5¾ x 3½ inches.

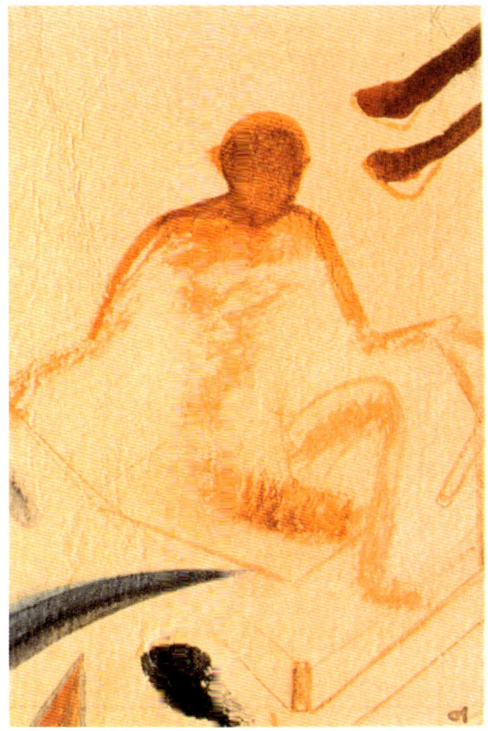

FIG. 5 Nilima Sheikh, *Untitled*, 1995, watercolor on paper, 5¾ x 3½ inches.

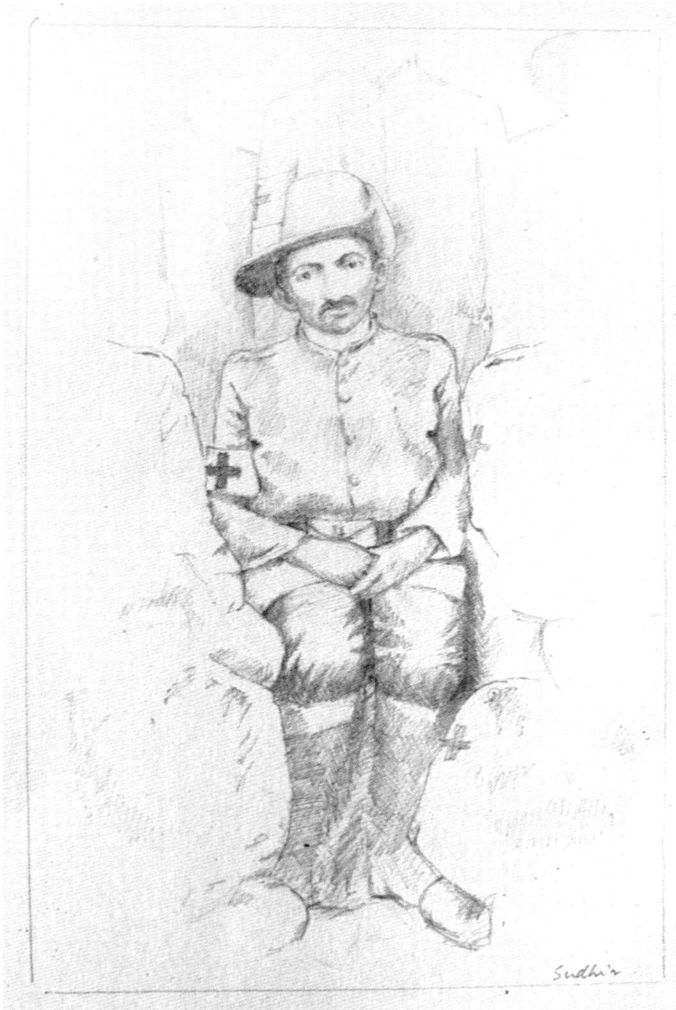

FIG. 6 Sudhir Patwardhan, *Gandhiji No. 1*, 1995, pencil, 5¾ x 3½ inches.

ideology of Hindutva."[9] But that section was flanked by two others that highlighted emerging artistic approaches to the question of communal violence: one emphasized the movement of Indian artists into installation and photography-based practice, and the other focused on artists' engagements with urban space. Those were also the two most important formal shifts in Indian contemporary art in the 1990s. While the works included in this exhibition may have been more uniformly focused on issues of political import, *Ways of Resisting* also reads as an excellent summary of artistic practice over the decade, in general. The exhibition therefore stands as confirmation of the seamless connection between secularist activism and artistic practice.

Sahmat-sponsored exhibitions do not differ in structure from others routinely staged in India. The works of art shown in *Ways of Resisting* were familiar to viewers from exhibitions in commercial galleries, as were the artists who participated in *Postcards for Gandhi*. As architectural historian Arindam Dutta has observed, these events do not resemble the sort of public artistic interventions that constitute political art in other parts of the world.[10] Sahmat's art exhibitions have so far confirmed rather than subverted the reflexive nature of much of contemporary art production, in which works of art point back to their makers. Sahmat is clearly invested in the signature of the artist as a potent site of meaning and value.

M. F. Husain: Citizen, Artist, Exemplar

The potential fruits of that investment are nowhere clearer than in Sahmat's defense of M. F. Husain. Beginning with the 1996 campaign by Hindu nationalist groups against the artist's so-called nude goddesses, Sahmat has spearheaded the public defense of Husain's work. The organization has simultaneously pursued three distinct arguments. One provides a classic liberal defense of Husain's freedom of expression, both as a person and invoking a legal exception established in Indian case law, as an artist.[11] The second follows the example of *Hum Sab Ayodhya* by establishing the art historical precedents for Husain's images. In a series of articles, historians of art have argued that Hindutva's sensitivity to eroticism is actually quite new.[12] A third set of arguments presents Husain as an exemplary artist-citizen who should be honored, not reviled, for his role in the development of a modern art responsive to the visual culture of the Indian people. This last argument was made most eloquently in the Bharat Ratna petition described above, which was sent in the midst of the last, decisive attack on the artist, the campaign that led Husain to place himself in voluntary exile.

That petition lauded Husain's versions of Hindu iconography, noting that his work with the *Ramayana* and the *Mahabharata* was grounded in a vision of those epics as almost infinitely flexible and adaptable to a variety of historical contexts. It noted how Husain recognized the diversity of the Indian nation and its "syncretic civilization," and he helped to shape the imperative faced by the modern Indian artist: "to evolve a uniquely modern language consistent with the complexity of [Indian] civilizational narratives." But finally, and most interestingly, the petition argues that "Husain is such an iconic figure that we could use the very iconography of Maqbool Fida Husain, *of the person himself*, to forward ideas about Indian visual culture in the framework of a dynamic public sphere." This is the crux of the argument, as it captures the way that Sahmat treats the ideology of artistic expression as a useful social fact. Instead of pursuing forms of art that might expose the relationship of subjectivity to expression, artist to work, as problematic, Sahmat's actions keep those links intact and marshal them for political effect.

Presenting M. F. Husain as an exemplary artist-citizen, Sahmat also defines art as a field of political and ethical possibility, an expressive domain in which the potential meanings of culture can be freely explored. It is worth noting that this strategy departs from other models for the relationship between art and politics. That includes the leftist cultural organizations that are Sahmat's precursors, like the Progressive Writers' Association. But it may also be this attitude, combined with a view of artistic practice as the site where a critical subjectivity and bodily discipline meet, that accounts for Sahmat's prestige in the Indian art world.

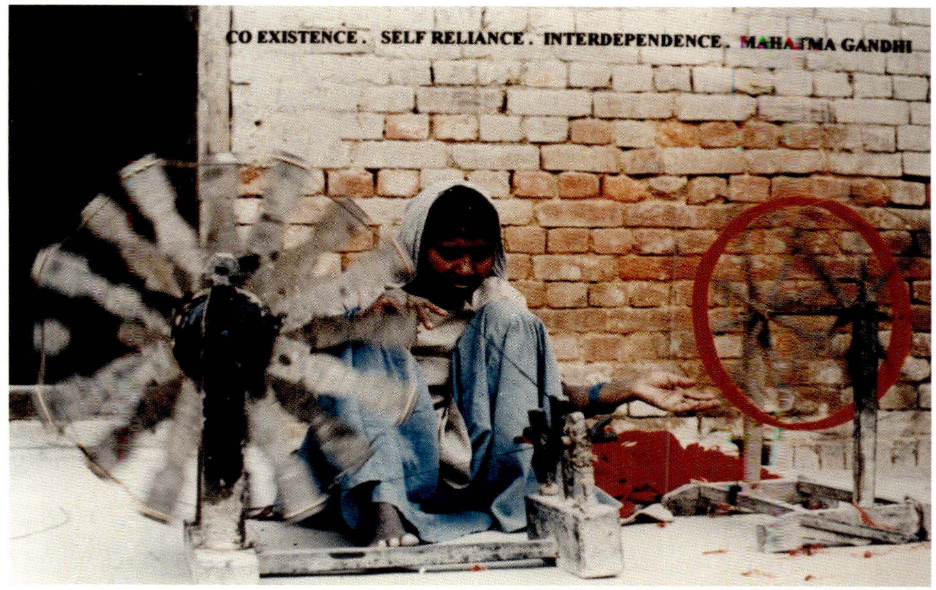

FIG. 7 Rummana Hussain, photograph of a woman in Saidanpur, Barabanki, 1995, 3½ x 5¾ inches.

Karin Zitzewitz is assistant professor of art history and visual culture at Michigan State University. She received her PhD in anthropology from Columbia University in 2006. Her forthcoming book, *The Art of Secularism: The Cultural Politics of Modernist Art in Contemporary India*, traces the effects of the rise of Hindu nationalism in India upon the profoundly secular practices of art. She collaborated with Mumbai gallerist Kekoo Gandhy on a memoir, *The Perfect Frame: Presenting Modern Indian Art* (2003). She has published articles in *Third Text* and *Visual Anthropology Review*.

Rebecca Zorach

Accumulations in Space and Time: Sahmat's Gifts for India

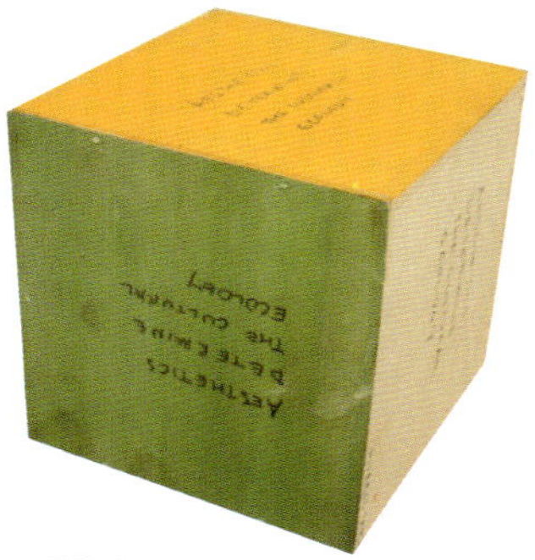

FIG. 1
Michael Morris, *Aesthetics Determine the Cultural Ecology*, 1997, mixed media, 5 x 5 x 5 inches.

FIG. 2
Ilona Lovas, *Untitled*, 1997, mixed media, 5 x 5 x 5 inches.

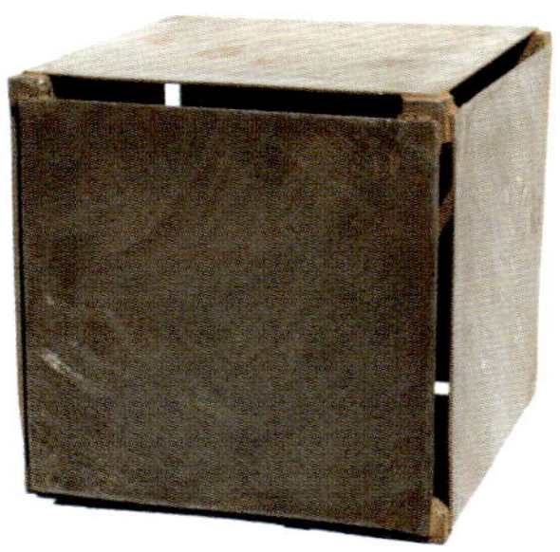

Among the array of projects produced by the indefatigable Indian collective known as Sahmat, the 1997 *Gift for India* makes itself legible as part of the global contemporary art world—perhaps one could say a global dialogue on socially and politically engaged art practice. It is formally sophisticated, and many of the participants were international. As a project honoring the fiftieth anniversary of India's independence, *Gift for India* was presented at Lalit Kala Akademi Galleries in New Delhi and incorporated contributions by multiple artists, each starting from the basic medium of a five-inch cube. Artists made cubes out of many different media. They built on, decorated, deconstructed, or filled the cube; they used it as a space for scrawling pointed political messages or creating subtle visual associations; a few radically changed its shape. The basic structure was an intimate version of a minimalist cube—a lineage visible in Michael Morris's *Aesthetics Determine the Cultural Ecology* (**FIG. 1**) or Ilona Lovas's lightly textured metal cube (**FIG. 2**).

In Vivan Sundaram's introduction to the *Gift for India*'s project catalogue, he connects the project to earlier Sahmat interventions, such as *Artists Against Communalism: Images and Words* (1991) and *Postcards for Gandhi* (1995). Sundaram's rubric for all these projects is "mail art"—he thus ties them to a set of practices in play since the 1960s that use the postal system as the medium or vehicle for art. This strategy is just one of several strategies through which Sahmat has creatively exploited old-technology networks—print media, public and vehicular installations (on bicycles, auto-rickshaws, and taxis) and the mail—to provide effective communication to a large and far-flung population with limited access to the internet.[1] For example, in *Images and Words*, part of the 1992 project *Artists Against Communalism*, participants were invited to send images and text on eleven-inch squares that were arranged on canvas panels in grids of three by three. The panels were displayed informally on bamboo easels that were easily transported to allow for open-air installation in thirty different cities in 1991–92 (**FIG. 3**).[2] The combination of text and image and the variety of levels of complexity and sophistication made the work accessible; its portable format allowed a broad public to engage in discussion.

Many of the cubes in *Gift for India* were overtly political in their content. They display political messages (**FIG. 4**), presented as meaningfully empty boxes, prisons, or, as in K. S. Radhakrishnan's *Free to Struggle*, a platform from which to seek freedom (**FIG. 5**). But it might seem, looking with the jaundiced eye of the contemporary art world, that the formal structure of the project had no particular political force. Many of the participating artists played with the notion of the cube as container, or used an idiom of the gift—as in the wrappings, stamps, and mailing addresses in Carlos Altamirano's *Terra de mi casa* (**FIG. 6**). As an accumulation of gifts, the project addressed not only mobility and movement across borders but also generosity as a key theme. As a feature of contemporary art, generosity has potential to serve as a challenge, subtle or more overt, to market economies (and by extension, perhaps, to the speculative and simulacral logic of the late capitalist art market).[3] But can the simple idea of the gift really bear this much ideological ambition? Generosity seems easily reduced to an undistinguished virtue that has long been an assumed feature of art practices. The artist, after all, has always given something to the viewer—even if he or she also holds something back.

In fact, I would argue that the form of the exhibition was as important as the content of the cubes, not because it was an accumulation of gifts but because it was an accumulation of individual expressions: it performed pluralism against communalism.[4] The term *communalism* has specific resonance in South Asia, where it refers to ethnic or religious nationalism—the political and sometimes violent privileging of one particular community. *Gift for India* works against this formation. Its metaphor is one of donation, but also of architecture: the cubes are building blocks of a national and international community distinct from the "communal"—in principle infinitely inclusive and extensible. As accumulation, the cubes suggest a basic ground of commonality (most participants stuck to this format even as a few altered it) that is equal and antihierarchical. Like the gift, pluralism is a value we might not have expected to find threatened, or, conversely, deeply politicized. But in the context of the rise of Hindu nationalism in India, pluralism has come to constitute a very assertive statement.

CLOCKWISE FROM TOP LEFT

Panel from *Images and Words.* Work by (from left to right and top to bottom): Ramlal Dhar, Abid Alami, Prayag Jha, Manmohan Bawa, Virendra Prabhakar, J. K. Chillar, Debes Ray, Nirmal Kapoor, and V. K. Asthana.

Vijayan Kannampilly, *Untitled*, 1997, watercolor on cardboard box, 5 x 5 x 5 inches.

K. S. Radhakrishnan, *Free to Struggle*, 1997, bronze, approximately 8 x 8 x 12 inches. Collection: Lalit Nirula.

Carlos Altamirano, *Terra de mi casa*, 1997, mixed media, 5 x 5 x 5 inches.

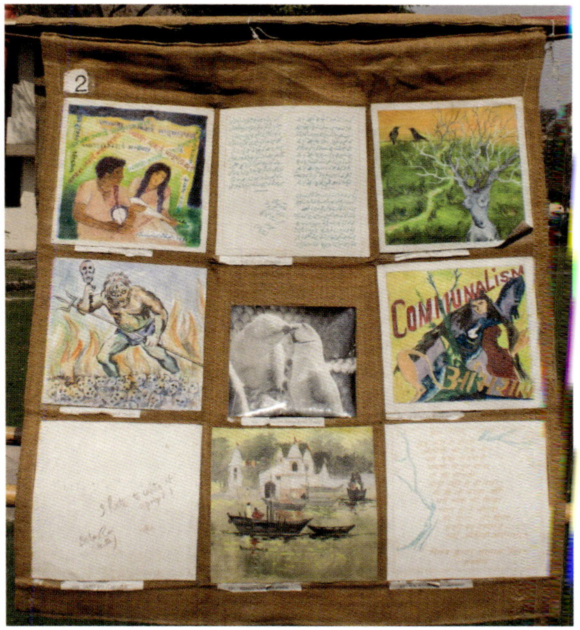

FIG. 3

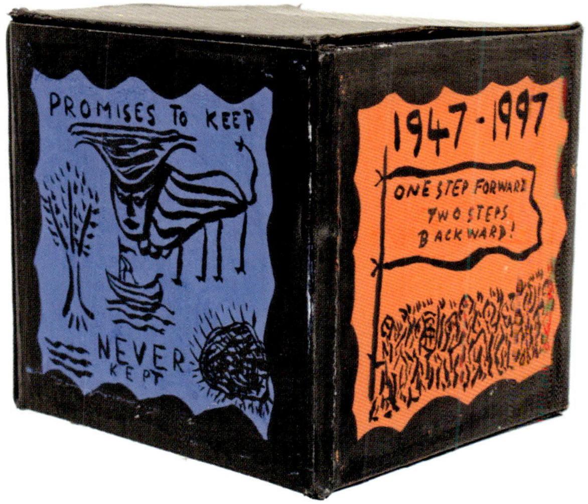

FIG. 4

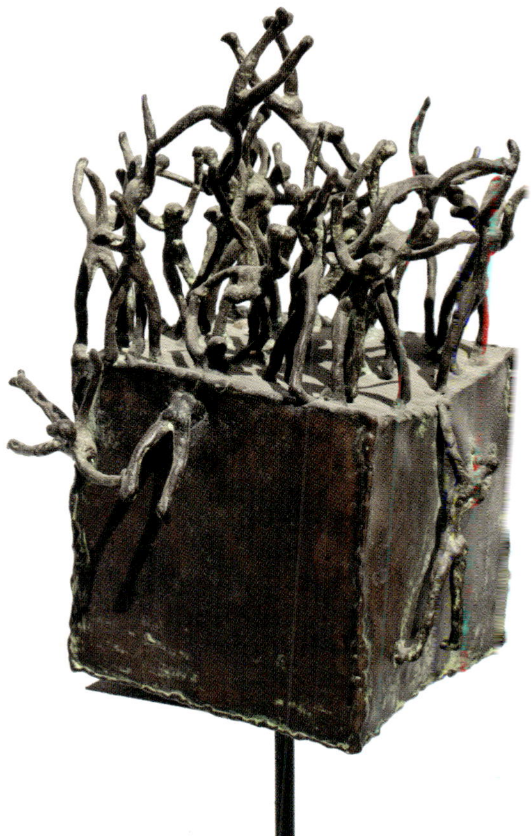

FIG. 5

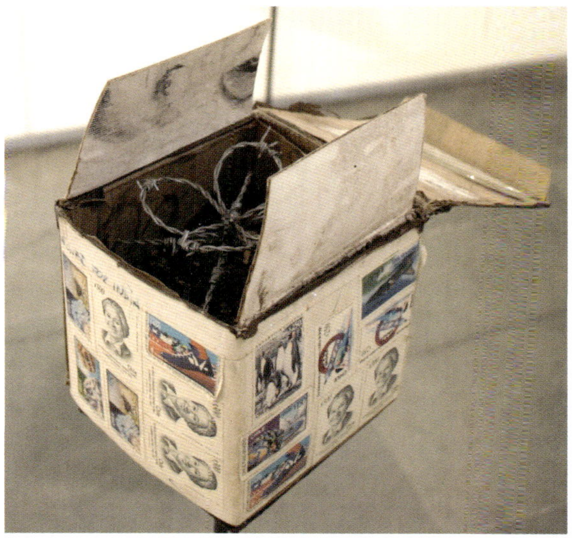

FIG. 6

FIG. 7 Work from *Hum Sab Ayodhya*, as installed at *Image, Music, Text: 20 Years of Sahmat*, M. F. Husain Gallery, Jamia Millia Islamia University, New Delhi, 2009.

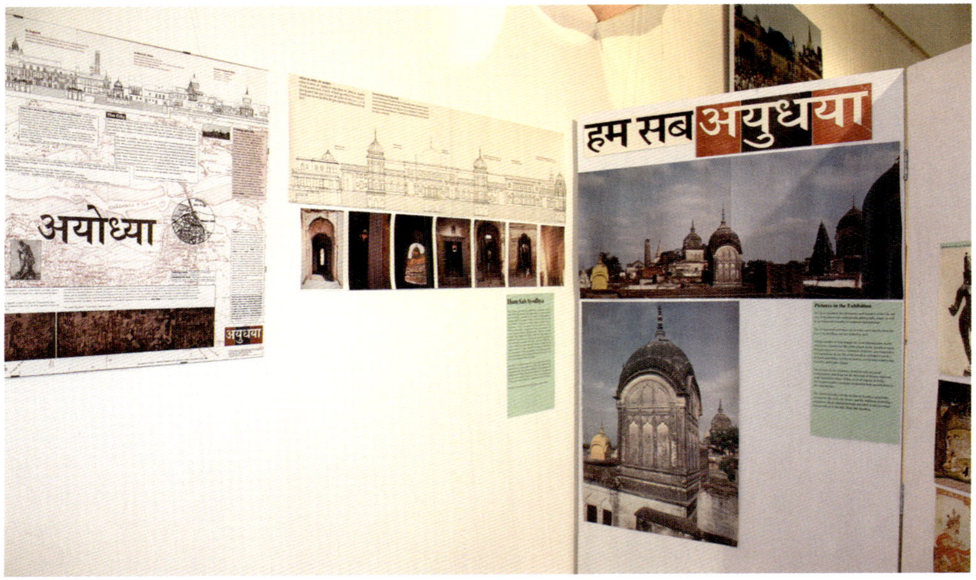

The structure of the *Gift* is more or less infinitely extensible. One can always add another five-inch cube. Each one constitutes a space to be occupied creatively by an individual artist.[5] The question, though, is what about a space, actual or conceptual, that's limited? A space for one person to occupy that another person absolutely cannot? Pluralism works fine, we might say, until somebody pulls out a gun. The "gun" might of course be ideological and conceptual, but might also be actual, as in the events that prompted the founding of Sahmat.

Since its founding, Sahmat has also found itself responding to communal violence that specifically targets cultural production, old and new. In 1992 Hindu nationalists used the cover of an orchestrated political "riot" to demolish the sixteenth-century Babri Masjid (mosque) in the city of Ayodhya in Uttar Pradesh. For nationalists the demolition was a symbolic and actual reconquest, the settling of an old score: they believed the mosque stood on the proper site of an older Hindu temple and hence represented a hated Muslim victory over Hinduism. For liberal thinkers in India it was a vicious attack on cultural heritage in a country whose history and present have embraced many faiths and whose challenge is to maintain a pluralistic, civil public culture. While from an American perspective the actions of Hindu nationalists may seem like the extreme products of an exotically violent political culture, they are barely removed from the furies whipped up by Christian nationalists in our own context.[6] We have only to look to the public outrage over plans for an Islamic community center in lower Manhattan (near the site of the September 11 attacks), to the bizarrely tenacious claims that President Barack Obama is a Muslim, or to the small-scale attacks on mosques around the country, for evidence of a similar fervor that is not, indeed, so far removed from the halls of power.

If the United States does indeed have similar problems, what we don't have is a cultural organization like Sahmat that can bring together artists and intellectuals to move quickly and creatively to respond to incidents like the mosque's demolition. Sahmat produced performances, discussions, and a body of visual displays that contained, as architectural theorist Arindam Dutta describes it, "a plethora of historical, political, social, and anthropological details testifying to the complexity of society in the Ayodhya region."[7] Again, the aim was pluralist: "a picture of pluralist syncretism in opposition to the monolithic mythicisms being forwarded by Sangh [Hindu nationalist] ideologues."[8]

A strategy of portable displays combining images (photographs, prints, and drawings) and texts, similar to *Images and Words*, was used in 1993 for *Hum Sab Ayodhya*. This exhibition was the companion piece to *Muktnaad*, a series of performance works that responded to the demolition of the Babri Masjid **(FIG. 7)**.[9] Sahmat's creative forms of display lifted scholarly documentation out of the realm of documentation; to the Hindu nationalists *Hum Sab Ayodhya*'s arguments actually constituted blasphemy. The exhibition was targeted in a variety of ways: it was vandalized by Hindu nationalists in Faizabad,[10] police shut down the show in Delhi, and legislators leveled charges of criminal conspiracy against the state at Sahmat. The pretext was a portion of one text panel titled *Ram Katha* that mentioned, in a measured scholarly tone, the *Dasaratha Jātaka*, dating to between the fourth and second centuries BCE, in which Rama and Sita are presented as brother and sister. Hindu nationalist ideologues seized upon this reference as blasphemy and Sahmat was indicted for "fomenting communal unrest."[11] The *Ram Katha* text panel was confiscated and banned—a ban finally lifted by Delhi's High Court in 2001.[12]

Sahmat's efforts at assembling and disseminating evidence for a diverse and rich history of the cultural life of the Indian subcontinent might be likened to the Tucumán Arde project of 1968 in Argentina. Responding to an economic crisis in the northern province of Tucumán (where a new, privatizing government had shut down eleven large state-owned sugar mills), artists and cultural workers created an installation to display documents and information that were the product of their research on the political and economic situation in the province.[13] Like some of Sahmat's work, it was also shut down quickly by the state. While documentation (for example, photographic records of ephemeral performances, or the graphic presentation of research undertaken by artists) has come to be a familiar idiom in post-1960s art practice, it has often been presented in a vein of irony, fiction, and invention. When the issues at stake are deadly serious, documentation might appear to be activism rather than "art." What is especially distinctive about Sahmat's interventions into the interpretation of cultural tradition is that they construct activist art as activist art history.

What's significant here is not just that Sahmat relies on a notion of a secular public sphere in political terms—for example, for purposes of free speech—but also that this secular context has been key to modern notions of what art can and cannot do, notions that artists and intellectuals have continued to rely on through the shifts within postmodernity and the rise of new nationalisms. The assumption that religious images may convey a variety of meanings, and do not incarnate fixed truths, is a key basis for the secular assumptions of modern art in general. It makes images manipulable by artists. (Of course they always were, but it makes this creative flexibility central to the accepted vernacular definition of what artists do.) Art historians have long viewed the establishment of modernity in tandem with a process of secularization—the expansion of nonreligious subject matter, the disenchantment of art, but also art's arrogation of some of the social and reflective functions of religion, its capacity to raise important questions and process cultural conflicts. In the West, Judeo-Christian iconography has been reduced to an occasional resource for artists (often in the context of a religious commission) and largely abandoned by "serious" artists.[14] But in India the postcolonial context gave a different valence to traditional religious imagery; it was a resource for the forging and tempering of a new national visual culture. Representations of the Hindu pantheon suggest not only "Hinduness" but also "Indianness." Thus the painter and filmmaker

FIG. 8 Ram Rahman poses with a cutout of M. F. Husain at a photo booth created for *Husain @ 95*, Jamia Millia Islamia University, September 17, 2010.

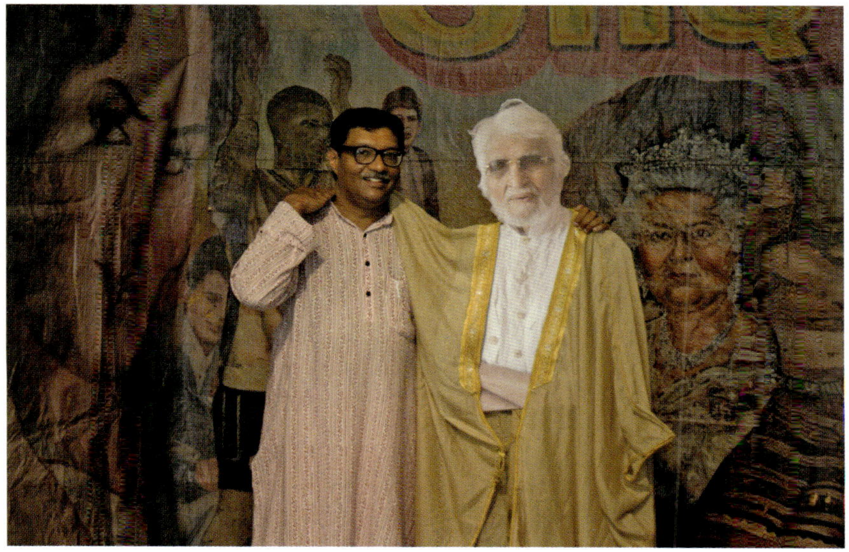

M. F. Husain, long the epitome of cultural aspirations for a secular and modern India, used images drawn from the Hindu pantheon as part of a pan-Indian glossary of iconography to dip into and manipulate to his own ends—even as his use of nudity and eroticism indicated a complex relationship both to Indian religious sculpture and to the nude as a central theme of the Western tradition.[15] The nationalists' newly aggressive cultural strategy resulted in attacks on M. F. Husain, beginning in 1996, highlighting his Muslim background and framing their indignation in communal terms. This "Picasso of India" was subjected to a reign of terror. His works were vandalized, nationalists demonstrated against his exhibitions, criminal charges were leveled against him, his house was attacked, and effigies of him were burned. Sahmat's work in support of Husain included statements, elaborate birthday celebrations, and the conference *Iconography Now!* Both grounded in the Husain case and theoretically ambitious, the conference addressed questions of tradition, meaning, and politics. In 2010, the year before Husain's death, Sahmat's celebration of his birthday included a series of photographs in which participants posed with a life-size cutout portrait of Husain (FIG. 8). A simple performance, it was also an accumulation of evidence of support for the embattled artist and for what he represented within the Indian public sphere.

Hindu nationalist attacks on the Babri Masjid, Sahmat's *Hum Sab Ayodhya*, and M. F. Husain refuse aesthetic distance: they attempt to close the (modern) gap between image and god, assuming that if religious images do not perhaps physically embody the gods (or maybe they do), then at the very least the things we do with or to them *are done to* the gods. Discussing a Buddhist Jataka in which Rama and Sita are brother and sister cannot be merely a historical illustration—it is an affirmative statement about their relationship. Painting Saraswati in the nude is a direct dishonor to the goddess. Whether Hindu nationalists use these claims cynically—manipulating the mass media to stir up emotion, exploiting the fact in particular that visual media have the potential to be ripped from context and transmuted into spectacular media controversy—is not really important. By insisting on a fixed meaning for religious images, they attack a whole arena of cultural agency—the idea that meaning is not fixed once and for all but may be ambiguous and multilayered; that icons can accrue new connotations; that artists, with their work, can "critically intervene in the ongoing social processes."[16] By attacking these ideas directly, however, they attribute new agency to the work of artists who persist in challenging orthodoxy. For Sahmat, this new capability has perhaps been an opportunity embedded within the crisis: an opportunity for a cultural practice to demonstrate its potential power through the (obviously painful) violence of the responses it prompts.

The formation of the group Sahmat itself performs as both a political and an artistic statement. Sahmat literally, by its acronym, is a "trust." A trust is a fund, but "trust" is also a style of social relationship (and this is highlighted by the phonetic meaning of the word *sahmat*, agreement or compact[17]). The social form of the trust or compact becomes both aesthetic and political through the organization's activities and thus comprises a social form that is a work of art in its own right, as well as a living creative memorial for a particular individual—brilliant street theatre pioneer Safdar Hashmi—and a reminder that his slaying was the result of communal violence. Not a monument but a trust, the group followed from the spontaneous coming together of artists and intellectuals to protest the political killing. While commemorating Hashmi the individual, the organization has not made him its central focus, but rather has engaged in a strategy of proliferating and accumulating cultural production and documentation and both promoting and modeling pluralism. What I would like to suggest with the notion of accumulation is that Sahmat has functioned through accumulation of different kinds—accumulation through space (the assembling of evidence, the numerical building up of support), and an effort at shining light on processes of accumulation through time. Part of the challenge enacted on the level of representation is to argue that cultural meaning itself does and should accumulate, that iconography operates through visual ambiguity, allusion, and citation, the divergent and convergent functioning across time of varying historical and individual artistic styles, and the syncretic layering of meanings. Sahmat has done this by diving energetically and creatively—using the tools of the artist—into a series of image wars of vital importance to historians and critics as well as to artists.

Rebecca Zorach is professor of art history at the University of Chicago. Her writing and teaching clusters around two poles: art of the European Renaissance, and art, politics, and theory since the 1960s. Zorach is currently writing a book on experimental spaces in the Black Arts Movement, and at work on a project, *Never The Same*, to compile interviews and archival materials documenting socially and politically engaged art in Chicago. She lives and works in Chicago.

Notes

1. India ranks third in sheer number of internet users, but only because of the size of its population. Actual penetration (percentage of population using the technology) is only a little over 10 percent. http://www.internetworldstats.com/top20.htm.

2. Sahmat, *Sahmat 20 Years, 1989–2009: A Document of Activities and Statements* (New Delhi: Sahmat, 2009), 24.

3. These potential challenges have been examined in the collection of essays *What We Want is Free*, edited by Ted Purves (Albany, NY: SUNY Press, 2004).

4. In politically engaged art circles elsewhere, "communalism" might be misinterpreted to mean something positive. In the context of relational aesthetics and participatory art forms, the creation of community is often a goal. At the same time critiques of "community" have become familiar, and revolve around a sense that (at least as used in the art world) it has an excessively affirmative character. Miwon Kwon, for example, in *One Place after Another: Site-Specific Art and Locational Identity* (Cambridge, MA: MIT Press, 2004), criticizes the "integrationist" spatial logic of US public art policy from the 1980s (67) and community art projects that, reflecting a "model of social harmony and unity" (72), seek to represent a community and often fail to account for divergences within a community. According to Critical Art Ensemble, community "contradicts the politics of difference." See Critical Art Ensemble, "Observations on Collective Cultural Action," *Art Journal*, vol. 57, no. 2 (Summer 1998): 72–85.

5. The fact that they also depend upon one another for community is also suggestive of the way Jacques Rancière describes the project *Je&Nous* by Campement Urbain in his "Aesthetic Separation, Aesthetic Community": *Art&Research, A Journal of Ideas, Contexts, and Methods*, vol. 2, no. 1 (September 2008), http://www.artandresearch.org.uk/v2n1/ranciere.html. *Je&Nous* (not yet realized) was a plan to reinforce community by creating a single-user space: a safe place for one person at a time to enter for purposes of solitary contemplation, but one that depended on the will of the community to maintain and hence, ideally, would produce that community at the same time that it produced solitude.

6. For a discussion of current Christian nationalism (synonymous with Dominionism), see Michelle Goldberg, *Kingdom Coming: The Rise of Christian Nationalism* (New York: W. W. Norton, 2006).

7. Arindam Dutta, "Sahmat, 1989–2004: Liberal Art Practice against the Liberalized Public Sphere," *Cultural Dynamics*, 2005, 17: 193–226.

8. Ibid.

9. See *Muktnaad, Hum Sab Ayodhya: A Selection of Reports, Editorials, Discussion, Comments from the Press* (New Delhi: Sahmat, 1994).

10–11. Ibid., 207.

12. *Sahmat 20 Years*, 45.

13. On Tucumán Arde, see Luis Camnitzer, *Conceptualism in Latin American Art: Didactics of Liberation* (Austin, TX: University of Texas Press, 2007) and Miguel A. López, "How do we know what Latin American Conceptualism Looks Like?," *Afterall* 23 (Spring 2010): 5–21.

14. The presumed misuse of iconography has been a theme in US cultural politics as well, apparent in unsuccessful efforts to remove Chris Ofili's *The Holy Virgin Mary* from the 1999 *Sensation* exhibition at the Brooklyn Museum, and the successful forced removal of David Wojnarowicz's *A Fire in My Belly* from the National Portrait Gallery's *Hide/Seek* exhibition because its depiction of ants on a crucifix was deemed offensive to Christians by some Republican members of the US Congress. See Lawrence Rothfield, ed., *Unsettling "Sensation": Arts Policy Lessons from the Brooklyn Museum of Art Controversy* (New Brunswick, NJ: Rutgers University Press, 2001); Blake Gopnik, "National Portrait Gallery Bows to Censors, Withdraws Wojnarowicz Video on Gay Love," *Washington Post*, November 30, 2010, http://www.washingtonpost.com/wp-dyn/content/article/2010/11/30/AR2010113006911.html.

15. This "most flamboyant artistic personality of post-Independence India" epitomized "the very entity of modern Indian art." Tapati Guha-Thakurta, "Art History and the Nude: Art, Obscenity and Sexuality in Contemporary India," in *Iconography Now* (Sahmat, 2006), 9–34, 13.

16. "Artists' protest statement in support of M. F. Husain," October 18, 1996, *Sahmat 20 Years*, 93–94, 93.

17. The Sanskrit root *sam* is cognate with the Greek root *sym* and Latin *com* (as in community).

Sahmat: Project Participants

***Artists Alert* (1989)**
Participating artists: K. M. Adimoolam, Krishen Ahuja, Akhilesh, Vasudevan Akkitham, Altaf, Navjot Altaf, Amit Ambalal, Amitava Banerjee, Maitreyi Banerjee, Prabhakar Barwe, Manjit Bawa, Bishen Bhardwaj, Veena Bhargava, R. B. Bhaskaran, Jyoti Bhatt, Harinder Singh Bhatti, Pulak Biswas, Usha Biswas, Shobha Broota, Arpana Caur, Jayashree Chakravarthy, Jagdish Chander, Kanchan Chander, Suneela Bindra Chopra, Bijon Chowdhury, Dhiraj Chowdhury, Jogen Chowdhury, Walter D'Souza, Devraj Dakoji, Pratibha Dakoji, Amitava Das, Biman Das, Jatin Das, Dharmanarayan Dasgupta, Robin David, Ajay Desai, Meera Devidayal, Jagdish Dey, Atul Dodiya, Ajit Dubey, Laxma Gaud, Siddhartha Ghosh, K. Ganesh Haloi, Somnath Hore, M. F. Husain, Rummana Hussain, Nirmal Kapoor, Naresh Kapuria, Kishori Kaul, Bhupen Khakhar, Krishen Khanna, K. Khosa, Devayani Krishna, Kanwal Krishna, Lalitha Lajmi, Madan Mahatta, Sheila Makhijani, Nalini Malani, Robin Mandal, Alex Mathew, Anjoli Ela Menon, Leila Mukherjee, Meera Mukherjee, Mrinalini Mukherjee, Reddeppa Naidu, Badri Narayan, Naren Nath, Akbar Padamsee, Jyoti Pandya, Prashant Panjiar, Mukul Panwar, Madhvi Parekh, Manu Parekh, Gieve Patel, Jeram Patel, Nagji Patel, Sudhir Patwardhan, Ashok Prajapati, Om Prakash, Surya Prakash, Pushpamala N., Ram Rahman, Mona Rai, Raghu Rai, A. Ramachandran, Raghavendra Rao, D. L. N. Reddy, Ravinder Reddy, Rekha Rodwittiya, Shyamal Roy, Suhas Roy, Jehangir Sabavala, Piraji Sagara, G. R. Santosh, B. C. Sanyal, Paritosh Sen, Himmat Shah, Parthiv Shah, Shamshad, Satish Sharma, Archana Shastri, Lalu Prasad Shaw, Gulammohammed Sheikh, Nilima Sheikh, Ketaki Sheth, Deepak Shinde, Vilas Shinde, Siddharth, Arpita Singh, Gurcharan Singh, Paramjit Singh, Prem Singh, Raghubir Singh, Tejbir Singh, K. G. Subramanyan, Anupam Sud, Sudha, Vivan Sundaram, B. V. Suresh, J. Swaminathan, Soni Taraporevala, Vasundhara Tewari, S. G. Vasudev, Umesh Verma, S. S. Vohra, Yusuf, Moti Zharotia.

***Chauraha:* All India Street Theatre Festival, Delhi (1989)**
Participating theatre groups: Chennai Kalai Kuzhu (Chennai), Duggar Manch (Jammu), Indian People's Theatre Association (Patna), Jagar Ladhau Lok Kala Aghadi (Maharashtra), Jan Kala Manch (Bhavnagar, Gujarat), Jana Natya Manch (Delhi), Praja Natya Mandali (Andhra Pradesh), Ritwik (West Bengal), Samudaya (Karnataka).

***Chauraha:* All India Street Theatre Festival, Delhi (1990)**
Participating theatre groups: Aavahan (Bhilai, Madhya Pradesh), Abhinaya (West Bengal), Garage Studio (Ahmedabad, Gujarat), Goregaon Cultural Unit (Mumbai), Jana Natya Manch (Delhi), Progressive Writers' Association Theatre Group (Tamil Nadu), Rang Chetna (Trichur, Kerala), Sahas (Cuttack, Orissa), Vihan (Banaras, Uttar Pradesh).

***Chauraha:* All India Street Theatre Workshop (1991)**
Resource persons: Ramgopal Bajaj, Rati Bartholomew, Bhaskar Chandavarkar, Chandralekha, Rang Chetana G. P. Deshpande, Sudhanva Deshpande, Hasan, Alpana Khare, Aishwarj Kumar, Sonal Mansingh, Sadanand Menon, Dadi Pudumjee, M. K. Raina, Joy Sengupta, Tripurari Sharma, R. S. Shelke, Madan Gopal Singh.

***Janotsav* (1989)**
Coordinators of Janotsav workshops:
Music: Kajal Ghosh, Madan Gopal Singh
Photography: Parthiv Shah
Fine Art & Graphics: Amit Paul, Pratibha Dakoji
Theatre: Habib Tanvir, Ashish Ghosh
Street Theatre: Rati Bartholomew, Jana Natya Manch
Environmental Projects: Romi Khosla, National Institute of Science, Technology and Development Studies (NISTADS)
Painting: Vivan Sundaram, Shamshad
Literature and Poetry (Hindi and Urdu): M. M. P. Singh, Gauhar Raza
Dance: Bharat Sharma, Madhavi Mudgal
Video/TV: Sashi Kumar, Centre for Development of Instructional Technology (CENDIT)
Puppetry & Creative Writing (English): Dadi Pudumjee, Randhir Khare
Newsletter: Anil Chandra, Indian Institute of Mass Communications (IIMC)

Children's Books

PED
Author: Safdar Hashmi
Illustrations: Mickey Patel

RED FLOWER
Author: Safdar Hashmi
Illustrations: Mona Rai

BANSURIWALA
Author: Safdar Hashmi
Illustrations: Arpita Singh

HOLI
Author: Safdar Hashmi
Illustrations: Mohandas N. N.

GADBAD GHOTALA
Author: Safdar Hashmi
Illustrations: B. V. Suresh

KITABEN
Author: Safdar Hashmi
Illustrations: Surendran Nair

SARE MAUSAM ACCHHE
Author: Safdar Hashmi
Illustrations: Nilima Sheikh

DUNIYA SABKI
Author: Safdar Hashmi
Illustrations: Bindia Thapar

NATAK KI DUNIYA
Author: Safdar Hashmi
Illustrations: Bindia Thapar

BAGH KI SAIR
Author: Safdar Hashmi
Illustrations: Vasudevan Akkitham

BAPU
Author: Uma Shankar Joshi
Illustrations: Madhavi Parekh

CHAMPA
Author: Haku Shah
Illustrations: Haku Shah

BAPU KA AITIHASIK MUKADMA
Author: Mulk Raj Anand
Illustrations: Shamshad

IDGAH
Author: Premchand
Illustrations: Jehangir Jani

SITARA GIR PADEGA
Author: Madhukar Upadhyaya
Illustrations: Sanjay Sharma

TOTA KAHANI / THE STORY OF THE PARROT
Author: Rabindranath Tagore
Illustrations: *Patuas* from Bengal

VIR PURUSH / THE BRAVE LITTLE MAN
Author: Rabindranath Tagore
Illustrations: *Patuas* from Bengal

BRISHTI PARE TAPAR TUPUR / DAYLIGHT IS FADING
Author: Rabindranath Tagore
Illustrations: *Patuas* from Bengal

Artists Against Communalism

***AAC* Delhi (1991)**
Participants: Javed Akhtar, Manjit Bawa, Arpana Caur, Hari Prasad Chaurasia, Fahimuddin Dagar, Dagar Bandhu, Jatin Das, Astad Deboo, Gopi Gajwani, Moloyashree Hashmi, Shanti Hiranand, Ali Sardar Jafri, Bansi Kaul, Amjad Ali Khan, Asad Ali Khan, Sabri Khan, Shafat Ahmad Khan, Krishen Khanna, Yamini Krishnamurthy, Sharon Lowen, Birju Maharaj, Sonal Mansingh, Joy Michael, Rajan & Sajan Mishra, Madhup Mudgal, Shubha Mudgal, Vishnu Nagar, Bansi Parimoo, Indrani Rahman, M. K. Raina, Rahi Masoom Raza, Raja & Radha Reddy, Bhisham Sahni, Leela Samson, Kiran Sehgal, Uma Sharma, Gulammohammed Sheikh, Prayag Shukla, Arpita Singh, Paramjit Singh, Vivan Sundaram, J. Swaminathan, Habib Tanvir, Wadali Brothers, Jana Natya Manch, and Naya Theatre.

***AAC* Aligarh (1991)**
Participants: Manjit Bawa, Gopal Das, Rita Ganguli, Yunus Husain Khan, Sharon Lowen, Sonal Mansingh, Mrinalini Mukherjee, Dadi Pudumjee, Lalit Rao, Ale Ahmad Saroor, Shaharyar, Pt. Narendra Sharma, Vivan Sundaram, and Naya Theatre.

***AAC* Mumbai (1991)**
Participating artists: Shamim Ahmed, Javed Akhtar, Kishori Amonkar, Aarti Ankalikar, Kankana Banerjee, Ranjit Barot, Neela Bhagwat, Hari Prasad Chaurasia, Baharuddin Dagar, Fahimuddin Dagar, Wasifuddin Dagar, Zahiruddin Dagar, Astad Deboo, Ashwini Bhide Deshpande, Sitara Devi, Nida Fazli, Dhruv Ghosh, Nayan Ghosh, Shobha Gurtu, A. K. Hangal, M. F. Husain, Ali Sardar Jafri, Pt. Jasraj, Dileep Jhaveri, Satish Kaleskar, Ulhas Kasalkar, Prabhakar Kaslekar, Amjad Ali Khan, Sultan Khan, Randhir Khare, Kartik Kumar, Sonal Mansingh, Mehol, Shubha Mudgal, Amol Palekar, Raghunandan Pansikar, Prabodh Parikh, Daya Pawar, Dadi Pudumjee, Lalit Rao, Raghunath Seth, Pt. Ravi Shankar, Shiv Kumar Sharma, Gulammohammed Sheikh, Maya Upadhyaya, and C.R. Vyas.

***AAC: Images and Words* (1991)**
Participants: V. G. Abhimanue, Sam Adaikalasamy, Balbhadra Agarwala, Fatima Ahmed, Krishen Ahuja, Ajmal Ajmali, Akhilesh, Javed Akhtar, Vasudevan Akkitham, Abid Alami, Altaf, Navjot Altaf, Amarkant, Amit Ambalal, Amitabh, Anand (P. Sachidanandan), B. Anoop, V. K. Asthana, Kirat Babani, Bashir Badr, Ramesh Bakshi, Nazeer Banarsi, Manabendra Bandyopadhyay, Anandamoy Banerjee, Anuradha Banerjee, Maitreyi Banerji, Jitendra Singh Baoni, Waseem Barelvi, Alif Ahmed Barq, Abbas Batliwala, Hemi Bawa, Manjit Bawa, Manmohan Bawa, Harish Bhadani, Mahendra Bhalla, P. Bhaskaran, R. K. Bhaskaran, Jyoti Bhatt, Bireswar Bhattacharjee, Dilip Bhattacharya, Malini Bhattacharya, Harcharan Singh Bhatty, L. M. Bhaud, Tapan

Bhowmik, G. S. Bhullar, Bharat Bhushan, Abdul Bismillah, Pulak Biswas, Swapan Biswas, Usha Biswas, Neeta Borker, Bilash Bose, Gulabdas Broker, Shobha Broota, Ajeet Caur, Arpana Caur, Bachint Caur, S. K. Chaddha, Sadhan Chakraborty, Jagdish Chander, Kanchan Chander, Anil Chatterji, Sukumar Chatterji, Surjit Singh Chaudhury, Chanchal Chauhan, Bal Chhabda, Chillar J. K., Sunila Bindra Chopra, Bijon Chowdhury, Dhiraj Choudhury, Jogen Chowdhury, Medini Choudhury, Shail Choyal, Peter Colaco, Dinesh Dadhichi, Prafulla Dahanukar, Naina Dalal, Amitava Das, Biman Das, Jatin Das, Nirmalendu Das, Debrata De, Jagdish De, Ashapurna Debi, Ajay Desai, Arvind M. Desai, Sanjay Desai, G. P. Deshpande, Chandrakant Devtale, Ramlal Dhar, Santokh Singh Dhir, Shiv Doblia, Atul Dodiya, Ajit Dubey, Vinay Dubey, Kartar Singh Duggal, Manoj Dutta, B. S. Elias, S. R. Faruqui, Nida Fazli, Mridula Garg, Balwant Gargi, Ramesh Gaur, Kishore Ghosh, Rajat Kumar Ghosh, Sankho Ghosh, Subha Ghosh, Phal S. Girotia, Olivinho J. F. Gomes, Adam Gondavi, Sheela Gowda, Hari Om Gulati, Prabir Gupta, Subodh Gupta, Gurpreet, R. M. Hadapad, Muzafar Hanafi, Sudhir Hasamnis, Chandana Hore, Reba Hore, Somnath Hore, Satakadi Hota, Harbhajan Singh Hundal, M. F. Husain, Owais Husain, Rummana Hussain, B. Ingle, Ali Sardar Jafri, Jagdish, Raj Jain, Habib Jalib, Ali Jawed, Gurmukh Singh Jeet, Ramahari Jena, Prayag Jha, Dileep Jhaveri, Samar S. Jodha, Hema Joshi, Rajesh Joshi, Meena Kakodkar, Kamal Kansara, Nirmal Kapoor, Naresh Kapuria, Prakash Karmakar, Basant Kashyap, Nand Katyal, Bhushan Kaul, Rajinder Kaul, Amarjit Kaunke, Prabhjyot Kaur, Surjit Kaur, Jagdish Kaushal, Dinkar R. Kaushik, Krishen Khanna, Randhir Khare, Shuja Khawar, Saghar Khyami, Shri Kishorewala, Valson Kolleri, K. N. Kulkarni, K. S. Kulkarni, Meenu Kulkarni, Shakuntala Kulkarni, U. Vijay Kumar, Punathil Kunhabdullah, Prithpal Ladi, Shanu Lahiri, Lalitha Lajmi, Ram Lal, Rajiv Lochan, Yurika Lochan, Promilla Luthra, Amritlal Madan, Jayanta Mahapatra, Madan Mahatta, Sheila Makhijani, Nalini Malani, Robin Mandal, Anjana Mehra, Tyeb Mehta, Ushakant Mehta, Arvind Membro, C. D. Mistry, Isha Mohammad, Wasi Mohammad, Mrinalini Mukherjee, Kaushik Mukhopadhyaya, Ashok Mullick, Veer Munshi, B. R. Musafir, M. K. Muthuswamy, Rakesh Nagar, Vishnu Nagar, Sachida Nagdev, Bharat Naik, Surendran Nair, Vasudevan Nair, Jagdish Nandwana, Badri Narayan, T. Narayan, Neena Nehru, Nisreen, Ashokan Paduval, Naren Panchal, Jyoti Pandya, Mahendra Pandya, B. R. Panesar, Khumar Panipatti, Prashant Panjiar, Mukesh Papiani, Madhavi Parekh, Manu Parekh, Bansi Parimoo, Ratan Parimoo, Avinash Pasricha, Gieve Patel, Jeram Patel, Amaresh Pathak, Devilal Patidar, Ramesh Chandra Patkar, Malati Pattanashetti, D. P. Pattanayak, Sudhir Patwardhan, Ashit Paul, Neeraj Paul, S. Paul, Pavanan, Virendra Prabhakar, Vishnu Prabhakar, K. Prabhakaran, Ashok Prajapati, Brahm Prakash, Uday Prakash, Nawab Punathil, Pramod Pushkarna, Ram Rahman, Mona Rai, Sampurna Rai, Gargi Raina, Basav Raj, Indira Raj, A. Ramachandran, V. Ramesh, Raghavendra Rao, Rekha Rao, Balbir Singh Rathi, Manu Rathod, Balvir Rawat, Anand Shankar Ray, Debes Ray, Pratibha Ray, Gauhar Raza, P. T. Reddy, T. Sudhakar Reddy, N. N. Rimzon, K. K. Rishi, Rekha Rodwittiya, Samir Roy, A. G. Ryan, Jehangir Sabavala, Naveen Sagar, Bhisham Sahni, Kashinath Salve, Soni Sanjeev, G. R. Santosh, Dayal Sarbapriya, K. Satchidanandan, Shukla Sawant, Savinder Sawarkar, Amarnath Sehgal, P. S. Sehrai, Mrinal Sen, Nabaneeta Dev Sen, Orijit Sen, Haku Shah, Parthiv Shah, Prabha Shah, Sumant Shah, Shaharyar, Shamshad, Gauri Shankar, Sandeep Shankar, M. Shanthamani, Asha Sharma, Bulbul Sharma, Natraj Sharma, O. P. Sharma, Sanjay Sharma, Satish Sharma, Shyam Sharma, Suresh Sharma, M. Shashidharan, Archana Shastri, Gulammohammed Sheikh, Nilima Sheikh, Khushbash Sherawat, Shibu, Jin Sook Shinde, Vilas Shinde, J. S. Shraddha, Shriprasad, Jaydev Shukla, Jayesh P. Shukla, Prayag Shukla, Shuvaprasannna, Shrilekha Sikander, Arpita Singh, Bhagwan Singh, Dayanita Singh, Gurcharan Singh, Gurdial Singh, Harbhajan Singh, Maheep Singh, Namita Singh, Narenderpal Singh, Paramjit Singh, Prakash Singh, Prem Singh, Rameshwar Singh, S. K. Singh, Thakur Dilip Singh, S. N. Sinha, Vrundavan Solanki, Mahinder Soni, Sreejith, Vivan Sundaram, B. V. Suresh, J. Swaminathan, Ghulam Rabani Taban, Habib Tanvir, Jaidev Thakore, Nita Thakore, N. Thiagarajan, Vasudha Thozhur, Rajendra Kumar Tiku, Vinod Tiwari, Atiq Ullah, Kishore Umrekar, Carlos Valles, R. Varadarajan, Venkatesh Vasudevan, Hemant Vayangarhkar, Vasantharao Venkatarao, Umesh Verma, Rajesh Vora, Asghar Wajahat, Yusuf, Paul Zacharia, and Zahoor Zargar.

Special banners at auction of *Images and Words* exhibition panels (1992)
Participating artists: Altaf, Navjot Altaf, Prabhakar Barwe, Bal Chhabda, Meera Devidayal, Mehli Gobai, Owais Husain, Rummana Hussain, Prabhakar Kolte, Shakuntala Kulkarni, Lalitha Lajmi, Nalini Malani, Aryana Mehra, Pritam Patil, Smin Punegar, Pushpamala N., Deepak Shinde, Jinsook Shinde, Vilas Shinde, Lakshman Shreshta, Srilekha Sikander, and Praful Vahanukar.

Ayodhya: Demolition of the Babri Masjid and After

***Anhad Garje, Delhi* (1993)**
Participants included: Keshav Badge, Kankana Banerjee, Gopal Das Baul, Kartik Das Baul, Randasi Baul, Nitai Das, Abdul Rab Fakir, Allan Fakir, Fakirni, Shobha Gurtu, Shanti Hiranand, Shubha Mudgal, Bunger Khan, Hafiz Khan, Jaffar Husain Khan, Gulam Husain Niyazi, Naseeb Pyare, Eltaf Husain Sarahang, Bhai Dilbagh Singh, and Gulbagh Singh.

Posters by artists: Manjit Bawa, Gopi Gajwani, M. F. Husain, Nalini Malani, Akbar Padamsee, Manu Parekh, Orijit Sen, Haku Shah, Shamshad, Gulammohammed Sheikh, Nilima Sheikh, Arpita Singh, Vivan Sundaram.

***Anhad Garje, Bombay, Gujarat, and Lucknow* (1993)**
Participating artists: Kishori Amonkar, Keshav Badge, Kankana Banerji, Bhakto Das Baul, Neela Bhagwat, Hemant Chauhan, Atul Desai, Shobha Gurtu, Shanti Hiranand,

Pt. Jasraj, Sweta Jhaveri, Bungar Khan, Jafar Husain Khan, Shubha Mudgal, Nasib Pyare, Eltaf Husain Sarahang, Bhadra Savai, Madan Gopal Singh, C. R. Vyas, Wadali Brothers, Nasib Wali, and Warsi Brothers.

Hum Sab Ayodhya **(1993)**
Resource Persons: Aijaz Ahmad, Athar Ali, Rajinder Arora, Benoy Behl, Prakash Bhakuni, Ravindra Bhan, Vani Bhan, Indira Chandrasekhar, Prashant Dhawan, Irfan Habib, Suvira Jaiswal, Vivekanand Jha, Samar Jodha, Vijay S. Jodha, Geeta Kapur, Bhupen Khakhar, Ravinder Kumar, Alex Mathew, Arun Mathur, Surendran Nair, K. N. Panikkar, G. N. Pant, Madhu Prasad, Rajendra Prasad, Ram Rahman, M. K. Raina, K. T. Ravindran, Rajat Ray, Shounack Ray, Sanjog, Arshiya Sethi, Parthiv Shah, Gulammohammed Sheikh, Anisha Shekhar, P. K. Shukla, Kulwant Singh, Snehanshu/team, Sushil Srivastava, Vivan Sundaram, Romila Thapar, and Asad Zaidi.

Muktnaad **(1993)**
Performers (individuals and groups): Girija Devi, Sitara Devi, Guru Kelucharan Mahapatra, Rajan & Sajan Mishra, Madhavi Mudgal, Palakkad K.V. Narayanaswami & Padma Narayanaswami, Swami Pagaldas, Umayalpuram Sivaraman, Mandolin Srinivas, IPTA (Indian People's Theatre Association) Patna, Naya Theatre, Habib Tanvir.

Participants (individuals and groups): Janaki Abraham, Dinesh Abrol, Imran Ahmad, Shabi Ahmed, Akhilesh, Vidya Das Arora, Mohammad Aslam, Baharuddin, Akshaya Bakaya, Pritam Bali, Sudip Banerjee, Pablo Bartholomew, Devdas Baul, Manmohan Bawa, Manu Bhandari, Malini Bhattacharya, Mihir Bhattacharya, Amitava Bhowmick, Gurcharan Bhullar, R. S. Bisht, Indira Chandrasekhar, Manini Chatterjee, Aditi Chowdhury, Bijon Chowdhury, Amitabh Dasgupta, Manjira Datta, Ramesh Dixit, Partho Dutta, Mehr Afsan Farooqui, Meenakshi Ganguli, Nanak Ganguly, Yubaraj Ghimire, Siddharth Ghosh, Adam Gondavi, Ravindran Gopinath, Prabir Guha, Joyoti Gupta, Ruchira Gupta, Suman Gupta, Sohail Hashmi, Rummana Hussain, Leela Dhar Jaguri, Ajay Jaitley, Vijay Singh Jodha, S. Kalidas, Lima Kanungo, Geeta Kapur, Prakash Karmakar, Girish Karnad, Kartik, Shaji Karun, Rajinder Kaur, Mohd. Farid Kazmi, A. Khan, Alpana Khare, Romi Khosla, Pixie Lemac, Arvind Krishna Mehrotra, Farida Mehta, Sadanand Menon, Kristine Michael, S. C. Mishra, Neelanjana Mukhia, Javed Mulick, Babli Nagpal, Chitra Padmanabhan, S. K. Pande, K. N. Panikkar, Prabhat Patnaik, Damini Pola, Ponnappa, Kalpana Prasad, Madhu Prasad, Ram Rahman, Mahua Raichandani, Kadammanitta Ramakrishnan, Radhika Ramaseshan, G.K. Govind Rao, Nina Rao, Sajeda Rashid, Anuradha Marwah Roy, Sudha Sachdev, Bhisham Sahni, Kalpana Sahni, K. Satchidanandan, H. C. Satyarthi, Maya Satyarthi, Lakshmi Sehgal, Sabina Sehgal, Sethu, Mukesh Shah, Parthiv Shah, Shamshad, Jugnu Sharde, Rajendra Sharma, Rajesh Sharma, Ramchandra Sharma, K. M. Shrimali, P.K. Shukla, K. Marul Sidappa, Siddhalingaiah, Hisamul Islam Siddiqui, Madan Gopal Singh, Ratan Singh, Sheetla Singh, Sushil Srivastava, Vivan Sundaram, P. Sunderarajen, Prakash Upadhyaya, Urfi, S. G. Vasudev, Rajendra, Rooprekha Verma, Neera Vyas, Yadav, Kalam Natya Manch, Sewa, Jana Natya Manch, Prayog, IPTA (Indian People's Theatre Association), Prerna, Vishal Natya Manch, Rashtriya Ekta Kala Manch Ensemble, Puppet Theatre, Alternative Living Theatre, and students and teachers of Patna Art College.

Tribute to Gandhi

Postcards for Gandhi **(1994–95)** Exhibition of postcards in six cities: Delhi, Mumbai, Chennai, Bangalore, Calcutta and Ahmedabad.

Participating artists: V. G. Abhimanue, K. M. Adimoolam, Ravi Agarwal, Ajaykumar, Vasudevan Akkitham, Navjot Altaf, Amit Ambalal, Abul Kalam Azad, Vijay Bagodi, R. B. Bhaskaran, Jyoti Bhatt, Tapan Bhattacharyya, Arpana Caur, Barry Chan, Jagdish Chander, Kanchan Chander, Bijon Chowdhury, Jogen Chowdhury, Walter D'Souza, Amitava Das, Jatin Das, Sunil Das, Subha De, Atul Dodiya, M. J. Enas, Gopi Gajwani, Siddhartha Ghosh, P. Gopinath, N. S. Harsha, Rummana Hussain, Nand Katyal, Surjeet Kaur, Bhupen Khakhar, Krishen Khanna, Bharti Kher, Yunus Khimani, Shakuntala Kulkarni, Ram Kumar, Vijay Kumar, Rajiv Lochan, Chitrabanu Majumdar, Sheila Makhijani, Nalini Malani, Robin Mandal, Alex Mathew, Shami Mehndiratta, Veer Munshi, Sashidharan Nair, Surendran Nair, Badri Narayan, R. M. Palaniappan, Amlan Paliwal, Madhavi Parekh, Manu Parekh, Jeram Patel, Nagji Patel, Sudhir Patwardhan, K. Prabhakaran, Prakash, Pushpamala N., Jayanti Rabadia, Ram Rahman, Mona Rai, A. Ramachandran, Judy Blum Reddy, P. T. Reddy, N. N. Rimzon, Rekha Rodwittiya, Indrapramit Roy, Suhas Roy, Jehangir Sabavala, Tara Sabharwal, Shukla Sawant, Orijit Sen, Haku Shah, Parthiv Shah, Shambhavi, Shamshad, Bulbul Sharma, Gulammohammad Sheikh, Nilima Sheikh, Shibu N., Deepak Shinde, V. M. Shinde, Vilas Shinde, Shuvaprasanna, Prem Singh, Sanjiv Sinha, K. G. Subramanyan, Anupam Sud, Vivan Sundaram, B. V. Suresh, Jaidev Thakore, Roy Thomas, Vasudha Thozhur, R. Varadarajan, Umesh Verma, Viswanathan, Yusuf, and Babu Xavier.

Gift for India **(1997)**
Participating artists from India: Molly Abhimanue, V. G. Abhimanue, Ayisha Abraham, Vasudevan Akkitham, Amit Ambalal, Abul Kalam Azad, T. M. Azis, Eleena Banik, Jitendra Baoni, Arup Kumar Barua, Hemi Bawa, Pooja Broota, Shobha Broota, Arpana Caur, Jagdish Chander, Kanchan Chander, Sukumar Chatterjee, Bhagwan S. Chavan, Vidya Chitre, Suneela Bindra Chopra, Arunanshu Chowdhury, Gautam Das, Samir Das, Subha De, Meera Devidayal, Manisha Doshi, Nicola Duruvasula, M. J. Enas, Rajan Fulari, Sumati Gangopadhyay, Pramod Ganpatye, Manisha Gera, Shilpa Gupta, Subodh Gupta, Suman Gupta, Archana Hande, Rummana Hussain, Shridhar Iyer, Kavita Jaiswal, Jehangir Jani, Tushar Joag, Joejo, Hem Jyotika, Durga Kainthola,

Sahmat: Project Participants

Bharati Kapadia, Vijayan Kannampilly, Naina Kanodia, Ratnabali Kant, Sachin Karne, Ravi Kumar Kashi, Nand Katyal, Rajnish Kaur, Bhupen Khakhar, Yunus Khimani, Shakuntala Kulkarni, Sushil Kumar, S. Kundu, Lalitha Lajmi, Shantanu Lodh, Madan Mahatta, Pavan Mahatta, Sheila Makhijani, Nalini Malani, Anita Malhotra, Robin Mandal, Alex Mathew, Vijay Saraf Meenagi, Mekhala, Neeta Mohindra, Prashant Mukherjee, Kaushik Mukhopadhyay, Veer Munshi, S. Lakshmana Murthy, Peter Nagy, Surendran Nair, Anuradha Nalapat, Babu Namboodiri K., P. K. Nandakumar, Shruti Nelson, Madhavi Parekh, Manisha Parekh, Manu Parekh, Nagji Patel, Virendra Patel, K. S. Radhakrishnan, Mimi Radhakrishnan, Ram Rahman, Gargi Raina, M. K. Rajan, Chameli Ramachandran, N. N. Rimzon, Rekha Rodwittiya, Indrapramit Roy, Samir Roy, Sanjay Roy, Sharmila Sawant, Amitabh Sengupta, Haku Shah, Kavita Shah, Neehal Shah, Parthiv Shah, B. O. Shailesh, Shambhavi, Shamshad, Bulbul Sharma, Natraj Sharma, Gulammohammed Sheikh, Nilima Sheikh, Jin Sook Shinde, Vilas Shinde, Shrilekha Sikander, Anjum Singh, Sanjeev Sinha, Praneet Soi, P. Srinivasan, K. G. Subramanyan, Vivan Sundaram, Shyam Sunder, B. V. Suresh, Vasundhara Tewari, Nita Thakore, Roy Thomas, R. Varadarajan, Darshan Vora, Manoj Vyloor, and Yusuf.

Participating artists from outside India:
Australia: Lyndell Brown, Pip Cozens, Neil Degney, Edwin Easydorchik, Bonita Ely, Charles Green, Noelene Lucas, Janis Somerville, Rodney Spooner, Robin Stieger, Judith Wright
Brazil: Dora Longo Bahia, Angele Freiberger, Jeanette Musatt
Chile: Carlos Altamirano, Ian Szydlowski
Canada: Gwen Curry, Debora, Daniel Dion, Mansaram, Eric Metcalfe, Michael Morris, Bryan Mulvihill, Su Schnee, Vincent Trasov, Henry Tsang, Richard Turner
Costa Rica: Kaisu Koivisto, Cecilia Paredes
France: Philippe Bouriette, Rajendre Dhawan, John Felton, Agathe de Filippi, Chantal Georgens, Anne Rochette, Sarkis, Wade Saunders, Christopher Taylor, Viswanadhan.
Germany: Johannes Brus, Inge Mann, Peter Nagel, Julia Neuenhausen, Siegfried Neuenhausen
Hong Kong: Choi Yan-Chi
Finland: Ilona Lovas
Indonesia: Nindityo Adipurnomo
Hungary: Heri Dono, Mella Jaarsma, Agus Suwage
Israel: Judith Guetta, Simcha Shirman
Kenya: Archana Hebbar
Japan: Andrew Wamae
Macau: Konstantin Bessmertny
Mexico: Vida Yovanovich
Netherlands: Kate Bowes
New Caledonia: Rene Boutin, Luc Harring, Shibu Natesan, Bernd Strik
Pakistan: Elizabeth Dadi, Iftikhar Dadi
Peru: Juan Enrique Bedoya, Anamaria McCarthy
Philippines: Imelda Cajipe Endaya
Puerto Rico: Rosa Irigoyan
Thailand: Kamin Lertchaiprasert, Pinaree Sanpitak, Vasan Sitthiket
UK: Rasheed Areen, Ranjana Appoo, Mark Cazalet, Stephen Cox, Alison Harper, Timothy Hyman, Carl Jaycock, Richard Lannoy, Alnoor Mitha, Prafulla Mohanti, Ranjana Thapalyal
USA: Ray Barrie, Lynda Benglis, Eric Bowen, Abraham David Christian, John Cross, Linda Cross, Zarina R. Hashmi, Alfredo Jaar, Mary Kelly, Marta Violette Kot, Azyz Sharafy, Paul Smith, Richard Turner
Vietnam: Vu Dan Tan

Art on the Move (2001)

Participating artists: Arunkumar H. G., Eleena Banik, Nicola Durvasula, M. J. Enas, Subba Ghosh, Jehangir Jani, Tushar Joag, Reena Saini Kallat, Manjunath Kamath, Bharti Kher, Sonia Khurana, M. Sovan Kumar, Prashant Mukherjee, Kaushik Mukhopadhyaya, Veer Munshi, Mahua Ray, and L. N. Tallur.

Ways of Resisting (2002)

Participating artists: Altaf, Navjot Altaf, Pablo Bartholomew, Suranjan Basu, Arpana Caur, Sheba Chhachhi & Sonia Jabbar, Atul Dodiya, Walter Emilio D'Souza, M. J. Enas Probir Gupta, Rummana Hussain, Jehangir Jani, Jitish Kallat, Riyas Komu, Nalini Malani, Veer Munshi, Surendran Nair, Akbar Padamsee, Prashant Panjiar, Sudhir Patwardhan, Pushpamala N., Gargi Raina, Ram Rahman, Sahir Raza, N. N. Rimzon, Inder Salim, Savi Savarkar, Parthiv Shah, Tejal Shah, Nataraj Sharma, Gulammohammed Sheikh, Nilima Sheikh, Arpita Singh, and Vivan Sundaram.

There was group participation from Open Circle (Mumbai), Vistaar (Bangalore), and Voices against Violence (Vadodara). Alongside the exhibition, there was continuous screening of video documentaries by Manjira Datta, Saba Dewan, Madhushree Dutta, Shohini Ghosh, Suma Josson, Gopal Menon, Anand Patwardhan, Gauhar Raza, Rahul Roy, Teesta Setalvad, and others.

The Making of India (2004)

Participating artists: M. Angley, Yusuf Arakkal, Kriti Arora, Arunkumar H. G., Abul Kalam Azad, Sabrina Moutishi Banerjee, Eleena Banik, Pablo Bartholomew, Manisha Gera Baswani, Veena Bhargava, Jyoti M. Bhatt, Vinayak Bhattacharya, Shobha Broota, Arpana Caur, Samir Chakraborty, Kanchan Chander, Vidya Chitre, Jogen Chowdhury, Samit Das, Rakhi De, Ajay Desai, Devendra, M. J. Enas, Gopi Gajwani, Hema Guha, Subodh Gupta, Harshvardhan S., Saba Hasan, Pooja Iranna, Raja

Jaikrishen, Jehangir Jani, Rotabrata Joarder, Hem Jyotika, Ranbir Kaleka, Jitish Kallat, Reeni Saini Kallat, Ratnabali Kant, Bharati Kapadia, Naresh Kapuria, Sachin Karne, Nand Katyal, Krishen Khanna, Nawal Kishore, Riyas Komu, M. Sovan Kumar, S. Prasanna Kumar, Nupur Kundu, Subrata Kundu, Shantanu Lodh, Sheila Makhijani, Manmeet, George Martin, Merlyn, Neeta Mohindra, Prasanta Mukherjee, Veer Munshi, Babu Namboodiri K., Madhavi Parekh, Manisha Parekh, Manu Parekh, Ashim Purkayastha, Pushpamala N., Ram Rahman, Sukanya Rahman, N. N. Rimzon, Tara Sabharwal, Piyali Sadhukaan, M. S. C. Satya Sai, Inder Salim, Gigi Scaria, Anshuman Sen, Mithu Sen, Haku Shah, Parthiv Shah, Shamshad, Ajay Sharma, Gulammohammed Sheikh, Nilima Sheikh, Anjum Singh, Arpita Singh, Paramjit Singh, Prem Singh, Premalya Singh, Vivan Sundaram, Deepak Tandon, Roy Thomas, Umesh Verma, Viswanadhan, and Ankita Yadav.

Making History Our Own **(2007)**

Participating artists: V. G. Abhimanue, Yusuf Arakkal, Kriti Arora, Kahini Arte-Merchant, Arunkumar H. G., Abul Kalam Azad, Eleena Banik, Pablo Bartholomew, Tapan Bhattacharya, Vinayak Bhattacharya, Shobha Broota, Arpana Caur, Samit Das, Meera Devidayal, Anita Dube, M. J. Enas, Mahula Ghosh, Gauri Gill, Sunil Gupta, Pooja Iranna, Jehangir Jani, Hem Jyotika, Manjunath Kamath, Sonia Khurana, Tamal Krishna, Shakuntala Kulkarni, Lalitha Lajmi, Nitin Mukul, Veer Munshi, Peter Nagy, Anuradha Pathak, Ashim Purkayastha, Pushpamala N., Ram Rahman, Sukanya Rahman, Gargi Raina, Aditi Singh Reddy, Biswajit Saha, Inder Salim, Tanmoy Samanta, Gigi Scaria, Mithu Sen, Shamshad, Bulbul Sharma, Gulammohammed Sheikh, Nilima Sheikh, Anjum Singh, Arpita Singh, Paramjit Singh, Kavita Sukhani, Vivan Sundaram, Kiyomi Talaulicar, Deepak Tandon, and Zarina.

Free Speech and In Defense of Husain

For Husain at 94 **(2009)**

Participating artists: Hafeez Ahmed, Aji V. N., Navjot Altaf, Arunkumar H. G., M. S. Prakash Babu, Eleena Banik, Richard Bartholomew, Sandeep Biswas, Shobha Broota, Arpana Caur, Kanchan Chander, Pallav Chander, Amitava Das, Aurogeeta Das, Samit Das, Ajay Desai, Venktesh Desai, Meera Devidayal, Anju Dodiya, Atul Dodiya, Priyanka Dua, Vibha Galhotra, Akash Gaur, Ashim Ghosh, Gauri Gill, Subodh Gupta, Sunil Gupta, Archana Hande, Saba Hasan, Samjo Husain, Raja Jaikrishan, Jehangir Jani, Vijay S. Jodha, Megha Joshi, Durga Kainthola, Ranbir Kaleka, Rashmi Kaleka, Jitish Kallat, Bharati Kapadia, Showket Kathjoo, Nuzhat Kazmi, Alexis Kersey, Bharti Kher, Bari Kumar, Nida Mahmood & Raoul Chandra, Mithila Maniketh, Alex Mathew, Anjolie Ela Menon, Pravat Mishra, Neeta Mohindra, Veer Munshi, Mira Nair, Kavita Nayyar, Satish Panchal, Birendra Pani, Prashant Panjiar & Itu Chaudhuri, Madhavi Parekh, Manisha Parekh, Manu Parekh, Sudhir Patwardhan, Meher Pestonji, Kanishka Prasad, Pushpamala N., Habib Rahman, Ram Rahman, Mona Rai, Gargi Raina, Rekha Rao, Inder Salim, Tanmay Santra, Gigi Scaria, Vijay Sekhon, Joydip Sengupta, Kaushik Sengupta, Haku Shah, Parthiv Shah, Shamshad, Mukesh Sharma, Gulammohammed Sheikh, Nilima Sheikh, Anjum Singh, Arpita Singh, Paramjit Singh, Prem Singh, Kaushal Sonkaria, Vivan Sundaram, Kiyomi Talaulicar, Tanmaya Tyagi, Viswanadhan, Gazanfar Zaidi, and Tabassum Zaidi.

Photography Credits

Janotsav, pages 55–60: Parthiv Shah

Artists Against Communalism, pages 69–72: Parthiv Shah, Ram Rahman

Images and Words, pages 77–81: Parthiv Shah, Madan Mahatta, Ram Rahman

Slogans for Communal Harmony, pages 83–91: Parthiv Shah

Anhad Garje, pages 99–105: Ram Rahman, Parthiv Shah

Ayodhya: Demolition of the Babri Masjid and After, pages 113–125: Ram Rahman

Muktnaad, page 124: Parthiv Shah; page 125: Pablo Bartholomew

Gift for India, pages 142–45: Ram Rahman; pages 146–51: Anil Rane

Art on the Move, pages 152–59: Ram Rahman

Ways of Resisting, pages 162–70: Ravi Pasricha, Pablo Bartholomew, Ram Rahman

History and Culture, pages 176–79: Ram Rahman

The Making of India, pages 181–85: Ram Rahman

Making History Our Own, pages 194–203: Ram Rahman

In Defense of M. F. Husain, pages 217–21: Ram Rahman

Husain @ 95, pages 230–31: Ram Rahman

Posters and books photographed by Lalit Narayan Bunty

Art photographed by Ram Rahman

PRINTED IN CHINA